**GERMAN REUNIFICATION: A REFERENCE GUIDE
AND COMMENTARY**

GERMAN REUNIFICATION: A REFERENCE GUIDE AND COMMENTARY

by
Jonathan Osmond

With contributions by

Rachel Alsop, Karen Henderson, Charlie Jeffery, Ian Jeffries,
David Spence and Graham Timmins

GERMAN REUNIFICATION: A REFERENCE GUIDE AND COMMENTARY

Published by Longman Group UK Limited, Westgate House,
The High, Harlow, Essex, CM20 1YR, United Kingdom

Distributed exclusively in the United States and Canada
by Gale Research Inc., 835 Penobscot Building, Detroit,
Michigan 48226, USA

ISBN 0-582-09650-2

© Longman Group UK Limited 1992
All rights reserved. No part of this publication
may be reproduced, stored in a retrieval system, or
transmitted in any form or by any means, electronic,
mechanical, photocopying, recording or otherwise,
without either the prior written permission of the Publishers or a
licence permitting restricted copying issued by the Copyright Licensing
Agency Ltd, 90 Tottenham Court Road, London W1P 9HE

A catalogue record for this publication is available from the British Library

Typeset in Times 10 on 12pt

Printed in Great Britain by BPCC Wheatons Ltd, Exeter

For Magda Sztajerwald

CONTENTS

Preface	ix
Notes on Contributors	xiii
Maps	
Germany in 1945	xiv
The German Democratic Republic before reunification (as on January 1, 1990)	xv
The Federal Republic of Germany from October 3, 1990	xvi

Part I
Revolution and Reunification

Chronology of events 1989–92	3
The shape of Germany before 1949	15
A brief history of the German Democratic Republic	18
The collapse of the communist regime in the GDR	23
The democratic GDR and the reunification of Germany	57

Part II
Politics, Economy and Society

The integration of eastern Germany into the European Community (*David Spence*)	93
Electoral volatility in united Germany (*Charlie Jeffery*)	115
East German politicians and parties in the new Federal Republic (*Karen Henderson*)	133
The impact of reunification on the east German economy (*Ian Jeffries*)	152
Trade unions and German reunification: the social dimension (*Graham Timmins*)	170
The experience of women in eastern Germany (*Rachel Alsop*)	185

Part III
Reference Section

Directory of German reunification	201
Tables of governments, election results and economic indicators	243
A 10-point plan for overcoming the division of Europe and Germany — speech by Chancellor Kohl in the *Bundestag*, Bonn, November 28, 1989 (*abbreviated text*)	256
Treaty between the Federal Republic of Germany and the German Democratic Republic establishing a Monetary, Economic and Social Union, Bonn, May 18, 1990 (*text*)	260
Treaty on Unification of the German Democratic Republic and the Federal Republic of Germany, Berlin, August 31, 1990 (*abbreviated text*)	275
Treaty on the Final Settlement with Respect to Germany [Two-Plus-Four Treaty], Moscow, September 12, 1990 (*text*)	287

CONTENTS

Treaty between the Federal Republic of Germany and the Union of Soviet Socialist Republics on Good-Neighbourliness, Partnership, and Co-operation, Bonn, November 9, 1990 (*text*) 292

Bibliography 297

Index 303

PREFACE

Amongst all the extraordinary images which remain with me of Germany in the last three years, the one which seems to linger most vividly is a very mundane one. On a rainy day in the leafy suburbs of west Berlin I was having lunch in an Italian restaurant. The few customers were sitting at tables along the window and I was at the far end of the room, already eating and with a newspaper spread out in front of me. A couple in their early fifties came into the restaurant, shunned the dozens of empty tables in the room, and came to sit opposite me, side by side. We exchanged civil greetings, but otherwise they showed no signs of wanting to enter into conversation. Nor did they have any obvious interest in the nondescript view out of the window.

I did not need to ask, but I knew from their clothes and their behaviour that these were east Berliners or possibly Potsdamers having a quiet afternoon out. Their choice of table was due to their east German experience. For them empty tables meant no service, probably shortage of staff or food or both. They sat instead at the otherwise least occupied table, mine. The extraordinary thing was not that as strangers they did not behave as locals might — tourists and immigrants all over the world do things inexplicable to the native inhabitants — but that they did not know the ordinary modes of behaviour *in their own city*, perhaps a bus ride from their home. In fact in this one trivial respect their conduct was more different from that of west Germans than the latter's conduct would be from, say, mine as a visitor from Britain or from that of the Italian owners. It struck me that if east Germans had to adapt in such humdrum matters — and adapt they no doubt quickly would in instances like this — how many other areas of life of much greater importance were going to prove difficult? And how one-sided was the process going to be? Would west Germans also have to alter their behaviour and perceptions? I thought I knew the answer to that.

German reunification means learning that you can sit at an empty table and still get served. It means remembering that if you want chicken you do not ask for a "Broiler". It means no longer having to queue in a bookshop for a plastic carrier basket before you can look around. It means this and that for ordinary people, and it also means traffic jams where there were none, unemployment, race hatred, and discovering that your friend has been supplying information on you to the security service. For west Germans it means unwelcome tax increases and for some pressure on housing and jobs. It is also part of the new shape which has come upon European and world politics, a shape which is still far from settled and which has its own dangers. German reunification includes the most trivial aspects of two groups of people coming together who have lived forcibly separate lives for over 40 years, it brings in its train often devastating problems of personal and family adjustment, and it raises questions of global significance. This book hopes to go some way in portraying these features and the many in between.

"Reunification" is really the wrong word. Though it might apply appropriately to families and to the city of Berlin, it is not an accurate representation of the overall political result of recent events. The two German states of 1949–90 were never "unified", so they cannot be "reunified". The state of Germany as it exists now has never existed before. The shape of

PREFACE

"Germany" has indeed always been a fluid one, and the current manifestation is only one solution of many which have been tried. "Reunification" stands in the title of this book solely in order to avoid confusion with Bismarck's "unification" of 1871, which was itself only a partial organization of the German-speaking peoples of central Europe. For the purposes of this book "German reunification" is shorthand for the entry of the German Democratic Republic into the Federal Republic of Germany on October 3, 1990, according to Article 23 of the Basic Law of the Federal Republic and Article 1 of the Unification Treaty of August 31, 1990.

The book is divided into three parts. Part I provides a summary chronology of recent events, followed by a brief discussion of the historical background and a detailed account of developments from the last years of the German Democratic Republic through to the situation in united Germany in the spring of 1992. The emphasis is on the political, but in order to explain the politics there is also considerable reference to economic and social matters. Part II comprises a series of essays, each of which goes into more detailed discussion of crucial aspects of German reunification. The themes range from the international context (David Spence), through German politics (Charlie Jeffery and Karen Henderson) and the economy (Ian Jeffries), to social aspects of reunification in eastern Germany (Graham Timmins and Rachel Alsop). Part III is a reference section, allowing the reader easy access to compact information on individuals, political parties, institutions, regions of Germany, the composition of governments, election results and economic indicators. The text of four major treaties is provided in full or in abbreviated form, and there is also a bibliography of recent work in English and German.

The purpose of the arrangement of the book is to allow the reader to approach the subject from a variety of different angles, general and detailed. The resultant duplication of some information in different parts of the book is therefore quite deliberate. Also, in order to facilitate moving from one section to another, **bold type** is used on first mention in each section of Part I to indicate an entry in the Directory in Part III. Neither the account in Part I nor the essays in Part II contain detailed source references, but the Bibliography provides an indication of the main and most easily accessible published works in English and German which were used in the compilation of the book.

Published material is the main source used in the preparation of the book, but it is of very varied kinds. East and West German newspapers have, of course, been indispensable, not only mainstream publications like the *Frankfurter Allgemeine Zeitung* in the West and the former official party mouthpiece, *Neues Deutschland*, in the East, but also the many often short-lived products of the turbulent time. Official publications from Bonn and Berlin, including statistical material, have also been used, as have reports by economics research institutes such as the *Deutsches Institut für Wirtschaftsforschung*.

Many of the main participants in events have now written their accounts or given lengthy interviews which have been written up by others. They include the last four heads-of-state of the GDR, Erich Honecker, Egon Krenz, Manfred Gerlach and Sabine Bergmann-Pohl; the man who negotiated German unity on the West German side, Wolfgang Schäuble; the last communist prime minister of the GDR, Hans Modrow; the governing mayor of (West) Berlin when the Wall was opened, Walter Momper; the man placed in charge of the archives of the *Stasi* relating to individuals, Joachim Gauck; and two former prominent members of the old *Politbüro*, Günter Mittag and Günter Schabowski. We also have eyewitness accounts of the *Volkskammer* committee to investigate corruption and abuse of office (by Volker Klemm) and of the meetings of the Round Table (by Uwe Thaysen). From the citizens' movements in the GDR individuals such as Jens Reich and Wolfgang Ullmann have published their views in book-form. Many others — from all political sides — have contributed shorter pieces or given interviews in books and periodicals. Another — highly controversial — participant in debate has been the east German psychotherapist, Hans-Joachim Maaz, who in his books *Der Gefühlsstau* ("The backlog of feelings") and *Das gestürzte Volk* ("The people turned upside down") has painted a desperate and highly personal account of psychological distress in the former GDR.

Important though these published sources are, it is important to have witnessed events and to have talked to ordinary people in east and west Germany. I found particularly in the former GDR that every time I had begun to form an impression of what I thought was current "popular opinion", the next conversation I had knocked it for six. This is a salutary lesson for an historian. Apart from impromptu contact with Germans east and west, I was also fortunate to have been in Berlin on the night of November 9, 1989 and — from the east Berlin side — to have observed the scenes at the Brandenburg Gate. The next day I spoke to Central Committee members leaving the obviously fraught meeting inside SED headquarters and in the evening I attended the SED mass meeting in the Lustgarten, addressed by Egon Krenz. I was again in Berlin for the March 1990 elections, finding in the Alliance 90 headquarters on the Friedrichstrasse a surprisingly buoyant response to a disastrous electoral performance. Many other visits — not just to Berlin but to Brandenburg, Saxony, Thuringia and Bavaria, for instance — have also contributed to whatever understanding I have of recent events. Similarly, the other contributors to this book have their own direct experiences of these extraordinary times. They have visited Germany east and west, sometimes for longer periods of research and have had the opportunity to carry out systematic interviews (Rachel Alsop of prominent women's representatives, for instance). David Spence was himself a participant, in that he was Secretary of the European Commission's Task Force for German Unification.

The emphasis throughout the book is on developments in East Germany both before and after unification. This is not because West German politics and society do not have their own interest and they are discussed here as appropriate, but because the crisis came from within the GDR and the consequences of unification are being felt most keenly in the eastern *Länder*. This is the reason, for instance, that in Part I there is a brief history of the GDR, but not of the Federal Republic. The course of the revolution in the GDR can only be explained against this background, whereas to include details of the history of the Federal Republic would be to overburden the book with extraneous material. The information is as far as possible up-to-date to May/June 1992.

I should like to acknowledge my thanks to all those who helped in the preparation of this book: to the individual contributors, who were impressively prompt in their submissions; in particular to Karen Henderson for many helpful suggestions and interesting discussion on the former GDR; to John Harper of Longman for proposing the book in the first place and for expediting its production; to Nicola Greenwood, who coped so well with the copy-editing as the material came in in bits and pieces; to the British Council and the German Academic Exchange Service for enabling me to undertake research in the former GDR in the spring of 1991; to colleagues at the Humboldt University in Berlin and the University of Leipzig who were so hospitable to me during that time, particularly to Professor Volker Klemm, to Herr Eckbert Schauer, and to Professor Günter Nötzold; to the staff of the Confederation of British Industry, who made it possible for me to attend the London conference on Germany in November 1991, addressed by — amongst others — Frau Birgit Breuel of the *Treuhandanstalt* and Herr Jürgen Möllemann, Federal Minister of the Economy; to The Economist

PREFACE

Intelligence Unit — particularly to Charles Jenkins, David Young and Vlad Sobell — which provided me with research material and travel funds over the years I wrote its quarterly reports on East Germany; to the *Gesellschaft für Deutschlandforschung* and the *Forschungsstelle für gesamtdeutsche wirtschaftliche und soziale Fragen* which enabled me to visit Berlin on numerous occasions over this period and to hear the views of prominent participants in events and academic commentators; to Judy Batt, who first steered me in the direction of the GDR, without realizing what it might lead to; to Janet Dittmer and to Mick Traynor in Friedenau who over several years have put me up and put up with me more often than I had a right to expect; to Günther Lottes and Gerhard and Susanne Waldherr, who made my stays in Regensburg so enjoyable and fruitful; to Martin Cherry, for friendship and proof-reading; and most of all to my wife, Magda, and to my sons, Alexander and Laurence, for being so patient during the months when work kept me late in my university office, and Conrad, for waiting considerately until the book was finished before making his own appearance.

All of these have helped the book to take shape, but none is responsible for its faults. The accounts and views expressed here are mine and — with some editorial intervention on my part — those of the other authors. They and I hope that this book will contribute to an understanding amongst English-speaking readers of the German situation, and that we might even generate a response from those in Germany who are more directly living through what we — like Christopher Isherwood at an earlier less hopeful date — can see only through a cold lens.

NOTES ON CONTRIBUTORS

Jonathan Osmond is Lecturer in History at the University of Leicester. He has published articles on German agricultural history in several collections and his book *Rural Protest in the Weimar Republic: The Free Peasantry in the Rhineland and Bavaria* appears shortly. He covered GDR affairs for the Economist Intelligence Unit from 1983 to 1990 and has contributed to S. White (ed.), *Handbook of Reconstruction in Eastern Europe and the Soviet Union* (1991), and B. Szajkowski (ed.), *New Political Parties of Eastern Europe and the Soviet Union* (1991).

Rachel Alsop is a postgraduate in the Department of European Studies at the University of Bradford. Currently researching in Berlin, she is completing a doctoral thesis on the effects of German unification on female employment in eastern Germany.

Karen Henderson is Lecturer in East European Politics at the University of Leicester. She is completing a doctoral thesis on political structure in Czechoslovakia and the GDR 1970–85 and is a contributor to S.Whitefield (ed.), *The New Institutional Architecture of Eastern Europe* (forthcoming).

Charlie Jeffery is Lecturer in Politics and Deputy Director of the Centre for Federal Studies at the University of Leicester. His main research interests are in voting behaviour and federalism in Germany and in the National Socialist era in Austria. His publications include (ed. with P. Savigear), *German Federalism Today* (1991), and "Voting on Unity: The German Election of 1990", in *International Relations* (1991).

Ian Jeffries is Lecturer in Soviet Economic Institutions at the University College of Swansea. His publications include (ed.) *The Industrial Enterprise in Eastern Europe* (1981), (ed. with M. Melzer) *The East German Economy* (1987), *A Guide to the Socialist Economies* (1990) and (ed.) *Industrial Reform in Socialist Countries: from Restructuring to Revolution* (1992).

David Spence works for the Commission of the European Communities in Brussels. He was Secretary of the Commission's Task Force for German Unification. His publications include *Enlargement Without Accession: The EC's Reponse to German Unification* (1991), of which his contribution to this volume is an abbreviated and revised version.

Graham Timmins is Lecturer in European Politics at the University of Huddersfield. He is a specialist in German and eastern European affairs and has published several articles on the former GDR. He is completing a doctoral thesis on "German Unification and Organised Labour".

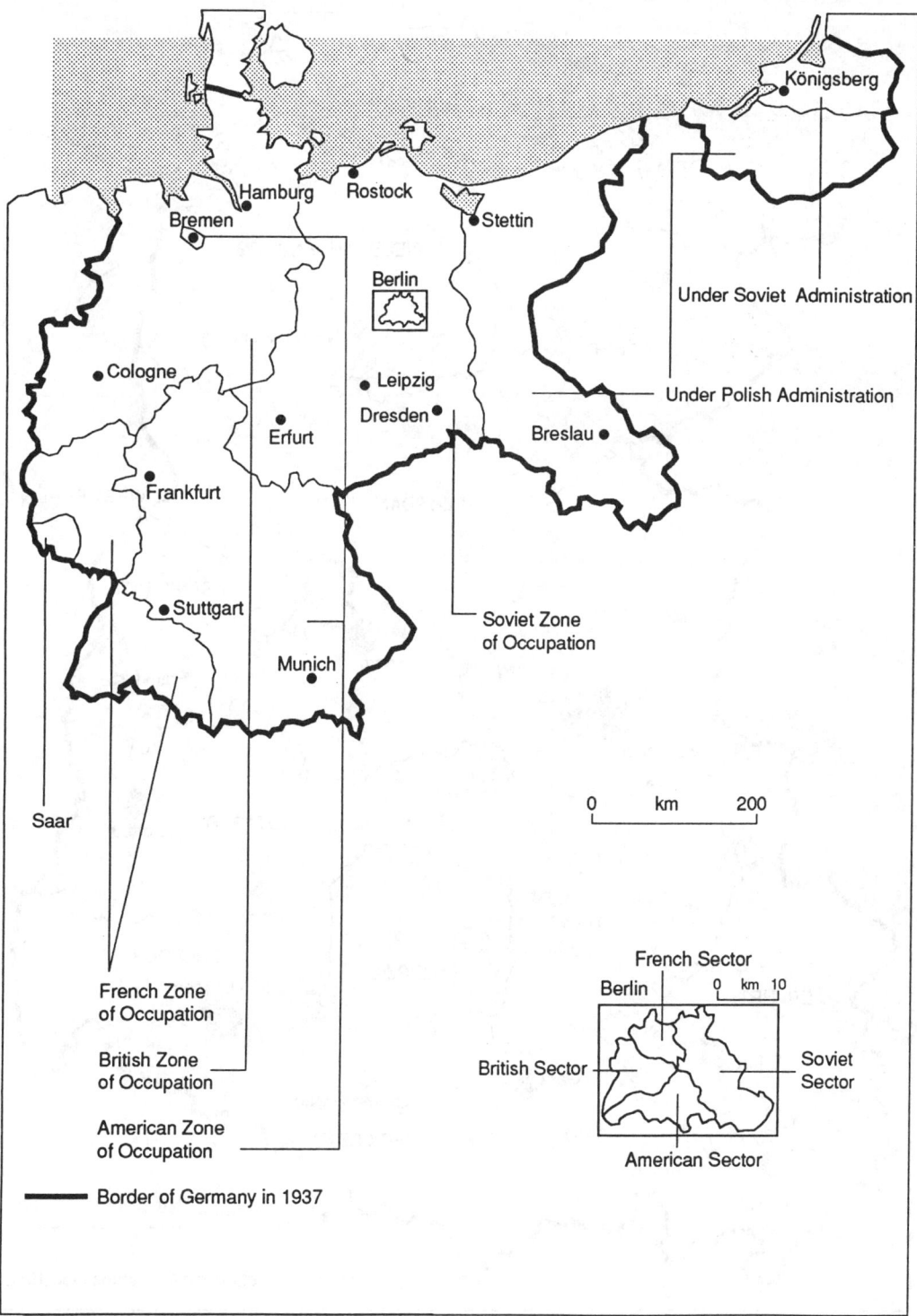

Germany in 1945

The German Democratic Republic before reunification (as on January 1, 1990)

The Federal Republic of Germany, October 3, 1990

I REVOLUTION AND REUNIFICATION

CHRONOLOGY OF EVENTS 1989 – 92

Bold face indicates entry in DIRECTORY.

1989

January 1. New foreign travel regulations come into effect in GDR, but meet with little enthusiasm.

January 15. Eighty arrests follow **Leipzig** demonstration; official growth in GDR 1988 net material product announced as 3 per cent (target: 4.1 per cent); real growth nearer 1.7 per cent.

January 19. Erich **Honecker** declares Berlin Wall will last another 100 years.

January 23. Honecker announces cuts in armed forces and military spending.

January 29. Elections to West **Berlin** Chamber of Deputies result in **CDU** defeat, **Republican** advance, and eventual formation of coalition government of **SPD** and **Alternative List**, with Walter **Momper** (SPD) as Governing Mayor.

February. Politbüro sends deputation under Günter **Mittag** to investigate alleged shortcomings in Dresden party organization of Hans **Modrow**.

February 5–6. Would-be escaper Chris Gueffroy shot dead by GDR border police in Berlin; this and later incidents provoke West German protests.

March 3. GDR *Volkskammer* approves electoral law giving local voting rights to certain categories of foreigners.

March 13. In West Germany television interview former GDR spy chief, Markus Wolf, speaks out for reform; demonstration in Leipzig for right to emigrate broken up by *Stasi* (State Security Service).

April 1. Revised travel regulations introduced in GDR in wake of criticism, but still very limited in scope.

May 2. Hungarians begin to dismantle border with Austria.

May 7. Local elections in GDR show slight increase in votes against single "National Front" list; unofficial observers accuse authorities of falsifying results to disguise real level of opposition.

June 5. Tiananmen Square massacre applauded by GDR authorities; popular demonstrations reject this.

June 11. Honecker attends reconsecration of renovated Greifswald cathedral.

June 18. West German elections to European Parliament show sudden advance of Republicans and other parties of the extreme right.

June 22–3. SED Central Committee meets in East Berlin; Joachim Herrmann, party secretary for agitation and propaganda, delivers hardline report, singling out Hungarian reforms for criticism.

June 29. "Soviet Forces in Germany" renamed "West Group of Soviet Forces".

July 8. Honecker falls ill at Warsaw Pact summit in Bucharest and is forced to return home.

July 10. After hospital treatment for gall bladder complaint, Honecker goes on holiday.

July 31. West Germans announce that so far in 1989 over 46,000 GDR citizens have legally migrated to West Germany.

August 8. West German mission in East Berlin forced to close under pressure of would-be emigrants.

August 13. West German embassy in Budapest similarly closed.

August 18. Honecker undergoes further surgery.

August 19. Several hundred GDR citizens break through Austro-Hungarian border.

August 22. West German embassy in Prague forced to close.

September 1. Honecker leaves hospital for convalescence.

September 11. Hungarians allow GDR citizens to cross to Austria; **New Forum** founded.

September 12. **Democracy Now** founded.

September 19. Meeting of Evangelical Synod in Eisenach calls for reform.

September 20. Manfred **Gerlach**, leader of **LDPD**, encourages questioning and new ideas.

September 21. New Forum denied official recognition.

September 25. Honecker takes up work again.

September 30. **Genscher** in West German embassy in Prague announces agreement on emigration of refugees; that night trains begin to leave for West Germany via the GDR.

October 1. **Democratic Awakening** (DA) founded.

October 6. President Gorbachev arrives for celebrations of 40th anniversary of the GDR.

October 7. Anniversary parade in East Berlin; Gorbachev warns "He who comes too late is punished by life"; Demonstrations throughout GDR meet with armed force; **Social Democratic Party** (SDP) founded.

October 9. Mass demonstration in Leipzig; Gewandhaus conductor Kurt Masur intervenes to help prevent bloodshed; in Dresden mayor Wolfgang **Berghofer** agrees to meet a delegation of protesters.

October 10–11. Politbüro meets to discuss crisis; Alfred Neumann's proposal that Günter Mittag be dismissed is rejected.

October 12. Politbüro issues appeal to solve problems with concerted strength.

October 14. Egon **Krenz** makes plans with Willi **Stoph** for removal of Honecker.

October 15. Krenz, Günter **Schabowski** and Harry Tisch meet at latter's home to finalize plans.

October 16. Over 100,000 people march through Leipzig demanding reform.

October 17. Politbüro votes to remove Honecker, Mittag and Herrmann.

October 18. Special meeting of Central Committee; Honecker, Mittag and Herrmann removed from all party offices; Krenz elected new General Secretary of **SED**; Krenz announces a "turning point" (**Wende**).

October 23. About 300,000 people demonstrate in Leipzig; other demonstrations take place elsewhere.

October 24. **Volkskammer** elects Krenz as Chairman of Council of State (26 votes against, 26 abstentions) and of National Defence Council (eight against, 17 abstentions).

October 26. In Dresden Hans Modrow and Wolfgang Berghofer address meeting of 100,000 people; Helmut **Kohl** and Krenz discuss the situation by telephone.

October 27. Amnesty announced for those who had fled illegally; appeal that they return.

October 29. West Berlin mayor Momper and (East) Berlin party secretary Schabowski meet in East Berlin.

October 30. Demonstration of over 200,000 in Leipzig.

November 1. Krenz holds talks with Gorbachev in Moscow.

November 2. Dismissal/resignation of **Margot Honecker** (education minister), Tisch (FDGB chairman), Gerald Götting (CDU chairman), Heinrich Homann (NDPD chairman) and of first two of SED district party secretaries; Krenz in Poland.

November 3. Krenz announces *Politbüro* action programme; departure from *Politbüro* of five members, including Erich Mielke (head of state security); resignation of mayor of Leipzig.

November 4. Largest protest demonstration yet: approximately one million take to the streets of East Berlin.

November 6. New travel law fails to meet demands of people; mass demonstrations continue.

November 7. *Volkskammer* committee rejects new travel law; Stoph government resigns, but continues in caretaker capacity.

November 8. Meeting of Central Committee (to November 10); *Politbüro* resigns and new election held; votes for and against made public; Krenz re-elected General Secretary; Modrow joins *Politbüro* and is recommended as new prime minister.

November 9. At press conference Schabowski announces opening of borders to West Berlin and the Federal Republic; throughout night thousands of people cross between two states in both directions; there is dancing on the Berlin Wall.

November 10. GDR citizens pour across the borders; Kohl interrupts visit to Poland to speak at rally in West Berlin, meeting hostile reception; Krenz addresses SED rally in East Berlin, with mixed reaction; Lothar **de Maizière** elected chairman of (East) CDU.

November 12. Central Committee calls for an extraordinary party congress.

November 13. Horst Sindermann (SED) resigns as *Volkskammer* chairman; Günter Maleuda of the farmer's party (DBD) elected in his stead, defeating **Gerlach** (LDPD); Modrow elected new prime minister on show of hands (one vote against).

November 16. Academy of Science rehabilitates disgraced members; change of editorship at *Neues Deutschland*.

November 17. Modrow forms new government; Ministry of State Security (*Stasi*) abolished and replaced by Office for National Security.

November 18. Modrow government approved by *Volkskammer*: 28 ministers — SED (17), LDPD (4), CDU (3), **DBD** (2) and **NDPD** (2); commissions established to propose constitutional and electoral reforms; in East Berlin and other cities large demonstrations continue against the SED's leading role and for free elections; 15,000 attend New Forum rally in Leipzig.

November 20. Rudolf Seiters, head of Chancellor Kohl's office, meets Krenz in East Berlin.

November 22. *Politbüro* proposes "**Round Table**" discussions.

November 23. Mittag expelled from SED.

November 24. New customs regulations come into force, to prevent goods in GDR being bought up by foreigners; **Green Party** founded.

November 26. Otto Graf Lambsdorff (**FDP** chairman) meets leaders of LDPD and DA in East Berlin.

November 27. 200,000 demonstrate in Leipzig.

November 28. Kohl announces 10-point plan for German unity.

November 30. Alfred Herrhausen, chief executive of Deutsche Bank, murdered by **Red Army Faction** in Bad Homburg.

December 1. *Volkskammer* excises from the constitution the SED's leading role.

December 2. SED members demonstrate outside the Central Committee building, demanding resignation of leadership.

December 3. Krenz, *Politbüro* and Central Committee resign; 25-strong provisional committee replaces them; Honecker and others expelled from SED; Mittag and Tisch (FDGB) arrested; Human chain of protest formed across GDR.

December 4. CDU leaves "Democratic Block" led by SED; calls for German unity begin to be heard at the continuing demonstrations.

December 5. Honecker and Mielke under house arrest at Wandlitz; Modrow and Seiters (on behalf of Kohl) agree on hard-currency fund to assist GDR citizens and on lifting of currency and visa requirements for citizens of the Federal Republic.

December 6. Krenz resigns as Chairman of State Council and National Defence Council; provisionally replaced in former capacity by Gerlach (LDPD).

December 7. First meeting of Round Table, bringing together old parties, new groups and parties, and church representatives.

December 8–9. SED party congress; Gregor **Gysi** elected party chairman, Modrow and Berghofer as deputy chairmen.

December 11. US, British and French ambassadors to Federal Republic and Soviet ambassador to GDR meet in Control Commission building in West Berlin.

December 13. Contacts established between SDP and West German SPD.

December 15–16. CDU holds special congress in East Berlin.

December 16–17. SED resumes party congress and renames itself SED-PDS (Party of Democratic Socialism); DA forms itself as a political party; Wolfgang **Schnur** elected chairman.

December 17. West German president Richard von **Weizsäcker** meets Gerlach in Potsdam.

December 18. Second session of Round Table.

December 19–20. Kohl visits Dresden and holds talks with Modrow; they decide to form "contractual community" between the two German states; Kohl receives rapturous welcome in Dresden.

December 20–22. President Mitterrand of France visits GDR.

December 22. Brandenburg Gate reopened by Kohl and Modrow.

December 31. 1989 total of GDR citizens leaving for Federal Republic stands at nearly 350,000.

1990

January 2. President Havel of Czechoslovakia, visiting Berlin, envisages confederation of two German states.

January 3. Opposition groups threaten to leave Round Table if Modrow does not abandon plans for state security office; six parties and groups, including SDP, DA and New Forum, form electoral pact; large demonstration in East Berlin, led by SED-PDS, against neo-Nazism and racism.

January 8. At Leipzig and other demonstrations the calls for German unity dominate.

January 11. Modrow presents government programme to *Volkskammer*, abandoning plan for state security office; constitution altered to allow foreign participation in GDR enterprises; Krenz and Schabowksi resign from *Volkskammer*.

January 12. SDP meets in Berlin and changes name to **SPD**.

January 13. Price rises announced for children's clothes and other items.

January 15. Stasi headquarters stormed by protesters.

January 16. Modrow visits West Berlin.

January 20. **German Social Union** (DSU) founded in Leipzig.

January 21. Berghofer, mayor of Dresden, and 39 colleagues leave SED-PDS; Krenz and Schabowski expelled from SED-PDS.

January 22. Modrow offers opposition parties role in government.

January 23. First meeting in East Berlin of German–German Economic Commission; party symbol removed from SED-PDS headquarters in East Berlin.

January 27–28. New Forum agrees its constitution, but not as a political party.

January 28. Volkskammer elections brought forward from May 6 to March 18; proposal for Government of National Responsibility announced, to include opposition parties.

February 1. Modrow presents declaration on "path to German unity", proposing neutral confederation; new liberal travel law comes into force, also allowing GDR citizens to buy West German Marks.

February 4. SED-PDS changes its name to **PDS** in order to break clearly from the old ruling party; **FDP** founded in East Berlin.

February 5. Opposition parties furnish eight ministers without portfolio in Modrow government; CDU, DSU and DA form **Alliance for Germany** to fight March elections.

February 7. New Forum, Democracy Now and **Peace and Human Rights Initiative** form **Alliance 90** to fight elections.

February 10. In Moscow Kohl meets Gorbachev, who agrees that Germans themselves should take decision on unity.

February 11. FDP, **LDP** and **DFP** form liberal electoral alliance, **League of Free Democrats**; first East German Green Party congress approves its programme.

February 13. In Bonn Modrow and Kohl agree on commission to prepare monetary and economic union.

February 14. In Ottawa two German foreign ministers and those of USA, USSR, UK and France agree to hold **"Two-Plus-Four"** conference on German unity; Green Party and **Independent Women's Association** form electoral alliance.

February 15. Kohl rejects neutral Germany.

February 18. First congress of DSU in Leipzig.

February 20. New electoral law.

February 25. First SPD congress in Leipzig elects Ibrahim **Böhme** as chairman and Willy Brandt as honorary president; Modrow elected honorary president of PDS.

March 5. Round Table agrees "social charter" as basis for inter-German talks.

March 7. Modrow tries to enlist Gorbachev's help in preserving property relations in the GDR.

March 12. Last session of Round Table.

March 14. Preliminary Two-Plus-Four talks begin in Bonn; Schnur resigns as chairman of DA, because of former *Stasi* links.

March 18. Elections to *Volkskammer*: CDU victory (163 seats) but even with allies no overall majority (192 seats out of 400); SPD 88 seats; PDS 66 seats.

March 19. DSU and CSU representatives meet near Hof in West Germany; Deutsche Kreditbank founded in East Berlin.

March 20. West German cabinet plans to abolish special measures for incoming GDR citizens; three liberal parties (LDP, FDP, DFP) propose merger.

March 21. Böhme elected chairman of SPD delegation in *Volkskammer*.

March 23. Mass grave of victims of Stalinism discovered at Fünfeichen, Neubrandenburg.

March 24. Honeckers prevented by popular protest from moving to government house in Lindow.

March 25. First Lufthansa flight from Frankfurt am Main to Dresden.

March 26. Böhme gives up SPD party posts and *Volkskammer* seat, pending investigations into alleged co-operation with *Stasi*; CDU leadership proposes Lothar de Maizière as prime minister; treason charges against Honecker and others dropped.

March 29. Demonstrations in several cities press for investigation of possible *Stasi* pasts of *Volkskammer* members; coalition negotiations begin between CDU and SPD.

March 30. Böhme, de Maizière and Gysi cleared of collaboration with *Stasi*.

April 1. **Bundesbank** proposal of 2:1 exchange rate meets with GDR protest.

April 2. CDU fraction proposes de Maizière for premiership; Böhme resigns from SPD leadership.

April 3. Coalition talks between Alliance for Germany parties, SPD and liberals; Honecker transferred to Soviet military hospital in Beelitz, Potsdam.

April 5. First meeting of newly-elected *Volkskammer*; Sabine **Bergmann-Pohl** (CDU) elected president; abolition of State Council approved; 100,000 demonstrate in Berlin against 2:1 exchange rate.

April 9. Coalition cabinet formed; de Maizière (CDU) prime minister; **Meckel** (SPD) foreign affairs; **Diestel** (DSU) interior; **Romberg** (SPD) finance; **Eppelmann** (DA) defence and disarmament; 11 ministries for CDU, seven for SPD, three for liberals, two for DSU and one for DA.

April 12. New government approved by *Volkskammer*.

April 18. De Maizière delivers government declaration to *Volkskammer*, proposing German unity, democracy, and exchange rate for wages, pensions and savings of 1:1.

April 23. Bonn government proposes 1:1 exchange rate for wages and first tranche of savings and otherwise 2:1 rate.

April 24. Kohl and de Maizière agree on currency, economic and social union from July 1, 1990.

April 25. In Cologne assassination attempt on Oskar **Lafontaine**, SPD chancellor candidate in West Germany.

April 27. Negotiations begin on state treaty between two Germanies.

April 29. De Maizière in Moscow talks with Gorbachev; GDR farmers protest against worsening agricultural situation.

May 2. Terms of state treaty on currency union published in Bonn; East Berlin government announces measures to alleviate agricultural crisis.

May 5. First Two-Plus-Four meeting in Bonn.

May 6. In GDR local elections CDU, SPD, DSU and PDS all lose ground; advances by liberals, farmers' party and citizens' groups; CDU still well ahead.

May 13. SPD wins state elections in **North Rhine-Westphalia** and **Lower Saxony**, depriving CDU of majority in West German *Bundesrat*.

May 18. State treaty on currency, economic and social union of the two Germanies signed in Bonn by respective East and West German finance ministers, Walter Romberg (SPD) and Theo **Waigel** (CSU).

May 20. Lafontaine urges vote against state treaty, fearing economic collapse in GDR; in conflict with Hans-Jochen Vogel, party chairman.

May 21. Renewed mass farmer protests in GDR.

May 22. DSU fraction in *Volkskammer* votes for dismissal of Interior Minister Peter-Michael Diestel (DSU); Diestel and de Maizière resist.

May 31. Volkskammer decides that finances of all parties to come under government supervision and that GDR state symbol be removed from all public buildings.

June 1. Karl-Marx-Stadt renamed Chemnitz.

June 2. PDS demonstration in Berlin against *Volkskammer* vote, fearing eventual disbanding of party.

June 6. Susanne Albrecht, long-sought suspected terrorist, arrested in East Berlin; other arrests follow, showing how GDR had provided a haven.

June 9. Wolfgang **Thierse** elected new chairman of SPD in GDR.

June 11. De Maizière meets President Bush in Washington.

June 12. Gorbachev proposes initial German dual membership of NATO and Warsaw Pact; rejected by USA and Federal Republic.

June 13. PDS discloses party funds of M 1.08 billion.

June 14. West German SPD leadership agrees to vote for state treaty.

June 15. Agreed between German governments that claims can be made for property in GDR confiscated since 1949, but not during occupation of 1945–49.

June 17. Volkskammer expunges socialist character of GDR constitution and approves ***Treuhandanstalt*** (Trust Agency) law, paving way for privatization; DSU attempt to push through immediate German unity fails.

June 18. De Maizière received by President Mitterrand in Paris.

June 21. Volkskammer approves state treaty.

June 22. **Bundestag** approves state treaty; in **Bundesrat** only representatives of Lower Saxony (SPD) and **Saarland** (SPD and Lafontaine's state) vote against; Checkpoint Charlie dismantled; Two-Plus-Four talks continue in Berlin.

June 23. Anti-fascist demonstration in East Berlin ends in violence against police.

June 25–26. Parliamentary chairwomen Bergmann-Pohl (GDR) and Süssmuth (Federal Republic) visit Israel.

June 29. West German President Weizsäcker favours Berlin as new German capital; Detlev **Rohwedder** of Hoesch named as next chairman of *Treuhandanstalt*.

June 30. Interior Minister Diestel leaves DSU, complaining of rightward drift; followed by other leading figures.

GERMAN REUNIFICATION

July 1. From midnight currency, economic and social union of two Germanies; Deutschemark currency in GDR; inter-German border open.

July 2. GDR shops reopen with western goods and new prices.

July 6. Warning strike of 120,000 metalworkers in Berlin and **Brandenburg**.

July 8. West German victory in football World Cup in Rome celebrated in both German states.

July 10. In **Bonn** and Berlin negotiations on second state treaty of unification.

July 14–16. Kohl with Gorbachev in Moscow and the Caucasus; talks result in Gorbachev's acceptance of all-German NATO membership.

July 16. Treuhandanstalt begins work under Executive President Reiner **Gohlke**, formerly of *Bundesbahn*.

July 17. Polish foreign minister takes part in Two-Plus-Four session in Paris; discussion of Oder-Neisse German-Polish border.

July 19. De Maizière insists on two separate territories for all-German elections; opposed by SPD and liberals.

July 23. Dispute continues in GDR government over timing of unification and mechanism of elections; SPD threatens to leave coalition.

July 24. Liberals announce withdrawal from coalition.

July 26. Parliamentary committees from GDR and Federal Republic recommend joint electoral territory for all-German elections; no decision yet on 5 per cent hurdle.

July 27. SPD decides to remain in coalition.

August 6. Under growing economic pressure in GDR, de Maizière announces that he and Kohl favour bringing all-German elections forward to October 14; protest from other parties and requirement for constitutional amendment force retreat.

August 12. FDP organizations in GDR and Federal Republic join to form first united party (others will follow suit).

August 15. General Secretary of GDR CDU, Martin **Kirchner** removed from office on suspicion of having collaborated with *Stasi*; mass demonstrations by GDR farmers; in East Berlin Agriculture Minister Peter Pollack pelted with eggs; de Maizière sacks Finance Minister Romberg (SPD) and Agriculture Minister Pollack (independent, nominated by SPD); Economics Minister Pohl (CDU), Justice Minister Wünsche (independent) and Foreign Minister Meckel (SPD) also resign; cabinet crisis leads to SPD withdrawing from coalition.

August 20. Reiner Gohlke resigns as Executive President of *Treuhandanstalt*; to be replaced by Supervisory President Rohwedder.

August 23. Volkskammer approves by necessary two-thirds majority the accession of the GDR to the Federal Republic of Germany at midnight on October 2/3.

August 24. Bundesrat approves unitary electoral law with 5 per cent hurdle for parties to enter *Bundestag*.

August 31. GDR and Federal Republic sign 900-page unification treaty in East Berlin.

September 12. Two-Plus-Four talks concluded in Moscow; wartime allies abandon remaining responsibilities in Germany.

September 13. German-Soviet co-operation treaty signed; Soviet troops to withdraw from East German territory by 1994; Germany to contribute DM 15 billion to USSR.

September 28. GDR Housing Minister Axel Viehweger (FDP) resigns after admitting contact with *Stasi*.

September 30. Federal Constitutional Court in Karlsruhe rules electoral law unconstitutional on grounds of unfairness to GDR parties.

October 1. East and West German CDU unite.

October 3. At midnight GDR joins the Federal Republic of Germany; Berlin capital of Germany (although government still in Bonn).

October 5. New *Bundestag* meets, with 144 delegated members from GDR; approves revised electoral law; de Maizière, **Krause**, Bergmann-Pohl, **Ortleb** and Walther join Kohl cabinet as ministers without portfolio.

October 12. Assassination attempt in Baden on Interior Minister Wolfgang **Schäuble** leaves him crippled.

October 14. Elections to five reconstituted East German *Landtage* give CDU victory in four (53.8 per cent of vote in **Saxony**); SPD ahead only in Brandenburg (38.3 per cent); SPD loses ground in Bavarian election.

October 19. Police raid PDS headquarters in Berlin.

October 20. Colonel Joachim Krase (d. 1988), formerly deputy head of military intelligence service (MAD), revealed as *Stasi* spy.

October 25. *Bundestag* passes third supplementary budget, raising expenditure from DM 312 billion to DM 396 billion to pay for unification costs.

October 26. Gysi admits PDS illegally transferred DM 100 million to USSR; denies prior knowledge.

November 1. Last of five new *Land* governments formed in Brandenburg: **Stolpe** (SPD) leads coalition of SPD, FDP and Alliance 90; other governments: **Gies** in **Saxony-Anhalt**, **Biedenkopf** in Saxony, **Gomolka** in **Mecklenburg-West Pomerania**, **Duchac** in **Thuringia** (all CDU, leading coalitions with FDP, except Saxony — CDU alone).

November 12. CDU leadership in Bonn declares that German unity will be financed without tax increases.

November 14. Germany and Poland sign border treaty, reaffirming Oder-Neisse line.

November 15. Alternative List (Greens) leaves coalition with SPD in West Berlin government over treatment of squatters in East Berlin.

November 19–21. CSCE meeting in Paris declares end of Cold War and divided Europe.

December 2. Elections to all-German *Bundestag* won by Kohl coalition: CDU/CSU 319 seats (43.8 per cent of vote); SPD 239 (33.5 per cent); FDP 79 (11.0 per cent); PDS 17 (2.4 per cent); Alliance 90/Greens 8 (3.9 per cent); CDU tops poll in election to Berlin House of Representatives (CDU 40.3 per cent; SPD 30.5 per cent) and seeks to form grand coalition; in East Berlin SPD ahead (SPD 32.1 per cent; CDU 25.0 per cent; PDS 23.6 per cent).

December 3. Coalition negotiations begin (lasting until mid-January); Economics Minister Helmut **Haussmann** resigns; Lafontaine declines leadership of SPD.

December 5. Vogel re-elected parliamentary chairman of SPD, but does not wish to continue as party chairman.

December 9. De Maizière denies renewed accusations of past *Stasi* activity.

December 11. Finance ministers of five new *Länder* and Berlin demand higher funding; renewed aspersions about *Stasi* past force Böhme to resign from SPD executive.

December 17. De Maizière resigns from government and deputy party leadership because of allegations of *Stasi* complicity; SPD executive proposes Björn **Engholm**, minister president of **Schleswig-Holstein**, as next party chairman, succeeding Vogel.

December 20. Newly elected *Bundestag* meets in Berlin *Reichstag*, with 519 members from west Germany and 143 members from east Germany.

December 31. 642,200 unemployed in former GDR; 1.8 million on short-time.

1991

January 13. Minister President of **Baden-Württemberg** Lothar Späth (CDU) resigns over illegal expenses affair; succeeded by Erwin Teufel (on January 22).

January 16. Kohl cabinet announced; few major changes; FDP retains control of Economics Ministry (Jürgen **Möllemann**); posts for East Germans: Günther Krause (CDU) transport, Angela **Merkel** (CDU) women and youth, Rainer Ortleb (FDP) education.

January 17. United Nations' Gulf War against Iraq begins; Kohl, just reappointed Chancellor, pledges that no German troops will participate.

January 20. *Landtag* election in **Hesse** gives SPD narrow victory; Hans Eichel (SPD) to become Minister President.

January 24. CDU-SPD grand coalition *Land* government formed in Berlin; Eberhard **Diepgen** (CDU) elected Governing Mayor.

January 29. Bonn government promises financial assistance to USA and Israel in Gulf War.

January 31. *Bundesbank* raises interest rates.

February 6. Federal cabinet drafts bill to regulate property claims in east Germany.

February 12. Federal government promises additional support for eastern *Länder*, including immediate DM 5 billion.

February 19. Federal Environment Minister Töpfer announces programme of ecological reconstruction in eastern Germany, costing DM 17 billion in 1991.

February 26. Government coalition parties agree on tax increases from July 1, 1991.

February 28. Ceasefire ends Gulf War.

March 5. Unions and employers agree on wage increases for 1.7 million public service workers in east Germany from July 1, 1991, taking pay to 60 per cent of west German levels.

March 25. EC announces aid to east German *Länder* and east Berlin worth DM 6.2 billion.

April 1. Military organization of Warsaw Pact dissolved; President of *Treuhandanstalt* Rohwedder murdered in Düsseldorf by Red Army Faction.

April 8. Lifting of visa regulations for Polish visitors to Germany.

April 11. *Treuhandanstalt* rejects claims that fraud had cost it millions.

April 14. Birgit **Breuel** takes over as president of the *Treuhandanstalt*.

April 15. Expert committee predicts good medium-term growth prospects for eastern *Länder*.

April 21. CDU suffers heavy defeat in *Landtag* election in **Rhineland-Palatinate**, Kohl's home state; government passes to SPD (Rudolf Scharping elected Minister President, May 21).

April 23. Chancellor Kohl announces his support for Berlin as seat of parliament and government; Constitutional Court declares that property confiscations in the Soviet Occupation Zone 1945–49 must stand.

May 16. *Bundesbank* President Karl Otto **Pöhl** announces his early retirement, citing personal reasons.

May 21. Arrest of former GDR prime minister Willi Stoph, former GDR defence minister Heinz Kessler and two others on charges of ordering shootings on the former inter-German border.

CHRONOLOGY OF EVENTS 1989–92

May 29. Björn Engholm elected chairman of SPD in place of Hans-Jochen Vogel.

June 2. **Hamburg** election sees SPD success and CDU decline; Henning Voscherau (SPD) remains mayor; Federal CDU leadership rejects SPD call for a referendum on Bonn or Berlin as seat of government; Dresden neo-Nazi leader Rainer Sonntag shot dead in the city.

June 3. Red Army Faction terrorist Susanne Albrecht sentenced to 12 years' imprisonment.

June 6. Harry Tisch sentenced to 18 months' imprisonment for embezzlement of GDR union funds.

June 20. *Bundestag* votes by a majority of 18 in favour of Berlin as future seat of parliament and government.

June 24. Federal Transport Minister Krause (CDU) rejects accusations of malpractice with regard to motorway service station concessions.

July 1. Tax rises to help finance German unity come into effect for one year; eastern command of *Bundeswehr* dismantled.

July 4. Werner **Münch** (CDU) elected successor to Gerd Gies (CDU) as Minister President of Saxony-Anhalt.

July 9. Governing parties agree to Economics Minister Möllemann's demand for cuts in subsidies and tax concessions totalling DM 33.33 billion 1992–94; former leader of GDR CDU, Gerald Götting, sentenced to 18 months imprisonment suspended for misappropriation of CDU funds.

July 31. Helmut Schlesinger takes over from Pöhl as president of *Bundesbank*, with Hans Tietmeyer as deputy.

August 9. Federal and European Minister in Saxony-Anhalt, Brunner (FDP), resigns because of former *Stasi* connections (followed on August 13 by Agriculture Minister Mintus (CDU)).

August 12. Finance Minister Waigel confirms increase in VAT would be limited to 1 per cent, up to 15 per cent.

August 15. *Bundesbank* raises interest rates (Lombard rate from 9.0 per cent to 9.25 per cent, discount rate from 6.5 per cent to 7.5 per cent).

August 17. Remains of the Prussian kings Frederick William I and Frederick II (the Great) reburied at Sanssouci palace in Potsdam.

August 19–21. Abortive putsch against Gorbachev in the USSR.

September 6. De Maizière resigns deputy chairmanship of CDU and all other party posts.

September 29. In **Bremen** election CDU and extreme right **German People's Union** (DVU) gain ground.

September–October. Racist attacks increase on foreign refugees in east and west Germany.

October 7. Treaty of good neighbourliness signed with Czechoslovakia.

November 23. Ulf **Fink** defeats Kohl's candidate, Angela Merkel, in election for presidency of CDU in Brandenburg.

November 29. *Bundestag* agrees budget of DM 422.1 billion for 1992, requiring new borrowing of DM 45.3 billion.

December 19. *Bundesbank* raises interest rates by 0.5 per cent (Lombard rate to 9.75 per cent, discount rate to 8.0 per cent).

December 23. German government recognizes independence of Croatia and Slovenia.

December. Mikhail Gorbachev resigns.

1992

January 7. Former mayor of Dresden, Berghofer, admits in court that he falsified May 1989 election results.

January 20. Former border guard, Ingo Heinrich, sentenced to three-and-a-half years imprisonment for shooting Chris Gueffroy at Berlin Wall in February 1989.

January 28. Chancellor Kohl nominates Bernhard **Vogel** (CDU) as Minister President of Thuringia, replacing Josef Duchac (CDU).

January. German unemployment reaches 3.24 million (6.3 per cent of workforce in west, 16.5 per cent in east).

February 7. Treaty on European Union signed at Maastricht.

February 10. Former *Stasi* head Mielke goes on trial for two murders committed in 1931.

February 14. Bundesrat approves rise in VAT to 15 per cent from January 1993, after Brandenburg government (SPD-led) breaks ranks on SPD anti-increase policy.

March 4. IG Metall demands 9.5 per cent pay rise for metalworkers.

March 5. SPD threatens to block ratification of Maastricht treaties unless changes negotiated.

March 13. Minister Presidents of all 16 *Länder* demand role in negotiations about contributions to EC.

March 18. Bundesbank warns that tax rises inevitable if public spending not cut back.

March 19. Berndt **Seite** (CDU) replaces Alfred Gomolka (CDU) as Minister President of Mecklenburg-West Pomerania.

March 31. Defence Minister Gerhard Stoltenberg (CDU) forced to resign over illegal arms shipments to Turkey; to be succeeded by CDU general secretary Volker Rühe.

April 5. In *Landtag* election in Baden-Württemberg CDU vote slumps and Republicans become third party with 10.9 per cent; in Schleswig-Holstein extreme right German People's Union (DVU) wins 6.3 per cent but SPD holds onto overall majority of *Landtag* seats.

April 27. Genscher announces resignation from foreign Ministry; public service workers' strikes begin in Western Germany.

April 28. FDP parliamentary party rejects Kohl's and Lambsdorff's nomination of Irmgard Schwaetzer as new foreign Minister; Klaus Kinkel chosen instead.

May 4. Public service workers' strikes intensify.

THE SHAPE OF GERMANY BEFORE 1949

A glance at the central European pages of any historical atlas will reveal medieval and early modern "Germany" as a coloured composition worthy of Jackson Pollock. Even into the 19th century the territory comprised numerous, sometimes tiny, city states, bishoprics, duchies, principalities and electorates. The lands of each of them were also divided, with many complicated territorial enclaves and exclaves. Some of the states were of greater size and importance — such as **Brandenburg**-Prussia, **Saxony, Bavaria** and Austria — and some areas were governed by external monarchies — Denmark and Sweden, for instance. Most, but not all lands thought of as "German" were within the Holy Roman Empire of the German Nation (a 14th-century designation), but this territory also included many other peoples — Italians, Danes, Poles, Sorbs, Czechs, French, Dutch and others. Even those whom we might latterly describe as "Germans" were various indeed in language, culture and — since the Reformation — in religious confession. The territorial extent of states familiar to us today also altered continually through war, treaty and inheritance. In 1807, for instance, Bavaria did not hold some of its present-day Franconian lands in the north but did stretch southwards through the Tyrol and down to Lake Garda in present-day Italy. In the same year the Kingdom of Saxony was much larger than, and of a different shape from, the Free State of Saxony reconstituted in 1990. The territory now known as the Rhine Palatinate, and the birthplace of Chancellor Helmut Kohl, bears scant relationship to the land known as the Palatinate fought over in the Thirty Years War (1618–48).

It took Napoleon to abolish the Holy Roman Empire (1806), to redraw the map of central Europe and to reduce the number of German states. His alterations were then largely adopted by the Vienna settlement of 1815, leaving 38 states (39 from 1817). Two larger polities dominated the new German Confederation: Prussia, which stretched from the Prussian heartlands in the far north-east, through Silesia and Brandenburg to the newly acquired Rhine Province in the west; and the Habsburg Empire ("Austria"), which within the Confederation held Bohemia and Moravia, Austria itself, the Tyrol and Illyria. Outside the Confederation the Habsburgs ruled wider stretches of southern and south-eastern Europe, including Hungary and northern Italy. Of the other German states, the most significant were the Kingdoms of Bavaria, Württemberg, Saxony and Hanover (in personal union with the British crown until Victoria's accession in 1837) and the Grand Duchies of Baden and Hesse.

Before the 19th century it is therefore difficult to define what might be meant by "Germany". Certainly there was a literary culture uniting the German-speaking lands, but this had been primarily fostered during the 18th century and reached a highpoint in the talents of Goethe (1749–1832) and Schiller (1759–1805). Also the Napoleonic Wars generated a myth of the "Wars of Liberation", which was fostered by some philosophers, writers and political figures, not always in accord with the historical facts. Nationalism also often went hand-in-hand with new liberal notions. Thus when Hoffmann von Fallersleben in 1841 wrote the "Song of the Germans" on the then British island of Heligoland he sang of "unity and justice and freedom" as well as of German women and German wine and of "Germany above all else" ("Deutschland über alles"). Also when he described the borders of his Germany as "from the Maas to the Memel" (from the Meuse in present-day France, Belgium and the Netherlands to the border between Lithuania and Russia) and "from the Etsch to the Belt" (from the Adige in Italy to the sea channels of Denmark), he was not advocating drastic expansion but describing where Germans lived.

In the event the nation state of Germany which emerged in the 19th century was far less ambitious in extent; it was a so-called "small German" solution, excluding even the major power of Austria. It derived from the Customs Union of 1834 and took shape in the 1860s under the aegis of Bismarck's Prussia. Wars against Denmark (1864), Austria (1866) and France (1870) expanded Prussia's influence and the borders of what was in January 1871 to become the German Empire. This "Second Reich" (after the "First Reich" of the Holy Roman Empire) was therefore only one of many possible forms of German state and it was to last only until 1918. In the wake of defeat in the First World War a republic was declared — the "Weimar Republic" after the **Thuringian** city where the National Assembly convened — which faced under the Versailles Treaty of 1919 substantial territorial losses in the west, north, south-east and north-east. Henceforth, East Prussia was separated from the rest of the Reich by the so-called Polish corridor, and the **Saarland** in the west was detached from the Reich, pending a later plebiscite.

These territorial concessions were but one of the issues which preoccupied Adolf Hitler after he had taken power in 1933 in the so-called "Third Reich". He set about revising the conditions of the Versailles Treaty and further expanding German territory. At first the other European powers acquiesced, as Germany annexed Austria and the Sudetenland fringes of Czechoslovakia in 1938 and the remainder of the Czech lands in 1939. Hitler's onslaught on Poland in September 1939 provoked Britain and France to declare war, but did not save Poland from dismemberment by the Germans and their temporary Soviet allies. During the course of the war the boundaries of the Greater German Reich were expanded to exert a rule of terror over most of central and eastern Europe. Within the Reich the boundaries between the German states had been abandoned in favour of *Gaue* (provinces) which for all the Nazi pseudo-traditional rhetoric only partly conformed to historical divisions. Once again the shape of Germany was an arbitrary one.

The defeat of Hitler's Reich led to the occupation of Germany and Austria by the armed forces of the United States, the Soviet Union, Britain and France. The cities of **Berlin** and Vienna, both within Soviet-controlled territory, were divided into four occupation zones. The Austrian Republic was to be freed from occupation in 1955 and to develop as a separate German state. The Soviet zone of Germany and the three western zones were to become the respective bases of the two German republics of the post-war era.

The Germany of 1945 was not only occupied but further reduced in size, primarily in the east. The Soviet Union retained the Polish territory it had annexed in 1939 and compensated the Poles by extending the borders of the refounded Polish state to the Oder and western Neisse rivers. The western allies had understood that the eastern Neisse had been intended, which would have left a large portion of Silesia within German territory, but they did not prevent the Soviet plan. Large numbers of Germans were expelled from East and West Prussia, eastern Brandenburg and Pomerania, and from Silesia. As far as many of these people and the west German authorities were concerned, the lost territories were "under Polish" or "under Soviet administration", and appeared as such on west German maps for many years afterwards. During the process of German reunification in 1990 the issue came alive again, with demands being raised that the claim be not abandoned to the "frontiers of 1937", that is, to the position after the return of the Saarland to Germany in 1935, but before the annexation of Austria in 1938.

From 1945 each of the occupying powers had its own policies with regard to its part of Germany, but there was no initial intention (except perhaps on the part of the French) permanently to divide the country. However, once the British and Americans had created a common economic zone called "Bizonia" in 1947 (later joined by the French) and introduced currency reform in 1948, the gulf between the western powers and the Soviet Union widened considerably. The beginnings of the Cold War and specific quarrels over Berlin led to separate political and economic development in the west and east. It was in fact the West Germans who first established a separate state by promulgating the Basic Law of the Federal Republic of Germany in May 1949 and holding elections in August. They resulted in a narrow victory for the **Christian Democratic Union** and **Christian Social Union** (CDU/CSU) and the appointment in September of Konrad Adenauer (CDU), the former mayor of Cologne in the Weimar Republic, as Federal Chancellor.

Although the West Germans moved first, the intentions of the political leaders in the Soviet zone and their Moscow mentors had already become clear. On October 7, 1949 the German Democratic Republic was established and the Soviet Military Administration in Germany was dissolved. By the end of the year diplomatic recognition had been accorded by the Soviet Union and by the new socialist states of Eastern Europe and the Far East. The GDR was — until 1990 — to be firmly bound into the structures of Soviet-dominated communism.

A BRIEF HISTORY OF THE GERMAN DEMOCRATIC REPUBLIC

The pre-history of the German left

The GDR was founded in 1949 on the territory of the Soviet occupation zone, but it had deeper German roots as well. During the last quarter of the 19th century the **Social Democratic Party of Germany** (SPD) had grown to become the largest socialist party in the world. In 1891 at Erfurt in **Thuringia** it adopted a Marxist programme, but in general the party pursued political and economic change through legal reformist activity. On the eve of the First World War the SPD had about one million members and the trade unions associated with it about 2.5 million. The city of **Berlin** and the industrial cities of **Saxony** were heartlands of German Social Democracy. The SPD was also by now the largest party in the *Reichstag*, but the political system did not permit it any role in government. Despite an internationalist and anti-imperialist programme, the SPD parliamentary party approved funds for the German war effort in 1914. This helped to provoke a split in the party in 1917, when the left formed the **Independent Social Democratic Party of Germany** (USPD). It was from within the radical left of the USPD that the **Communist Party of Germany** (KPD) emerged at the end of 1918, after revolution had brought down the German dynasties and propelled the SPD and USPD into power. When Communist uprisings took place in Berlin and Munich in 1919, they were quelled with a savagery sanctioned by the SPD, and this was one of the factors which led to a deep gulf between the parties of the left in the ensuing years.

After elections in early 1919 the SPD governed nationally in coalition with the Catholic Centre Party and the liberal German Democratic Party, but this arrangement did not survive the political and economic crises of the early republic and the SPD played at most a minor role in government until 1928–30. At municipal and *Land* level, however — most notably in the largest state of Prussia and its capital of Berlin — the SPD did lead coalitions and initiated major programmes of social welfare.

In the hyper-inflation year of 1923 the states of Thuringia and Saxony were the scenes of attempts by the KPD, in local coalition with the SPD, to take Germany back onto a revolutionary path. The entry of Communists into the state governments moved the Reich government to adopt the reserve powers of SPD Reich President Ebert and remove the KPD influence. Thereafter the KPD, under the leadership of Ernst Thälmann and increasingly directed from Moscow, attacked the SPD for its reformism and collaboration with bourgeois parties and state institutions. By the final years of the republic the KPD line, derived from Stalin, was to denounce the SPD rather than Hitler's National Socialists as the main enemy — as so-called "social fascists".

From 1930 parliamentary government was all but dead in Germany, as Chancellor Brüning used President Hindenburg's powers to rule by decree. The SPD tolerated much of his legislation, but was excluded from power. Meanwhile, the political extremes of right and left made strong advances, benefiting from the economic depression and mass unemployment. The Nazis gained strength from an apprehensive and impoverished middle class, and the KPD won support from the working-class unemployed. In the November 1932 elections the Nazis won 196 *Reichstag* seats and the KPD 100, drawing closer to the SPD's 121.

Although the KPD and SPD had jointly more seats than the National Socialists, the feud between them weakened their resistance to the Nazi threat. When Hitler was appointed Chancellor in January 1933, both parties were banned, trade union offices were destroyed, and Social Democrats and Communists were despatched to concentration camps, where many — including Thälmann — died, or were forced into exile. Some underground opposition activity continued, carried out by such zealots as the young Erich **Honecker**, but it was of little effect. Honecker himself was arrested in 1935 and spent the rest of the Third Reich in gaol. The Soviet Union was the destination of many Communists, including future GDR leaders Wilhelm Pieck and Walter Ulbricht. They and others were schooled in the harsh world of Stalinism and many did not survive the purges. In 1943 in Moscow Ulbricht helped to found the National Committee for a Free Germany, in preparation for the reconstruction of Germany after the defeat of the Third Reich, and the introduction of a Communist system.

The pre-1945 experience defined the emergent socialist state in a variety of ways. The GDR derived from a long tradition of German revolutionary socialism which had then been distorted by Stalinism. The inability of the left to stop Hitler was, though, seen by many Social Democrats as a reason to join forces with the Communists. The Communists were only too keen to assert their authority on an amalgamated political left. The sufferings of both Social Democrats and Communists at the hands of the Nazis and the barbarism of the Hitler regime also gave to the GDR a specific "anti-fascist" purpose and rhetoric which it maintained to the last.

Soviet occupation and the amalgamation of the left

The Soviet Military Administration in Germany (SMAD) purged heavily implicated Nazis from positions of power and confiscated large industrial and agricultural property. Much industrial and transport equipment was dismantled and removed to the Soviet Union by way of reparations. As the political exiles returned, SMAD permitted the KPD and the SPD to regroup, and approved the formation of two non-socialist parties, the **Christian Democratic Union** (CDU) and the **Liberal Democratic Party of Germany** (LDPD). These were later joined in the so-called National Front of all parties by the **Democratic Farmers' Party of Germany** (DBD), by the **National Democratic Party of Germany** (NDPD), a party for ex-officers, ex-Nazis not implicated in war crimes and the middle class, by the **Free German Trade Union League** (FDGB), and by the **Free German Youth** (FDJ).

Although the ruling party for most of the GDR's history was often loosely termed "the Communist Party", it was in fact an amalgamation of the two previously warring factions of the German left, the SPD and the KPD. In recognition of the alleged new harmony, the party which emerged in April 1946 was called the **Socialist Unity Party of Germany** (SED). At its head stood the joint chairmen, Wilhelm Pieck of the KPD and Otto Grotewohl of the SPD. At the foundation of the party, the SPD membership stood at around 679,000 and the KPD's at 619,000. This apparent pre-eminence of the SPD did not prevent the KPD element from acquiring a rapid dominance of the party. Communists were more likely than their Social Democratic allies to be appointed or promoted to party posts and in January 1949 the principle of parity between the two was abandoned. Furthermore, the party soon became a more centrally directed organization, with real power in the hands of the small *Politbüro*. This had a Communist majority and here, as in the rest of the party, the Social Democrats found themselves pushed into a subordinate position. The other parties of the SED-dominated National Front were also forced into an orthodox line, but they maintained a function of providing a political home for those who, for reasons of religion, class or ideology, were thought unsuitable for membership of the SED.

In the autumn of 1946 local and regional elections were held in the Soviet zone, and the SED achieved a substantial plurality but no overall majority. However, in the one place — Berlin — where the SPD had been able to retain an existence separate from the KPD, it became clear how the Communists had hijacked the German left in the Soviet zone. The SED came third behind the SPD and the CDU in Berlin as a whole, and second to the SPD in the Soviet sector. It was evident that if the SED was going to shape a new Germany, that Germany might have to be part only of the old Reich.

The Ulbricht era 1950–71

On the foundation of the GDR in October 1949 Wilhelm Pieck (formerly KPD) became president and Otto Grotewohl (formerly SPD) prime minister, but they were not the men who dominated the early history of the state. Walter Ulbricht was elected to the *Politbüro* in January 1949 and as General Secretary of the SED in July 1950. He then shaped it in his image, as a disciplined, orthodox Marxist-Leninist party. All the debate which there had been about a specifically "German" socialist path, distinct from the Soviet model, was now abandoned and those who did not conform were purged from party membership.

The first major crisis of the GDR came in the summer of 1953, after the death of Stalin. The raising of work norms by at least 10 per cent provoked an uprising of workers in East Berlin and other cities on June 17. It was explained officially as the work of paid criminal elements from West Berlin, and was violently suppressed by Soviet troops. The new norms were retracted, however, and Ulbricht himself survived by pinning the blame on others and purging them from the leadership.

In the 1950s the GDR began to establish itself as a distinct independent state, although it relied heavily on Soviet tutelage. In 1950 the GDR joined the Council for Mutual Economic Assistance (CMEA, "Comecon", or RGW in German). In 1954 the Soviet Union recognized the sovereignty of the GDR. In 1956, after the Federal Republic of Germany had joined NATO, the GDR formed its own **National People's Army** (NVA) and Ministry for National Defence, and joined the Warsaw Treaty Organization.

The East German economy in the 1950s faced massive problems of reconstruction and the perceived need to compete with and overtake the economic performance of the Federal Republic. In mid-decade a so-called "new course" allowed some private enterprise to continue, but this was replaced by a concerted drive for full socialization. Centralized state planning was instituted on a seven- (later five-) year basis; most industry was nationalized; and a programme of agricultural collectivization was launched, culminating in the almost complete eradication of individual peasant farming by 1960.

Political repression and evidence that the economy of the Federal Republic was providing opportunities and a standard of living impossible in the GDR led to emigration westwards of over a hundred thousand GDR citizens each year. The city of Berlin was the favourite route, and in 1961 the Ulbricht regime decided in consultation with the Soviet Union to seal it off. On August 13, 1961, a wall was built between the Soviet sector and West Berlin and around the territory of West Berlin. At the same time the frontier between the GDR and the Federal Republic was tightly sealed.

The 1960s saw new twists and turns in an attempt to speed economic advance. Production incentives were introduced and aspects of the economy were decentralized. In 1965 nine new industrial ministries replaced the overall Economic Council. From 1968, however, partly in response to the events in Czechoslovakia which GDR troops had helped to halt, centralized planning returned to the forefront.

The GDR under Honecker 1971–89

The years 1970–71 saw significant changes for the GDR. Ulbricht responded only reluctantly to overtures being made by the new Social Democratic Chancellor of the Federal Republic, Willy Brandt, to reach an accord between the two German states. He was also not in favour of proposals for a four-power agreement on Berlin. Ulbricht's concern was that the separate identity of the GDR, enforced by the Berlin Wall and fostered in such aspects of GDR life as sport (the GDR fielded a separate Olympic team in 1968), would be eroded by closer contacts between the Germanies and a more relaxed situation in Berlin. His stance, combined with a worsened economic situation in 1970, led both domestic critics and the Kremlin to drop him. In May 1971 Ulbricht was replaced as First Secretary of the SED by Erich Honecker, his long-time protégé.

Brandt's *Ostpolitik* (eastern policy) led from meetings with prime minister Willi Stoph in Erfurt and Kassel in 1970 to detailed negotiations on the character of future inter-German relations. In December 1972 the two Germanies signed the so-called Basic Treaty, in 1973 both were admitted to the United Nations, from 1973 the GDR began to receive diplomatic recognition by foreign states (Britain in 1973, the USA in 1974), and in 1974 the GDR and the Federal Republic established permanent missions (below embassy status) in Bonn and (East) Berlin respectively. The agreements between the two German states did nothing to alter the Federal Republic's constitutional claim to act on behalf of all Germans, nor the GDR's insistence on its status as a sovereign state, but they did open the way for increased trade, some relaxation of travel restrictions, and co-operation in numerous other fields.

Meanwhile, the Soviet Union, United States, Britain and France signed in September 1971 the Four Power Agreement on Berlin. This went a long way towards regularizing the status of the city and avoiding the tensions of 1948 and 1961. The western powers conceded that West Berlin was not strictly part of the Federal Republic of Germany, while the Soviet Union pledged to keep open the transit routes to that part of the city. West Berliners were also to be allowed greater access to the territory of the GDR.

The constitution of the GDR, as amended in 1974, enshrined a multitude of political and human rights which were blatantly ignored in practice. It also entrenched the irreversible alliance of the GDR with the Soviet Union and the leading political role of the SED. This meant that the GDR was governed by a complex interaction between party and state on the basis of "democratic centralism". Most state functions at national and local level were also covered by party secretaries. Constitutionally, the parliament or People's Chamber (***Volkskammer***) was the highest organ of state, but since there were no freely contested elections, it was a rubber-stamp for the ruling party. The presidency of the GDR was abolished in 1960, and the head of state was the Chairman of the State Council (*Staatsrat*). This post was occupied from 1976 to 1989 by Erich Honecker. The Council of Ministers (*Ministerrat*) was officially the government of the GDR, but it was overshadowed by the SED party apparatus. The prime minister (Chairman of the Council of Ministers) was Willi Stoph from 1976 to 1989.

The economic troubles of the early 1970s were eased somewhat by the new centralized policies, but with a time lag the oil crisis hit the GDR too, as the Soviet Union increased its prices to its allies. Domestic industrial production in the GDR was inadequate and the ties to the CMEA partners made it difficult to develop strong exports to earn hard currency. Debt to the West was growing alarmingly.

The 1980s began in economic and political gloom. High debt levels and poor economic performance combined with international tension over Afghanistan, Poland and the stationing of new nuclear weapons in Europe. Within the GDR there arose a dissident church-based peace movement, which gathered considerable support before being weakened by police repression, the forced emigration of many of its activists and eventually by a diminution of super-power tension. This peace movement was, however, a precursor of what was to emerge later.

By the mid-1980s the economic and political situation of the GDR was apparently much improved. It is no coincidence that what was to be the highpoint, the year of 1984, with record economic performance and a proposed Honecker visit to the Federal Republic, was the 35th anniversary of the GDR. Early in the year large numbers of citizens were permitted to emigrate, in an attempt to rid the country of malcontents. The economy did seem to be on the upturn, with a reported record growth rate of 5.5 per cent in Net Material Product. A hard-currency trade surplus was achieved, and foreign debt stabilized so much that Western credit was once more forthcoming. The only disappointments for Honecker were that the GDR had to boycott the Los Angeles Olympics and that in its dying throes, the old Kremlin leadership instructed him not to accept the invitation to visit the Federal Republic.

With hindsight it can be seen that much of this achievement was contrived and based on weak premises. The GDR economy did pick itself up out of the recession of the early 1980s, even if allowance is made for the deliberate falsification of statistics which has since been admitted. However, the recovery, particularly on the hard currency side, was based largely on the import, processing and re-export to the West of oil products. The rest of GDR industry was less dynamic and was building up problems for the future. Lignite production, for instance, was boosted strongly — from 278 million tonnes in 1983 to 312 million tonnes in 1985 — but stagnated thereafter as mining became more difficult, and meanwhile exacerbated the dreadful pollution associated with it. Other industries were starved of investment as money was pumped recklessly into already out-dated microtechnology. The provision of the population with consumer goods, however, did not improve sufficiently, and staple prices for food, accommodation and transport could only be kept down by increasing the large state subsidies. These, it has since been conceded, were funded by hard-currency borrowing not revealed in the state budgets of the Ministry of Finance.

Erich Honecker meanwhile adopted the role of world statesman. His initial setback over the visit to the Federal Republic was overcome when he set forth for **Bonn** in September 1987. This was a personal triumph for him and for his perception of the GDR, but it was, of course, the same Mikhail Gorbachev who allowed him to travel who was later to be his undoing. The Bonn visit was one of many around the world, including several to NATO countries. As the 40th anniversary of the GDR approached, Honecker could look with some pride on the international acceptance of the GDR, on apparent economic advance and on a successfully imposed social and political peace.

THE COLLAPSE OF THE COMMUNIST REGIME IN THE GDR

The origins of the crisis

On July 11, 1989 the official party newspaper of the **SED,** *Neues Deutschland*, announced in a brief report that after treatment in hospital the General Secretary of the Central Committee of the SED and Chairman of the State Council of the GDR, Erich **Honecker**, had the previous day gone on his annual holiday "according to plan". The GDR was a planned economy and a planned society, so it was fitting that even in a minor personal emergency the country's leader should stick to the rules. If Erich Honecker's vacation went according to plan, however, it was just about the only event of 1989 which did. The year which was on October 7 supposed to crown 40 years of socialist achievement instead saw the beginnings of a spectacular collapse of the GDR and the first hints that it might no longer be viable as an independent state.

Honecker's gall-bladder complaint and his advancing years (77 in the summer of 1989) contributed to the crisis of confidence at the top and the personnel changes of the autumn, but only as part of a general transformation. In order to understand the developments of 1989, one must look at both the international and domestic situation of the GDR in that year.

Influences from outside the GDR

The international context was defined primarily by the appointment back in March 1985 of Mikhail Gorbachev as General Secretary of the Communist Party of the Soviet Union. Although it took some while for Gorbachev's new approach of *glasnost* (openness) and *perestroika* (restructuring) to establish itself even in the Soviet Union, the publicity given to him — not least on the West German television viewed by most East Germans — had a major impact on perceptions in the GDR. For Honecker and his closest associates in the SED leadership the problem was that they were defiantly loyal to the Soviet Union, but now the Soviet Union was itself changing. Honecker soon came to dislike Gorbachev (and Boris Yeltsin even more), but he had to maintain the stance of undying friendship. For Gorbachev the sham must have been even more painful.

In one important respect Gorbachev did Honecker a big favour. The latter's proposed visit to the Federal Republic had been called off humiliatingly at the last minute in 1984 at the behest of the old Kremlin leadership. Gorbachev, who as late as 1986 was himself opposing too close a contact with the West Germans and advising Honecker against going to **Bonn**, eventually gave his blessing to a rescheduled trip, which took place in the autumn of 1987. This gave Honecker an opportunity to demonstrate the independent identity of the GDR and its international respectability. Although both Germanies maintained their stances of principle and constitutionality, Honecker was in practice received with the dignity of a visiting foreign head-of-state. This, coupled with the large West German loans which were negotiated in the mid and late 1980s, suggested that the GDR could foster good relations with the Federal Republic without giving any political ground.

The SED leaders' approach to *glasnost* and *perestroika* was a complicated one. On the first count they could by 1989 point to concessions on travel to the west and to a greater element of public discussion in the electoral procedure (both minimal in their real impact), while in practice forbidding any real opening up of debate. It had even come to the point where revered communist authorities and Soviet publications were perceived as potentially dangerous. In January 1988 (and again a year later) unofficial demonstrations on the anniversary of the murders in 1919 of the early communists Rosa Luxemburg and Karl Liebknecht were broken up by the security forces. The demonstrators had dared to take up as a slogan Luxemburg's insistence that "freedom is always the freedom of others who think differently". In early 1988 issues of the Moscow-published *Neue Zeit* failed to be delivered to subscribers, and in November the Soviet German-language magazine *Sputnik* was withdrawn from sale because of the tone of its articles. Particularly offensive to the SED was a discussion of Hitlerism and Stalinism. The official announcement was that the Ministry for Post and Telecommunications had deleted *Sputnik* from its list of approved periodicals, but it later transpired that this was untrue. Honecker had intervened directly to ban the magazine.

Perestroika was countered in a rather different way. The SED leadership argued that while it respected and applauded the Soviet Union's own policies in the advancement of socialism and world peace, these were not appropriate to the GDR. The reason was that the GDR had already since the late 1970s conducted a thorough reform of its economic structures and did not on this occasion need to follow the Soviet example. As *Politbüro* member Kurt Hager famously put it in an interview with the West German magazine *Stern* in March 1987, "If your neighbour re-papered his flat, would you feel bound to re-paper your flat too?" Hager later said that he regretted the way in which he had expressed his views and the way in which they had been interpreted in the west. His intention, he said, had not been to suggest that the GDR was distancing itself from the Soviet Union, but merely that each state was finding its own way towards socialism. The reception to Gorbachev was not uniform in the *Politbüro*. If Honecker, Hager, **Mittag** and Mielke were hostile, others found hope in the new Soviet Union. Günter **Schabowski**, for instance, reports that when Gorbachev came to power he was an unknown to most of the *Politbüro* but came to appeal to the younger members like himself because of the more open way in which he spoke.

Amongst the population at large the example of Gorbachev came to be a powerful one, and it was not clouded by the negative aspects of his policies experienced by the peoples of the Soviet Union. In the GDR, where — as Honecker rightly insisted — economic performance and provision of goods were far in advance of the Soviet Union, there was no conflict between approving Gorbachev's political reforms and deploring the economic collapse and suppression of nationalisms. If the East German system were opened up, economic prosperity and consumer choice might be expected from the west, without the traumas of the Soviet Union. The enthusiasm was akin to that in western countries and was manifested — to Honecker's embarrassment — by the "Gorbi" shouts from the marchers at the October anniversary celebrations in 1989.

The Soviet Union was not the only ally of the GDR to be undergoing transformation. Well before Gorbachev the Poles had attempted through Solidarity to forge a democratic path and, although this had been temporarily curtailed by martial law from 1981 to 1983, public debate in Poland in the 1980s was far freer than in the GDR. The political upheaval of 1988–89 — with the institution of "round table" talks, the legalization of Solidarity, limited free elections, and the appointment of Tadeusz Mazowiecki from Solidarity as prime minister in September 1989 — could not fail to show the people of the GDR that change was afoot and, importantly, that the Soviet Union was not about to snuff it out with force. The apparent economic disaster of Poland was less encouraging, but another ally seemed to have that aspect under better control. Hungary had for years operated a limited market economy, which was familiar to the citizens of the GDR from their holidays there. In 1989 the Hungarians also displayed their commitment to greater contacts with the west by in May dismantling their physical border with Austria.

This decision by the Hungarians has rightly been seen as the catalyst for change in the GDR. The significance was that thousands of East Germans each year holidayed in Hungary and might now be able to use the new "green" border to emigrate unofficially. This was not at first permitted by the Hungarians, because East German holders of West German passports issued at the Federal German embassy in Budapest (under Federal German law East Germans had automatic Federal German citizenship if they sought it) did not have an appropriate visa and could not therefore leave the country. During the summer, however, the pressure built up, as more and more GDR citizens flocked to the impromptu camps on the Austrian frontier. These were now not just holiday-makers who saw a window of opportunity, but also people who had travelled to Hungary with the express purpose of emigration. On several occasions groups of them forced their way across, leading to a growing potential for violence. The West German government, meanwhile, exhorted the Hungarians to allow the people to leave and accompanied their moral encouragement with financial promises. From September 11 the Hungarians let the East Germans through. This provoked cries of outrage from East **Berlin**, with accusations that the Hungarians, in cahoots with the West Germans, were engaged in a "trade in human beings". At *Politbüro* meetings the talk was of the Hungarians having betrayed their GDR allies. The official attitude towards those leaving the country was just as vehement. An official communiqué declared that "We do not mourn after them". This contentious phrase was, according to SED secretary for agitation and propaganda Joachim Herrmann, inserted into the original draft by Erich Honecker himself.

Other would-be emigrants took refuge in the West German embassy in Warsaw, and even more serious were the events in Prague. The Czechs — along with the Romanians — were regarded as some of the few trustworthy communist allies left, but this did not prevent difficulties arising in the Czech capital. In August the West German embassy had to be closed because it was full of East Germans. The reintroduction of visa requirements for East German travel to Czechoslovakia and promises from East Berlin of amnesty and favourable treatment of those returning home voluntarily failed to defuse the situation. West German Foreign Minister Hans-Dietrich **Genscher** then managed at the end of September to negotiate an agreement with the Czechs and the East Germans. On September 30, to tumultuous acclaim which was to stand him and his **Free Democratic Party** in good stead in the coming year, he announced in the Prague embassy that those in refuge there would be allowed to leave by train for the Federal Republic. East Berlin's one stipulation was that the trains make a detour through the territory of the GDR. This perverse roundabout trip was meant to save the face of the SED, but in fact it achieved the opposite. When it became known in Dresden in early October that the sealed trains would pass through, large crowds gathered at the railway station, some in the hope of joining the exodus. There was violence, injury and damage as the security forces waded in.

One other event of international consequence needs to be added to the picture. In June 1989 the Chinese leadership had clamped down on the student reform movement in the bloodbath of Tiananmen Square, and the Honecker regime had shown alacrity in its approval of the measure. Various *Politbüro* members, later including Egon **Krenz**, visited China and expressed their support for the Beijing regime's approach to dissent. The message was intended as much for domestic consumption as for the Chinese, implying an open threat to those who might be contemplating mass protest in the GDR. In this regard, however, it backfired, since many people in the GDR were appalled by the Tiananmen massacre and by their government's condoning it. They were if anything spurred on by the incident to greater criticism of the system. Also, it is likely that many within the SED hierarchy now shied back from confrontation with dissidents; they had seen the bloody consequences of sending in the troops, and they realized the implications for the GDR's international position if such events were to be repeated in the centre of Europe. From the fact that serious force was not used in **Leipzig** in October 1989 it can be assumed that the Chinese incident informed developments in the GDR.

Domestic compliance and dissent

The East German revolution could not have taken place as and when it did if it had not been for the current international constellation, particularly the changed attitude on the part of the Soviet Union and the Hungarians' border policy. That it did take place, however, was due to deep stresses within the GDR itself. Here it is difficult to generalize, because while it is possible to list the issues which frustrated people — lack of freedom to travel, lack of freedom of speech and political expression, poor supply of consumer goods, militarization of schools, environmental pollution, surveillance and harassment and so on — this does not mean that everybody saw things in the same way or had the same priorities. The mass protests which were eventually the characteristic of the revolution in the GDR in the autumn of 1989 had diverse and indirect origins. Like those elsewhere in central and eastern Europe, they represented a coalition of protest which was of short duration.

Social life in the GDR was controlled and regimented, with a high degree of petty interference in people's lives. It has even been suggested — by the psychotherapist Hans-Joachim Maaz — that annoying and frustrating people was an unconscious or even deliberate tactic on the part of those in authority to deflect opposition into a feeling of helpless outrage. Opposition was also neutralized by the ways in which the system divided people from each other. No-one could speak completely openly with their colleagues, workmates, friends or acquaintances; there was always — except perhaps under the influence of alcohol — a reserve which had to be maintained in case one's companion was an "unofficial collaborator" with the **Stasi**. Even more laming perhaps was the knowledge that he or she harboured the same suspicions in return. Meanwhile everybody, or nearly everybody, went through the motions of mouthing loyalty to socialism and to the GDR, or retreated into public conformity and sullenness.

The full extent of this damage to the society has yet to be revealed, but some cases have shocked — that of Vera Wollenberger of the "Church from Below" and later of the Greens, for example. She discovered from her *Stasi* file that her husband had been informing on her for years. He was an "unofficial collaborator" under the code-name "Donald". Other instances were revealed of fathers informing on sons, and friends upon friends. The cumulative effect of this suspicion was to dampen or thwart overt dissent, but it was an explosive issue once it came into the open. On the one hand there was a genuine joy of liberation on the part of people who knew that they had been subject to chicanery, and on the other the horror of discovering that matters had been worse than they had even imagined.

Those who did take the step of declaring themselves critical of the system (and there were many degrees of this, of course) were very few. Some prominent writers could combine a critical stance with public acclaim within the GDR. Others — like the singer Wolf Biermann in the 1970s — had provoked the authorities to bar them from the country. This was the experience of one of the founders of **New Forum**, Bärbel **Bohley**, who was expelled from the GDR for a time in 1988. The general effect of official policy towards dissenting intellectuals was to weaken potential opposition. They and their complaints could usually be exported to West Germany, and there was less of that curious interlocking of party bureaucrats and dissenters which was to be found in Budapest, Warsaw and Prague.

Less formulated dissatisfaction was also exported. During the 1980s the numbers of people who were allowed officially to emigrate westward increased enormously, especially — as in 1984 — when the GDR wanted to stage national celebrations without foreign criticism or unpleasant incident. The effects of these departures were various. If those who were more determined left, then it might be assumed that those who stayed were the more docile and compliant. It also meant, however, that those who did go were on average younger and more highly qualified, thus denuding the GDR of talented people.

Emigration also had dreadfully disrupting effects on families and friendships, which were exploited to the full by the authorities, especially when the departure had not been officially sanctioned. Part of the anger could be diverted away from the state toward the person who had so inconsiderately left his or her relations, friends and colleagues in the lurch. The situation for those remaining could be very serious. If, for instance, one spouse left behind the other in a house which they owned jointly (house ownership was not general in the GDR, but far from unknown), a half share of the property was forfeit to the state. The deserted partner could therefore be forced to sell up and move. This was only one of the various penalties which could directly or indirectly be imposed in the authorities' revenge on those left behind. Individuals could also choose deliberately to inflict harm in this way. It is a sign of the deep dissatisfactions which there were, however, that despite these potential negative consequences, the numbers of applications for permission to leave continued to grow through the 1980s, creating a sense of uneasy impermanence in many families.

All these aspects of emigration came to the fore in 1989 when the exodus via Hungary and Austria began, and they help to explain the response of so many who did not leave. All the ambiguities of choosing to leave or not, the bitterness of those left behind, the determination not to be manipulated any longer by the regime, the industrial, transport, social and medical crises which developed as vast holes in the workforce began to appear, all these prompted the response which was to echo at the growing mass rallies in Leipzig and elsewhere: "We are staying here!" Most East Germans wanted after all not to leave their homes and families, but simply to have unrestricted access to West Germany and the wider world.

Another slogan of the Leipzig marchers quickly captured the world's imagination — "*We are the people*". Confronting the SED bureaucrats, who assumed in the name of "the people" a perpetual right to personal power, the demonstrators declared their sovereignty. They claimed a right to democratic participation which the political structures of the GDR had not hitherto allowed. This was an issue which had already excited controversy earlier in 1989. In May local elections had been held throughout the GDR, and opposition groups had dared to place observers at polling stations in order to monitor the staged ritual of approving the National Front. That they did so was partly the consequence of minor but much-publicized reforms in the system of selecting candidates announced by the chairman of the electoral commission, Egon Krenz.

The electoral system of the GDR meant that a "yes" vote to the uniform official list of candidates could be registered simply by placing the voting slip straight into the ballot box. Anyone using the voting cabin was presumably objecting to the list in some way or another. It required some courage and sense of purpose to expose oneself in this way to later criticism or harassment from the authorities. The monitors' observations on this occasion of voter refusal to return the official list unchallenged conspicuously did not tally with the published results, and there were protests against ballot-rigging, which continued monthly through the rest of the year. As significant, however, was the fact that even the official results indicated an increased willingness on the part of the electorate to vote against the approved candidates. It may seem extraordinary that those in charge of conducting the elections — the mayor of Dresden, Wolfgang **Berghofer**, for instance — felt the need to fiddle statistics which already indicated support of over 90 per cent, but they had to present the near unanimity required by the party and by Honecker in particular. Anything less would have laid them open to the charge that their own party organization was failing to maintain public morale.

Many of those protesting against the bogus electoral returns had a history of critical dissent on other issues, such as militarism and environmental pollution. These matters were not easily raised in public in the GDR, but there was one forum for discussion which was to play a significant role in the east German revolution — the church.

The churches in the GDR could not fulfil quite the same role as an alternative national focus as the Catholic church did in Poland, but they did continue a long central German Protestant tradition and they provided the one public arena which was not entirely subservient to the SED. Most practising Christians in the GDR belonged to one of the Protestant churches grouped together since 1969 in the Federation of Evangelical Churches in the GDR (*Bund der Evangelischen Kirchen in der DDR* - BEK). Estimates of membership in the late 1980s have been of about seven million people, though this is a high figure difficult to verify for the period of communist rule. It contrasts with the much smaller Roman Catholic community of some one million.

The relationship between church and state was not an easy one, but a *modus vivendi* was achieved in the 1970s and 1980s. In 1971 the BEK had declared that "We want to be a church not against, a church not besides, but a church in socialism", and in 1978 there took place an historic meeting between Erich Honecker and the BEK leadership, which led to a degree of autonomy for the churches in the pursuit of "basic humanitarian aims". The church rarely intervened in political matters, but practising Christians could pursue a form of political career in the **Christian Democratic Union** (CDU), one of the block parties of the GDR.

The accommodation between church and state and the role of the CDU were not without their critics. Many who in the church found — not exclusively for religious reasons — a forum for discussion of contentious political and social issues and of personal moral dilemmas felt that the institution had compromised too much with the SED regime. This distrust applied even more strongly to the CDU. Nevertheless, the churches did give a focus for dissenting voices and were the origin of several of the new political groupings which emerged in 1989. It is no coincidence that the mass demonstrations in Leipzig in the autumn of 1989 began each week after Monday evening religious services, nor that many of the emergent politicians of the revolution in the GDR were pastors of the evangelical churches.

The incapacity of the old regime

Against the buffeting of external and internal problems practically every step taken by the GDR leadership in the course of 1989 brought crisis nearer. In fact, the problem was usually that the regime was scarcely able to act at all. The response to the crisis of 1989 can only be understood against this background of a debilitating degeneration which had been taking place in the SED itself. From top to bottom the ruling party was in a paralyzed state — a situation which had its origins in the very nature of SED rule but also in an increasing failure to recognize reality.

Two of the main principles of the SED were party discipline and collective action. The first proved to be a straitjacket in the face of difficulty, preventing potentially influential figures from voicing criticism; the second was in any case a myth. The process of top-level decision-making in the GDR had always been difficult to pin down, and the memoirs, interviews and statements under interrogation of leading participants have only partly clarified the situation. One thing is plain: Erich Honecker was the principal well-spring of authority, in close collaboration with Erich Mielke and Günter Mittag, although the latter denies this. Honecker was at the head of the party secretariat, the *Politbüro*, the Council of State and the National Defence Council. Only the Council of Ministers was not his preserve, but that was scarcely a limitation.

Since the **Wende**, leading figures of the old regime have described the deliberations of the leading councils of the GDR and the overwhelming impression is that little of consequence was ever decided or even debated. Matters which were not deemed appropriate for detailed discussion — or in some cases even mention — by the *Politbüro* included the economy, the GDR's foreign debt, the environment, the *Stasi*, and in 1989 the exodus of citizens via Hungary — precisely those issues which needed urgent attention. Indeed over the years — according to Joachim Herrmann — the amount of discussion actually declined appreciably. This meant that *Politbüro* members had no experience of debating complex issues and coming to difficult decisions. They were usually faced with measures already decided by Honecker and his close associates or — more usually — they were simply not informed. Again and again the hearings of the ***Volkskammer***'s investigation committee of November 1989–February 1990 were told by former senior members of the decision-making bodies of the GDR that they did not know what was going on. This applied particularly to the economy (Mittag's responsibility) and the *Stasi* (Mielke's). This could be put down to a desire to escape blame, but in fact most of those interrogated — **Margot Honecker** being a determined exception — were all too willing to admit blame, even if they maintained that they had no remit in this or that specific matter.

These senior men were deliberately kept in the dark. Their areas of responsibility were very specific, so as to prevent them from gaining an overall picture, but also all too vague. There was such an overlapping of authority between the party secretaries, the ministers, the *Volkskammer* spokesmen, the Central Committee departmental leaders, the district secretaries and the *Stasi* that it was never entirely clear who was responsible for what. In many instances the underlying answer was that the *Stasi* was. An example of this was given by Wolfgang Herger, from 1985 SED Central Committee departmental leader for questions of security and a member of the highly-secretive National Defence Council. Herger told the *Volkskammer* investigation committee that when on taking office he telephoned Mielke to ask for information on certain matters he was told, "You're responsible for the political work, the party work; you're not to concern yourself with operational matters in the Ministry of

State Security". Similarly Egon Krenz, who was actually party secretary for security and also a member of the National Defence Council, claims that he was allowed no say in "operational matters".

It was assumed by several *Politbüro* members who were not on the National Defence Council that this was the body which was the powerful one in the state. It had authority, as its name suggests, over strategic matters of national security and its composition was not officially disclosed. In fact, the National Defence Council comprised 12 *Politbüro* members — amongst them Hager, Kessler, Krenz, Mielke, Mittag, Sindermann and **Stoph** — plus five members of the SED Central Committee, foremost amongst them the Council's secretary, *Generaloberst* Fritz Streletz. By all accounts the meetings of the National Defence Council were as anodyne and pre-programmed as those of the other party and state bodies. There was, for instance, no discussion of *Stasi* matters.

Even if one views the protestations of ignorance and non-involvement with scepticism, it is evident that — to say the least — channels of communication amongst the political leaders were poor. This applied particularly to the *Stasi* fiefdom of Mielke, who conducted his business with Honecker in private discussions after meetings of the *Politbüro* and the National Defence Council, but also to other major areas. Hans Reichelt, Minister for the Environment, subsequently complained that he had no means of acting upon his limited knowledge of the disastrous ecological state of the GDR, because Günter Mittag refused to allow discussions of the environment to interfere with economic priorities. In fact he refused to allow discussions of the environment at all.

The lives led by senior figures were also extraordinarily isolated from each other and from the reality of life in the GDR. *Politbüro* members had houses on the Wandlitz estate north of Berlin, but it appears that there was practically no contact between most of them. As Schabowski put it, they did not visit each others' homes and they did not even meet while mowing the lawns; gardeners did that for them. Outside the estate their opportunities for discussion were also limited and when they did snatch the occasion for some more open words, they changed the subject when Mittag or Honecker joined them.

Wandlitz boasted a shop and other facilities for *Politbüro* members and their families. Western goods were available at subsidized prices, and some families made great use of the opportunity. Professor Volker Klemm of the *Volkskammer*'s investigation committee reports, for instance, that Günter Mittag's daughters bought 10 imported colour televisions in 1988 and that in the crisis month of November 1989 the Sindermann family spent over M 23,000 in one day (November 8), including over M 7,000 on gold jewellery. The revelation of these practices, of the large private houses built from public funds, and of the huge over-stocked hunting estates commandeered by the party leaders fuelled a sense of outrage in the population in the winter of 1989–90 which was instrumental in the final collapse of SED authority. During the period of SED power, however, the way in which the senior figures lived effectively deterred them from forming cliques against Honecker (until the last, that is), bought them off with consumer privileges, and protected them from experiencing real life in the GDR.

The crisis in the party

The example of *glasnost* elsewhere, the emigration crisis and the apparent ossification of the leadership had their effects not only upon the population at large, but also upon those who were in the privileged position of SED party membership. The real implosion of the SED came after the ouster of Honecker and later Krenz, but even before the change of regime there were signs that all was not well in the party.

In the first instance there was friction between the district (*Bezirk*) party leaderships and the centre. This was not exactly a new phenomenon. Regional policy, whether it affected local economic activity, urban renewal, computerization or cultural programmes, had for decades depended upon the cordiality or otherwise of links between the district leadership and the SED in Berlin. By 1989, however, several of the district secretaries were becoming frustrated at the rift between the behaviour and pronouncements of the *Politbüro* and the reality of life as they saw it in their areas. The district leaderships were the ones which had to face the immediate problems of long-term economic stagnation, emigration of skilled labour and mass demonstrations.

One district leadership in particular was a thorn in the side of the top men in Berlin. In Dresden, Hans **Modrow**, the district party secretary, had over the years gained a local reputation for modest living and fair dealing and was seen in West Germany as a potential communist reformer. Modrow was not, on the other hand, well liked by Honecker and his close associates. Time and again he had been passed over when it came to nominations for the *Politbüro*; he had not even been made a candidate member. In 1989 Modrow felt pressure being exerted upon him. In February he was subjected to investigation of his local party by a delegation led by Günter Mittag, and in September he invoked the hostility of Honecker and others by persevering with a visit to Stuttgart, despite recent tensions between the two German states over the emigration issue and the cancellation of a visit by a West German **SPD** delegation. Modrow's role was soon to become a crucial one, but at this stage the conflict between the centre and the Dresden district was only an extreme form of a general and growing problem.

Some members of the Central Committee of the SED were also showing signs of concern about the general situation in the GDR. On October 6 the deputy minister of culture, Hartmut König (who was later to help Egon Krenz compose his memoirs), and Jochen Willerding of the **FDJ** wrote to Honecker asking for a meeting of the Central Committee to be held within two weeks. Several others, including the author Hermann Kant, made similar requests. They were not exactly complied with, since the Central Committee meeting was called for November 15–17. However, when the crisis at the top broke, one day's notice was given of a meeting on October 18.

Many ordinary SED members, particularly younger ones, also feared for the future of the party and the GDR if some sort of change were not instituted soon. We do not as yet have detailed evidence on disquiet within the party, but we can gauge it in part from expressions of relief when Honecker finally did go and from the pressures for change which were immediately brought to bear from within the ordinary party membership on his successor Krenz. Krenz himself recounts how in early October his friend and colleague Walter Friedrich from the Leipzig Central Institute for Youth Research, which was allowed to carry out investigations into public opinion, warned him: "In my opinion comrade Honecker should resign soon. I am firmly convinced that not 50 per cent but about 90 per cent of all comrades would welcome this. Comrade Honecker has very largely lost his earlier prestige amongst the people."

We also have Schabowski's account of disillusionment within the SED and within the youth organization, the **Free German Youth** (FDJ). According to Schabowski, when the FDJ was making arrangements in early 1989 for its Whitsun meeting in Berlin it was unusually difficult to find accommodation for non-Berlin FDJ members in the capital, even with SED members. Those who did take in the young people reported (as they were presumably required to do) that the latter's political motivation was zero. They "just wanted to see Berlin" and put up with the fact that they had to "trudge past Hony". One should not read too much into these views, which were no doubt those of generations of FDJ youngsters before them. What is significant, however, is that criticism was being expressed more openly and that FDJ leaders were being posed awkward political questions which they now felt they had to confront. Another sign of stress was that the FDJ symphony orchestra, which was due to perform Beethoven's Ninth at the celebrations, declined to play in blue FDJ uniform. Honecker allegedly responded, "Then they should drop the whole thing", and there was no performance.

The conspiracy against Erich Honecker

If the SED was to salvage anything from the growing crisis, there had to be a change in the leadership. Honecker was seen by many of his senior comrades, even it seems by those who professed the greatest loyalty, as having become a dangerous liability. His secretive power, his obstinacy in the face of evident change, and his increasing incapacity through ill health meant that any response to the crisis was predicated on his removal. We now have several accounts of this process, which bore fruit on October 17–18, 1989, but their differing interpretations must warn us from too definitive an account at this stage. If we are to believe Horst Sindermann, for example, the main conspirators against Honecker were Stoph, Krenz, Hermann Axen and Sindermann himself. This contrasts somewhat with the group described by Schabowski: Krenz, Lorenz, Tisch and Schabowski himself, with Stoph drafted in as spokesman at the *Politbüro* meeting. The fact that the stories do not entirely mesh is, of course, partly because certain people are in retrospect trying to cast their own role in a favourable light. This is not the only reason, however. The plot against Honecker had to be conducted against the background of the lack of personal contact typical of *Politbüro* membership noted above. It also had to be conducted in strictest secrecy so that Honecker could not through his associates get wind of his opponents' plans and act against them. Because of the code of party discipline, he would in such a confrontation still have the upper hand. The discussions between the various plotters were therefore very piecemeal, with one individual sounding out opinion from one group of *Politbüro* members and another from another. It would have been quite possible, therefore, for one person to develop an inflated sense of his own importance in the scheme.

Mittag and Honecker in the face of the crisis

Because of its dependence on Erich Honecker, even when he was personally absent through illness, the *Politbüro* reacted very tardily to the signs of crisis in the summer and autumn of 1989. A large number of its members became uneasy about the inadequate response, and it was from this unease that the conspiracy began against Honecker and also against Mittag and the propaganda secretary, Joachim Herrmann. Personal resentments played a part. Egon Krenz, who had long been billed in the western media as Honecker's "crown prince" was not permitted in August 1989 to deputize for the General Secretary during his convalescence. Instead he was instructed to take four weeks holiday, while Günter Mittag stepped in. In constant contact with the sick Honecker, Mittag made no significant change in party policy. For this he was later castigated by Alfred Neumann, Krenz, Schabowski and others, but in his memoirs he defends his actions vigorously. He claims that he refused to panic and that he kept lines of communication open with Budapest and did not ban travel to Hungary, so as not to escalate the emigration problem. Much of the criticism levelled against him, he claims, was that he was not hardline enough in the face of "counter-revolutionary forces", but this sounds like self-justification in the post-GDR climate. Mittag also maintains that in September Krenz specifically supported him in his actions, by saying "Günter, I would have acted in exactly the same way".

It was under Mittag's chairmanship in early September that the *Politbüro* first openly debated the crisis in the GDR. The meeting began with Mittag presenting figures on the number of GDR citizens currently in Hungary (about 120,000) and painting a picture of the West Germans being in charge in the refugee camps. He rejected a ban on travel to Hungary because he feared that that would only make matters worse. There followed conventional attacks from Erich Mielke and Horst Sindermann on the machinations of the imperialists, and a promise from Mielke to delay the processing of applications to travel to Hungary. However, other *Politbüro* members began to voice their disquiet. Werner Krolikowski, the Central Committee secretary for agriculture, asked whether the time had not now come for the *Politbüro* to issue a statement to the people. Schabowski took up this proposal but warned against simply repeating the old clichés. He offended Krolikowski by saying, "Spit it out then, what you want to say in the statement, Werner!"

Schabowski then went a good deal further. He proposed not only that the statement offer new travel regulations to the population, but also address all the economic problems of the GDR. He demanded that the national press and television now adopt a more sober and honest tone, in order to reflect more accurately the real situation in the country. Schabowski was by and large supported by Lorenz, Walde and Böhme, the party secretaries for Karl-Marx-Stadt, Cottbus and Halle, and even to a certain extent by Kurt Hager. It was Hager, however, who scuppered the debate by insisting that it could go no further on such fundamental issues in the absence of the General Secretary. Schabowski describes this outcome of the meeting as "a case of German misery" and a missed chance. As he puts it in his memoirs, the leadership of the GDR "sank again into silence".

On September 25 Honecker returned to work, and the sense of stagnation continued. Rather than confronting the serious situations in Hungary, Czechoslovakia and at home in the GDR, Honecker directed his now reduced energies towards the final planning of the 40th anniversary celebrations. His only concession to the crisis was to authorise the notorious transport via the GDR of refugees from Prague to the Federal Republic, and this was because he wanted the trouble cleared up before the festivities in October. In the event, of course, the disturbances at the railway station in Dresden only drew more attention to the problem.

Mikhail Gorbachev and the 40th anniversary of the GDR

Anniversaries played an important role in the GDR, marking out the separate socialist identity of the state. Sometimes — as with the Luther quincentenary in 1983, the fortieth anniversary of the officers' plot against Hitler in 1984, or the 25th birthday of the Berlin Wall in 1986 — they displayed a shift of political emphasis, to be judged according to the prominence given to the occasion. Less ambiguous were the anniversaries of the GDR itself, and October 7, 1989 was the 40th. Honecker, who enjoyed being fêted at home and abroad, planned the affair as a giant international affirmation of the achievements of the GDR. In the event the celebrations played no small part in his dismissal and the demise of the state itself.

One pitfall of political anniversaries is the very fact that they draw attention to longevity. They can actually draw out latent frustration and criticism. So it was in the GDR in 1989, especially since the festivities were planned against such an inauspicious background. There was an evident dichotomy between the images of the GDR being peddled in public — of a caring democratic state glowing with economic prosperity — and the reality known to the population. Added to this were the lingering problem of emigration and the examples of reform being attempted elsewhere in eastern Europe. The star guest in October was also the most important proponent of reform, Mikhail Gorbachev.

Three aspects of the anniversary precipitated a show-down: the public reception received by Gorbachev; Honecker's own behaviour; and the suppression of the unofficial demonstrations. It could not be hidden from anyone — least of all from Erich Honecker — that the crowds accompanying the motorcade on the morning of October 6 and in the march past in the evening adulated not him but his Soviet guest. The FDJ members in particular chanted not "E-rich!" as they had done in the past, but "Gor-bi!" Günter Mittag was heard to leave the platform muttering, "That was a scandal. It should have been organized differently".

The party meetings with Gorbachev were not exactly comfortable. On the afternoon of October 6 Honecker and Gorbachev had both given long ceremonial addresses, and Honecker's had been marked by the almost complete absence of any reference to current difficulties. The furthest he went was to say that any problems would be solved by the GDR itself by socialist means and that questions regarding the development of the GDR would be dealt with by the party conference (due in the spring of 1990). Gorbachev's reply was not confrontational, but where Honecker had attacked the "revanchist" policies of the Federal Republic, Gorbachev spoke of international co-operation, human communication, and good Soviet relations with the Federal Republic.

The next day the two men held private discussions at Schloss Niederschönhausen, prior to a meeting with the *Politbüro*. Günter Mittag tried to get himself invited to join them. He failed, and was left outside in the adjoining room, but at this stage the other members of the *Politbüro* were under the impression that Mittag was with Honecker and Gorbachev, and this did not improve the general attitude towards him. Krenz and Stoph in particular resented the General Secretary's reliance upon Mittag. Honecker emerged from the private meeting looking displeased and did not react to Mittag's questioning glance.

It was during Gorbachev's speech to the assembled *Politbüro* members that he used the phrase which was to become famous: "He who comes too late is punished by life." The interpretations of this remark vary. Schabowski maintains that Gorbachev was referring primarily to the problematic situation in the Soviet Union, whereas Krenz claims that Gorbachev looked round at his audience as if to see if he had been properly understood. In other words, he meant the comment to be a spur to action.

Honecker replied with another eulogy on the achievements of the GDR. When he had concluded, according to Schabowski, Gorbachev looked up, smiled and made a quiet tutting sound, as if to say "Was that all?" At a reception in the evening Schabowski and Krenz spoke with members of the Soviet delegation and allegedly criticized Honecker's speech and promised that there would soon be changes. Gorbachev then left for the airport and, according to information given to Krenz who was not present, urged those who were seeing him off to "take action!" Schabowski is sceptical about this, since it was Mittag and Axen who accompanied Gorbachev, and these were hardly the men from whom the Soviet president could expect radical change. Schabowski does make the point, however, that despite the obvious tension surrounding Gorbachev's visit and his exasperation at Honecker's obduracy, there was in no sense any planning between the *Politbüro* plotters and the Russians.

On the surface the public occasions of October 6–7 had gone smoothly, but not far from the official podia there had been serious disturbances. At the time the members of the *Politbüro* were led to believe that the protest demonstration of some 15–20,000 people on the Alexanderplatz had been dispersed peacefully, but in fact shortly afterwards — during the evening reception in the Palace of the Republic — police and *Stasi* had laid into the demonstrators in the streets of the Prenzlauer Berg district to the north of the city centre. There had been injuries and arrests. It was not only in Berlin that there had been conflict; disturbances were reported in the districts of Leipzig, Dresden, Karl-Marx-Stadt, Halle, Erfurt and Potsdam. Honecker and Mielke tried in their instructions to district party leaderships to pass off the occurrences as the work of "rowdies", whose violent behaviour disturbed ordinary citizens, but clearly a new stage in the crisis of the GDR had been reached.

Krenz, Schabowski and the removal of Honecker

On the morning of Sunday, October 8, 1989 Krenz and Schabowski were due to attend a meeting called by Erich Mielke in the headquarters of the *Stasi* in the Normannenstrasse. They heard the Minister for State Security report on the events of the day before and claim that the national day had generally passed off without disturbance. During the briefing Krenz passed Schabowski five type-written pages which turned out to be a draft *Politbüro* statement on the current crisis, including the problem of emigration. The general tone of the document was modest enough, but it went far further than Honecker was ever likely to do in addressing the causes of discontent in the GDR. Later, in Krenz's office in the Central Committee building Schabowski tried to persuade Krenz to liven up the statement, but he was reluctant to do so. It had to be presented to the *Politbüro* by Honecker and it had to gain support from other members of that body.

That afternoon the draft reached Honecker at Wandlitz and he telephoned Krenz to voice his displeasure. He was not prepared to present the document to the *Politbüro*. Krenz tried to persuade him, but all he got was an appointment to talk with the General Secretary the following day. Now that Honecker had been confronted with the draft, however, Krenz and Schabowski had to assure themselves of adequate support from the *Politbüro*. Not all members should be approached, for fear of word getting back to Honecker, and not all who were contacted should be apprised of the ultimate intention of removing the General Secretary. Krenz and Schabowski therefore had to assess the possible attitudes of the various *Politbüro* members. Krenz said that Siegfried Lorenz, party secretary for the Karl-Marx-Stadt district, was already aware of the plan, and that he, Krenz, thought he could win over Kurt Hager, Willi Stoph, Erich Mielke and Werner Krolokowski. Schabowski undertook to contact Werner Jarowinsky, Harry Tisch of the **FDGB**, and Hans-Joachim Böhme, party secretary for the Halle district. Alfred Neumann — "big Ali", as Schabowski calls him — was thought to be so antagonistic to Günter Mittag that he could be relied upon for support.

When Krenz was summoned to Honecker's office the following lunchtime he received a stern warning that the *Politbüro* would not approve his draft statement. Honecker did not, however, prevent the document being circulated to *Politbüro* members. Instead he tried at the meeting the next day (October 10) to weaken Krenz's position by giving the impression that the draft had his, Honecker's, approval while at the same time attacking Krenz indirectly through his criticism of another document about the current mood of young people in the GDR. He then proposed that a sub-committee of Mittag, Herrmann and Krenz produce a final version for publication, and he threw Mittag some documentation of his own for inclusion. He was obviously hoping that Mittag and Herrmann would be able to modify the statement before it was issued to the official news agency and *Neues Deutschland*. Krenz meanwhile had suggested that Schabowski be added to the team and Honecker had agreed without enthusiasm. When the four men met later, Herrmann and Mittag were cautious about altering the document, and only a few phrases were incorporated from Honecker's material. Schabowski takes this as a sign that they knew change was afoot and did not want to be caught on the wrong side.

This had all been a tricky manoeuvring on both sides about a *Politbüro* statement which in truth did not go very far to meet public unrest. With regard to emigration it continued to speak of "provocation" and "the imperialism of the Federal Republic", although it did take a new tone about those leaving the country. The relevant passage read:

> Socialism needs everybody. It has room and prospects for all. It is the future of the coming generation. And for that reason it is not a matter of indifference to us that people who worked and lived here have renounced our German Democratic Republic.

This was very different from Honecker's barb that "we do not mourn" and from one published only 10 days before in *Neues Deutschland* that "one should weep no tears after them". Elsewhere in the statement standard SED platitudes were mixed with hints that new possibilities were open:

> Together we want to discuss all the basic questions of our society which are to be solved today and tomorrow. Together we want to find an answer as to how we are to overcome the not easy challenges of the coming decade in the spirit of the humanist ideals of socialism. [...] It is a matter of economic efficiency and its use for all, of democratic co-operation and engaged collaboration, of a good range of available goods and payment in accord with achievement, of media which are in contact with real life, of possibilities to travel and a healthy environment. It is a matter of the contribution of our republic to securing peace in the world. It is literally a matter of everything which serves to benefit the people. We want to cross the threshold of the next century in a strong socialist GDR. [...]
>
> We possess all the necessary forms and forums of socialist democracy. Our appeal is that they be used even more thoroughly. But we also state openly that we are against suggestions and demonstrations behind which lurk the intention of misleading people and changing the constitutional basis of our state.

Source: *Neues Deutschland*, October 12, 1989.

There is no doubt that Krenz and Schabowski were trying to confront the crisis by engaging in more open discussion, but so much of what they said was wrapped up in SED jargon that the population might well be sceptical. At this stage, of course, the conspirators had to tread fairly carefully, because Honecker was still at the helm, but even after he had gone the tone of official SED pronouncements was always at least three steps behind popular opinion. The conditioning of those who had risen through the old system generally prevented them from taking the bold steps which were required, and they suffered too from the fact that their public credibility was near zero.

The *Politbüro* meeting on October 10 also witnessed the first signs of an overt challenge to the top leadership. Alfred Neumann, whose contempt for Günter Mittag's handling of the economy was of long standing, launched into a catalogue of criticisms of the party secretary for the economy. He accused him of ineptitude in the economic sphere and he was particularly scathing about the senselessness of putting so much investment into micro-technology. He also maintained that Mittag had during Honecker's absence been indecisive in the face of "counter-revolutionary activities". Neumann proposed that Mittag be relieved of his duties. Other *Politbüro* members then weighed in, putting the propaganda secretary Joachim Herrmann to the test as well, but Defence Minister Heinz Kessler suggested that Neumann's proposal be dropped. It was, but the attack on Mittag and Herrmann was a sign of what was to come in earnest only a week later. It had also perhaps subdued them in the matter of the *Politbüro* statement, although Mittag claims that he was trying to alter the document but was effectively outmanoeuvred by Schabowski.

Meanwhile Honecker continued to behave as if nothing were amiss, and the momentum against him increased. On October 11 he summoned the SED district secretaries and Central Committee secretaries (among them Krenz and Schabowski), and gave an account of the deliberations of the *Politbüro* which to Schabowski was as if Honecker had been at a different meeting. The General Secretary then blamed the problems of the GDR on NATO. This gloss on the current situation no longer satisfied several of the district secretaries. Günther Jahn of Potsdam indirectly hinted that Honecker might resign, and others — Johannes Chemnitzer of Neubrandenburg, Siegfried Lorenz of Karl-Marx-Stadt and Werner Walde of Cottbus — described the worsening situation in their districts. Hans Modrow of Dresden cited in particular the disturbances at the city's railway station and asked whether the *Politbüro* even knew what was happening in the republic. He spoke of a "failure of the leadership". Schabowski supported him, but Honecker seemed impervious to criticism and accused Modrow of setting himself up against the party leadership. He concluded the meeting by saying that the duty of the party was to ensure that counter-revolution had no chance in the GDR. As the participants dispersed, Krenz spoke with Modrow and Lorenz about possible personnel changes at the top. Modrow also thanked Schabowski for what he had said at the meeting. The latter suggested: "We must have a word sometime", and Modrow agreed.

On October 13 Honecker had another meeting, this time with the chairman of the National Front of the GDR and the chairmen of the other block parties — the **NDPD, LDPD, DBD** and CDU. Also present were Mittag and Herrmann. Honecker was trying to recoup his position by presenting a unified SED front, but Krenz, who was supposed to be there, gave his excuses. The official report of the meeting was standard stuff, but one of the party leaders was already breaking ranks, and tried in vain to get some more critical observations incorporated into the communiqué drafted by Herrmann. This was Manfred **Gerlach**, chairman of the LDPD, who had already the previous month called publicly for new ideas in the GDR. According to his own account, he now spoke for 30 minutes, criticizing the way the SED was handling the situation. He demanded dialogue with the new political groupings New Forum, **Democracy Now** and **Democratic Awakening**, and proposed more lenient (though still very limited) travel and citizenship regulations. He did not, however, receive support from the other party leaders.

The intrigues at the top were not just a matter of personal feuds, for the situation in the country was reaching a very dangerous stage indeed. Each week the mass demonstrations were growing in size, especially in Leipzig, and there was a real threat of a "Chinese solution". Such violence against the populace would have taken the crisis to new heights both domestically and internationally. The next large demonstration was now due on Monday, October 16, and on the Friday evening before Krenz telephoned Schabowski to tell him that he and Streletz, secretary of the National Defence Council, had persuaded Honecker to sign an order that no force be used against the Leipzig demonstrators. Honecker had apparently wanted to send a few tanks to warn the marchers off, and it was the danger of this kind of response which helped to stiffen the resolve of Schabowski and Krenz that the General Secretary be displaced at the *Politbüro* meeting on the Tuesday morning.

It was arranged that Krenz and Schabowski meet on the Sunday evening at the house of the trade union leader Harry Tisch in Wandlitz. Tisch had already indicated that he was willing to be part of the move against Honecker. He, like Neumann, was particularly keen to be rid of Mittag as well. As he allegedly put it to Schabowski, "The schemer must go. He is Honecker's evil spirit. His economic policy is destroying the trade unions too". At Tisch's house, where Schabowski was amazed by the book-shelves full of beer-mugs, Krenz reported that he had spoken to prime minister Stoph the day before, and Stoph was willing to propose Honecker's dismissal at the *Politbüro* meeting. Stoph, who now had his chance to get back at the man who had so often humiliated him and who had preferred Mittag and Mielke as confidants, had also made it clear that he was intending to resign after the next party congress. Stoph's reported suggestion of Krolikowski as his successor — which was immediately quashed by Schabowski and Tisch — and Tisch's nomination of himself for the job only show how completely out of touch these men were with the rate of change in the GDR.

While Tisch, who was going to Moscow the next day on other business, was entrusted with telling Gorbachev what was to happen, there were several incidents which kept nerves on edge. A telephone call from Krenz to Schabowski, which was couched in covert language for fear of its being intercepted, led to a misunderstanding about Stoph's intentions. Schabowski's impression was that Stoph was now insisting that Honecker be allowed to stay on as Chairman of the Council of State. Otherwise Stoph would not co-operate, which would have endangered the whole enterprise. However, it later transpired that Stoph was in fact proposing himself as Honecker's successor in that capacity, another indication of the air of unreality which afflicted these ageing party hacks. The second incident was that Honecker contacted Schabowski (as Central Committee secretary for Berlin) to say that he wished to visit the Bergmann-Borsig factory. Schabowski advised him not to: "Erich, I don't think any purpose would be served by you going there. With the mood as it is, you would just be placing yourself in a bad situation." Honecker replied, "If that's what you think …" and hung up. Finally, as Schabowski made some final approaches to *Politbüro* and Central Committee members, he had an argument with Werner Krolikowski. Schabowski was telling him of Stoph's plan and urging him to support the motion when Krolikowski, who had evidently not forgotten the altercation in the *Politbüro* in September, made it clear that he did not like being told what to do. The two parted coolly, and Schabowski cites this incident as yet another example of how unprepared they all were in this risky adventure.

The proposed meeting between Schabowski and Modrow had not yet taken place, but Modrow was taking his own steps. On the Tuesday morning, shortly before the *Politbüro* was due to meet, Modrow telephoned Honecker. Honecker's report of the conversation is that Modrow wanted a meeting to resolve differences between them. Modrow describes his intention as being to persuade Honecker to step down. What would have come of the meeting, arranged for Friday, October 20, must remain speculation. Within the hour it became redundant, as indeed did Erich Honecker.

The *Politbüro* met at 10 o'clock. Honecker shook everybody by the hand as usual, and the minutes of the last meeting were read out. What followed varies somewhat in the accounts available. According to Schabowski, Honecker began to address the first item on the agenda when Willi Stoph interrupted him, and Honecker let him speak: "I propose the motion that comrade Honecker be relieved of his function as General Secretary and also that comrades Mittag and Herrmann be relieved of their functions." According to Krenz, Stoph did not interrupt but responded to Honecker's request for further agenda items. Stoph then not only proposed Honecker's dismissal but also Krenz's appointment.

According to Schabowski, Honecker at first appeared to be trying to ignore the proposal, but protests forced him to allow discussion. Krenz takes a different line, expressing his respect for Honecker's willingness to give free rein to expressions of opinion. This is also the import of Honecker's own account. Whatever the case, one by one the speakers all voiced their agreement with the motion. Even Mittag, Herrmann and Mielke joined in, but with rather different emphases. Mittag — according to Schabowski, Krenz and Honecker, but decisively not in his own recollection — commented that Honecker's dismissal was overdue. Herrmann took the blame upon himself for the failings in SED media policy, while Mielke made the extraordinary comment: "I can tell some tales." The implication was that he had material on Honecker which he could use against him. Some of this has indeed emerged since. Each of the 25 members present spoke (the one absentee, Kessler, a close comrade of Honecker, was away in Nicaragua) and then all — including the three targets — voted in favour of the motion. It was also decided that Krenz would be recommended to the Central Committee as the next General Secretary. Almost $18^{1}/_{2}$ years after its inception, the Honecker era was at an end.

Egon Krenz's false start

Strictly speaking, the *Politbüro*'s decision on Honecker's departure from the post of General Secretary was a recommendation to the Central Committee, which was due to meet the next day, October 18. There was no real danger of the Central Committee overturning it, but it was important how the change was presented and received. Schabowski, who had drafted a resignation speech for Honecker to deliver, was also concerned that it be clear that Honecker was leaving *all* his offices, despite the fact that the Central Committee did not have disposition over his roles as chairman of the Council of State and of the National Defence Council.

Honecker's speech, in which he cited health grounds as the reason for his resignation, did conform to Schabowski's wishes in this regard, but Honecker went beyond the draft by naming Krenz as his suggested successor. Honecker denies making a unilateral decision, claiming that Krenz proposed the insertion himself, citing Stoph's motion at the *Politbüro*. Schabowksi, however, saw this action as the kiss of death for Krenz's leadership (the phrase he uses is "the curse of the pharaoh"); from the very beginning Krenz was unable to define a new era in GDR politics, because he was linked too much with that of Honecker. Although there may be some truth in this, it is really another example of how the old leadership — including the main rebels against Honecker — underestimated how far the whole system was already compromised. Krenz's position was not helped by Honecker, but neither would it have been very much stronger if his name had emerged independently from the Central Committee meeting. "The laughing horse", as he was colloquially known, was too familiar a figure to the population of the GDR.

The Central Committee dutifully approved the resignation/dismissal of Honecker, Mittag and Herrmann, and those members — among them Hans Modrow — who tried to use the occasion for a more far-reaching discussion of current problems were frozen out. Instead it was decided that Krenz should appear on television to speak to the people at large. Both Modrow and Schabowski are critical of Krenz's performance, which merely repeated the wording of his address to the Central Committee and adopted the conventional style of the SED bureaucracy rather than a more human approach. Schabowski uses the English word "flop" to describe the broadcast, and Modrow claims that from this point the people of the GDR and even the SED itself were set against Krenz as General Secretary.

Krenz's speech was published the following day in *Neues Deutschland* alongside an announcement thanking Erich Honecker for his life's work and conspicuously not thanking

Mittag or Herrmann. Most of it was formulated in the old style, and even the celebrated reference to a *Wende* ("turning point" or "change") did not look very radical: "With today's meeting [of the Central Committee] we shall introduce a *Wende*, above all we shall again seize the political and ideological offensive." Krenz appealed at length to all the established socialist ideals of the GDR and to all the various sections of the population, but he did eventually draw attention to problems of the economy, the environment, emigration and the standing of the party among the population. The words used, however, were conventional: "contradictions", "questions", "a complicated situation"; for his public audience there was little more than a promise of "dialogue", again a term which had over the decades become denuded of meaning.

The citizens' movements

If the events in the upper reaches of power in the GDR were remarkable, what was happening in the country at large was even more so. In the whole of its history the GDR had only once witnessed popular protest on a large scale and that was back in 1953. In the autumn of 1989, however, the dam burst and hundreds of thousands if not millions of people became involved in a process which overturned the structures of the state. The fact that the popular mobilization was in a broad sense "successful" and almost entirely peaceful, however, should not blind us to the fact that at the time the outcome was far from certain. All those who marched through the streets or who formed new political organizations were taking great personal risks and had no way of knowing where their actions might lead. This, of course, means that they showed great courage, but it also means that we should not assume that all events were leading to one inevitable conclusion. Indeed, during the autumn and winter of 1989–90 many different solutions to the underlying crises were debated and explored.

There was unanimity on the desirability of democracy in the GDR, but diverse approaches to it within the citizens' movements. In early October 1989 the main new organizations jointly issued a declaration, in which there was a call for UN-supervised free elections with compulsory use of the voting booth to preserve confidentiality. However, many within the new movements hoped to generate a level of democratic participation which went beyond casting a secret ballot. They hoped to involve the views of as many people as possible in the formation of the new order. Their purpose was not to replicate forms of party political behaviour in western Europe, but to engage in more direct, popular "basis democracy". In this respect many within the opposition to the SED shared the latter's public scepticism of or contempt for "bourgeois" parliamentary politics, which were seen as a system in which party bosses negotiated deals above the heads of the electorate and lined their own pockets at the same time.

Apart from the fundamental democratic principle, reflected in the names of two of the prominent new groupings — Democracy Now and Democratic Awakening — there were several other important strands present in the citizens' movements of the GDR, all of them familiar from the "alternative" politics of West Germany, but even more challenging in the East German context. They co-existed in one form or another in all the new organizations, but they were also represented separately by groups with a particular emphasis.

One such was the ecological issue, which had provided a focus for dissenting activity in the 1980s and which had aroused the wrath of the authorities, exemplified by the raid on the Zion church in Berlin in 1987. It found expression in late 1989 in the formation of the **Green Party**. Another was the question of women's rights in and contributions to society. The main organization founded to promote this specifically female perspective was the **Independent Women's Association**. A third was an anti-militarist attitude, strongly present in church circles and with important parallels in West Germany. It derived from a cognizance of the aggressive German past, a fear of the consequences of nuclear proliferation (particularly in the German centre of Europe), and an hostility to the way in which military values were instilled in the youth of the GDR from an early age. The organization which most fully embodied this current of thinking was the **Peace and Human Rights Initiative**, which had been founded illegally as far back as 1986. It survived as a separate movement through the revolutionary upheaval in the GDR, and also provided an input of ideas and personnel for the largest of the citizens' movements, New Forum.

New Forum

The very choice of the name New Forum was meant to stress an opening of public debate, rather than a fragmentation into sectional political interests. This idea of the broad public forum was indeed a feature of developments elsewhere in central and eastern Europe, with Solidarity in Poland, Democratic Forum in Hungary, and Civic Forum in Czechoslovakia. Even Bulgaria and Romania were to have their "forum" parties, although these were of much less significance.

The broad perspective of New Forum was both its strength and the cause of its eventual downfall. In the heady, dangerous days of October and November 1989 New Forum was able to give a name and a series of objectives to the marches in the streets of Leipzig, Berlin and the other cities of the GDR. It had been launched in September and had attempted in vain to use the constitutional provisions of the GDR to gain official recognition. The tactic was in part to expose the system as the corrupt sham that it was. Continuing illegality was no bar, however, to the swelling of the numbers espousing New Forum's demands for democracy, economic reform and ecological repair. The idea of the "forum" also carried over into the **Round Table** discussions which sprang up all over the GDR and were eventually to form a link at national level between government and opposition. New Forum was to suffer, though, a fate similar to that of Solidarity and the Czech Civic Forum, but sooner and more comprehensively. Differences of opinion soon surfaced within a movement which was very disparate and had no tradition or mechanisms of internal discipline. When free elections loomed, factions consolidated themselves into political parties. New Forum, though it was to play a part in the electoral process, refrained from constituting itself as a political party. Whereas Solidarity and Civic Forum did have experience of winning elections before breaking into their component parts, New Forum never did.

An intriguing question, but one which is not easy to answer, is how far the leaders of the citizens' movements — foremost among them New Forum — truly represented the views and aspirations of the mass following. Indeed, perhaps the designations "leaders" and "following" themselves distort the reality. Throughout the revolution in the GDR political "leaders" of the opposition had to respond to the actions and demands of those on the streets. This was indeed part of the credo of those who spoke for New Forum. Although individuals with evident political ambition did soon emerge and helped to shape political parties in preparation for elections, many who represented the general cause of democracy within New Forum and some of the other citizens' movements refused to cast themselves in the role of a political leadership. No-one of the calibre of Václav Havel emerged; nor was there an energetic populist figure like Lech Wałęsa.

As for the social composition of New Forum there is still a great deal of investigation to be done. The indications are, though, that manual workers were markedly under-represented, with only about 12 per cent of the membership, but this is a term which is itself fraught with difficulty. The line between support and eventual membership was a vague one. New Forum was an organization of younger adults: over one-third of members were in the age group 26–35 years. The significant presence of artists and intellectuals in the leadership — Bärbel Bohley and Jens **Reich**, for instance — was not exactly representative of GDR society, but — along with the activities of many pastors — did reflect the concerns of those who were amongst the first to march the streets.

Although the declared aims of New Forum and the other citizens' movements were forward-looking democratic ones, the mass mobilization was also, of course, a *protest* against the existing system and a call for retribution. As soon as Honecker was ousted, there were calls for the arrest and trial of the old guard of the SED, and these mounted as the revelations of corruption and self-enrichment emerged from November onwards. Krenz, Schabowski and those who remained from the old *Politbüro* were called upon to resign. Only Hans Modrow managed to retain a measure of public support.

The main target of popular hostility, however, was the *Stasi*, the embodiment of the worst practices of the SED regime. The Ministry of State Security itself was abolished in mid-November, but the protests continued against preserving any form of it in a successor organization. Their highpoint was reached in mid-January 1990 when the *Stasi* headquarters in the Normannenstrasse in Berlin were stormed by a crowd. Similar events were to occur in other cities. Once inside the building, the protesters hurled furniture and equipment through the windows and destroyed documents, and it is likely that former *Stasi* members were amongst those inciting the crowd, with this very purpose in mind. Certainly *Stasi* officers did their best to remove or shred documents while they had time.

The Krenz regime and the end of the Berlin Wall

Despite his disastrous start, Egon Krenz tried to redeem his promises of dialogue. He made a point of visiting ordinary factory workers and of talking to church leaders, and these meetings no longer had quite the self-congratulatory tone of the past. Krenz and his other senior comrades were constantly exposed to popular criticism. The change at the top also did nothing to dampen the weekly demonstrations. In fact it encouraged the calls for democratic reform, and hundreds of thousands marched the streets. On November 4 East Berlin excelled even Leipzig in numbers, with up to one million on the move. Similarly, the problem of emigration intensified rather than diminished, and the cautious new travel law of November 6 failed to satisfy anyone, not even the *Volkskammer*. Before November 9, according to Krenz's own estimate, more than 300,000 GDR citizens had left for the West by one means or another. Krenz had not yet benefited from having removed Honecker, and the problems which he faced were indeed getting worse.

No political change was possible without a substantial clear-out of the old personnel, and this began in early November. *Politbüro* members — including Mielke and Tisch, ministers — including Margot Honecker, district party secretaries — including Hans Albrecht (Suhl) and Herbert Ziegenhahn (Gera), and the chairmen of other political parties — Gerald Götting (CDU) and Heinrich Homann (NDPD) — began to disappear from office, and then on November 7 the Stoph government resigned, followed the next day by the entire *Politbüro*. The Central Committee elections to replace the latter brought in a reduced line-up blessed by some but not many new faces, although for the first time abstentions and votes against successful candidates were announced. Some of those chosen were unable to take office because they had meanwhile been spurned by their district party organizations, but the main figures held on. They were Krenz, Schabowski and — new to the *Politbüro* — Hans Modrow. He was proposed as the new prime minister (chairman of the Council of Ministers), replacing Stoph, and was approved by the *Volkskammer* on November 13.

The opening of the Berlin Wall

That was only after the most extraordinary event in the whole history. On the evening of November 9 (by strange coincidence a notorious German anniversary — of the Berlin revolution of 1918, of Hitler's abortive putsch in 1923, and of Reich Crystal Night, the anti-Jewish pogrom of 1938) Schabowski announced at his regular international press conference that henceforth citizens of the GDR would be allowed to travel out of the country with a minimum of formalities. Krenz had decided that the only way to defuse the situation was to take a radical step, and that meant abandoning all the previous regulations restricting travel. The irony was, of course, that the Berlin Wall had been built in 1961 to stem an outward flow of population; now it was to be opened with the same purpose in mind. The Stoph government had prepared a document which allowed for both temporary visits and permanent emigration to be approved at short notice and without specific reasons being given. Krenz had presented it to the Central Committee meeting that afternoon and there had been some discussion. Schabowski had then told Krenz that he must leave for the press conference at 6.00 p.m. and Krenz had given him the two sheets of paper which contained the new dispensations.

Some confusion has surrounded the announcement and the expectations behind it, but it does now appear that both Krenz and Schabowski knew the significance of what they were doing, even if they initially expected people to go through the usual channels of applying for permission to travel. The only misunderstanding lay in the fact that Krenz had intended the borders to be open from the morning of November 10, while Schabowski announced to the assembled journalists that the new rules applied immediately. There was in fact an ambiguity in the document, which explains Schabowski's reaction to the question put to him: paragraph 2 began with the words "with immediate effect", while paragraph 3 specified that "the attached press release is to be published on November 10".

The effect was electrifying. During the evening and into the night there was a rush to the border crossings along the Berlin Wall and some tension between the crowds and the bewildered border guards, before the latter yielded to the popular pressure and allowed people to cross to West Berlin. Visas were issued on the spot or forgotten altogether. West Berliners too joined in, crossing in droves into the east of the city, in many cases without any controls whatever. There was dancing on the Wall by the Brandenburg Gate and celebration in the underground trains and all-night cafés of West Berlin.

The milling of people in Berlin and the storm of Trabant cars westwards through the Wall and through the other border points between the two Germanies were flashed across the world and were instrumental in encouraging what was to come soon afterwards in Prague and Bucharest. Suddenly the cruellest monument of the division of Europe had been breached and the possibilities for change in eastern Europe were unbounded. If 200 years earlier the storming of the Bastille had been the symbol of the French Revolution, so now the opening of the Berlin Wall was the symbol of the revolutions of 1989.

The event may have been of international significance, but it was also very specific to the city of Berlin. Only two years earlier West Berlin and East Berlin had each staged completely separate celebrations of the 750th anniversary of the founding of the city. Now the joy of unity was particularly keen. The feeling of being hemmed in was one which had primarily affected East Berliners, but also West Berliners, albeit in a different and less drastic way. Now the barriers were down, the city could rediscover its identity. As the popular West Berlin newspaper, the *Berliner Zeitung*, put it in its banner headlines on November 10, "Berlin is Berlin again!"

That was the positive side, but in the months to come the two parts of the city joined together only uneasily. Very quickly, it seemed, the Berliners' mood of relief and euphoria gave way to grudging antagonisms. If on the weekend after the opening of the Wall hundreds of thousands of East Berliners were greeted with cheers, "welcome money" from the German government, and free gifts from supermarkets and fast-food chains, the complaints soon began in West Berlin about shops, buses and trains being overcrowded with short, pasty-faced people in bleached denims. The pressure also hit the already constrained housing and jobs market in the West.

For the East Berliners and East Germans in general the reverse stereotype developed of the arrogant West German who carried large amounts of money and expected everything to be available to him and to be done his way. The notions of the "Besser-Wessi" (the westerner who [thinks he] is better) and the "Mecker-Ossi" (the easterner who is always complaining) followed not long after the fall of the Wall and have plagued the process of reunification. They reflect popular experience to a limited extent, but they have been deliberately fostered by the tabloid press in both parts of Germany and by publishers of unfunny joke books about "Ossis" and "Wessis".

The end of the Krenz interregnum

Krenz and Schabowski, indeed all apart from Modrow, had little time left. The gamble of opening the Wall did not succeed in its purpose of bolstering the GDR and the communist regime. Rather it accelerated the problems of the state. Admittedly, most of the East Germans who took the opportunity to travel westward did so as visitors rather than emigrants, but the numbers of those leaving permanently did not diminish, and the open border presented all kinds of new economic problems. In any case, releasing the people from their previous captivity satisfied only one of their major demands. It also did not necessarily generate gratitude to the new leadership of the SED, which still lacked popular legitimacy. Many East Germans, most of whom had not been permitted to travel even *near* to the border with West Germany let alone across it, now saw the watch-towers, fences and razed land for the first time. Their response was anger at rather than thankfulness to their political masters. Also to experience the consumer world of the Federal Republic, even as a window-shopper, and to see the condition of the infrastructure there was to foster comparisons with home and to increase expectations for the future. The marches in the cities continued. On November 27 some 200,000 demonstrated in Leipzig, and on December 3 a human chain of protest was stretched across the country.

For the SED the process of collapse was a rapid one. The Central Committee was racked by disagreement about the way forward, every day seemed to bring forth new scandals about the past — most notably that of the dealer in hard currency and arms, **Schalck-Golodkowski** — and the *Politbüro* no longer had control over decisions taken by district party organizations and leaderships. It was fast becoming an irrelevant institution. On December 1 the *Volks-*

kammer, now under a non-SED chairman (Günter Maleuda of the DBD) and beginning to function as a real parliament, excised the leading role of the party from the constitution. Two days later, under pressure now from within the party membership, the entire SED leadership resigned. It was replaced not by a structure of the old kind, but first by a provisional committee and then at an emergency party congress on December 8–9 by a 100-strong committee chaired by Gregor **Gysi**. Former leading members were expelled from the party and some, including Honecker, Mittag and Tisch, were arrested. Meanwhile Krenz had ceased to be head of state on December 6, less than two months after his displacement of Honecker. Manfred Gerlach of the LDPD took over in a provisional capacity.

The government of Hans Modrow

A recast coalition of the block parties

The focus had already by now shifted to Hans Modrow, the prime minister. On November 13 he had been charged by the *Volkskammer* with the formation of a new government, and he had recognized that this must be an administration seen to be separate from the disintegrating power structures of the SED. His complicated negotiations with the SED and with the other block parties were made no easier by the fact that until a new cabinet was officially installed, the outgoing prime minister, Willi Stoph, peevishly denied Modrow the use of his office, although he himself was no longer to be seen there. Stoph even had the gall to describe a meeting between Modrow and outgoing ministers on November 14 as a "breach of the constitution". The prime minister designate therefore conducted his business from the hotel "An der Spree".

The composition of the Modrow government (see Part III, Table 7) certainly had a new look to it, but with 17 out of the 28 ministries the SED was still in the majority. There was also more than a sprinkling of familiar old ministerial faces — eight in all — like those of Foreign Minister Oskar Fischer and Foreign Trade Minister Gerhard Beil, leaving aside some long-term SED and *Stasi* figures who had not previously been in the cabinet. Even some of the representatives of the block parties, which were now jostling for a greater share of power, were leftovers from Stoph's team. Hans Reichelt of the DBD clung onto the environment portfolio despite having less than a glowing record, while the decision to leave Hans-Joachim Heusinger (LDPD) at the Ministry of Justice must rank as a crass mistake. By January these two were forced to resign, as were Gerhard Schürer (SED), head of the State Planning Commission since 1966, and the new Finance Minister, Uta Nickel (SED), who was embroiled in allegations of financial impropriety. Another prominent new female member of the government, Professor Christa Luft of the SED, gained perhaps greater credibility as she tried to wrestle with the economic difficulties of the GDR, but she could do little to stop the slide into disaster. One largely unknown face, as deputy prime minister with responsibility for church affairs, was the newly elected chairman of the CDU, the lawyer and musician Lothar **de Maizière**.

Although his cabinet still suffered from over-reliance on figures from the past, the government declaration which Modrow made to the *Volkskammer* on November 17 did carry a new tone. There was a recognition of the role which ordinary people had played in the democratic upheaval and of the importance within socialism of individuality and tolerance:

> The democratic renewal, a tumultuous process with many facets and contradictions, was begun by hundreds of thousands of the people, who have taken to the streets with integrity and on their

own initiative. The will for renewal of our socialist society and its state has embraced millions of citizens and has thus become a political force, so that political parties and social groups have emerged with self-confidence. [...]

Individuality is what we should respect here, I believe. Political and ideological tolerance are indispensable elements. A socialism which can develop into an achievement-oriented society through the work of its citizens should be able, depending on its economic results, to provide social security for all. Thus we ask all citizens to support this government. We need those who are prepared to do so to give us the benefit of their trust, and I know that with that I am asking a lot. Therefore I want to make it clear here: this government will make only those promises which it can actually keep.

At last there was a fuller recognition of the scale of the economic problems facing the GDR, although the implicit apportioning of most of the blame to Günter Mittag, Harry Tisch and Joachim Herrmann was rather disingenuous:

These facts are clear: the national economic plans were not balanced honestly, the competition of the district collectives was sometimes directed towards unrealistic goals, and trade union participation was robbed of its democratic character. Through a biased and autocratic investment policy the disproportions between industry and its suppliers have increased considerably and the state of the fixed assets fund has deteriorated markedly. The planned productive performance between 1986 and 1990 remains some way behind target, as do the anticipated receipts in the state budget. The sums allocated for consumption and social policy have already been reached or exceeded, as a result of which the ratio of purchasing power to saleable goods has consistently worsened. The continued raising of credits from banks in capitalist countries has also governed the resources of the GDR, which has led to great strain in foreign trade, having a negative effect on the domestic market and on investment possibilities.

The media were unable to represent these facts and circumstances because the journalists only had at their disposal facts which were embellished, falsified or unsuitable for analysis. Most who attempted to reveal the truth failed, or were prevented from doing so.

The programme of reforms which was outlined was still conceived within a state socialist context, but one now imbued with democratic and decentralized mechanisms:

Firstly, reforms of the political system, together with legislative measures to strengthen the rule and security of law. These include in particular an electoral law, a law on the Council of Ministers and a media law. Proposed amendments to the criminal law can follow relatively quickly. The travel law, possibly to be called the pass[port] law, will be submitted after discussion.

Secondly, there is the matter of an economic reform which must aim to raise the autonomy of the economic units, in order to increase their performance significantly, to reduce central direction and planning to a required reasonable level and — this is perhaps the most complex task — to implement the performance principle to an ever greater extent. [...] A careful, unprejudiced examination of the policy on subsidies and prices is in this context a special task.

Thirdly, educational reform is needed. [...]

Fourthly, we need a long-term programme — to be realized and re-examined year by year — with the aim of reconciling the economy with ecology more than has hitherto been the case. And I might add that in this area the GDR is not as bad as — through unnecessary secrecy — it appeared to be. [...] Urgently required is a new energy concept which leads to a reduction in the use of fossil fuels and in energy input.

Fifthly, an administrative reform which aims to democratize the leadership and administration of the state, to make its work more intelligible and, not least, to reduce considerably the financial and personnel costs of the administration.

Source: *Neues Deutschland*, November 18/19, 1989.

THE COLLAPSE OF THE COMMUNIST REGIME IN THE GDR

Crisis in the economy

Scarcely veiled by these noble pronouncements was the anticipation of major difficulties in the economic and social sphere. Four of the five proposals for reform held potentially explosive consequences. Freedom of travel, which was already becoming reality, meant further emigration and commuting to work in West Germany, both depleting skilled labour resources. An economic reform based on the reduction of subsidies and an increase in prices would place sudden burdens on a cushioned pattern of consumer expenditure and make many industries uncompetitive. Ecological improvement — the need for which was seriously underplayed — would be impossible without closing polluting industries and spending large sums of money on cleaning up. And "to reduce considerably the financial and personnel costs of the administration" meant cutting jobs. Measures were suggested to relocate people in productive areas, but the lurking menace of unemployment throughout the society was not addressed.

The open border was already exacerbating economic problems. Whereas East Germans visiting the Federal Republic had only limited financial resources with which to buy western goods, GDR shops were now subject to swarms of shoppers taking advantage of the low, heavily subsidized prices. On November 24 the government introduced new customs controls to curtail this practice, but in doing so appeared to be placing the blame for the economic difficulties on foreigners, specifically on Poles. New Forum took exception to this use of foreigners — many of whom were residents in the GDR — as scapegoats and published an appeal for "More Solidarity!". Unfortunately, the blaming of outsiders was to become a more general problem as difficulties mounted.

The Modrow government made much of its commitment to "stabilizing" the economy, and the former prime minister still maintains in his memoirs that if only a limited amount could be achieved, a much worse situation was nevertheless avoided. On December 9, 1989 he met the general directors of the centrally controlled combines and representatives of district-managed industry, with a view to maintaining production and introducing measures of reform. It was agreed that the combines should have more powers to make their own decisions, including over foreign trade deals. However, the central planning system was not abandoned; indeed, the intention was still to present a plan for 1990 to the *Volkskammer*, albeit late — in April. Modrow appears ambivalent about the wisdom of this, but he defends his decision to leave the general directors in place on the grounds that there was what he calls a slight economic recovery in the first quarter of 1990.

The Round Table

The greater number of non-SED ministers in Modrow's cabinet did nothing to assuage the criticism which was coming from what we might call — in imitation of a West German concept — the extra-parliamentary opposition. After all, the formation of a new government without an election having been held, and its inclusion of a few more ministers from the old block parties were scarcely convincing signs that the GDR had taken a new democratic turning. There were indications even from within the block parties that they recognized that there was a democratic deficit, or at least that too close a co-operation with the SED was now more of a liability to them than an advantage. Criticism came from within the LDPD itself about the re-appointment of Heusinger, and on December 4 the CDU announced that it was leaving the so-called Democratic Block. The LDPD followed suit shortly afterwards.

The old parties were all electing new leaderships and reconstituting themselves, and they faced now an ever-growing welter of new foundations. These included the citizens' movements already mentioned, plus a refounded Social Democratic Party (**SDP**, later SPD), the **United Left** (VL) and many others (see Directory). The seven main opposition groups — that is, the Peace and Human Rights Initiative, New Forum, Democracy Now, Democratic Awakening, the SPD, the Green Party and the United Left — were already part of a "contact group" which had existed surreptitiously since October 4, 1989. During November the group had been meeting weekly to discuss the issues facing the GDR and how to deal with the SED. Already the notion of a "round table" discussion between all parties and organizations had been mooted, in imitation of the "round table" talks in Poland and Hungary. This was variously conceived as a way of conciliating opposing views and as a way of confronting the SED and the other block parties and challenging their claim to power.

The formation of the Modrow coalition made the founding of the Round Table a realistic cause, and it was at this point that the churches of the GDR once more played a vital role. On November 21, three days after the new government had officially taken office, the Protestant bishops Gottfried Forck of Berlin and Werner Leich of Eisenach agreed to sponsor the Round Table, and they were backed by the Catholic church as well. There is some confusion as to the process by which invitations were issued to the eventual participants. The CDU paper *Neue Zeit* reported that the bishops assumed that the Round Table would be co-ordinated by Democracy Now, which had first suggested the idea, while *Neues Deutschland* gave the impression that the SED was the main mover, a claim which was patently untrue. Although the block parties had apparently received some sort of invitation by November 28, since they discussed it at length on that day, the official invitation from the Federation of Evangelical Churches was published on November 30:

> In agreement with the secretariat of the [Catholic] Berlin Conference of Bishops and the [Protestant] Working Community of Christian Churches, the secretariat of the Federation of Evangelical Churches extends an invitation to Round Table talks on December 7, 1989 at 14.00 in the communal hall of the United [Moravian] Brethren in the Dietrich Bonhoeffer House, Ziegelstrasse 30, Berlin.
>
> Taking part in the Round Table discussion will be two representatives each from the new parties and groupings.
>
> Source: U.Thaysen, *Der Runde Tisch*, p.34.

By the time the Round Table met as planned for the first time the position of the SED had been further eroded. It no longer had a constitutional "leading role", nor was it any longer headed by General Secretary Krenz, though he had not opposed the Round Table. The Round Table therefore began as a rather chaotic confrontation between the new organizations and the governmental parties, the latter bolstered by two of the "mass organizations". These were the FDGB and the Union of Mutual Peasant Aid (*Vereinigung der gegenseitigen Bauernhilfe* — VdgB), both of which were SED-controlled. Because of this over-representation of the SED position there was some haggling at the first meeting, the result of which was a balancing of the FDGB against participation by the Independent Women's Association. This meant that the two sides each had 19 seats, with New Forum and all of the block parties occupying three seats each and all the other participating organizations two each. To complete the Round Table — which was in fact rectangular — there were three churchmen to chair the debates, three speakers from the press and one pastor representing the Sorb minority in the GDR. None of these had a vote. The first three sessions took place in the cramped conditions of the Bonhoeffer House, but thereafter the Council of Ministers made conference rooms available at the Schloss Niederschönhausen, with far better facilities.

All the problems of the GDR were now up for discussion: the lack of political freedoms, the failings of the economy, the catastrophe of the environment, and much else besides. But there were certain fundamental concerns which had to be debated, and they were — at length and in earnest. Firstly, the Round Table had to recognize that — like the government which was under fire — it had no democratic legitimation. Therefore it could in principle take no definitive decisions. However, since no body in the GDR had democratic legitimacy — not even the *Volkskammer*, since it had been elected under a less than free system — certain steps had to be taken by somebody. The Round Table was the obvious forum, since it brought together representatives — albeit unelected — from the government and the opposition. At the first meeting it was decided that new *Volkskammer* elections should be held on May 6, 1990.

It is perhaps surprising that in a supposedly "revolutionary" situation another five months were set aside before the people were to be allowed to have their say, but the new organizations wanted sufficient time to get themselves sorted out and to mount a proper campaign. They also saw an appropriate symbolism in holding free elections one year after the fraudulent local elections which had helped to launch the opposition movement. In any case, the very fact that the citizens' movements were sitting down opposite the SED-led government was an indication that avoidance of outright "revolution" was a priority. At the Round Table, in the *Volkskammer*, even within the SED itself, everything was conducted with the intention of maintaining the constitutional framework of the GDR and avoiding violent upheaval.

The second fundamental issue was the *Stasi*. It had been abolished as such by Modrow, but in its stead was the not dissimilar Office for National Security (*Amt für Nationale Sicherheit*). This became known amongst its opponents as the "*Nasi*". Through the rest of December and into January 1990 the oppositional groups were determined to open up the history of the *Stasi* and to discuss the ways in which it was or was not being dismantled. They wanted to safeguard the interests of its victims and to prevent the wilful destruction of incriminating documents. They also wanted the abolition of the *Nasi*. Their concerns were not just with exposing the past and bringing malfeasants to justice; there were pressing fears about the present too. The SED and its surveillance apparatus were far from dead, and there was no guarantee that there would not be a reassertion of SED power through overt or covert means. In late December the violence which racked Romania and the barbarism of the *Securitate* there were a potent danger signal.

Modrow took note of the opposition to the *Nasi* but persevered with plans to replace it with an "Office for the Protection of the Constitution". He justified this on the grounds that every state had to have security services to safeguard its interests, but his motivation is unclear. He may simply have misjudged how popular antagonism to the *Stasi* carried over to any successor organization. He was under extreme pressure of work and appeared physically exhausted to observers at the time. However, the comments in his memoirs betray more than this. He appears more critical of those who attacked *Stasi* premises than of the *Stasi* itself, and this suggests that he was not himself hostile to the old apparatus. He wanted merely to make it more acceptable and to use it as before to support the state socialism of the SED.

Modrow took his proposals to the *Volkskammer*, but was forced to withdraw them. The opposition members of the Round Table threatened otherwise to withdraw from the discussions, and this would have left the government very exposed. After Modrow had reluctantly conceded came the attack on the Normannenstrasse, which gave further evidence both of the strength of popular feeling against the *Stasi* and indirectly of the continuing power of that institution.

Noises off: the West German approach and East German popular opinion

The labours of the Round Table were predicated on the continuing existence of the GDR. Both the old parties and the new were endeavouring with varying levels of enthusiasm to construct a truly democratic German Democratic Republic. The extent to which it was to continue as a socialist republic was debatable, and here there were divisions as much within the two main sides at the table as between them. Democratic Awakening, for instance, had more in common ideologically with the CDU and LDPD than it did with the United Left or New Forum. However, events in the wider world were beginning to suggest that there was another possible outcome of the upheaval in the GDR. Since the GDR had been a state defined by its political stance and by its loyalty to the Soviet Union, was there any longer a justification for its separate existence, now that the politics had changed and the Soviet Union was itself in a state of flux? Could a reformed, democratic GDR maintain itself as an independent state? What would it mean to have separate democratic "German" states in the centre of Europe, with free passage of people between them? Could the GDR survive as a kind of Austria: separate, different, yet German? The opening of the Berlin Wall had pushed the question of German reunification up the political agenda, though it was not yet at the top of it.

Since the changeover from Honecker to Krenz and particularly since the assumption of office by Modrow, there had been frequent contact between the leading politicians of the two German republics. This was not new, but the context was. On the East German side there was a greater openness in discussion, and for both states there were many serious issues of mutual concern which needed immediate attention. Amongst them were the problems caused to both countries by mass emigration, and the questions of economic and currency relations across a more open border.

In the Federal Republic events in the GDR had naturally been followed with interest and the opening of the Wall on November 9 was the occasion of public celebration, at least in Berlin and in border areas. Chancellor **Kohl** had been caught out rather in the first instance. He had had to interrupt an important visit to Poland of all places, and experienced difficulty flying out because of the autumn weather. The irreverent Berlin *tageszeitung* headed its report "Kohl in the fog". On his return he had then had a very rough ride from a West Berlin audience at a meeting outside the town hall in Schöneberg. It looked as though he was handling the crisis badly. This, however, was a lowpoint not reached again until the spring of 1991, by which time circumstances had changed beyond recognition. In the intervening period Kohl and his advisors appeared to master the problems of inter-German relations with aplomb.

At the end of November Kohl put forward a 10-point plan to the **Bundestag** (see Part III), in which he declared that "Reunification — that is regaining national unity — remains the political goal of the Federal government", but this phrase came only towards the end of a document which concentrated on matters of migration, transport and communications, economic reform, investment, democratic elections, and the situation in Europe at large. It was in any case only a restatement of a constitutional fact of life in the Federal Republic. Kohl picked up Modrow's mention of a term which might describe inter-German relations in the future, a so-called ***Vertragsgemeinschaft*** (contractual community), which would maintain the separate statehoods of the GDR and the Federal Republic, while forging ever-closer economic, cultural and political bonds.

The first sign that events were turning in Kohl's favour was when he visited Modrow in the GDR just before Christmas 1989. In the streets of Dresden he was accorded an ecstatic welcome from crowds who had already begun to chant not "we are the people" at their demonstrations, but "we are one people". Modrow found himself discussing with Kohl provisional arrangements for links between the two Germanies. At this stage actual political unification was seen to be a long way off, even by Kohl. Modrow, of course, had no intention of surrendering the identity of the GDR, and Kohl had to tread fairly cautiously if he were not to excite fears and resentments in the GDR, in Poland, in the Soviet Union and even in the western world.

Contacts between the two Germanies were developing in a number of respects. West German political parties were putting out feelers to their potential counterparts in the GDR. Prominent international visitors, such as Presidents Mitterrand and Havel paid visits to the GDR, the latter giving his blessing to some form of future German confederation. This was an important concession from another country which — like Poland — was sensitive about the notion of an expanded Germany. Economic talks began between the two Germanies in January. And meanwhile the ordinary human contacts were increasing as more border crossings were opened — including one at the Brandenburg Gate itself. In the new year visa regulations were lifted altogether for Germans, if not yet for foreigners.

What was most remarkable, however, was how the tone of debate and of the demonstrations had changed, in the south of the GDR in particular. While the protests on behalf of democratic renewal and against the *Stasi* continued, they were already merging with demands for German unity. New political parties were being formed with this purpose at the top of their programme and existing parties were beginning to debate possible forms of German unification. This is a process not easy to explain, because it involved so many different, sometimes apparently contradictory elements.

There were already severe economic strains in the GDR in early 1990 and the notion that the strength of the Deutschemark and the West German economy might pull the GDR out of its problems clearly had some appeal. However, this was a motive which was to play a stronger part later. What seems to have been of critical importance in swaying public opinion in January was the way in which the entire system as it had existed in the GDR was being discredited day by day and week by week, at a time when still there had been no electoral confirmation of the changes. Indeed, there remained the question of how much change there really had been. Those who were finding a political voice hostile to socialism saw an SED prime minister in power and devising a new state security service, and a planned economy limping from crisis to disaster. The best way to be rid of both was, perhaps, to abandon the state which they supported.

Another ingredient was a resurgence of identities distinct from and in opposition to the "GDR" identity. In **Saxony** in particular, which had been at the forefront of the protest movement, nationalist claims were at the same time affirmations of regional defiance. Saxon pride and resentment of Berlin could well be accommodated in an enlarged Federal Republic. The political party which best expressed this aspect was the newly formed **German Social Union** (DSU), which campaigned for the re-establishment of the *Länder* in the GDR and for German unity. The DSU sought and found many admirers not only in the **Christian Social Union in Bavaria** (CSU), which it most resembled politically, but also in Chancellor Kohl's CDU. Kohl's Minister of the Interior, Wolfgang **Schäuble**, describes how moved he was at the founding congress of the DSU in February 1990. He also tells how the General Secretary of the DSU, Peter-Michael **Diestel**, circulated copies of the *third* verse of the Song of the Germans — "Unity and justice and freedom" — because he feared that, "Otherwise they'll all sing the first verse; it's the only one they know". The strains of "Deutschland über alles" echoing from Leipzig might well have given the Russians, French and British pause for thought, let alone the Poles and Czechs.

Two notes of caution must be sounded here, however. Although the marchers greeted Kohl and later visitors with enthusiasm, although the placards and banners favouring unity proliferated, although Saxon coats-of-arms were sported on the backs of Trabants and Wartburgs and the "DDR" symbol was replaced by "D", one should not assume that these were the only emotions present, that everybody in the GDR wanted unity and that everybody who lived in Saxony felt "Saxon" again or still. In fact, among party members and ex-party members and among those who had committed most to the pro-democracy movement, there was anxiety about expressions of nationalism and a certain disorientation of identity. Those in their 30s and 40s in particular had grown up as "citizens of the GDR" and had homes and jobs there. They might look sceptically at their fellow citizens who very suddenly, it seemed, had turned nationalistic and regionalistic at the same time. Perhaps the latter were using the rhetoric to cover up deeper problems.

If *German* nationalism had been forcibly discouraged in the GDR, it had not been fostered either in the Federal Republic. Apart from on sporting occasions, the invocation of German pride was generally frowned upon. To be Bavarian or to be European was quite acceptable, but to flaunt "Germanness" was more controversial, especially amongst the young. On their frequent travels about Europe and the world they often faced residual hostility to their nationality. As for the GDR, for most West Germans it was unwelcoming, dismal foreign territory. Many had been there far less than they had to Italy or France, and many not at all, except perhaps in transit to West Berlin. At no stage after the autumn of 1989 was there any great enthusiasm for reunification. It was a matter of principle for those on the political right, but neither in January and February of 1990 nor later were West German towns and villages buzzing with excitement about German unification.

The Government of National Responsibility

The Modrow government was now under pressure from all sides — over the *Stasi*, over German unity, over price rises and other problems in the economy — and the coalition was under threat. Modrow's own party was also in crisis and could be little support to him. It had changed its name in December to the SED-PDS (**Party of Democratic Socialism**) and became the PDS in February 1990; it was expelling prominent members such as Krenz and Schabowski, and it was losing many others, including Modrow's close associate Wolfgang Berghofer, mayor of Dresden, on January 21, 1990. Its symbol — a social democratic and communist handshake — was removed from the frontage of the party headquarters in central Berlin, because — so it was said — the refounded SPD wanted its hand back.

Modrow's response was dramatic. Indeed, January 1990 can be seen as a major turning point, after which German reunification was the likely immediate solution rather than a possible long-term outcome. On January 22 he offered the opposition parties and groupings a part in government, on January 28 he announced the formation of a non-party Government of National Responsibility and the bringing forward of the *Volkskammer* elections to March 18, and at a press conference on February 1 he presented his conception of the path to German unity, entitled "For Germany, one fatherland":

Europe is entering a new stage of its development. The post-war chapter is being closed. The preconditions for a peaceful and neighbourly co-operation of all peoples are taking shape. The union of the two German states is moving onto the agenda.

The German people will find its place in building a new peaceful order, the result of which will be the overcoming of the division of Europe into hostile camps and the division of the German nation. The hour has come to draw a line under the Second World War, to conclude a German peace treaty. Through it all problems will be settled which are bound up with the aggression of Hitler Germany and the collapse of the "Third Reich".

The steps towards German union which Modrow proposed were fourfold:

– Conclusion of a treaty on co-operation and good neighbourliness as a contractual community, which should straightway contain essential confederative elements, such as economic, currency and transport union and co-ordination of the law.
– Formation of a confederation of the GDR and the FRG with common organs and institutions, such as a parliamentary commission, a *Länder* chamber, common executive organs for particular areas.
– Transfer of rights of sovereignty of both states to the organs of power of the confederation.
– Formation of a unified German state in the form of a German Federation [*Föderation* or *Bund*], by means of elections in both parts of the confederation; the convening of a unified parliament, which would decide on a unified constitution and a unified government resident in Berlin.

Source: *Neues Deutschland*, February 2, 1990.

This document was a remarkable transformation of Modrow's position, but it did contain terms which made it unacceptable to the West Germans. The most important of these related to the Warsaw Pact and NATO. Modrow stipulated military neutrality for the GDR and the Federal Republic as they proceeded to form a federation, and suggested that in the longer term the presence of foreign troops on German soil and German membership of a military alliance were open to question. These conditions were rejected by Chancellor Kohl, who wished to make it clear to his NATO allies that the Federal Republic's continuing loyalty was not to be doubted. Also unacceptable to the Bonn government was the proposed running order of events. Despite the fact that the *Volkskammer* poll had been planned and even brought forward, there was a suggestion that the democratic element of elections might follow confederation rather than precede it. Kohl was determined not to treat in detail with a non-elected GDR government. And the assumption that Berlin would be the seat of government was one which begged many questions indeed.

The ground was opening for negotiation, however, just as the political system in the GDR was opening up further to new ideas. From February 5 the stranglehold of the old parties was finally broken, as eight representatives of the new parties and movements entered the cabinet as ministers without portfolio (see Part III, Table 8). The Round Table had effectively pushed its way into the government itself, although it continued to meet separately as well until March 12.

This new "Government of National Responsibility", within which all members were required to let party membership rest, was meant to represent the broadest coalition of forces, acting in the national interest. Because of the forthcoming elections, however, it coincided with a stepping up of party political activity and the formation of electoral agreements in anticipation of March 18. On the right was the **Alliance for Germany**, in the centre the liberal **League of Free Democrats**, and on the libertarian left, representing the citizens' movements, **Alliance 90**. Outside these three main pacts were the PDS, the SPD (formerly SDP), and a plethora of smaller parties.

The proximity of the elections led to a marked cooling in the relationship between Kohl and Modrow. Indeed one of the main sources of bitterness which surfaces in the memoirs of the last communist prime minister of the GDR is the way in which in February and March 1990 he was frozen out by his West German counterpart. He criticizes Kohl again and again for not keeping the promises of financial assistance to the GDR which he gave in December 1989, and then for treating the head of government of the GDR in an offhand manner in the run-up to the *Volkskammer* election, as if he simply did not matter any more. Modrow attributes this change first of all to the reception which Kohl received in Dresden in December, which encouraged him to think about rapid German unification on West German terms, and then to Kohl's party-political electoral considerations in early 1990. He describes how on February 3 at the World Economic Forum in Davos Kohl and his wife were personally very hospitable:

> The Kohls treated me so nicely and attentively, as if I had visited their family 10 times at their home. But there was no longer the aspect of political togetherness, of peaceful getting together. The Chancellor showed interest, made remarks, but without giving any indication of his conception of the further steps in relations between the FRG and the GDR.
>
> Source: H.Modrow, *Aufbruch und Ende*, p.128.

When Modrow visited Bonn 10 days later the atmosphere was businesslike and frostier. Kohl made it clear that he was interested in the other members of Modrow's coalition, and — in Modrow's eyes — he distanced himself from the GDR prime minister.

One might make two comments about the impression which Modrow conveys. Firstly, not having had any experience of free elections himself, he does not seem to have understood that it was perfectly normal for Kohl to be distancing himself from his political opponent and concentrating his attentions on his electoral allies. Secondly, at no point does Modrow even register the fact that whereas Kohl's position was the product of a general election in the Federal Republic, he — Modrow — was an unelected functionary whose position derived originally from a dictatorship. This difference seems to have got lost in Modrow's self-perception as a representative of the people of the GDR, who certainly needed representing. Much as one might applaud the service which Hans Modrow performed in the final stages of the GDR and the general dignity with which he conducted himself, this fundamental point does not seem to have sunk in.

Reforms of the East German economy, January–March 1990

Both before and after the restructuring of the government, one of its principal concerns had been the future of the East German economy. A lot had been said about reform, decentralization and adaptation, but in practice little had been achieved. Meanwhile the prospects for all sectors of the economy looked ever bleaker. Therefore, in the months from January to the eve of the *Volkskammer* election in mid-March several measures were taken to try to remedy the situation. Their purpose was to open up the economy of the GDR to domestic, West German and foreign investment, and to make the economy more flexible in its decision-making and more responsive to demand. However, it was also clear that the political leadership of the SED-PDS/PDS, the bureaucracy, and the managers of the enterprises had no immediate intention of relinquishing planning or general socialist ownership. The legislation regarding joint ventures, limited liability and joint-stock companies, private enterprise and public trusteeship was not at this stage intended to challenge radically the fundamental economic organization of the GDR. It did, however, provide the mechanisms which were to be used later by non-communist governments.

The purpose of the Joint Venture decree of January 25, 1990 was to admit foreign capital into the GDR in order to stimulate the economy, without permitting the feared sell-out of domestic industry. It allowed foreign investment in the founding of a concern in the GDR of between 20 and 49 per cent of the total, and a higher proportion — effectively anything below 100 per cent — if this was seen to be in the interests of the national economy, or was in small and medium-sized concerns. GDR participants in such joint ventures could include combines, individual concerns, institutions, co-operatives, and private individuals. In practice these regulations presumably meant that foreign investors could buy into existing GDR concerns, provided that there was officially a new enterprise founded, but the state's scrutiny was intended to prevent a swamping of the GDR. In reality, of course, the immediate external interest in investing in the GDR proved to be less dynamic than had been hoped or feared.

On March 1, 1990 the decree on the conversion of people's combines, concerns and institutions into capitalized companies took the process a stage further. All enterprises could now be transformed into either limited liability companies (*Gesellschaften mit beschränkter Haftung* — GmbH) or joint-stock companies (*Aktiengesellschaften* — AG). Excluded from the provisions were services and parts of the infrastructure such as the postal service, railways, waterways and roads. There were also other possibilities for co-operatives and private companies. On March 7 a bill was passed by the *Volkskammer* regulating the foundation of private enterprises, which was meant to foster the development of small and medium concerns, especially in the fields of trade, transport, services and tourism.

In mid-March a further crucial step was taken, with the founding of the ***Treuhandanstalt*** (Trust Agency). Its statute of March 15, 1990 was published just before the elections:

> Tasks, Rights and Duties of the *Treuhandanstalt*
>
> (1) The *Treuhandanstalt* exercises trusteeship over that property of the people which, until its conversion according to the decree of March 1, 1990 on the conversion of people's combines, concerns and institutions into capitalized companies [...], is held in the funds of the people's combines, concerns and institutions. Excepted is that property of the people in the legal control of concerns and institutions subordinate to towns and communities, that which is in areas to be organized as state enterprises, and that used by the LPGs [*landwirtschaftliche Produktionsgenossenschaften* — agricultural co-operatives].
>
> (2) On conversion, the *Treuhandanstalt* [...] assumes control of those parts of the business and those shares which belong to the people, of the capitalized companies formed.
>
> (3) The substance of the trusteeship is the administration of the property of the people in the general interest.
>
> Source: P.Koppe, *Unternehmensgründung und Unternehmensbeteiligung in der DDR* (Munich: Rehm, 1990), p.154.

It should be noted that through the complicated legal jargon, which is made even more opaque by the different conceptions of "property" in the GDR, two points are clear. Firstly, this was not a privatization. Most property in the GDR now passed into the trusteeship of the *Treuhandanstalt*, which thereby became the largest holding company in the world. Whether concerns had been converted into capitalized companies or not, they were in the main to be administered by the *Treuhandanstalt*, which was accountable to the *Volkskammer*. In those businesses which had private capital too the *Treuhandanstalt* administered the other "public" part. Secondly, the prime criterion for the *Treuhandanstalt* was not economic viability or profitability, but "the general interest". This might, of course, include viability and profitability, but it also included matters of employment, the environment, national security, strategic matters and so on.

In other words, the government and the bureacucracy of the dying communist-led regime in the GDR had devised a means by which — they hoped — an overwhelmingly socialized economy could continue to function. That their hopes were dashed, and so soon, was due primarily to the election campaign of February–March 1990 and the eventual verdict of the voters.

THE DEMOCRATIC GDR AND THE REUNIFICATION OF GERMANY

The *Volkskammer* elections

The election campaign

As befitted the novelty of free elections in the GDR, the campaign saw a colourful variety of numerous parties and party alliances engaged in a lively and foreshortened electoral contest. On February 20 the *Volkskammer* passed the electoral law, which provided for a smaller chamber of 400 members (previously 500), chosen by proportional representation under the Hare-Niemeyer procedure, as in the Federal Republic. However, no 5 per cent hurdle was implemented, so small parties stood a chance of representation. Parties were permitted to present common lists, which allowed the various electoral alliances to function. The country was divided into 15 districts, but voters were to be able to cast their ballot at any polling station, with the results counted nationally.

The next day, February 21, the *Volkskammer* passed bills on political parties and associations and on freedom of assembly. The following day the 30-strong electoral commission was convened. It comprised representatives from the various parties and organizations, under the presidency of Petra Bläss of the **Independent Women's Association**. Its immediate function was to decide which parties and party alliances were to be permitted to stand in the elections. They had to register with the *Volkskammer* by February 26, and no fascist, militarist or similar organizations were to be tolerated. On March 9 the commission announced the results of its deliberations: 24 lists were to appear on the ballot paper (one of which, the Europe Union of the GDR, did not in the event put up candidates).

All the old block parties stood — including what had been the **SED** under its new legend of **PDS** — although the **LDP(D)** was part of the **League of Free Democrats** and the **CDU** campaigned alongside **Democratic Awakening** and the **DSU** in the **Alliance for Germany**. Of the "mass organizations" of the old system, the **Democratic Women's League of Germany (DFD)** stood in its own right and the **Free German Youth** (FDJ) was hidden away in the **Alternative Youth List**. The other principal contenders were the **SPD, Alliance 90** — which grouped together **New Forum, Democracy Now** and the **Peace and Human Rights Initiative** — and the **Green Party**, which joined forces with the Independent Women's Association. There were many small left-wing parties, including revivals of the **KPD** and even of the **USPD** from the days of the Weimar Republic. Enthusiasts for malt and hops could — at least in the Rostock district — cast their vote for the **German Beer Drinkers' Union**. This was not just an East German phenomenon; it had companions in the Friends of Beer parties in the Czech Republic and in Poland.

In early March the political posters spread through the GDR. Some were cheap impromptu efforts, but others looked professional and showed inventiveness and humour. There was in the main a refreshing lack of the simpering politicians' portraits so typical of West German elections, but then most East German campaigners were relatively unknown. One face which was used frequently was that of Wolfgang **Schnur** of Democratic Awakening, but this was unfortunate, since he had to resign four days before the poll because he had worked with the *Stasi*. He was not the only party leader to come under such suspicion; both Ibrahim **Böhme** of the SPD and Lothar **de Maizière** of the CDU were accused of similar complicity, but for the time being they survived.

The Green Party, Democratic Awakening — which had adopted the tag "social + ecological" — and even the **DBD** went for the environmentalist slant. A Green Party poster showed a child's painting of a garden, with the caption "We have only borrowed the earth from our children"; and the DBD espoused "Eco-agrarian production", which was in some contrast to everything it had promoted in the past. The **German Forum Party** too, part of the League of Free Democrats, displayed a large green tree on its placard, with the motto "The centre". On the right the new DSU and the old **NDPD** both played the nationalist card, with "The path to German unity" and "For the German future" respectively. The SPD was more cosmopolitan, with "The better concept: a European Germany". Women's issues were highlighted by many of the parties, including, of course, the DFD. Its message of "Through women more democracy", however, accorded ill with its SED past.

The CDU took many approaches, stressing particularly the prospect of a united Germany in a united Europe, the social market economy, small business, and social welfare. However, there was some skulduggery in **Berlin** which produced counterfeit CDU leaflets pledging "reincorporation of our eastern territories", "abolition of the PDS (SED)", "the formation of élites", and "drastic raising of rents and abandonment of costly social services". These, of course, were no part of CDU policy.

By far the wittiest and most pointed campaign was that of the PDS, which still had a lot of money to spend. Its contributions included the photograph of a telephone receiver surrounded by small ads from the newpspapers offering land for sale and posts for doctors. The caption read "No connection under this number". The German word for telephone connection is *Anschluss*, also the term used to describe Austria's annexation by Hitler in 1938. Another variant was a poster showing simply an outline map of the GDR and the phrase "A shame to throw it away!" The change in the PDS was exemplified by the further text below, "For a social market economy, achievement-oriented and humane". The appeal to the potential victims of capitalism was an overtly defeatist slogan: "For the weak a strong opposition". The PDS was now more in touch with reality.

Although much of the impetus behind the elections, exemplified by the poster campaign, came from within the GDR itself, the main running was made by West German interlopers. The CDU, the SPD and the **FDP** sent in all their big guns: Chancellor **Kohl**, former chancellors Brandt and Schmidt, Foreign Minister **Genscher**, and many more. Already at the time the complaint went up in the GDR — not just from the other parties — that the democratic renewal in the country was being hijacked by the seasoned politicians from the west.

Early opinion polls — of uncertain reliability in this fledgling democracy — gave the SPD a substantial lead, providing encouragement too to the West German party. It had seen support for Helmut Kohl's CDU in the Federal Republic falter during 1989 in the Berlin and European Parliament elections, but it had not yet experienced any fillip for SPD fortunes. It looked now as though the GDR might provide it. In the event, the reverse occurred. The opinion polls began to register a swelling of support for the CDU, especially after it formed the Alliance for Germany with Democratic Awakening and the DSU. On March 1 the Alliance was recording 24 per cent support in the polls, the SPD 53 per cent and the PDS 11 per cent. By March 7 the figures were 30 per cent for the Alliance (21 per cent for the CDU alone), 34 per cent for the SPD, and 17 per cent for the PDS. No other parties really came into the frame.

The main reason for the swing towards the Alliance was its clear commitment to German union on terms which looked favourable to the citizens of the GDR. On March 1 the Alliance parties held a press conference to announce their "immediate programme". It took place in **Bonn** not in the GDR, which aroused criticism from the PDS. The programme promised German unity under the terms of Article 23 of the Basic Law of the Federal Republic; in other words, the GDR would "join" the Federal Republic. The Deutschemark would be introduced at a rate of 1:1 for savings, wages and pensions. This pledge, which Kohl backed with his personal authority at election meetings in the GDR, was contrary to the advice of Karl Otto **Pöhl** of the *Bundesbank*, but it appealed to a GDR constituency which felt hoodwinked and exploited by the communist regime.

Kohl's advantage over all opposition was that he was able to use his office as chancellor to make such undertakings and also to negotiate a favourable attitude on the part of the four powers (the USA, USSR, United Kingdom and France) which still held rights in Germany. Indeed, Kohl had already in February received an assurance from President Gorbachev that German unity was a matter for the Germans themselves, and on March 14 preliminary **Two-Plus-Four** talks began in Bonn. Kohl could deliver, whereas the SPD could not. In fact, many within the West German SPD — its chancellor candidate Oskar **Lafontaine** in particular — appeared reluctant to envisage early German unity and more concerned about halting the continuing flood of East German migrants into West Germany.

Election victory for the CDU

The result of the elections exceeded Kohl's wildest hopes. The Alliance for Germany only narrowly failed to win an absolute majority of votes and of seats in the new *Volkskammer* (see Part III, Table 11 and also Jeffery essay in this volume). It achieved this victory despite the long-term complicity of the eastern CDU in the old regime and its scant involvement in the revolution of 1989. The western CDU, which in the past winter had been equivocal about whether it should throw its lot in with the compromised eastern CDU or the new DSU, saw its sponsorship of the Alliance for Germany — which combined both — handsomely vindicated. The CDU emerged by far the strongest party in the Alliance, with 40.8 per cent of the vote, bolstered by the DSU's performance in **Saxony** and **Thuringia** (6.3 per cent of the vote overall). It looked as if the same kind of relationship might develop as between the CDU and the Bavarian **CSU** in the Federal Republic. Even the admitted former *Stasi* involvement of Democratic Awakening chairman, Wolfgang Schnur, had damaged only his party (a mere 0.9 per cent of the vote) and not its allies.

The election result was a clear break from the communist system on the part of most of the electorate, but the PDS did hold on to a respectable 16.4 per cent of the vote, helped by the recent performance of outgoing prime minister Hans **Modrow** and new party chairman Gregor **Gysi**. It still had the backing of those whose lives had been wedded to the former ruling party and of those who saw it as the best defender of the positive socialist aspects of the

GDR against encroaching capitalism and the spectre of unemployment. Most voters, though, used their first democratic opportunity to reject their former rulers.

The Social Democrats — with 21.9 per cent — could take little comfort from the vote. There was clearly a communist core to their left which they could not yet hope to attract, but more seriously they had failed to make a convincing moderate socialist appeal to a broad swathe of public opinion. The very term "socialism" had become anathema to so many. Far from latching onto the pre-Nazi social democratic past of Saxony and Thuringia, those were the very areas which had swung most strongly toward the CDU and DSU. The SPD also suffered during the later stages of the election campaign from allegations that its leader, Ibrahim Böhme, had been involved with the *Stasi*. Shortly after the poll he was forced to lay down his party offices temporarily, pending investigation. This resignation later became permanent.

Poor results saw the beginning of the end for two of the block parties, the NDPD (0.4 per cent) and the DBD (2.2 per cent), but the LDP(D) managed to survive by allying with the other liberals — who received in all 5.3 per cent of the vote — and eventually formed part of an eastern FDP. The NDPD was later to do the same, and the DBD was to find a final resting place in the CDU. New Forum and the other citizens' initiatives which had spearheaded the revolution of the previous autumn paid the price for not having party organizations to match those of the parties supported by West German counterparts. Their message of a humane democratic GDR sorting out its own problems before considering German unification also failed to satisfy by this juncture. Alliance 90 won only 2.9 per cent of the vote, and the Green Party and Independent Women's Association only 2.0 per cent between them.

Because of the system of pure proportional representation, even the weaker parties found some seats in the new *Volkskammer*, so it was a varied assembly which gathered to debate the future of the democratic GDR on April 5, 1990. Its first task was to elect its own president, and on the second ballot Sabine **Bergmann-Pohl** of the CDU reached 214 votes. She thereby became not only the president of the parliament but also acting head-of-state, since it was decided under the next item on the agenda to transfer to her the powers of the retiring chairman of the Council of State, Manfred **Gerlach**, and to postpone the election of a state president. In her first official address to the *Volkskammer* its new president declared, "The tender seedling of democracy is now entrusted to us. Let us through our labours take spring into the land!"

The government of Lothar de Maizière

De Maizière did not form a government immediately after the elections. Indeed, for a brief period it seemed that he might not aspire to the post of prime minister at all, and three weeks passed before he had constructed a cabinet. The electoral arithmetic left the Alliance for Germany, with 192 seats, just short of half the chamber and well adrift of the two-thirds majority needed for the constitutional changes which were envisaged. The PDS was ruled out as a coalition partner — although the CDU had lived quite happily with the SED for decades before — and the liberal faction was not large enough by itself to boost the Alliance to a two-thirds majority. De Maizière therefore had to win the support of the SPD.

This was made difficult by the inclusion in the Alliance for Germany, and thus of necessity in the new government, of the DSU. The DSU had made furious attacks on the SPD during the election campaign and was already drifting markedly rightward. The SPD accused it of being too much like the far-right **Republicans**, who had made inroads into West German politics in the course of 1989. De Maizière managed the delicate balancing trick and in the end included both the DSU and the SPD, plus the liberal **BFD**, in his new broad coalition government (see Part III, Table 9). The DSU was given the ministries of the Interior and Economic Co-operation, the SPD Foreign Affairs, Finance and five others (including that of Agriculture, for which the SPD nominated an independent). The BFD took three ministries, there was one further independent, and Rainer **Eppelmann**, Wolfgang Schnur's replacement, was given Democratic Awakening's consolation prize of one ministry. It was the one he wanted, though: that of Defence and Disarmament. The remaining 11 cabinet posts were taken by the CDU.

Negotiations on monetary union

The success of the East German CDU made Kohl's task much easier than it might otherwise have been. De Maizière and Kohl had agreed before the end of April that the two Germanies would enter monetary, economic and social union on July 1 (the date often mentioned at the time was July 2, since July 1 was a Sunday). There would be a currency exchange rate of 1 Mark = 1 Deutschemark for wages, pensions and the first tranche of private savings. Otherwise the rate would be 2:1. The decision on the exchange rate was — candidly admitted by Wolfgang **Schäuble** — taken for political and pyschological reasons, rather than on economic grounds. Unlike, say, the Polish and Czech currencies which could find their own realistic and downward international level, the East German Mark was to be drastically over-valued in order to maintain morale and — it was hoped — keep the population in the east. The problem was to be, of course, that the effect on the East German economy was in any case going to drive East Germans to seek work in the West.

Negotiations began at once on the details of the so-called "state treaty" (*Staatsvertrag*) on monetary, economic and social union. Indeed, unbeknown to the East Germans the Federal Ministry of the Interior in Bonn had already begun in February to work out the legal implications of German unity *beyond* monetary union. At this stage the East German side was led by the up-and-coming Günther **Krause** (CDU), de Maizière's parliamentary secretary, and the West German side by Hans Tietmeyer of the *Bundesbank*, although naturally many others — especially on the West German side — were drawn into the discussions. The talks were concluded with extraordinary rapidity, in awareness of the mounting economic crisis in the GDR but with perforce inadequate information on the GDR side. On May 18 in Bonn the "state treaty" was signed by the respective finance ministers of the two Germanies, Theo **Waigel** (CSU) of the Federal Republic and Walter **Romberg** (SPD) of the GDR (see Part III for text). With this act — in theory at least — the social market economy, with its free competition and its social legislation, was in the second half of 1989 to operate in the GDR.

At this stage the West Germans were sanguine about the financing of German unity. They assumed that the East German economy would respond generally positively to monetary union and that western investment would pour into the east. Therefore the amount of public finance which Theo Waigel was prepared to commit at this stage was preposterously low. The five-year German Unity Fund, to be raised on the capital markets, was only DM95 billion, with this figure to be supplemented by DM20 billion from savings within the West German budget (see also *Costs of unification* below). These figures were determined largely by wilful optimism and by political considerations. The Federal government did not believe it dare make tax demands on the West German electorate, and it was probably right.

The state treaty also left another hostage to fortune. It was recognized by the negotiators that one of the biggest problems facing the East German economy and society was going to be that of property rights. There were going to be many demands for the restitution of houses, businesses and land lost by one means or another to the communist state. However, there was disagreement about the extent to which restitution could be contemplated. According to Schäuble, Lambsdorff and Genscher (both FDP) wanted all expropriations — including those of 1945–49 — now to be reversible, whereas de Maizière refused point-blank to be party to a document which made possible a return to the position before 1945. There would, he said, be no support for this in the GDR and it would also bring conflict with the Soviet Union. The GDR negotiators also wanted to build into the treaty some protection of tenancies and building rights, so as to prevent greedy western speculators buying up everything in sight. This was not acceptable to West German economic interests, so the whole question of property rights was left out of the treaty. It did not, however, thereby disappear.

Politics in the GDR in the summer of 1990

De Maizière and, by proxy, Kohl had meanwhile faced another electoral test. In early May local elections were held in the GDR, and there were some changes (see Part III, Table 12). Turnout, though still high, was well down on the near complete participation in March, from 93.4 per cent to about 80 per cent. The elections confirmed the dominance of the CDU over its rivals, but it lost considerable ground. Even more so did its partners in the Alliance for Germany. The DSU, which was by this stage visibly fragmenting into right and left wings, lost nearly half its support, and Democratic Awakening ceased to be of any significance. The other two big parties also had to concede some ground, the PDS more than the SPD. Alliance 90, including New Forum, continued its decline. The gainers were — appropriately for these local elections — local citizens' groups and independents, and also the liberals of the BFD. There was also, at the expense of the CDU and DSU, an advance made by two farmers' parties, the old DBD and the new **Farmers' Association of the GDR**. Their success emphasized the growing crisis in GDR agriculture, even before the strains of economic union.

Other issues refused to die, and brought the coalition parties under pressure. Of particular importance was the lingering question of the *Stasi*. The DSU parliamentary fraction turned against its Interior Minister, Peter-Michael **Diestel**, accusing him of soft-pedalling on the *Stasi* and working together with former *Stasi* members. The position was not helped by the revelation that the *Stasi* had over many years provided a safe haven in the GDR for wanted alleged terrorists of the West German **Red Army Faction**. Diestel refused to bow to pressure and was backed by de Maizière. However, at the end of June Diestel and some of his colleagues resigned their party membership. Diestel obviously felt himself to be under personal threat, since he and Rainer Eppelmann were armed when they appeared in public. Their fears were not irrational, in view of the assassination attempts on Lafontaine and Schäuble in 1990 and the murder of **Rohwedder** in 1991. The DSU, meanwhile, also caused trouble by trying to pre-empt de Maizière and Kohl in mid-June by proposing in the *Volkskammer* that there be *immediate* German political unity. The proposal fell, but was symptomatic of the frenetic chaos of the time.

The form of that unity was contested too between de Maizière, the SPD and the BFD. The former wanted two separate electoral territories for the all-German elections, whenever they might be. The effect of this would be to bolster the DSU, to face the SPD with difficult competition from the PDS, and perhaps to endanger the parliamentary survival of the liberals in the GDR. The SPD and BFD argued for one electoral territory with the same rules as in the present Federal Republic, namely a 5 per cent hurdle before any ***Bundestag*** seats could be claimed. The coalition was falling apart, until temporary agreement was reached on one electoral territory, with perhaps a lower threshold than 5 per cent to assist the parties in the GDR which did not exist in the Federal Republic.

De Maizière's problems were not over. He and Kohl, faced by the evidence of mounting economic chaos in the wake of the currency union and fearful of losing all-German elections if they were held as late as December, tried to bring the date forward to October 14, shortly after the unification date of October 3 which was now becoming firmer. De Maizière announced the plan without apparently consulting Kohl, and the extent of their panic was revealed. To bring forward *Bundestag* elections was, however, a matter of constitutional significance and the West German SPD promised to block the manoeuvre.

As the elections approached, de Maizière began to flex his political muscles against his recalcitrant coalition partners. In late July he seemed not to mind when the liberals from the BFD left his coalition over the questions of the timing of unification and electoral law. However, his right-hand man Krause, who was away on holiday at the time, was appalled, because it meant greater reliance on the SPD. This did not matter for much longer, for in mid-August de Maizière sacked all three of his economics ministers, Romberg (finance — SPD), Pohl (the economy — CDU) and Pollack (agriculture — independent proposed by the SPD), the latter having been treated ignominiously by angry egg-throwing farmers. The impression given was that de Maizière was trying to push the blame for the economic mess onto his ministers. He was, however, also settling his scores with the SPD. The dismissal of Romberg led to the SPD quitting the coalition. With such a short time to go before unification, de Maizière compounded the indignity of his ex-ministers by not even bothering to replace them. State secretaries dealt with the remaining economic tasks, and in the run-up to the signing of the unification treaty de Maizière acted as his own foreign minister.

The negotiation of unity

The negotiation period for the second treaty between the two Germanies, the unification treaty, was not very much longer than that for the state treaty on monetary union. Because of a desire to proceed as quickly as possible and the need to co-ordinate the process with the international negotiations and the timing of the *Bundestag* elections, less than two hectic months — July and August — were available, although a good deal of preliminary work had been done. The talks were led on the East German side by Günther Krause and on the West German side by the Minister of the Interior (since this was an internal German matter), Wolfgang Schäuble (CDU). It is Schäuble who has given us the blow-by-blow account in his *Der Vertrag: Wie ich über die deutsche Einheit verhandelte* (The Treaty: How I negotiated German unity — see Bibliography).

There were many complicating factors, of which several may be mentioned here. Firstly, both sides of the discussion were coalitions. On the East German side it was a particularly fractious coalition of inexperienced politicians with strong opinions. On the West German side there was perhaps more cohesion, but there was similar strength of opinion and more skill in coalition manoeuvre. Schäuble reports, for instance, how even at the very last stage the agreement was threatened with complete collapse by the opinions of the FDP. Secondly, the West Germans had to take account of the fact that their state was a federal republic; the wishes of the **Länder** had to be given proper regard, and they were of great variety. Throughout his account Schäuble expresses his general annoyance with the West German *Länder* (he does have kind words to say at times!), but this was not least because most of them were by governed by the Social Democrats. This was a third complication: the treaty had to be passed by the West German **Bundesrat**, which had an SPD majority. The SPD opposition had to be included in the debate or it could scupper the final agreement. On this point Schäuble is unapologetically partisan, and he is particularly scathing about the behaviour of the SPD's chancellor candidate Oskar Lafontaine. Lafontaine never ceased to point out the pitfalls of unification as devised by the CDU. Most of what he predicted — widespread closures of industry, mass unemployment, social tension — was, like the prophecies of Cassandra, to come about, and like Cassandra, Lafontaine was reviled for his views. He eventually suffered electorally as a result.

At times the negotiations took a tragi-comic turn. In a desperate attempt to make unity a blend of east and west rather than simply a take-over by the Federal Republic, Lothar de Maizière raised the symbolic matters of the name of the new state, its flag and its national anthem. He proposed the German Federal Republic (*Deutsche Bundesrepublik*), which would have meant changing all the paperwork in the west as well as in the east. As for the flag he had, according to Schäuble, no specific alternative to suggest, but he did propose that the new German national anthem be the first verse of the GDR's anthem followed by the third verse of the Federal Republic's. This would mean Johannes R. Becher's "Risen from ruins, And turned to the future, Let us serve you for the best, Germany united fatherland [...]" — words in recent years unsung in the GDR of the SED because of the fourth line — followed by Hoffmann von Fallersleben's "Unity and justice and freedom, For the German fatherland! [..]". The tune would still be Haydn's familiar *Kaiserhymne* from "Deutschland über alles", which would mean trimming a line from the GDR contribution or perhaps skipping through the words in a rather undignified manner. The West Germans were polite about de Maizière's suggestions and then allowed them to drop from the agenda.

Where there was common ground on the seriousness of the issue was over another symbolic and also practical matter: the location of the German capital and the seat of government. Here de Maizière was adamant for Berlin, for a variety of reasons, one of the strongest of which was the need to display the integration of the territory of the GDR into the Federal Republic. To have the capital in Bonn, way in the west, would be to give the message to the citizens of the GDR that they had been annexed and even deprived of their capital city. In West Germany at this stage such a proposal was very controversial and probably not capable of generating a majority in the *Bundestag*, so Schäuble — though himself in favour of Berlin — did not want the issue incorporated into the treaty. In the end a compromise solution was adopted which leant more de Maizière's way: the unification treaty did specify Berlin as the capital, but the question of the seat of parliament and government was left to be resolved after the establishment of German unity. This it was in June 1991, but only after a heated campaign on both sides, an emotional *Bundestag* debate, and a victory for Berlin by only 18 votes.

Several major issues of principle lay behind the inter-German discussions. The first, strongly represented by Schäuble, was that the unification treaty had to be accepted by both German parliaments *as a whole*. This was not just a matter of expediency; Schäuble did not want there to be any opportunity for amendments which would alter the Federal Basic Law by the back door. This was one of the reasons why the controversial issue of abortion rights was left for later discussion (see Alsop essay in this volume). Another principle, contested between Schäuble and some of his cabinet colleagues, was whether Federal law should apply to the GDR automatically, unless otherwise specified, or whether GDR law should continue, unless otherwise specified. Schäuble preferred the latter interpretation, but had to back down, especially in view of the contrary opinion of the Ministry of Justice.

On the East German side, as de Maizière's position on national symbols showed, there was generally a concern that not everything of value in the GDR be lost. This applied particularly to social provisions. Even Krause — of whom Schäuble remarks, "In contrast to the prime minister, Krause never gave a sign of the desire to save anything at all from the old GDR for the new Germany" — gave a long list of questions about practical financial, economic and social matters which were worrying people in the GDR. Krause, it might be said, was apparently becoming anxious about a breakdown of social stability and possible violence in the GDR. He did not share the extremely pessimistic views of Diestel, but by August he was — in Schäuble's view — beginning to panic. The desperate situation in the agricultural production of the GDR led him personally to take suitcases of money to the farmers, and he threatened several times either to resign and to go back to his academic post or to flee to the west.

The voluminous unification treaty, signed on August 31, 1990, was in effect an extension of the laws of the Federal Republic into the territory of the GDR, but on a wide range of points there were clarifications to be made and temporary arrangements to be implemented (see Part III for abbreviated text). The West German Basic Law had to be altered in some respects, most notably in its provisional character. There was henceforth no implication that "other parts of Germany" might join the Federal Republic. This was a message that the unification of Germany was now regarded as complete and that there was no expectation of lost territories in the east being regained.

The international context

German unification was not just a matter for the Germans themselves. The two states were each strategically crucial for the military and economic alliances of east and west, the Warsaw Treaty Organization (Warsaw Pact) and the Council for Mutual Economic Assistance (CMEA) on the one hand, and the North Atlantic Treaty Organization (NATO) and the European Community (EC) on the other. Furthermore, there was an historical legacy which required attention if the two German states were to be united. There had been no peace treaty with Germany after the Second World War, the city of Berlin was subject to the Four Power Agreement of 1971, and the four powers (the USA, the USSR, the United Kingdom and France) still had residual rights and large concentrations of troops in Germany as a whole. There were also the questions of the confiscations of property in the Soviet Occupation Zone by the Soviet Military Administration from 1945 to 1949, a united Germany's eastern border with Poland and the extension of European Community membership to eastern Germany. All these matters had to be settled before unification could become a reality.

The Soviet Union

The main concern of the governments in Bonn and East Berlin was whether the Soviet Union would allow the absorption of its ally in perpetuity, the GDR, into the Federal Republic, and if so on what terms. The evidence by 1989 was that President Gorbachev was applying the so-called "Sinatra doctrine" of allowing the communist states of eastern Europe freedom of manoeuvre to do it "their way", but the complete disappearance of the GDR and the possible extension eastward of NATO territory was perhaps too much to expect of him. However, without the agreement of the Soviet Union the responsibilities of the four powers would not be abrogated.

Throughout the early phase of the revolution in the GDR **Krenz** and Modrow had naturally kept in close contact with the Soviet leadership about developments in the GDR. By February, when even Modrow had come out in favour of moving toward German union, the West Germans were anxious to know the attitude of Gorbachev. Therefore on February 10, 1990 Chancellor Kohl spoke with the Soviet leader in Moscow. He was assured that the Germans themselves should decide upon their future without outside interference, but it was far from clear that this decision could include the incorporation of the GDR into the area of NATO responsibility. This, however, was from Kohl's point of view a *sine qua non*.

On June 12 Gorbachev showed that he was still reluctant to surrender the territory of the GDR entirely. He proposed that Germany should initially have dual membership of NATO and the Warsaw Pact. This suggestion was rejected emphatically by the United States government and by the Federal Republic. Only a month later Gorbachev gave way. By this time Russia and several other Soviet republics had declared their sovereignty and it was the future of the Soviet Union which now concerned him more than the terms of German unity. In mid-July Kohl held talks with Gorbachev in Moscow and the Caucasus, the result of which was Soviet acceptance of a united Germany's right to choose its own alliances, in other words of all-German NATO membership. It was, however, specified that while Soviet troops remained in the former territory of the GDR, NATO structures would not be extended to that region. Although Gorbachev had really little bargaining power by this stage, Kohl could present his visit as a triumph of personal diplomacy. He could also, when later under criticism, claim that he had used the brief opportunity available to him to gain Soviet approval. Had German unity not been achieved in 1990 and the *coup* against Gorbachev in August 1991 been successful, the chance might have been lost.

Another telling point in Germany's favour with regard to Gorbachev in 1990 was the desperate financial plight of the Soviet Union. The Bonn government offered financial assistance, in particular to help pay for the rehousing of Soviet troops departing from eastern Germany. The initial figure agreed in September was DM15 billion. This was part of a package including the German-Soviet co-operation treaty of September 13, under which Soviet troops would leave by 1994, and was followed up by the Treaty on Good-Neighbourliness, Partnership and Co-operation, signed in Moscow on November 9, 1990, one year to the day after the opening of the Berlin Wall (see Part III for text).

There was one other problem, regarding property rights in the GDR. On March 7, 1990, just before he left office, Hans Modrow tried to enlist Gorbachev's help in preserving property relations in the GDR. He was concerned that the country would be swamped by claims for restitution of property confiscated, surrendered or compulsorily purchased since 1945. He knew that the Soviet Union would not be keen to have the actions of the occupying force from 1945 to 1949 challenged by claims for restitution or financial compensation. Gorbachev did not intervene, but the occupation period remained an open question. In June the governments of the GDR (now led by de Maizière) and the Federal Republic agreed to exclude the 1945–49 period, but this was challenged in the courts by property claimants. Eventually on April 23, 1991 the Federal Constitutional Court in Karlsruhe declared against them, saying that property confiscations in the Soviet Occupation Zone 1945–49 had to stand.

THE DEMOCRATIC GDR AND THE REUNIFICATION OF GERMANY

The Two-Plus-Four Talks

Although the Soviet Union was the external power which most had to be conciliated, a general agreement on the status of Germany was essential. Even the French and British had their concerns about the prospect of German unification (see Spence essay in this volume). The Americans were more positive, but they were concerned about Germany's commitment to NATO and the future of United States troops in Germany. At the Open Skies Conference in Ottawa in mid-February 1990 President Bush declared of the United States and the Federal Republic: "We both want a united Germany which enjoys full sovereignty. A united Germany which is a full member of the Western community and of the NATO Alliance, including participation in its integrated military structures. A united Germany which is, as the Federal Republic has been for over 40 years, a model of freedom, tolerance and friendly relations with its neighbors."

Bush proceeded to announce a programme of Two-Plus-Four talks which would draw together the two German republics and the four former occupying powers. The first official meeting would be held in Bonn on May 5, preliminary discussions having been held in the same city in mid-March. Negotiations, which in the event proved fairly problem-free, continued in June in Berlin, in Paris in July, and in Moscow in September. The GDR's position was represented by its inexperienced Foreign Minister Markus **Meckel**, who had difficulty in competing with the wily Hans-Dietrich Genscher. Since Meckel departed the government in mid-August, Lothar de Maizière's was the name which appeared for the GDR on the Treaty on the Final Settlement with Respect to Germany, which was signed in Moscow on September 12, 1990 (see Part III for text). This document was in effect a belated peace treaty concluding the Second World War. It brought to an end the wartime allies' remaining responsibilities in Germany and it pledged Germany to recognize the Oder-Neisse border with Poland and refrain from making any territorial claims whatsoever against other states.

Poland

The country with the most immediate apprehension about German unification was Poland. It had good cause, since nearly one-third of its territory comprises lands detached from Germany after 1945: most of former East Prussia in the north-east, most of former Pomerania in the north-west, most of Silesia in the south-west and parts of other former Prussian provinces in-between. The GDR had in 1950 signed the Görlitz Treaty with Poland, confirming the Oder-western Neisse border between the two states, and in 1970 the Federal Republic under Chancellor Brandt had signed a treaty recognizing this same western border of Poland. However, Brandt's move had not been without its right-wing critics in the Federal Republic, and the constitutionality of the treaty was often called into question. At that stage their noisy refusal to abandon claims to the lost territories did not make much difference, since the Federal Republic had in any case no border with Poland. With German unification this was going to change, and the issue surfaced once more.

From a Polish perspective there were several worrying indications. In the first place, the 1949 Basic Law of the Federal Republic specified that it applied "for the time being" to the named *Länder* of the Federal Republic. It was to apply to "other parts of Germany [...] after their accession". This phrase was now in 1990 to apply to the territory of the GDR, but it might also be used to hold open a claim to former German territories now in Poland. Secondly, Chancellor Kohl appeared over-willing to accommodate those in West Germany who demanded the return of eastern lands, particularly Silesia. He had in the past addressed the annual gathering of Silesians, and when he visited Poland in November 1989 he was given a warm welcome from the remaining German-speaking community there. Placards appeared declaring "You are our chancellor too!" Kohl also refused to commit himself on the Oder-Neisse border, saying that it was a matter for the parliament of a united Germany to decide.

Kohl's equivocation, though unsettling for the Poles, was really to do with domestic Federal politics. At home he had in 1989 been fending off a political challenge from the right, and he had his eyes on the forthcoming Federal election. Once the CDU and its allies had won in the GDR in March, however, he felt rather more confident about clarifying matters with Poland and declared that this was the price which had to be paid for German unity. On July 17, 1990 the Polish foreign minister, Krzysztof Skubiszewski, took part in the Two-Plus-Four session in Paris to ensure that the German-Polish border was to be inviolable, and the final Two-Plus-Four Treaty in September did include a clause committing Germany and Poland to a binding treaty to this effect. The treaty was accordingly signed by Genscher and Skubiszewski in Warsaw on November 14, 1990. It reaffirmed the border and it also recognized the pain on both sides caused by the events of the past.

The European Community

Since the normalization of relations between the Federal Republic and the GDR in the Basic Treaty of December 1972 the GDR had enjoyed an unusual status with regard to the European Communities. Though not a member, it conducted its trade with one member — the Federal Republic — without tariff barriers. This was because the Basic Law of the Federal Republic did not recognize the GDR as a "foreign" country, and inter-German transactions came under the heading of domestic, not foreign trade. For the East Germans this naturally held many advantages, not least because the West Germans supported inter-German trade through an interest-free credit system known as the "swing". Some commentators even described the GDR as a surrogate member of the European Community, but this was a great exaggeration, since there was little evidence of East German goods in any quantity moving through the Federal Republic into other EC member states.

Even before 1989 links between the GDR and the European Community had been developing, as association agreements between the EC and central and east European states and EFTA countries were explored. Once the prospect of German unification arose, however, the individual EC states and the Community as a whole had to deal with the potential status of east Germany *within* the Community (for detailed discussion of these issues see Spence essay in this volume). Individual states like France and Britain had their concerns about the power of an expanded Germany within the Community, and favoured a slow process toward unification. Jacques Delors of the European Commission, and the European Council — meeting in December 1989 in Strasbourg — were, however, more favourably disposed to rapid German unification and incorporation of east Germany into the European Community. Delors in particular saw it as an opportunity to promote support for greater European integration.

The process by which the former GDR was to become part of the Community raised many fundamental issues within the apparatus and laws of the Community (see Spence), but the eventual outcome was relatively straightforward and uncontroversial. Eastern Germany became part of the Community not by accession as a new member but by virtue of the expansion of the territory of a member state — the Federal Republic. The question of the number of German members in the European Parliament has for the moment been shelved. That of the obligations of the former GDR under existing international agreements is being dealt with by the European Commission. For the east Germans themselves probably the most important aspects are the method and timing of the implementation of European Community law and standards in east Germany. It was agreed that there should be varying periods of transition, in order to allow east Germany to accommodate itself gradually to the regulations, much in the way that newer members like Spain and Portugal were still doing.

Because of the run-down of its economy and attendant social problems, the eastern part of Germany qualifies for financial aid from the European Community. In March 1991 it was announced that a package of DM6.2 billion would be made available in the period up to 1993. This comprises DM4.35 billion for regional and agricultural measures and DM1.85 billion for employment measures.

The unification of Germany

At midnight on October 2–3, 1990 the German Democratic Republic ceased to exist. Its territory joined the Federal Republic of Germany and, under the terms of the unification treaty, the united city of Berlin became once more capital of the country, over 45 years since it had lain in rubble at the end of the Third Reich. On a new public holiday, replacing October 7 in East Germany and June 17 in West Germany (the anniversary of the 1953 uprising in the GDR), Germans in all parts of the country celebrated the conclusion of a tumultuous political year, but it was in Berlin that the festivities were most spectacular.

On October 4 the *Bundestag* met symbolically in the Reichstag building, but this did not yet mean that Berlin was to become the seat of German government. The following day the *Bundestag* continued its business as usual in Bonn. To give the former GDR parliamentary representation in the period pending a new election, the east German parties nominated members to the *Bundestag* in accordance with their proportional strength in the old *Volkskammer*. In all, 144 nominees entered the *Bundestag*, including members of the PDS like Hans Modrow and Gregor Gysi. Five delegates — Lothar de Maizière, Sabine Bergmann-Pohl, Günter Krause (all CDU), Rainer **Ortleb** (FDP) and Hansjoachim Walther (DSU) — were invited to join Chancellor Kohl's government as ministers without portfolio.

The immediate political impact of "the five new federal states", as the former GDR came to be called, was to bolster the ruling coalition in Bonn. After elections to the five new **Landtage** in October (Berlin had to wait until December for its poll) the CDU formed governments in four of the eastern *Länder*, either on its own — in Saxony — or in coalition — in Thuringia, **Saxony-Anhalt** and **Mecklenburg-West Pomerania**. Only in **Brandenburg** could the SPD lead a coalition. The elections (see Part III, Table 13) confirmed the strength of the CDU in Saxony and Thuringia and the ongoing decline of its partner, the DSU. The liberals made good progress, especially in Saxony-Anhalt, where Genscher's impact was felt, and the SPD could take consolation from its Brandenburg result. Alliance 90 benefited from its contacts with the growing Green movement, and the PDS fell back, but only slightly. Apart from the regional dominance of the CDU within the former GDR, the results meant that the Christian Democrats and their partners now regained a majority in the *Bundesrat*, Germany's second chamber. They had lost this in May 1990 when the SPD had seized control in Lower Saxony.

The Bundestag *and all-Berlin elections*

In one very important respect the west German system did not apply immediately in east Germany. After much heated debate and a ruling by the Constitutional Court in Karlsruhe on September 30, it was decided that for the first all-German elections to the *Bundestag* on December 2, 1990 the territories of the two former states should be treated as separate electoral regions. The effect of this was that the normal minimum of 5 per cent of the vote before seats could be taken in the *Bundestag* applied not to Germany as a whole, but to the two separate parts. This allowed those parties which were specifically of the former GDR to gain the parliamentary representation which would have eluded them under a nationwide 5 per cent requirement. The Court had ruled that this would be unfair.

The campaign now began in earnest, with Kohl hoping to ride high on his achievement of German unity within one year of **Honecker**'s fall and without major diplomatic problems. His opponent, Oskar Lafontaine, continued to berate the chancellor for having botched the process of economic integration, with dire consequences to come.

In the elections on December 2 the CDU and the FDP performed well in the former GDR, and the SPD very badly (see also Jeffery essay in this volume). The CDU polled 43.4 per cent, which was marginally up on the elections in March 1990 to the now redundant *Volkskammer* and, together with the sharply diminished vote of the DSU, slightly above the combined result of the CDU and CSU in west Germany. The FDP put in a very strong showing in east Germany: 13.4 per cent, compared to 10.6 per cent in west Germany. The popularity of foreign minister Genscher, himself born near Halle and the hero of the Prague embassy in September 1989, played a major part in this.

The SPD in east Germany did improve on its showing in March 1990 (from 21.9 per cent to 23.6 per cent), but this was a dismal result for a party which had initially emerged so confidently in the course of the changes in the GDR. It is probable that Lafontaine did not recover in east Germany from the impression which he had given of being half-hearted about unification. In east Germany the SPD also had to its left a party taking votes. The PDS managed 9.9 per cent, a substantial drop from the 16.4 per cent in March 1990. The east German **Greens**, backed by the citizens' movements which spearheaded the revolution, just squeezed in with 5.9 per cent, embarrassing their west German counterparts, who did not. The far-right Republicans failed to make any impact in east Germany; their 1.3 per cent was less than the 2.3 per cent in west Germany.

On the same day as the *Bundestag* elections, the process of restoring regional representation throughout Germany was completed, as the newly unified city of Berlin went to the polls. Berlin, which is for the moment at least a separate *Land* within the enlarged Federal Republic, now once more had a parliament of its own. Until just before the election West Berlin had been ruled by a coalition of the SPD and the **Alternative List**. This had then fallen apart acrimoniously over the treatment of squatters in East Berlin. East Berlin had been ruled by a coalition also headed by the SPD. In these new elections, however, the SPD performed badly, and the CDU and FDP made strong advances. They did not quite have an overall majority between them, and the outcome of negotiations was a grand coalition between CDU and SPD, with Eberhard **Diepgen** (CDU) replacing Walter **Momper** (SPD) as governing mayor.

The SPD's losses were primarily in West Berlin, although it gave ground slightly even in East Berlin. They formed part of the general poor performance of the party in the national elections, but were also due to the controversial SPD-Alternative List government of the western part of the city. The CDU did well in east and west, although there was still a large difference between the two. The CDU did, however, overtake the PDS in the former "capital of the GDR". The PDS still had over 20 per cent of the vote in East Berlin, but its position, as in the rest of east Germany, was being eroded. The FDP could be pleased with its showing; it had not been represented in the West Berlin parliament before this election, but it recovered in both parts of the city. The combined forces of the Green alliances in East and West amounted to nearly 10 per cent of the vote. The final message from this election was that the appeal of the far-right Republicans had ebbed for the moment at least. Despite fears of extremism in both West and East, the Republicans could only muster 3.7 per cent in West Berlin (previously 7.5 per cent) and 1.9 per cent in East Berlin (total for Berlin 3.1 per cent).

This completed the initial political integration of east Germany into the enlarged Federal Republic of Germany. The former ruling party was rewarded for its 40-year custody of the country by being displaced by its former subordinate party, the CDU. Erich Honecker, it was announced rather blatantly on election day, was to be charged with multiple manslaughter, in connection with the shooting over the years of escapees at the inter-German border.

In this, as in so many other respects, the past casts a long shadow over "the five new federal states". Both the PDS and the East German CDU have been beset by scandals of misappropriation of party funds, and all the old block parties have come under fire for trying to hold onto their large property holdings in the east. And again and again spy cases are revealed and accusations made about the past *Stasi* associations of public figures. The most prominent to fall was Lothar de Maizière himself in mid-December, just missing out on appointment to Helmut Kohl's new cabinet. The only major political survivors were Günther Krause and two other new ministers in Bonn, Angela **Merkel** and Rainer Ortleb. Meanwhile three of the five new minister presidents of the new *Länder* (**Duchac**, **Gies** and **Gomolka** — all CDU) have been forced to resign and a fourth — Manfred **Stolpe** (SPD) — has come under attack for his *Stasi* contacts. It will be a long while before political life in the east of Germany fully frees itself from its recent history (see Henderson essay in this volume).

After the euphoria, Germany faced a bleak position in the new year of 1991. The true scale of the collapse of east Germany now became clear and difficult decisions had to be made. At the end of January the *Bundesbank* raised interest rates, and in February it was announced that, contrary to all Kohl's earlier pledges, taxes would be raised from July 1, 1991, appropriately on the anniversary of currency union. Kohl had one unfortunate justification for his action, namely the explosion of war in the Gulf. Germany, constitutionally forbidden from engaging troops anywhere in the area, except perhaps in NATO-member Turkey, was stung by foreign criticism into raising its financial contribution to the war effort.

Revolution, reunification and the economy

The political crisis of the German Democratic Republic derived in large measure from its economic crisis, and the problems did not depart with unification. Indeed, in many respects they grew worse as the old system was exposed to market forces (see also Jeffries essay in this volume).

The East German economy 1989-90

The economy of the GDR before the revolution of 1989 was primarily industrial — manufacturing, mining and electricity generating 72.3 per cent of Net Material Product in 1988, the construction industry 7.4 per cent — but with a surprisingly large agricultural sector (9.8 per cent of NMP). The economy was almost entirely state-owned, with only about 3.5 per cent of NMP deriving from private enterprises, and those operating under strict limitations. Energy for both industrial and private consumption came primarily from indigenous supplies of lignite in the southern part of the country. The mining and burning of lignite caused severe ecological and health damage, which was evident to anyone visiting the area. Poor air quality, a coating of brown dust everywhere, and dying trees all testified to the problem.

The GDR managed a full range of products, with an emphasis on engineering, vehicles, chemicals, optics and some consumer goods. The supply of the latter to the population was quite inadequate, however, in terms of both quantity and quality. One major feature of the GDR economy which came to have deleterious effects both on the state budget and upon the adaptability of industry and agriculture was the high level of subsidy on a wide range of goods and services. Most of these were staple food products and fares, but some items were included — such as cut flowers — which scarcely came into these categories. The result of these subsidies, which reached 18.5 per cent of state expenditure in 1988, was to keep most staple prices at 1950s levels. The budget could not carry this; it was admitted after the **Wende** that the neatly balanced budgets of the GDR had in fact themselves been surreptitiously subsidized from hard currency borrowing which did not appear in the accounts. The effect on production of the artificially low prices was that there was no incentive to produce goods in response to demand; producers were guaranteed their income. Some curious anomalies resulted; bread, which was heavily subsidized, was cheaper than animal feedstuffs, so bread intended for human consumption was fed to pigs. The pigs were then bought by the state and sold at a loss.

At the end of 1988 the GDR party and governmental apparatus had once more gone through the motions of approving the next year's plan and state budget. Both were presented with a greater clarity and detail than they had been in previous years, suggesting that changes in attitude were taking shape, but they showed no sign of a change in policy. Despite clear evidence from even the official figures that the apparent economic upturn of the mid-1980s was a thing of the past and was being followed by a remorseless downward trend (see Part III, Table 17), the planners stuck to quantity growth with an emphasis on expensive new technology. In fact, this development programme of autarky in microtechnology, a project dear to the heart of Erich Honecker, had for years been drawing much needed investment away from dilapidated industries, without really being able to modernize production techniques on a significant scale.

The economy at this juncture was characterized by outdated plant, manned by disgruntled and under-used workers on long shifts, producing goods according to plan rather than according to demand. If the plan looked in danger of not being fulfilled, short-cuts were taken or statistics manipulated. Production was often delayed or halted because of supply bottlenecks, and the whole production process was marked by enormous damage to the environment.

For most of 1989 the official statistics maintained their usual fictions, with NMP growth from January to September reported at 4.0 per cent in comparison with the same period of 1988, gross industrial output up 4.4 per cent, net industrial output up 6.0 per cent and labour productivity up 6.1 per cent. Retail trade turnover was claimed to have risen by 4.0 per cent and net money incomes by 3.1 per cent. These figures were far from comforting, however, since they showed little improvement in the general position. In the autumn things did not only get worse, but it was now admitted that they were getting worse. Gross industrial output in November fell in comparison with November 1988 by 2.5 per cent, and growth in NMP by the end of the year was only 2.1 per cent. Over 40 per cent of main plan targets were admitted to be behind schedule, and the state budget was M5–6 billion in deficit.

The reasons for this dramatic decline were a greater honesty in the figures themselves, the political chaos of the last quarter of the year, and the drain on the labour force of emigration. Already in the summer the exodus via Hungary, Czechoslovakia and Poland had begun to deplete the workforce in key areas. It was precisely younger, skilled workers and professionals who were the first to leave, opening crucial gaps which were to become very serious indeed by the end of the year. At that point some 350,000 men, women and children had left the country altogether, reducing the work force by at least 2 per cent, and worse was to come. In the first 10 days of 1990 over 15,000 left the GDR to settle in the Federal Republic and this rate showed no signs of abating.

The first half of 1990 saw the downhill slide begin (see Part III, Table 18). In all sectors of the East German economy concerns faced shortages of supplies, critical gaps in the workforce, and competition from western producers. This was either because the latters' goods were being sold in the GDR or because East Germans in Berlin and near the border were doing their shopping in the Federal Republic. In the early summer western consumer goods, foodstuffs, alcohol and tobacco were being sold on the streets of the GDR, often from mobile stalls. Second-hand cars were being driven to the GDR for sale.

All these problems were exacerbated by the monetary union of July 1, 1990. From that date all wages and salaries had to be paid in Deutschemarks and concerns' debts were converted at a rate of 2:1. The GDR's CMEA trade partners also now had effectively to pay for goods in hard currency. All these aspects placed great strain on the viability of industry and agriculture, but of more immediate importance were the removal of price subsidies and the swamping of the East German market with western produce. The food and consumer goods industries almost overnight found that their produce was replaced by western alternatives more attractive to the population. West German suppliers saw the GDR as a huge untapped market and tried to relieve the East Germans of their now converted savings.

By the last quarter of 1989 gross industrial output was down by 1.0 per cent. The first half of 1990 had seen the position worsen. In the third and last quarters of 1990 output was half that in the equivalent periods of the previous year. The year-on-year outcome was of a fall in gross output of about 20.0 per cent (see Part III, Table 18). The fall in output was accompanied by an accelerating laying off of workers or placing them on short-time. Unemployment, which had officially been nil under the old regime, rose from 7,000 (0.1 per cent) in January 1990 to 757,200 (8.6 per cent) a year later (see Part III, Table 19 and also Jeffries and Timmins essays in this volume). As significant was the level of short-time working, which in many cases amounted to unemployment, funded from the West German budget. In July 1990 there were 656,000 short-time workers; by January 1991 there were 1,841,000. Within the category of short-time there were changes too. At the end of December 1990 41 per cent of short-time workers had had their working hours cut by more than half. Only a month later this proportion had risen to 50 per cent.

The support of short-time workers by the Federal Labour Institution (*Bundesanstalt für Arbeit*) became a matter of controversy. It was suggested by some entrepreneurs that it was discouraging people from looking for new opportunities. As the president of the Federal Association of German Industry (BDI), Heinrich Weiss, put it in February 1991, "I cannot expect from someone who is receiving 92 per cent of his net wage for not working that he start looking for a new job with any great ambition". However, the political effect of withdrawing state support would be unacceptable to the government, so it devised a scheme to extend the short-time provisions beyond the original deadline of June 1991, while insisting that workers in such a position participate in a retraining scheme.

Besides unemployment, there has been a significant reduction in the total labour force in east Germany. This may be as much as 15 per cent (1.3 million). This is due to emigration, commuting to West Germany, early retirement, dismissal of working pensioners and foreign workers, and unemployment itself. This will ease the position in the longer-term, as overmanned sectors of the economy trim down, but in the mean time unemployment, with its accompanying social tensions, remains high.

Throughout 1991 and in 1992 the German government was desperately picking on any signs of economic improvement in the east German economy. There were some to be found, for instance in the unemployment figures for June 1992. They showed unemployment in east Germany down a fraction to 1,123,000 (13.8 per cent), although the position was considerably worse than this in Mecklenburg-West Pomerania in the north, with 16.2 per cent. Estimates at the same time from Jürgen **Möllemann** at the Economics Ministry were for growth in the east German economy in 1993 of between 9 and 11 per cent, but this is, of course, from a very poor basis and also includes the growing incomes of eastern commuters to west Germany.

The costs of unification

At the forefront of the unification issue were and still are the questions of how much it will cost and who will pay for it. They are economic questions which allow no simple answer, but they are also political questions which have been exploited by all participants in the process. In the early stages of the debate it appeared that the East German economy, in crisis as it was, could nevertheless be integrated into the West German economy without major upheaval. The two Germanies were after all the economic leaders in their respective European camps. Well before economic and currency union, however, it became clear that the task was going to be much greater and much more costly than this. The massive depletion of the East German labour force and the reluctance of West German and other western business to invest in the GDR threatened to undermine the East German economy before the process of unification was even agreed. Currency union then itself posed problems, with politically-determined exchange rates and sudden competition from West German produce. Industry and agriculture were collapsing, the state budget of the GDR was proving inadequate, and at the same time it was becoming clear how huge the task was going to be of modernizing the infrastructure of the GDR and repairing the environmental damage.

These problems were to be faced at the same time as the political parties geared up for first the *Volkskammer* elections in March 1990 and then the *Bundestag* elections in December. Chancellor Kohl, whose position in West Germany had been slipping, knew that he needed to win the GDR vote for the CDU. This would make the negotiation of unity easier and it would stand him in better stead in the eventual all-German elections. He and his colleagues in West and East Germany had to make economic promises before March and then deliver enough of them before December. Kohl also had to consider the impact on his West German constituency of a high bill for unification. As for the SPD opposition, its chancellor candidate Oskar Lafontaine tried to exploit Kohl's earlier weakness, to seize the initiative in the GDR by emphasizing the social welfare and democratic socialist credentials of his party, and to present what he claimed was a more honest costing of unification. He also took account of West German concern about the numbers of East Germans entering the Federal Republic by suggesting that the incentives for them to do so should be withdrawn and that the money be spent on rebuilding the GDR from within. As is now known, Kohl's strategy succeeded where Lafontaine's failed, but in the process the public costings of unification were manipulated and underestimated. Only after the elections of December 1990 did the Bonn government admit its mistakes.

Before the March *Volkskammer* election Kohl made a promise that the exchange rate between the two German currencies would be on a 1:1 basis, at least for personal savings. This was contrary to the advice given publicly to Kohl by the president of the Bundesbank, Karl Otto Pöhl, who argued for a lower, more realistic rate. Meanwhile, the East German CDU leader, Lothar de Maizière, promised that no-one in the GDR would lose by unification. The clear message of both was that a victorious CDU would use the resources of the booming West German economy to guarantee the savings, jobs and wages of the citizens of the GDR. It was a message which contributed to the CDU landslide win.

The figure for the costs of unity agreed between the two Germanies was DM115 billion over five years (DM22 billion in 1990; DM35 billion in 1991; DM28 billion in 1992; DM20 billion in 1993; and DM10 billion in 1994). DM20 billion was to derive from savings in the West German budget, particularly in the hitherto existing costs of the division of Germany. The remaining DM95 billion, known as the German Unity Fund, was to be raised on the capital markets, half by the Federal government and half by the *Länder* of the Federal Republic. Thus unity was to be achieved at no direct cost to the West German tax-payer, with only a very modest increase in public borrowing, and without antagonizing the *Land* governments of West Germany.

Lafontaine cast doubt upon the figures, when he suggested that DM100 billion per annum was a more likely cost — five times as much as that agreed between finance ministers Waigel and Romberg. He was not the only one to do so. Most independent analyses came out with much higher estimates than those in the inter-German agreement. Already in June 1990, before currency union, a commentary in the *Süddeutsche Zeitung* suggested an extra borrowing requirement in the second half of 1990 of about DM43 billion, in 1991 of DM66 billion and in 1992 of DM70 billion, thus well exceeding in three years the total amount allocated for five.

The crunch came with currency union on July 1, 1990. It was not so much the 1:1 exchange rate for the initial tranches of personal savings which caused the problem. There was something of a spending spree on western goods, but not to the degree feared. It was the 1:1 rate for wages and the 2:1 rate for industry's obligations which were too much to bear. The former, necessary perhaps to keep workers, nevertheless placed huge pressures on concerns now facing western competition, especially when unions began to press for wages nearer West German levels. The latter made the debts of East German industry soar in real terms. The effect of this was to land the **Treuhandanstalt** and ultimately the West German government with the entire amount of approximately DM120 billion.

This burden was from the past, exacerbated by the terms of the currency union, but it covered nothing of the costs of the future. East German agriculture alone in 1991 needed in the region of DM19 billion to survive, over half the amount deriving from the German Unity Fund in that year. A study by the Institute for Ecological Economic Research added then the costs of environmental improvement and restructuring in the fields of energy, transport, waste disposal and water. The estimate is of as much as DM38–47 billion per annum for 10 years. Since new investors in East German industry are not to be held responsible for existing environmental damage (so-called *Altlasten* — "old burdens"), these costs will have to be borne primarily by the public purse. As unemployment and short-time working in the former GDR have risen they have posed a burden on the Federal exchequer. Compensation is payable to those claiming back property confiscated by the communist regime, if that property cannot simply be returned. And another vast sum will have to be paid for the relocation of the capital in Berlin and in the reallocation of federal functions around the cities of the newly united Germany. The indications are that there is no hurry at the moment to take this expense on board. The move to Berlin is not expected to be complete until after the end of the century, and a decision was taken, for instance, not to move the Constitutional Court from Karlsruhe to **Leipzig**.

To add to the political problem, in the run-up to the all-German elections in December 1990 Kohl and his ministers made firm undertakings that there would be no tax increases to fund unity. Like President Bush before them, they then had to eat their words. Very soon after the elections Finance Minister Waigel was talking about forms of environmental taxation which might contribute, along perhaps with a privatization programme in West Germany. In January increased borrowing of DM20–30 billion in 1991 was announced, and in mid-February 1991 the new Economics Minister, Jürgen Möllemann, was admitting that the government had "got its sums wrong" and that tax rises were inevitable. An emergency package of an extra DM30 billion over three years was announced to give assistance to the five east German *Länder*.

From July 1, 1991 a series of tax increases came into effect for one year, placing extra duties on petrol and raising personal taxation. Although these were announced as temporary, the pressure on public finances continued in 1992. Value Added Tax is to rise to 15 per cent from January 1993, and Finance Minister Theo Waigel again warned that unless there is sufficient private investment in eastern Germany, further tax and duty increases will be necessary. Transport Minister Günther Krause announced in July 1992 his intention to increase fuel duties and possibly to introduce an annual motorway fee as in Switzerland. These proposed measures he justified not only on financial but also on ecological grounds. Many government programmes have been trimmed or cut altogether in 1991–92, including German participation in the European Fighter Aircraft consortium.

It is impossible to put one clear figure on the eventual cost of unification. To give some idea of the scale, in 1992 the estimated net transfers to the east, excluding the railways, postal service and — importantly — the *Treuhandanstalt* were in mid-year expected to be about DM180 billion. This contrasts sharply with the DM115 billion originally set aside in mid-1990 for *five* years.

The privatization of the east German economy

The body whose task it has been to privatize economy of the GDR, the *Treuhandanstalt*, was the creation of the Modrow regime, but its purpose soon changed after his fall from office. The de Maizière administration had a stronger free-market orientation, and the *Treuhandanstalt's* purpose came to be the disposal of socialized and state property either into private ownership or into insolvency. Its remit was a large one. It could order enquiries into the operations and finances of concerns and it could make funds available to restructure them. In the longer term its purpose was to sell them off. The process moved very slowly to begin with. By mid-July 1990 a quarter of the approximately 8,000 concerns involved had still not been transformed into capitalized companies, and of those now legally GmbH or AG, many did not yet have full complements of chairmen, boards and management. Another problem was that companies put in large claims for restructuring funds. The *Treuhandanstalt* had to make controversial choices about which businesses were viable in the longer term and should be supported for the time being. For the month of July 1990 alone claims totalled over DM17 billion, of which 41 per cent were approved.

The slow progress made by the *Treuhandanstalt*, the emphasis which it was forced to place on keeping ailing industries going rather than on selling them, and the accusations made that bureaucrats and managers still in place from the old system were hampering advance all took their toll, and only four weeks after his appointment Reiner **Gohlke** resigned. He said that the task of privatization was more difficult than he had originally assumed and that the GDR economy was in chaos. Gohlke was replaced by Detlev Rohwedder, chairman of Hoesch steel and already chairman of the *Treuhandanstalt*'s supervisory board. Despite voicing many qualms himself about the efficacy of the Treuhandanstalt in the face of its enormous task, Rohwedder was persuaded by the West German government to carry on into 1991 and he took the privatization priority further.

Even at the end of 1990 the progress made by the *Treuhandanstalt* was very limited. In addition to the "old" debts of East German industry, the *Treuhandanstalt* had paid out DM28 billion in liquidity credits, unsure how much of this would ever be repaid by ailing companies. Its revenue so far from the proceeds of sales was only DM2.5 billion, so the original aim of financing the whole operation through sales was a long way off. In October 1990 Detlev Rohwedder had estimated the assets of the *Treuhandanstalt* at DM600 billion, but this now seemed an over-estimate. By the end of the year the number of firms sold off was in hundreds rather than thousands.

The controversial actions of the *Treuhandanstalt* made it the focus of much popular discontent. Whenever a business was allowed to go under or dismiss a large proportion of its labour force, the *Treuhandanstalt* came under fire. On the other hand it was criticized for moving in too bureaucratic and cumbersome a manner when investors were seeking to purchase property. One tragic consequence of the attacks on the *Treuhandanstalt* — not, of course, intended by those who criticized — was that members of the terrorist Red Army Faction took it into their heads to court sympathy and cause chaos by murdering Detlev Rohwedder. He was shot in Düsseldorf on April 1, 1991. His death, coming after previous terrorist murders and lone attempts on the lives of west German politicians, created public outcry.

If his death was meant to hamper privatization, Rohwedder's successor, Birgit **Breuel**, soon saw to it that this was not the outcome. Breuel, a punchy proponent of the free-market economy, made it her purpose to promote the image of the *Treuhandanstalt* and to step up its programme of privatization within Germany and abroad. The results have been impressive, even if a large number of problem cases remain and the financial receipts of the *Treuhandanstalt* have been low. In its summary balance-sheet of June 1, 1992 the *Treuhandanstalt* reported that it had privatized 7,613 concerns and parts of concerns (the original 8,000 had been broken up several times, so this does not mean that nearly all had been sold); 13,374 hectares of agricultural land; and 7,000 lots of real estate. Particular emphasis had been placed on creating a new *Mittelstand* (middle class) of *small* businesses, and to this end 25,000 retail and trade outlets, 1,700 pharmacies, 550 bookshops, 600 cinemas and more than 300 hotels and restaurants had been sold to the *Mittelstand*. However, total receipts by the *Treuhandanstalt* were only DM29.3 billion, and its debts stood at DM117.5 billion (end 1991).

Despite high-profile campaigns abroad to attract foreign interest, it had not been as forthcoming as had been wished, but nevertheless by March 1992 nearly 350 concerns, representing DM10,833 billion and nearly 100,000 jobs, had found foreign purchasers. The largest numbers were going to British (66), Swiss (64) and French (48) firms.

Property claims

One of the main reasons why most East German concerns failed to excite immediate interest on the part of western investors was the question of property rights. Would-be purchasers were afraid that any property they might acquire would subsequently be claimed back by a former owner expropriated by the previous regime. The two German governments tried to regulate this matter in an agreement signed in June 1990. Under it no claims could be made for the restitution of property confiscated during the occupation period 1945–49. Property confiscated since without compensation would in principle be restored to the original owners or their heirs. If, however, land or premises had been converted into public amenities (for instance, a housing estate) or been absorbed into some larger economic enterprise, compensation would be given instead. Also, if GDR citizens had acquired property in an honest manner, the original owners would similarly receive compensation in lieu of the property itself. This was to avoid acrimony over East Germans being evicted from their homes, farms or businesses by returning former owners.

By the beginning of 1991 this agreement was seen as not having been enough to encourage investment, and new regulations were drafted by the Ministry of Justice and laid before the *Bundestag* in February. It was noted that the *Treuhandanstalt* and the new *Land* governments had been faced with great difficulties over the property question. More than a million restitution claims had been received for 1.5 million properties. At least 9,000 claims related to small and medium-sized businesses which were now part of combines in the hands of the *Treuhandanstalt*. Estimates of the extent of the claims ranged from 40 per cent to nearly one half of all property in the former GDR. The purpose of the new bill was to simplify procedures both for claimants and for those wishing to buy East German properties and businesses. The *Treuhandanstalt* was to have greater scope in making suitable sale or rental arrangements for each individual case. Another change was the inclusion of the years of the Third Reich (1933–45) within the time for which claims could be made, thereby including widescale expropriation of Jewish owners. The occupation years were still excluded.

Investment in the GDR

After the initial flurry of business interest in the GDR dating from the breaching of the Berlin Wall, most West German companies came to view the GDR primarily as an extended domestic market rather than as a focus for major investment. The President of the (West) German Chamber of Trade and Industry (DIHT), Hans-Peter Stihl, criticized the GDR's remaining legislative barriers for this, but in addition to any effect from this quarter there were the general uncertainties and the unwillingness to get involved before some of the mess was sorted out. As far as the added market of about 16 million people was concerned, it could largely be supplied from existing capacity in West Germany.

This applied less to certain financial, service and infrastructural sectors. The large West German banks, particularly the Deutsche and the Dresdner, moved in smartly to develop a network of branches throughout the GDR — often in prefabricated accommodation, and Allianz insurance pre-empted its competitors by taking 49 per cent (the maximum at that stage) of the state-run insurance system. The three electricity giants of the Federal Republic also stepped in to take over the GDR power network; RWE of Essen, Bayernwerk of

Munich, and PreussenElektra of Hanover were on their way towards an agreement with the GDR, but they ran up against difficulties with the West German monopolies commission. Nearly half of the gas monopoly, Verbundnetz AG, was sold to Ruhrgas AG and BEB Erdgas, with the remainder being offered to seven other German and foreign interests, including Wintershall AG and British Gas plc. Lufthansa was to have taken over the East German airline, Interflug, but then withdrew from negotiations and Interflug was wound up. The West German Telekom section of the Bundespost and the East German Deutsche Post planned a crash programme to develop the woefully inadequate East German telephone system. The aim was to instal 100,000 instruments in 1990, and through glass-fibre cables to increase the inter-German capacity to 600,000 calls per day. They planned further to build modern telephone exchanges in nine cities, so that not all calls had to pass as hitherto through East Berlin or Magdeburg.

Although the emphasis in West German involvement in the East German economy has been on infrastructural problems, some major companies have set manufacturing projects in motion. Car-makers have been in the forefront. Volkswagen, spending DM5 billion, plans an assembly plant producing 250,000 cars per year from 1994. This will be at Mosel, north of Zwickau, the town renowned for manufacturing the two-stroke Trabant. Daimler-Benz negotiated the takeover of the IFA works at Ludwigsfelde, south of Berlin. This would cost DM1 billion, with a further DM1–2 billion set aside for other investment. Opel, the German subsidiary of General Motors, plans to spend DM1 billion on a 150,000 cars per annum plant at Eisenach. This would replace the Wartburg production in the town, which has been axed by the *Treuhandanstalt*.

There are problems for all investors in east Germany. Even though the German government has made it clear that investors are not financially responsible for the environmental clean-up required, most have refused to take over the premises and plant of the East German companies; they are instead developing new greenfield factories. This leaves the problem of the old sites. Other forms of new enterprise have also developed, particularly in the retailing and service sector. Here West German companies have established their presence in the towns and cities of east Germany, and some small East German entrepreneurs have been launching their own businesses. In 1990 an estimated 227,000 firms were founded. Most of these were very small, however, and have difficulty in the face of experienced west German competition.

Agriculture

East German agriculture was overwhelmingly socialized, with nearly 95 per cent of agricultural land organized in co-operatives (LPG) or state farms (VEG). Private production, including that on the individual plots of co-operative farmers, did, however, contribute significantly to the supply of eggs, livestock, fruit and vegetables. The mid-1980s had seen record cereal harvests (11.66 million tonnes in 1986), but there had been a decline since then (10.80 million tonnes in 1989). In any case, yields were only moderate in comparison with West Germany, some 15 per cent lower in the case of wheat.

Revolution and unification threw the agricultural sector of the GDR into deep trouble. For a long time protected by subsidy from the rigours of the market, it faced an immediate slump in demand. Once the doors opened to West German foodstuffs on July 1, 1990, consumers avoided domestic produce. Rightly or wrongly, they considered it of inferior quality, and even price cuts failed to move it. In fact, in many shops GDR products were not available. West German milk went on sale, while GDR farmers poured theirs onto the fields. In the summer of 1990 it looked as though the total collapse of agriculture was imminent. Funds were lacking for all aspects of business, including paying wages, and the de Maizière government had to step in with emergency measures to hold the situation in check. These included a deal with the USSR to supply agricultural produce, particularly pork, from surplus production.

The agriculture of the GDR also suffered from structural problems which will take a long and painful time to solve. First, there were proportionately more people working in agriculture than in West Germany, 14 full-time workers per 100 hectares of land, compared to only seven in the West. Some of these were in ancillary functions in the co-operatives, but even so overmanning was high and unemployment soon bore down heavily on agriculture. Second, agricultural production was divided too rigidly into arable and livestock, which made for expensive and artificial flaws in the system and for over-specialized agricultural workers. Third, the environmental damage done by and to agriculture has been bad for productivity and is bad for marketing in an increasingly environmentally-conscious Europe. And fourth, as the privatization process got underway, so the unclear property relations in the agricultural sphere become a problem. Strictly speaking, members of co-operatives did not surrender ownership of their land, but only the use of it. This meant that larger co-operative farms might once more be divided up in ways which were not economically rational.

The Bonn government and the European Community have had to make transitional arrangements to prevent the collapse of East German agriculture. EC rules are to be introduced gradually in the region, and the government has used intervention buying, production cutbacks, and the export of foodstuffs in an attempt to ease the transition.

Ironically, the performance of East German arable production was very good in 1990. The cereal harvest of 11.83 million tonnes was a new record, exceeding even 1986. This, and the drop in domestic demand for fodder grain, has led to excess stocks. East German and West German grain production together make Germany the leading producer of barley in the European Community and second only to France in wheat.

Reports in mid-1992 indicated mixed fortunes in east German agriculture. East German food had recovered a good deal of its market amongst the population, partly because people were used to local specialities, partly because of price, and partly because large numbers of people deliberately sought out east German produce as a gesture of solidarity. Meanwhile, the structure of production has changed dramatically. Some 600,000 people have left agricultural employment (meaning unemployment for many), and many small concerns have started up. About 16,000 family farms have appeared, although they are on average markedly larger than the average in the old *Länder* of the Federal Republic — 90 hectares and 30 hectares respectively.

Transport

The transport infrastructure of the GDR was quite woeful. Despite a programme of electrification in the 1980s, the railways of the *Deutsche Reichsbahn* moved unbearably slowly. The new partnership with the Bundesbahn has a huge task ahead, and in 1992 the two organizations were running a total debt of DM55 billion. In mid-July 1992 transport minister Krause announced that privatization of the railway system will begin in 1994, with the formation of the Germany Railway (*Deutsche Eisenbahn* AG). Three subsidiary public companies will be responsible for passenger services, freight, and track maintenance.

The state of the urban and inter-urban roads of the region also testified to the reluctance of the old regime to let people travel anywhere. From the opening of the inter-German border the pitted two- or even one-lane remnants of 1930s motorways were overburdened by increased domestic traffic and by that of West German visitors. Traffic congestion increased and the accident rate soared, as East Germans bought new and used western cars in large numbers. Since then road-building programmes have proliferated all over the former GDR.

Finance

In the course of the revolution in the GDR the previous state monopoly on banking was broken up, and from October 3, 1990 the finances of the "new *Länder*" fell under the general budget of the Federal Republic. Even before unification the major West German banks began to move into East Germany in order to set up premises and to capture personal and business accounts. They were very cautious at first, however, to fund investment.

The political change also unlocked huge demand on the part of the East German population, and people did have savings to spend. Under the old regime staple goods had been very cheap and all others difficult to find. Excess income therefore found its way into savings accounts (about M163 billion at the end of April 1990), which were in large measure converted into Deutschemarks on July 1, 1990.

In the course of 1990 it became clear that even before the revolution the state budget of the GDR had been more frail than the official picture had led to believe. The surpluses announced had been based on a high degree of hard-currency borrowing. Gross debt at the end of 1989 was approximately $22.3 billion, and by March 1990 it had increased to about $32 billion. During 1990 the ability of the East German government to remain within the strictures of the economic union agreement broke down, and several supplementary budgets in Bonn were required. The crisis of the municipal and *Land* governments of East Germany in 1991 was even worse, and major help from Bonn was and is needed to prevent them from breaking down entirely.

Energy and the environment

The GDR was heavily dependent on its sole large indigenous energy resource, lignite or brown coal. In 1988, 85 per cent of electricity production was from this source, a proportion which had actually been rising during the 1980s. Nuclear energy provided nearly 10 per cent of the total, a fall from 12 per cent in 1980. Both these sources pose major problems. Lignite reserves, though still plentiful, are increasingly difficult to exploit, and the mining of them and the burning of the fuel have caused massive environmental destruction. Nuclear power is not a satisfactory alternative because the safety levels at the power stations have been discovered to be quite inadequate. For these reasons, both a series of lignite power stations and the nuclear reactors at Greifswald and Rheinsberg have been closed down.

Pollution levels in the GDR were higher in most respects than in the Federal Republic because of lignite mining and use, uranium extraction, oil pollution at military installations, over-use of artificial fertilizers, and concentrated livestock production. In certain regards, like domestic waste from consumer products, recycling, and pollution from car exhaust emissions, the GDR had some advantages, but unfortunately with the advent of the capitalist consumer society these are rapidly being lost.

All these environmental problems cannot be tackled at once, but in February 1991 the Federal Minister of the Environment, Klaus Töpfer, announced a programme called "Ecological construction" to improve conditions in east Germany, at a cost in 1991 of DM17 billion. Its range included reducing carbon dioxide emissions, imposing increased fees on producers of industrial and possibly domestic waste, extending and constructing sewage plants, and clearing some of the worst polluted sites in the new *Länder*.

Foreign trade

The communist regime of the German Democratic Republic made analysis of its foreign trade performance very difficult indeed, far more so than did its partners in the CMEA. The statistics issuing from East Berlin were incomplete and implausible. In the first place, trade was not broken down by country into imports and exports. This made it very difficult to assess the GDR's overall trade balance and the relationship between its CMEA and non-CMEA transactions. The problem was compounded by the fact that even the turnover figures country-by-country did not correspond to OECD mirror figures on a discernible pattern of exchange rates. This led to discrepancies between the relative trade volumes derived from western and from GDR statistics. According to the East Germans, for instance, Switzerland was their main capitalist trading partner after West Germany, whereas the OECD figures showed France taking that place. More seriously, the trade account with the Federal Republic of Germany assumed a rough parity between the two German currencies, an assumption which was far from reality. The result was that inter-German trade appeared lower down the list of trade turnover than other observations suggested.

There were other complications. Trade with CMEA was largely on a barter basis and the money figures put on deals were sometimes in transferable roubles, sometimes in Valuta Marks (the GDR's foreign trade accounting unit, not entirely equivalent to the domestic Mark), and sometimes in the currency of the trading partner (Forints, Zloty etc.). In all instances it was not necessarily the case that actual money had changed hands; a notional value was being placed on complex deals. Furthermore, an undisclosed amount of trade with the USSR appears to have been in hard currency.

The trade pattern alleged by the old statistics was as presented in Part III, Table 21. Socialist countries (primarily CMEA) accounted for 69.1 per cent of the GDR's foreign trade turnover in 1988, the industrialized countries of the capitalist world 27.6 per cent, and the developing countries 3.3 per cent. These proportions had been roughly stable for about two decades, although since 1983 the proportion of trade with the socialist world had risen once more after a decline before that. Within non-socialist trade that with developing countries had been in relative decline. The statistics showed the ostensible dominance of trade with the USSR (37.5 per cent of total trade turnover in 1988), with Czechoslovakia (8.2 per cent) and the Federal Republic of Germany (7.0 per cent) a long way behind. Trade with other OECD states seemed of scarcely any significance.

These statistics, like those on the domestic economy, were bogus. They probably had as their main purpose a fudging of the crucial importance of inter-German trade to the GDR economy. With the ouster of Erich Honecker and the economic manipulator Günter **Mittag** and then of SED rule entirely, the figures were entirely recast by the renamed Statistical Office of the GDR. Closer estimates could now be made of the structure and development of foreign trade in the last years of the GDR.

Part III, Table 22 shows the position in 1988–89, as now recalculated. The difference is remarkable. In 1988, turnover with West Germany at 19.7 per cent of the total was much closer to that with the USSR (24.5 per cent) than the 7.0 per cent and 37.5 per cent respectively published under the old regime. The position narrowed further in 1989 to bring trade with West Germany (20.6 per cent of the total) very close indeed to that with the USSR

(22.9 per cent). Other hard currency trade also figured much more prominently than had ever been admitted in the past, with CMEA partners Bulgaria and Romania much lower down the list than they had been before. In fact in value terms "western industrial nations" (including West Germany) took 48.5 per cent of GDR exports in 1989 and provided 53.1 per cent of GDR imports. Nearly one third of GDR trade was conducted with the European Community. Naturally these new figures do not alter the fact that in volume terms the GDR traded vastly more goods within the CMEA than with other countries, but the old figures did not present the picture in volume terms either. The worth to the GDR of its western trade, particularly that with West Germany, was grossly underestimated in the statistics, for political reasons.

The structure of GDR exports and imports according to categories of goods has also been reclassified by the Statistical Office. In 1989, 36.5 per cent of exports and 31.6 per cent of imports were machinery, vehicles and transport equipment; 18.7 per cent of exports and 18.6 per cent of imports were finished goods; 12.1 per cent of exports and 9.0 per cent of imports were chemicals; and 8.3 per cent of exports and 14.5 per cent of imports were fuels and lubricants. The only changes of any consequence in the second half of the 1980s had been a rise in the importation of machinery and transport equipment, and a halving of exports and imports of fuels and lubricants. This last can be explained by the fact that the GDR used to depend for large hard currency earnings on the import, refining and re-export of mineral oil. This trade declined as price relationships became less favourable.

GDR engineering exports were most important for the other CMEA countries and the developing countries, much less so for developed countries, which provided a good deal of plant. Within the CMEA, particularly in relations with the USSR, the GDR had a role of providing relatively advanced quality equipment in exchange for raw materials and semi-finished goods. Exports to the developed countries (primarily West Germany) were — after oil re-exports declined from 1986 — largely finished goods, for example, furniture, toys, and clothing.

By 1989 GDR foreign trade was as sluggish as the rest of the economy, with exports as judged by the new statistics rising by 4.3 per cent in value and imports by 2.1 per cent. In dollar and volume terms these increases must have been even more marginal. The GDR's deficit with OECD countries (including West Germany) rose from $471 million in 1988 to $707 million in 1989, partly due to increased imports from France, Italy and Austria. Trade with West Germany saw exports up 6.1 per cent in Deutschemark terms and imports up 12.0 per cent, but in dollar terms exports were down 1.2 per cent and imports up 4.3 per cent. This was a continuation of the undynamic path of recent years. GDR trade with other CMEA countries saw exports down by 0.2 per cent and imports by 3.2 per cent.

Analysis of foreign trade in 1990 was complicated by the political developments of that year. From July 1 currency and economic union and from October 3, 1990 full political unity meant that the contention over the decades by the West Germans that inter-German trade was not foreign trade became an undisputable reality. This, and the transition to full Deutschemark accounting, complicated assessment of performance in 1990 in relation to previous years. The GDR Statistical Office published figures for foreign trade in the period January-July 1990 inclusive, expressed now in Deutschemarks (see Part III, Table 23). Exports in that period were worth DM21.2 billion, imports DM17.4 billion. This represented in comparison with the same period of 1989 a fall in exports of 8 per cent and in imports of 24 per cent. However, these assessments now excluded West Germany and left the country-by-country breakdown looking like an exaggeration of the old communist statistics: 79 per cent of exports were to CMEA countries, and 69 per cent of imports were from them. The USSR accounted for 42.1 per cent of turnover, and Czechoslovakia for 9.5 per cent.

In the first half of 1990 (before economic union) GDR exports to West Germany were worth DM3.93 billion, up 12.4 per cent on the same period in 1989. Imports more than doubled (up 116.3 per cent) to DM7.85 billion. Combining these two sets of figures the West German share of total turnover in the first half of 1990 was an estimated 26.3 per cent, the Soviet share 31.0 per cent, both figures up markedly on the corresponding ones for 1989. The surge in West German supplies to the GDR was, of course, a result of the open border and the huge demand for consumer goods in the GDR. The figures for the first half of 1990 show massive increases in West German deliveries of foodstuffs, cars, clothes, tobacco and a whole range of other goods.

In non-German trade in the months January–July 1990 GDR exports only increased in food and livestock (by 20 per cent), items which were being replaced in the GDR itself by West German produce. GDR exports of fuels and lubricants were down 53 per cent. Imports of food were cut by 43 per cent, and of engineering and electrical products and vehicles by 30 per cent. The whole process represented the integration of the GDR into one German economy.

From July 1, 1990 inter-German trade was no longer foreign trade for the GDR. West German produce flooded the GDR market, while East German concerns strove to fulfil remaining export orders, especially to CMEA countries. The unleashing of demand in the GDR and the stimulation of demand in West Germany also meant a large increase in total German imports. In November 1990 the western part of Germany had a trade surplus of DM762 million, compared to DM10.6 billion in November 1989. Eastern Germany had a surplus of DM2.5 billion, but this figure now excluded West German supplies and includes the final phases of filling previous CMEA orders.

It had been thought by the Federal German government before the full economic consequences of economic union became apparent that the former GDR would — through its former CMEA contacts — have an important role in developing German trade with the states of central and eastern Europe and with the Soviet Union. In fact, as the revised statistics show, GDR trade with the CMEA was not quite as important as had been assumed. Furthermore, the collapse of most east German trade under the new currency conditions, however, plus the massive political and economic upheavals to the east and south have meant that this function has not yet been of great significance. Indeed, there is a danger that much of the expertise and many of the contacts will have been lost. Nevertheless, German economic influence has been spreading rapidly in the east of Europe, and will, no doubt, continue to do so.

The social consequences

German unification has meant many changes for people in the GDR, ranging from the freedom to travel to the freedom to be cast into unemployment. In general it has produced a mobility, especially amongst the young, unknown in that region, and something of the "wild east" phenomenon to be experienced elsewhere in the former communist states. There is money to be made, but there are also dangers of falling into poverty. For individuals and families the immediate problems have been employment and housing. Unemployment or short-time working have propelled many into seeking work in west Germany on a permanent or temporary basis or into trying to found their own businesses. Women, whose importance in the labour market of the GDR was greater than in the Federal Republic, have found themselves in particular difficulty as far as jobs are concerned (see Alsop essay in this volume). Meanwhile rents on flats have risen perhaps five-fold, putting pressure on those whose incomes have suffered. The question of property claims is still far from solved, and practically every day there are newspaper reports of east Germans being forced out of their homes by west German claimants. These are all new pressures on east Germans and require adaptability, but it should be said too that for most people the standard of living has improved. Their money has real worth, because there are things to buy with it.

Adaptation to new ways of thinking is something which is very difficult to pin down. In many respects, especially amongst the young, there is no very great difficulty in dropping all the jargon of the old days and adopting western styles. For those who knew the GDR for longer the problem is greater. People are cast upon their own resources far more, having to find work for themselves, arrange their own insurance and make their own provisions for child-care. One sad feature of the situation is that many people — particularly women and the elderly — no longer feel safe on the streets of the cities. There has certainly been an increase in crime (bearing in mind, though, that pilfering from the workplace was endemic in the old system), if not to the extent feared. It is, however, the *feeling* that the streets are not safe that is new. The fact that this is a widespread phenomenon in western societies is no consolation.

A person's relation to the old system is a complicated matter which cannot be generalized, but there are inevitably problems for individuals, families and other relationships about past behaviour, especially as people make use of the right to see the *Stasi* files kept upon them. For some the revelation of betrayal by family and friends has caused great distress. It is also true that many of the personnel changes taking place in the economy, in public employment and in educational institutions are coloured by personal scores being settled. The way in which, for instance, the CDU has suddenly become a respectable party while the former SED is no longer, has undoubtedly caused injustices and proked resentments (see also Henderson essay in this volume). Past party membership is, however, not always a clear cut matter. The man in charge of the *Stasi* files, Joachim **Gauck**, has remarked, for instance, that west German employers are often looking askance at east Germans who did *not* belong to the FDJ, the SED or one of the block parties. They are wondering, he suggests, whether their rejection of conformity is what the company now wants.

Labour unrest

West German resentments about the costs of unification have manifested themselves in a variety of ways, but not least in the increasing labour unrest in west Germany in the early months of 1992. As competition from east German labour has increased and wages have been held back allegedly in order to reduce the cost of German unity, so trade unions in west Germany (see also Timmins essay in this volume) have responded with strike action. Metalworkers extracted a pay deal well ahead of the rate of inflation, and for several weeks public service workers brought disruption to west German cities by halting transport, rubbish collection and other services. In fact, if one wanted to find visible evidence in the prosperous cities of western Germany away from the inter-German border that something dramatic had occurred in the country since November 1989 this was one of the few examples.

Right-wing extremism

Another example has been more disturbing, and, understandably, this nastier aspect of life in the new Germany has been given prominence in the international press. The incidence of racist attacks and the growth of neo-Nazism causes concern about the future of Germany. One of the problems is that neo-Nazism as a political standpoint or simply as a matter of style was a means within the old GDR of registering hostility to the system. Secondly, the constant official rhetoric of "anti-fascism" and "anti-racism" never really *explored* these phenomena in the way in which many West Germans did, and it also equated them with the Federal Republic. This robbed the anti-fascist stance of much of its credibility. Thirdly, the GDR was by its very nature a society isolated from cosmopolitan influence, not just since 1949, but since 1933, when racism became an official philosophy. Now that the society is more open, but beset by social and economic problems, the appeal to unemployed young men of aggressive group behaviour against identifiable scapegoats is unfortunately great.

These scapegoats are various. They include the "socialist" guestworkers in the former GDR from Vietnam and Mozambique. They include the numerous Romanians and gypsies who have migrated to Germany. And they include the Poles, who have freer access to Germany and are in many cases operating small impromptu businesses. There were ugly scenes at the border when Poles were first admitted into Germany without a visa requirement in April 1991. In addition there has been a large influx of refugees from many parts of eastern Europe and from the middle east. The temporary accommodation given to them while their pleas for asylum are investigated has been subject to some horrific gang attacks, especially in the autumn of 1991. Hoyerswerda, between Dresden and Cottbus, was the scene of one of the nastiest of these, and the refugees had to be bussed to west Germany.

West Germany itself has witnessed many similar events, which suggests that there are more influences at play than simply the working out of the residual problems of the GDR. Unemployment, housing shortage and the visible presence of large numbers of Turks, Yugoslavs, gypsies and settlers from eastern Europe have encouraged gang violence and political mobilization of the right in the west too. This political aspect is something which west Germany can offer the east Germans ready-made. Small far-right groups have long been established in west Germany and they experience occasional waves of electoral popularity. In west German *Land* elections since unification the **German People's Union** (DVU) and the Republicans have both scored electoral successes. There are also small neo-Nazi groups such as the **German Alternative** which have been seeking to gain ground in east Germany and have found a particular foothold in Dresden.

This said, the right-wing organization and violence is a minority matter, and the outrages have caused public dismay. There have also been large demonstrations *against* racism. Sometimes, as in January 1990, after there had been desecration of Jewish cemeteries in East Berlin, they were used by the PDS to mobilize people in the party's cause, but there have been other less cynical occasions, such as the mammoth march through the centre of Berlin and similar events elsewhere in Germany in November 1991.

The media

The media in the old GDR were rigidly controlled by the political apparatus. Foreign material was strictly vetted and rarely allowed into the country. Alongside this paucity of critical information, however, was set the fact that most of the population of the GDR could and did watch West German television. This was of great significance when western reports showed the protests against the regime in the autumn of 1989, the fall of the Berlin Wall, and the demonstrations in favour of unification in 1989-90.

The political changes in the GDR saw rapid transformation of the media. In mid-November the editorship of *Neues Deutschland* passed from Herbert Naumann to Wolfgang Spickermann, one of his former editorial team. There was no wholesale changeover in staff, but the tone of the paper began to alter. The emphasis was still on the SED's role in a socialist GDR, but there was more open reporting of developments and discussion of problems. From December 4, 1989 the paper appeared no longer as "Organ of the Central Committee of the SED" but as "Central Organ of the SED", reflecting the growing demands within the party for greater democracy. Two weeks later, at the time of the extraordinary party congress, this last reference to the party was dropped, and *Neues Deutschland* became simply a "Socialist Daily Newspaper". In practice, of course, it was still tied to and financed by the SED-PDS (later PDS). To complete the changes, a friendlier format was introduced on February 19, 1990, with a wider variety of articles and text broken down into smaller sections. While Modrow was still prime minister, *Neues Deutschland* had a continuing function as the principal newspaper of record, but on the changeover to de Maizière it became more and more the representative voice of the PDS in opposition. Because of this and because of the dramatic decline in party membership, circulation dropped sharply.

Similar changes overtook the other party newspapers, but the main alteration was the huge incursion of West German material. This did not just mean that West German (and other western) papers and periodicals became freely available in the GDR; they swamped the market. Western publishers began to buy out their East German counterparts (including the purchase of the SED publishing house by the late Robert Maxwell) and publish regional editions of their own papers. The Munich-based *Süddeutsche Zeitung*, for instance, began to issue a Saxon-oriented version. These developments endangered the survival of local initiatives which had sprung up in the aftermath of the *Wende*. An important innovation, however, was the launch of a popular tabloid designed with the east German market in mind. This was *Super*, a tawdry sex and scandal sheet which was enormously popular for a time, but then lost circulation and by July 1992 faced closure. *Super*, east German editions of *Bild* and other popular east German publications have made a point of stirring up resentment amongst the east German population, not so much from a concerned as from a commercial point of view.

The television service also responded to the changes with many staff departures and a new, more open tone to programmes of current affairs. From mid-March 1990 the two channels were renamed from DDR1 and DDR2 to DFF1 and DFF2 and permitted to show commercials. They continued into the period of German unity, but they now have a primary function of reflecting local and regional interests and problems.

As in so many other respects, the political revolution in the GDR had, in the media, consequences not found elsewhere in central and eastern Europe. Although the press, television and radio all changed significantly and expressed the new freedoms, they almost immediately began to be replaced by West German products. The one aspect of German culture which probably means that distinctive newspapers and television channels will continue in eastern Germany is that already in West Germany the press and television were more decentralized than in, say, the United Kingdom.

Conclusion

German reunification is still new, and it is impossible yet to draw firm conclusions about its consequences. As the following six essays show, there are still many unanswered questions with regard to the international situation, the political choices of the electorate and the actions of politicians, the economy, and the prospects for working people, especially women. What has been achieved is in many senses remarkable, not least for its peacefulness, but one must be careful about the rhetoric of the successful. The groundwork was laid not by politicians in Bonn, but by people on the streets in Leipzig risking their careers or their lives, and that democratic impulse has in large measure been squandered.

The problem was that the former GDR needed and generally wanted western assistance, but has suffered under the pressures of the free market and the take-over of much decision-making by west Germans. The population of the old Federal Republic, on the other hand, has from the outset been reluctant to make substantial sacrifices on behalf of the east Germans. It has often been suggested — especially outside Germany — that Chancellor Kohl should early on have made a "blood, toil, tears and sweat" speech, appealing to German nationalism for sacrifices in the name of a unity achieved remarkably peacefully and easily. The problem was that such a fund of patriotism was — because of Germany's history in the 20th century — at a low level. Kohl was probably right in judging that he could not handle the matter in this way. However, the early misrepresentations of the true costs of unity — recognized immediately by all who were familiar with the situation in the GDR — were inexcusable.

The situation as it now stands in mid-1992 is that the west Germans are no more enthusiastic about reunification than they ever were, but they are getting used to it. The east Germans have many resentments about the way in which they have been treated first by the old regime and now by the westerners, but they do not in the main regret reunification. Many indeed have found the new situation full of exciting possibilities for personal development and advancement. Also, as the problems mount elsewhere in central and eastern Europe, most east Germans recognize that the problems they face are common to other peoples, who do not have the advantage of wealthy western relations. Many peoples, including European peoples, would be glad to have the problems the Germans have, but the economic sacrifices which are currently required disproportionately from east and west Germans are certainly fuelling discontent on both sides. Racism and right-wing violence are unfortunately commonplace elsewhere in Europe too, but for historical reasons they have a particularly destructive role in Germany. The positive side is that there are many in Germany who — aware of the horrors of the past — are prepared to mobilize *against* racist outrages.

In 1992 the continuing political identity of the GDR has been manifest in two important political respects. The PDS, which seemed to be on a downward trail set to end in obliteration at the next *Bundestag* elections, put in a remarkable performance in the district (*Bezirk*) elections in Berlin on May 24, 1992. The successor to the SED won 29.7 per cent of the vote in east Berlin and was the strongest party in six out of the 11 districts. The fact that it scored only 0.9 per cent in west Berlin puts its all-German prospects into perspective, but it clearly still has a function as a repository of protest in east Germany.

Another example are the new Committees for Justice, founded on July 11, 1992 by the perhaps surprising partnership of Peter-Michael Diestel (CDU) and Gregor Gysi (PDS). The Committees are meant as a new form of citizens' movement in the new *Länder*, representing east German interests in a united Germany which allegedly pays them too little heed. Diestel, who ran into difficulty with his original party, the right-wing DSU, in 1990, now has problems with the CDU. He resigned from his post of parliamentary leader of the CDU in the Brandenburg *Landtag* after conflict with the chairman of the Brandenburg CDU, Ulf **Fink**, and, seeing himself as a spokesman for the east, he has teamed up with the leader of the PDS. They have gathered together a number of prominent churchmen, artists and intellectuals in order to represent the citizens of the former GDR. According to Diestel: "We want to participate actively in politics and help to shape it. Perhaps one day we shall also appear as a party, in order to be electable. But at the moment our thoughts do not yet go that far."

The response of other politicians to the initiative has been varied, but generally hostile. CDU figures like Fink and CDU General Secretary Peter Hintze have been very critical, and thought has been given to Diestel's exclusion from the party. Even amongst those who agree that the government has been shamefully negligent of east Germany, like Vera Wollenberger of Alliance 90, the new movement attracts adverse comment. She sees in it an attempt — by Gysi in particular — to give the old forces of the GDR a new political platform.

So the problems of east Germany still have their spokesmen, and the west German politicians cannot assume that their views will automatically hold sway in the east. Indeed, a new dimension altogether has been added to German politics. Erich Honecker and his comrades used to pride themselves on having created a workers' state, a dictatorship of the proletariat. Their lasting achievement has been to preserve that proletariat within east Germany. West Germany was, of course, never quite the classless society which some claimed it was — it only appeared so in contrast to Britain — but the class element of German society, curiously mingled with the regional dimension, now once more plays an important role.

So far the German government has managed to ride out the process of unification and the problems which have followed from it. There are major social dislocations and economic problems, but still the west German economy has the strength to provide support for the east. Compared to the carnage of Yugoslavia, the miseries of Romania and Albania, the break-up of Czechoslovakia, the governmental instability of Poland, and the incalculable capacity for disaster in what was the Soviet Union, the Germans have much to be grateful for. The easterners marched in rebellion, and the westerners stepped in to distribute the prizes. As Wolfgang Schäuble put it, "Of course we were lucky, but that isn't against the law."

II POLITICS, ECONOMY AND SOCIETY

THE INTEGRATION OF EASTERN GERMANY INTO THE EUROPEAN COMMUNITY[1]

David Spence

This essay provides an account of the issues posed by German unification for the European Community. It describes the deliberations behind the scenes and looks at the concerns of member states about the implications of an enlarged Germany for the Community and the overall balance of power in a wider Europe. The deepening of the Community resulting from the Maastricht summit of December 1991 and its potential widening to include the EFTA countries and several countries of eastern and central Europe have led to calls for a major debate on the kind of Community likely to emerge in the next century.

German unification reset the agenda of the Community along the lines of those valid at the establishment of the original European Coal and Steel Community (ECSC), namely to provide a framework of increased European integration to ensure limits to Germany's power. Indeed, the 1991 inter-governmental conferences on political, economic and monetary union owed much in their timing to the political response of other Community governments to the challenge of German unification, a response which supported not only the process of German unification but also the wider process of European integration.

Early European responses to developments in Germany

When the Berlin Wall was breached and German unification became a possibility the idea initially sounded alarm bells throughout Europe. Some feared a revival of German desire for hegemony in Europe as a whole and certainly within the Community. Indeed, it seemed possible for a short time that a worrying price to the Soviet Union for its agreement for German unification would be simultaneous withdrawal of West Germany from NATO and

---

[1] An earlier and longer version of this essay, with more detailed discussion of the internal workings of the European Community, was published by the Royal Institute of International Affairs as *Enlargement Without Accession: The EC's Response to German Unification* (RIIA Discussion Papers, no. 36, London, 1991). The author would like to thank Dr Helen Wallace, under whose direction that earlier publication appeared.

East Germany from the Warsaw Pact. The foreign policy of a resulting unitary German state might lean heavily towards the neutralism much canvassed in West Germany in the late 1980s.

Within the Community the economic facts pointed to seemingly inevitable conclusions. The new Germany, with a population of nearly 80 million, would be one-third larger than any of the other three larger member states — Britain, France and Italy. Unification could take Germany's share of Community output from 24 to 26 per cent, even before allowance was made for an increase in east German productivity. It would not stretch the imagination too far for the new Germany to pass from Willy Brandt's famous description of it as "an economic giant but a political dwarf" to giant status on both counts.

Chancellor Kohl and the then Foreign Minister Hans-Dietrich Genscher responded to such worries. In a speech at the University of Edinburgh on May 23, 1991, Kohl spoke of German integration into Europe as the legacy of Adenauer "to stop once and for all German policy vacillating between the East and the West", stressing that "Europe will be a federal Europe — it will not be a unitary Europe". However, the idea of Germany as the strongest state in a yet-to-be-defined federal union was precisely what many people had feared. It was a theme which led to a revival of the old British argument about the nature of federalism. Contrary to continental views, the British seemed to believe that federalism was a by-word for centralism, while the continental Europeans have always stressed the decentralizing principle of "subsidiarity" at the heart of federalist theory.

Indeed, in March 1990 the then British Prime Minister, Margaret Thatcher, convened a private seminar at Chequers to assess the implications of German unity. The seminar included an analysis of the German character and whether it had changed since the Second World War. Its conclusions, when leaked, were hardly conducive to close Anglo-German relations. The note of the meeting listed a series of uncomplimentary features of the German character including "angst, aggressiveness, assertiveness, bullying, egotism, (and) inferiority complex". It concluded that as far as German official policy of support for the European integration process was concerned, it might well be a tactic designed to mislead other member states. The idea that Germany seriously believed in European federalism as an alternative to nationalism was "not wholly convincing, given that the structure of the EC tended to favour German dominance". While this private discussion did not represent British policy, it provided a flavour of a debate that was not confined to Britain at that time.

As for the European Community, heads of state and government had declared at the European Council of December 1989 that:

> "We seek the strengthening of the state of peace in Europe in which the German people will regain its unity through peaceful self-determination. This process should take place peacefully and democratically, in full respect of the relevant agreements and treaties and of all the principles defined by the Helsinki Final Act, in a context of dialogue and East/West co-operation. It also has to be placed in the perspective of European integration."

In a speech the following month to the European Parliament Jacques Delors, President of the European Commission, underlined the Commission's support for the unification process and predicted correctly that the integration of eastern Germany would be very fast. But initial disagreements between Germany and other member states on the implications and on the desired speed of unification now loomed. While the Germans clearly believed that a window of opportunity had suddenly been opened, other states, particularly Britain and France, hoped that matters would proceed more slowly. After all, German unification would stand simultaneously as the end of the Cold War and the final settlement of the Second World War, and there was a great deal at stake that went beyond the enlargement of the Community. However, a coalition quickly emerged on the Delors line that German unification could be a catalyst for further European integration.

The problem for the Community was its commitment to completing the internal market by the end of 1992 and to consolidation of the achievements of the Single European Act. In force since 1986, the Act had deepened the supra-national elements of Community business, setting a new agenda for integration. Majority voting had become the rule in many key policy areas. Community legal competence now included issues unforeseen in the original treaties, such as environmental policy, and member states were committed to foreign policy co-ordination and to moves towards economic and monetary union. All this meant that the Community was in a period of introversion. The Community response to the Turkish and Austrian applications for membership had been to delay. Indeed, the Commission had indicated that no application for membership could be considered until the internal market had been completed. Deepening the Community, it was believed, had priority over widening it. True, discussions on a new form of associate membership for EFTA countries had begun, as had bilateral trade negotiations with the countries of eastern and central Europe, including the GDR, but Community enlargement was not on the agenda in the short term.

To counter this, the Germans could argue that the Community had always maintained a positive stance on German unification. They could also argue that France and Britain had a particular status as two of the four powers with rights and responsibilities with regards to Germany and to the city of Berlin. In signing the 1952 Treaty on Germany the four — the United Kingdom, France, the United States and the Soviet Union — had also agreed to work towards a unified Germany with a liberal democratic constitution. Now the question had left the realms of hypothesis, debate about German unification in France and Britain led to a period of unease in their relations with the Federal Republic, not least as these two former occupying powers had to adjust to the consequences of Germany regaining sovereignty and becoming a "normal" nation state.

British and French initial doubts about the role of an enlarged Germany added to more general concerns in the Community about German power. Member state governments were rueful that Chancellor Kohl's 10-point programme was expounded with no prior Community consultation and made no reference to the sensitive issue of the Polish–German frontier. The announcement of the 10-point programme also came shortly after *Land* and European Parliament elections had seen an increase in Germany of support for the radical right-wing Republicans and German People's Union (DVU). The possibility of rapid unification was therefore greeted with ambivalence and in some quarters outright hostility. Nicholas Ridley, the British Secretary of State for Trade and Industry, was quoted as believing that European economic and monetary union was "a German racket designed to take over the whole of Europe" and that giving up sovereignty in the present circumstances, far from being a sure way to control German hegemony, was actually the reverse. His view was that if one gave up sovereignty in the present Community "you might just as well give it to Adolf Hitler". Shortly after making these remarks Ridley was forced to resign. The affair, occurring in the same week as the leaked information about the Chequers seminar, caused the British government some embarrassment and contributed to tension in Anglo-German relations during this crucial period. Another area of concern was reflected in an interview with Margaret Thatcher, published by *Der Spiegel* in March 1990, in which she expressed concern at Chancellor Kohl's reluctance to make a firm commitment on the inviolability of the Polish border. This issue, along with the Two-Plus-Four negotiations and the question of Germany's NATO membership, preoccupied British ministers and senior officials.

As for France, President Mitterrand's hasty visit to Poland in November 1989 and to the GDR in December, his publicly expressed doubts about Chancellor Kohl's 10-point plan, and his December visit to Kiev made unconditional French support for rapid German unification far from certain. Just as Delors was to turn German unification to the advantage of the Community, Mitterrand used the event to reinforce the orientation which French policy had taken in the wider European framework. French policy had long been characterized by the belief that consolidation of the Community would bind Germany into a framework of checks and balances to its potential hegemony. Indeed, in French thinking consolidation implied inclusion of a specific Community dimension to security issues. The strategy was to concentrate on strengthening the West European Union as a precursor to an independent European foreign policy and strengthening its links with the European Community as a means to this end. This would imply a redefinition of Europe's role in NATO and would conveniently get round the problem of France's continued ambivalence about it.

German unification could thus be part of Mitterrand's grand design. He claimed to have no reservations about German unification, as he stressed in a speech in Copenhagen on the day after the opening of the Berlin Wall, but he had previously said the process might take 10 years. His reiterated point was that the process should strengthen European integration, take other countries' interests into account and be placed in the framework of broader European developments. However, further European integration did not seem to be Chancellor Kohl's main priority and there was growing German reluctance to speed up the process of European economic and monetary union. This was a source of grave concern to the French. Now that providing a framework to dilute German power was becoming the priority, Mitterrand had to negotiate hard to ensure linkage between agreement to German unification and acceleration of the European integration process.

Jacques Delors was amongst the first to recognize that German unification provided a potential catalyst for the next phase of efforts to accelerate European integration. If an enlarged Germany posed challenges for the Community and for the balance of economic power between its members, here was an opportunity for the Commission to use member states' worries to speed up progress on economic, monetary and political union, within which Germany would be even more tightly bound into the Community.

At the Strasbourg meeting of the European Council on December 8–9, 1989, German unification had received the Council's blessing on condition not only that it respect the Helsinki Final Act, but that it be "placed in the perspective of European integration". The Council also agreed that the inter-governmental conference on economic and monetary union would start as early as December 1990. Agreement on a second inter-governmental conference was to follow at the Dublin European Council in April 1990. The rapid convening of the two conferences resulted in good part from recognition of the implications of German unification, though the further implications of the democratization of other central and east European countries also began to impinge. The prospect of several new applications for Community membership was a distinct reality and the Community needed to opt for deepening before widening.

It seems likely too that the coincidental timing of a French presidency of the Council during the second half of 1989 played a significant role. French policy on economic and monetary union had been to achieve as much progress as possible during its own presidency. The French view was that economic and monetary union would replace the power of the *Bundes-*

bank with the pooled power of a European central bank. The nearly unanimous view that German unification implied a need to accelerate European union was a heaven-sent opportunity to focus minds on preparatory talks and to settle a starting date for negotiations. The ground for this was cleared by a meeting of heads of state and government over dinner in Paris on November 18, 1989.

Margaret Thatcher had originally hoped for German support in resisting an early start to the inter-governmental conferences, but German agreement to the date of December 1990 for the start of the conference on economic and monetary union was the price Chancellor Kohl paid to the French President in order to quell his publicly expressed doubts about the rapid unification of Germany and Kohl's 10-point plan. Once persuaded, Kohl and Genscher made a virtue of necessity. They frequently used the open fears about German unification to stress their view of the vital link between German unity and further European integration. As the CDU's foreign affairs spokesman, Karl-Heinz Hornhues, was later to put it, "some countries want political union because they fear the dominance of a united Germany; we should exploit that fear before it diminishes".

Debates within the Community on the means of integration

Integrating the new German *Länder* was to be an enlargement of an unusual kind. Two sets of issues had to be resolved before detailed negotiations could begin. First, the question of the legal route to integration of the GDR into the Community had to be addressed. Would this be a new accession or the simple expansion of an existing member state? Second, what would be the legal, institutional and administrative consequences? Both questions required more than strictly legal answers.

The process by which the GDR would join the Community obviously resembled an accession. Moreover, there was near unanimity in Germany and elsewhere in the Community that, as with previous accessions, the economic integration process would take years. Indeed, Spain and Portugal were still covered by a transitional period to full membership, lasting from 1986 until the end of 1995 and even longer for some specific areas of Community policy. However, it would be unthinkable to retain a transitional period for so long in what was to become a part of the Federal Republic. It was politically more expedient to treat German unification not as an accession, but as an expansion of the territory of an existing member state. This meant making a series of legal assumptions much debated in the European Parliament and the Commission.

For the European Parliament only an accession treaty requiring its assent under the provisions of Article 237 (EEC) would suffice. Primary legislation was therefore necessary. The Council and the Commission could not accept this view. It implied a much longer negotiation process than political reality was likely to allow. Primary legislation would require the agreement by the Council on a negotiating mandate for the Commission, direct negotiations with the GDR and subsequent ratification by each national parliament. A new accession would also provide an exception to the Community's self-imposed rule that new accessions would only be considered after 1992.

The problem for the European Parliament arose because any alternative to conventional accession would exclude it from the negotiation process and remove from it the right under the assent procedure to the last word on what was negotiated. It would then lose the opportunity to pronounce on the political desirability of the integration of the GDR into the Community and, by implication, German unification itself. However, the parliament was subsequently able to turn to its own advantage the refusal of the Commission and the Council to contemplate the accession option. Although the decision on this was settled by the two German states, the Commission and the Council of Ministers, the parliament secured a special inter-institutional agreement and some concomitant new rights. These were to guarantee it an enhanced role in the deliberations.

There was a parallel between the legal means used to unify the two Germanies and the route chosen to integrate the GDR into the Community. Instead of proceeding to an accession treaty, the Community could conclude that the references in the European Community treaties to the Federal Republic of Germany assumed no fixed territorial definition. Thus, this existing member state could simply redefine its territory without implications for primary legislation. In this hypothesis, Article 227 (EEC), which defines the territory of the Community by listing the member states, would not need revision. There would be no need to invoke Article 237 on new accessions, nor for assent from the European Parliament, ratification by member states and formal negotiations between the Community and the GDR. While any member state could request treaty amendment under Article 236 (EEC), there would be no legal obligation involved. In fact, no state saw a need to do so and political consensus on the issue was reached at the Dublin European Council in April 1990.

For Community decision-makers three legal and administrative issues had to be settled before the detailed work could begin. The first was the effect on the institutions; in particular, the question of whether the new geographical and economic realities made necessary a revision of the voting arrangements in Council and the representation of the new *Länder* in the European Parliament. Such a revision would require amendment of Articles 138 and 148 (EEC) and of the ECSC and Euratom treaties. The second issue concerned the implications under international law of merging the two states; whether the Federal Republic legally inherited the GDR's international rights and obligations in areas where competence had already been ceded to the Community. Third, transitional arrangements would be inevitable for the new *Länder* and these would have to be agreed by the Council of Ministers.

The institutional questions were of immediate concern to the European institutions. Voting in the Council of Ministers is weighted according to a political formula which considers France, Germany, Italy and the United Kingdom as equal members for voting purposes. Though a substantial increase in the German population might imply a corresponding change in the voting weights, member states were grateful for Germany's decision not to request a review of these arrangements. This calmed political anxieties and avoided the major public debate which the consequential primary legislation would have implied. It was certainly wise of the Federal Republic, because it created a reservoir of goodwill on which it might draw in the subsequent negotiations. It also avoided setting a precedent for other potential members, such as Turkey, where the population principle might prove embarrassing.

The question of an increase in the number of German Commissioners was relevant, but also left to rest. It too would have required primary legislation, and would have put an end to the gentlemen's agreement on the appointment of two Commissioners from the larger member states. The question of a streamlining of the Commission and the possible reduction of the total number of Commissioners was later on the agenda of the inter-governmental conference.

As for the European Parliament, Article 137 (EEC) could be interpreted as justifying an increase in the number of members of the parliament as a result of a population increase in a member state — in this case of 30 per cent. Alternatively, a redistribution of existing seats could perhaps provide the necessary democratic legitimacy. However, no coefficient between population and representation is fixed in the treaty, and the possibility of setting precedents for future enlargement was serious. No immediate change was requested by the German government. The question of a uniform electoral procedure is now on the Community agenda and will certainly include discussion of the link between population and the number of MEPs. Meanwhile there is disquiet in eastern Germany about the lack of voting representatives in the European Parliament, since it was agreed for the time being that the new *Länder* be represented by 18 observers with no voting rights. The only alternative short of a treaty change would have been the resignation of 20 current office-holders and a redistribution of the 81 seats to include full members from the new *Länder*.

The second major issue concerned the law of succession of states. The decolonization process of the 1950s and the assumption by new states of the responsibilities of former colonial powers provided a legal framework. The Commission's legal service inferred from the "doctrine of moving treaty frontiers" that the legal personality of the Federal Republic would not change with its enlargement and that the Community would inherit those international treaties where Community competence existed. This came as some surprise to the legal advisers of the Federal Republic, whose assumption had been that the Foreign Ministry would remain responsible for the potential renegotiation of all such treaties. The Community clearly does act as a recognized international entity in areas of Community competence, so there was no extensive debate and the Commission view swiftly prevailed.

A more important question was whether the Community would consider the treaties of the GDR void on unification or respect obligations under them. Insofar as such treaties did not contradict Community policy there would be no legal consequences, but in early 1990 the full extent of the treaty framework of the GDR within the CMEA (Comecon) was known neither to the West German government nor the Commission. However, the political question of *Vertrauensschutz*, that is the respecting of the "legitimate expectations" of the GDR's trade partners, was considered crucial. There were three main reasons for this. First, the Community was currently preparing for a negotiation of European (association) Agreements with three of the GDR's trading partners, Hungary, Poland and Czechoslovakia. An immediate raising of tariffs on their exports to the former GDR would be contrary to the spirit of these negotiations. Second, and more importantly in terms of practical politics, a sudden imposition of the common external tariff on east German imports would jeopardize those countries' transition to market economies. Third, it was recognized that east German industry would in any case suffer from the sudden arrival of market economics and it was important to maintain east German CMEA markets to ensure that a further burden was not imposed on east German industry. The Commission therefore decided to opt for *Vertrauensschutz*. The detail would be the subject of negotiations between the Commission and the German authorities and subsequently between the Commission and member states. The Germans had in any case included the *Vertrauensschutz* principle in the draft treaties on economic and on political union.

The third major question concerned measures exempting the former GDR from certain Community legislation on a transitional basis. Given the decision to recommend that unification be considered as the expansion of an existing member state, Community law would normally be applicable immediately and in its entirety. This meant that the transition question was relevant to substantive treaty law and to secondary legislation. It was evident that the treaties would not permit the existence of a planned economy denying the very basis of the Community's four freedoms. Equally, the Federal Republic would not be able constitutionally to fuse with the GDR without the introduction of a market economy and concomitant legal structures. The same principle applied to secondary legislation. If the GDR could not apply existing Community directives and regulations, derogations would have to be negotiated and agreed by the Council of Ministers under the relevant voting arrangements, depending on the treaty basis of individual items of legislation to be amended. In sum, agreement had to be reached whereby primary legislation would not be required and transitional measures could apply to only part of a member state.

Preparation within the Community institutions

As these implications of German unification emerged, a co-ordinated response by the Community institutions became necessary. The Strasbourg European Council of December 1989 had asked the Commission to prepare a paper outlining the essential elements of a Community response. Within the Commission, initial responsibility remained with the President and a small group of Commissioners known internally as the "group of four". These four — Delors, Bangemann, Christophersen and Andriessen — ensured that the Commission's strategy "Europeanized" the process of German unification, thereby stressing the importance of its contribution to European integration itself.

In January 1990 a further special group of Commissioners was set up with Vice-President Bangemann in the chair. Commissioners, senior German politicians and officials were to address the Commission on individual policy areas likely to require derogations from secondary legislation. The "Bangemann Group", as it became known, met for the first time on February 9 and then weekly until July 1990. The German Permanent Representative, Jürgen Trumpf, and his senior officials in Brussels became regular visitors to the 13th floor of the Berlaymont. On March 23 Chancellor Kohl himself addressed the Commission in a meeting lasting two hours.

The Commission strategy took account of three concerns. First, German unification should not take place to the detriment of European integration and in particular it should not jeopardize the completion of the internal market by 1992. Second, the advantages to member states of increased trade and the new German market were to be underlined. Finally, in light of the approaching negotiations on new roles for the Commission resulting from the inter-governmental conferences, the opportunity was to be used to demonstrate the effectiveness of the Commission in orchestrating a fast-track "accession".

Meanwhile, on February 15 the European Parliament had agreed to set up its own "temporary committee to consider the impact of the process of German unification on the European Community". The committee met for the first time on March 1 under the chairmanship of Gerardo Fernandez-Albor, a Spanish Christian Democrat, with the British Socialist, Alan Donnelly, as rapporteur. The committee's brief, agreed on March 13, 1990, was to consider the institutional aspects of German unification, the overall political context, both in the Community and within Germany itself, and the impact on sectoral policies.

The committee's strategy was to insist that the European Council's likely overruling of the parliament's view on the accession question did not diminish the role the parliament intended to play. From the outset, the committee adopted a high profile, both within the parliament and in its relations with the German government and the Commission. The Commission's Secretary-General, David Williamson, attended the first meeting and promised extensive collaboration. Invitations to the two German governments and parliaments to participate in the work were immediately issued. The East German *Volkskammer* began sending representatives on April 19, but before this the committee had taken evidence from Gerry Collins (President of the Council), Irmgard Schwaetzer (then West German Minister of State for Foreign Affairs) and the "group of four" Commissioners.

The final stage in the preparation process was the special meeting of the European Council in Dublin on April 28, 1990. The Commission had now to provide the analysis requested in Strasbourg in December. Its communication to the Council was based on deliberations in the Bangemann Group and preliminary observations by the Commission's services. The paper gave a brief analysis of the East German economy and of the advantages of unification for Europe as a whole. It then set out a strategy for the gradual incorporation of the GDR into the European Community. The health of the East German economy seemed impressive when compared with the situation in other CMEA countries. Gross National Product, judged on the GDR's own figures, was higher per head than in Ireland, Greece or Portugal. The Commission's analysis of the economic prospects was optimistic:

> "In general terms, we are likely to see vigorous economic growth in the German Democratic Republic, generating high demand throughout the Community, and an increase in imports from the other member states. This additional growth will be reflected in additional (Community) revenue."

In retrospect, it is clear that the Commission's paper misjudged the economic situation in the GDR and the short-term results of unification.

The Commission paper argued that German unification would offer "an opportunity for reinforcing and speeding up European integration". As to how the Community should proceed, the Commission formally recommended that the procedures used for accession should not apply. The integration of the GDR was, however, to be comparable to an accession, with two exceptions. First, many of the economic adjustments would occur before formal integration into the Community by virtue of the projected treaty on monetary, economic and social union. Its implementation on July 1, 1990 would provide the basis for harmonizing legislation in areas of Community competence. The second difference was that the process of integration would not involve negotiations with the GDR itself, but with the Federal Republic as the existing member state.

The Commission foresaw three stages of integration. The first interim stage would commence with the implementation of monetary, economic and social union. The second transitional phase would begin with unification itself, and the final stage would be determined when the *acquis communautaire* became fully applicable in the new *Länder*.

During the first phase, the Commission argued, the gradual adoption by the GDR of Federal German legislation would provide the precondition for membership of the Community — a market economy. The Commission would ensure that the Community's competition and state aids requirements were being met. At the same time, the Commission saw this phase as the period when the price, credit and monetary system would be totally overhauled, VAT introduced and the tax and social security system adapted.

On the transitional phase, the Commission pointed to major problems which were the subject of the subsequent negotiations in the Council. Since 1992 was to see the end of intra-Community controls on free movement, December 31, 1992 would have to be the target date for the expiry of transitional measures. There would also be important implications for the Commission's proposals on relations with the GDR's main trading partners in the East. The Commission's aim was to ensure that problems foreseeable in the transition period would not affect Community policy on free movement and free competition. The various policy areas affected included the internal market, transport, fisheries, agriculture, the structural funds, the environment, social affairs, and trade policy; in short, the whole gamut of Community policy.

Preparing the transitional measures for eastern Germany

The Dublin European Council accepted the Commission's views on how best to integrate the GDR into the Community and the phasing proposed. It required the Federal Republic to keep the Community informed of developments between the two Germanies and the Commission to be fully involved in these discussions. This marked a considerable success for the Commission in raising its profile, since it was now guaranteed a formal right to influence the inter-German negotiations on monetary union and was later even granted an official seat at the discussions on the Treaty of Unification. The Commission thus became the prime source of information for member states, which allowed it formally to set the Community agenda thereafter. The European Council also granted the GDR full access to the European Investment Bank, Euratom and the loan facilities of the European Coal and Steel Community. This accompanied continued support from the Community within the G-24 framework and participation in Eureka.

The European Council confirmed that the transitional measures would recognize "all the interests involved" and should be "confined to what is strictly necessary and aim at full integration as rapidly and as harmoniously as possible". This went some way to allaying fears that German unification would jeopardize aid and investment in the less prosperous member states.

The Dublin European Council's conclusions allowed the Commission to formalize co-ordination arrangements between its services. Previously, arrangements had featured German unification on the weekly agenda of the Commission and the Bangemann Group meetings. In addition, a high-level steering group was now created. Composed of all directors-general, this "inter-service group" was chaired by the Secretary-General himself. The operational level was handled by the Task Force for German Unification under the chairmanship of Carlo Trojan, the Deputy Secretary-General, which met for the first time on May 8, 1990. The two priorities of the Task Force were analysis of the areas of Community competence affected by German monetary, economic and social union and ensuring that the Commission was seen to be influencing the interim stage in which the GDR would come into the Community.

The Secretary-General of the Commission, David Williamson, and his deputy, Carlo Trojan, formed a Commission delegation to Bonn where discussions with Hans Tietmeyer (head of the West German team for the intra-German negotiations) in the margins of the Two-Plus-Four talks on May 5 led to several amendments to the draft treaty on monetary, economic and social union. It was one of several such meetings. They led to the Commission's adopting an official role in the later negotiations on the unification treaty. Either the Deputy Secretary General or a senior member of the Commission's legal service attended all sessions of the negotiations to ensure that the implications for Community law were correctly assessed.

The Community legislative requirements resulting from German monetary, economic and social union were threefold. The Commission proposed setting up a *de facto* customs union between the GDR and the Community with special provisions for agriculture, industrial products and ECSC products. These proposals were made on June 20, 1990, with the intention of aligning the Community legal framework immediately after monetary union on July 1. A further legislative proposal empowered the Commission to issue Euratom loans for projects in the GDR. The GDR was thus becoming a *de facto* member of the Community before unification and certainly before the Community had had time to consider all the implications and settle the transitional measures.

At this stage, the Task Force was planning for the initial report on the implications of monetary union to be followed in autumn 1990 by a more detailed assessment of the implications of unification. It seemed likely that even a fast-track route to unification would still allow the Commission time to complete the analysis so that proposals for derogations could be made in January 1991. The negotiations with the Council would then proceed during the spring.

Each directorate undertook extensive fact-finding sessions in Brussels, Bonn and the GDR. The example of agriculture, though exceptional in its extent, illustrated the work being undertaken by the Commission services at this juncture. As of the first week of June 1990, seven agricultural working groups met permanently in Brussels to review the whole gamut of agricultural legislation. Meetings ended in late July with a draft of a major submission to Council and the European Parliament.

Meanwhile, the timing for unification had changed. It was now assumed that a "fast track" to unification required the Commission to make its proposals by September and the interinstitutional negotiations to be completed in the minimum three months necessary for the co-operation procedure to function. Since all-German elections were planned for December 2, unification and general elections would, it was believed, take place on the same day. However, events in Germany continued to accelerate. In early August, the German government informed the Commission that the link between the election and unification no longer held. The Two-Plus-Four talks were due to end formally on September 12 and there would thus be no legal hindrance to implementation of the Treaty of Unification on October 3. It was therefore decided to complete the Commission's examination of the proposals for transitional measures on August 21 and to send them immediately to the Council of Ministers and the European Parliament. This allowed informal preparation of negotiating strategies in member states and a preliminary discussion in the parliament's ad hoc Committee before receipt of the proposals could be acknowledged and the formal work of the parliament could begin.

Given the impossibility of completing negotiations before the date set for unification, the Commission included in the proposals a set of emergency interim measures. This allowed it to authorise temporary implementation of the proposed transitional measures before member governments had had time to analyse the implications or the Council had debated the contents. This meant giving the Commission very extensive powers for the interim period. Member states and national parliaments had been presented with a fait accompli not so much by the Commission, but by the mounting pressures in Germany for unification. These could not be held back without enormous political cost to the German government. Collapsing confidence was leading to a haemorrhage in East Germany as its citizens moved to the West in search of work. The fast track to unification meant either that the Community institutions must accept the Commission's proposals for interim measures or that the new Germany would be in immediate breach of its obligations under the treaties. There would thus be a legal vacuum during the period of negotiation of the transitional measures. There was hardly an alternative to immediate implementation of interim measures.

The European Parliament's temporary committee had begun its work long before the Commission had embarked on formal preparations, and the Commission had often declared the need for collaboration. Drawing on these declarations, the parliament requested an inter-institutional agreement to be decided by a "trialogue" of the Community's presidents. Enrico Baron Crespo from the Parliament, Jacques Delors for the Commission and Gianni de Michelis, the Italian Foreign Minister, for the Council, met on September 6. The resulting inter-institutional agreement limited the validity of the emergency interim measures to the end of 1990. The parliament agreed to hold two readings of the legislation on the interim measures in the September plenary session, on September 11 and 13 respectively. The Council agreed in turn to consider the parliament's amendments and reach its common position on September 12. The Commission's re-examined proposal would then be presented to the General Affairs Council scheduled for September 17. This implied a 27-day period between Commission proposal and Council acceptance and left the Federal Republic and the Commission 15 days to implement the interim measures before unification.

The agreement also covered arrangements for consideration of the transitional measures. It was settled that the parliament's view would be on both the package as a whole and the detailed proposals. This was a political agreement, which the parliament clearly intended to substitute for the assent procedure which would have been required for a normal accession. The Council agreed not to take a final decision on any legislative proposals until after the second parliamentary reading and committed itself to completing its own first reading in time for a second parliamentary reading in November.

The transitional measures

The terms of monetary union and the immediate Community measures had provided the basis for incorporating the GDR into the Community by ensuring equal treatment of Community and German firms in the GDR, establishing reciprocal free trade, the applicability of the common agricultural policy, Community rules on company law, freedom of establishment, competition, VAT and customs and excise. Nevertheless, a good deal of secondary legislation still required amendment.

With the exception of the environmental legislation and certain pharmaceutical directives, on which derogations were permitted until 1995, the transition period was set to end on December 31, 1992. The Commission's policy was based on three premises. First, the *acquis communautaire* should be the baseline to be achieved by 1992. Second, transitional measures should be proposed only where objective legal, social or economic reasons left no alternative. Third, the derogations would be temporary and cause minimum disturbance to the functioning of the common market.

The presidency was held by the Italian government for the duration of the negotiations. It was decided at the end of August 1990 to set up two special Council working groups composed of officials from the permanent representations. One group concentrated on agriculture and reported to the Special Committee for Agriculture, while the other analysed the rest of the relevant policy areas. The split between agriculture and the rest reflected both the size of the problems involved and traditional institutional arrangements. It led to poor co-ordination on the vital issue of the international implications of German unification and to a situation in which the package in its entirety came under question. These problems arose because difficulty with the agricultural part of the package became linked with parallel negotiations over the Community's position in the GATT (General Agreement on Tariffs and Trade) discussions. The negotiating tactics of member states in the deliberations on Community policy in the GATT round were influenced by the practical split in the procedures for German unification. The British were to use it to their own advantage in seeking a Community line on GATT which accorded with their priorities for reform of the Common Agricultural Policy. The Germans later came under pressure to relax their support for the French position on reform. Agreement on German unification was part of the bargain. For the Spanish it was possible to argue that the logic of the Common Agricultural Policy contradicted Community efforts to preserve *Vertrauensschutz* for European CMEA countries. It thus allowed the Spanish the potential to split off agricultural interests from the main negotiations and simultaneously to link *Vertrauensschutz* to a request to review Spanish and Portuguese arrangements during their own transition period. In effect, they requested application of the same principle of respect of legitimate expectation.

There had been considerable discussion in Germany earlier in the year about which ministry should co-ordinate policy and lead negotiations. The outcome was reflected in the German Permanent Representation, where the lead was taken by the Economic Counsellor, on secondment from the Federal Ministry of Economic Affairs, rather than the Political Counsellor, whose department was the German Foreign Office. The lead in the negotiations was taken by a delegate from the Ministry of Economic Affairs, Hans-Dieter Kuschl. He prepared the terrain in Bonn by holding frequent co-ordination meetings to determine an inter-ministerial line. Thereafter German officials, led by Kuschl, travelled frequently to Brussels to attend the negotiations. There was usually an official from the East German Ministry of Economic Affairs in attendance. East German officials had no negotiating rights, but were called upon to give expert advice where necessary. Much of the preparatory work was done during the dawn hours or late at night. On days when no negotiations took place, co-ordination and prior negotiation took place by telephone between Kuschl and his opposite numbers in the Commission and the German Permanent Representation.

A major question was how the Commission and the Germans would ensure the correct application of the transitional measures. The question arose soon after the implementation of the interim measures in September 1990, as the detail of what member states had agreed on a provisional basis became clear. The basis of the transitional measures, allowing exceptions to internal market and other standards, was that these should be strictly limited to former GDR territory.

The interim measures had consisted of a Council directive and a Council regulation. The two measures authorised the Commission to apply the transitional measures proposed before the completion of the legislative process. Both measures obliged the Commission to report to the parliament and the Council on how it intended to verify the application of Community law and to ensure proper management of Community income and expenditure. There were legitimate concerns about how the Commission and the German authorities would police an area of German territory with no physical frontiers. The run-up to the deadline on the derogations coincided with a period when the frontiers between member states themselves were destined to disappear. It would be ironic if precisely at a time of relaxation of border controls, the Community were obliged to increase controls to ensure the application of Community law in the territory of the former GDR.

The German authorities were reluctant to introduce measures requiring stricter control procedures in Germany than in other member states. The Commission, too, was keen that any specific controls should not provide precedents that might retard the progress towards a frontier-free Europe and, conceivably, to the postponement of implementation of the

Schengen Agreement, a limited exercise in opening frontiers between a core of member states of which Germany was one.

Concern about the influx of goods from the east

On October 16, 1990, the Commission set out its position in a report to the Council and the European Parliament on the measures envisaged to control the identified risks. Goods conforming to Community standards were naturally to be allowed full circulation within the Community, but there were four broad categories of non-standard products liable to escape from the territory of the former GDR: those produced within the framework of the derogations; those imported from third countries to which the same derogations on standards would apply; those on which Community duties would not be paid; and problems specific to agricultural products.

Member states and parliamentarians were particularly exercised by the risk that the derogations would allow abuse. Sub-standard goods might find their way from the new *Länder* to Community markets. In addition, since the derogations included the lifting of quantitative restrictions and external tariff constraints, it was conceivable that a flood of east European goods might cross through east Germany. The effects on markets of cheap sub-standard products from either the former GDR or CMEA countries were potentially serious.

The Commission argued that the current methods of control would suffice. Technical controls at the place of production for foodstuffs or authorisation for pharmaceuticals would be the logical and usual complement to identification by labelling. As for imports, the end-use relief scheme provided the framework. The end-use regulation ensures that final consumption or incorporation of the goods into other products acquiring Community origin are subject to authorisation, the obligation to keep precise records, inspection and stiff penalties in cases of infringement. By requiring the German government to enhance the controls already applied in the Federal Republic and by reiterating member states' rights to control goods in transit and at the final point of importation, the Commission was able to satisfy the concerns of both Council and European Parliament. Its acceptance of a complaints procedure allowing rapid action over cases of infringement completed the framework of controls.

The German government was obliged by amendments to the proposed derogation to report to the Council and European Parliament on the implementation of the transitional measures. The question of control was the subject of a special session of the parliamentary Budget Committee in Potsdam on June 24, 1991. Though the European Parliament's temporary committee concluded its formal work in December 1990, its members were convened to follow up the transitional measures and visited Bonn and Berlin in June 1991. Meanwhile, questions were regularly put to the Commission and the Council in the European Parliament. Vice President Bangemann responded on behalf of the Commission to a wide range of questions during the parliamentary session in Strasbourg in June 1991, commenting that there had as yet been no case of a complaint being made by a member state about inadequate control procedures.

Problems of procedure within the Community

The Council reached a common position on the package on November 6, 1990. This was transmitted to the parliament the next day. The package would come under review at the second November session of the parliament. In the meantime, the temporary committee considered a series of further amendments and agreed to propose some of them for vote in plenary session. The major sticking points concerned "comitology" (the kind of committee of Commission and member state officials set up to control implementation of the measures) and a so-called flexibility clause designed to foresee situations where the transitional measures proved either insufficient or incorrect. The formula finally agreed allowed the flexibility clause to amend derogations where they had proved incomplete, but not to add new ones. If additional derogations were required, a new Commission proposal would be necessary. This would necessitate the agreement of the Council and the parliament and remove altogether the flexibility of a decision by committee. The Council voted unanimously to reject an amendment on the committee structure.

In short, the European Parliament had agreed to accept a committee structure where it would have little power to influence the implementation of the measures, though it had ensured that new derogations would trigger the full legislative procedure anew. This seemingly simple solution was the result of extensive bargaining between parliament and Council, the Commission acting as mediator between the two. As extraordinary as it may seem to the uninitiated, comitology and flexibility were the two issues around which the process of legal integration of the former GDR into the Community might have come unstuck.

Areas of agreement and of concern

The Commission's package of August 21, 1990, contained 21 specific legislative proposals plus the two interim measures. For many issues apparently relevant at first sight there were no negotiations, since there was no question of a derogation from Community legislation. Thus, for example, Community legislation was already applicable in the field of competition policy, free movement of persons and capital, financial services and public procurement. These areas had been covered by the two treaties on German union. As for state aid, flexibility was proposed for shipbuilding and the steel industry, but, despite some British concern, the issues were hardly contentious. However, legitimate concerns of member states regarding the continuation of aid to Berlin and the former frontier area between the two Germanies had surfaced early on in the process. They were settled by Sir Leon Brittan's commitment to ensure that the Germans phased out the aid in due course.

In fact it took until May 1991 for agreement to be reached with Germany on the phasing-out process for this special aid. Under the circumstances there was general sympathy for the dilemma of the German government in a field where the business plans of large numbers of small and medium-sized firms were totally dependent on tax breaks that had been in existence for decades. The special aid schemes are now to be phased out by the end of 1993. After some initial concern at the very generous conditions offered by the *Treuhandanstalt* to investors in the new *Länder,* the Commission agreed that, providing there was equal treatment of German and other member state companies, the existing incentives might continue.

In most areas of Community policy it was remarkable how few contentious issues there were. In the field of the internal market, for example, the Task Force's analysis showed that 80 per cent of existing Community legislation could be applied immediately. The main problems for the negotiators over the remaining 20 per cent were those of control and flexibility discussed above. Derogations in the field of health and safety legislation concerned the Germans alone and were thus of no major concern to other member states. As for research and development and telecommunications, minor derogations in the telecommunications area were the only legislative adjustments deemed necessary. Interestingly and ironically, the most important of these concerned the use by the Soviet military in eastern Germany of the wavelengths reserved for mobile telephones by a Community regulation on standards. In the energy field, long before the Commission had made its proposals, the Kohl government had called upon the east Germans to close down nuclear installations which clearly did not reach Community safety standards. There was no question of a derogation in so sensitive an area.

In transport it was agreed that international and cabotage quotas for road haulage would be adjusted in the coming review in 1991. Other transport issues included the validity in the Community of GDR driving licences, rules governing the professions, where a derogation of one year was requested by the Germans, and questions of the applicability of scrapping premiums for obsolescent rivercraft. These were not issues of major concern to other member states.

The fisheries regime did not require amendment of the arrangements on internal resources, with the exception of an adjustment of the quota for the cod catch in the Svalbard area. There was a minor conflict over the basis used by the Commission for the calculation, one delegation arguing that the reference years for total allowable catches should not be 1976–85 as the Commission had argued, but 1973–86. The Germans did not request an adjustment of other catches and quotas, so no negotiating issues arose. There would have to be adjustments to the Community's aid programmes within the fishing industry and also to the multi-annual guidance programmes. Again, this was not the stuff of major conflict, though there was undeniable concern on the part of some member states.

Environmental policy, however, was an area of great concern. Negotiations on these issues took up a good deal of time in the Council working group. The Commission's belief was that even the relatively long derogation period until the end of 1995 would probably be insufficient to remedy the catastrophic environmental situation in the GDR. Nevertheless, the German authorities took the view that they would be able to fulfil their obligations under the transitional arrangements and meet the timetable. Member states were particularly exercised by the risk that, despite the exclusion of new installations from the derogations, there would be potential for misuse. It was argued that an old plant could undergo major overhaul, thus rendering it to all intents and purposes new, and yet it might retain the classification old and thus benefit from a derogation. The effect of this would be the production (possibly for export) of goods at prices competitive only because they did not meet expensive standards of environmental protection. Much time was spent in finding a suitable definition of old and new plant. It was finally agreed to accept a reference to the strict German legislation in the area as a basis for the Community view.

The Commission also spent considerable effort on ensuring that member states with their own difficulties in applying Community environmental legislation should not profit from the situation. They could do this by using the relatively long transitional periods given to the former GDR as a justification for special treatment involving extension of their own periods of transition. The Commission was sympathetic to German concerns that even the five-year derogations to air and water pollution standards might not suffice. Future requests for extensions to the timescales of the derogation will doubtless be considered in the light of progress in achieving Community standards. However, member states will need to be sure that derogations in specific areas are not simply serving to guarantee market shares. This has been mooted, for example, in the field of waste disposal.

The structural fund provisions caused much debate within the Commission and between member states. Responsibility for the funds is spread across the fields of social affairs, regional affairs, and agriculture. General co-ordination is provided by a separate Directorate General whose task is the "co-ordination of structural instruments". The internal debate was later mirrored in the Council working group. It was generally agreed that the necessary data was not available for the correct application in the new *Länder* of the structural fund principles for assessing eligibility, but there was a reluctance to accept blanket solutions dispensing with tight rules set out in the structural fund regulation. In practice, however, the alternatives were very limited. The fears of member states, that sloppy application of the rules would create bad precedents, were countered by the German and Commission delegations. The point was that these were extraordinary arrangements, never to be repeated. There could be no question of setting precedents. Nor was there a risk, as was feared by certain southern Community members, that the distribution of the structural funds would disadvantage them. The funds voted were additional.

However, this was the case for the special arrangements designed to take the new *Länder* to the time when an overall renegotiation of the structural funds will be necessary, namely in 1993. Then, assuming no change in the overall amount attributed to structural funds, there may well prove to be a slightly smaller proportion of the funds available for countries traditionally receiving high levels of support. But since an increase in the structural funds will be part of the political price for agreement in the inter-governmental conferences, the question may well never be put in this form.

The negotiations concerning external relations were complicated. No exemptions from existing Community treaties were proposed, which were therefore to apply immediately upon unification. Some treaties needed to be renegotiated with third countries to allow for the increase in size of the Community market. Textile treaties under the Multi-Fibre Agreement were a case in point. However, such issues were not contentious.

Balancing the interests of eastern Europe and of the Iberians

Reference was made above to *Vertrauensschutz* or respect of legitimate expectations, in the field of trade with European CMEA countries and Yugoslavia. Basing itself on this principle, the Commission proposed the suspension of customs duties on goods imported from European CMEA countries and Yugoslavia. The suspension would be valid in the first instance until the end of 1991, with a possible one year renewal to be decided. The principle was acceptable to member states, though the question of how to ensure the just application of the derogation was, as we have seen, difficult for delegations to resolve. A later practical question concerned a German request to include anti-dumping duties in the suspension of import duties. The Commission at first argued that special conditions in this particular case might be considered a precedent by CMEA countries in other negotiations with the Community. Member states and the Commission came, however, to accept the German view, on condition that the suspension of anti-dumping provisions would be limited to existing anti-dumping duties. It would apply only to fixed quantities of goods listed in the proposals as being subject to trade agreements. In any case, all such goods were to be limited to consumption in the new *Länder*.

The matter then became complicated further when it was realized that agricultural products accounted for a considerable share of the total trade between the CMEA and the GDR. Did *Vertrauensschutz* and the suspension of import duties now mean that the instruments of the Common Agricultural Policy were not to apply? In particular, would agricultural imports now be possible outside the regime of levies and price-fixing current in the Community? The details of this thorny problem were debated in the Council. The Commission was under pressure to give precise lists of the products concerned and the quantities likely to be involved. There were two views. On the one hand the Commission, in the shape of the directorate-general responsible for external relations, had been making "positive noises" to successive delegations from CMEA countries expressing their concern at the effects on their export markets in the ex-GDR. On the other hand, the idea of major derogations in agricultural policy was unthinkable in the directorate-general responsible for agriculture.

Informal consultations took place between the directorate-general for external relations and representatives from CMEA countries. Both the Commission and the European Parliament were coming under pressure from the Soviet Union, Poland and Hungary not to take measures which would upset the balance of their trade. For the directorate-general for external relations there was to be no exception to the principle of *Vertrauensschutz*. All sectors, whether agriculture, steel or textiles (and pressure was great from all quarters) were to be fully incorporated into the transitional measures. The new proposal seemed to meet the concerns of most member states, though Mediterranean countries were keen to find out from the Commission whether there was a balance between "southern" and "northern" goods benefiting or suffering from new conditions of competition in the new *Länder*. It was at this point that the Spanish delegation produced the legendary rabbit from the hat.

The Spanish were justifiably concerned that the arrangements would have serious implications for Spanish access to the new Community market, now that it was to be open to traditional imports from all former east European trading partners, as well as all imports from Community member states *with the exception of* Spain and Portugal. Their access to Community markets in general was still subject to the transitional period applicable until the end of 1995. Here, of course, the difficult discussion on accession versus expansion of an existing member state had ironically come full circle. Until German unification Spain and Portugal had been able to export goods to the GDR, a third country, without the imposition of import duties. Since there was to be no accession treaty for the GDR and no long-term phasing-in of Community legislation as had been the case for Spain and Portugal, Spanish and Portuguese exports to the former GDR, as to the rest of the Community, would now attract part of the community external tariff and partial levies. Moreover, such exports would be in competition with goods from CMEA countries for which the principle of *Vertrauensschutz* was to lead to a suspension of the external tariff. Spain could thus plead a loss of advantage. Under these circumstances it was unlikely that the package of transitional measures would be acceptable.

The European Parliament, discreetly lobbied by the Spanish and the Portuguese, was proposing an amendment. The parliament had also concluded that offering a mere year's suspension of import duties would not assist the beleaguered eastern and central European countries. The parliament's proposal was to extend the dispensation from one to two years. December 1992 rather than 1991 would thereby become the cut-off date for tariff-free access. Several governments, including the British, disliked the extension but were willing in the end to compromise.

The two issues of Spanish and Portuguese access to the new Community market in the former GDR and the extension of the time limit to the derogation now threatened to block the legislative process by compromising the timetable settled in the inter-institutional agreement. The Council was faced with two alternatives. Either there could be an amendment to the treaties of Spanish and Portuguese accession or the Council could decide to split the package by removing the external and agricultural elements and letting the parliament consider the remainder of the package in second reading. This would be in the hope of finding an alternative solution to the Spanish and Portuguese problem.

The debate on agriculture

Two procedural commitments in the inter-institutional agreement were of relevance here. First, the agreement on timing and second, the parliament's right to an opinion on the whole and the parts of the package in a single second reading. There was also a substantive, though extraneous problem arising from disagreement between member states over agricultural trade within the GATT. The earliest settlement possible for the outstanding agricultural issues would be at the Agricultural Council on November 5–6, 1990. The package as a whole could therefore not reach the parliament until after November 6. The time was already unreasonably short for the parliament's committees to deliberate on amendments for second reading. In addition, there was no certainty that the Agricultural Council would be able to settle the outstanding issues raised by German unification, since the negotiating environment was soured by dissension over the Community's position within the GATT.

The GATT round was a thorny issue on the agenda of both the Agriculture and Foreign Affairs Councils in the autumn of 1990. The problem was to agree a Community position on agriculture. It was well-known that Germany was supporting France in resisting drastic reductions in agricultural support. It was similarly well-known that Britain was keen to use the GATT discussions as a means of achieving long-sought reforms of the Common Agricultural Policy. To the British it seemed reasonable that the Germans should modify their position on agricultural subsidies as the price of general agreement to German unification. The Germans were asked to abandon support for the French position on the issue. Since agreement was not forthcoming, there was no guarantee that the GATT issues would be resolved in time. A threat therefore hung over the German unification negotiations that the final decision on the agricultural and trade policy components would be delayed until a compromise could be reached on the GATT mandate to the Commission.

The second procedural commitment in the inter-institutional agreement concerned the integrity of the package. A way out of the deadlock over agriculture could lie in splitting it. In this case, the Council's common position, settled except for agriculture at the Transport Ministers' Council on October 30, could already go to the parliament. Legally, agriculture and trade do not require second readings. Though this would be an effective way out of the dilemma, the Commission was unwilling to envisage a contradiction of the "whole and the parts" commitment to the parliament.

Once again, agriculture was proving the major difficulty in reaching Community consensus. Senior Commission officials believed that the Community would be much criticized if it left the impression that the only hindrance to the integration of the new *Länder* into the Community was agriculture. The subject was all the more delicate since the interim period had seen upheavals in the agriculture of the GDR and there had been some abuse of the situation by Community traders anxious to benefit from cheap beef prices in the GDR. The abuse had led to market distortions throughout the Community.

The solution to the Spanish and Portuguese dilemma came in a new proposal from the Commission under the terms of the accession treaties for those countries. It gave Spain and Portugal equal access for agricultural products to the former GDR market for the period in which the derogation from the external tariff was allowed to European CMEA countries and Yugoslavia. The Council was on this basis able to settle almost all the outstanding issues. There was however a subsequent last-minute request from the Portuguese delegation for the Community to consider anew the question of free movement of workers and the transitional period applicable to Portugal under its accession arrangements. Again, the special and different nature of the GDR's integration into the Community has to be stressed. Considerations such as those affecting the free movement of Portuguese workers during the Portuguese transitional period simply did not apply to the former GDR. Common sense demanded that the Community take account of this, so the Community agreed to look at the issue again in 1991.

Spain and Portugal had expressed their readiness to agree to the new Commission proposal covering their specific concerns and thus to accept the whole package of measures. However, in December once again just as final agreement seemed complete, a further request arrived from the Spanish and Portuguese delegations. The new Commission proposal had provided for extension of the terms offered to the CMEA countries to Spain and Portugal, that is, continuation of tariff-free exports to the former GDR within the quantities of "traditional" (agricultural) trade flows. The Spanish now required that *all* products allowed duty-free entry from CMEA countries should form part of the new Spanish and Portuguese duty-free arrangements. This appeared to be more a question of principle than of real concern about market access in specific areas. By this late stage it was in any case clear that trade flows between CMEA countries and the new *Länder* were in steep decline, as west European products replaced those exported from the GDR's trading partners. The further modification met with little resistance. Once this issue was resolved, there were no further issues to discuss and the final package was therefore approved by the Council of Ministers on December 4, 1990.

Conclusions

This essay has described the process by which the former GDR was eased into the legal framework of the Community and has illustrated the speed and effectiveness with which Community institutions can act under pressure. Though German unification must be considered a *sui generis* operation, it is worth looking at the implications for further developments in the European Community. There are three broad areas of relevance. They concern Germany's role in Europe, the lessons for future enlargement of the Community and the institutional implications.

Attention throughout the Community has been more than usually focused on the Federal Republic since unification. Perhaps the most important lesson for member states has been the short-term failure of German monetary and economic union. It is now clear that integrating two such divergent economies and imposing one currency at an exchange rate decided for political purposes has had far-reaching and negative effects on the weaker of the two economies involved. Faced with an economy superior in virtually every respect, the former GDR has been in almost permanent economic crisis since July 1, 1990. It has been clear too that some of the major assumptions of market economics simply do not hold in conditions where important economic variables change for political and social reasons. By 1992 the crisis was not restricted to eastern Germany. April 1992 saw widespread strikes in western Germany as the trade unions voiced strong opposition to the German government's attempt to limit wage increases. The reason, as government spokesmen continually reiterated was both the need to prevent galloping inflation and the need to ensure solidarity with the new *Länder*.

It has proved impossible to retain factors of competitive advantage such as wage rates, rents and house prices in a system where comparability is easy because of the single currency and the single market, not only for production and consumption but also for social benefits. It has not been possible, for example, to prevent wage rates in east Germany rising towards those of west Germany. Despite the official pegging of salaries at approximately 60 per cent of west German rates, pegging prices in the same way was clearly out of the question. Raising real wages in eastern Germany was both in the interest of east German workers, since consumer prices are broadly the same in all parts of Germany, and most west German workers, whose wage rates would otherwise be undercut by eastern workers. Importantly, however, the advantages to investors of the lower cost economy of eastern Germany were correspondingly reduced. Add this to the vexed issue of property ownership and the recipe is quite simply lack of investment and economic inertia.

As for economic management, the German government was reluctant to raise tax rates or to redirect infrastructure investment from west to east Germany. The resulting fiscal deficit of 5 per cent of Gross Domestic Product and consequent rises in inflation and interest rates had serious consequences. The effects were visible not only in the Federal Republic but also in other Community member states tied to the fortunes of the German economy by the European Monetary System.

What of the implications for the wider process of European integration? In the German case, appeals to a new "national interest" made possible the acceptance of huge transfers of resources at least until the consequent belt-tightening in the west became painful, but it is unlikely that a similar "European interest" could be conjured up should comparable problems arise with European economic and monetary union. Indeed, even in the German case the sacrifices of the west were made grudgingly. As expectations in the east became determined by rights and obligations created precisely because of the integration of the two economies, the social costs in terms of a decline in national unity became menacing. Despite the swift progress on the two inter-governmental conferences, the lessons have not been lost in the negotiations between member states on the content of economic and monetary union and the speed with which it can be attained.

As to German views on further European integration, the evidence from the integration of the two Germanies has not led the German government to increased circumspection. As has already been pointed out, Germany under Chancellor Kohl and former Foreign Minister Genscher remained among the most pro-federalist of member states. When Genscher announced his resignation in April 1992, some observers began drawing worrying conclusions for the future of European integration. The fact that the debate about ratification of the Maastricht agreements was most vociferous after the signing of the treaty rather than, as in the British case, before, made all the above problems coincide with a fundamental questioning of the European Community in the Federal Republic.

Though the lessons of German unification have led to a stricter German attitude on the necessary degree of economic convergence between member states to be attained before economic and monetary union can be countenanced, the federalist rhetoric remains. As sincere as it may be when used by senior politicians, two themes of continuity in German foreign policy lie behind it. The first, evident since the Second World War, consists in stressing the need to submerge German autonomy within wider Community and NATO structures. This seems to counteract any suggestion that German economic power will produce an aggressively independent political orientation in government, which would raise all the bogeys of the past.

The second theme concerns Germany's role in the wider Europe. The Germans have already begun to take their new role seriously. As early as February 1990, Genscher commented that:

> "The world rightly expects that the united Germany will take on more responsibility. We know this, we accept this, because we want it too. We shall avail ourselves of this wider role which falls upon us, not out of an outdated nation-state interest — in pursuit of national power — but as good Europeans and in co-operation with the European Community."

Both Kohl and Genscher actively promoted the idea of a rapid widening of the Community to encompass the newly enfranchized states of eastern and central Europe. The united Germany has an obvious policy interest in maintaining the stability and increasing the prosperity of its eastern neighbours. One concern is immigration, where there are already signs of German intolerance, all the more ominous with the evidence of right-wing radicalism in the new and the old *Länder*. Thus, the German call for European federalism and Community enlargement remains in line with Germany's traditional domestic and foreign policy objectives. It also fits squarely with the role Germany traditionally maintained in the European balance of power. While its function as economic locomotive of the Community has been temporarily diminished, its role as mediator between East and West has been enhanced. To this extent it can be concluded that Germany's overall high-political aims were successfully achieved both by the outcome of the Two-Plus-Four negotiations and the smoothness with which the GDR was integrated into the Community. As the pace of enlargement now quickens, Germany's pivotal economic role will be crucial, provided domestic tensions do not reset the German political agenda.

A fundamental difference should be borne in mind when comparisons are made between the expansion of the European Community to include the former GDR and the potential enlargement of the Community to encompass Poland, Hungary and Czechoslovakia. These countries (with difficulty in the last case) have retained a specific sense of national identity, whereas the death-wish of the GDR was the striking feature of the months preceding unification. The pressures for enlargement have not, of course, been brought about by German unification, but the apparent ease with which one of the most hard-line of the communist states was accepted into the fold will make it difficult for wary Community member states to resist the pressure for further enlargement. After all, if the major argument against this was not incompatibility but simply cost and national interest, the reasoning would look dubious. It would be as if the rhetoric of the west European welcome of the end of communism in Europe were to find no practical outcome beyond technical assistance and gradual market access. This is not the stuff of which political dreams are made. Though Germany was a special case, the flexibility shown by the Community may not remain an exception.

This essay has shown that a major issue such as German unification has today to be treated as a Community issue rather than in terms of traditional nation-state perspectives. It demonstrates how much the essential nature of Europe's international relations are evolving. Everybody, from Community officials to senior politicians in the member states was prepared to make exceptions in order to facilitate the process. But the role of the European Commission was crucial in anticipating the acceleration of the process and linking it to further European integration, thereby redefining the Community's agenda and increasing its stature. Despite the initial concerns, by mid-1990 there was general agreement that the operation had to be smooth and fast. It remains to be seen whether the situation in the former Soviet Union and in central and eastern Europe will bring about the same degree of institutional flexibility.

ELECTORAL VOLATILITY IN UNITED GERMANY

Charlie Jeffery

The result of the *Bundestag* election of December 1990 was a comprehensive victory for the government parties of the German unification process, the CDU-CSU and the FDP. Having together gained almost 55 per cent of the vote, spread evenly across eastern and western Germany, the Christian and Free Democrats now possess a decisive *Bundestag* majority over an opposition divided between the Social Democratic SPD, the ex-Communist PDS and the Greens/Alliance 90 (see Table 1). On this basis, their position in government is certainly secure until the next *Bundestag* election in 1994. It has even been suggested that they built up such a strong position in the 1990 election that there is no realistic chance of a change in government in 1994. The argument of this essay is that such a conclusion is premature. By placing the outcome of the 1990 *Bundestag* election into a longer-term perspective which considers trends in voting behaviour in both western and eastern Germany prior to December 1990, it suggests that voting patterns in the new Germany will be characterized by a high degree of volatility and unpredictability for the foreseeable future.

The first section of the essay examines the changing nature of voter–party relationships in West Germany during the 1980s. This period saw an increasing volatility of West German electoral relations, as previously stable patterns of voting behaviour became subject, at least in part, to a process of dealignment. Partial dealignment was reflected in an increasing sensitivity of individual voting decisions to the influence of the most significant political issues of the time. Together partial dealignment and increasing issue-orientation introduced new elements of unpredictability in West German voting behaviour which, by the end of the 1980s, had undermined a hitherto unusual level of stability in the party system.

If voter–party relationships in western Germany were undergoing a process of *dealignment* prior to the 1990 *Bundestag* election, the situation in the former GDR was more one of *non-alignment*. This situation is examined in the second section of the essay, which discusses voting behaviour in the GDR *Volkskammer* election of March 18, 1990. In the absence of a democratic electoral tradition East German voters on the whole lacked any clear sense of affinity to the parties standing for election. As a consequence, their electoral decisions were highly volatile, subject almost exclusively to the short-term influence of political issues.

The third section shows that these trends were confirmed in the patterns of voting behaviour underlying the results of the 1990 *Bundestag* election. The confirmation of these trends reflected in part the unusual nature of the election as a single-issue ballot dominated by the question of unification. But it was also a manifestation of a heightened electoral volatility arising from the unification of two electorates with highly divergent characteristics and interests within a single, common electoral framework. It is argued that the features of this framework for electoral politics in the new Germany will persist in future elections, serving to reinforce the process of dealignment in western Germany and to confirm the non-alignment of the eastern German electorate. The electoral success of the government parties and the weakness of the opposition in December 1990 were therefore based on unstable, volatile foundations. This casts a considerable degree of uncertainty on the future electoral performance of the German parties and by no means excludes a scenario of radical change in 1994.

Table 1: *Results of the* Bundestag *election, December 1990*[1]

	Germany		Election Area West % vote Bundestag		Election Area East % vote		
	% vote	seats	1990	1987	Bundestag Dec. 1990	Landtage[2] Oct. 1990	Volkskammer March 1990
CDU[3]	36.7	268	35.5	34.5	41.8	43.6	40.8
CSU	7.1	51	8.8	9.8	-	-	-
SPD	33.5	239	35.7	37.0	24.3	25.2	21.9
FDP[4]	11.0	79	10.6	9.1	12.9	7.8	5.3
Greens (West)	3.9	0	4.8	8.3	-	-	-
Greens (East) / Alliance 90[5]	1.2	8	-	-	6.0	6.9	4.9
PDS	2.4	17	0.3	-	11.1	11.6	16.4

[1] "Second"/party list votes, excepting the GDR *Volkskammer* election, where voters had only one vote.
[2] No *Landtag* election was held in East Berlin in October. These figures therefore exclude East Berlin.
[3] The CDU stood, alongside the German Social Union (DSU) and the Democratic Awakening (DA), as part of the Alliance for Germany in the GDR *Volkskammer* election.
[4] At the GDR *Volkskammer* election: League of Free Democrats (BFD).
[5] Greens and Alliance 90 stood separately at the *Volkskammer* election and in certain of the *Landtag* elections.

A party system in flux: West Germany in the 1980s

From centrism to polarization

One of the roots of this uncertainty lies in what has been termed the "upheaval" experienced in the party landscape of West Germany during the 1980s. Prior to the 1983 *Bundestag* election, the West German party system had exhibited an unusual degree of stability for well over a decade, characterized by the electoral supremacy of the two large *Volksparteien* ("people's parties"), the CDU-CSU and the SPD, and the key "balancing" role played by the small FDP. From 1969 onwards the Christian and Social Democrats were each able consistently to attract over 40 per cent of the vote. The vote-winning capacity of these "people's parties" was based on the projection of a moderated ideological profile which could generate an appeal across broad sections of the electorate. Neither, however, was able to broaden out its electoral base sufficiently to win an absolute majority in this period. This invested the third party in the *Bundestag*, the FDP, with a key role. With just a modest share of the vote, normally 6–10 per cent, the FDP was able to assume the role of powerbroker, whose support was needed for the formation of either CDU-CSU or SPD-led coalition governments. Functioning in this way as the indispensable "linchpin" of a "two-and-a-half" party system, the Free Democrats exerted a centripetal force on the *Volksparteien* which served to concentrate party competition on a moderate centre ground. During the 1980s this neatly balanced, centrist party system was thrown out of equilibrium. The breakthrough of "New Left" politics as a parliamentary force after 1983, in the form of the Greens, served as the catalyst for change. The emergence of the Greens, mainly at the expense of the SPD, seemed to presage a polarization of West German party politics. The inroads they made into the SPD vote were sufficient in both 1983 and 1987 to rule out numerically the possibility of an SPD-FDP coalition. This destroyed the Free Democrats' hitherto pivotal position and tied them in practical terms, at least until such time as the SPD regained its lost electoral support, to a continuation of the coalition formed in 1982 with the CDU-CSU. The loss of votes to the Greens also caused a partial, if ambivalent, abandonment by the SPD of the electoral middle ground in an attempt to recover its electoral strength by competing for the New Left vote.

A rudimentary two-bloc party system thus emerged, tending to a polarization between the SPD and Greens on the left and the CDU-CSU and FDP on the right. Further evidence of the potential for polarization surfaced after 1986, when a fifth party, the far-Right Republicans, scored notable successes in local and European elections. The main losers to the Republicans were the Christian Democrats, particularly in the Bavarian domain of the CSU. The electoral potential of the far right was, in all probability, too localized to secure nationwide representation in a *Bundestag* election. Nevertheless, the prospect of even minor losses threatened to destabilize existing coalition dynamics on the right and provoked a rightward shift, especially in the CSU, in the attempt to outflank the Republicans' appeal.

Foundations of the Volkspartei *vote*

The reasons for the destabilization and polarization of the West German party system can be traced primarily to a decline in the integrative electoral capacities of the SPD and CDU-CSU. The two great *Volksparteien* found it increasingly difficult during the 1980s to maintain the allegiance of the broad sections of the electorate which had guaranteed their supremacy in the "two-and-a-half" party system. This can be seen most obviously in the decline in the combined *Volkspartei* share of votes cast at *Bundestag* elections from a highpoint of 91.2 per cent in 1976 to just 81.3 per cent in 1987 (see Table 2). The combined losses of the *Volksparteien* were, however, even greater when one considers the decline in voter turn out experienced in this period. Taking this into account, the combined decline in *Volkspartei* support, expressed as a percentage of the electorate as a whole, fell from 82.7 per cent in 1976 to just 68.8 per cent in 1987.

The *Volksparteien* were not, therefore, just losing votes to other parties, but also failing to mobilize voters to go to the polls. The SPD was evidently the major loser in this process, suffering pronounced falls in its share of votes cast and in its support in the electorate as a whole. In the case of the CDU-CSU, though, the figures hardly indicate, notwithstanding substantial fluctuations, any unambiguous downward trends. However, Table 2 simplifies voter–party relations somewhat by giving an indication only of *net* electoral change. Additional survey evidence points towards an increasing *gross* fluctuation in voting patterns. In other words, more and more voters were changing their choice of party from election to election, although most of these inter-party migrations cancelled each other out, and were therefore "hidden", in the net election results. One estimate suggests, for example, that the proportion of voters who had switched party allegiance since the previous *Bundestag* election had risen from 24 per cent in 1980 to 38 per cent in 1987. Such findings indicate that the outward maintenance of even the high and broadly stable vote share of the CDU-CSU — not to mention the decline of the SPD — disguised an increasing inability of these parties to rely on the support of the same voters from election to election. Whatever the net figures, fewer and fewer people were casting their votes consistently for the same party.

Table 2: *Electoral performance of the* Volksparteien *1976–1990*

	Bundestag elections				
	1976	1980	1983	1987	1990
% vote:					
CDU-CSU	48.6	44.5	48.8	44.3	44.3
SPD	42.6	42.9	38.2	37.0	35.7
CDU-CSU + SPD	91.2	87.4	87.0	81.3	80.0
Turnout	90.7	88.6	89.1	84.4	78.5
% electorate:					
CDU-CSU	44.1	39.4	43.5	37.6	34.8
SPD	38.6	38.0	34.0	31.2	28.0
CDU-CSU + SPD	82.7	77.4	77.5	68.8	62.8

An explanation of the declining integrative capacities of the *Volksparteien* requires some initial consideration of the foundations which had underpinned the previous cohesion of their vote. Both the CDU-CSU and the SPD have traditionally been able to rely on the support of core voter groups whose allegiance was based on divisions of interest rooted in the structural cleavages of German society: the Christian Democrats typically among observant Catholics and the Social Democrats among unionized manual workers. These core groups have, however, while generally retaining the strength of their party allegiance, declined in absolute size amid long-term trends towards secularization and the modernization of the economic structure. The consolidation of the electoral strength of the CDU-CSU and SPD therefore depended on their ability to branch out from their core voter groups and become genuine "people's parties", capable of attracting a broader coalition of electoral support. Both parties, the CDU-CSU from the foundation of the Federal Republic, the SPD some 10 years afterwards, attempted this by abandoning the sharp ideological identities which had characterized and narrowed the appeal of their respective precursors in the Weimar Republic, in order to broaden their electoral potential as moderate parties of popular integration.

The high and relatively stable vote shares won by the CDU-CSU from the 1950s and the SPD from the second half of the 1960s suggests a high degree of success for this strategy. It indicates that they were able to supplement the structurally rooted party loyalties of their declining core electorates with rising levels of support from new voter groups. Moreover, the stability of the *Volkspartei* vote also indicates that these new voter groups were developing enduring loyalties to their chosen *Volkspartei*. This phenomenon, also witnessed in other western democracies, can be explained by the concept of *party identification*, which suggests that voters may develop stable and persistent attachments of an affective, or psychological nature to political parties. It has been found that such a sense of party identification does not only structure voters' decisions in a limited sense, but also, and more broadly, their general view of the world of party politics. In other words, party identification can promote long-term stability in individual voting behaviour. Survey evidence suggests a progressive strengthening of party identification in West Germany in the 1960s and 1970s, particularly in the case of the *Volksparteien*. By 1980, for example, around two-thirds of CDU-CSU and SPD voters expressed a "strong" sense of identification with their party. The strength of these affective attachments provides an explanation for the persistent electoral supremacy of the CDU-CSU and SPD — despite the decline of their core electorates — which underpinned the stability of the "two-and-a-half" party system into the 1980s.

The Volksparteien *in an era of issues*

However, during the 1980s trends were identified which suggested a partial breakdown, or *dealignment*, of these affective, partisan ties between voters and parties. Evidence accumulated which pointed towards a growing popular disillusionment with the party system as a whole (in the German term, *Parteienverdrossenheit*), but most particularly with the CDU-CSU and the SPD. Lacking in internal democracy and allegedly consumed so much by the concern to broaden electoral support that they had abandoned any clear ideological or programmatic profile, the two *Volksparteien* had become remote from the electorate, unresponsive and increasingly irrelevant to changing political concerns. The malaise was deepened by a series of party political scandals involving at best the abuse of public office, at worst outright corruption, which confirmed the apparently remote and self-serving image of the *Volksparteien* and intensified further the sense of popular alienation.

A consequence of this growing alienation was the emergence of rather more sceptical and detached attitudes towards parties in general and the *Volksparteien* in particular. This scepticism was reflected in a weakening of party identification, in the partial dealignment of established voter-party bonds. The proportion of *Volkspartei* voters professing a strong, long-term identification with their party fell steadily during the 1980s, opening the way for less predictable short-term factors to play an increasing role in influencing voting preferences.

Of particular importance here was a tendency towards a more *issue-oriented* voting behaviour. Increased issue-orientation added a new element of volatility to voter-party relationships by placing an emphasis on the "issue images" projected by the parties: their policy positions on key issues, their actual or perceived competence in dealing with the problems surrounding those issues, the ability of their leaders to articulate the issues effectively. In other words, voters were less likely to make their decisions near-automatically on the basis of a long-standing sense of party identification, and were more likely to make a short-term judgement in favour of the party whose issue image best reflected their own palette of issue preferences at that point in time.

From the perspective of the West German *Volksparteien*, the combination of weakened party identification and heightened issue sensitivity represented a dual problem. Firstly, they could no longer rely fully on the allegiance of the broad coalitions of support which had previously supplemented their core electorates to sustain their electoral hegemony. Secondly, and following from this, they now needed to project issue images which could guarantee sufficient support from issue-oriented voters to maintain their electoral predominance into the future. Both the CDU-CSU and the SPD failed to resolve these problems convincingly. The result was a decline in their capacity for electoral integration, which, in turn, undermined the stable dynamics of the "two-and-a-half" party system.

The ratlose Riesen: Volkspartei *politics in the 1980s*

In a recent book Rudolf Wildenmann evoked the image of the *Volksparteien* as "*ratlose Riesen*", as "baffled giants", reacting with head-scratching perplexity to increasing popular disillusionment with political parties and associated changes in patterns of voting behaviour. The sense of "bafflement" was most severe in the case of the SPD. In many senses the Social Democrats were classic victims of the trends towards dealignment and issue-sensitivity outlined above. At the heart of the problem was the emergence of the Greens. The Greens succeeded in attracting support from, in particular, younger and well-educated voter groups who had previously shown a strong sense of identification with the SPD. Their defection was, in large measure, issue-motivated. It reflected the inability of the SPD to respond to and articulate the "New Politics" issues which had emerged to prominence since the late 1960s and the Greens' success in appealing to the New Politics agenda.

The emergence of the Greens plunged the SPD into a crisis of identity and direction. The central problem was to find a way to appeal to, and regain the support of New Left, "green" voters while not simultaneously alienating its traditional, Old Left, core electorate of unionized manual workers. The problem was exacerbated in the 1987 election, which saw not only further losses to the Greens, but also for the first time substantial losses in the Social Democratic core electorate. This led after 1987 to an intensified strategy debate in which a new generation of party modernizers won the upper hand. The result was the emergence of a strategy which, for the first time, gave equal, if not greater prominence to New Left issues, particularly in environmental policy, than to traditional SPD concerns in social and economic policy.

This modernized strategy was confirmed in the emergence of Oskar Lafontaine, Minister-President of the Saarland and the most prominent party modernizer, as the prospective Chancellor Candidate for the forthcoming *Bundestag* election, scheduled (at that time only for West Germany) for December 1990. Lafontaine, dismissive of the articles of faith of the trade union wing of the party, sought party renewal in an opening up of the party to green issues and in a willingness, ultimately, to consider a return to government in coalition with the Greens.

Throughout most of 1988 and 1989, the prospects for this modernized SPD seemed favourable. Both the party and Lafontaine held substantial opinion poll leads over the CDU-CSU and Chancellor Helmut Kohl. In addition, a more genuine potential for government co-operation with the Greens had emerged by the start of 1989 following the success of their pragmatic, "realist" wing in gaining ostensible control over the direction of the party in December 1988 and the formation of an apparently viable "Red-Green" coalition in West Berlin in January 1989.

At the same time as the SPD seemed at last to have hit upon a solution to its identity crisis, the CDU-CSU entered its own period of "bafflement". The heightened gross fluctuations in voting behaviour which were noted earlier showed that the Christian Democrats too were increasingly unable to maintain a stable basis of support under the impact of declining party identification and the trend towards issue voting. The instability of CDU-CSU support was, for many in the party, confirmed in the abrupt decline and deep trough in popularity experienced by the party after its 1987 *Bundestag* election success. The party fell clearly behind the SPD in opinion polls and lost ground in a succession of *Land* elections. Support was ebbing away both at the centre, mainly to the FDP, but also to the SPD, and on the right to the Republicans, amid deepening popular criticism of the lacklustre and gaffe-ridden leadership by Helmut Kohl of party and government and of the government's handling of health, taxation and immigration policy issues.

This vulnerability on both flanks mirrored in milder form the SPD's crisis of identity, and provoked an often acrimonious inner-party debate which focused on the alleged blandness of the party's public profile and which was increasingly directed against Kohl's leadership. The main protagonists in this debate were centrist "modernizers", who hoped to open up the party leftwards to embrace "softer", "modern" themes, and right-wing traditionalists who aimed to assert a more clear-cut conservative and nationalist party identity. Unlike the SPD, no real attempt was made after 1987 to resolve this emerging identity crisis beyond the marginalization by Kohl of the leading modernizers amid platitudinous statements of the necessity of party unity.

The condition of the West German party system prior to the emergence of national unification on the political agenda was therefore one of flux. The old certainties of the "two-and-a-half" party system had been undermined by the changing patterns of voting bahaviour which had eroded the electoral hegemony of the *Volksparteien*. In the face of an increasingly dealigned, issue-sensitive electorate, both the CDU-CSU and the SPD had been forced to question their party's identity and direction, with the SPD coming up, apparently, with the most electorally plausible answers.

A case of non-alignment: the *Volkskammer* election of March 1990

The Stunde Null

The voter–party relationships which underlay the results of the GDR *Volkskammer* election of March 18, 1990 were inevitably of an extraordinary nature. Prior to March 1990, the last free election held throughout the GDR's territory had been in November 1932. In the intervening years of Nazi dictatorship, Soviet occupation and communist rule, any firm voter–party ties established in eastern Germany before 1932 had withered away. In this sense the March 1990 election was a "*Stunde Null*", a "zero hour", in which voter–party relationships were essentially non-aligned.

In the absence of established party alignments East German voters displayed an unusual sensitivity to political issues in the months before the March election. This sensitivity was magnified by the acute sense of disorientation and uncertainty which dominated GDR politics amid the disintegration of the communist regime and the subsequent emergence and intensification of calls for unification with West Germany. Against this background of rapid and fundamental political change, the agenda of issues at stake itself underwent substantial modification in the pre-election period. In addition East German voters were faced, after over 40 years of single-party domination, with the problem of choosing from the wide range of parties standing for election, each of which was attempting, not always successfully, to keep pace with events and clarify its position with regard to the changing agenda. The consequence of this fluid and rather chaotic interaction between issues, voters and parties was an extreme volatility of voting intentions in the run-up to what was, ultimately, probably the most open and unpredictable ballot in German electoral history.

A total of 23 parties, several of which were united in electoral alliances, stood for election in March 1990. Only five of these parties and party alliances had a sufficient nationwide profile to suggest a realistic chance of significant electoral support: the PDS, the part-reformed and renamed reincarnation of the GDR communist party, the SED; the Alliance 90, which combined several of the citizens' initiatives, notably New Forum, which had played a prominent role in anti-Communist opposition in 1989; the East German SPD, formed in October 1989; and two party alliances formed only in February 1990, the Christian Democratic Alliance for Germany and the League of Free Democrats. The SPD, the Alliance and the Free Democrats received the support and co-operation of their equivalent parties in the West. The East and West German Social Democrats were the first to establish extensive inter-party co-operation in mid-December 1989. The full-scale input of the West German Christian and Free Democrats into the GDR election campaign was only secured when the Alliance for Germany and the League of Free Democrats were formed in February 1990.

Table 3: *Volatility in voting intentions in the GDR, November 1989 – June 1990*[1]

	Institut für Jugendforschung polls			*Allensbacher Institut für Demoskopie* polls			*Volkskammer* election, March 18, 1991	*Forschungsgruppe Wahlen* polls		
	End Nov. 89	Start Feb. 90	Start March 90	End Feb. 90	Early March 90	Pre-election		April 90	May 90	June 90
Alliance for Germany	10	17	31	21	34	45	48.0	38	44	45
SPD	6	53	34	48	37	27	21.9	34	26	39
League of Free Democrats	23	3	4	5	5	5.5	5.3	7	8	5
PDS	31	12	17	18	12	12.5	16.4	14	12	5
Alliance 90	17	3	1	-	-	-	2.9	5	6	4
Others	13	12	13	8	12	10	5.5	2	4	2

[1] The *Institut für Jugendforschung* polls provided separate results for the constituent parties of the electoral alliances Alliance for Germany, League of Free Democrats and Alliance 90. For the sake of comparability, composite figures are given here.

Sources: Peter Förster, Günter Roski, *DDR zwischen Wende und Wahl*, Berlin: Linksdruck, 1990; Dieter Roth, "Die Wahlen zur Volkskammer in der DDR. Der Versuch einer Erklärung", *Politische Vierteljahresschrift*, Vol. 31, No. 3, 1990.

The volatile and unpredictable nature of the relationship between the electorate and these parties is clearly illustrated in Table 3, which sets out the findings of a series of pre- and post-election opinion polls alongside the *Volkskammer* election results. Although the pre-election polls had methodological shortcomings which cast some doubt on the accuracy of their findings, they still give a broad indication of changing East German voting intentions before March 18. Three features are particularly noteworthy. Firstly, the clear and decisive shift away from the SPD and towards the Alliance for Germany in the last weeks of the election campaign. Secondly, the stabilization of PDS support at around 15 per cent in early 1990. And thirdly, the dwindling of the Alliance 90 vote into insignificance after its apparent early popularity.

The changing agenda: from opposing the communists to unifying the Germanies

The poor performance of the Alliance 90 may seem surprising given the prominent role played by its component groups, especially New Forum, in mobilising anti-communist protest in the autumn of 1989. However, support for New Forum in that period reflected far more a broad identification with its anti-communist opposition stance than any specific, positive popular commitment to its programme of participatory democratic reform. Never much more than a focal point of opposition to the SED-regime, New Forum became increasingly irrelevant for most East Germans as soon as debate in the GDR had moved beyond how to get rid of the communists and become preoccupied with the question of unification. In other words, New Forum fell victim to rapidly changing issue priorities: when the issues moved on, it was left behind.

The issue which came ultimately to dominate the *Volkskammer* election campaign was national unification. Moreover, a broad consensus developed remarkably quickly in favour of the general principle of uniting with West Germany. Some 48 per cent of East Germans were in favour of unification in November 1989. The figure rose to 76 per cent in February 1990 and 91 per cent by election day. The questions confronting the East German electorate therefore revolved less and less around whether or not to pursue national unity, and increasingly around how, when and by whom it might best be brought about. In this situation the western-sponsored parties had an inherent advantage: they could point to the aid their western partners could offer in bringing the desire for unity to fruition. This advantage was reflected in the growing combined share of popular support the western-sponsored parties, the Social Democrats and Christian Democrats in particular, were able to attract. Conversely, the only "indigenous" East German party which proved capable of maintaining a significant popular presence was, on the strength of its continuing support within the ex-communist "establishment", the PDS.

Up to February 1990 the SPD, as indicated by its commanding lead in the opinion polls, was able to put forward the most plausible answers to the questions posed by unification. It had the pedigree of being one of the first forces to call for national unity at the end of 1989. Subsequently it developed a clear conception of how the GDR might be incorporated into the West German economic and political order in a gradual, medium-term process which would provide a measure of protection for GDR citizens against social and economic dislocation. And it could, if elected, call on the experience of its powerful West German sister party in steering the process towards unity. However, as demonstrated in the abrupt swing away from the SPD and towards the Allaince for Germany from late February onwards, this commanding lead was less secure than the SPD, confident of victory in March, imagined.

The vulnerability of the SPD's lead had three main sources. Firstly, it had won its advantage in part by default; it was the only party which had, at that time, developed an issue image broadly in line with popular issue preferences. Others, notably the Alliance for Germany, would follow. Secondly, poll findings suggested that voting intentions were as yet by no means firmly established. Fewer than 50 per cent of professed SPD supporters had made a firm voting decision by February 1990. Most voters were apparently reserving for themselves the option of switching their party allegiance before election day. The third source of the SPD's vulnerability lay in Bonn or, perhaps more precisely, in Saarbrücken.

The West German SPD, notwithstanding the enthusiastic efforts of its elder statesman Willy Brandt, displayed an ambivalent, even critical attitude towards unification in early 1990. This reflected the growing influence of Oskar Lafontaine, its prospective chancellor candidate for the next Bundestag election. Born in 1943, Lafontaine was representative of a post-war, "post-national" generation which had never known a united Germany. He was slow to grasp the significance of events in the GDR after the autumn of 1989, assuming initially that Germany would remain divided into two states. Moreover, once the momentum behind unification had become obviously irreversible by the start of 1990, he proved either unable or unwilling to articulate and appeal to the needs and aspirations of East Germans. He seemed rather to remain bound to the narrower context of West German politics, stressing, most notably in his own campaign for re-election as Minister President of the Saarland in January 1990, the potential material disadvantages unification might bring for West Germans. Lafontaine's apparent lack of enthusiasm for unification implicitly weakened the East German SPD's claim to possess a reliable and effective partner in the West. It also contrasted starkly to the unequivocal support given by prominent West German Christian Democrats, in particular Chancellor Kohl, to the Alliance for Germany following its formation on February 5, 1990.

Victory at the last minute: The Alliance for Germany and rapid unification

Despite the lateness of its formal entry into the election campaign, the Alliance for Germany was therefore able to rely on the unambiguous support of its western partners. Moreover, and crucially, those partners were also in government in the West, able to swing the full political and economic weight of the Federal Republic behind the Alliance's campaign message. This incorporated a clear-cut promise of rapid unification, beginning as soon as possible with the incorporation of the GDR into a German economic and currency union, and followed quickly thereafter by the absorption of the GDR into the constitutional order of the Federal Republic.

The wholehearted Christian Democratic commitment to rapid unification offered a clear alternative to the SPD-East's medium-term strategy (whose credibility was, in any case, undermined by the ambivalence towards unification conveyed by the SPD-West), and has generally been seen as the decisive factor in explaining the abrupt reversal of Social and Christian Democratic fortunes in the last weeks before the March election. In the month or so before polling day, the election campaign became increasingly polarized between the differing speeds of unification proposed by Alliance and SPD. The key factor here was undoubtedly the question of currency union by the introduction of the Deutschemark (DM) in eastern Germany.

The SPD proposed a slow and cautious approach which would see the implementation of currency union only when measures had been taken to safeguard the economic interests of the GDR citizens. The contrasting commitment of the Alliance for Germany to the rapid introduction of the DM was motivated by two factors. Firstly, it was seen as a form of incentive which might serve to stem the continuing flow of migrants from east to west. Secondly, in a more positive sense, it was also viewed as a way of administering a "shock therapy" to the East German economy, which, within the framework of monetary stability provided by the DM, would "root out" inefficient branches of production and create the foundations for a prosperous future free market order. Such thinking evidently struck a chord with the East German electorate, over 90 per cent of which was, by March 1990, in favour of the introduction of the DM "as soon as possible". The preference of the East Germans for rapid currency union was accompanied by an awareness that any adjustment to a free market order would bring short-term disadvantages. This eminently realistic assessment of immediate prospects was, however, balanced by a belief that economic revival and rising living standards would follow in the long term. The abrupt exposure to the discipline of a market economic framework inherent in the Alliance's plans for rapid currency union offered a more direct route than the SPD's gradualist strategy to the prosperity most people expected in the long term. Rising Alliance and declining SPD support in the last weeks before the March election can therefore be attributed to the perception that rapid currency union represented the best means on offer of realising long-term economic hopes.

A further advantage accrued to the Alliance in that it was adjudged to possess significantly more competence than the SPD in managing the problems of transition. This can be attributed above all to the impact created by Helmut Kohl in his addresses to Alliance rallies in the final stages of the campaign. Playing on his capacity, as leader of the West German government, to "deliver the goods", Kohl evoked an upbeat and optimistic vision of unification by offering protection for East German savings and pensions and promising currency union under highly generous terms.

The dramatic swing to the Alliance, which was emphatically confirmed in the final election results, was therefore a vote for the future, an investment in the presumed capacity of the Christian Democrats to deliver future prosperity more effectively and more quickly than its competitors, particularly the SPD. The scale and speed of the pro-Alliance swing testifies to the extreme volatility of voting intentions in an electorate which lacked established party alignments and was overwhelmingly oriented around current political issues. Following its belated creation just six weeks before the election, the Alliance succeeded in projecting an issue image sufficiently attuned to the aspirations of the East Germans to "mop up", even at the last minute, previously undecided voters. The SPD, pledged to a slower pace of unification and hampered by the apparent ambivalence of its western partner, was the major loser, unable to retain the high, but never firmly committed levels of support it had attracted in February 1990.

This picture of non-aligned issue-orientation is confirmed in the relative insignificance of group-based patterns of voting behaviour in March 1990. Beyond an affinity of the relatively small proportion of voters with a religious affiliation to the Alliance for Germany and of the formerly privileged groups of the Communist regime with the PDS, there existed no clear-cut party alignments based on a sense of collective group identity. In the remainder of the electorate issue-based voting predominated. This was seen most obviously in the "inverted" profile of the manual worker electorate, a majority of which voted for the future prosperity promised by the Alliance rather than the "natural" representative of manual worker interests, the SPD.

The extreme issue-orientation of the East German electorate inevitably raised doubts about the ability of the parties which stood in the March election to retain their vote shares in subsequent elections. These doubts could be seen on both general and specific levels. Firstly, in general terms, those issues considered most important by the electorate at any one point in time may subsequently lose their significance and/or be superseded by new priorities. The impermanence of priorities places a premium on the parties' ability to "keep up" and adapt convincingly to changes in the issue agenda. As the example given above by New Forum/Alliance 90 shows, such an ability is by no means assured. Secondly, and more specifically, the victory of the Alliance for Germany in March 1990 was based on its success in appealing to, and raising expectations about, an optimistic vision of the future. Its future electoral performance therefore depended on its ability to meet those expectations. If the Christian Democrats failed to make obvious progress towards the realization of the rosy future vision they had projected, the continued commitment of its supporters from March 1990 could not be guaranteed.

In both these respects, the results of the *Volkskammer* election could not be seen as a firm predictor of party performance in the all-German election subsequently called for December 2, 1990. An early indication of this was given in opinion surveys carried out in the GDR after the March election, against the background of ongoing controversies concerning currency union and growing fears about the parlous state of the GDR agricultural sector. These surveys (see Table 3) indicated a continuation of the unpredictability and volatility which characterized East German voting intentions in the run-up to the March election, and augured for another issue-dominated ballot in December.

Issues, voters and parties in the new Germany

Electoral volatility in December 1990

Much has already been written about the first all-German *Bundestag* election of December 2, 1990. The intention here is not, therefore, to rehearse the finer details of the election campaign and outcome. Rather, this section attempts to place the patterns of voting behaviour underlying the December 1990 results into a longer-term perspective. It shows that the tendencies towards a volatile relationship between voters and parties in both eastern and western Germany were confirmed and reinforced in the December election. It then goes on to explain why these tendencies were consolidated in December 1990 and, from that basis, to offer insights into potential future developments in electoral politics in unified Germany.

A high level of volatility in western German voting behaviour is not immediately evident if one compares the 1990 election results with those of 1987 (see Table 1). Party vote shares, with the exception of the Greens, remained broadly stable between 1987 and 1990, and therefore do not indicate especially high net changes in voting behaviour. However, a comparison of gross changes in voting patterns (the extent to which individual electoral decisions were changed compared to the previous election) in 1987 and 1990 does provide clear evidence of a continuing dealignment of voting behaviour in western Germany. The results of a survey carried out by the Mannheim *Forschungsgruppe Wahlen* on election day in 1987 suggested that 75.8 per cent of voters (or, taking turnout into account, 63.9 per cent of the electorate) had voted for the same party as in the previous election in 1983. The equivalent figures for repeat voting in 1990 fell to 71.1 per cent of voters and, taking into consideration the marked decline in turnout in 1990, just 55.9 per cent of the electorate as a whole. In other words, barely half of the western German electorate cast a vote for the same party in 1990 as in 1987.

This increased electoral volatility, while affecting all parties, was reflected most significantly in the continued decline in the ability of the *Volksparteien* to sustain their previously high levels and broad base of electoral support. The SPD was once more the major and most obvious loser. While the CDU-CSU equalled its 1987 result, the SPD again suffered a decline in its share of the vote compared to the previous election (see Table 2). Particularly striking here were the further losses it incurred in its core electorate of unionized manual workers.

These have been attributed to the failure of the New Left image projected in 1990 under the leadership of Oskar Lafontaine to appeal clearly to the aspirations of the manual worker Old Left, and indicate that the 1990 election failed yet again to provide a solution to the identity crisis which dogged the SPD during the 1980s.

Table 2 also shows that both *Volksparteien* continued to be affected by falling turnout in western Germany in 1990. Taking the heavy fall in turnout between 1987 and 1990 into account, combined *Volkspartei* support, seen as a percentage of the electorate as a whole, fell, at 62.8 per cent, to its lowest ever level since 1949. Some care is needed in evaluating this relationship between declining turnout and falling *Volkspartei* support. Most commentators have seen the marked decline in turn-out in 1990 as a phenomenon which reflected a generalized lack of interest on the part of the electorate in an election campaign whose outcome was seen to be highly predictable. However, a detailed breakdown of the election results indicates that falling turnout had a disproportionate impact on both the SPD and the CDU-CSU: those electoral districts where turnout fell most sharply were also those in which both the CDU-CSU and the SPD suffered above-average losses. This apparent correlation between falling turnout and falling *Volkspartei* support suggests a further decline in the capacity of the *Volksparteien* to mobilize past voters to reaffirm their support from one election to the next. It also confirms the general trend towards the erosion of stable, long-term voter–party alignments and their replacement by more volatile, short-term, inter-election factors as the determinants of electoral decisions in western Germany.

There is also considerable evidence to suggest that the extreme volatility which characterized voting behaviour in the GDR in March 1990 was maintained in December. Again, this is not immediately evident from the data presented in Table 1, which sets out the results of the December election alongside those of the elections to the newly constituted eastern German *Länder* parliaments (*Landtage*) on October 14, 1990, and those of the *Volkskammer* election in March. Although the fluctuations in individual party vote shares between March and December were not especially high in absolute terms, they remain significant enough, relative to the short period of time involved, to suggest a high level of net electoral volatility.

Additional figures which take into account gross electoral change confirm the impression of high volatility. Only 71 per cent of voters cast their vote for the same party in December as they had done in the *Landtag* elections just two months beforehand. Taking the turnout rate of 74.7 per cent in December into account, this means that a mere 53 per cent of the eastern German electorate as a whole cast a vote for the same party in December as in October. These high levels of both net and gross volatility within such a short timescale indicate an unusually high susceptibility of voting decisions to the influence of short-term factors.

Voting on unity

The December election saw, therefore, in western Germany a reinforcement, and in eastern Germany a confirmation, of the tendency towards a form of voting behaviour shaped to a decreasing extent by stable, long-term voter–party alignments, and to an increasing extent by more unstable, short-term factors. The explanation for this lies in part in the extraordinary, single-issue character of the election. The overriding preoccupation of German voters in December 1990 was national unification. The election marked in one sense the culmination of the formal unification process which had been pursued with remarkable speed during 1990. But it was also, at the same time, the starting point from which the practical process of managing the fusion of two economies and two societies with widely divergent characteristics would be launched. The election therefore represented an opportunity for the electorate both to look back and give its verdict on the events of 1990, but also to look ahead and mark out its vision of the future Germany.

In these circumstances it is not surprising that unification dominated the political agenda in both east and west, even to the extent of marginalising the issues which had persistently structured political debate in western Germany prior to 1990. Moreover, pre-election survey findings suggest that national unity was not an issue whose implications would be judged neatly around the criteria which otherwise help to shape voting patterns. Overwhelmingly endorsed by some 85 per cent of western Germans and 95 per cent of eastern Germans by August 1990, unification evidently had a resonance which cut across "normal" bases of voter-party alignments. This popular enthusiasm for unification reflected in part the sense of euphoria which surrounded the achievement of unity after over 40 years of division. But it also reflected a belief common to a majority in both east and west that unification, after a brief and inevitably difficult period of transition, would bring long-term benefits for all.

The overwhelming preoccupation of the all-German electorate with unification-related issues provides the background against which voting behaviour in December 1990 needs to be assessed. Voting decisions were unusually responsive to the unification issue images projected by the parties contesting the election. The merits of party policies on unification, perceptions of party competence, and the personal qualities of leading party figures all played a central role in influencing voting behaviour. In these circumstances, the German voter was more likely than ever before in the history of the Federal Republic to cast votes in accordance with short-term judgements concerning these party issue images rather than on the basis of persistent voter-party alignments.

Seen against this background, the government parties of the unification process, the CDU-CSU and the FDP, enjoyed an electoral advantage from the outset. They were able to point to a record in government during 1990 which had hurdled with remarkable speed and skill both internal and external obstacles to the realization of popular aspirations for unity. In addition, the Christian/Free Democrat government was adjudged to have a decisive competence advantage over a hypothetical SPD-led alternative in dealing effectively with the transitional problems arising from the incorporation of eastern Germany into the Federal Republic. And finally, both the CDU-CSU and the FDP proved highly successful in enhancing their parties' appeal by focusing their campaigning on the qualities of their foremost leaders, Helmut Kohl and Hans-Dietrich Genscher.

In the case of the FDP, the success of this tactic is hardly surprising. Genscher's prominent role in the external aspects of the unification process in 1990 was easily grafted on to his enduring popularity as an effective Foreign Minister in western Germany and his credentials as an easterner by birth to maximize his and his party's appeal. Kohl, however, enjoyed neither widespread personal popularity nor a reputation for effective leadership before 1990. Indeed, his position as leader of the CDU-CSU — and by implication as Chancellor as well — had come under challenge amid the divisive strategy debate conducted in the party after 1987. Whether unification "saved" Kohl or not is a matter of conjecture. What is certain is that he suddenly discovered an unlikely and inspirational "can-do" style in 1990, which both generated popular support across east and west and (consequently) reunited the CDU-CSU firmly behind his leadership. Assuming the self-styled mantle of "Chancellor of all Germans", he mobilized electoral support both by playing on his achievements in leading the Germans to unity and by capturing the popular mood through the projection of a somewhat nebulous, but undeniably optimistic vision of a future Germany firmly embedded in a prosperous and peaceful, post-Cold War European order.

The opposition parties during 1990, the SPD, the Greens (standing together in December with the Alliance 90 in the east) and the PDS conspicuously failed to project issue images in line with popular preferences. Most obviously they were, as opposition parties, unable to claim credit for the realization of national unity. More crucially they failed to adapt to the overwhelming popular endorsement of unification during 1990. All three parties displayed an ambivalent and critical attitude to the unification process of 1990. In the case of the Greens and the PDS this reflected, for different reasons, a belief that unification had been carried through wholly on western terms and had failed to recognize the "positive" achievements of the GDR. The reasons for the SPD's ambivalence are rather more complex and merit further attention.

If unification can be seen to have "saved" Kohl's CDU-CSU, it "doomed" the SPD of Oskar Lafontaine. The promising outlook which existed in 1989 for Lafontaine's modernized SPD evaporated rapidly during 1990. With the collapse of the GDR and the move towards national unity, the SPD was saddled with an image, a leader and policies which had been chosen in response to the changing agenda of West German politics. With its ponderous intra-party machinery it was unable to arrest the momentum and change direction to adapt effectively to the new context of all-German politics. The Social Democrats consequently conveyed the impression that their outlook remained essentially West German throughout 1990 and that they were unable or unwilling to respond positively or imaginatively to the challenges posed by unification.

This apparent ambivalence towards unification was clearly illustrated in the SPD's ultimately disastrous campaign in the East German *Volkskammer* election of March 1990, and was confirmed in its central campaign themes in December. In contrast to Kohl's evocation of a broad, positive vision of national unity, Lafontaine and the SPD sought to draw attention to the potential pitfalls, arguing that the supposedly reckless pace of unification in 1990 would inevitably result in severe economic disadvantages for both eastern and western Germans. While subsequent developments have broadly confirmed the SPD's arguments, they were, back in December 1990, unproductive. As was noted above, most Germans fully expected to encounter problems in the short term, but felt that these would be succeeded and outweighed by long-term benefits. In failing to appeal to this optimistic vision of the long term future, the SPD's arguments did little more than invest the party with a negative and carping image which both confirmed the inability shown in the *Volkskammer* election to articulate convincingly the aspirations of eastern Germans, and limited its support in the west.

The new framework for German electoral politics

This analysis has accounted for the high degree of electoral volatility in December 1990 by focusing on the fluidity of relationships between voters and parties in the circumstances of an essentially single-issue election. It would be wrong to infer from this that electoral relations will somehow stabilize at a lower level of volatility at the next *Bundestag* election in 1994. Unification has placed German electoral politics into an entirely new framework. The characteristics of this new framework militate against any new alignment and stabilization of voter–party relations.

The new framework for German electoral politics has two central features. Firstly, unification has combined two electorates which have, and will retain for the foreseeable future, clearly divergent, even opposed values and interests. Willy Brandt's famous and oft-repeated vision of "joining together what belongs together" is gradually revealing itself as over-optimistic, even naïve rhetoric as the two Germanies uneasily come to terms with the realities of unification. This can be seen on at least two levels. Most generally, east and west Germans have divergent political and social cultures which arose from their separation and socialization in two utterly different forms of society. In a more concrete sense, eastern and western Germans have different, and potentially conflicting material interests: the eastern Germans to escape the economic morass bequeathed by Communism and worsened, at least temporarily, by the stumbling attempts so far made to create the foundations of a market order in the east; and the western Germans to ensure that the absorption of the former GDR does not endanger their own economic stability and success.

These "fault-lines" between east and west were partially submerged amid the optimistic reception of unification during 1990, but have since come to be expressed in an emerging sense of irritation and tension between easteners and westeners. This divergence of east and west has fascinating implications when it is considered alongside the second feature of the new framework for electoral politics in united Germany: the nature of the party system. The party system of the new Germany is, following the success of western parties in sponsoring and, in most cases, later merging with sister parties in the east during 1990, essentially that of the old West Germany. These territorially expanded incarnations of the West German parties now face the problem of projecting an appeal capable of mobilising support simultaneously in two electorates with divergent values and interests.

The problem is exacerbated by the trend towards dealignment among western German voters and by the non-aligned nature of the eastern German electorate. As a result the (West) German parties are confronted with the daunting task of expanding from a western base to appeal to a capricious eastern electorate without alienating a western electorate which has itself lost much of the former strength of its party attachments. This potential danger applies in particular to the SPD and the CDU-CSU, for whom the east–west dimension adds to the severe integrative difficulties they already face within their restive western electorates.

The SPD is ostensibly in the most precarious position. In 1990 it manifestly failed to "spread" its appeal from west to east. But, at the same time, the December election showed that it is still no nearer to a solution to its crisis of identity and direction in western Germany. In December the modernized SPD succeeded in regenerating support in the New Left, green electorate, but only, as was pointed out above, at the expense of far greater losses in its traditional manual worker electorate. The SPD is therefore now faced with a dual identity crisis on both east–west and New Left–Old Left dimensions.

The CDU-CSU also faces integrative problems in the new Germany. These are less obvious than those of the SPD but, potentially, just as serious. Although the CDU-CSU succeeded in 1990 in generating a broad appeal across east and west, this appeal was based primarily on its presumed capacity to deliver future prosperity and well-being for all. The reality of life in unified Germany is so far proving to be very different as eastern Germans face economic collapse and as western Germans are burdened with higher taxes as the government struggles to finance the costs generated by the demise of the eastern economy. To maintain the coalition of eastern and western support in 1994 the Christian Democrats will need to be able to point to clear evidence of economic revival.

In addition, the Christian Democrats have by no means overcome the crisis of identity and direction which had emerged in western Germany by the end of the 1980s. Unification served to paper over and defer rather than to solve this crisis. As the dust thrown up by unification settled, the CDU-CSU's electoral vulnerability in the west re-emerged in the series of *Landtag* elections held during 1991, reopening the intra-party debate on the strategy needed to maintain and stabilize the party's electoral capacity.

Table 4: *Popular support for the CDU and SPD in eastern Germany during 1991*

	Bundestag result	January	February	April	July	August	September	November
CDU	41.8	39	34	28	29	30	33	30
SPD	24.3	26	34	38	41	44	39	38

Source: EMNID surveys published in *Der Spiegel*.

Tables 4 and 5 give some indication of the scale of the integrative problems faced by the CDU-CSU and the SPD in the new Germany. Table 4 shows the results scored by the two *Volksparteien* in the regular opinion polls conducted by EMNID in eastern Germany during 1991. The decline in support experienced by the CDU after December 1990 is remarkable. Against the background of continued economic decline in the east, the Christian Democrats lost a full third of their popular support in the five months between the December election and April 1991, and had barely recovered from that level by the end of the year. Equally, if not more, striking is the improvement of the SPD's performance from the 24 per cent share of the vote it received in December 1990 to a high point of 44 per cent in the opinion poll of August 1991. It is doubtful, though, whether the Social Democrats should be reaching metaphorically for the champagne bottles with a view to the 1994 election. Their surge in the polls reflects far more an anti-CDU backlash than any firm commitment to the alternatives they offer. The fluidity of SPD support is indicated in the downward trend in the party's popularity which set in after August 1991 and which continued into 1992. More generally, it is certainly too soon to make any plausible predictions of future electoral performance on the basis of these poll findings. However, what these polls do show is the continuing sensitivity of eastern German voting intentions to current issues, particularly concerning the economy. It is this issue which will undoubtedly prove decisive in the east in 1994.

Table 5: Länder *elections in western Germany during 1991*

	Hessen Jan. 91		Rhineland Palatinate April 91		Hamburg June 91		Bremen Sept. 91	
	%	±	%	±	%	±	%	±
CDU	40.2	−1.9	38.7	−6.4	35.1	−5.4	30.7	+7.3
SPD	40.8	+0.6	44.8	+6.0	48.0	+3.0	38.8	−11.7
FDP	7.4	−0.4	6.9	−0.4	5.4	−1.1	9.5	−0.5
Greens	8.8	−0.6	6.4	+0.5	7.2	+0.2	11.4	+1.2

An indication of the situation facing the *Volksparteien* in the west since the 1990 election is given in Table 5, which reproduces the results of the four western *Länder* elections held during 1991. With the exception of the election in Hesse, the CDU-CSU and SPD experienced unusually high fluctuations in their vote shares compared to the previous election in the relevant *Land*. These fluctuations can be attributed above all to the impact exerted by specific issues in each of the elections: in Rhineland-Palatinate the controversies stirred up by the raising of taxes by the government just months after Chancellor Kohl had insisted they would not be raised; in Hamburg the effective management of the local economy by the sitting Social Democratic city government; and in Bremen, the economic ineffectiveness of the Social Democratic administration, combined with an anti-immigrant backlash which benefited a locally popular far-right party, the German People's Union.

The continuing issue sensitivities of voters in both east and west clearly pose severe problems for the *Volksparteien* in maintaining a stable base of support in either part of Germany. The real test will come, however, when CDU-CSU and SPD next come to face these two volatile electorates simultaneously in the 1994 *Bundestag* election. The *Volksparteien* will then face a situation with important similarities to that which they faced in West Germany during the 1980s. As party identification weakened and as issue sensitivities increased in the 1980s, the CDU-CSU and SPD were forced, to a greater or lesser degree, to adjust their programmatic stance and party image to incorporate new issue priorities. As Stephen Padgett has argued, these adjustments, often made incrementally and haphazardly, tended to blur and dilute rather than clarify party identities and thus militated against any potential realignment and restabilization of voter–party relationships around new issue affinities. The relationship between weakening party identification and adjustments to party identity thus becomes a self-reinforcing cycle.

In the electoral context of the new Germany, the *Volksparteien* now need somehow to "spread" their appeal across both east and west. In the attempt to project party appeal across such a highly differentiated national electorate, a further dilution of party identity seems likely. In this case, the *Volksparteien* will inevitably run the danger of spreading that appeal too thinly and appealing to neither electorate effectively. This, in turn, will tend to accelerate the process of dealignment in the western German electorate, to confirm a permanent non-alignment of the eastern German electorate and therefore to prevent the emergence of new, stable all-German voter–party alignments. As a consequence, a keen, short-term issue-sensitivity will emerge as an enduring feature of electoral politics in the new, unified Germany.

EAST GERMAN POLITICIANS IN THE NEW FEDERAL REPUBLIC

Karen Henderson

A crucial element in the creation of stable democracies in the previously communist states of Eastern and Central Europe is the formation of a functioning party system which can represent the citizens' voices in parliamentary decision-making. As in most other issues affecting the new democracies, the position of the former GDR is fundamentally different from that of its erstwhile allies, as it has taken over ready-made west German structures. In the federal German elections of December 1990, the east Germans returned representatives in a seemingly orderly party constellation; and in October 1990 they had elected five east German *Land* parliaments whose governments merged easily into the west German landscape of the *Bundesrat*.

However, the impression of a well-balanced democratic party system is partly illusory. In some respects, the alienation of the average citizen from democratic party politics is as problematic among east Germans as, say, Poles or Czechs. It is, however, at first sight far less evident because the region inherited a well-functioning government from West Germany. Yet two particular difficulties emerge. One concerns the parties' programmes. Can programmes which have been largely framed according to a west German political agenda reflect the aspirations of east Germans, people who differ markedly both in their historical experience and the actual material conditions of their everyday lives? This is an issue where west German politicians will be required to adapt. The second difficulty, however, directly relates to east German politicians and concerns their lack of authority. By what right, the average citizen might ask, do these individuals exercise power on their behalf? Who can judge whether they have the political competence to alter the west German agenda to the benefit of their constituents?

These are problems which were largely avoided during the numerous elections which took place in 1990. Throughout Eastern Europe, the first free elections of 1990 were "plebiscites on democracy". They were a complex form of referendum about the democratic future of the countries, in which the overriding desire of the majority of the population was formally to reject the discredited communist parties (however they might have been renamed), and the system of rule over which they had presided. In March 1990, the way the east Germans rejected communism was through a substantial vote for the CDU, the party whose label was most closely identified with a policy of rapid German unification. They were not only rejecting their past, but also selecting a ready-made model for their future. In December

1990, when they went back again to the polling stations some two months after the goal of unity had been achieved, one might have expected more complex issues to predominate, yet they did not. The recent escape from communism was still foremost in the minds of many voters and they used the election to place their seal of approval on their previous decision and to vote for the "unity Chancellor" Kohl.

A somewhat simplistic view of the east German issue was also not discouraged by the main political parties. The CDU insisted that unification, and fairly rapid equalization of living standards east and west, could be achieved without raising taxes. So, simultaneously, the west Germans were offered a continuation of their own status quo and the east Germans were offered change. In tandem with this, the SPD's policy, as it penetrated the public consciousness, was a mere denial of the CDU's attractive vision: unification without tax increases was not feasible. So the west Germans feared they were going to have to pay for it, while the east Germans were left with the impression that the SPD did not really want it. The Social Democrats failed to put across a competing vision of a united German nation making noble sacrifices for a common future. The question of concrete policy choices which the extraordinary situation of the country entailed was suspended for the duration.

This was the issue which finally had to be addressed in 1991, and this was when the illusion of the orderly east German party system began to crumble. A very basic analysis of the west German and the east German party system reveals a common core with a divergent periphery. Both parts of the country have the CDU and the SPD as the major parties, with the FDP, in between them politically, demonstrating lesser support. In west Germany, this core is flanked on the left by the Greens, who lost their *Bundestag* representation in December 1990, and on the right by the Republicans, who failed to gain national representation at the same time. In east Germany — as perhaps befits a smaller territory in a stage of transition — the periphery made it into the *Bundestag* in the form of the old communists (PDS) and the Greens/Alliance 90 (citizens' movements).

The PDS and Alliance 90 are the specifically east German parties, and it would therefore be easy to view them as the divergent factor in a comparison of the party system in east and west Germany. In practice, however, this is misleading, since the reality of everyday life can be more readily characterized by peripheral merging of interests with a gaping chasm in the middle. Accordingly, in 1991 the crisis surrounding the parties in the former GDR did not manifest itself in a surge of support for the parties which were (in west German terms) extra-systemic; it was far more visible in the core of the party system, namely in the malfunctioning of the major west German parties under east German conditions. The crucial difficulty lay at the level of the individual politicians in east Germany, whose competence and integrity increasingly came under attack.

A party system has been established, but its efficacy is dependent on the politicians who people it. In order to create a truly unified Germany, the party leaderships have to succeed in integrating into it both the new east German electorate, and their party machines, and the east German politicians.

The new political actors

The politicians and parties in the new German *Länder* can be located in two quite separate spectra: that of the former GDR, and that of the Federal Republic. They have an identity anchored in each, and part of the current problem stems from the merging of the two very different sets of criteria involved. In trying to categorize both politicians and parties, these elements intermingle.

The politicians in east Germany can be divided into several main groupings. Firstly, there are former members of political parties in the GDR. These were members of the communist SED and the four minor (or "block" parties), though now there is a firm distinction between ex-communists in the PDS and members of the CDU or FDP. A less clear distinction is between those who were rank-and-file party members and those who were functionaries. Additionally, there is a small amount of cross-membership, largely involving ex-SED members who have joined, or wish to join, a party other than its successor, the PDS. Secondly, there are politicians who had no political experience before autumn 1989. A smaller sub-category is formed by individuals, mostly church leaders, who gained political experience in public life in the GDR without being in a party. Thirdly, there are west Germans who have chosen to work in politics in east Germany, and they include a sub-group of politicians who originally came from the GDR. The main difference between these categories is their level of political experience. However, whereas the third category, west Germans, have both political experience and political authority, there is no automatic correlation between these two factors among the politicians of the former GDR.

Four main party groupings can be distinguished which returned deputies from the new *Länder* to the *Bundestag* elected in December 1990. Firstly, there are parties with predecessors in the GDR and the Federal Republic: the Christian Democratic Union (CDU) and the Free Democratic Party (FDP). Both became all-German parties in late summer 1990, when they united with East German counterparts which each contained large remnants of two of the GDR's four minor parties as well as one or two new parties. Secondly, there is one party with only a predecessor in the Federal Republic: the Social Democratic Party of Germany (SPD). The East German partner with which it merged shortly before unification had existed for less than a year. Thirdly, there is one party with only a GDR predecessor: the Party of Democratic Socialism (PDS). This consists largely of the rump communist Socialist Unity Party of Germany (SED), with the addition of a few new left-wing recruits, and its 17 seats in the *Bundestag* were almost all won in the eastern electoral territory. Fourthly, there are parties with no predecessors: Alliance 90 and the Greens. Representing only citizens' movements and parties formed during or after autumn 1989, and standing together on a single list in eastern Germany, they obtained eight seats in the *Bundestag*. The west German Greens, with whom they were not at that point formally linked, failed to obtain 5 per cent of the vote in the western electoral territory.

The third and fourth categories are parties and groupings specific to eastern Germany, and which are marginalized on the left wing of the Federal Republic's political system. This is something of an irony, since they represented the two opposing ends of the political spectrum in the GDR during the revolutionary period.

The problem in characterizing the political parties in east Germany derives in part from the fact that the groupings of politicians and the groupings of parties do not pair up neatly. Far from it: the number of possible permutations yielded by a matrix of both sets of groupings is illustrated, for example, by the fact that even the 17 *Bundestag* deputies returned by the PDS in December 1990 contained representatives of all three groupings of politicians. So even the two sets of very broad categories above produce, when combined, many varying political profiles. These would be even more numerous if the groupings had not been reduced to a minimum by lumping together, for instance, the current CDU with the FDP, and former SED functionaries with rank-and-file members of the minor block parties. The variety results from the fact that individual politicians in eastern Germany have both a previous personal identity with reference to the GDR and a new, party identity in the united Germany. Reconciling the two is one of the problems faced by all the political parties today.

The Politicians

Political participation in the GDR

To understand the current political structure in east Germany, it is necessary to have a brief look at its origins in the communist period. The GDR was generally thought of as a one-party state ruled by the SED. This party was formed from the forced merger of the communist KPD and the social democratic SPD which took place in the Soviet occupation zone after the war. In the same period, a Christian Democratic Union (CDU) and Liberal Democratic Party (LDP, later LDPD) were also founded, and these found similar constituencies to their west German counterparts, the CDU and FDP. By 1947, however, they had been largely subordinated to the SED, and in 1948, the communists attempted to weaken them further by instigating the formation of two further parties, the National Democratic Party of Germany (NDPD) and the Democratic Farmers' Party (DBD). All five parties were members of a "Democratic Block", which stood for elections on a single list which also included social organizations such as the Trade Unions. The voter was thus effectively deprived of any element of real choice. So, to an extent, was any aspiring politician, whose legal activity was restricted to the framework of the Democratic Block which had been imposed by the SED.

The fact that the GDR had four parties apart from the communists was usually overlooked in characterizing the country's political system since the multi-party arrangement was designed to achieve monolithism rather than pluralism. The block parties, as the four minor parties were called, were not expected to produce any policy initiatives of their own, but merely to serve a "transmission belt" function in propagating the SED's policies among the population at large. They were targeted at groups such as Christians (CDU), independent craftsmen or small businesspeople (LDPD), former soldiers or rank-and-file Nazis (NDPD) and rural agricultural workers (DBD); these were people who might be quite prepared to participate fully in socialist society, but would baulk at calling themselves communists.

The precise aims of the SED in prolonging the life of these puppet parties, and whether these parties were rational instruments for achieving these aims, is open to question. It is not a question which needs to be answered here, because in the united Germany it pales into insignificance in comparison to a second, much more urgent one: what were the motives which led hundreds of thousands of GDR citizens to join the block parties? This issue is crucial, for however minor their role may have been under the communist system of rule, these people now constitute a majority of the membership of the political parties in east Germany as a whole. In the CDU and FDP — that is, the major parties in the coalition government in Bonn — an overwhelming majority of east German members are "blockis". And these former members of the block parties now enjoy a status in the German political system which is dramatically higher than that of former SED members.

The motives for joining a block party are explained in a number of different ways. Firstly, it was accepted in all socialist countries with a formal multi-party system that there should be no poaching of each others' members. Consequently, joining a block party was a fail-safe method of avoiding pressure to enter the SED. This was, in itself, no very creditable reason for joining a party, since it represented the desire to avoid complications and lead a quiet life.

It also applied largely to people working in professional spheres where party membership might be expected.

Secondly, joining a block party was a declaration that one did not oppose the GDR's system of socialism, although not personally an adherent of Marxist-Leninist doctrine. It precluded any role in top-level decision-making, or certain careers (most notably military ones), but it did allow a degree of professional advancement and participation in public life at a lower and middle-ranking level. Again, this type of membership was essentially a personal life strategy.

Thirdly, for some citizens, joining a block party was simply the second best option to SED membership. Official doctrine accentuated the SED's character as a party led by the working class, but genuine workers were less easily enticed than professionals by the promotion prospects whose achievement was facilitated by political activity. Hence the desired quotas of workers, and young people, which local SED organizations were expected to recruit did not always correspond to the demand from potential members. As a result, some would-be communists were channelled into other parties, where their participation was considered more conducive to the goals of a fully integrated socialist society. Christians, some agricultural workers and people who were not state employees were considered more suitable human material for the CDU, DBD, LDPD and NDPD. Here, their willingness to co-operate with the communist regime could help maintain the facade of a multi-party system, and they, in turn, could enjoy some privileged access to information and contact networks on the peripheries of power. This phenomenon is almost impossible to quantify, since it is a motivation to which no-one today admits.

Finally, there were also positive motivations for block party membership. Convinced Christians, for example, felt that in a society where open oppositionists were excluded — often literally, by coerced emigration — more could be achieved in moderating the day-to-day hardships of life in the GDR by winning small concessions in the local community or workplace through low-level committee work as a CDU member. Three questions arise here, though. Is this merely retrospective justification for a decision largely prompted by personal self-interest? Secondly, at what level in the block party hierarchy did the promotion of SED policies predominate over personal social conviction? And lastly, how different is this from the motivation of many rank-and-file SED members who were indifferent to ideology but wished to make a personal contribution to the well-being of the society in which they lived?

Differentiating between the various types of block party members is highly problematic. At first sight, it may seem simple to ask what individuals actually did during their time in the block parties, but such judgements have a large subjective element. Most political activity is based on compromise, and the citizens of socialist countries had to make many compromises unfamiliar in the west. Also, there is a very thin dividing line between helping one's fellow human beings and favouring one's friends and allies. Under the constraints of East European socialism, and the extreme personalization of daily life which developed there in the 1970s and 1980s, this line is harder to draw than elsewhere.

The political framework in transition

The turbulent months from October 1989 until the first free elections to the *Volkskammer* parliament in March 1990 radically altered the framework of political participation in the GDR. New actors began to enter the political scene, and for existing party members the rules and the scope of the game altered beyond recognition. Participation was no longer limited by the restraints of the communist system: dissidents became politicians, the passive became active, and existing party members had to reveal their true allegiances. Yet amidst the turmoil of a country in transition, it is possible to identify the main landmarks for the recruitment of politicians to the democratic party system now functioning in east Germany. Using these, the time from 1989 to 1991 can be divided into five overlapping periods, throughout which individual personalities rise and fall like shooting stars as their competence in the newly emerging system is tested.

The first period lasted approximately until the end of 1989. This can be characterized as the time when democratic development was carried out in a purely GDR context. The institution which formed its landmark was the Round Table. This was established in Berlin on December 7, 1989, as the first formal mechanism for consultation between the old political forces in the GDR and the new democratic forces which had emerged in the revolution of that autumn. Round the table sat, in equal numbers, representatives of the old political parties, and representatives from the new citizens' movements and parties which had been founded within the previous three months.

Although the Round Table met until the week before the only free elections to the *Volkskammer* parliament on March 18, 1990, it had by this time already become a partially ossified body. This happened because it was too complex to renegotiate its composition to include the new parties which were still springing up all around; and also because the political decisions it reached had ever-diminishing importance as it became clear that the Federal Republic of Germany was a major actor in the GDR's political future. Yet the Round Table's members were the politicians of the first hour, a strange but wholly East German mixture of the old regime and the dissident opposition. Wolfgang Schnur, Chairman of the citizens' movement Democratic Awakening, emerged to be both, and had to resign on the eve of the *Volkskammer* election when it became known that he had worked for the Stasi secret police. Others survived the course and became active members of the first *Bundestag* to be elected in all Germany in December 1990: people such as citizens' movement representatives Ingrid Köppe (New Forum) and Wolfgang Ullmann (Democracy Now); the Social Democrat Markus Meckel; and the leader of the SED successor party, PDS Chairman Gregor Gysi.

The second period had the democratically elected *Volkskammer* as its landmark. This was the phase when West German parties entered the East German political scene as major actors, which meant that it was substantially different in character from the preceding period. From the fixing of the election date in December, and more particularly after it was moved forward by seven weeks at the beginning of February, a key issue for all east German politicians was the formation of electoral alliances and the selection of candidates. The Social Democratic Party of the GDR, which had been formed in October 1989, appeared to be the main contender for power; it was bolstered by its early links with its west German counterpart, whose name it adopted in January 1990. Yet the crucial event of the period was probably the success of Chancellor Kohl in bringing about an alliance of three centre-right parties, the "Alliance for Germany", whose commitment to unification by the speediest possible means, and whose support from the Chancellor, the man in the strongest position to deliver it, led to an unexpectedly decisive election victory.

The March 18 *Volkskammer* elections brought a second wave of east German politicians into prominence. Foremost were the members of the new coalition government of the GDR, who represented, put simply, all the parties with "sisters" in the Federal Republic. Some were former block party members, some were new to political life. Their careers were chequered, and none was appointed to Chancellor Kohl's new cabinet in January 1991.

The man of the hour was the new Minister President of the GDR, Chairman of the

CDU-East, Lothar de Maizière. Yet, although he went on to become Deputy Chairman of the All-German CDU and a member of the *Bundestag* in December 1990, his political skill was questionable and recurrent allegations of informal collaboration with the *Stasi* were a persistent problem, so that he finally withdrew from politics in the autumn of 1991. De Maizière's formal deputy as Minister President, and Minister of the Interior, was Peter-Michael Diestel, who represented the new centre-right party, the DSU (German Social Union). A controversial figure who had yet to learn the political art of discretion, Diestel was disowned by his own party for insufficient rigour in disbanding the *Stasi*. He swapped to the CDU in time to become their candidate for the office of Minister President of Brandenburg in the October 1990 *Land* election there, which his growing unpopularity helped them to lose. He then temporarily left the limelight as leader of the opposition in the Brandenburg parliament. The third group supported by Kohl's government, the citizens' movement Democratic Awakening, was represented by their new Chairman, Rainer Eppelmann, as Disarmament and Defence Minister. Pastor Eppelmann's name was already well-known in the west, as he had been an active pacifist and dissident long before the events of 1989, and then a Round Table member, but he caused puzzlement by his insistence on adhering to contracts to buy Russian armaments during the dying days of the GDR National People's Army. However, after his party merged with the CDU, he was elected to the *Bundestag* in December 1990, and remained active in the CDU in the *Land* of Brandenburg.

The SPD's ministers, who were all new to political life, resigned from the government in August 1990 after de Maizière dismissed, *inter alia,* their Finance Minister Walter Romberg for alleged incompetence. The SPD Foreign Affairs Minister, Marcus Meckel, was later elected to the *Bundestag,* and the Labour and Social Affairs Minister, Regine Hildebrandt, re-emerged in a similar post in the government of Brandenburg — the only east German *Land* to be led by the SPD after the October 1990 elections.

The FDP's east German sister, the League of Free Democrats, faired worst of all: they had made the mistake of putting forward an old LDPD member, Kurt Wünsche, as Justice Minister, although he suffered from the stigma of having twice occupied the identical post in the GDR. He was forced to resign in August 1990, but problems continued with allegations that their Construction Minister, Axel Viehweger, had had *Stasi* links. Viehweger was nonetheless later elected to the *Land* parliament of Saxony for the FDP, and was still denying the *Stasi* allegations and insisting on keeping his seat there after the FDP expelled him from the party in November 1991.

When German unification took place, 144 *Volkskammer* members were delegated to the *Bundestag* in Bonn, and five east Germans joined Kohl's cabinet as ministers without portfolio. Their presence was largely symbolic, but the lacklustre performance of the inexperienced politicians in the recent GDR government was reflected by the fact that its only member to reach Bonn was Lothar de Maizière, whose inclusion was largely a matter of decorum. The same probably applied to the former *Volkskammer* president, Sabine Bergmann-Pohl, whom it is hard not to regard as the token woman. The third CDU minister, Günther Krause, had been instrumental in negotiating the Unification Treaty as de Maizière's parliamentary state secretary, and was known to be Kohl's favourite east German politician. The final two ministers were the largely unknown Hansjoachim Walther (DSU) — the only new politician of the five — and the FDP's Rainer Ortleb. Neither of these parties could delegate a minister from the former GDR government: both the DSU's ministers had left the party protesting about its alleged right-wing shift, and the FDP's problems have been outlined above.

Of the five ministers without portfolio, only Krause had undoubtedly obtained his place in Bonn on the basis of proven political competence. It is fair to ask, however, whether the problems of de Maizière's parliamentary colleagues stemmed in the main from the fact that they were inexperienced and untested politicians, or from the daunting nature of the tasks they faced. Krause, in negotiating the Unification Treaty, was dealing with the political establishment in Bonn and the drafting of a complex set of legal provisions. While taxing, this was probably a more manageable task than those confronted, for example, by ministers Romberg (Finance) and Diestel (Interior), who had to cope on a day-to-day level with the monstrous administrative machines left behind by the old regime, and the thousands of individuals who worked with them.

The third period began before the December 1990 elections, and its landmark was the new *Länder* parliaments elected on October 14, 1990. The elections were important in two respects: it was the first occasion on which west Germans actually obtained elected office on the territory of the former GDR, and it also gave the new east German politicians their first opportunity to enter permanent rather than temporary political roles.

Of the five new east German *Länder,* one produced a Social Democrat Minister President, and one a west German: Manfred Stolpe in Brandenburg and Kurt Biedenkopf in Saxony. These were to become the most respected spokespeople of the east Germans. Stolpe was the Consistorial President of the Protestant Church of Berlin-Brandenburg and the deputy Chairman of the League of Churches, and he was a rare phenomenon in east German politics: he had experience of the political arts of negotiation and compromise, without being tainted by identification with the former regime. At 56, he was older than many of the new entrants into the world of politics, and the fact that he had not joined the SPD until July 1990 gave his decision the air of quietly considered conviction. Biedenkopf was also in his fifties, and had been General Secretary of the Federal Republic's CDU in the 1970s. An academic as well as a *Bundestag* deputy, he had gone to Saxony to work as a guest professor early in 1990, and he was personally distanced from Kohl to the extent that he easily slipped into the role of the competent west German dedicated to promoting the interests of his east German consituency.

The remaining three Minister Presidents — Alfred Gomolka in Mecklenburg-West Pomerania, Gerd Gies in Saxony-Anhalt and Josef Duchac in Thuringia — were rather colourless CDU members from the block party days. By March 1992 all three had been forced to resign, and two were replaced by west Germans. In addition, each Minister President headed a *Land* government of up to a dozen members, and up to a third of these — usually including the Minister of Justice — were initially west Germans. The spate of ministerial resignations which gradually followed as *Land* deputies were checked for former *Stasi* allegiance was a major embarrassment to all political parties.

The fourth period for the recruitment of east German politicians revolved around the landmark of the first *Bundestag* election to take place in all Germany, in December 1990. This was also the first time that east Germans had been elected to roles which entrusted them with running the lives of west as well as east Germans. Most of the deputies elected from the new *Länder* were east Germans, and for Chancellor Kohl the major question was which ones to select for his new cabinet. Günther Krause, who had refused the chance of becoming Minister President in his home *Land* of Mecklenburg-West Pomerania, was an obvious choice, and he was appointed Minister of Transport. Coalition politics also dictated that there should be an FDP minister from the new *Länder,* and so the deputy Chair of the all-German FDP, Rainer Ortleb, became Minister of Education. Finally, it was advisable also to select a woman. Since Sabine Bergmann-Pohl had not shone as a politician, she was demoted slightly to being a state secretary in the Ministry of Health, while Angela Merkel became Minister for Women and Youth. Merkel had been deputy spokesperson of the former GDR government, and since she had entered politics by joining Democratic Awakening after the revolution, she had no problems with a dubious block party past. The choice of her office was also significant: an inevitable controversy was brewing over the need to harmonize the liberal east German abortion laws with the (themselves contentious) west German provisions, and it was probably felt politic to involve an east German woman in this process. By late 1991, it was in fact Merkel — the only east German minister without a block party past — who replaced Krause as the west Germans' east German politician. Krause's star waned as he was attacked for possible involvement in business scandals, and he began to appear less sure-footed in negotiating the obstacle race of Bonn politics.

The fifth and last period, like all the others, overlaps with those which preceded it. Yet it is also different, for it has no landmark other than the united Germany itself. It began in the early months of 1991, when the elections in eastern Germany were over and east German politicians had been appointed to permanent ministerial office and other posts within their parties. The area's political system had been established, and hard truths about the problems facing the newly united Germany finally had to be faced: the west Germans had their taxes raised, contrary to Kohl's elections promise, and the east Germans were confronted with ever-increasing unemployment rates which seemed to make a mockery of the CDU's earlier contention that in a united Germany, no-one would be worse off and many would be better off. More significantly, however, the spontaneous mass recruitment of east Germans to democratic political life had stopped. The realities of the new party system in east Germany gradually became clear as each party had to arrange itself as best if could with the human resources it had already gathered. Parties with a membership base rooted in the GDR era continued to be plagued by the past sins of their members, while the new parties struggled with an inadequate infrastructure of party organizations. And the polity in Bonn had to come to terms with the needs and demands of the country's new citizens. The real problem of unification was only just beginning.

The Parties

The CDU

Chancellor Kohl's CDU was placed in a strange situation in 1990, insofar as its East German partner was thrust upon it by the GDR electorate in the *Volkskammer* election. Kohl had been dubious about endorsing the East German CDU as his partner in the GDR for fear it would make him an easy target for criticism at home, since he would have been dealing with an old structure of the SED regime, rather than one of the forces of the revolutionary renewal. In addition, a number of newly formed centre-right groupings which were modelling themselves on the West German Christian Democrats amalgamated in February 1990 to form the DSU, and its members were adamant in their opposition to the old block party CDU, and extremely reluctant to enter into any alliance with individuals tainted by socialism. However, Kohl finally persuaded them to join in the "Alliance for Germany", since sole endorsement of the DSU, or of the DSU together with the citizens' movement Democratic Awakening, could have handed the GDR to the SPD by splitting the Centre Right vote.

In reality, though, almost half the GDR's electorate, in its headlong flight towards unification, did not appear to share west German reservations about former block parties, and 40.8 per cent voted for the CDU compared to 6.3 per cent for the DSU and 0.9 per cent for Democratic Awakening. From then on, it was obviously both desirable and feasible for the west German CDU to gloss over the GDR past of its east German namesake. The voters had chosen Chancellor Kohl's partner for him. The received wisdom is that Kohl had to achieve an alliance between the DSU and CDU because the latter's substantial organizational infrastructure would otherwise have deflected too many votes from the Christian Democrat camp. Whether this is actually true is one of history's great unknowns. After all, the LDPD had had an organizational infrastructure as strong as that of the CDU-East, yet only achieved 5.3 per cent of the vote in the March 1990 election when it stood in a single-list alliance with two other, untainted liberal parties. It also seems apparent that the CDU vote in March 1990 was a vote for Kohl and unification, and not for the old CDU block party. And in view of the problems posed by the party's past in 1991, it is at least worth positing that Kohl may have made a mistake in the early months of 1990 when he decided that co-operation with the CDU-East was indispensable. Had he, early in 1990, wholeheartedly endorsed the DSU and its forerunners as the unification forces with which he wished to deal, in hindsight he might well have turned the tide in their direction. Had he totally disowned the CDU-East as well, he might have succeeded in condemning it to oblivion. How the DSU's party structures would have coped with victory, and whether the CDU members would have eventually joined them, is another question. But had this situation arisen, the problem scenario faced by the CDU in 1991 would certainly have been very different.

As with all parties, in the year after the elections it was hard to obtain precise membership figures for the CDU, with the General Secretary, Volker Rühe, talking in July 1991 of 80,000 to 100,000 members in the new *Länder* (compared to 660,000 in the old Federal Republic). The key issue, however, was membership trends. The generally accepted number of CDU-East members at the time of its merger with the CDU-West lies between 130,000 and 140,000. Therefore, there was clearly a loss of members after unification, but even more worrying were the proportions of old block party members to new members. According to Rühe, of the 21,000 new members who joined the CDU after unification, at least 4,000, or maybe as many as 7,000, had left by August 1991. This meant that the party was still dominated by the old "blockis", who constituted well above 80 per cent of members in the east German *Länder* as a whole. Such figures are the background to the crises the party faced in the former GDR in 1991.

In the year after the successful *Bundestag* elections in 1990, the CDU's task was to achieve a functional balance in eastern Germany between various factions in the party: these were, broadly speaking, old block party members, new east German members, and west Germans. However, the west German influence can in no way be regarded as a unified force, since CDU members from the old Federal Republic who chose to become involved in politics within east Germany were to an extent self-selecting; they were not all initially emissaries from Bonn who had been selected for the role by Chancellor Kohl.

The first shock of the year for the old block party members was the redundancy of a majority of full-time party functionaries. This impeded the work of many local party groups, where members were less used to the idea of party work being done on a voluntary basis than their west German counterparts. The real shock waves, however, hit the *Land* parliaments when the results of *Stasi* checks on their deputies became known. This process started in May in Mecklenburg-West Pomerania, where four of the nine deputies who were revealed to have had *Stasi* links belonged to the CDU. A worse scandal developed five weeks later in Saxony-Anhalt, when the CDU Minister President, Gerd Gies, was forced to resign for having attempted to pressurize colleagues by threatening to make false accusations of *Stasi* complicity. He was succeeded by the *Land's* west German finance minister, Werner Münch, who reshuffled his cabinet to remove a further two CDU ministers whose block party pasts had been questioned. But he was still left presiding over a contingent of six ministers which contained ex-members of all four GDR minor block parties. Two of these then had to resign when past *Stasi* links were revealed, and Münch ended up with a cabinet composed half-and-half of west and east Germans.

With the results of *Stasi* checks on other *Land* parliaments still outstanding, the events in Saxony-Anhalt set the scene for an all-German CDU row about the state of the party in east Germany which erupted at the end of August 1991. The main protagonist for change on the west German side was the then General Secretary Volker Rühe, whom many east German politicians accused of interference and insensitivity to problems in the former GDR. It became clear that however urgent the need for party renewal in the new *Länder* — and this was recognized by many of the native politicians there — too blatant intervention from Bonn could be counter-productive. Chancellor Kohl was left in a difficult position. While it appeared that the CDU in the eastern *Länder* was being weakened by the continued functioning of old contact networks between the former block party members, which discouraged new blood in the party, there was no simple formula for eradicating the problem. Proposals like that of erstwhile dissident Rainer Eppelmann, who suggested that anyone who had had political office in the GDR before November 1989 should take a back seat for three or four years, would have had far-reaching ramifications for the work of the party, and even risked a split. An alternative strategy, which was gradually being implemented on an *ad hoc* basis, was to lower the profile of the old CDU members by introducing west Germans into prominent positions in the new *Länder*. Yet this was too reminiscent of a takeover from outside, and not necessarily conducive to the promotion of new politicians in east Germany.

This dilemma was illustrated by the balance amongst the highest office-holders in east Germany. After Gies's resignation in Saxony-Anhalt, two of the four CDU Minister Presidents came from the west, and both of these — Biedenkopf in Saxony and Gies's successor Münch — were also likely to assume the post of CDU chair in their respective *Länder* in the near future. A third chair of a CDU *Land* organization, in Mecklenburg-West Pomerania, was occupied by the Federal Transport Minister Krause, an east German closely identified with Kohl, and a fourth — in Brandenburg — was vacant following the resignation of Lothar de Maizière from political life. Against this background, the contest for the chair of the Brandenburg CDU became an interesting display of the divergent strands within the party. Since the party was in opposition in the *Land* parliament, local politicians were aware of their need for a chair who could project an effective political presence to oppose the popular SPD Minister President Stolpe, but no such person could be found within their own ranks and they turned to the west German Ulf Fink, a deputy in the Berlin parliament who had been born in Saxony. He was also vice-chair of the DGB Trade Union Federation, and chair of the CDA, the Christian Democrat labour organization. He therefore represented the reformist wing of the CDU, like many other west Germans active in the new *Länder*, and his candidacy was not supported by Bonn. It came as no surprise, then, when two weeks before the voting took place, Kohl's new favourite east German, Angela Merkel, announced her candidacy. While she maintained this had been her own decision, it was clear that she had the backing of both Rühe and Kohl; the latter stated openly that it would be a good thing in the prevailing situation if a politician of east German origin took over the post, and that he would also like to see a woman in the function. The manoeuvre, however, was far too transparent, and when the internal election took place in November, Fink gained almost twice as many votes as Merkel.

The incident was significant as an illustration of the cross-currents in east German politics: Bonn supported an east German from its own camp, whereas the local CDU preferred a west German of their own choosing. The numerical majority of the old block party members was such that change could only take place with them, and not without them. By the beginning of 1992, however, the need for the renewal of the CDU in eastern Germany was becoming increasingly evident. The second of the three east Germans to head CDU *Land* governments, the Minister President of Thuringia, Josef Duchac, finally resigned after repeated questioning of his activities in the old block party CDU and dissatisfaction with his performance among his ministerial colleagues. His replacement was a west German, the former Minister President of the Rhineland-Palatinate, Bernhard Vogel, and the decision clearly appeared to have been reached in Bonn, and not in the Thuringian capital, Erfurt. The CDU had broken the promise of its slogan in the *Landtag* election of October 1990, "A Thuringian for Thuringia". This was a sign of the growing unacceptability of old block party CDU members as the former GDR began to come to grips with its past.

At the heart of the CDU's dilemma in the new *Länder* is the question of political authority, which is influenced by both its politicians and its policies. Their fundamental problem was that by the end of 1991, the party had failed to produce a single east German politician who commanded widespread respect. At a federal level, the east German ministers Krause and Merkel owed their prominence largely to their backing from Chancellor Kohl, rather than to any popular acclaim for their personal political achievements. Merkel had, in December, been elected as deputy to the national party chairman, Helmut Kohl, her defeat in Brandenburg notwithstanding. It is hard not to view this as "double tokenism": it was the perceived need to have a politically untainted east German woman in a position of prominence rather than her popular appeal to the east German electorate which determined the appointment. By normal western standards, it is quite remarkable that the deputy chair of the ruling party in the most powerful country in Europe should be occupied by an individual who had been involved in political life for less than two years.

Given the lack of popular east German politicians among the ranks of the CDU, its future electoral support in the eastern *Länder* is thus likely to depend not so much on east German politicians as on the policies of Kohl's federal government — though the party may also be assisted by the dissonant west German voices within it demanding more socially oriented policies for the former GDR. An interesting light is shed on all this by psephological analyses of the 1990 elections. They suggest that, in terms of policy positions, the east Germans are actually more left-wing than the CDU, and nearer to the SPD, or even the PDS. Their vote for the CDU was therefore determined largely on an assessment of political *competence*, rather than any traditional criteria of left or right, and their point of reference in making political choices was the old regime, which had proved itself to be singularly incompetent. The SED regime had declared that all its policies were "for the good of the people", yet it produced a standard of living far inferior to that of the Federal Republic. As a consequence, in 1990, any theoretical judgement of a party's declared policies was subordinate to the question of whether a party could, in general, implement political changes which would increase the citizen's well-being. In other words, the CDU's continued success would be contingent on its efficacy in realizing the people's hopes for the future.

This is important in viewing developments within the CDU in east Germany. What emerges is that the aura of competence which brought the CDU to power there appears to surround only its west German politicians. This is scarcely surprising, since in the former GDR the major source of political authority is the proven success of the Federal Republic. As long as this is true, the party's best electoral strategy may in fact be — in the short term at least — to replace as many office-holders from the old block party as possible with "imports" from the old Federal Republic.

The FDP

The Free Democrats are in the interesting position of having more members in the former GDR than in the Federal Republic. In the west they are a relatively compact party with fewer than 70,000 members, which is only about half as many as the SPD and CDU in comparison to the percentage of votes they gain. In the east, however, the fact that the FDP incorporated two former block parties endowed it with well over a hundred thousand members. Despite a steady loss of members throughout 1991, it still remained larger in the east than in the west.

This organizational and numerical strength of the east German FDP is not without its political drawbacks. It is extremely difficult for the east German Free Democrats who came to the party from the two independent, post-1989 liberal parties to make any impression amid the sea of "blockis". Although the former comprise some third of the FDP deputies from the new *Länder* in Bonn, at the level of *Land* parliaments they begin to disappear completely. Given that the party's membership base is already disproportionately large in relation to its electoral strength in the former GDR, joining the FDP would not appear a particularly easy route for an east German anxious to play an active role in political life.

The party also has a further difficulty with its political profile. It may well have reached its zenith in the *Bundestag* elections of December 1990, when it obtained over 13.4 per cent of the vote — more than it has ever gained at federal level in the old *Länder*. At this point, unification was still the dominant issue in the electorate's mind, and the FDP was heavily identified with the achievements of its foreign minister, Hans-Dietrich Genscher. This was demonstrated by the party's strong showing in Genscher's birthplace, the land of Saxony-Anhalt and the city of Halle. The latter returned the first directly elected FDP deputy in decades, the former LDPD functionary Uwe-Berndt Lühr, who also became the national party's General Secretary towards the end of 1991. Since December 1990, however, one of the most prominent figures in the all-German FDP has been the federal economics minister, Jürgen Möllemann, and his policies — and the economic policy of the FDP as a whole — are not perceived as being particularly sympathetic to the social needs in the new *Länder*. For former GDR citizens alienated by any form of socialism, the reformist wing of the CDU and the doctrines of social catholicism have a far greater potential appeal.

Additional bad publicity has been gained by controversy over the FDP's retention of the property from the old block party, as well as *Stasi* allegations against prominent FDP members in the east. In some cases, like that of Axel Viehweger, the former de Maizière government minister, or Gerd Brunner, former minister in Saxony-Anhalt, this was exacerbated by refusal to retire gracefully from their seats in the *Land* parliaments.

Nevertheless, in spite of these problems, the party is not threatened by an existential crisis: it has so much fat in terms of members that it could lose three-quarters of them and still be left with a healthy core to run an election campaign and supply candidates for political office. Yet, like the CDU, its popular profile was dominated by the performance of west rather than east German politicians.

The SPD

The SPD had been forcibly merged with the commiunist KPD in 1946 and its identity lost, so that the east German Social Democrats were able to emerge as a new, untainted party in October 1989. However, after its unexpected defeat in the *Volkskammer* elections, the summer of 1990 saw the party in disarray. Its chairman and leading candidate in the *Volkskammer* election, Ibrahim Böhme, was forced to resign as a result of *Stasi* allegations, and the party's participation in de Maizière's government, controversial in itself, was not a success. Failure to participate could have been equally damaging, however, by guaranteeing even earlier marginalization in the unification process. On top of this, the all-German SPD's chancellor candidate for the December 1990 elections, Oskar Lafontaine, never obtained any rapport with the east German electorate, and the *Land* elections of October 1990 were lost badly.

Membership is also a fundamental problem for the SPD in the new *Länder*. The fact that it inherited no membership base from a GDR party means that it is many times smaller than the CDU, the FDP and the PDS. Estimates of membership in east Germany during 1991 put the membership at somewhat below 30,000. Since the party has over 900,000 members in the old Federal Republic, this means that east Germans have to be overrepresented at a national level in proportion to their membership in order to retain any east German profile in the party at all.

Since the SPD is not in power either in Bonn or in most of the east German *Länder,* any assessment of the party must rely less on the developments which have taken place since the December 1990 elections, and more on its latent ability to become a governing party. A number of questions affect the SPD's chances of becoming a major political force in the new *Länder*. The most obvious is overcoming structural problems and building up its party organization. While numerically weak, it does at least have the advantage of being untainted by the past to an extent that the mass membership parties are not. There may have been isolated resignations of SPD deputies in *Land* parliaments after their earlier *Stasi* contacts were revealed, but this whole procedure undermined it to a lesser extent than the other three major parties (CDU, FDP and PDS). Its members can also claim that they did not collaborate with the SED regime at a more mundane, everyday level in the way the block parties did. In practice, this also means that the SPD is not riddled by contact networks between old members from GDR times, and theoretically this should make the party more easily permeable for new members. If the simmering discontent in the new *Länder* about social problems such as unemployment should become mobilized in party activity, the SPD is the most likely beneficiary.

The SPD may also benefit from the fact that it was not in office during the formative phase of democratic political life in eastern Germany. This has granted it a breathing space in which some east German Social Democrats will emerge as authoritative and competent politicians with a track record of serving the interests of their constituents. They may then be able to assume high office on the basis of proven merit and popular support among their own electorate, rather than artificial promotion by a Bonn leadership perceiving the need to provide balanced representation of east Germans.

A second crucial issue for the SPD is capturing the party's natural constituency. In the early post-revolutionary days, before the *Volkskammer* election, there was a widespread belief that the East Germans might tip the scales of the West German party balance in the SPD's favour. This was because the GDR contained regions which had been traditional SPD strongholds in the inter-war period, largely because of their working-class profile and the overwhelming preponderance of Protestants over Catholics. However, 40 years of communism had actually distorted the social fabric of the GDR to the point where traditional criteria such as class and religion did not seem to apply.

Soviet-style socialism had alienated the working class to the extent that twice as many of them voted for the CDU as for the SPD, while amongst white-collar and managerial employees the difference was far less marked. These latter groups also had a greater tendency to vote PDS. This is indicative of the fact that conservatism, defined as a desire to preserve current social status, has a radically different effect on voting behaviour in east and in west Germany. In the GDR, the SED was the party of privilege, and in the new Germany, the working class therefore voted for the party that appeared nearest to being its opposite. This was the CDU. Only the self-employed, who lacked any real GDR identity, showed similar voting patterns east and west.

The effect of religious affiliation on voting patterns has not been distorted to the same extent by the GDR, and thus poses less of a problem for the SPD. Nearly two-thirds of Catholics in the new *Länder* voted CDU, but there have always been far fewer of them in this region than in western Germany. Protestants initially appear to constitute a greater problem, since they were far more likely to vote CDU in the former GDR than in the old *Länder*. However, the key factor to be borne in mind is the question of religious self-definition: in the former GDR, the term "Protestant" tends to denote only Protestants who attend church regularly, and such people are more inclined to vote CDU in west Germany too. Since religion was discouraged in the GDR, conformist pressure militated against the indifferent majority declaring a purely nominal Christian affiliation. Consequently, in the former GDR over half the population has no religion at all; and in 1990 this group was only slightly more likely to vote CDU than SPD.

It is therefore probable in the long term that the religious composition of the new *Länder* will work in the SPD's favour. Controversy over abortion serves to highlight the Catholic orientation of the CDU in the west, which will remain alien to the vast majority of former GDR citizens. The far more crucial issue for the SPD is gaining the working-class vote. It is possible that overall improvements in the standard of living will sustain confidence in the CDU, as it did in the Federal Republic in the 1950s; but it is also possible that, as western-type social stratification establishes itself in the east, the SPD will be able to raise its profile as the protector of the working people through trade union work. Additionally, the party has a chance to present itself as representing the interests of the socially weak in general, and this group currently encompasses a large proportion of all east Germans when they are compared with west Germans.

Another difficulty for the party will be merging the interests of its constituents east and west. Average SPD voters in the old Federal Republic still enjoy a standard of living superior to that of most east Germans, with the result that unification served to catapult many of them, overnight, to being the middle rather than the lower income groups in German society as a whole. This is likely to involve some degree of psychological adaptation. This is nowhere near as enormous as the adaptation processes that unification entailed for the east Germans. Yet the east German worker at least had some material and political comforts to compensate for the disruption of their everyday lives caused by unification. The west German worker had none. No national euphoria appears to compensate for a decline in living standards caused by tax increases and rising rents, and demands for wage increases are the consequence.

The final question of crucial importance to the SPD is the fate of the PDS. Since the latter is unlikely to survive the next *Bundestag* elections, the distribution of its 11 per cent of the vote is significant, and much of it is likely to come to the SPD. However, the fate of the PDS's members, past and present, is also vital, as will be discussed below.

What the SPD has been left with is a hard core of 30,000 members with a far stronger middle-class bias than their counterparts in the west. Precisely because it is composed of people who suffered personal disadvantage from their failure to compromise with the communist regime, they will find it hard to welcome and integrate socialists who did compromise: only a tiny percentage of their current membership was once in the SED. Yet, somehow, they have to triple their size even to match the CDU and FDP in the new *Länder*, to say nothing of matching the strength of the SPD in the old Federal Republic. At a time when political recruitment in the former GDR has reduced to a trickle, this will be a hard task.

The PDS

Before November 1989, the SED had 2.3 million members, which represented well over four-fifths of the GDR citizens belonging to a political party. By late 1991, only about 180,000 of these remained in the PDS. This has two implications which affect not only the PDS but also the general party constellation in eastern Germany.

Firstly, the dropout rate from the SED/PDS was immeasurably greater than that from the minor block parties. It lost the low-level careerists and all its reluctant members. Therefore, although the rump PDS contained many elderly diehard communists who were simply unable to come to terms with the changes which had taken place around them, it can reasonably be assumed that the party also contained a substantial proportion of east Germany's most committed socialists. Many of them were experienced in the complexities of politics, since skill in compromise was inherent to survival in a body such as the SED. There were indications in the year after the *Bundestag* elections that some of these remaining PDS politicians at *Land* and federal level might be making informal approaches to the SPD to see if they might continue their political lives in a left-oriented party which has a future in the new state. It is probable that the SPD will be forced, both short and long term, to rebuff them because of the stigma which is attached to PDS membership. Nonetheless, this may entail the loss to east German politics, and to the SPD, of a fair part of a generation of those socialists most willing to involve themselves in the political process.

Secondly, there is the question of the two million SED members who have withdrawn from politics. A large proportion of them undoubtedly joined the communist party for careerist reasons, and would not have been in a political party at all in a society where non-affiliation was an acceptable mode of behaviour. But others differed from rank-and-file members of minor parties in one respect only: they were acceptable to the SED because they happened to have no Christian beliefs, and were employed in the large state sector of the economy. Even if the SED's claim to be a party of the working class was a statistical sleight-of-hand, it still embraced hundreds of thousands of workers who were prepared to undertake everyday tasks in the organization of their community. Elsewhere, such people might well have become Social Democrats. The spectre that emerges from this is that the legacy of the SED regime may in fact have neutralized politically much of the SPD's natural constituency. A chance of fate has allowed many minor party members a smooth transition into the democratic processes of the Federal Republic, while excluding the majority of previously active citizens, who were in the SED. The extreme clash of political cultures inherent in German unification, as well as the strong, functioning infrastructure of the Federal Republic's political life, has made the erstwhile communists expendable to the former GDR in a way they are not elsewhere in the new democracies of central and eastern Europe. The SED and PDS have therefore played a role in weakening the SPD which may be politically more significant than any strength they themselves retain.

With its 180,000 members, the PDS was easily the largest party in east Germany, but nonetheless had seemingly insuperable problems. Two sets of factors can be identified in its decline: those internal to the party, and external influences. Internally, the structure of the party's membership base was unfavourable. About half the membership was approaching pensionable age or older, and a sociological analysis showed likewise that over half of its members remained in the party because they regarded it as their political home from tradition, or because of its identification as a GDR party. Such members are bound to be an encumbrance in forming a political mission of relevance to the changing conditions in Germany. The party had difficulty establishing its new direction: its traditionalists sought to play a role in parliamentary politics through the creation of some sort of left-wing coalition, whilst the reformist stream clearly saw its role in opposition. Additionally, attempts to ensure the PDS's survival by extending its field of operation to the old *Länder* came to nothing. The problem of the party's general lack of appeal there was exacerbated by the fact that the few west Germans to join the party caused what can only be described as a clash of political culture between the left in east and west. It is also difficult to believe that even a dynamic, united PDS would have been able to find an appropriate gap in the political spectrum of the new Germany. For the socialist-oriented citizens wishing to build a better future, the SPD could be a more effective agent of everyday working-class political participation, while the Greens and Alliance 90 provide a more credible focus for radical opposition to the Federal Republic's established structures. This meant that the PDS was indispensable only to those whose political perspective looked essentially back to the past, embracing both nostalgia for the GDR and the need to defend their role in building it.

It was against this unfavourable internal situation that external pressures began to take their toll on the party. Its failure to break whole-heartedly with the past found little understanding among the public at large. This was particularly true in the case of politicians accused of working with the *Stasi*. From the early days of 1990, the people of the GDR had simplified the daunting task of freeing themselves from the SED legacy by associating the *Stasi* with all that was fundamentally evil in the system. Establishing degrees of complicity with the regime in a country where politics embraced the whole of the society where every citizen lived was so complex an undertaking that *Stasi* links had become the litmus test for determining ultimate guilt. While *Land* deputies of other parties sometimes denied *Stasi* allegations, only PDS members made attempts to retain their seats by admitting and *justifying* their contacts with the *Stasi*. The situation began to verge on the unreal in the case of higher SED functionaries, exemplified by former Prime Minister Hans Modrow. The test of whether or not someone had worked for the *Stasi* ceased to function at this level, since such people were more likely to have received information from the *Stasi* than to have provided it.

While the political pedigree of the PDS was unacceptable to the popular culture which had developed in the former GDR since 1989, it also now had to face a second political culture in which it was an anathema: that of the old Federal Republic. Too impatient to wait for the PDS's inevitable demise at the hands of the east German voters, the new authorities emanating from Bonn began to exert pressure on the organizational base of the party. The decisions of the *Treuhand,* which was entrusted with unravelling the financial affairs of the

SED/PDS, at one point even seemed to be pushing the party towards a state of bankruptcy from which it could scarcely expect to emerge.

The Greens and Alliance 90

The fate of the alternative political movements in Germany remained one of the most open questions in the year after the *Bundestag* elections. The Greens and Alliance 90, standing on a joint list, managed to obtain over 5 per cent of the vote in the eastern territory in December 1990 and thus obtained eight seats in the *Bundestag*. Shortly afterwards, the Greens joined with their counterparts in the west to form a single party, and in September 1991, Alliance 90 also became a political party in its own right. This was a controversial decision which was forced on the citizens' movements by the fact that the Unification Treaty only gave them a year to come into line with the provisions of the Federal Republic's Party Law. Some members of New Forum considered that political parties were a negative influence on a parliamentary democracy and refused to join the new party.

The major problem facing the Greens and Alliance 90 is that neither is likely to surmount the 5 per cent barrier at the next federal election if they cannot join together in the intervening period, but it will be a hard task for them to reach the level of consensus necessary to do this. The west German Greens have long been prone to factionalism, and their political priorities are very different from those of the east Germans in Alliance 90. However, the refusal of Alliance 90 to unite with a west German partner with the same alacrity as other political groups in the new *Länder* has an underlying cause with significance for understanding the position of east German politicians in general. For these "revolutionaries of the first hour" the electoral advantages of merging with the Greens are predominantly technical: they derive from the Federal Republic's election laws. They are not underpinned by the need to "borrow" political authority from a west German party whose achievements are acknowledged by east German voters. The respect granted to the Greens/Alliance 90 group in the *Bundestag* stems from their own achievements in the autumn of 1989, whereas for most east German deputies acceptance in Bonn is a consequence of their incorporation in party structures which form an integral and long-established part of the Federal Republic's political system. (The PDS, lacking either achievements from GDR times or west German patronage, benefits from neither respect nor acceptance.) The distinct profile of the east German *Bundestag* members from the citizens' movements has also been accentuated by the failure of the Greens to obtain 5 per cent of the vote in the west German electoral territory in December 1990, thereby leaving the east Germans as the sole national representatives of the alternative political movement.

In addition, the electoral need of the Greens to unite with Alliance 90 in order to secure the requisite spread of support throughout the Federal Republic and re-enter the *Bundestag* as representatives of the west Germans means that they are dependent on their east German allies to an extent which other parties are not. The relationship between the Greens and Alliance 90 is thus marked by a degree of reciprocity between east and west lacking elsewhere in the political system. A union between the two groups will require a balanced policy debate and a degree of compromise between the aspirations of citizens in the old and new *Länder* of a kind which did not take place in other parties. Yet, whatever solution is finally reached, it appears increasingly unlikely that the next *Bundestag* will include a group of deputies specifically representing the interests of former GDR citizens.

Conclusion

The parties in east Germany have been formed largely by chance. The party *system* was externally imposed: it grew up in a different society, at a different point in history. Yet the human resources it contains in the new *Länder* bear a heavy imprint from the stratification of the communist era. They cannot be classified politically by the criteria familiar in the west. Most east German politicians became members of all-German parties in the early months of rapid change after the upheaval of autumn 1989, and some talk openly of the way their party membership was determined almost accidentally. They sometimes have difficulty identifying with the more ritualistic elements of polarized policy dispute between government and opposition: like their electorate, their judgement can be pragmatically issue-orientated, and their perceptions of the urgent needs of the new *Länder* can transcend party divisions in a manner alien to the old Federal Republic. In Bonn, particularly, many east Germans feel themselves to be outsiders and find it hard to reconcile the generous facilities with which they are provided as *Bundestag* deputies with the technologically primitive conditions in which their constituents have to tackle the urgent economic, social and administrative problems in the new *Länder*.

Two at first sight contradictory conclusions can be drawn about the role of east German politicians in the new Federal Republic. The first is pessimistic. At a federal level, they have found it extremely difficult to slot into a system which has functioned smoothly for over 40 years. The initial, formal welcome for the representatives of the east was gradually superseded by a more critical examination of both their competence and their political integrity. The latter related to a GDR past whose complexity was hard for west Germans to comprehend. The former was a skill normally acquired through decades of political activity, during which only the most resilient gradually surmounted the hurdles on the way to high political office. It is scarcely surprising that so many east Germans, catapulted to prominence, fell at the first hurdles they encountered.

A more optimistic prospect may, however, emerge at *Land* level. The German federal system may prove fortuitous for the integration of east German politicians. It provides the opportunity for genuine political power to be exercised at a level where the experience of 40 years living in the GDR, or at the very least an intimate knowledge of local problems, is invaluable. Although there has been a gradual trend towards top positions in the east German *Länder* being occupied by west Germans, this is in itself an integrative process, since the individuals concerned are using political skills gained in the old Federal Republic to represent the interests of their east German constituents. In addition, the *Länder* governments provide a half-way house where east German politicians may acquire both the political competence and the popular authority which will equip them for higher office in the near future. The chances of east German politicians should therefore improve markedly, if gradually, over the next few years. At the same time as they acquire political experience, a natural selection process will mark out the high-fliers. These will then emerge into a Federal Republic which has itself subtly changed its political agenda as the west Germans come to terms with the impact of unification.

THE IMPACT OF REUNIFICATION ON THE EAST GERMAN ECONOMY

Ian Jeffries

The economy of the German Democratic Republic before 1989

Natural resources and labour

The German Democratic Republic started off in generally worse shape than the Federal Republic, having suffered greater wartime destruction and having to pay heavy reparations to the Soviet Union. Although it inherited a rather unbalanced industrial structure, with weak development of chemicals, iron and steel, heavy engineering and shipbuilding, for instance, the GDR, alongside Czechoslovakia, was unusual in that it was an advanced, industrialized country before the start of the socialist era.

The GDR was on the whole poorly endowed with raw materials, but two important exceptions were lignite (brown coal) and potash, both heavy polluters unfortunately. Thus the GDR was heavily dependent on imports of fuels and raw materials, especially from the Soviet Union. The oil price "shocks" of 1973–74 and 1979, although the increases were lagged due to the pricing system of the CMEA (Comecon), caused the response of some substitution of lignite for oil and reform measures to improve resource utilization.

There was full employment in the GDR and the labour shortage spurred both economic reform and the building of the Berlin Wall in 1961 to staunch migration to the Federal Republic. Although the GDR had the highest standard of living in the socialist bloc, it was always the wealthier West Germany which provided the comparison. The GDR tried in vain to catch up, seeking legitimacy largely through rising living standards. The GDR saw itself at the forefront of the battle between socialism and capitalism and this ideological factor severely constrained the limits to which economic reform could be undertaken. Right to the very end Erich Honecker refused to follow President Gorbachev's advice to relax political and economic control, even after a new mass migration of people westwards had started in 1989. Ironically, it was partly to stem this tide of emigration that the Berlin Wall was then opened in November 1989.

Economic policy and organization

The GDR's was a command economy, with the most important decisions taken centrally. Nevertheless, there were phases of reform. The New Economic System from 1963 to 1971 was the first comprehensive reform and the most radical in Eastern Europe in the early 1960s outside of Yugoslavia. Many observers interpreted the GDR reform as a laboratory experiment conducted on behalf of the Soviet Union. But although decision-making was decentralized to a limited extent and there was greater reliance on "economic levers" such as taxes and prices to steer the economy more indirectly, the essentials of command planning were maintained. This was especially the case after the 1968 amendments, involving greater control over key areas.

The period 1971–79 then saw recentralization. Erich Honecker, who replaced Walter Ulbricht as first secretary of the Socialist Unity Party of Germany (SED) in May 1971, set three leading tasks: the "chief task" *(Hauptaufgabe)* was to improve the supply of consumer goods; "intensification" *(Intensivierung)*, a term first used in the early 1960s, was stressed again, the idea being to increase output largely through the more efficient utilization of inputs, especially through technical progress; and there was to be an active social policy, including a massive housing programme and numerous individual measures such as pension increases. The slogan summing up and linking these priorities, "unity of economic and social policy", was coined and promoted at the Ninth Party Congress in May 1976. The 1970s economic system did not, however, solve the GDR's problems, which were exacerbated by the oil shocks.

An "economic strategy for the 1980s" was developed by Honecker at the Tenth Party Congress in April 1981, essentially involving a further stress on "intensification". Radical economic reform was eschewed and instead intensification was sought through the "perfecting" *(Vervollkommnung)* of the economic mechanism. For example, plan targets henceforth stressed input savings; a payroll tax was imposed to encourage labour efficiency; and the combine *(Kombinat)* was made the main production unit.

The combine was a horizontal and vertical amalgamation of enterprises under the unified control of a director general. The idea was to streamline the planning process. The combines' activities covered the whole spectrum of activities from research and development to marketing. The vertical element involved the incorporation of the most important supplier enterprises, with the aim of improving the severe supply problems which typically afflicted command economies. The GDR's industrial structure thus became highly monopolistic, characterized by giant production units. The centrally directed combines in industry and construction varied in size from 2,000 to 80,000 employees, with an average of 25,000 people and 20–40 enterprises. There were 127 of these in 1986, while there were also 94 combines in regionally directed industry. The private non-agricultural sector was encouraged in later years, but even so in the mid-1980s it only accounted for 2.3 per cent of industrial output. Private manufacturing trades were allowed to employ up to 10 people, but the actual average number of employees was only three.

In agriculture, which employed about 11 per cent of the labour force, production was dominated by the agricultural producer co-operatives *(Landwirtschaftliche Produktionsgenossenschaften* — LPG), which accounted for some 87 per cent of land used for agricultural purposes and 84 per cent of the agricultural labour force. The state farms *(volkseigene Güter)* thus played a much smaller role than in the Soviet Union, many of them being involved primarily in research and breeding. The co-operative farm was a giant unit, covering on average 1,369 hectares (and 4,608 hectares for those in crop rather than livestock production) in the mid-1980s. The average crop unit employed 240 people and comprised 500 former farms, while the average livestock unit employed 110 workers and had 1,500 head of livestock. However, GDR agricultural productivity was only about 40 per cent of the West

German level. Private farming, including both private farms and private plots within the co-operatives, accounted for a little over 9 per cent of agricultural land and was important for certain commodities, such as meat (more than 20 per cent of total output), fruit (30 per cent) and vegetables (11 per cent).

The GDR leadership's reluctance to raise retail prices was overcome in 1979, when the prices of already highly taxed quality industrial consumer goods such as televisions, washing machines and cars, were planned to go up in line with rising costs. But the prices of staple foodstuffs, children's clothing, housing rents and transport fares continued to be held down. Bus and train fares, for instance, had not been changed since 1949, while rent took only 3 per cent of urban household income. The necessary subsidies put considerable strain on the state budget.

Economic performance in the 1980s

In order to monitor the economic performance of the GDR, the Central Intelligence Agency (CIA) compiled a series of figures for Gross National Product (GNP) calculated as far as possible on a Western basis. It confirmed a long-term economic decline. The average annual rate of GNP growth in the period 1971–75 was 3.1 per cent. In 1976–80 it was 2.3 per cent, and in 1981–85 it was down to 1.9 per cent. Thereafter, the figures for the individual years were 1.5 per cent in 1986, 1.7 per cent in 1987, 1.1 per cent in 1988, and 1.2 per cent in 1989. These Western estimates were consistently well below the official GDR ones, but even the official figures for the growth of Net Material Product (which excluded so-called "non-productive" services) showed a deteriorating economic performance during the second half of the 1980s. In the early 1980s the official growth rate had been well above 4 per cent, except in 1982, when it dipped to 2.6 per cent. From 1984, a year with the 1980s peak growth figure of 5.5 per cent, the trend was downward. Official NMP growth (based on 1985 prices) was 5.2 per cent in 1985, 4.3 per cent in 1986, 3.3 per cent in 1987, 2.8 per cent in 1988, and 2.1 per cent in 1989.

In the late Honecker era, according to the official figures, the CMEA and other socialist countries accounted for 69.1 per cent of the GDR's foreign trade, the Soviet Union alone for 37.5 per cent (both 1988). As revised official statistics published in 1990 showed, these figures underestimated the real value of western trade for the GDR, but there is no gainsaying the vast importance of CMEA markets for the viability of concerns and for employment in the GDR. The GDR's role in the now defunct CMEA was mainly to supply relatively high-quality, high technology capital goods, such as machine tools, industrial robots and computers, in return for fuels and raw materials, especially from the Soviet Union. To the west the GDR benefited from substantial concessions in its trade with the Federal Republic, which did not regard the GDR as foreign territory. For example, GDR exports to West Germany were allowed in free of tariffs and levies (although there were quotas on certain items), while the so-called "swing" credit provided an interest-free overdraft facility up to a certain limit (raised from DM 600 million to DM 850 million in July 1985). With other Western countries the GDR usually demanded counter-trade agreements, and it was isolated among the East European CMEA countries in not allowing joint equity ventures with Western companies. In Europe as a whole only Albania shared this distinction.

The 1980s were a period when the GDR had to contend with severe foreign trade and payments problems. It was successful in reducing its net hard currency debt from $12.5 billion in 1981 to $6.5 billion in 1985, but foreign debt rose again thereafter from $7.9 billion in 1986, to $10.4 billion in 1988 and $18.5 billion in 1989. Reduced capital goods imports and sluggish investment in general only stored up trouble for the future, since the capital stock was rapidly becoming obsolete. This was despite the limited but highly publicized new investment in key technologies such as computers and industrial robots. In all, the economy was in no shape to cope with the shock of political collapse in 1989–90, the loss of eastern markets, and the intense West German and international competition which were to be consequent upon German economic and monetary union in 1990.

Economic policy from November 1989 to June 1990

The Modrow government

With Honecker having been ousted in October, the appointment of Hans Modrow as prime minister on November 13, 1989 represented the beginnings of a marked shift in economic policy. His interim government implemented a number of market-oriented policies. Modrow himself talked in terms of a "market-oriented planned economy". In a November speech to the *Volkskammer* (People's Chamber) he thought there should be "no planning without the market, but no unplanned market economy ... This does not mean that central planning will be abolished, but a real socialist planned economy needs the market". Modrow spoke out against party interference and the "arbitrary ordering around of the economy to its detriment". Prices should reflect costs, the prices of basic commodities should reflect "economic reality" and "idiotic" subsidies should be abolished. Specific measures included the announcement on November 21 that half the state-decreed plans for individual branches of the economy and also 10-day and monthly targets for enterprises were to be abolished. In January 1990 the State Planning Commission was replaced by an Economic Committee comprising directors, economists and political groups. And at the Congress of the Free German Trade Union League (FDGB), held in the first days of January 1990, union independence from party and state was proclaimed, and demands were made for the right to strike and increased worker participation in enterprise decision-making (see also Timmins essay in this volume).

The private sector was to be encouraged. Modrow thought that the state sector should dominate areas such as energy, heavy industry and transport, while the private sector would play an important role in such sectors as the small-scale manufacture of consumer goods. Christa Luft, the new minister for the economy (from the SED), talked of the prospects of "widespread" privatization, while the deputy minister for foreign trade, Christian Meyer, envisaged a "tidal wave" of small and medium-sized enterprises, although at this stage it was considered whether they should be limited to a ceiling of 300 employees. Meanwhile the smaller enterprises nationalized in 1972 were to be offered back to their original owners. A trust agency, the *Treuhandanstalt,* was established on March 1, 1990 to handle the dismemberment of the combines. Its functions included restructuring, credit guarantees and liquidation. Privatization was also mentioned, but this function only became important in the post-Modrow era. The Modrow directive envisaged transforming the combines into joint stock companies by affixing the suffix AG *(Aktiengesellschaft)* to their corporate names and setting up East German citizens as their shareholders.

There was to be a phased price reform, including the gradual reduction of subsidies for many consumer goods, with income compensation. In January 1990 it was announced that price controls were to be removed in stages. The plan was to reduce the huge annual sum spent on subsidies, amounting to around M51 billion, in three stages. As a first step it was announced that the subsidies on items like children's clothes and shoes were to be reduced by M1.2 billion, with the corresponding price rises compensated for by an additional monthly allowance of M45 for each child up to 12 years of age and M65 for each child aged 13 and over. On February 19, 1990 the Round Table, set up in December 1989 and comprising government and opposition, voted to abolish M30 billion of food subsidies and to make a compensatory payment of M150 per person. This was revoked three days later, however, because of the consequent panic buying in the shops. Electricity and lignite prices were increased on January 3, 1990, with the aim of avoiding power cuts. The government planned to reduce drastically the output of lignite and to double nuclear energy's share of electricity from the then 10 per cent with the help of Western technology.

A banking reform was also set underway. This included plans for the state bank *(Staatsbank)* to become an independent central bank on April 1, 1990, losing its previous commercial functions to the *Deutsche Kreditbank*. The Foreign Trade Bank *(Aussenhandelsbank)* was to lose its monopoly of foreign exchange and credit activity. Both GDR enterprises and foreign companies were to be able to buy shares in GDR commercial banks, while these banks in would, in turn, be permitted to buy shares in enterprises.

An immediate problem with regard to foreign trade was the availability of many heavily subsidized and therefore cheap goods and services in a GDR with open borders. A number of measures were taken to deal with the situation. For example, on November 22, 1989, the export of antiques was banned, while two days later it was decreed that only GDR citizens and authorised foreigners working in the country were allowed to buy a whole range of goods, including children's clothing, car parts and cameras. On January 4, 1990, West Germans were forbidden to place bulk orders for services such as dry cleaning, shoe repairs and tailoring.

In a November 17, 1989 speech to the *Volkskammer*, Modrow made an ideological breakthrough as regards private foreign capital. He announced that "the GDR is open to suggestions by our capitalist partners that were earlier treated cautiously or ignored ... Joint ventures, direct investment, profit transfers, pilot projects to preserve the environment are no longer foreign words to us". A 49 per cent maximum stake in a joint venture by a "foreign" (including West German) partner was suggested at first, but on January 12, 1990, the *Volkskammer* agreed to a higher percentage when this was "of interest to the economy", for example, in areas of new technology. Minister of the Economy Christa Luft was in favour of small West German companies being allowed to set up wholly-owned subsidiaries in East Germany.

In a February 4, 1990 speech Chancellor Kohl said that substantial economic aid was necessary before the election, but the aid did not materialize. The then West German foreign minister Hans-Dietrich Genscher, too, thought that instant and comprehensive aid to the GDR was needed. On January 24 the Federal Republic did actually announce a DM6 billion low-interest credit to modernize the GDR economy, but on February 5 Christa Luft called for a DM10–15 billion grant to compensate the GDR for the difficult post-war conditions; this was needed to boost economic growth and facilitate the move towards partial convertibility of the GDR Mark. Her request was rejected by the West Germans, but they promised to start releasing credits for small and medium-sized enterprises and to provide DM20 million for urban restoration. At the start of January 1990 the DM100 per annum "welcome money" given to GDR visitors to West Germany was replaced by a DM2.90 billion "foreign currency fund", the Federal Republic providing DM2.15 billion. GDR citizens were allowed to exchange up to M200 a year on favourable terms, namely M100 at parity with the Deutschemark and the other M100 at 5:1. The proceeds of the fund were to be used for infrastructural and tourism projects in the GDR. Concessions were also made to West German visitors to the GDR. As of December 24, 1989, they no longer needed visas and were not forced to exchange DM25 a day at parity.

The de Maizière government

The change in government to a CDU-led coalition from April 1990 accelerated the changes which were already in train. It also meant that the structures set up by the Modrow administration were now used with a more expressly free-market purpose. This applied particularly to the *Treuhandanstalt,* which moved from a priority of restructuring *(Sanierung)* to one of privatization *(Privatisierung)*. On June 17, 1990, a new *Treuhandanstalt* law was passed by the *Volkskammer* to this effect. Along the same lines the two German governments had agreed two days beforehand that claims could be made for the restitution of property in the GDR nationalized after 1949.

Prime Minister de Maizière and his advisers were meanwhile now working with Chancellor Kohl towards early economic union of the two Germanies, with political unity not far behind. On April 24, 1990, Kohl and de Maizière agreed that July 1, 1990 should be the date of economic, monetary and social union, and negotiations began within days between the respective finance ministers, Theo Waigel for the Federal Republic and Walter Romberg for the GDR. A state treaty *(Staatsvertrag)* on economic, monetary and social union was signed in Bonn on May 18.

German monetary, economic and social union

Monetary, economic and social union took place on July 1, 1990. The term "union" is misleading because what actually happened was that the Mark of the GDR was replaced by the Deutschemark, with the West German *Bundesbank* in control of monetary policy, and the GDR adopted West Germany's "social market economy". As with the European Community, monetary union is conventionally seen as the final stage of countries coming together. Exchange rate adjustments are used to ease the transitional stage of uniting unequal economies. Speedy German union, it was argued, would bring benefits in, for instance, the assurance of a sound, convertible currency. Much reference was made at the time to the currency reform of June 1948 which, coupled with the abolition of most price controls and rationing, was the prelude to the West German "economic miracle" *(Wirtschaftswunder)* of the 1950s. It was argued from this example that instant monetary union was necessary, despite the obvious differences in circumstances, such as the fact that the early post-war economy had not been a command economy.

In some respects there has been a phasing in of the social market economy, for example with regard to housing rents and environmental standards. The general achievement of West German environmental standards was set for the year 2000, but emission standards for new investment projects applied from the beginning of July 1990, and 1996 is the target date for adaptation by existing lignite power stations and for air and water standards. Nuclear safety rules applied straight away and the last nuclear reactor (at Greifswald) was closed on December 15, 1990. Two new nuclear power plants are to be built. West German income and corporate taxes were delayed until January 1991, while privatization would obviously take time. In effect the West German economy was to swallow up a relatively inefficient economy something like one-tenth its own size.

The terms of monetary union

The final conversion ratios between the Mark of the GDR and the Deutschemark were more generous than had been generally anticipated. The *Bundesbank* had recommended 1:1 for personal savings up to M2,000 and 2:1 for everything else, while the previous black market rate had fluctuated in the range 5–10:1. The economist Holger Schmiedling (see Bibliography) has argued that on the basis of the competitiveness of GDR exports to the West, calculated according to the Mark value of domestic inputs necessary to earn DM1 of exports, the Mark of the GDR was worth only DM0.23. It should be borne in mind, however, that the nominal wage ratio before monetary union was not greatly out of line with the labour productivity ratio. A typical GDR industrial worker (in Marks at a conversion ratio of 1:1) earned about one-third the Deutschemarks of his West German counterpart per month. Estimates of the average GDR – West German productivity ratio varied, but one at the lower end of the range (30 per cent) was given by the Federal Minister of Finance, Theo Waigel. According to the Federal Statistics Office, in the second half of 1990 the average gross monthly wage in the GDR was DM1,357, that is 37 per cent of the West German level, while productivity was only 28.5 per cent of that in West Germany. Some economists have argued that the initial conversion ratio is not important, since wage rises would in any case have to be sufficient to staunch labour migration to West Germany.

The terms for converting the Mark of the GDR into the Deutschemark were as follows. *Individual savings:* the exchange rate was 1:1 for individuals aged 60 years or more for savings up to M6,000, for those aged 15–59 years for savings up to M4,000, and for those below 15 years for savings up to M2,000. These terms applied to savings held at December 31, 1989, while for deposits legally accumulated during the first half of 1990 the conversion ratio was 3:1. Remaining savings and cash in circulation were exchangeable at 2:1. *Wages and pensions:* the exchange rate was 1:1. *Corporate debt:* the exchange rate was 2:1. This "debt" was owed internally and was the result of enterprises formerly having to transfer the bulk of their net revenue to the state budget and thereby being forced to resort to bank credit. There was thus no clear relationship between the debt owed by individual enterprises and their economic viability, and there was the danger that viable enterprises would be bankrupted unnecessarily.

Monetary and fiscal effects

Before economic union there was uncertainty about the possible effect on consumption and savings of the generous conversion of GDR savings and wages into Deutschemarks. There were fears of inflation and of a decline in the value of the currency. In 1987 East German savings deposits amounted to M141.9 billion, and cash in circulation was M15 billion. As it turned out, however, there was no inflationary East German spending spree, due to factors such as the threat of unemployment, an obvious incentive to save, and the attraction of interest earned in Deutschemarks. There was, however, an initial massive switch in expenditure away from East German products and towards West German and foreign goods. This began to moderate in 1991, but even so the Deutsche Bank reports that west German deliveries to eastern Germany amounted to DM207 billion in that year, while the reverse flow was only DM38 billion. This was one of the causes of the rapid rise in unemployment in east Germany. The effects of monetary union on individual East German prices were very diverse, with the once heavily taxed consumer durables like cars and television sets coming down in price and the once heavily subsidized commodities like basic foodstuffs going up.

Inflation has so far been largely contained in both halves of Germany. The German Institute for Economic Research *(Deutsches Institut für Wirtschaftsforschung* — DIW) has estimated that monetary union led to a 13.5–14.0 per cent increase in the money supply (M3) and an increase in productive potential of 11 per cent. The *Bundesbank* has, nevertheless, raised interest rates several times, in October 1989, November 1990, January 1991, August 1991 and December 1991. In all the Lombard rate (the rate at which banks receive unlimited, emergency loans from the *Bundesbank*) has risen from 7 per cent to 9.75 per cent and the discount rate (the rate at which banks receive limited loans from the *Bundesbank* collateralized with short term bills) from 5 per cent to 8 per cent. The most recent rises in interest rates were in response to a west German inflation rate of 4.4 per cent for the year to July 1991, the highest since the end of 1982 and a peak for 1991. The average rate for 1991 was 3.5 per cent, the highest since 1981. This was after the west German inflation rate in 1990 had come down to 2.7 per cent from 2.8 per cent the previous year. Annual inflation reached 4.8 per cent in March 1992, falling to 4.6 per cent in April.

One casualty of developments since monetary union was the West German government's initial optimism that the taxpayer would not be subjected to higher levies to pay for reunification. For example, as of 1 July, 1991, there applied a one-year 7.5 per cent personal and corporate income surcharge, the insurance tax went up from 7 to 10 per cent and the petrol tax was also raised. Because of the potential political damage, the government also blamed the increased costs of aid to the Soviet Union and Eastern Europe and the contributions to the Gulf War. The then *Bundesbank* chairman Karl Otto Pöhl had always been less optimistic than the government about the prospects of not having to raise taxes to finance unification and continually stressed the need to control spending. In its March 1992 report the *Bundesbank* urged the government either to restrain spending or face the possibility of having to raise taxes again. The strains began to show in the spring of 1992 with a serious outbreak of strikes and strike threats in west Germany. This was directly related to the question of the distribution of the burden of financing reunification.

The German Unity Fund had originally been established to finance unification without a rise in taxes. DM115 billion had been set aside over the period 1990–94, DM20 billion of this coming from West German budgetary savings and DM95 billion from borrowings on capital markets. In August 1991 it was announced that a further DM6 billion a year was to be added to the fund for 1992, 1993 and 1994. In February 1992 it was agreed that VAT would increase from 14 to 15 per cent in January 1993 and that the extra revenue, amounting to DM33.6 billion over the period 1992–94, would go into the fund. The overall German budget deficit was given as 3 per cent of GNP in 1990 and 3.3 per cent in 1991, but the figures exclude the borrowing of organizations such as the *Treuhandanstalt*.

As for the inflation rate in east Germany, the Deutsche Bank estimated it at minus 4 per cent for the whole of 1990, although plus 9.8 per cent in the second half of the year, and plus 14.2 per cent in 1991. The DIW figures were minus 2.7 per cent for 1990 and plus 12 per cent for 1991. The five institutes' figures were plus 0.2 per cent and plus 13.6 per cent respectively. Forecasts for 1992 are around the 12 per cent mark.

It is difficult to estimate the financial cost to West Germany of unification. The Federal Finance Minister, Theo Waigel, said on June 26, 1990 that "only a soothsayer or a swindler can estimate the costs of German unity". As regards the overall value of West German official transfers to East Germany, in June 1991 the former *Bundesbank* president Karl Otto Pöhl estimated that DM150 billion would be transferred from West Germany to East Germany in 1991. Transfers may amount to up to two-thirds of East Germany's GNP. The DIW has estimated that the net transfer of public funds (that is, taking into account the increased tax receipts in west Germany resulting from the rise in demand from east Germany) was DM105 billion in 1991, rising to an estimated DM125 billion in 1992, almost a half of east German GNP. In its March 1992 report the *Bundesbank* provided figures which showed that in 1991 net transfers from west to east Germany amounted to over DM139 billion (5.5 per cent of west Germany's national product) and were likely to rise to DM180 billion in 1992 (6.5 per cent). In 1991 DM60 billion went to private households, meaning that west Germany financed one-third of consumption in east Germany. For 1992 the forecast was a rise to DM85 billion and 40 per cent respectively. By contrast in 1991 east Germany contributed only 3.5 per cent of all tax revenue compared with its 20 per cent of the total German population. In the same year east Germany received DM3.5 billion from the European Community, but because of Germany's increased overall contribution the Community's net contribution was only DM1 billion.

The capital needs of east Germany are truly staggering. The Munich-based IFO economics institute has estimated that DM210 billion would be required up to the year 2000 to produce the same quality of environment as in west Germany. For example, sewage disposal needs more than DM100 billion, and the modernization of the road and rail network would take more than DM200 billion. According to Siebert's calculations (see Bibliography), the total capital required for restructuring in eastern Germany amounts to some 25 per cent of west Germany's GNP.

It is important to bear in mind that the West German economy was generally in an excellent shape to take on the burden of supporting her poorer twin. Indeed West Germany benefited both from the aforementioned switch in demand and from the inflow of young, relatively skilled and mobile workers. A 4.5 per cent growth rate was achieved in West Germany in 1990 and 1.5 percentage points were officially accredited to reunification. The current account has also been transformed by reunification. In 1989 the Federal Republic recorded a surplus of DM107.6 billion on the current account of the balance of payments. This fell to DM77.4 billion in 1990, although the figure included east Germany for the second half of the year. This turned into a deficit of DM34.2 billion in 1991. Despite the prospect of modest growth of around 1.5 per cent in 1992 in west Germany and the labour unrest, there is still official confidence in the underlying strength of the west German economy and in the east German economy's prospects in the longer run.

Effects on output and employment

There is general agreement that the short run for east Germany is and will be very difficult, due to such factors as the relatively obsolete capital stock and the large number of uneconomic enterprises. But there is some dispute about the more distant future. There are pessimists who fear a southern Italy "Mezzogiorno" situation of a permanent relatively depressed region. This might be a danger, since migrants with the best alternative options could leave along with their human capital, but most observers and participants see the long-run prospects as excellent. In April 1991 Chancellor Kohl said "I am convinced that in four to five years east Germany will be transformed into a flourishing landscape". The "long run", however, may not be on the near horizon. The DIW estimated in early 1992 that it will take 20 years for east German living standards to match those of west Germany, while Prognos of Basle has suggested that by the year 2010 east German per capita GNP will be around 87 per cent of west Germany's. The picture varies substantially between sectors, being relatively bright in activities such as construction, services, textile machinery and computers, and rather dim in areas such as lignite, consumer electronics and clothing. The motor car industry, however, shows that west German and foreign investment can bring about a fundamental transformation, helping the districts of the former GDR where Trabants and Wartburgs used to be produced, Zwickau and Eisenach respectively.

Table 1: *East Germany: estimated rates of growth of GNP and GDP[1] (%)*

	1990	1991	1992
German Institute for Economic Research (DIW)			
GNP	−13.3	−20.0	15.0
GDP	−14.0	−23.5	10.5
Deutsche Bank			
GNP	−14.0	−31.0	10.0
GDP	—	−35.0	6.5
Five institutes (Berlin, Essen, Hamburg, Kiel and Munich)			
GNP (autumn 1990 report)	−15.0	−10.0	—
GNP (autumn 1991 report)	—	−20.0	10.0-15.0
GNP (spring 1992 report)	−14.4	−30.3	10.5
Federal government report, January 29, 1992			
GNP	—	−16.0	10.0

[1] GNP includes income earned by east Germans working in west Germany, whereas GDP does not.
Sources. *DIW Economic Bulletin,* March *1992, vol. 29, no.1.* Deutsche Bank, *Unification Issue,* October 28, 1991, no. 61; November 19, 1991, no. 63. Deutsche Bank, *Focus Germany*, January 20, 1992, no. 70; April 2, 1992, no. 77. *Financial Times,* October 22, 1991; December 24, 1991, April 14, 1992.

Estimates of the effects of reunification on east German national income are difficult, because of the problem of converting GDR statistics to a west German basis and because of the traumatic effects on the eastern economy. Table 1 shows some of the estimates made by different forecasters, but the same organization understandably often revises its own figures over time. For example, the Deutsche Bank and the five institutes have revised the 1991 output figure from around minus 20 per cent to around minus 30 per cent. The early consensus that the turning point would be mid-1991 changed for a while to autumn 1991 or spring 1992 or even later. A complicating factor was predicting the end of what proved to be a short Gulf War. The DIW has estimated that the fall in total output in the east did not stop until the second quarter of 1991. There seemed to be a bottoming out sometime during the summer of that year. Some sectors, especially construction and services, actually showed signs of expanding and these will lead the overall recovery of the economy. Estimates vary, as Table 1 indicates, but east German GNP may be judged to have fallen by around 14 per cent in 1990 and up to 31 per cent in 1991. A *rise* of perhaps 10 per cent may be expected in 1992.

The industrial sector was particularly badly affected, output falling by more than 50 per cent in the second half of 1990 and by around 30 per cent for the whole of the year. The *Bundesbank* report of December 1991 noted that even industrial production was beginning to recover slowly: "The eastern German economy has probably passed its low point even if the recovery is not yet broad-based or self-sustaining." The Deutsche Bank put the fall in industrial output in 1991 at 55 per cent, with a predicted 20 per cent increase in 1992. The percentage falls in the output of individual sectors in 1991 were as follows (with estimates for positive growth in 1992 in brackets): precision engineering and optics −81 (+1); office equipment, data processing −74 (+2); electrical engineering −68 (+21); non-ferrous minerals −65 (+61); mechanical engineering −63 (+11); foundries −61 (+9); wood processing −59 (+13); chemicals −51 (+8); food, beverages and tobacco −49 (+30); textiles −48 (+6); iron and steel −38 (+9); motor vehicle construction −30 (+12); steel construction −30 (+31); oil processing −14 (+6); and printing −12 (+32).

The Deutsche Bank has also provided some interesting general statistics for 1991, which indicate the scale of the problem. East Germany's GNP amounted to only 7.4 per cent of the West German level (8.3 per cent in the second half of 1990) and 6.9 per cent of all-German GNP. Meanwhile per capita GNP was 29.3 per cent of the West German level. The productivity of east German workers was only a shade less than 30 per cent of that of their west German counterparts. There were also signs of significant structural shifts within the suffering economy. Manufacturing industry as a percentage of east German gross value added fell from 65 per cent in 1988, to 44 per cent in the second half of 1990 and to only 34 per cent in 1991, while the respective figures for services show increases from 7 per cent, to 17 per cent and to 24 per cent.

Table 2: *Unemployment and short-time working in east Germany, 1990–92*

	Unemployed		Short-time		Total	
	000s	%	000s	%	000s	%
Jan. 1990	7	0.1	—	—	7	0.1
April	65	0.7	—	—	65	0.7
July	272	3.1	656	7.4	928	10.5
Oct.	537	6.1	1,704	19.1	2,241	25.2
Jan. 1991	757	8.6	1,841	21.0	2,598	29.6
April	837	9.5	2,019	22.7	2,856	32.2
July	1,069	12.1	1,611	18.1	2,680	30.2
Oct.	1,049	11.9	1,200	13.5	2,249	25.4
Jan. 1992	1,343	16.5	520	5.8	1,863	22.3
Feb.	1,290	15.9	—	—	—	—
March	1,200	15.5	—	—	—	—

Source: *Monatsberichte der Deutschen Bundesbank*, 1990–92.

Unemployment has increased rapidly, as is shown in Table 2 (see also Alsop and Timmins essays in this volume). There was full employment in the Honecker era, but unemployment rose from 142,096 (1.6 per cent) in June 1990 to a short-term peak of 1,068,600 (12.1 per cent) in July 1991. In addition there were those on short time *(Kurzarbeit)*; 229,975 in June 1990 and 1,611,000 in July 1991. By December 1991 unemployment was 1,037,709 (11.8 per cent) and a million were on short time. January 1992 saw a big increase in unemployment to 16.5 per cent due to the end of short-time working for many and a reduction in the figure for those considered capable of gaining employment (from 8.8 million to 7.9 million). For some "short time" really meant that no time was actually worked, but on average these workers were employed for half their normal time at first. This proportion then gradually fell to 40 per cent. Estimates of peak unemployment have varied a great deal, but a figure of 1.5 million by the summer of 1992 became representative. However, more recent estimates suggest a lower figure.

Figures from the Deutsche Bank also show changes in the labour force which affect overall unemployment levels. At the end of 1991 around 450,000 east Germans commuted to work in west Germany, nearly 400,000 were involved in job creation schemes, some 450,000 were retired early (at 55 on two-thirds final pay), about 450,000 were participating in vocational training programmes and around 175,000 constituted "hidden unemployment", mainly married women. Employment fell from 9,861,000 in 1989, to 8,916,000 in 1990 and to 7,250,000 in 1991. Regional unemployment is an acute problem, given the frequent local dependence in the former GDR on large-scale plants.

West German regulations allow the unemployed or people temporarily laid off to be paid about two-thirds of their previous wage, specifically 68 per cent for one year if married and 63 per cent if single. The percentages then fall to 58 per cent and 52 per cent respectively. The short-time work arrangement operating in east Germany before the end of 1991 involved the payment of 68 per cent of the previous wage by the state plus an additional 22 per cent by the enterprise, thus bringing the total up to 90 per cent.

While unemployment has soared, the creation of new jobs and businesses has, nevertheless, been rapid. In April 1991 *The Economist* estimated one million jobs and 300,000 businesses since the start of 1990. The DIW, however, has pointed out that while 360,098 enterprises were registered and 46,390 deregistered between the start of January 1990 and the end of March 1991, these figures included, for example, businesses reconstituted or split off from larger ones. Net new-business creation probably amounted to at most 100,000 units. By the end of August 1991 only 175,000 of the 435,000 net registrations could be considered to be new businesses.

Contributory factors to the crisis

There are several important factors which have contributed to the economic collapse in east Germany. Firstly the GDR provided a legacy of, by Western standards, a generally inefficient economy with a typically obsolete capital stock. The instant exposure to competition from advanced Western economies was bound to be traumatic. To make matters worse, monetary union involved one of the world's strongest currencies. Thus unlike Poland, say, east Germany has been unable to devalue its currency in order to make itself competitive.

Secondly, trade with the former CMEA collapsed despite temporary subsidization and tariff concessions. According to the Deutsche Bank, in 1991 east German exports to CMEA countries fell by 60 per cent, with exports to the Soviet Union down by 45 per cent, to Bulgaria by 91 per cent, to Hungary by 86 per cent, to Romania by 85 per cent, to Czechoslovakia by 81 per cent, and to Poland by 66 per cent. Total east German exports fell by 7 per cent in 1990 and by 53 per cent in 1991. But due to factors such as generous export guarantees, the Soviet Union's share of east German exports (excluding intra-German trade) actually increased: 40.3 per cent in 1989, 46.7 per cent in 1990 and 54.7 per cent in 1991, when the share of all the former CMEA countries was over two-thirds. The link with the former Soviet Union was especially important in terms of jobs. The East Berlin Institute for Applied Economic Research reported that, in 1988, 260,000 workers were directly employed in industrial exports to the Soviet Union and 220,000 indirectly. The total of 480,000 accounted for 15 per cent of all employment in GDR industry. The Federal government's estimate is that in 1989 around 850,000 jobs in the commercial sector were directly dependent on intra-CMEA trade as a whole and a further 500–600,000 jobs in ancillary industries and other producing sectors were at least partly dependent.

Thirdly, East Germany's "cheap labour" advantage has been rapidly eroded by nominal wage rises far in excess of productivity increases. The Halle Institute for Economic Research has estimated that in 1991 unit wage costs in east German industry were about 70 per cent higher than in west Germany. By the end of 1990 east German wages were around half the west German level and Karl Otto Pöhl, writing in early July of that year, put the figure at 60 per cent. It should be noted, however, that east Germans work longer hours, have fewer fringe benefits and take shorter holidays. West German and east German trade unions have merged and have often faced demoralized, unorganized and demotivated enterprise management lacking a secure future. The mighty IG Metall's aim, for example, is parity in pay in East and west Germany by 1994 and in working hours by 1998 (see also Timmins essay in this volume).

The closing east German-west German wage gap may appear to at least help staunch the flow of labour westwards, but this is not necessarily so. The Berkeley survey data used by Akerlof and his colleagues (see Bibliography) show that few workers wish to migrate for higher west German wages, most preferring to work in east Germany or wait for new jobs there if unemployed. The real cause of most migration seems to be the lack of employment in east Germany and not the east–west wage differential. According to the Akerlof study, "higher wages will cause more migration by increasing unemployment than they will by closing the wage gap". One controversial remedy suggested is temporary wage subsidy of east German labour, the idea being that a lower real wage would encourage employers to offer more work and thus induce more people to stay in the East. Akerlof's team favours what they call a "self-eliminating flexible employment bonus programme", the value of the bonus falling to zero as wages in east Germany approach those in west Germany. The programme would bring benefits in the form of increased investment, lower unemployment, speedier privatization and reduced migration. The budgetary cost, they argue, would be low, perhaps even negative because of the savings in unemployment benefits and the tax revenue raised. The critics (they include the *Bundesbank* and the Deutsche Bank) of this scheme and others like it argue that there is the danger of such subsidies becoming permanent, of preserving the existing economic structures by hindering the necessary adjustments, and of wage rises following on from the subsidies.

Despite initially falling output and rising unemployment, private households in east Germany are better off in real terms than before reunification. This is due to factors such as rising wages and massive transfers from west Germany. The DIW has calculated that real income per head rose by 11.5 per cent in 1990 and probably remained roughly constant in 1991. In 1992 a perceptible increase can be expected. Real disposable income per capita is likely to be about a quarter above the pre-unification level. It is also worth bearing in mind that these figures underestimate the actual increase in living standards, because of factors such as improvements in the quality and availability of goods.

The privatization of the east German economy

The Treuhandanstalt

The *Treuhandanstalt,* the trust agency or holding company set up in March 1990, has the task of dismantling and privatizing the state-run economy of the GDR. The *Volkskammer* passed a law reconstituting the *Treuhandanstalt* on June 17, 1990, entrusting it not only with the combines and enterprises, but also property belonging to organizations such as the *Stasi* and army. The old political parties of the GDR have also under protest had to surrender much of their property to the *Treuhandanstalt*. On July 13, 1990 the new management board was convened for the first time and in October the *Treuhandanstalt* was given its full legislative mandate to privatize the east German economy. All told, 40 per cent of east Germany's surface area and 50 per cent of its workforce became the *Treuhandanstalt's* responsibility, with a mandate to build a private sector and secure the livelihoods of four million people. The *Treuhandanstalt* deals not only with privatization, but also restructuring, credit guarantees to provide temporary protection for enterprises, and liquidation. Its first task was to keep the 8,000 companies in business, and it assumed responsibility for the debt owed to the east German banks.

The present president of the executive board of the *Treuhandanstalt* is Birgit Breuel, who became a member of that board in October 1990 and president on April 13, 1991. The original holder of her post was Reiner Gohlke, the former chairman of the *Bundesbahn*. He resigned in August 1990 and was replaced by Detlev Rohwedder, head of the West German company Hoesch and originally chairman of the supervisory board of the *Treuhandanstalt*. In this latter capacity Rohwedder was replaced by Jens Odewald, chairman of the West German Kaufhof department store chain. It was Rohwedder's assassination by the Red Army Faction on April 1, 1991, which brought Breuel the most important post.

The *Treuhandanstalt* was initially endowed with the ownership rights of some 8,000 "large" enterprises (those with more than 250 employees) employing more than four million people in total, the high number of enterprises being the result of the splitting up of the combines. This dismemberment of combines has actually continued, which explains why at times there have been more enterprises on the books of the *Treuhandanstalt* than there were at the start, despite sell-offs. Originally enterprises were obliged to draw up Deutschemark balance sheets by 31 October 1990 in readiness for privatization, but this date proved to be unrealistic and several extensions were granted.

The smaller industrial enterprises nationalized in 1972 quickly began to be returned to former owners. Service establishments such as shops and restaurants were also subjected to a rapid process of privatization. A subsidiary of the *Treuhandanstalt* was set up to deal with this so-called "small privatization". By April 30, 1991 the larger retail stores and smaller hotels had all been privatized, while figures of 76 per cent and 62 per cent applied to small stores and pharmacies and restaurants respectively. In March 1992 the *Treuhandanstalt* reported that it had privatized nearly 15,000 retail outlets.

There are various exceptions to the general remit of the *Treuhandanstalt*, causing a certain amount of confusion and dispute. Enterprises controlled by municipalities and the former *Bezirke* (districts) plus the land belonging to them have become the trustee ownership of the Federal government and thus not the *Treuhandanstalt*. Municipalities are then able to apply for these enterprises. Public buildings are the property of the relevant political authorities, while publicly-owned housing has been awarded to the municipalities. The railways and the postal service are deemed special property.

Actual privatization of the large enterprises speeded up after a slow start. In mid-January 1991 it was reported that more than 450 enterprises had been privatized, raising DM2.5 billion in sales revenue, and in mid-April 1,261 (403 in the last quarter of 1990 and 858 in the first quarter of 1991). By the end of August 1991 nearly 3,400 had been sold off, raising DM12.5 billion, but only 156 had been sold to foreigners. By the end of 1991 France accounted for 44 enterprises, Switzerland 42 and the United Kingdom 26. The then Foreign Minister Hans-Dietrich Genscher reported in May 1991 that only 5 per cent of all investment had come from outside Germany as a whole.

The *Treuhandanstalt* report of March 1992 revealed that in the previous 21 months the *Treuhandanstalt* had privatized around 5,500 manufacturing and service companies, leaving 5,800 still in its administration, and nearly 15,000 retail outlets, securing over DM100 billion in investment in east Germany and over one million jobs. The proportion of the workforce employed by *Treuhandanstalt* companies had fallen from 50 per cent to 22 per cent. Some 250 non-German companies (these exclude foreign-owned companies in west Germany) had invested more than DM10.5 billion, most of this — DM8.5 billion — in 1991.

Investors in east Germany face many obstacles, such as a poor infrastructure, particularly of transport and communications, severe environment damage, and European Community competition rules. Concern has been shown by the European Community about the problem of monopoly in sectors such as banking, electricity, gas and airlines. For example, the east German airline Interflug attracted the attention of Lufthansa among others at first, but was closed down by the end of April 1991 partly because of delays caused by European Community intervention. The Community has also queried west German subsidies to west German firms investing in east German sectors such as motor vehicles. Foreign investors in east Germany, of course, have no problems in repatriating profits, the Deutschemark being a sound, fully convertible currency. But foreign and west German investors in east Germany have had to be spurred on by substantial concessions. In May 1991 Foreign Minister Hans-Dietrich Genscher revealed that an investor putting DM100 million into east Germany would receive up to DM57.3 million in such forms as grants, subsidies, tax write-offs and special depreciation rates. (See also Spence essay in this volume)

Claims to nationalized property

The initially slow start to privatization was caused by a number of factors, but a major one was the early stress on returning property to former owners. The uncertainty and long delays in establishing ownership claims proved to be a major deterrent to investment in east Germany. The agreement of June 15, 1990 between the West German and East German governments provided a basis for the settlement of property claims. However, the occupation period of 1945–49 is unaffected because of agreements made with the Soviet Union, and on April 23, 1991, the German constitutional court confirmed that land and property seized between 1945 and 1949 could not be reclaimed by the former owners. Those who left after 1949 or their heirs had the right in principle to reclaim the assets left behind. Property was to be returned "as far as this is possible, taking into account the social and economic realities that have developed over the last 40 years". This means, for example, that firms which became part of larger units or land used in road and housing schemes are not available for physical restitution. The same applies to farms that became part of larger production units, although working farmers have the right to reclaim their land from co-operative or state farms.

The legislation has been substantially amended a number of times in order to encourage investors. For example, in March 1991 the *Bundestag* approved legislation giving priority to any investor judged to have the best programme for investment and for sustaining and creating jobs. Former owners would be compensated financially if they were not successful in their claim for property restitution. The size of the investment pledged and the number of jobs secured has in many cases taken precedence over the *Treuhandanstalt* getting the highest price, and in any case a former owner has at least to match any other offer. Investors are generally compelled to retain their new company's assets for five to seven years as a rule. The new policy covers the Nazi property seizures of 1933–45 as well as the post-1949 socialist ones.

Forms of privatization and restructuring

The *Treuhandanstalt* has been criticized for not varying the privatization process enough to include, for example, a greater use of auctions and public share offerings. A decision was made to encourage more management buy-outs and foreign sales, the latter in earnest after April–May 1991. During a visit to London in November 1991, Birgit Breuel talked about greater contracting out to independent investment banks, flotation on stock markets and large-scale public tender for groups of small enterprises. On January 7, 1992, the Sachsenmilch dairy company of Dresden became the first east German company to be listed on the German stock exchanges. The *Treuhandanstalt's* March 1992 report mentioned 900 management buy-outs, though most of these were small. Over half of them had fewer than 20 employees.

In March 1991 the *Treuhandanstalt* agreed to undertake a "socially acceptable regional policy" and to form special cabinets with the five new east German *Land* governments in order to enhance the integration of structural and regional policies. Thus the effects on regional unemployment are now given increased emphasis, although this policy is controversial. The closing down of enterprises which dominate entire regions, such as those in mining, steel, chemicals and shipbuilding, would be devastating in terms of a particular area, removing the core of employment which might act as a foundation for growth.

Restructuring is also now given greater priority, this being controversial too because some argue that the private sector should perform this task. In July 1991, in an equally disputed move, the government, employers and trade unions agreed to set up job-creation enterprises, and the critics fear for a permanently subsidized east Germany. The *Treuhandanstalt's* role is to provide start-up help, premises, machines and managerial personnel for these enterprises. Activities include urban renewal projects, public works, environmental clean-ups and the retraining of workers. The number of enterprises actually declared bankrupt by the *Treuhandanstalt* was 983 by the end of 1991, although most were small. Formal policy is for a case-by-case approach to the old debts of enterprises, but the *Treuhandanstalt* has in reality assumed the bulk of the debts of enterprises sold off and of the substantial ecological liabilities.

East German agriculture

The *Treuhandanstalt* administers two-thirds of the forested area of the former GDR and almost 30 per cent of the agricultural land. Agricultural producer co-operatives (LPG) were to perform a division of net assets and reconstitute themselves in corporate form by the end of 1991. The land itself belongs either to private individuals, only some of whom are actually co-operative farmers, or is currently being administered by the *Treuhandanstalt* in the case of land expropriated in the period 1945–49. According to DIW figures, the land belongs to co-operative members (22 per cent), non-members (47 per cent) and to the *Treuhandanstalt*

(24 per cent). According to the Deutsche Bank, by the autumn of 1991 one-third of co-operatives were still structured as before, another third had drawn up private enterprise solutions, 17 per cent were working on such a strategy, and 15 per cent had declared bankruptcy.

The DIW and the Deutsche Bank have both been critical of the policy of attempting to establish the family-run farm as the dominant model. While not recommending the continuance of the present production co-operatives, they argue that there are competitive advantages in larger units, though not as large as the current ones. In the event, the return to privatized, individual agriculture has been slowed by property claims, lack of business skills, a shortage of funds, and the uncertainty of life outside the co-operatives. According to the Deutsche Bank, as of autumn 1991 perhaps only as few as 10 per cent at most of co-operative farmers were attracted to the idea of reclaiming property and starting private businesses, with many favouring voluntary co-operatives or limited liability companies.

East German agricultural output was adversely affected by the substantial initial switch by consumers towards west German and foreign products in 1990, but 1991 saw a gradual and partial reversal of this trend. The Deutsche Bank views the medium and long term as quite favourable. The European Community's Common Agricultural Policy provides a general protectionist shield for east Germany, but since east Germany has to abide by existing Community quotas set for individual products such as milk and sugar, some considerable output reductions are necessary, 30 per cent in the case of milk compared to 1989, for example.

Conclusion

Whilst personally welcoming German unification, it is not churlish to ask whether the speed at which it was attained and much of the associated short-run pain was strictly necessary. Rapid economic and monetary union, it was argued by those who promoted it, was essential to staunch the flow of east Germany migrants *(Übersiedler)* westwards, and political unification had to follow quickly in case the political situation deteriorated in the Soviet Union. Chancellor Kohl eagerly cited as evidence the announcement of the Soviet coup of August 19, 1991, although he fell silent once it was clear that the coup had failed.

It can, however, be argued that there was nothing inevitable about the extremely rapid pace of reunification. The former president of the *Bundesbank* Karl Otto Pöhl had warned against rapid monetary union, stressing the need for prior structural change, the phasing in of a competitive market economy and the introduction of conventional monetary policy. Pöhl was not even consulted when the then Federal Economics Minister Helmut Haussmann announced on February 6, 1990, that German economic and monetary union was to take place. Political pressure forced an acceptance of the situation, but Pöhl restoked the controversy on March 19, 1991, when he said "we introduced the Deutschemark with practically no preparation or possibility of adjustment, and, I would add, at the wrong exchange rate ... So the result is a disaster, as you can see. I am not surprised, I predicted this". East Germany, he said, had been rendered "completely uncompetitive". But Pöhl did accept that monetary union was inevitable: "I am not criticising the decision. But the outcome was predictable." Pöhl himself decided to retire early, and he was succeeded as president by Helmut Schlesinger on August 1, 1991.

It could also be argued that economic and monetary union could have been slowed by the earlier ending of the special financial inducements granted to migrants and by the giving of substantial aid. Indeed Chancellor Kohl had said on February 4, 1990, that substantial economic aid was necessary before the March election in the GDR, but this never materialized. The fact that an election was also imminent in the Federal Republic also subjected events to short-run political expediency. East Germany's economic problems became a dominant consideration, but the extent of the collapse after economic and monetary union gives fuel to the argument that a more gradual process would have been desirable. The West German government underestimated the cost of reunification, and the argument over the distribution of this burden has been a bitter one.

There is also considerable debate about the extent to which the state should intervene in east Germany's economy. As we have already seen, individual measures such as wage subsidy and the involvement of the *Treuhandanstalt* in restructuring enterprises prior to privatization are controversial. The more laissez-faire economists believe that as much rein as possible should be given to market forces. But there are many critics of the old *Ordnungspolitik,* which merely provides a framework for the operation of market forces in the form of a sound currency, a basic infrastructure and competitive market conditions. At the other extreme are the advocates of massive state involvement in such forms as large-scale job retraining and creation. While the theoretical debates continue, the state has in practice generally taken a more interventionist role as the recession in the east German economy has deepened and symptoms of social unrest have multiplied. The increasing number of racist attacks and the election successes of the extreme right in western Germany (profiting not just from the strains of unification but also from concern over the large number of asylum seekers in Germany) do not leave the responsible politicians unmoved.

TRADE UNIONS AND GERMAN REUNIFICATION: THE SOCIAL DIMENSION

Graham Timmins

The social tensions of German reunification

In her opening speech to the new *Bundestag* on December 20, 1990, its president, Rita Süssmuth, called for tolerance and fairness in attempts to remove the feeling on the part of east Germans of being "foreigners in their own country" and to exercise solidarity between the two parts of Germany. Willy Brandt, in a statement designed to invoke memories of the euphoric reaction to the opening of the Berlin Wall on November 9, 1989, argued that "sometimes the walls in people's heads stand for longer than those made of concrete". German unification has resulted in immense social disparity between the eastern and western regions of Germany. The emergence of the mutually derogatory terms *"Ossis"* (east Germans) and *"Wessis"* (west Germans) in the popular vocabulary represent the social tensions that have grown out of the process of economic and political unification. Article 106 of the German Basic Law commits both federal and state institutions to the task of achieving unity in living conditions throughout Germany. However, according to one opinion survey, the majority of east Germans are unconvinced that they will attain comparable living standards to those in western Germany in the near future. Moreover, this opinion has strengthened since unification.

Table 1: *Expectations of living standards in Germany*
(West and east Germans were asked to respond to the statement "Citizens of the former German Democratic Republic will remain second class citizens in the united Germany for some time to come".)

	West Germans		East Germans	
	autumn 1990	spring 1991	autumn 1990	spring 1991
Agree	33	39	75	84
Don't Agree	47	45	15	9
Don't Know	19	15	8	7

Sources: *Spiegel Spezial* No. 1 (1991) and *Spiegel* No. 30 (1991).

The popular optimism that accompanied the political events in the German Democratic Republic in 1989 quickly became a feeling of desperation for many during 1990 as they were confronted with the sobering impact of marketization. Whilst not always comparable with West Germany in terms of the quality of provision, relatively wide and open access to social welfare and educational facilities together with economic subsidy of housing, transport and food guaranteed a minimum standard of living for all. Disaffected by the "consumer rush" that accompanied the opening of the Berlin Wall and the introduction of the Deutschemark into the GDR economy, a large number of east Germans have begun to question the advantages that unification is assumed to have brought them (see Table 1). The blind rejection of everything that is east German has led many to conclude that rather than October 3, 1990 symbolizing unification, the GDR was subject to "annexation" *(Anschluss),* and that the socialist hegemony to which they had been exposed since 1949 had been replaced by a capitalist variant. In addressing this accusation, it is often argued that the current rise in neo-fascism in eastern Germany and the lack of understanding of democratic practices can be put down to political socialization under the old communist leadership. This argument, although true in part, reduces the significance of socio-economic disparity between the eastern and western German states and distorts attempts to assess accurately the social problems to which unification has given rise. The initial priority following the collapse of the communist leadership was the implementation of democratic elections in the GDR and it was therefore inevitable that attention was focused on the development of the party system. Once this objective had been achieved, much of the attention switched to the importance of industrial relations and the role of organized labour in the process of unification. Within this context three aspects will be examined here: the demise of the east German trade union movement and the merging of east and west German labour under the authority of the (West) German Trade Union Federation *(Deutscher Gewerkschaftsbund* — DGB); the collapse of the east German labour market and the issue of wage parity; and the political problems of labour representation in the east German states. The significance of organized labour in the reconstruction of the West German economy in the post-war period and its contribution to the "economic miracle" is generally acknowledged. However, its role in German unification is clouded with controversy. The objective of this essay is therefore to provide an overview of trade union policy regarding unification and to assess the motives behind the DGB's platform, before concluding with some tentative suggestions as to what the future may hold for German trade unionism.

The demise of the FDGB and trade union unification

From 1945 to 1989 the Free German Trade Union Federation *(Freier Deutscher Gewerkschaftsbund* — FDGB) had acted as a "transmission belt" for the GDR leadership, communicating official policy to the masses and administering state social insurance provisions. It was this collusion with the ruling Socialist Unity Party *(Sozialistische Einheitspartei Deutschlands* — SED) that left the FDGB devoid of legitimacy and authority as the east German system imploded in the autumn of 1989. As political demonstrations spread throughout the GDR in 1989, the FDGB was noticeable for its absence, the leadership in a state of paralysis as the convulsions gripping the country intensified. Attempts to assert independence from within were stamped upon by the long-standing chairman of the FDGB and member of the *Politbüro,* Harry Tisch, who maintained on October 16, 1989 that "whoever wants to use the unions in order to oppose the state in the GDR is in the wrong country". Tisch was then forced to resign on November 2, 1989. His successor, Annelis Kimmel, a long-standing SED activist whose period in office was to last just five weeks, showed herself equally incompetent in restoring any credibility to the FDGB leadership, which was fast becoming left behind by grassroots initiatives demanding democratic reform and the establishment of independent unions. The financial crisis which was gradually enveloping the FDGB as members either left or withheld their union contributions intensified with every exposure of administrative abuse of power or corruption, charges of which went right to the top. It was discovered that Tisch had sanctioned a payment of 100 million marks to the Free German Youth (*Freie Deutsche Jugend* — FDJ) for a festival in 1988. Investigations revealed that only half of the amount had been used by the FDJ, leaving the remaining 50 million unaccounted for. On December 2, 1989 Tisch was arrested and a day later expelled from the SED in a belated attempt to cleanse the party apparatus. Tainted by these scandals, the FDGB leadership was forced to resign collectively on December 9, to be replaced by a "preparatory committee" headed by Werner Peplowski, chairman of the Printers' and Paper Workers' Union *(IG Druck und Papier)*.

The new FDGB leadership was given the brief of preparing for an extraordinary congress which had been set for January 31, 1990. In a declaration calling for a thorough reform of the FDGB into a federation of free, independent unions, the leadership set out its three central objectives: the establishment of strong independent unions, the co-ordination of individual unions by the FDGB, and the protection of union rights under a trade union law. The problem was that these proposals had been taken without significant consultation with the mass membership and assumed that the FDGB had a chance of being rescued. It was apparent that the FDGB leadership had failed to appreciate the changing environment, most significantly that the pace of events was being determined from below rather than from above and that the state was therefore not in a position to guarantee protection for the FDGB structure.

At the extraordinary congress Helga Mausch, a member of the National Democratic Party *(Nationaldemokratische Partei Deutschlands* — NDPD), was elected chair of the FDGB, mainly due to the fact that she was not an SED member. In an attempt to purge its political legacy, the congress appointed a committee to investigate past incidents of corruption, developed a new set of rules to prevent future abuses of power, demanded a union law to protect union rights (which would be asserted via a general strike if necessary) and launched an action programme calling for social security for the employed and unemployed. The FDGB leadership assumed that it had been able to stem its decline at the congress and moved to consolidate its position by introducing a bill into the *Volkskammer* on February 20, 1990 which was passed on March 6, 1990, shortly before the national elections. The new union law was designed to provide legal protection for the unions during the process of German unification and an element of co-determination in shaping the east German economy. Mausch, in outlining her vision of the future role of the FDGB, argued that "whether there will be a market economy here which is worthy of the attribute 'social' depends heavily upon how the trade unions are able to co-determine and protect the interests of labour".

The landslide victory of the Alliance for Germany, campaigning on a platform of rapid unification and monetary union, in the elections on March 18, 1990, swept away the political support base for the FDGB within the *Volkskammer*. When details of the proposed monetary union at a rate of 2:1 became public, the FDGB responded by calling for mass protest demonstrations. On April 5, 1990, over a million union members turned out on the Alexanderplatz in East Berlin to protest against the proposed conditions for monetary union. The turnout, in suggesting revived support for the FDGB, distorted the actual political trend.

The FDGB platform was shared by a number of "losing" political parties, most significantly the Party of Democratic Socialism (*Partei des Demokratischen Sozialismus* — PDS), the successor to the SED, and the FDGB thereby offered itself as a platform for opposition to the democratically elected *Volkskammer*. The implicit danger of such a move was marginalization, and as the momentum leading to unification increased this danger was realized as the initiative swung to the West German DGB.

The DGB's initial reaction to events in the GDR was one of caution with most contact being conducted via the FDGB. However, following the congress in February 1990, attempts to reform the FDGB structure were welcomed by the DGB, which released a "declaration on German unity" on March 7, 1990, supporting the construction of free and independent unions in the GDR. Practical support for reform was provided by individual unions in the form of technology and trade union expertise. However, in supporting democratic reform of the FDGB, there was concern within the DGB that its reputation could be tarnished should its involvement with the FDGB appear too close. The assumption made by Helga Mausch, that the FDGB would constitute an equal partner with the DGB, set alarm bells ringing throughout union circles in the Federal Republic. Mausch had failed to appreciate that the construction of independent unions in the east would be impossible without assistance from western sister organizations. Moreover, Mausch exposed her lack of understanding as to how the DGB policy-making process operated. At the 14th DGB national congress in May 1990 the two biggest West German unions, the metalworkers *(IG Metall)* and the Public Services and Transport Workers' Union (ÖTV), accounted for half of the 525 delegates present. Any policy adopted by the DGB would have to take into account the positions of these two powerful unions. The assumption that the DGB could operate as a go-between for the FDGB with the individual unions was both naïve and politically suicidal.

The suspicion that the FDGB was attempting to legitimize its authority via a partnership with the DGB led to a formal break in relations on April 27, 1990 when DGB chairman, Ernst Breit, announced that all co-operation with the FDGB was to be ended. Aware of the threat this presented, the FDGB leadership responded with a last-ditch attempt to recapture the political initiative by calling for 80 per cent pay increases, a reduction in the working week to 38 hours and a guarantee that the liquidity of businesses, institutions and organizations would be maintained following currency union on July 1, 1990. Mass industrial action was threatened should their demands not be met. That Minister President de Maizière felt confident enough to reject the demands out of hand showed the real measure of power and influence that the FDGB now had among east German labour.

The fatal blow to the FDGB leadership came from below when, on May 9, 1990, the chairmen of the 20 individual unions making up the FDGB announced their decision to oust the leadership and replace it with a Federation of Trade Union Chairmen, represented by an advisory committee *(Sprecherrat)* headed by Peter Rothe, chairman of the Rail Workers' Union. In a declaration published in the trade union newspaper *Tribüne* on May 10, 1990, the FDGB was condemned as politically discredited and it was announced that Helga Mausch had been instructed to prepare an extraordinary congress at which the FDGB would be officially dissolved as a precursor to trade union unification.

Peter Rothe opened negotiations on the issue of union mergers with the DGB immediately and on May 22, 1990 at the 14th DGB national congress in Hamburg a motion calling for trade union unification within the framework of the DGB was passed and the DGB Federal Executive Committee instructed to oversee the process of unification. The final chapter for the FDGB came on September 14, 1990 when the delegates to the extraordinary congress voted almost unanimously (there being two abstentions) to dissolve the FDGB as of September 30, 1990, transferring full authority for co-ordination of union activities in the eastern states to the DGB and with the individual unions being advised to dissolve themselves and merge with their partner organizations in the west.

Table 2: *Trade union membership 1990–91*

	Membership 1990	1991	Growth %	East Germans number[1]	%
Construction Workers (IGBSE)	462,751	838,000	81	346,000	41
Mineworkers (IGBE)	322,820	576,000	78	250,000	43
Chemical, Paper & Ceramic Workers (IGCPK)	675,949	900,000	33	205,000	23
Rail Workers (GdED)	312,353	533,300	71	223,000	42
Education & Science (GEW)	189,155	370,000	96	180,000	49
Horticulture, Agriculture & Forestry Workers (GGLF)	44,054	140,000	218	95,000	68
Commerce, Banking & Insurance Workers (HBV)	404,695	713,000	76	313,000	44
Wood & Plastic Workers (GHK)	152,731	241,500	58	88,500	37
Leather Workers (GL)	42,615	70,000	64	27,500	39
Printing & Paper Workers, Artists & Musicians (IG Median)	184,720	231,000	25	46,000	20
Metalworkers (IGM)	2,726,705	3,689,000	35	989,000	27
Food-Processing Workers (NGG)	275,203	402,200	46	127,000	32
Public Service & Transport Workers (ÖTV)	1,252,599	2,076,000	66	876,000	42
Police (GdP)	162,780	204,000	25	39,000	19
Postal Workers (DPG)	478,913	604,000	26	125,000	26
Textile & Clothing Workers (GTB)	249,880	440,400	76	190,400	43
German Trade Union Federation (DGB)	7,937,923	12,028,400	51	4,150,400	35
German Salaried Employees' Union (DAG)	503,528	600,000	19	100,000	17
Christian Trade Union Federation (CGB)	304,741	309,000	1	7,000	2
German Civil Service Federation (DBB)	800,000	1,000,000	25	200,000	20
Total Trade Union membership	9,546,192	13,937,400	46	4,457,400	32

[1] These figures are approximations and are open to wide fluctuations given the present volatility of the east German employment market.

Sources: M.Kittner (ed.), *Gewerkschaftsjahrbuch 1991;* E.Hubner and H.Rohlfs (eds.), *Jahrbuch der Bundesrepublik Deutschland 1991/92;* M.Fichter, "From Transmission Belt to Social Partnership? The Case of Organised Labour in Eastern Germany" in *German Politics and Society* 23 (1991); and data obtained from *dpa Sozialpolitische Nachrichten* and individual unions.

The legal and organizational implications of the mergers, which centred on the problems as to whether former FDGB functionaries should be taken over and if the memberships would be accepted on a mass basis or be required to make individual applications, were left to the responsibility of the individual unions and resulted in a variety of unification strategies. The fact that not all east and west German unions matched up in terms of their jurisdiction over representation led in some cases to accusations of membership poaching, the most public conflict being that between the Mineworkers' Union (IGBE) and the Public and Transport Workers' Union (ÖTV). Despite such problems, the process of trade union unification had by the end of 1990 been more or less completed. Of the 9.6 million FDGB members registered in 1989, roughly 45 per cent have since joined the new all-German unions, which is a high figure in view of mounting unemployment (see Table 2).

According to the influx of east German labour into the individual unions and the proportional split between east and west German memberships, unification has affected unions to varying degrees. However, one common problem facing the union leaderships is that of integrating the interests of two quite disparate labour forces within one organization.

It is often claimed that the strength and solidarity of the West German trade union movement is based upon the organizing principles of the *Einheitsgewerkschaft,* a politically neutral trade union, and the *Industriegewerkschaft,* with a union membership based upon an industrial branch and not on occupation or skill. This solidarity is then translated into effectiveness through participation in the work's council *(Betriebsrat)* and the principle of co-determination *(Mitbestimmung).* However, during the 1980s the union leaderships came under increasing pressure from their memberships. Despite the high density of union organization, they were unable to prevent unemployment from rising to above two million, the highest level in the post-war period. Moreover, the Neue Heimat scandal, involving the housing co-operative owned by the DGB, which resulted in heavy financial losses, seriously damaged the credibility of the DGB and led to accusations that it had become far too diverse in its activities and that the unions ought to resort to and concentrate on their traditional role of representing labour at the workplace. These pressures opened a debate on the need to reassess the role of trade unions in German society which, given the advent of feminism and green politics in Germany, threatened the unions' status as a progressive force in society. The trade union hierarchy came to appear bureaucratic, timid and lacking in vision.

Whilst the Neue Heimat scandal had raised calls for the trade unions to remove themselves from politics, unification has put them into the political limelight more than ever and has magnified their predicament. Like all other organizations, the trade union leaderships were caught cold by the suddenness of political collapse in the GDR. The manner in which they respond to the new challenges thrust upon the unions is therefore central in attempts to redefine their role in Germany as a whole.

Unemployment and claims for wage parity

On July 1, 1990, the Deutschemark was introduced into the GDR. Whilst the exchange rate of 1:1 was attractive to the East German consumer in that it boosted purchasing power, it almost immediately rendered a large proportion of the East German economy uncompetitive and led to a collapse in both its internal retail market and its export markets in the Soviet Union and Eastern Europe. Six months on from monetary union in January 1991 Kurt Biedenkopf, premier of the CDU government in Saxony, described his state as being on the verge of disintegration. He argued that the federal government, despite having put internal unity at the top of its agenda for the national elections in December 1990, had done little to realize this task and he said that the east German states were facing bankruptcy.

In May 1990 a "unity fund" of DM115 billion to ensure the assimilation of the east German states into the west German economic system over a five year period had been announced, with any additional costs being financed by an anticipated "growth dividend". On February 12, 1991 Economic Minister Jürgen Möllemann admitted that the government had underestimated the economic problems of unification and announced an extra DM24 billion over two years as part of a Joint Programme for Eastern Regeneration *(Gemeinschaftswerk Aufschwung Ost)* which was designed to support local authorities' expenditure, to finance infrastructural investment, to extend incentives to new investors and to create new jobs in the region. *Aufschwung Ost* also had the effect of antagonizing the west German population as, contrary to pre-election promises, the increased financial burden of unification was to be met by tax increases. This move, together with a soaring budget deficit, forced the Bundesbank into increasing interest rates and led to its chairman, Karl-Otto Pöhl in an apparently spontaneous outburst, to describe monetary union as having been a "disaster".

Table 3: *Unemployment and short-time statistics 1990-92*

	West Germany				East Germany			
	Unemployed		Short-time		Unemployed		Short-time	
	(000)	(%)	(000)	(%)	(000)	(%)	(000)	(%)
Jan. 1990	2,191	7.5	90	0.3	7	0.1		
April 1990	1,915	6.6	65	0.2	65	0.7		
July 1990	1,864	6.4	30	0.1	272	3.1	656	7.4
Oct. 1990	1,687	5.8	39	0.1	537	6.1	1,704	19.1
Jan. 1991	1,874	6.3	93	0.3	757	8.6	1,841	21.0
April 1991	1,652	5.5	145	0.5	837	9.5	2,019	22.7
July 1991	1,694	5.7	146	0.5	1,069	12.1	1,611	18.1
Oct. 1991	1,599	5.4	173	0.6	1,049	11.9	1,200	13.5
Jan. 1992	1,875	6.3	215	0.8	1,343	16.5	520	5.8

Sources: Monatsberichte der Deutschen Bundesbank, 1990–92

The collapse of the east German economy had a devastating effect on the labour market. East Germans were unaccustomed to unemployment, having experienced "employment as a right" for the preceding 40 years under the communist leadership, but the shock was intensified by the magnitude of the upheaval, which is without parallel in post-war European history (see Table 3). Unemployment surged, though several factors complicate our estimation of it. In two areas they have acted to diminish and in two others to increase the number officially unemployed.

Emigration has certainly taken many out of the east German labour market. Estimates suggest that approximately one million people emigrated to west Germany between May 1989 and January 1992. However, this figure does not take into account the number moving back to the east German states after a temporary period in the west. Another way in which the unemployment statistics have been kept down is the widespread practice of short-time working. The west German state has provided a wage subsidy for firms encountering a fall in business, in order to allow them to reduce production whilst preventing redundancies. By early 1991 perhaps half of the east German workers on short-time were actually unemployed. This situation had arisen out of the special conditions for short-time payments in the east German states, whereby the state in extreme situations would be allowed to pay the wages of an entire company in order to avoid bankruptcy and an escalation in unemployment. Originally intended for the first 12 months following economic union, these special conditions were extended to December 1991.

Unemployment levels have been accentuated by the prior differences in employment rates between east and west Germany. The proportion of the labour supply in employment in the GDR (83 per cent) was high in comparison to the Federal Republic (69 per cent) and can be put down primarily to the high number of women in employment. Nearly 80 per cent of women were in employment in the GDR compared to 57 per cent in the Federal Republic. One conclusion to be drawn from this is that production in the GDR was labour intensive and that under market conditions the proportion of labour supply in employment would fall to a lower natural rate. The trend in unemployment seems to bear out this assumption, given that 61 per cent of all unemployed in the eastern states are women (see contribution by Alsop in this volume).

Structural unemployment has also played its part. Although not unknown in market economies, this phenomenon in the east German context is based upon the thesis that planned and market economies developed different employment structures in the post-war period. In 1988 the proportion of the workforce engaged in manual assembly operations was 11.8 per cent in the GDR compared to 4.3 per cent in the Federal Republic, while the proportion in machine-based manufacturing was relatively low at 12.9 per cent in the GDR compared to 15.7 per cent in the Federal Republic. Moreover, looking at a comparison of sectoral employment, it is revealed that 10 per cent of the GDR workforce was employed in agriculture, compared to 3.9 per cent in the Federal Republic; and that only 8.1 per cent and 9.3 per cent were employed in the wholesale/retail and service sectors respectively, compared to 13.0 per cent and 18.0 per cent in the Federal Republic. These differences have led to the bizarre situation in which there is a simultaneous surplus and shortage of labour depending upon the occupation and sector examined.

Throughout 1991 competing estimates of between 30 and 50 per cent unemployment were presented, but whilst there were great differences in the number of unemployed predicted there was a general consensus that the rise in unemployment would bottom out in the latter part of 1992. It has been suggested that the most pessimistic predictions are now unlikely to be realized given the benefits expected to be derived from the *Aufschwung Ost* programme.

Implicit in the criticism launched against the Kohl leadership was the mistaken assumption on the part of the government that the market would regulate the economic process of unification. It was envisaged that the public sector would be required to provide financial support for a transitional period only and that investment funds from private sources would increasingly predominate, an attitude summed up in the OECD summary for 1990–91: "The proposed plan for monetary union foresaw only a short-lived and limited contraction of output and employment in Eastern Germany to be followed by vigorous expansion of economic activity by massive private investment." The *Treuhandanstalt* (Trust Agency), which had been established to co-ordinate the rationalization and privatization of the 8,000 east German state-owned concerns, soon encountered a number of obstacles inhibiting private investment, the most serious of which were: inadequate economic infrastructure in the former GDR; the lack of financial expertise for valuation purposes; the issue of property rights; market uncertainty in Eastern Europe; and administrative delays. The result of this was that a large proportion of the *Treuhand's* budget was wasted on holding up unviable concerns through liquidity payments, pending assessment of their economic viability.

However, the lack of private investment has been increasingly attributed to rising wage levels. In 1989 both labour productivity and wage levels in the GDR were roughly one-third of those in the Federal Republic. In assessing the conditions for investment in eastern Germany, it was argued that a well trained and relatively cheap labour force would be a strong attraction to would-be investors. However, during 1990 labour productivity dropped as industrial output plummeted by 53 per cent. Wage levels, on the other hand, rose to 38 per cent of those in western Germany and by the end of 1991 were on average 65 per cent of the west German wage.

A number of explanations have been offered for this rapid rise in east German wages, notably by the American research team of G. Akerlof (see Bibliography). They argue that wages were increased in compensation for the removal of food, transport and rent subsidies following economic union, and for higher wage deductions in the form of social insurance payments. A psychological "fairness factor" also came into play in that it is not possible to link wage increases to labour productivity in the transport and services sector. Many east Germans felt that it was unwarranted that they should be punished economically for the SED leadership's mismanagement of the economy over the preceding 40 years. Strong union pay bargaining in the east German states was also based upon the assumption that a large number of enterprises would not survive the process of economic transition. Given that unemployment benefit in Germany is paid on a progressive scale according to wage level prior to redundancy, it was logical for the unions to press for the highest possible increases before the enterprises went bankrupt. The unions could also argue that wage increases were a means of reducing migration to the west. Whilst this would benefit the social dimension to unification in the east, it would also protect west German wage levels from the pressures of undercutting, for example in the construction industry. Finally, there was a lack of resistance by employers to union wage demands. Many east German managers were unused to aggressive union collective bargaining and, on the assumption that they too would eventually lose their jobs and that the increased wage costs would be met by the *Treuhand*, they had little motivation to resist the unions.

The *Bundesbank* has consistently maintained that in order to maintain an element of competitiveness and avoid a complete collapse of the labour market in the eastern states, wage increases must be determined by labour productivity, a view shared by the government, employers' associations and numerous economic research institutes. This attitude tends to disregard the fact that economic union was driven by political rather than economic motives. The primary concern in introducing the Deutschemark was to stem the flood of economic migrants entering the Federal Republic from the GDR. As one banner on show at the Leipzig Monday demonstration prior to the *Volkskammer* elections in early 1990 succinctly phrased the problem, "If the Deutschemark doesn't come to us, we'll go to it!"

At the DGB congress in May 1990 the mineworkers' leader Heinz-Werner Meyer succeeded Ernst Breit as chairman of the DGB. In his keynote speech to the congress Meyer mapped out the DGB's position as far as economic union was concerned. Despite the structural problems of marketization, the GDR was not to become the "poorhouse" of Germany and retraining was to be provided for workers made redundant during the transitional phase. The first part of the platform was translated into the demands that currency union be at a 1:1 exchange rate for wages and pensions, and that the financial burden of unification not be placed upon German labour in the guise of low wage settlements. In December 1990 the

DGB federal executive committee announced its negotiating and campaign programme for the following year, entitled "Shaping Social Unity". The priority for the DGB and the individual unions during 1991 was set down as the achievement of "a large step towards an environmentally and socially acceptable paritization and improvement in work and living conditions in Germany". The most controversial proposal contained in the programme was that of wage parity between eastern and western Germany. Meyer reasoned that wage parity was essential for social stability in eastern Germany. Given the argument that economic union had been introduced in order to stem the flood of economic migrants into the West, the existence of a unitary labour market in Germany made wage parity necessary if the outward flow of skilled labour from the eastern states was to be avoided.

In a report published in January 1992 the German Institute for Economic Research (DIW) estimated that only 600,000 East Germans (7 per cent of the total labour force), a number much lower than had been originally anticipated, had emigrated to western Germany during the period from July 1990 to January 1992, with 100,000 of this number having made the relatively short trip to West Berlin. Furthermore, there is little evidence to suggest that many east Germans are seriously contemplating a move to the west. In a survey conducted by the DGB's own research institute during 1991 it was discovered that whilst two-thirds of east Germans would consider retraining or working in a different occupational field in order to find employment, only 13 per cent said they would consider moving to a new area to find work, with 17 per cent answering "perhaps" and 70 per cent answering that they would not consider a move in order to find work. The empirical data at first glance therefore appears to contradict the reasoning behind demands for wage parity. However, what also emerged from these two studies was that, of those who had emigrated to the west, 65 per cent were under the age of 35, 83 per cent were male and 89 per cent had completed either an apprenticeship or had higher or further educational qualifications. Whilst it is therefore necessary to be tentative in drawing conclusions from these two studies, it appears to be the case that, although the size of migration is less than expected, those migrating appear to be young, male and skilled.

The DGB has repeatedly warned of the dangers of social tension should the east–west gap become too large and maintains that wage increases in 1990 were instrumental in avoiding the political confrontation of what was feared at the time would be a "hot autumn". In condemning the accusations from employers' associations that excessive wage demands were the cause of long-term unemployment, that the trade unions were calling for rapid wage parity in a deliberate attempt to destroy jobs and that the trade unions, rather than economic mismanagement, were the cause of all economic problems, Meyer argued that such arguments had been used by employers as ammunition for attacks on trade union behaviour long before unification and that "the tune has changed but the song remains the same".

Klaus von Dohnanyi, a prominent member of the SPD federal executive committee and until 1988 mayor of Hamburg, is better placed than most to comment on the economic situation in eastern Germany. Since July 1990 he has been chairman of the supervisory board at the heavy industrial plant TAKRAF AG in Leipzig. In his book, *Das Deutsche Wagnis* (The German Venture), written shortly before unification, he argued that economic reconstruction in the east German states is as much a political challenge as it is economic. In concluding that wage paritization in the near future based upon labour productivity is almost impossible to imagine, he warns of the political dangers that will arise should insufficient attention be given to the social tensions of unification which unemployment and disparity in wages may provoke: "Should the social gap between the GDR and FRG regions not become visibly smaller from year to year and its closure be possible within the near future, Germany will have to live with increasing political tension, the likes of which it has not experienced in the last 40 years."

The economic dilemma in the east German states can therefore be characterized as an extremely precarious balancing act. Should wages rise too quickly in the former GDR, there is a danger that the labour market could collapse completely as private investment is deterred, which in turn would destabilize the west German economy as the government is compelled to increase taxation and public borrowing in order to subsidize unemployment. On the other hand, should wages fail to rise quickly enough, this could lead to what skilled labour remains in eastern Germany emigrating, if not to western Germany then to other European countries where skills are in demand, a move which would seriously damage the process of economic reconstruction and, by continuing social disparity between east and west Germany, raise the political temperature in the country. The issue of wage parity is made more complex by the fact that employers and unions are not approaching the problem from the same perspective. In stressing the political consequences of social disparity, the unions have been accused of a "perception gap" between their wage demands and what employers can realistically afford. In summarizing this dilemma it can be argued that the awareness of political necessity cannot be allowed to cloud economic reality in eastern Germany, but that the social consequences of marketization must not be too extreme if the process is to be a success.

The economic research team from the University of California, Berkeley has offered a way out of this dilemma in the form of what is dubbed a "Self-Eliminating Flexible Employment Bonus Programme". The suggestion is that the state would reduce labour costs by providing wage subsidies in eastern Germany which would be gradually phased out as labour productivity increased. It is argued that this programme would increase the attractiveness of investment in the region, remove the state burden of financing unemployment as jobs were preserved and new ones created and comprise a "social contract" between the government and unions in the form of protection of jobs in return for restraint in wage negotiations. Klaus von Dohnanyi adds a caveat to the proposal of wage subsidy in arguing that marketization without access to markets is a meaningless exercise and that east German firms require some form of preferential treatment if they are to have any chance of breaking into the German domestic and international markets. The problem of such a proposal is apparent. Protecting east German companies from market competition is fraught with inherent dangers given the objective of making them competitive.

Wage subsidy on such a scale has been greeted with some cynicism in Germany. State subsidies have recently been reduced in order to meet the costs of unification and as the DIW has pointed out, once introduced, subsidies have a tendency to continue longer and be more expensive than they were originally intended. The basic argument against the Berkeley model is that it would prolong the process of economic transition in eastern Germany. It is unlikely that labour productivity will attain west German levels in the near future and may encourage the proliferation of labour intensive technology in the region, resulting in a scenario in which, according to the DIW, "the German economy would comprise a west German sector with high labour productivity and high wages and an east German sector with low labour productivity and subsidized wages. The attempted market-determined assimilation of the two economic sectors and living standards would be postponed until the distant future".

This is an attitude undoubtedly shared by the OECD. In its criticism of economic policy in the first year following economic union, the OECD summary for 1990–91 argues that the problems that arose were not a result of market forces, more the lack of them:

> "In the first year of union a critical task was the establishment of a functioning labour market and, in particular, encouragement of efficiency-oriented social partners. However, apart from inherited rigidities of the past, the generous provision of liquidity credits, payments for short-time working and limited management contracts have resulted in soft budget constraints and lack of concern by both management and unions for the competitiveness of enterprises. Taken together, this has contributed to the fall of labour productivity, and the damaging surge in wage costs. However, if budget constraints become more binding and firms' employment policy were to be related to future profitability, labour hoarding may diminish and productivity and competitiveness improve in the remaining enterprises."

Table 4: IGM "four-stage plan" in Mecklenburg-West Pomerania (% of west German rates)

	Blue-collar workers	White-collar workers
1 April 1991	62.6	58.6
1 April 1992	71.0	69.0
1 April 1993	82.0	80.0
1 April 1994	100.0	100.0

Source: *DGB Tarifbericht*, July 1991.

In rejecting mass wage subsidy as a means of attracting investment, the alternative proposal forwarded by the government and employers' associations is trade union restraint in wage negotiations. The trade unions, however, are intent on achieving wage parity by one means or another. In March 1991 the metalworkers' union *IG Metall* achieved an agreement in the eastern state of Mecklenburg-West Pomerania which would provide wage parity with west Germany on April 1, 1994. This "four-stage plan" (see Table 4) has been criticized as risky in the way in which it gives the green light for similar and perhaps more ambitious demands by other unions. Soon after the agreement in Mecklenburg-West Pomerania the Construction Workers' Union (IGBSE) and the Commerce, Banking and Insurance Workers' Union (HBV) announced that they wanted to achieve wage parity before the end of 1992.

The battle lines for the 1992 wage round were drawn by Hans-Peter Stihl, President of the German Chamber of Commerce, in late December 1991 when he announced that high labour costs were putting the German economy under pressure on international markets, and that union restraint in wage negotiations during 1992 would be the key to economic recovery. Against the background of the announcements in December 1991 by the Public Service and Transport Workers' Union (ÖTV) and Salaried Employees' Union (DAG) that they would demand 9.5 per cent and by *IG Metall*, HBV and the Civil Service Union (DBB) that they would be putting in demands for 10.5 per cent for the 1992 wage round, the opening shot was sounded when Economics Minister, Jürgen Möllemann, argued that wage rises of 6.7 per cent in 1991 had been damaging to the economy and should not be allowed to exceed 5 per cent in 1992, a figure later further reduced to 4 per cent by Klaus Murmann, President of the German Employers' Association. More controversial was Möllemann's suggestion that the government use legal measures to hold civil servants below this figure as a signal for other sectors of the economy.

The response from the unions was that wage demands had traditionally been formulated and negotiated on a responsible basis, and had been moderate given buoyant growth rates and profits during the 1980s. Angered by the apparent government interference in wage negotiations, a practice proscribed by the principle of "wage-setting independence", there was the suspicion that west German employers were using unification as an excuse to push down west German wage rates. The chairman of *IG Metall,* Franz Steinkühler, has fiercely maintained that wage levels are not responsible for the economic catastrophe in the east German states, and in rejecting the need for union restraint in wage negotiations had anticipated the perceived onslaught against the unions in December 1991, arguing that:

> "although labour has the bulk of the financial burden of German unity to shoulder, this has not stopped employers, conservative politicians and their academic 'auxiliary troops' from demanding wage sacrifices. Whilst workers in the west provide their contribution to unity in the form of solidarity tax, increased income tax and social insurance deductions and in the east through a slower process of wage paritization, employers are profiteering from unification as lavish increases in orders lead to large profits."

With employers and unions set on an apparent collision course, Heinz-Werner Meyer, speaking at the DGB Annual Reception in January 1992, concluded that whilst 1990 had been "The Year of Political Celebrations" and 1991 "The Year of Economic Collapse", 1992 would be "The Year of Social Crisis". Implicit in Meyer's statement was the political undercurrent of wage negotiations and it highlighted the problems facing the DGB in its role of representing the interests of east German labour.

Problems of labour representation in eastern Germany

The Institute for Empirical Psychology (IFEP) conducted a survey in the new federal states during February and March 1991 in order to test the perception of west German trade unions among east Germans and also to discover the expectations east German labour had of their unions. The results revealed that the stabilization of the economy and protection of jobs were the main expectations and that whilst it was true to see the trade unions as the main hope, the trust that east German labour was prepared to put in the trade union movement was highly dependent upon results. The east German membership has long been used to a paternalistic FDGB and has high expectations of west German trade unions, too high as far as the DGB is concerned.

Throughout 1991, as the DGB and individual unions developed their organizational structures in the east German states, a central task was to explain to east German labour the role of trade unions in a liberal democratic market economy. The DGB has remonstrated with east German workers, arguing that many in the region have had their perception of a trade union distorted by the FDGB, and that trade unions are not a form of "social repair shop"; their ability to influence policy is limited. This argument has done little to placate the rising tensions in the east German states, given the unemployment trends in the two parts of Germany. In an opinion survey conducted in eastern Germany by the Electoral Research

Group of Mannheim in December 1990, looking at the most important political issues, the most common problems listed were low wages (24 per cent), economic recovery (27 per cent) and unemployment (72 per cent). It is therefore not surprising that the collapse of the labour market had a detrimental effect on attitudes towards trade unions and has led to signs of tension within the union structures. At a seminar held in July 1990 looking at the issue of labour representation in the GDR, *IG Metall* was accused of "imperialism" and "centralism", whilst on other occasions west German union officials have been criticized for their arrogance in dealings with east German members.

Another question is what responsibility trade unions have in the representation of unemployed labour in the east German states. In a recent study by the DGB-financed research institute, the Hans-Böckler-Foundation, it is argued that the unemployed often have great expectations of trade unions and are disappointed that little attention is given to their situation. For their part, trade union officials are often unsure as to what function they are expected and able to perform. An internal paper produced by the DGB in May 1991 acknowledged the problem of unemployment in the east German states and the potential consequences it could have for the trade unions. It suggested that unemployment could lead to either mass protest or resignation by east German labour, but stressed that trade unions had a significant role to play in reducing unemployment through "active labour policy". The "emergency programme" announced in February 1991 demanding, among other things, infrastructural investment and the implementation of employment creation schemes, is claimed to have been the genesis of the government's *Aufschwung Ost* proposal. Klaus Grehn, former lecturer at the FDGB school in Bernau and president of the east German Unemployed Association (*Arbeitslosenverband* — ALV), is less positive in his appraisal of trade union activities in the region. Grehn claims that the ALV, founded at the beginning of 1990, now has approximately 3,500 voluntary workers in the eastern states who advise 30–40,000 people per month. It regards as central to its functions "the public discussion of the political significance of unemployment, its causes and its economic, social and medical consequences, and the development of 'counter-concepts to unemployment'", matters which the trade union movement, Grehn argues, has failed to address.

The re-emergence of the "Monday demonstrations" in Leipzig in March 1991 under the organizational banner of *IG Metall* provides an example of the controversy surrounding the role of the unions in the east German states. The government and employers' associations condemned the action as inflamatory, whilst other commentators saw it as a blatant attempt to channel protest away from potentially destabilizing political action. In the event, the demonstrations failed miserably to live up to their earlier counterparts.

The conservative attitude to trade unions is one of varying degrees of disdain, which ranges from treating them as a disruptive but functional entity, to that of a subversive and highly undemocratic phenomenon. In March 1991 CSU General Secretary, Erwin Huber, condemned what in his eyes was the irresponsible behaviour of the trade unions in the eastern states, accusing them of "incitement". Such a perspective is in direct contradiction to that of the radical left in Germany which condemns the trade union movement for its betrayal of labour's interests. In conforming to the values of the "corporate state", it is argued that the unions, acting as an "agent of order" in society, dilute the class tensions which could destabilize the political *status quo* and bring about political change.

There is a lack of consensus within the DGB itself as to the nature of trade unionism. Hermann Rappe, head of *IG Chemie*, views the trade union as an essential component to the functioning of the social economy in the form of a "social partnership", whereby the union provides a forum for the negotiation of interests between capital and labour. It is with this concept in mind that Heinz-Werner Meyer made the offer of co-operation in solving the problems of unification to the government in January 1991. As he put it,

> "The general responsibility for the future development of the new states belongs to the government. But it is the common goal of all political agents to achieve unity in living and wage conditions [...]. In order to alter the present situation it is necessary to combine the various political elements [...] in order to avoid serious confrontation."

This perspective assumes the existence of willingness on the part of government and employer to involve the unions in the policy-making process, and is implicit in acknowledging the inferior bargaining position of labour to that of capital. Furthermore, there is also the danger that the unions are seen to be compliant to the interests of capital, and as such jointly responsible for the failings of social policy. Whilst it is true that the vast majority of west German trade union members are not unduly concerned by the apparent corporatist role of their unions, this is based upon the affluence that west German labour has enjoyed in the post-war period. Now that the German economy is beginning to show signs of weakness, it remains unclear how long the west German worker can continue to enjoy his affluent status. A fall in west German living standards would have serious repercussions for the attitude of its members to the competence of the union leaderships. Should living conditions not rise quickly enough in the eastern states, the east German worker too will begin to question the effectiveness of union representation. The nightmare scenario for the trade unions is both developments happening simultaneously.

A contrasting perspective on trade unions is provided by Frank Steinkühler. The *IG Metall* head stresses the role of the union as a "counterforce" to the interests of capital. Whilst this much more confrontational attitude clearly distances the interests of capital and labour, the danger is in breaking the link altogether and of asserting a class interpretation of industrial relations in Germany. In appealing to the shrinking blue-collar working-class sector, little is done to entice the new emerging white-collar working class.

The internal conflict between the trade union as "social partner" and as "counterforce", seen against the background of the emerging post-industrial state in west Germany, is interesting enough. The added factor of the collapsing heavy industrial state in eastern Germany and the need to reconcile their quite different demands is fascinating in its complexity. The tripartite system of government, employer and trade union was an essential factor in the German economic miracle after 1945. The challenge that "zero hour" presented, the need to reconstruct the German economy out of the ashes of wartime destruction, had a cohesive influence on all parties and through the process of co-determination the benefits of co-operation have been maximized. In contrast to 1945, the atmosphere prior to unification in 1989 was one of economic stability and affluence. The situation in 1945 when labour had nothing to lose and everything to gain had been turned on its head by 1989. The political basis of co-determination has been weakened by the economic recession during the 1980s and unification has brought the relationship between labour and capital to breaking point. In advancing the social dimension to unification the DGB is attempting to reconcile the conflicting demands made upon it in western and eastern Germany. The danger is there that the concept of social partnership, much valued by the DGB, may be undermined by the class factor in eastern Germany. The structure and status with which the German trade union movement enters the next century will therefore be determined by its success in resolving the challenges of German unity.

THE EXPERIENCE OF WOMEN IN EASTERN GERMANY

Rachel Alsop

The objective of this essay is to examine the effects of German unification on women in the new federal states. The analysis focuses upon the changes occurring in the initial post-unification phase, although examination of the immediate problems will also identify potential long-term trends. The nature of German unification — the adoption of west German structures and practices in the new states — creates conflict between the expectations of east German women on the one side and the demands of the new social and economic system on the other. Research already indicates that women are the chief losers in the unification process, and the following discussion will thus concentrate upon areas where the process of adaptation is particularly problematic for east German women.

The labour market

Female employment in the GDR

To assert that women will be the chief losers in the unification process implies that women have gained something which they now stand to lose. Consequently before examining the post-unification position of east German women it is necessary to assess briefly the position prior to the collapse of the GDR, in particular with regard to the labour market. By international standards the rate of female paid employment was extremely high, matching employment levels only reached by men in western nations. Women in the GDR formed almost half the workforce. At the end of September 1989, 8.5 million GDR citizens were involved in paid labour, nearly 49 per cent of whom were female. Of the female working-age population 78 per cent was employed. If one adds women in training and studying to the figures, over 90 per cent of women were in some way "employed". Of particular importance was the high labour force participation rate of women with young children.

Despite the high rate of female involvement in the labour market, gender segregation occurred both on a horizontal and a vertical axis. Indeed, the high level of female labour force participation did not eradicate gender inequalities in the labour market. Women, as in the Federal Republic, were more likely to be working in lower paid, more routine jobs, with less scope for initiative and decision-making than their male counterparts. In 1988 women constituted almost two-thirds of the workers earning less than 1,000 marks per month and just over a quarter of those who earned more than this amount.

Women were also more likely to be employed in non-producing, white-collar jobs. In the latter years of the GDR the trend was growing for women to be employed in the service sector, as employment in industry and agriculture declined. Such developments reflected trends apparent in western economies, where the growth of the service sector has provided substantial employment for female workers. The expansion of the service sector in the GDR was, however, modest compared to that in the west.

Most female workers were employed full-time. There was little scope for flexible working hours, and part-time work was discouraged by the state. Women, however, constituted the majority of all part-time workers. At the end of the GDR era just over a quarter of all female workers were employed less than full-time. The number of women involved in this form of flexible employment was growing, with the majority of part-time workers employed between 25 and 35 hours per week. Areas of employment with a high number of female workers, such as the service and sales sectors, employed a comparatively large amount of part-time labour.

Women were severely under-represented in managerial positions. Where women did reach positions of power it was usually in middle and lower management and in fields of employment where there was a high level of female participation in the general workforce. Overall women made up just over a third of all managers and one in five in the industrial sector. In light industry where women represented 56 per cent of the entire workforce they constituted 44 per cent of the managers.

Systems of patriarchy — gender hierarchies in which men tend to play a dominant role and women a subordinate one — existed in both East and West Germany, yet the roles East and West German women played within the gender hierarchies were by no means identical. In the field of work the gains made by women in the GDR were most apparent. Of particular significance was the higher labour market involvement of women with children in the east than in the west. In the west the employment of women declined in their child-rearing years; this was not the case in the GDR. Women in the GDR were also on average better qualified than their western counterparts. At the end of the 1980s almost one-third of women in the west had no vocational qualifications or training compared to only just over 12 per cent in the GDR. In addition, more women were trained and worked in technical and managerial spheres than in the Federal Republic.

In the GDR women did not have to choose between a career and children, thus allowing the high employment rate of mothers. A network of institutional, financial and material provisions was created by the state to allow women to combine full-time employment and family responsibilities. Future erosion of women's access to collective childcare facilities and the increased care of children in the family unit will restrict their involvement in paid employment. In west Germany, on the other hand, the care of pre-school-age children, especially those below kindergarten age, tends to be undertaken primarily within the household unit. As childcare is predominantly the responsibility of women, access to the labour market is then restricted for women with children in their care. Women's labour force participation in the old *Länder* consequently adheres to a "three-phase model" — women work or study, leave the labour market to have and care for children and then return later to paid employment. On return to the labour market women usually suffer a devaluation of their skill and qualification levels.

If one compares the number of children in community childcare establishments in 1989 in the GDR and the Federal Republic the different methods become apparent, particularly with regard to the care of the children under three and of younger pupils in the after-school hours. In the GDR places existed for 80 per cent of children up to three years of age. In the Federal

Republic only two in every hundred children were cared for in crèches. In the GDR 81 per cent of six- to ten-year-olds had places in *Schulhorte,* providing care for pupils after school, compared to just 4 per cent in the west. With only half-day school this presents severe difficulties for mothers seeking full-time employment.

The attitude of women themselves towards their involvement in the labour market differs between east and west Germany. In the GDR the employment of women, even those with small children, was the norm. The transition to the market economy and movement towards the western system therefore involves a particularly difficult learning process for many women. The results of a survey conducted by the Institute for Applied Social Science (*Institut für angewandte Sozialwissenschaft* — Infas) in 1991, investigating the position of women in the new *Länder* in the process of German unification, indicate the importance of employment to east German women. Most of the women interviewed stated that working was a part of their lives they would not relinquish and ruled out the option of just being a housewife. Indeed, 61 per cent said they would not give up their jobs even if their partner was in a position to support them financially.

To understand the changing form of women's involvement in the labour market one must also be aware of the changing conditions behind female employment. In the GDR, in addition to an ideological commitment to promote the involvement of women in the labour market, a shortage of labour necessitated the full involvement of women in the economy. Consequently measures were introduced to increase women's involvement in the workforce and at the same time to increase the birthrate. The changing economic conditions engendered by the collapse of the GDR and the introduction of market economic forces will alter the nature of women's involvement in the labour force. The end of the shortage of labour and the beginning of a surplus of labour will, in particular, influence the nature of women's paid employment.

Women's employment since unification

Women workers have been disproportionately affected by the collapse of the state socialist system and the transition to a market economy. Since the collapse of the GDR women have made up the majority of the unemployed. At the end of 1991 women constituted 61.2 per cent of those registered unemployed, and the female unemployment quota lay at 14.7 per cent, 5.8 points above the male quota.

The labour market figures for January 1992 reveal dramatic increases for both male and female unemployment as the result of the expiry of special rules for employees working short time. The over-representation of women amongst the unemployed, however, had increased. Of the entire potential workforce, one in six were now unemployed; of the female workforce more than one in five were out of work. Women in January 1992 represented 61.6 per cent of the total unemployed, and the gap between male and female unemployment is constantly widening. The quota for female unemployment had by the end of January 1992 risen to 21.8 per cent, that is 9.2 points higher than the male unemployment quota. In October 1990 the gap between female and male unemployment had been just 1.4 points: 6.8 per cent female and 5.4 per cent male. Women are more likely than men to be employed in areas now requiring greater rationalization and to be made redundant because their firm has closed down.

The greater susceptibility of women to unemployment is coupled with a lower rate of re-employment. Men have a greater tendency than women to leave their jobs of their own accord, reflecting their greater chances of finding new employment. Women are also severely under-represented in work creation schemes (*Arbeitsbeschaffungsmassnahmen* — ABM). Although the structure of those involved is intended to reflect the structure of the unemployed, women only constituted 36.7 per cent of those taking part in December 1991 in the new *Länder*. Examination of the ABM places approved or offered by the employment offices reveal that the majority are in areas which traditionally employ a greater amount of male than female labour. Analysis of the distribution of male and female workers in ABM indicates the concentration of women in jobs in the social and administrative sectors. Men, however, have a greater tendency to be employed in the agricultural and horticultural branches or in the construction industry.

The gender division of labour and the higher tendency for men to find employment in work creation schemes is representative of the general re-employment of labour in the economy. Employment statistics indicate that women are less likely to find new employment than men. Scarcely more than 40 per cent of new employment was taken up by women in Brandenburg in November 1991. Moreover, two-thirds of women found employment in the service sector. Almost 70 per cent of the employment in this area was filled by female labour. Women, however, constituted only 15 per cent of those finding employment in manufacturing industries. Just under 18 per cent of women finding employment did so in this sphere.

Due to the existing sexual division of labour and gender inequalities in the east German labour market, economic restructuring and the accompanying changes in the employment structure are affecting male and female chances in the labour market differently. It is forecast that the east German economy will follow a course of adaptation to and approximation of the structure of the west German economy. The economic structure of the new *Länder* corresponds in many ways to that of West Germany approximately 20 years ago. If the trends of the last 20 years are then applied to the east German economy it is foreseen that in the new *Länder* the service sector will continue to expand and industry and agriculture to decline. Expansion of the service sector in western economies has created many jobs, predominantly part-time and for female workers. In the face of rising unemployment in the 1970s, the growth of the service sector in western nations to some degree cushioned women's greater susceptibility to unemployment in other branches of the economy. Thus, it is predicted that a growth of employment in the service sector will benefit women workers. As already stated, the majority of jobs in the east German service industries are already taken by women.

The reality of the situation in the east, however, only partially resembles the forecast. The numbers employed in the industrial and agricultural branches are declining rapidly. In the textile industry where women were well represented, one in three places had already been lost by the end of 1990. The service sector has not, however, begun to expand as expected. Reports issued in January 1992 indicate that more jobs are being lost in this area than are being created. Also many jobs had been lost in the administrative sector because of changes in the bureaucratic and political system, previous over-staffing and increased office rationalization. Consequently the decline of female employment has not as yet been offset by the expansion of the growth of tertiary sector employment.

The introduction of more flexible employment conditions should increase part-time employment for women. Within western economies there is a movement towards the existence of a smaller core of skilled workers and a larger periphery of less skilled, part-time, often female workers. Although the expansion of part-time labour will create jobs for women, one should, however, be aware of the disadvantages which accompany part-time work. Part-time work remains predominantly a female domain, with lower rates of pay, fewer legal rights, often poorer work conditions and limited career prospects.

The increasing rationalization of the industrial sector will force a shift from labour- to capital-intensive industries. Research in the west indicates that there is often a preference for male labour in capital-intensive production and for female in labour-intensive production, because of the cheapness of female labour. Rationalization will contribute to the increasing marginalization of female workers. There have already been cases in the new *Länder* where labour-intensive factories with a high proportion of female workers have been closed down, new, more technologically advanced machinery introduced and male workers re-employed.

Shifts in the sexual division of labour in the paid workforce are overwhelmingly to the benefit of male workers. Labour market analysis indicates that as a result of the economic difficulties and the high rate of unemployment, men are increasingly moving into traditionally female areas of employment. For example, in the banking and insurance branches the employment of men is increasing marginally faster than that of women (5 compared to 4 per cent). Men are also moving into the computerizing areas of the service sector. The increased competition between the sexes for jobs, however, only exists in the traditionally female areas. There is no evidence of the movement of women into traditionally male spheres of employment, such as the boom area of construction.

The over-representation of women in unemployment and their under-representation in new employment cannot therefore be attributed solely to the effects of changes in the economic structure. The specific preference of male to female labour in many areas of the economy should be placed within the context of gender relations in general. Although it is beyond the scope of this paper to offer a full analysis of the workings of patriarchy in Germany it is important to note that in both German systems prior to unification mechanisms existed which promoted the dominance of men over women in all social institutions. One need only look at the gender structure of the political and economic hierarchies in the Federal Republic and in the GDR to see that it was primarily men who held the reins of power.

Certain factors work to restrict the involvement of women in the labour market. Women tend to be less mobile than men, thus limiting the range of jobs available to them. More men than women travel from the new *Länder* to west Germany or to west Berlin to work. Women are 21 per cent of such commuters, one-third of those who commute to west Berlin and 16 per cent of those who travel to the old *Länder*.

Women's lack of mobility is a large obstacle to employment, especially for those women who live in rural areas where public transport is poor. A project in Luckenwalde in Brandenburg is, however, being set up to help combat women's limited mobility in the surrounding rural areas. The plan is to provide minibuses driven by women for women who wish to travel into the local town. The buses will operate on a more regular basis than the standard bus service. Such projects are rare as they are mostly dependent upon the investment of public money. At a time when public funds are already over-stretched the commitment to the promotion and support of women's issues in the political arena on both a state and national level together with the level of money available dictate the success of such initiatives. The "traffic-light" coalition in the state of Brandenburg has been particularly sensitive to the needs and demands of women within the state. The extent to which proposals and policies can become reality depends, however, at the end of the day upon the amount of money available in the state budget.

The family, housework and childcare

Housework

In west Germany domestic labour — housework and the day-to-day care of family members — is performed predominantly by women, unpaid, and within the household unit. Women's overwhelming responsibility for childcare and household tasks restricts their involvement in paid labour outside of the home. Women's relation to the domestic sphere not only limits their actual involvement in wage labour but also influences society's attitude towards women's commitment to employment. Thus, it is important to evaluate how unification will affect the interaction of women's domestic and wage labour in the new federal states.

In the GDR housework also remained predominantly in the private sphere, in spite of Marxist-Leninist ideology advocating the socialization of domestic tasks as one of the essential pre-requisites of female emancipation. Moreover, the performance of household tasks remained overwhelmingly the responsibility of women, despite women's labour market participation rate being virtually as high as men's. The state's support and promotion of the sexual division of labour in the home are indicated by the existence of a "housework day" — one day off work per month to "catch up" on household chores — predominantly for women. Men were, in general, only entitled to the "housework day" if they were single parents or if they cared for their wives within the home; in other words, if there was not a woman in the household able to perform the domestic tasks.

With regards to the division of labour in the households of the former GDR the Infas study revealed that 60 per cent of women spent 21 or more hours a week doing housework. 80 per cent of men, however, spent under 20 hours a week on domestic labour. In addition to the unequal distribution of time spent on domestic labour by men and women, the allocation of tasks tends also to be divided upon gender lines. The survey revealed that over two-thirds of east German women regard cooking and cleaning as their chores. This division of housework tasks in the east corresponds in general to that in the old Federal Republic. The Infas study, on comparing the results of the survey in the new *Länder* with those of a similar survey undertaken in North Rhine-Westphalia in 1985, concludes that the internal management of the household did not fundamentally differ from east to west. Even if men "helped out" in the home the management and planning of tasks in both east and west usually remained the domain of women.

The interaction of domestic and wage labour did, however, differ in certain key respects. Women in the east spent many more hours involved in paid labour, thus the demands upon their time tended to be greater. Households were in general less well-equipped with time-saving devices and the supply of goods and services in the east was poor compared to western standards. This all contributed to extra burdens upon the female domestic labourer. The increase in living standards following unification will bring with it the greater use of labour-saving devices in the home. Previous research has, however, indicated that such developments do not necessarily shorten the amount of time that women spend working in the home.

Social legislation and childcare facilities

An array of social legislation existed in the GDR with the primary aim of assisting women combine family and employment. The replacement of GDR legislation with western German legislation will make combining full-time work and a family more difficult. In addition to the housework day women were entitled to paid leave from work for one year to look after their first or second child and 18 months for the third or later child. As from the beginning of 1992 women in both the old and new *Länder* are able to take three years' leave. Payment is only provided for a maximum of 24 months and after the initial six months is income-related. The new legislation reflects the government's intention to promote the care of children under three years of age within the family which in turn restricts women's availability to take part in the paid workforce.

The restrictions placed upon women's participation in the labour force by their childcare responsibilities does not end when the children are of kindergarten or school age. Care for children is still needed in the school holidays, after school hours and when a child is ill. In the GDR both women and men were entitled to paid leave from work to look after sick children. The legislation applied to married couples with two or more children and to all single parents. The length of time allowed was scaled according to the number of children in the household. For one child a parent was allowed per year up to four weeks leave, six for two children, eight for three, 10 for four and 13 for five or more children. The legislation, however, expired on unification and the previous West German regulations now prevail in the new *Länder*. Now parents with insurance are entitled to eight days leave per year per child under eight to care for sick children. If the child is over eight or ill for more than eight days in one year the parent/s must make other arrangements. Although the law extends to both mothers and fathers the changes are of most significance to women as they are primarily responsible for the care of children. East German women have, however, commented that they are unwilling to take time off work to care for ill children as they fear this may jeopardize the security of their employment.

The participation of women with children in their care in paid labour outside the home is dependent upon the supervision of the children being undertaken by other people. In the GDR the overwhelming majority of pre-school age children had places in crèches or kindergartens. Care for younger pupils after school was also provided. In some instances, where women worked night-shifts, children were cared for overnight in *Wochenkrippen* (weekday crèches), returning to their families at weekends or when the mother was not at work. Community childcare was subsidized by the state and parental contributions were minimal. Since the collapse of the GDR childcare facilities in the new *Länder* have already begun to close. However, government officials maintain that childcare facilities are merging and that closures have not resulted in a large loss of places. In Brandenburg 90 per cent of children aged three and over still have kindergarten places and 60–70 per cent of under threes still have places in crèches. The widespread closure of firms has brought with it the closure of the in-firm childcare facilities. However, in the GDR the vast majority of childcare facilities were in the community and not linked to the place of employment. Consequently the closure of these facilities has not resulted in a dramatic increase in the loss of childcare places. The *Berliner Zeitung,* however, reported in June 1991 that *Schulhorte* places in east Berlin had been reduced by 20 per cent and crèche places by 10 per cent, and in February 1992 that 9,000 children were waiting for places in East Berlin alone. This compares to 30,000 in the west of the city. Fears for the continued existence of childcare places are therefore well-founded. Not only closures but increase in prices and the shortening of opening hours will restrict the availability of community childcare. The city of Berlin, for instance, is considering shortening the opening hours of state-subsidized childcare facilities in order to reduce expenditure. The price of places has also increased in an attempt to relieve state funding in this area.

The high unemployment figures may also lead indirectly to the reduction in the number of places available. Especially with the increase in childcare prices unemployed mothers may decide to care for their children in the family. Increased individual care of children will have two main consequences. Firstly, it will mean that the woman is no longer available for work and therefore is not officially unemployed. This would conceal the true number of unemployed women and seek to exclude women from the core of paid workers. Financially this would promote women's dependence upon their partners or in the case of single mothers their dependence upon the state. Secondly, the removal of children from childcare facilities may lead to a reduction in the number of childcare places available in future. This could in turn affect a woman's chance of finding employment again, as without a place in a childcare facility a woman may not be able to take up employment outside the home.

It is also possible that women will look to other family members, such as their own mothers, to take care of their children. With high levels of unemployment amongst older women and many forced into early retirement it may be that younger women will look towards the extended family to assist in their childcare difficulties. The effects of male unemployment upon the division of labour in households, especially in those where the female partner continues to work, is also an area of analysis which requires further attention.

The Federal Minister for the Family and Senior Citizens, Hannelore Rönsch, has indicated that part-time work is the only realistic possibility of combining the demands of family and employment, appealing to employers to increase the number of part-time jobs and to remove the disadvantages of part-time work. The use of flexible work methods to assist women with work and family responsibilities rules out any commitment on the part of the Federal government to the maintenance and support of the childcare system that existed in the GDR. Rönsch has also stressed the need for greater involvement of the private sector in the financing and running of childcare facilities. In-firm childcare facilities are advocated in conjunction with the growth of flexible labour forms — part-time work, job sharing, partial homeworking — as the solution to the dilemma of combining the rearing of children and paid employment.

The increasing need for the financing of childcare facilities to be undertaken by the private sector is echoed by Berlin's Senator for Youth, Thomas Krüger of the SPD. He advocates the building of childcare facilities by firms as this will be quicker than state initiatives, will relieve the city's finances and reduce the waiting list for places. The reaction of firms in the city has been mixed. A representative of Herlitz, the paper manufacturers, stated that the firm felt it was more in the interests of the child for childcare to take place in the vicinity of the home than at the workplace. The key factor in the expansion of private sector involvement will not, however, be the welfare of children but the economic viability of the cost involved.

The use of flexible labour and the increased involvement of the public sector in the provision of childcare facilities does not address the core problem at the heart of women's difficulties in combining childcare and employment — the overwhelming identification of women with the care of children. The measures advocated by the Federal government are aimed at assisting women with their dual roles as domestic and wage workers and do not attempt to redress the unequal division of labour between men and women in the household. Whilst women and men do not carry equal responsibility for the organization and carrying out of childcare and household chores, women and men will continue to enter the labour market on different terms. The promotion of greater equality in the sharing of housework and childcare would create the basis for equality between the sexes in the public sphere.

The abortion debate

So far this discussion has emphasized the effects of the introduction of west German structures in the new *Länder* and their impact on women in the public and private spheres. It has been shown how western practices have been assimilated into east Germany. Is there, however, any scope for the experience of over 40 years of state socialism to influence common German policy concerning women? A unified German policy on abortion was not included in the unification treaty. Instead it was decided that the separate legislation in force prior to unification would remain until the end of 1992, at the latest, whilst a common abortion policy was debated. Thus, the abortion issue exists as one area where there is a possibility of a "backflow" of influence from east to west.

Abortion was legalized in the GDR in March 1972. Women were able to opt to terminate their pregnancies up until the 12th week. Thereafter abortions were carried out only under medical direction. In the old Federal Republic, however, paragraph 218 of the Penal Code denies women the choice to terminate their own pregnancies. Abortion is not ruled out completely, but is only allowed under certain conditions and under medical approval. A woman is entitled to an abortion, for example, up to the end of the 12th week if she has been raped, up to 22 weeks of pregnancy if the child will be born with genetic or health damage, up to any time if it will physically endanger the life of the mother. Paragraph 218 also contains a clause which allows women to terminate their pregnancies if there is deemed to be a psychological and social need. Proof of the necessity of abortion in this instance is precarious and problematic. Many doctors are unwilling to advise abortions on these grounds as inadequate proof can result in the prosecution of both the doctors and women involved.

A special committee for the protection of unborn life was set up after unification to examine the abortion issue. The title of the committee reflects the majority viewpoint of the ruling conservative parties, with the emphasis upon the rights of the unborn child as opposed to those of the pregnant woman. Various proposals for a unified abortion policy were put forward. The suggestions ranged from that of the "Werner group", proposing a tightening of the existing paragraph 218, to that of the Greens in conjunction with Alliance 90, who called for the total abolition of paragraph 218, the time-limit on abortions to remain open and for counselling to be voluntarily undertaken. After much debate a "group motion" put forward by FDP and SPD members and supported by some politicians from the CDU, mainly east German, was passed in the *Bundestag* on June 25 1992. The proposal permits abortion up to the 12th week of pregnancy as with the legislation in the GDR, but differs in that counselling must now take place prior to the abortion.

The legislation also had to be approved in the *Bundesrat*. None of the east German states opposed the legislation, although the states of Mecklenburg-West Pomerania and Thuringia abstained during the vote. Although the legislation has been approved by both houses of the German parliament this may not, however, be the final word on the matter. The legislation must also be deemed to be in line with the constitution, which advocates the protection of unborn life. In 1975 legislation passed in the *Bundestag* to change the abortion legislation was declared by the Constitutional Court to be contrary to the principles of the constitution and was overruled. Members of the conservative parties have already brought the abortion legislation before the Constitutional Court, which has suspended implementation pending its ruling. Although unification and the east German experience have acted as stimuli to alter the west German abortion legislation, at the time of writing the exact extent to which women's access to abortion will change for both east and west German women is therefore still not entirely clear.

Women's reactions

Attitudes to full-time work

The discussion so far has indicated that the influence of the east German system on the form of the unified Germany is minimal. East German women, however, face an extensive re-organization of their lives, not least in their involvement in paid labour and in the interaction between their family and employment. A reduction in women's ability to take part in full-time labour will decrease their financial independence and could lead to greater economic dependence upon their partners, families or state benefits. A publication by the Federal Ministry for Women and Youth states, however, that "Women in the new German states want more time for their children than was wished and possible in the socialist system". "More time for their families" translates as decreased access to community childcare facilities and less involvement in paid labour. Are women really prepared to allow this erosion of their economic and social independence?

Conservative circles argue that women are willing to relinquish their "double burden" of work and family. It is argued that in the state socialist systems women were forced to work and, given the choice that a market economy allows, women will opt for increased involvement in the family sphere. Participation in paid labour would therefore be secondary to domestic responsibilities and secondary to male involvement in the workforce. Such an argument overlooks the vital contribution that women's wages made to the household budgets in the GDR and the importance attached to paid labour by women in east Germany. As stated above, the majority of east German women would be unwilling to give up work even if they did not need the money.

Research undertaken in the old GDR, however, indicated that many women with families certainly did want to work shorter hours. The demands of housework, family and full-time work along with the pressure to become involved in political and social activities put a great strain on women. The present decrease in women's participation in the labour force, the expected growth of part-time labour and the decline of female labour must therefore be considered within this context. Part-time labour may be a compromise solution to women's problems of combining work and family. However, representatives of employment offices indicate that the majority of east German women are looking for full and not part-time work. Women may ideally want to spend more time with their children but they do not seem willing to loosen voluntarily their "foothold" in the labour market and to lose the income provided by full-time work.

Demographic trends

One result of the unification of Germany has been a dramatic fall in the east German birth rate. In part the decline is the result of the migration of many young people to the west and the fall in the number of women reaching child-bearing age due to the introduction of the contraceptive pill in the 1960s. The fall in the number of babies born is, however, an expression of insecurity amongst both men and women about their economic position. Increasing unemployment and growing fears about the long-term possibilities of women being able to combine full-time work and family have caused many people to regard children as a luxury they cannot afford. According to a survey of local authorities and women's clinics in the new German states the birthrate has fallen by half in the last two years. For example, in Mecklenburg-West Pomerania the number of babies born fell constantly from October 1989 to September 1991. In the last quarter of 1989 over 6,000 children were born in the state; in the third quarter of 1991, however, scarcely more than 3,300. This tendency is representative of all areas of the former GDR.

The number of sterilizations in the new *Länder* has sharply increased. Reports indicate that in some areas sterilization has become the most common form of contraception. In some clinics where previously only two to three sterilizations were undertaken a year there are now three to four per day. As sterilization in the GDR was only allowed under medical direction and was relatively uncommon, the increase is partly the result of a backlog of women wishing to be sterilized. However, one must also take into account that in all the new *Länder,* with the exception of Brandenburg, contraception is no longer available free of charge. Sterilization is therefore a cheaper alternative to other contraceptive methods.

The organization of women

The fall in the birthrate and the increased number of sterilizations indicates that women in the new *Länder* may not be as quick to embrace a life of increased domesticity as conservative circles would lead us to believe. In the political arena, however, there has been little organized protest on the part of women against the changes to their lives since unification. Although lack of protest could be taken as support for the changes, one must bear in mind certain fundamental factors which limit women's involvement in such protest.

Both men and women, as a result of the structure of the East German system, have little experience of organized social and political protest. Unfamiliarity with the workings of the western capitalist system and involvement in trade union and pressure group activities hinders resistance to the changes in progress. Moreover east German women have little experience of organizing themselves to campaign specifically for women's issues. Feminist movements and action were regarded by the east German state as essentially bourgeois. Moreover, criticism of the gender hierarchy in the GDR amounted to an attack upon the workings of the entire system. Thus, open criticism of patriarchal structures did not occur.

In addition to this, the gains which were awarded to women in the GDR were not the results of women's own organized struggle but given to them by a male-dominated state structure. As the provisions were not the result of their own protest the implications of the withdrawal of GDR legislation may not be fully perceived until it is too late. Finally, the demands made on women's time and energies by their responsibilities for domestic labour in the family unit mean that many find it difficult to become involved in political activities. Consequently lack of organized protest on the part of women does not necessarily signify that women welcome the changes under way.

Women's differing experiences

For the purposes of this paper the analysis of the effects of unification upon women has focused upon women as a homogeneous group. The influence of factors which divide women — age, marital status, social status, ethnicity, physical health — has not been included. The absence of this analysis should not, however, undermine the importance of such factors in the examination of women's post-unification position. It is necessary to bear in mind that the changes in the social, economic and political systems will affect different groups of women to varying extents.

Single mothers, in particular, face difficulties in the adjustment to the new practices in east Germany. In the GDR the number of single parents was extremely high; the divorce rate being one of the highest in the world. The last official count in 1981 indicated that single parents constituted 18 per cent of family forms, although only one in a hundred single parents was a man. The numbers of single mothers was increasing and it is estimated that at the time of the collapse of the GDR over 20 per cent of families were headed by only one parent, namely the mother. In urban areas, particularly in east Berlin, the numbers are estimated as even higher. The existence of special legislation to assist single parents to continue participation in full-time employment meant that single parenthood was a viable option. Single parent families were not always the result of divorce or separations; in many cases women had chosen to have a child alone. Increased financial independence created through involvement in the labour market, combined with the support of the state meant that women were not dependent upon a partner for economic support.

The GDR was not, however, a paradise for single parents. Families with only one adult working member often had a lower standard of living as a result of only one wage coming into the household. Single parents also suffered isolation, having less time and opportunity to take part in leisure and social activities outside of the home. Moreover, despite the state's support of single parents, the nuclear family with two parents was still seen and promoted as the ideal and desired family form. Women choosing to bring up children alone often intended or hoped to settle with a partner later in life. Since unification, single mothers in the new Federal states must deal with additional difficulties. With the removal of GDR legislation, high unemployment and the erosion of state-provided community childcare facilities, the vast majority of single mothers is facing particular financial hardship. In the GDR, for instance, child maintenance money was guaranteed for each child until it was 18 years old. The west German regulations now in force in the new *Länder* guarantees maintenance contributions only up until the child's sixth year and for a maximum of 36 months. Single mothers' economic difficulties are compounded by their greater susceptibility to unemployment. Already by the end of September 1991 approximately one in six of single mothers were out of work. With the closure and rationalization of east German firms the array of social provisions and facilities attached to the workplace have also disappeared. A worker's social life often revolved around the workplace and fellow employees. Consequently the loss of access to "in-firm" leisure activities and social networks is felt by many east Germans, not least by single parents. It is important to remember that growing unemployment not only results in increasing financial hardship but also the collapse of networks of communication. Single parents, in particular, not only face worse material conditions in the post-unification phase but increased isolation and loneliness.

Conclusion

Analysis of women's position in the labour market up to January 1992 indicates that in the short-term the unification process and the initial transitional economic difficulties are having more adverse effects on women than on men. The greater susceptibility of women to unemployment and their difficulties in finding new work signify a long-term trend which will disproportionately reduce the number of women in paid employment in the new *Länder*.

The introduction of market economic forces and west German structures and practices in the new *Länder* means that female wage labour must now meet different demands. The conditions shaping women's employment have changed. In the GDR women's labour market participation was particularly influenced by the shortage of labour and concern over the birthrate. Consequently the state provided conditions for women to take part in the workforce on a full-time basis. In the new *Länder* a surplus of labour exists. Excess labour supplies, together with the trend towards more flexible work methods, provide the environment for the growth of individualized childcare methods and the more restricted involvement of women in the labour market. The identification of women with the domestic sphere combined with the present economic conditions will lead to the increased marginalization of women workers in the labour force. Women will increasingly have to make the choice between career and children. Decreases in the number of childcare places will limit women's availability to take part in the labour market. Consequently there will be a decline in the number of women of child-rearing age in full-time employment. The exclusion of many women from paid employment, the expansion of part-time labour and the increased individualization of childcare will all contribute to undermine women's economic independence.

III REFERENCE SECTION

DIRECTORY OF GERMAN REUNIFICATION

This directory lists the people, parties, organizations, institutions, places and terms which have played a notable part in the events of 1989-92. There is a bias throughout towards developments in the former GDR, since information on the old Federal Republic is more readily available elsewhere. The length of an entry does not, therefore, automatically correspond to its wider significance. In the descriptions of the German *Länder*, for instance, the towns listed are those of over 50,000 population in east Germany, but of over 100,000 in west Germany.

Bold face indicates a cross-reference to another entry.

Abbreviations: ch. = chairman/chairwoman; dep. = deputy; g.s. = general secretary; hon. = honorary; pres. = president; sec. = secretary.

Abwicklung (winding up). A term used to describe the closing down of enterprises and institutions and the dismissal of employees in the former GDR.

Alliance for Germany (*Allianz für Deutschland*). An electoral alliance formed in February 1990 by the **Christian Democratic Union** (CDU), **German Social Union** (DSU) and **Democratic Awakening** (DA) to fight the March election. It proved a means by which the West German CDU could balance support for its block party namesake with the potential of the new right-of-centre parties. The Alliance won 48.0 per cent of the vote and nearly half the seats in the **Volkskammer**, but most of the success belonged to the CDU. After the election the CDU prime minister Lothar **de Maizière** kept his promise to include his Alliance partners in government by appointing one DA and two DSU ministers, but they soon left those parties to become independent or to join the CDU. DA merged with the CDU in August 1990.

Alliance 90 (*Bündnis 90*). An electoral alliance formed in February 1990 by non-party citizens' groups **New Forum, Democracy Now** and the **Peace and Human Rights Initiative**. In the March election it performed disappointingly, with only 2.9 per cent of the vote and 12 seats in the *Volkskammer*. Its share of the vote fell back even further in the local elections in May. Increasingly Alliance 90 co-operated with the east German **Greens**, and improved upon its early electoral setbacks in the October elections to the east German *Landtage* and in the *Bundestag* election in December 1990. In the latter, in alliance with the Greens, it won 5.9 per cent of the vote and eight seats, and was, like the **Party of Democratic Socialism** (PDS), accorded "group" but not "fraction" status. It also won 11 seats in the **Berlin** House of Representatives. The membership of Alliance 90 in 1991 was approximately 2,000. In May 1992 Alliance 90 decided to unite with the Greens within a year, in order to improve the prospects of both in the 1994 *Bundestag* election.

Alternative List (*Alternative Liste* — AL). The electoral list in (West) **Berlin** corresponding to the **Greens** elsewhere in Germany and representing environmentalist and "alternative" politics. From January 1989, when it scored 11.8 per cent of the vote, to November 1990 the AL was in uneasy coalition with the **SPD** in the government of West Berlin, but then the issue of squatters' rights caused the AL to withdraw. In the election to the House of Representatives in December 1990 the AL's vote in west Berlin fell to 6.9 per cent, and — in competition with the **Alliance 90**/Greens list — it picked up only a 1.7 per cent share in the eastern part of the city. In elections in both Berlin and **Hamburg** the list often campaigns as the Greens — Alternative List (*Grüne — Alternative Liste* — GAL).

Alternative Youth List (*Alternative Jugendliste* — AJL). An electoral alliance of youth groups which stood in the March 1990 election to the **Volkskammer**. It included the Marxist Youth Association, the United Young Left, the Green Youth, and — most importantly — the **Free German Youth** (FDJ). This last was the youth organization dominated by the ruling **Socialist Unity Party**, and had been led in the past by both Erich **Honecker** and Egon **Krenz**. It had undergone reformist changes during the autumn of 1989 and its leader Eberhard Aurich had been replaced by Frank Törkowsky. He in turn was replaced in 1990 by Birgit Schröder. In the election the AJL achieved 14,615 votes, and it and the FDJ ceased to be of any significance.

Association of Working Groups for Employee Politics and Democracy (*Vereinigung der Arbeitskreise für Arbeitnehmerpolitik und Demokratie* — VAA). The party with the longest name and the lowest number of votes (380) in the March 1990 election.

Baader-Meinhof gang. See **Red Army Faction** (*Rote Armee Fraktion* — RAF).

Baden-Württemberg. *Population*. 9.46 million. *Area*. 35,751 sq km. *Capital*. Stuttgart. *Other cities*. Freiburg, Heidelberg, Heilbronn, Karlsruhe, Mannheim, Pforzheim, Reutlingen, Ulm. *Minister president*. Erwin Teufel (CDU). The south-westernmost *Land* of the Federal Republic, formed in 1951 from the previous *Länder* of Baden, Württemberg-Baden and Württemberg-Hohenzollern. Its main economic sectors are computers, motor cars (Mercedes Benz), aerospace, commercial services, agriculture and wine, and it had the reputation as the *Land* with the most dynamic economy of the old Federal Republic. Baden-Württemberg has long been dominated by the CDU, which in 1991–92 faced serious reversals. First, in January 1991 its prominent Minister President, Lothar Späth, was forced to resign over an expenses scandal. Then, in the April 1992 elections the CDU lost this last remaining west German *Land* where it had enjoyed an absolute parliamentary majority. Worse still, the extreme right **Republicans** took 10.9 per cent of the vote, primarily (but by no means solely) from the CDU.

Bavaria, Free State of (*Freistaat Bayern*). *Population*. 11.07 million. *Area*. 70,554 sq km. *Capital*. Munich (München). *Other cities*. Augsburg, Erlangen, Ingolstadt, Nuremberg (Nürnberg), Regensburg, Würzburg. *Minister president*. Max Streibl (CSU). By area the largest of the *Länder* in the old and in the new Federal Republic, Bavaria has a long history as a state. In its current form it derives from the post-Napoleonic settlement, but has since lost the Rhine Palatinate and gained Coburg. It was refounded after the demise of the Third *Reich*. Bavaria's economic strengths include agriculture, brewing, tourism, engineering and motor cars (BMW). Post-war Bavaria has been a political fiefdom of the **Christian Social Union** (CSU), associated for most of the period with the person of Franz Josef Strauss, who died in 1988. The CSU has declined electorally from its peak in 1974, but in October 1990 it retained its absolute majority in the *Landtag*.

Berghofer, Wolfgang (b. Bautzen, February 25, 1943), mayor of Dresden (SED), 1986–90. Berghofer was an associate of Hans **Modrow**, party secretary of the Dresden district, and in October 1989 he showed himself prepared to talk to opposition groups about the growing crisis. After **Krenz**'s fall, Berghofer became a deputy chairman of the **SED-PDS**, but he and a group of 39 associates resigned from the party on January 21, 1990. On May 23, 1990 Herbert Wagner of the **CDU** replaced Berghofer as mayor of Dresden. Berghofer then faced charges of electoral fraud in connection with the local elections of May 1989, and these he admitted in January 1992.

Bergmann-Pohl, Sabine (b. Eisenach, April 20, 1946), president of the *Volkskammer* (**CDU**), April–October 1990. A medical doctor who had been a member of the **CDU** since 1981, Sabine Bergmann-Pohl was propelled into prominence by being elected president of the *Volkskammer* on April 5, 1990. Acting head of state, she undertook a reconciliatory visit to Israel in June 1990 in the company of *Bundestag* president Rita Süssmuth (also CDU). Bergmann-Pohl entered the *Bundestag* after German unity, and joined Chancellor **Kohl**'s cabinet as minister without portfolio. She was elected on the CDU *Land* list for **Berlin** in December 1990, but did not receive a post in Kohl's reshuffled cabinet. Instead she became a state secretary in the Ministry of Health. In 1991 she published her memoirs as *Abschied ohne Tränen: Rückblick auf das Jahr der Einheit* (Departure without Tears: a Look Back at the Year of Unity).

Berlin. *Population.* 3.42 million (1991). *Area.* 883 sq km. *Governing mayor.* Eberhard **Diepgen** (CDU). Berlin, founded in the 13th century, was the capital city of Prussia and of the German *Reich* and has since October 3, 1990 been the capital of the Federal Republic of Germany. The city suffered devastating bomb damage in the latter stages of the Second World War. From 1945 it was under the control of Soviet, American, British and French forces, which each had their respective sectors of the city. "Berlin — Capital of the GDR" was the designation used in the GDR for East Berlin, the Soviet sector of Greater Berlin. It was not recognized as the capital city by the Western powers, nor in principle by the West German government. In practice, as the seat of government and administration, it adopted such a role. In return, the GDR and the USSR did not recognize West Berlin as part of the Federal Republic of Germany. Berlin was a bone of contention between the three Western powers and the USSR from the time it was occupied. The first Berlin crisis occurred in 1948, when the Soviet forces responded to currency reform in the Western zones of Germany by sealing off water and road routes to West Berlin, in an attempt to prevent the foundation of a separate West German state. The Western allies replied with a massive transport of food and fuel through the air corridors to West Berlin, which lasted until May 1949.

As a result of Walter Ulbricht's attempt to stem the flow of emigrants from the GDR, from August 13, 1961 until November 9, 1989 the Berlin Wall divided East from West Berlin. Passage in either direction was only via recognized border points. For GDR citizens permission to cross was hard to obtain; those who attempted to do so without permission risked being shot on sight. On the night of November 9, 1989 the Wall and the entire inter-German border was opened for GDR citizens to travel freely. With the signing of the **Two-Plus-Four** treaty and German unity from October 1990, the control of Berlin under the 1971 Four Power Agreement was superseded. The unification treaty specified that Berlin is now the capital of the Federal Republic, but it was not until June 1991 that the *Bundestag* by a narrow majority voted to return the seat of government and parliament to the city. The process is forecast to be a long and expensive one, involving a massive building programme. At the same time a large sports complex north of the centre of east Berlin is planned to support Berlin's bid to host the Olympic Games in the year 2000. Berlin is currently governed by a "grand coalition" of the **CDU** and **SPD**.

BFD (*Bund Freier Demokraten — Die Liberalen*). See **League of Free Democrats — The Liberals**.

Biedenkopf, Kurt (b. Ludwigshafen, Bavarian Palatinate, now **Rhineland-Palatinate**, January 28, 1930), Minister President of **Saxony** (CDU) from October 1990. Biedenkopf, who knew the territory of the GDR from school years in Merseburg in 1940–45, had already had a prominent career in academic life, industry and politics in the old Federal Republic before he involved himself in the affairs of the former GDR. He had been professor of law at the Ruhr University in Bochum (1964–70), general secretary of the **CDU** (1973–77), chairman of the CDU in Westphalia-Lippe, then **North Rhine-Westphalia** (1977–87) and member of the **Bundestag** (1976–84 and since 1987). In 1990 he became professor at the University of **Leipzig** and then in October 1990 he led the Saxon CDU to an overall majority in the *Landtag* elections.

Bohley, Bärbel (b. Berlin, May 24, 1945), co-founder of **New Forum**, September 1989. An artist and peace campaigner, Bohley came into conflict with the old GDR regime on several occasions. She was arrested in December 1983 and again in January 1988. Forced out of the country, she argued successfully to be allowed to return. In the autumn of 1989 she was a co-founder of New

Forum, the initial impact of which subsided as calls for German unity increased in the GDR. She remained critical of rapid union and the introduction of capitalism.

Böhme, Ibrahim (b. Heimen, **Saxony**, November 18, 1944 [?]), chairman of the **SPD** in the GDR, February–March 1990. Brought up in an orphanage, Böhme followed a variety of jobs and professions. He joined the **SED** in 1967, but left in 1976 in protest at the expulsion of singer Wolf Biermann. In the autumn of 1989 he was a co-founder of the **SDP** (later **SPD**) and took part in the **Round Table** discussions. In February 1990 he was elected SPD chairman, and looked a prospective prime minister as the SPD initially rode high in the opinion polls. The **CDU** was nevertheless victorious, and Böhme's defeat was compounded a week after the elections by accusations that he had been a *Stasi* informer. He temporarily laid down his party posts and *Volkskammer* seat, pending investigations. Although these initially showed no proof of his complicity, Böhme's position was irretrievably weakened and his health suffered. He resigned from the party leadership in April and from the party executive in December.

Bonn. *Population.* 290,000 (1991). A university city in western Germany south of Cologne, the birthplace of Beethoven and the capital of the Federal Republic of Germany from 1949 to October 2, 1990. The *Bundestag* and the Federal government still reside in Bonn, but in June 1991 the *Bundestag* voted by a narrow majority to move the seat of government to the new Federal capital, **Berlin**. The cost of the transition means that it is unlikely to be complete until after the turn of the century.

Brandenburg. *Population.* 2.61 million. *Area.* 29,059 sq km. *Capital.* Potsdam. *Other cities.* Brandenburg, Cottbus, Eberswalde-Finow, Eisenhüttenstadt, Frankfurt an der Oder, Schwedt. *Minister president.* Manfred Stolpe (SPD). One of the new *Länder* of the Federal Republic, comprising most of the pre-1933 Prussian province of Brandenburg, to the limit of the Oder-Neisse line, but excluding the city of **Berlin**. A province in 1945 and a *Land* from 1947, it was effectively abolished in 1952 and divided up into the districts of Potsdam, Frankfurt an der Oder and Cottbus. It was reconstituted by the *Volkskammer* law of July 22, 1990. The economic base of Brandenburg is varied, with a substantial agricultural sector alongside such industries as lignite mining (Cottbus district), chemicals (Frankfurt an der Oder) and metallurgy (Eisenhüttenstadt). Brandenburg is the only one of the east German *Länder* with an SPD-led coalition government, but minister president **Stolpe** has come under fire for his admitted contacts with the *Stasi*. Another matter of debate has been whether Brandenburg and Berlin should combine to form one *Land*. It has even been suggested in some quarters that in such an event the name of Prussia (abolished as a state in 1947) should be revived.

Bremen, Free Hanseatic City of (*Freie Hansestadt Bremen*). *Population.* 662,300. *Area.* 404 sq km. *Capital.* Bremen. *Other city.* Bremerhaven. *Mayor.* Klaus Wedemeier (SPD). The smallest of the three city states of Germany and indeed the smallest of all the *Länder*, Bremen was refounded as a *Land* in 1947. Comprising two separate territories, it was a United States occupation zone. Dominated by its docks, Bremen has undergone economic problems in recent years, especially in the shipbuilding sector. The *Land* election of September 1991 saw gains by the extreme right **German People's Union** (DVU).

Breuel, Birgit (née Münchmeyer, b. Hamburg, 1937), Executive President of the *Treuhandanstalt* (Trust Agency) since April 1991. The murder of Detlev **Rohwedder** necessitated finding a replacement for him as head of the *Treuhandanstalt*, and the choice fell upon Birgit Breuel, already one of his deputies. Having studied in Hamburg, Oxford and Geneva, Breuel joined the **CDU** in 1966 and she was elected to the **Hamburg** parliament in 1970. In 1976 she became economic spokesperson for the CDU and in 1978 she was appointed Minister of Economics and Transport in the government of **Lower Saxony**. She moved to the post of Finance Minister in 1986, remaining there until 1990. Her other experience includes the presidency of the board of the Hanover industrial fair and membership of several major company boards (Volkswagen, Norddeutsche Landesbank and Salzgitter). When she took over the *Treuhandanstalt* she applied to the task the energy and toughness for which she had acquired a reputation, and she emphasized even more than before under Rohwedder that the primary task of the *Treuhandanstalt* was to sell off east German industry as quickly and efficiently as possible.

Bundesbank (Federal Bank). See ***Deutsche Bundesbank*** (German Federal Bank).

Bundesrat (Federal Council — second parliamentary chamber). The *Bundesrat*, although a Federal institution, is the means by which the interests of the *Länder* are represented. Its approval is essential for the passage of laws affecting the *Länder* and it does have other rights of intervention. It is not directly elected, but comprises since German unity 68 nominees from the *Land* governments. The number of nominees from each *Land* roughly reflects the size of its population, the range being between three and six. In May 1990 the election in **Lower Saxony** gave a *Bundesrat* majority to the **SPD**, and this posed a potential difficulty for Chancellor **Kohl**'s proposals for the timing and nature of German unity. He had to ensure that the SPD would not block him in the *Bundesrat*. In the event there was no major problem and with the accession of the eastern *Länder* in October the **CDU** was once more in the majority. However, in April 1991 Kohl's home state of **Rhineland-Palatinate** was lost to the SPD, which thereby regained a 37 to 31 majority in the *Bundesrat*.

German unity has posed many problems for the federal nature of the state, which are expressed in the *Bundesrat*. There are questions of the equitable treatment of the *Länder* (implying financial transfers from west to east) and of relations with the European Community. In March 1992 the SPD threatened to block ratification of the Maastricht treaties if concessions to the *Länder* were not made. However, the SPD nominees do not always act in unison. In February 1992 **Brandenburg**'s representatives broke ranks to approve a VAT increase, because of the financial needs of the east.

Bundestag (Federal Diet — first parliamentary chamber). The *Bundestag* is the elected representation of the German people and the supreme organ of the Federal state. Its composition derives from proportional representation, with half its members elected for constituencies and the other half determined by the electors' second vote for party lists. However, to acquire seats in the *Bundestag* a party must achieve 5 per cent of the national vote or victory in three constituencies. This provision was introduced in order to prevent small, especially extremist parties from gaining a parliamentary foothold as they had done in the Weimar Republic. Before German reunification there were between 496 and 499 *Bundestag* seats (the number fluctuated slightly according to constituency wins) plus 22 (West) **Berlin** representatives nominated by the city government who had only observer status. In October 1990 the former east German *Volkskammer* added 144 delegates to the *Bundestag*, based on the relative strength of the parties in the last GDR elections. In December 1990 all-German elections to the *Bundestag* were held for the first time, with the result that the number in the chamber swelled to 662. The party composition was: **CDU** 270, **CSU** 49, **SPD** 239, **FDP** 79, **Alliance 90/Greens** eight, and **PDS** 17. This election was exceptionally based on separate electoral territories for east and west Germany, with a separate 5 per cent electoral hurdle in each. This was ordered by the Consitutional Court in order to give a chance to the native east German parties, but will not apply in future elections.

Bundeswehr (Federal Armed Forces). The *Bundeswehr*, including army, navy and airforce, comprised before German unification nearly 500,000 men and women, of whom nearly half were young male conscripts performing national service (civilian service is also an option). In addition there were about 176,000 civilian employees. Practically all of the *Bundeswehr* is under NATO command and under article 26 of the Basic Law it cannot wage aggressive war. It is also not to be deployed outside the NATO area and under the Paris Treaties of 1954 it cannot have nuclear weapons, although such weapons have been stationed on west German soil. Political control of the *Bundeswehr* lies with the Minister of Defence (in 1992 Volker Rühe of the **CDU**), and in periods of emergency or war with the Federal Chancellor. The *Bundestag* appoints an Armed Forces Commissioner (*Wehrbeauftragter*) to investigate complaints from members of the *Bundeswehr* and to report annually to the *Bundestag*.

The collapse of the GDR and the Warsaw Treaty Organization and the unification of Germany have presented the *Bundeswehr* with new challenges. In October 1990 it took over the army and all other forces of the GDR (see **National People's Army**, *Nationale Volksarmee* — NVA). This meant an additional 90,000 soldiers, 17,000 border troops, 47,000 civilian employees, 10,000 tanks and armoured vehicles, 2,500 artillery pieces, 400 fighter aircraft, 100,000 vehicles, 1.2 million firearms, more than 300,000 tonnes of ammunition, and all the land and buildings of the NVA. In order to cope with the change a new *Bundeswehr* Command East was established. Serving soldiers were investigated to see if they were suitable for further deployment (more than 20,000 former NVA soldiers applied to join the *Bundeswehr*), and decisions were taken to use or to abandon weapon systems and military installations. Less than half are to be kept. In July 1991 the *Bundeswehr* Command East was dismantled in order to accommodate the eastern forces in the standard command structure of the *Bundeswehr* (army, navy and airforce).

The war against Iraq in early 1991 placed the *Bundeswehr* in a difficult position. Troops could not be deployed directly because they would be outside the NATO area, but the German absence from the fighting occasioned some ill-informed criticism abroad. The Federal government tried to compensate by providing financial assistance to the war effort.

Carnations, The (*Die Nelken*). *Foundation*. December 1989/January 1990. *Leadership*. Brigitte Kahlwald (ch.); Michael Czollek (dep. ch.); Rainer Bartscher (dep. ch.). *History*. This small Marxist party came into being in the winter of 1989/90, holding its founding congress on January 13, 1990 in East **Berlin**. It tried to mobilize communists who had formerly been in the **Socialist Unity Party** (SED) or not in any party. Having originally been in close contact with the **United Left** (VL), the Carnations in February joined with it in an alliance to fight the March 1990 election. Between them they won less than 0.2 per cent of the vote and only one seat in the *Volkskammer*. *Programme*. Seeing themselves in the political tradition of the murdered early German communists, Rosa Luxemburg and Karl Liebknecht, the Carnations sought a new form of socialism in the GDR. They did countenance a form of market economy, but with worker participation in decision-making and within a socially determined general plan. They rejected a capitalist annexation of the GDR by the Federal Republic, which would bring mass unemployment and poverty.

CDU (*Christlich-Demokratische Union Deutschlands*). See **Christian Democratic Union of Germany**.

Christian Democratic Social Union (*Christlich-Demokratische Soziale Union* — CDSU). One of the 12 groups which formed the **German Social Union** (DSU) in January 1990.

Christian Democratic Union of Germany (*Christlich-Demokratische Union Deutschlands* — CDU). *Addresses*. Konrad-Adenauer Haus, Friedrich-Ebert-Allee 73-75, W-5300 Bonn 1; Postfach 1316, Jakob-Kaiser-Haus, Charlottenstrasse 53-4, O-1080 Berlin. *Foundation*. 1945 (in Soviet occupation zone); 1950 (in Federal Republic of Germany); merged October 1990. *Membership*. In 1991: 757,000 (including 111,000 in east Germany). *Leadership*. Dr Helmut **Kohl** (ch.); Peter Hintze (g.s.). *Former GDR leadership*. Gerald Götting (ch. 1966–89); Lothar **de Maizière** (ch. November 1989–October 1990).
History. The CDU in the GDR was one of the Democratic Block or National Front parties in alliance with the ruling **Socialist Unity Party** (SED). It was founded in July 1945 as a party to represent the Christian middle class, and was broadly equivalent to its West German counterpart. From 1947, however, under the leadership of Otto Nuschke, it entered into political alliance with the SED, and served to organize those career-minded Christians who had not chosen or not been chosen to join the SED itself. In the old GDR parliament the CDU had a number of seats (52) decided in advance by an allocation on the unified election list. The membership of the CDU in the GDR was at its height at the end of 1947 with 218,000. By the early 1960s only one-third was left (70,000), but after that the party grew steadily to 140,000 in 1987. This was a process encouraged by the SED, which determined membership of the block parties.

The relationship of the CDU with the churches in the GDR was not always a happy one. Although claiming to represent "socialist state citizens of Christian belief", the CDU came to symbolize compromise with the state rather more than defence of the Christian churches. When in the 1980s dissident groups protesting about militarism, nuclear weapons and pollution based themselves on the churches, the CDU became even more remote.

In November 1989 Gerald Götting was forced to resign as chairman and he was replaced by the lawyer and musician, Lothar de Maizière, who had not previously been active in the leadership. The party went through a period of crisis as it terminated its membership of the Democratic Block in December but remained in government with the SED. At a special party congress also in December the CDU rejected socialism and professed itself in favour of democratization and Germany unity. Its position at this stage was precarious, however, because it was open to charges of complicity in the old regime, and it faced electoral competition from both the newly founded **Social Democratic Party** (SPD) and from other parties on the right. When the **German Social Union** (DSU) was founded in January 1990 some CDU politicians in west Germany considered allying with the new party rather than with the eastern CDU.

However, a better solution was found with the formation in February 1990 of the **Alliance for Germany**, comprising the CDU, the DSU and **Democratic Awakening** (DA). With a massive input of west German CDU electoral campaigning and generous promises on the part of Chancellor Kohl, the Alliance scored a remarkable victory in the March elections. The CDU was the principle winner, with 40.8 per cent of the vote and 163 of the 400 seats in the *Volkskammer*. It performed particularly well in the southern parts of the GDR. Lothar de Maizière, who had been deputy prime minister with responsibility for church affairs in the last Modrow cabinet, formed a coalition government on April 9, 1990.

The succeeding months were then dominated by the negotiations towards first economic then political union between the two German republics. De Maizière was often depicted in the press as being under the thumb of Chancellor Kohl, but he did show initiative on occasions. In early August he embarrassed Kohl by revealing their intention (soon thwarted) to bring forward the first all-German elections, and in the middle of the same month he struck out at his coalition partners. He sacked several of his ministers and pushed the SPD out of the coalition.

The CDU had its own problems. In mid-August 1990 the general secretary of the party in the GDR, Martin **Kirchner**, was removed from office on suspicion of having collaborated with the *Stasi* (state security). There also remained the question of CDU property in the GDR, although in December 1989 the party had handed it over to the *Treuhandanstalt* (Trust Agency). Meanwhile, despite the accession to the CDU of first the **Democratic Farmers' Party** (DBD) in June and then DA in August, the membership was falling sharply, bringing the total in mid-1991 down to around 80,000. Thereafter it has grown to an estimated 111,000.

On October 1, 1990 the CDU of the GDR joined that of the Federal Republic. Following German unity two days later de Maizière became a deputy chairman of the federal CDU and a minister without portfolio in the Kohl cabinet. The united party then scored further electoral triumphs in the east German *Landtag* elections, in the elections to the **Berlin** House of Representatives, and in the elections to the new *Bundestag*. Chancellor Kohl formed a new coalition government in January 1991 of CDU, **Christian Social Union** (CSU) and **Free Democratic Party** (FDP). De Maizière was not a member of it, since he had fallen victim to another *Stasi* scandal, but two other east German CDU politicians were, Günther **Krause** and Angela **Merkel**.

If 1990 was a year of triumph for the CDU, 1991 began badly. Kohl's government was forced to announce tax rises to pay for German unification and for the Gulf War, and this contributed to the electoral loss of Kohl's home state **Rhineland-Palatinate** to the **SPD** in April and to a poor showing in **Hamburg** in June. In that same month Günther Krause, Minister of Transport, for a while came under intense pressure to resign because of his alleged role in the granting of motorway services franchises in the month before German unification. He survived, but so did the tensions between the eastern and western wings of the party. In late 1991 and early 1992 the CDU had mixed electoral fortunes, but the loss of its last remaining absolute *Landtag* majority in **Baden-Württemberg** in April was a bitter blow.

Organization. The CDU of the former GDR has now become part of the existing structure of the CDU in the Federal Republic. This comprises the federal party, the parties in the *Länder*, the district associations, and the local associations. The federal party congress, consisting of delegates from the *Länder* parties, normally meets every two years to decide policy and to elect the party chairman and the federal executive committee. A larger federal committee concerns itself with party matters between party congresses. In addition the CDU has eight associations for youth, women, employees, local government, small business and professional people, the economy, expellees and refugees, and the elderly.

Programme. The 1982 programme of the CDU in the GDR stressed Christian responsibility and democratic obligations. The bases of Christian Democratic thought and action were "loyalty to socialism, confident co-operation with the party of the working class ... and friendship with the Soviet Union". The CDU of the Federal Republic, of which the CDU of the former GDR is now a part, describes itself as a "broadly-based classless party amalgamating traditions of Christian social thinking, liberalism and modern conservatism". The CDU is broadly Christian and not tied to any one confession, but the accession of the GDR party has increased its Protestant component. Economically, the CDU is pledged to the social market economy, but has now adopted an ecological perspective as well.

Affiliations. **Alliance for Germany** (in the GDR from February 1990). Christian Democratic International; European Christian Democratic Union; European People's Party; European Democrat Union; International Democrat Union.

Christian League — The Party for Life (*Christliche Liga — Die Partei für das Leben*). *Foundation.* February 24, 1990. *Leadership.* Rudolf Taken. A small Christian party based in the south of **Saxony** which gained 10,691 votes (0.09 per cent) in the March 1990 elections to the *Volkskammer*. Its emphasis was on the family and the environment, and it had links with a party of the same name in **Baden-Württemberg**.

Christian Social Association (*Christlich-Soziale Vereinigung*). One of the 12 groups which formed the **German Social Union** (DSU) in January 1990.

Christian Social Party of Germany (*Christlich-Soziale Partei Deutschlands — CSPD*). One of the 12 groups which formed the **German Social Union** (DSU) in January 1990.

Christian Social Union (*Christlich-Soziale Union — CSU*). Founded in Leipzig in January 1990, the CSU was one of the 12 groups which formed the **German Social Union** (DSU) later that month. Imitative of, but not to be confused with the **CSU** in Bavaria (see next entry).

Christian Social Union in Bavaria (*Christlich-Soziale Union in Bayern — CSU*). *Address.* Nymphenburger Str. 64, W-8000 Munich 2. *Foundation.* 1945, remaining independent when **Christian Democratic Union** (CDU) founded 1950. *Membership.* 185,000 (1991). *Leadership.* Theo **Waigel** (ch.); Erwin Huber (g.s.). The principal party of the right in **Bavaria**, the CSU has governed there since the foundation of the Federal Republic and has also formed a part of every CDU-led coalition government in **Bonn**. Its charismatic and controversial leader for many years was Franz Josef Strauss, who stood for the chancellorship in 1980 and died in 1988. In Bavarian local elections in March 1990 the CSU lost ground, but in the *Landtag* election the following October it held on to an only slightly reduced overall majority (54.9 per cent).

Communist Party of Germany (*Kommunistische Partei Deutschlands — KPD*). *Foundation.* 1918. Banned 1933–45. Refounded 1945. In Soviet occupation zone merged with **SPD** to form **SED** 1946. Refounded January 1990. *Membership.* 5,000 (March 1990). *Leadership.* Klaus Sbrzesny. *History.* The KPD as refounded in 1945 was the dominant partner in the merger with the **Social Democratic Party** (SPD) to form the **Socialist Unity Party** (SED) in 1946. In January 1990 an attempt was made to revitalize the idea of the KPD, in rejection of the SED, now the **Party of Democratic Socialism** (PDS). The intent was to organize "all honest Communists". The party was refounded in **Berlin**, and in February held a congress in Frankfurt an der Oder, attended by 100 delegates. Its members were reported to be mainly young people not previously attached to any party. The KPD explored links with the **Carnations**, the German Marxist Party and the **United Left** (but not with the PDS), but stood independently in the March 1990 election. It polled only 8,819 votes, less than 0.1 per cent of the total. *Programme.* Humanism, peace and disarmament, social justice, and social ownership as the dominant form of ownership. Opposition to the absorption of the GDR into the Federal Republic, but willingness to countenance unification in a pan-European context.

CSU (*Christlich-Soziale Union in Bayern*). See **Christian Social Union in Bavaria**.

DA (*Demokratischer Aufbruch*). See **Democratic Awakening**.

DBD (*Demokratische Bauernpartei Deutschlands*). See **Democratic Farmers' Party of Germany**.

De Maizière, Lothar (b. Nordhausen a. Harz, **Thuringia**, March 2, 1940), Prime Minister of the GDR (**CDU**), April–October 1990. In the space of five months Lothar de Maizière emerged from relative obscurity as a lawyer, musician and lay church leader to be the prime minister of the GDR in April 1990. His path to prominence depended on the autumn 1989 revolution and the election campaign and **CDU** victory in the spring of 1990. Born the son of a lawyer, de Maizière joined the CDU as early as 1956. He studied first music (becoming a professional viola player), then law. From 1976 he was a member of the council of lawyers' associations, moving up to become a deputy chairman in 1987. He was involved in the defence of dissidents, and during this period came to know well Gregor **Gysi**, later chairman of the **SED**. De Maizière was also active within the evangelical church, becoming a vice president of the synod in 1986.

The autumn of 1989 brought crisis to all the political parties of the GDR, and when the long-standing chairman of the CDU, Gerald Götting, was forced to resign, de Maizière was elected in his stead in November. He was considered to be relatively untainted by the CDU's collaboration with the SED. Also in November de Maizière was appointed to the new **Modrow** cabinet as a deputy prime minister with responsibility for church affairs. During the run-up to the March 1990 elections, de Maizière resisted demands from Chancellor **Kohl** that the CDU withdraw from co-operation with the **SED-PDS**. He did, however, take his party into the conservative **Alliance for Germany** with the **DSU** and **DA**. The election result, more of a triumph for Kohl than for de Maizière, nevertheless propelled the latter into the limelight. For several weeks he appeared undecided as to whether to aspire to the premiership himself. However, negotiations began with the **SPD** and the Liberals on a grand coalition, and when the *Volkskammer* met on April 5, 1990 de Maizière was charged with forming a government. He announced his cabinet four days later.

Up to that point his relations with Chancellor Kohl had not been marked by cordiality, and in the lead-in to German unity he pledged his party to defending vigorously the interests of the GDR population. Once in power, his co-operation with Kohl increased as the two prepared the way for first economic then full political union. His government laid the ground for the abandonment of the socialist structures of the GDR, but was beset by mounting economic chaos. In the summer of 1990 this exacerbated conflict within the coalition and led to trouble with Kohl as well. In early August de Maizière embarrassed Kohl by announcing that the two of them planned to bring all-German elections forward. This was thwarted by West German constitutional requirements. Later in the same month de Maizière purged his cabinet of all three ministers in charge of the economy (Finance, Economy and Agriculture), prompting the departure from the coalition of the SPD. De Maizière did not reappoint ministers and took over the Foreign Ministry himself from Markus **Meckel**.

With German unity, de Maizière's post became redundant, and he joined Kohl's cabinet as minister without portfolio. On December 2, 1990 he was elected to the *Bundestag* on the *Land* list for **Brandenburg** and might have expected high office in the new government had not the shadows of the past closed in once more. Even before he became GDR prime minister, de Maizière had been touched by the *Stasi* scandal which brought down two other party leaders, Wolfgang **Schnur** (DA) and Ibrahim **Böhme** (SPD). He was accused of having been a collaborator with the *Stasi* under the code-name "Czerny". He denied this vigorously and survived. However, shortly after the all-German elections, renewed allegations were made in the press and although there was no concrete proof, de Maizière felt compelled to withdraw from public life. On December 17, 1990 he resigned from government and as CDU deputy chairman. Chancellor Kohl continued to express trust in him, and after his name appeared to have been cleared once more de Maizière returned to party activity. However, as access to the *Stasi* files was increased the suggestion that he had been an informer gained credence once again and he resigned all his CDU party offices in September 1991.

Democracy Now (*Demokratie Jetzt* — DJ). *Foundation.* September 1989. *Membership.* 836 (September 1990). *Leadership.* Wolfgang Ullmann (spokesman; b. 1929; minister without portfolio February–March 1990); Konrad Weiss, Hans-Jürgen Fischbek, Ulrike Poppe (spokespersons). *History.* DJ, one of the foremost citizens' movements in the GDR during 1989–90, originated in church circles in protest against the falsified election results of May 1989. It began on September 12, 1989 with the declaration of the "theses for a democratic restructuring in the GDR". A total of 15 of its leading members took part in the **Round Table** debates from December 1989 to March 1990. In February 1990 one of its leaders, the church historian Wolfgang Ullmann, joined **Modrow**'s "government of national responsibility" as a minister without portfolio. Konrad Weiss, a film director, joined the government commission responsible for drafting a new media law. Also in February DJ joined with **New Forum** and the **Peace and Human Rights Initiative** (IFM) to form the electoral pact, **Alliance 90**. This achieved a total vote of only 336,074 (2.9 per cent) and 12 seats in the *Volkskammer*.

DJ has never been a large organization. Registered membership never exceeded 1,000 and the broader circle of activists was at its height in the winter of 1989–90 only 3,000. Since then participation has fallen back significantly. DJ has been dominated by intellectuals in their late 30s and it fulfilled amongst the citizens' movements a theoretical and programmatic role. In December 1990 the paper *Demokratie Jetzt* was, in collaboration with IFM, retitled *Bündnis 2000*, and in January 1991 DJ formed a loose organizational liaison with IFM. DJ is represented in the *Bundestag* by Ullmann and Weiss.

Organization. DJ does not see itself as a political party, but as a citizens' movement. It has a central office in **Berlin** (shared with IFM), and offices in the east German *Länder*. It has also formed groups in **Bonn**, Frankfurt am Main and Cologne. *Programme.* A social and ecological market economy; democracy and the rule of law. DJ originally favoured a more gradual, three-stage path to German unity.

Democratic Awakening (*Demokratischer Aufbruch* — DA). *Foundation.* October/December 1989. Merged with **CDU** August 1990. *Membership.* Nil (55,000 in March 1990). *Leadership.* Wolfgang **Schnur** (ch. 1989–90); Rainer **Eppelmann** (ch. 1990; b. 1943; Minister for Defence and Disarmament 1990). *History.* DA had its origins in church circles in the summer of 1989, before the revolution itself in the GDR. An "initiative group" was formed in July, but a founding meeting was thwarted by the police on October 2. A delegates' meeting on October 29–30 provisionally constituted a party, which was then formally brought into being in **Leipzig** on December 16–17, 1989. The founders included the Rostock lawyer Wolfgang Schnur, the Berlin pastor Rainer Eppelmann, and the Wittenberg pastor Friedrich Schorlemmer. Schnur acted as chairman from October and was narrowly elected to that post in December. He, Eppelmann, Fred Ebeling and 13 others represented DA at the **Round Table** debates from December 1989 onwards.

The initial political location of the party was disputed, and — fearing a drift rightward — Schorlemmer took his Wittenberg group and other leading members of the party over to the **Social Democratic Party** (SPD) on January 18, 1990. Eppelmann became a minister without portfolio in the **Modrow** government of February 1990, and Schnur in the same month took DA into the **Alliance for Germany** with the **Christian Democratic Union** (CDU) and the **German Social Union** (DSU). However, on the eve of the March election Schnur was accused in the press of having in the past collaborated with the *Stasi* (state security). He strenuously denied this at first, alleging that he was the victim of a smear campaign. Under continuing pressure he admitted the charge and resigned on March 14, 1990. His successor, Eppelmann, failed in the short time available to undo the huge damage done to the party, and it achieved less than 1 per cent of the vote in the election and only 4 seats in the *Volkskammer*.

Eppelmann himself was made a minister in the **de Maizière** government. He insisted in the designation of his post that he was minister not just for defence but also for disarmament, but in a colourful period in office he continued to place arms orders for the **National People's Army** (NVA). The party meanwhile was disintegrating, and Eppelmann resigned from it to become an independent. In August 1990 DA merged with the CDU and by December 1990 Eppelmann was a CDU member of the *Bundestag* for a **Brandenburg** seat.

Programme. DA brought together a desire for German unity and the market economy with an insistence on social justice and environmental responsibility. It campaigned in the March 1990 election under the title "Democratic Awakening: social and ecological".

Democratic Farmers' Party of Germany (*Demokratische Bauernpartei Deutschlands* — DBD). *Foundation*. 1948. Merged with **CDU** June 1990. *Membership*. Nil (115,000 in 1987). *Leadership*. Günter Maleuda (ch. 1987-90; b. 1931; president of *Volkskammer* 1989–90). *History*. The DBD was one of the two parties in the GDR (the other being the **National Democratic Party**) which were set up at the instigation of the **Socialist Unity Party** (SED) to organize specific social groups. Founded in April 1948, the DBD was intended to draw the small peasantry and rural labourers into the communist sphere, and it played a crucial role in the collectivization of the late 1950s. It was one of the parties of the Democratic Block and the National Front, with 52 seats in the *Volkskammer*. It furnished government ministers, most recently Peter Diederich, who in the restructured **Modrow** government of February 1990 replaced his party colleague Hans Reichelt as Minister for Environmental Protection. In December 1989 the DBD chairman, Günter Maleuda, was elected president of the *Volkskammer*, narrowly defeating the expected victor, Manfred **Gerlach** of the **Liberal Democratic Party**.

The DBD's membership, like that of the other block parties, was rising from the mid-1970s, on SED encouragement. In 1987 it stood at 115,000. At the same time, however, the SED revived its interest in another organization for rural workers, the Union of Mutual Peasant Aid (*Vereinigung der gegenseitigen Bauernhilfe* — VdgB), as a means of infiltrating the SED into the agricultural sector. With about 425,000 members in 1984, the VdgB eclipsed the DBD, but in the revolution of 1989–90 the VdgB suffered a collapse of support because of its SED connections.

In the election of March 1990 the DBD took 251,226 votes (2.2 per cent of the total) and nine seats in the *Volkskammer*. As the economic crisis began to hit GDR agriculture hard in the spring of 1990, the protests of farmers grew and other small agricultural groups and parties were formed. The DBD united with these for the local elections in May and registered a marked improvement on its March result, 5.7 per cent of the vote. The DBD was losing members, however, and failing to find a distinctive new role to play in the transformed system. In June 1990 it merged with the **Christian Democratic Union** (CDU).

Programme. According to the party statute of 1987, "The DBD sees its most important obligation as being to help develop, advance and consolidate the alliance between the working class and the class of co-operative farmers". By February 1990 the DBD programme favoured democracy, a single statehood of the German nation in the framework of a peaceful Europe, and an ecologically-oriented socially just market economy. It continued to represent all those who worked on the land.

Democratic Women's League of Germany (*Demokratischer Frauenbund Deutschlands* — DFD). *Foundation*. 1947. *Membership*. 1,441,375 (1982). The "mass organization" for women under the old regime in the GDR, and therefore represented in the **Volkskammer**. In the March 1990 election the DFD won some 38,000 votes, 0.33 per cent of the vote, and one seat. It improved its performance in the May local elections to 1.24 per cent, but thereafter was of little significance.

Deutsche Bundesbank (German Federal Bank). *Address*. Wilhelm-Epstein-Strasse 14, W-6000 Frankfurt am Main 50. *President*. Helmut Schlesinger. *Deputy president*. Hans Tietmeyer. The *Bundesbank*, founded in 1957 in fulfilment of article 88 of the Basic Law of the Federal Republic, is the sole issuing bank in Germany. Its remit further includes the regulation of circulation, the supply and control of credit, the setting of prime interest rates, the regulation of minimum reserve levels in other banks, and the sale and repurchase of fixed-interest stock on behalf of state institutions. Profits from its foreign exchange dealings accrue to the Federal government, but the bank is meant to act as an autonomous body. This separation of government and central bank was intended to safeguard the currency against political interference and to prevent a recurrence of the hyper-inflation which Germany experienced in the early 1920s when the *Reichsbank* was in charge. However, the process of German unity brought into question the real autonomy of the *Bundesbank*. In early 1990 its then president, Karl Otto **Pöhl**, tried to argue against the exchange rates of GDR Mark:Deutschemark being proposed by Chancellor **Kohl**, on the grounds that they might threaten the Deutschemark, increase inflation and wreak havoc in the east German economy. The currency has weakened only slightly and inflation has not soared, but Pöhl's last prediction has proved accurate. In May 1991 Pöhl announced that he was retiring early for personal reasons, but the conflict over the currency and the murder of Detlev **Rohwedder**, president of the *Treuhandanstalt*, no doubt played their part in his decision. He was succeeded by Helmut Schlesinger, who will, it is assumed, give way on his retirement to his deputy, Hans Tietmeyer.

Diepgen, Eberhard (b. Berlin, November 13, 1941), Governing Mayor of Berlin (CDU), 1984–89 and from January 1991. A lawyer by profession, Diepgen joined the **CDU** in 1962 and was elected to the Berlin House of Representatives in 1971. In 1984 he took over as Governing Mayor when Richard von **Weizsäcker** left the post for that of Federal President. In January 1989 Diepgen was defeated by Walter **Momper (SPD)**, who formed a coalition with the **Alternative List**. The coalition collapsed in November 1990 and Diepgen's CDU was the victor in a united Berlin in the elections the following month. The results led to a grand coalition of CDU and SPD under Diepgen's leadership. He made a point of moving his office to the town hall in east Berlin, known popularly as the Red Town Hall (from its colour, not its politics).

Diestel, Peter-Michael (b. Prora, Rügen, February 14, 1952), GDR Minister of the Interior (initially **DSU**), April–October 1990. From his base as General Secretary of the DSU, Diestel, a lawyer, was appointed Minister of the Interior by Lothar **de Maizière** in April 1990. He very soon began to provoke public controversy and dissent from within his own party. He was accused of being too lenient with former members of the *Stasi*, even consulting them about how to dismantle the security apparatus. On May 22, 1990 the DSU parliamentary party voted for the removal of Diestel from office, but he and de Maizière refused to comply. On June 30 Diestel resigned from the party, but continued his ministerial career until the day of German unity. He did not enter the *Bundestag* either in October or December, but re-emerged first as CDU opposition leader in the **Brandenburg** *Landtag*, then as co-founder of the Committees for Justice (July 1992).

DSU (*Deutsche Soziale Union*). See **German Social Union**.

Duchac, Josef (b. Bad Schlag, Sudetenland, Czechoslovakia, February 19, 1938), Minister President of **Thuringia** (CDU), October 1990-January 1992. A chemical engineer in the rubber industry and a member of the East German **CDU** since 1957, Duchac was appointed plenipotentiary for Erfurt, then Thuringia in 1990. From October he led a coalition government in that *Land*, but had to resign in January 1992. He was replaced by Bernhard Vogel from west Germany.

DVU (*Deutsche Volksunion*). See **German People's Union**.

Ebeling, Hans-Wilhelm (b. Parchim, Mecklenburg, January 15, 1934), founder chairman of **German Social Union** (DSU), January–April 1990. Ebeling, pastor of the Thomaskirche in **Leipzig**, responded to the *Wende* in the GDR by founding in December 1989 the **Christian Social Party of Germany**. This he took into a merger with other groups, forming the DSU on January 20, 1990 with himself as chairman. The emphasis of the party was on "Christian values", German unity, the re-establishment of the old *Länder*, and the social market economy. On February 1, 1990 Ebeling, Lothar **de Maizière (CDU)** and Wolfgang **Schnur (DA)** met in West Berlin with Helmut **Kohl** to prepare a pact between their parties for the forthcoming *Volkskammer* elections. This **Alliance for Germany** was announced on February 5, 1990.

The DSU was not a full participant in the **Round Table** discussions, but it continued to gain ground in **Saxony** and **Thuringia** and performed creditably in the *Volkskammer* elections with 6.3 per cent of the vote and 25 seats. Ebeling became Minister for Economic Co-operation in the de Maizière cabinet, alongside his fellow DSU member Peter-Michael **Diestel** at the Ministry of the Interior. Ebeling left the DSU chairmanship in April 1990, and the party itself began to fall apart over Diestel's handling of the *Stasi* issue and other matters. Ebeling, Diestel and others felt that the DSU was moving dangerously towards the right and by the beginning of July they had left the party. Ebeling did not enter the *Bundestag* either after October 3 or after the elections of December 2, 1990.

Engholm, Björn (b. Lübeck, November 9, 1939), chairman of **SPD** from May 1991, Minister President of **Schleswig-Holstein** from 1988. Having studied in **Hamburg**, Engholm was a journalist and active SPD member. He was elected to the *Bundestag* in 1969 and in 1981–82 he had a short ministerial career under Chancellor Helmut Schmidt (education and science, then food and agriculture). From 1983 he concentrated his efforts on his native Schleswig-Holstein, where he led the SPD to victory in 1988 in the wake of the damage done to the **CDU** by the Barschel scandal. In April 1992 he held onto power in Kiel but with a reduced majority. Meanwhile in May 1991 Engholm had been elected chairman of the SPD, with the expectation that he would be chancellor candidate in the Federal elections of 1994.

Eppelmann, Rainer (b. Berlin, February 12, 1943), GDR Minister of Disarmament and Defence (initially **DA**), April–October 1990. A **Berlin** pastor, Eppelmann had been active in the peace movement, and he was strangely appropriate as the last Minister of Defence of the GDR, a post which he expanded to include specific mention of disarmament. Eppelmann's party base was the new **Democratic Awakening** (DA), which he helped to found in October 1989. On December 17 he was replaced as party chairman by Wolfgang **Schnur**, but he continued to play a prominent role as one of the DA representatives at the **Round Table** discussions and as a minister without portfolio in the **Modrow** "government of national responsibility" from February 1990. When Schnur resigned in disgrace on March 14 Eppelmann took over once more. In **de Maizière**'s cabinet Eppelmann had the task of supervising the dismantling of the **National People's Army** (NVA). The way he did this caused some surprise, as he continued to place large orders for weapons. Meanwhile, the DA was collapsing from within and Eppelmann resigned from it. By the *Bundestag* election of December 1990 he was a successful candidate for the **CDU** in Fürstenwalde, **Brandenburg**.

Farmers' Association of the GDR (*Bauernverband der DDR*). *Foundation.* March 9, 1990. *Leadership.* Karl Dämmrich. The Farmers' Association was formed to act on behalf of agricultural workers and its membership derived mainly from the communist Union of Mutual Peasant Aid (*Vereinigung der gegenseitigen Bauernhilfe* — VdgB). It formed a common list with the **Democratic Farmers' Party of Germany** (DBD) in the May 1990 local elections.

FDGB (*Freier Deutscher Gewerkschaftsbund*). See **Free German Trade Union League**.

FDJ (*Freie Deutsche Jugend*). See **Free German Youth**.

FDP (*Freie Demokratische Partei*). See **Free Democratic Party**.

Federal Armed Forces. See *Bundeswehr*.

Federal Bank. See *Deutsche Bundesbank* (German Federal Bank).

Federal Council. See *Bundesrat*.

Federal Diet. See *Bundestag*.

Feist, Margot. See **Honecker, Margot**.

Fink, Ulf (b. Freiberg, Saxony, October 6, 1942), chairman of the **Brandenburg CDU**. Although born in **Saxony**, Fink spent most of his life in West Germany, becoming chairman of the CDA, the trade union association linked with the CDU, in 1987. In November 1991 he stood for the chair of the CDU in Brandenburg, vacant since the withdrawal of Lothar **de Maizière**. He was challenged by Angela **Merkel**, who was clearly being supported by Chancellor Kohl. Kohl's manoeuvre backfired, since Fink, representing the reformist wing of the CDU, won easily.

Forum Party of Thuringia (*Forumspartei Thüringen*). One of the 12 groups which formed the **German Social Union** (DSU) in January 1990.

Free Democratic Party (*Freie Demokratische Partei* — FDP). *Addresses.* Thomas-Dehler-Haus, Baunscheidstrasse 15, W-5300 Bonn 1; Postfach 1335, Mohrenstrasse 20–22, O-1080 Berlin. *Foundation.* 1948 in western occupation zones; December 1989/February 1990 in GDR. Merged August 1990. *Membership.* In 1991: 140,000 (including 70,000 in east Germany). *Leadership.* Dr

Otto Graf Lambsdorff (ch., b.1926); Uwe-Bernd Lühr (g.s.). *Former GDR leadership*. Bruno Menzel (ch.); Peter Thietz (ch.); Jürgen Neubert (dep. ch.).

History. An FDP committee was formed in the GDR in December 1989. The party was founded on February 4, 1990. A week later it joined the **Liberal Democratic Party** (LDP) and the **German Forum Party** (DFP) in the **League of Free Democrats** (BFD) electoral alliance. This won 5.3 per cent of the vote and 21 seats in March 1990, and 6.7 per cent of the vote in May. The BFD then provided the basis for unity with the west German FDP in August 1990.

In the post-unification elections the FDP did particularly well in east Germany, reaching 13.4 per cent of the vote in the ***Bundestag*** election (10.6 per cent in west Germany). The membership was also in 1990 larger in east than in west Germany, but in 1991 the east German membership fell back sharply. Rainer **Ortleb** from the former GDR represents the FDP in Chancellor **Kohl**'s cabinet as Minister of Education, and the new General Secretary of the party is an east German, Uwe-Bernd Lühr.

Organization. The FDP is organized on a *Land* basis, with sub-groups as appropriate. The party congress, which meets annually and which all members are entitled to attend (though only delegates have voting rights), decides policy and elects the party leadership for a period of two years. *Programme*. The east German FDP proposed a social market economy, environmental protection, social security, and German economic and political unity. The stance of the long-established FDP in the Federal Republic is of economic and political liberalism, with a strong appeal to businessmen and farmers. *Affiliations*. League of Free Democrats (February–August 1990); Liberal International; Federation of Liberal, Democratic and Reform Parties of the European Community.

Free Democratic Union of Germany (*Freie Demokratische Union Deutschlands* — FDUD). One of the 12 groups which formed the **German Social Union** (DSU) in January 1990.

Free German Trade Union League (*Freier Deutscher Gewerkschaftsbund* — FDGB). The FDGB was until 1990 the monopolistic trade union organization of workers and other employees in the GDR. Originating in the early phase of reconstruction after the Second World War, the FDGB came to be inextricably linked with the ruling SED. The former Social Democratic tradition of the trade union movement was thus destroyed, as were rival Catholic and liberal unions. Conflict in labour relations was not admitted in the GDR, so the FDGB's function came to be supportive of state and party, with only limited scope for representing genuine grievances on behalf of the workforce. The FDGB consisted of 16 trade unions, in which were organized over 9 million members, that is over 90 per cent of eligible employees.

The revolution of 1989 soon brought change in the FDGB. Its chairman and *Politbüro* member since 1975, Harry Tisch, was one of the first casualties of grassroots pressure. He resigned at the beginning of November 1989 because, he said, he had lost the confidence of the members. Demands were made for his arrest on corruption charges. As other trade union leaders went the same way, Tisch's position was taken by Annelis Kimmel, former leader of the **Berlin** trade union organization. She too was replaced at the beginning of February 1990 by Helga Mausch of the **NDPD**. At the same extraordinary congress of the FDGB it was agreed that individual unions should have more autonomy and that the FDGB should remain only as a limited umbrella organization. As the economic crisis in the GDR developed in 1990, labour unrest began to overtake the previous role of the FDGB, and then amalgamation took place with the (west) German Trade Union League (*Deutscher Gewerkschaftsbund* — DGB). (See also Timmins essay in this volume.)

Free German Union (*Freie Deutsche Union* — FDU). One of the 12 groups which formed the **German Social Union** (DSU) in January 1990. Originating in the north of the GDR, its chairman was Martin Wisser.

Free German Youth (*Freie Deutsche Jugend* — FDJ). Originally presented not as a communist youth organization but as a free movement, the FDJ of the GDR was in fact from the outset a junior partner of the **KPD** and then the **SED**. Its first chairman, from 1946 to 1955, was the future GDR leader, Erich **Honecker**. Again, from 1974 to 1983 the leadership of the FDJ provided the training ground for high office, this time for Egon **Krenz**. He was followed by Eberhard Aurich. As the only officially permitted youth organization, the FDJ played an infiltrating role in all educational institutions and its members engaged in industrial and agricultural work. Its primary purposes were to indoctrinate young people in official ideology, to promote military training and to groom future members of the SED. Its 2.3 million members (1981) ranged in age from 14 years to over 24 years. (See also **Alternative Youth List**)

Gauck, Joachim (b. 1940), Special Commissioner of the Federal Government for the files of the former state security service (*Stasi*) relating to individual persons (from October 3, 1990). Gauck was a pastor in Rostock before joining **New Forum** in October 1989 and being elected to the *Volkskammer* for Alliance 90 in March 1990. In October he was given the daunting task of taking charge of the voluminous legacy of the *Stasi*, in which officers and informers had recorded in minute detail the lives of those upon whom they spied. Gauck argued successfully that individuals should be permitted to look at the files kept upon them and in the winter of 1991–92 many began to do so. What they discovered in many cases has led to the breaking of friendships and even family relationships.

Genscher, Hans-Dietrich (b. Reideburg, near Halle, March 21, 1927), Federal Minister of Foreign Affairs (FDP) 1974–92. Genscher has been one of the most prominent figures on the German political scene for over 20 years. First in **SPD**-led and then in **CDU**-led coalitions, he has occupied for the small **FDP** the important ministerial posts of the Interior (1969–74) and of Foreign Affairs (from 1974). From 1974 to 1985 he was Federal chairman of the FDP. During the crisis in the GDR and the lead-up to unification he played a crucial role, not just because he was Foreign Minister but also because he himself had his origins in the GDR, leaving in 1952. His association with the east stood him in good stead with the population of the GDR, especially when in a highly charged atmosphere he appeared at the West German embassy in Prague in September 1989 to announce that GDR refugees there could leave for the Federal Republic. Genscher was one of the negotiators of the **Two-Plus-Four** agreement, with his diplomatic experience rather overshadowing his idiosyncratic East German counterpart, Markus **Meckel**. Partly because of Genscher's high profile, the FDP polled extremely well in the former GDR in the *Bundestag* election of December 1990. It actually took a direct seat in Genscher's native Halle, its only such win in the whole of Germany since 1961. The successful candidate, Uwe-Bernd Lühr, was rewarded in 1992 by being appointed General Secretary of the FDP. On April 27, 1992 Genscher announced his resignation with effect from May 17. Health problems and a sense that his main task had been completed were the apparent reasons. His departure unleashed dispute in the FDP over his successor and problems within the CDU-CSU-FDP coalition.

Gerlach, Manfred (b. Leipzig, May 8, 1928), chairman of the State Council of the GDR 1989–90 (LDPD). From the final resignation of Egon **Krenz** in December 1989 to the first meeting of the democratically elected *Volkskammer* in April 1990 Manfred Gerlach was acting head of state (chairman of the State Council) of the GDR. As such, he had largely ceremonial functions. Gerlach had been prominent in GDR politics for a long time. From 1967 to 1990 he was chairman of the **LDPD**, the "liberal" party in alliance with the ruling **SED**, and was a loyal deputy to **Honecker**. In the autumn of 1989, however, Gerlach began to speak of the need for new ideas in the GDR and was the first leader of one of the "Democratic Block" parties to do so. The LDPD left the Block on December 5, 1989. Gerlach had meanwhile failed to be elected president of the *Volkskammer* on November 13, but he was elected acting chairman of the State Council on December 6. He had, unlike most other politicians of the old regime, survived into the new, but he was criticized for opportunism and an unconvincing sudden change of heart. On February 10, 1990 Gerlach gave up the LDPD leadership to Rainer **Ortleb** and on April 5 he was replaced as acting head of state by the new president of the *Volkskammer*, Sabine **Bergmann-Pohl**. From that point Gerlach retired from politics. In 1991 he published his political memoirs, *Mitverantwortlich: als Liberaler im SED-Staat* (Sharing Responsibility: as a Liberal in the SED State).

German Alternative (*Deutsche Alternative*). *Foundation*. May 1989. *Leadership*. Walter Matthaei (ch.). *History*. The German Alternative is a small neo-Nazi party, founded in **Bremen** but finding followers amongst the disaffected youth of the eastern *Länder*. It is reported to be organized in **Brandenburg**, Cottbus and, especially, in Dresden, where it derives from a breakaway group from the **Republicans**. The Federal chairman, Matthaei (b. 1916), was a member of the Nazi party and has close contacts with other current parties of the extreme right. *Programme*. "We are one people! We shall be one Reich again!" The German Alternative exploits and excites resentment against foreigners in Germany.

German Beer Drinkers' Union (*Deutsche Biertrinker Union* — DBU). *Leadership*. Andreas Häse (ch.). *Address*. Bertolt-Brecht-Strasse 1, O-2520 Rostock 21. A special-interest party which gathered 2,534 votes in the March 1990 *Volkskammer* election. All these were cast in the Rostock district, where the DBU had been founded in a Warnemünde pub on February 20, 1990. It campaigned for the rights of beer drinkers, for democracy, German reunification within a peaceful Europe and for a relaxation of the east German drinking and driving law, which forbade any consumption of alcohol. In the initial aftermath of economic union east Germany was flooded with the products of west German breweries, but then some of those east German breweries which had escaped closure began to reassert themselves in the market.

German Federal Bank. See *Deutsche Bundesbank* (German Federal Bank).

German Forum Party (*Deutsche Forumpartei* — DFP). *Foundation*. January 1990. Merged with West German **FDP** August 1990. *Leadership*. Jürgen Schmieder (ch. 1990); Lothar Ramin (ch. 1990). *History*. The DFP, founded in Karl-Marx-Stadt (now Chemnitz) in January 1990, was a breakaway liberal faction of **New Forum**. Its small membership was concentrated in the south of the GDR. It took part in the negotiations which resulted in the **Alliance for Germany**, but joined not that electoral pact but the liberal **League of Free Democrats** (BFD). The DFP merged in August 1990 with the West German **Free Democratic Party** (FDP). *Programme*. In favour of a social and ecological market economy and of German unity, without an extension of NATO into the territory of the GDR. *Affiliations*. League of Free Democrats (February–August 1990).

German Freedom Union (*Deutsche Freiheitsunion*). One of the 12 groups which formed the **German Social Union** (DSU) in January 1990.

German People's Union (*Deutsche Volksunion* — DVU). *Address*. Paosostrasse 2, W-8000 Munich 60. *Foundation*. 1971. *Leadership*. Gerhard Frey (ch.) The DVU is a neo-Nazi party founded by Frey, who is at the heart of many extreme-right organizations and publishes several scurrilous nationalistic newspapers. The DVU does not just declare itself against foreigners living in Germany; it also denies the genocide of the Jews and tries to rehabilitate the Nazi period. The DVU made some electoral progress in the European elections of June 1989 and then, profiting from xenophobia and the social difficulties of reunification, it reappeared to take parliamentary seats in **Bremen** and **Schleswig-Holstein** in 1991-92.

German Social Union (*Deutsche Soziale Union* — DSU). *Address*. Merseburger Strasse 82, O-7033 Leipzig, Germany. *Foundation*. January 1990. *Membership*. 12,000 (June 1990). *Leadership*. Hans-Wilhelm **Ebeling** (ch. 1990); Hansjoachim Walther (ch. 1990); Reinhard Keller (ch. 1991); Theodor **Waigel** (hon. ch., from Bavarian CSU). *History*. The DSU was founded in **Leipzig** in mid-January 1990 by Hans-Wilhelm Ebeling, pastor at the Thomaskirche. It drew together 12 small new parties or groups which had emerged since the revolution: the Christian Social Party of Germany; the Free German Union; the Progressive People's Party; the People's Union; the Social Citizens' Union; the German Freedom Union; the Christian Democratic Social Union; the Christian Social Association; the Young Union; the Forum Party of Thuringia, the Free Democratic Union of Germany; and the Christian Social Union.

Being founded later than many of the new parties in the GDR, the DSU was not represented at the **Round Table**, but it quickly gained support from the **Christian Social Union** (CSU) in Bavaria, and then helped to form the **Alliance for Germany** with the **Christian Democratic Union** (CDU) and **Democratic Awakening** (DA) in February 1990. In the March elections the DSU was overshadowed by the success of the CDU, but scored a respectable 6.3 per cent of the votes and 25 *Volkskammer* seats. The party furnished two ministers in the **de Maizière** cabinet: Ebeling (economic co-operation) and Peter-Michael **Diestel** (interior). Thereafter, however, the DSU began a very sharp electoral decline, ending up with only 0.9 per cent of the east German vote in the December 1990 *Bundestag* election and no seats. One of the main reasons for this was the furious infighting which beset the party. It was evident that it contained incompatible strands, which accused each other of leaning excessively to the right and to the left respectively. In May 1990 Diestel was called upon to resign by his own parliamentary party, on the grounds that he was being too lenient to the former *Stasi* (state security). He resisted this pressure, but resigned from the party in the summer, later to join the CDU. Other leading figures, including the founder Ebeling, also left the party, accusing their rivals of flirting with the far-right **Republicans**. In May 1991 the DSU tried to revive itself by drafting a new programme and electing a new leader, Reinhard Keller. The Bavarian CSU welcomed this and said that it was prepared to support the DSU politically and organizationally.

Organization. The DSU is active primarily in **Saxony** and **Thuringia**. Its organization was criticized by one of its former leaders: Hansjoachim Walther complained in the summer of 1990 that the list of members and associations was in such chaos that even he as chairman was not on it. *Programme.* The DSU was founded to promote German unity, Christian values, and a restoration of the old *Länder* in the territory of the GDR. *Affiliations.* Alliance for Germany (from February 1990); close ties with the Bavarian CSU.

Gies, Gerd (b. Stendal, May 24, 1943), Minister President (CDU) of **Saxony-Anhalt**, October 1990–July 1991. Gies was a veterinary surgeon and long-standing member of the East German **CDU**, becoming its chairman in Saxony-Anhalt in early 1990. He was elected to the *Volkskammer* in March 1990. From October he led a coalition government, but was forced to resign in July 1991 when it was found that he had put pressure on party colleagues to stand down by threatening to reveal alleged complicity with the *Stasi*. He was replaced by Werner **Münch** from west Germany.

Gohlke, Reiner (b. Beuthen, Upper Silesia, now Bytom, Poland, July 29, 1934), Executive President of the *Treuhandanstalt*, July–August 1990. Gohlke was from 1982 chairman of the board of the *Bundesbahn*, West Germany's nationalized railway. In mid-July 1990 he began work as head of the executive board of the *Treuhandanstalt*, but only a month later he resigned, saying that the economy of the GDR was in chaos. During his short tenure of office he had been criticized in some West German business circles for concentrating on restructuring rather than privatizing East German industry. His successor, Detlev **Rohwedder**, emphasized the latter course, but was murdered by terrorists in April 1991.

Gomolka, Alfred (b. Breslau, now Wrocław, Poland, July 21, 1942), Minister President (CDU) of **Mecklenburg-West Pomerania**, October 1990–March 1992. Gomolka taught geography at the University of Greifswald and had been a member of the East German **CDU** since 1960. He was elected to the *Volkskammer* in March 1990. When in October the most prominent regional politician, Günther **Krause**, decided that his future lay in **Bonn**, Gomolka became the surprise leader of the first democratic *Land* government of Mecklenburg-West Pomerania. He was forced to resign in March 1992 because of conflict within the *Land* CDU leadership, of which Krause, now Federal Transport Minister, remained the chairman. He was succeeded by Berndt **Seite**. Gomolka's departure meant that all three of the first native CDU minister presidents in east Germany resigned within 18 months of their election.

Green Party/The Greens, Green League (*Grüne Partei/Die Grünen, Grüne Liga*). *Foundation.* November 1989. *Membership.* 1,374 (1991); the Greens in west Germany total 38,000 (1991). *Leadership.* Judith Demba, Friedrich Heilmann, Viktor Liebrenz, Dorrit Nessing-Stranz, Henry G. Schramm, Christine Weiske (all committee members). *History.* During the 1980s unofficial ecological groups emerged in the GDR: for instance, the environmentalist library at the Zion church in **Berlin**, which staged its first exhibition in September 1986. These initiatives faced harassment by the security forces, including the violent entry of the Zion church premises in November 1987, which aroused protest at home and abroad. By 1988 there were up to 80 small ecological groups in the GDR, primarily in Berlin, Dresden, Erfurt, Halle, **Leipzig** and Schwerin, but the contact between them was limited. In order to counteract this, the Ark Network (*Netzwerk*

Arche) was founded in January 1988. However, allegations of "centralism" led to a split in the spring of 1988 between the Network and the environmentalist library. When later in that year and in 1989 talks did finally take place between the state authorities and the ecology groups, the Network was prominently represented.

In the revolutionary circumstances of October–November 1989 there were marked divergences of opinion in the "green" movement. Some activists wanted to represent an ecological standpoint within the other citizens' movements; others, particularly those from the Ark Network, wanted a separate green party. Out of the arguments emerged in November two new organizations, the Green Party and the avowedly non-political Green League. The Green Party published its first draft programme in December 1989 and held its first congress in Halle in February 1990, shortly after the founding congress of the Green League. At the **Round Table** debates the Green Party was represented by a total of 17 members and the Green League by 11.

The party contested the March 1990 election together with the **Independent Women's Association** (UFV), but only received 2.0 per cent of the vote and eight seats. In the autumn, in collaboration with **Alliance 90**, the position improved, and the *Bundestag* election brought 5.9 per cent and eight seats. This actually exceeded the performance of the longer established west German Greens, who did not reach the 5 per cent barrier.

The east German "Greens" (the Green Party changed its name in September 1990) are now associated with their west German counterparts, but also with what remains of the citizens' movements which carried the revolution of 1989–90. The forms of organization are loose, and in June 1991, for instance, the Greens of Thuringia proposed an amalgamation with the citizens' movements while remaining in the Federal Association of Greens. The political secretary of the west German Greens, Heide Rühle, meanwhile said that unity between them and the citizens' movements was some way off. The Green League still exists separately.

With lignite-mining and burning, old factory plant, intensive agriculture, and the polluted legacy of the Soviet army installations, the environmental damage in the former GDR is of enormous dimensions. Estimates of the cost of repairing it in the coming decades run into DM100 billions. Green politics can be expected to remain a live issue.

Organization. All party councils must comprise 50 per cent women. *Programme.* Environmental measures and disarmament. *Affiliations.* Common electoral list with Independent Women's Association (UFV) for March 1990 election. Common list with Alliance 90 in three of five *Länder* elections October 1990, and in *Bundestag* election December 1990. Contacts with Green League. Membership of Federal Association of Greens (*Bundesverband der Grünen*).

Greens — Alternative List (*Grüne — Alternative Liste* — GAL). See **Alternative List**.

Gysi, Gregor (b. Berlin, January 16, 1948), chairman of the **Party of Democratic Socialism** from February 1990. Gregor Gysi was born in Berlin to a partly Jewish family. His father, Klaus Gysi, had been a Communist before the Nazi period and after the war rose within the **SED** to become party secretary for religious affairs. A souring of relations with the churches, however, forced his resignation in July 1988. Gregor Gysi trained as a lawyer in the 1960s and joined the SED in 1967. From 1971 he practised as a lawyer and in 1988 became head of the council of lawyers' associations. He used his legal skills to defend dissidents in conflict with the authorities and this gave him a reputation for fair-mindedness and willingness to countenance reform. Gysi was a member of the group of party activists which engineered the downfall of **Krenz**, and he was a member of the temporary commission which succeeded him.

On December 9, 1989 Gysi was elected to the unenviable post of Chairman of the SED, and at the party congress waved a broom in the air to show his intentions. He led a party committee of 100 members, practically all of whom were new to the party leadership. Almost all of the old guard, including those who had instigated the "*Wende*" (turning point), were expelled from the party. Gysi tried to save the party by stressing its democratic potential (it changed its name to the PDS: Party of Democratic Socialism) and its break with the past. He fought a good election campaign in the circumstances, and the PDS emerged with 16.4 per cent of the votes and 66 seats.

Gysi entered the *Bundestag* after German unity on October 3, 1990 as a delegate for the PDS. Later that month he was forced to admit that PDS funds of around DM100 million had been syphoned off illegally to an account in the USSR. He denied any personal involvement and emerged relatively unscathed. On December 2, 1990 he was directly elected PDS member of the *Bundestag* for **Berlin**-Hellersdorf-Marzahn. Like so many politicians from the former GDR, however, Gysi in 1992 came under suspicion of having been an informer for the *Stasi* and his position was much weakened.

Hamburg, Free and Hanseatic City of (*Freie und Hansestadt Hamburg*). *Population.* 1.61 million. *Area.* 755 sq km. *First mayor.* Henning Voscherau (**SPD**). Hamburg on the river Elbe is one of the three city states of the Federal Republic. It has for centuries depended on shipbuilding, trade and fishing, but now also has a wide economic base of services, manufacture and finance. In June 1991 the *Land* elections saw the **CDU** fall to its lowest share of the vote since 1970.

Haussmann, Helmut (b. Tübingen, May 18, 1943), Federal Minister of the Economy (FDP), 1988–90. Succeeding his **FDP** colleague Martin Bangemann in December 1988, it was Haussmann who confronted the early problems of the collapse of the GDR economy. By the autumn of 1990 he was facing criticism even from within his own party and after the *Bundestag* election in December 1990 he informed Chancellor **Kohl** that he wished to resign. The FDP held onto his post, when Jürgen **Möllemann** took over in January 1991.

Hesse (*Hessen*). *Population.* 5.58 million. *Area.* 21,114 sq km. *Capital.* Wiesbaden. *Other cities.* Darmstadt, Frankfurt am Main, Kassel, Offenbach. *Minister president.* Hans Eichel (**SPD**). Hesse in its present shape is a state formed after the Second World War from former Hessian and Prussian territories. Its economic heart is the German financial centre of Frankfurt am Main. In January 1991 Hesse dealt a blow to Chancellor **Kohl** by narrowly voting out the previous **CDU** government.

Honecker, Erich (b. Neunkirchen, Prussian Rhine Province, now **Saarland**, August 25, 1912), General Secretary of the **Socialist Unity Party of Germany** 1971–89. Honecker was the second leader of the GDR, succeeding Walter Ulbricht as First Secretary (later General Secretary) of the SED in May 1971, and becoming head of state (chairman of the State Council) in 1976. Honecker supervised the entry of the GDR into the international community, while sparing little in the suppression of domestic political dissent. A *Politbüro* coup in October 1989 ousted Honecker and began the revolutionary process which culminated in the abolition of the GDR as a state and the assimilation of its territory into a united Germany.

Erich Honecker was born in the Saar region of western Germany to a Socialist then Communist mining family. In his autobiography he claims to have been impressed by the Russian Revolution, although he was only five years old at the time. He was involved in political activities during his youth, joining the **KPD** in 1929. In 1930–31 he was sent to train in Moscow. The accession of Hitler to power did not immediately affect the now detached Saar territory, but Honecker was active in the *Reich* too, using a variety of pseudonyms. He was arrested in 1935, and served 10 years' gaol in **Brandenburg**-Görden. After the war his career in the SED was rapid: he chaired the **Free German Youth** (*Freie Deutsche Jugend* — FDJ) from 1946 to 1955; he became a *Politbüro* member in 1958 and was responsible for security and defence; in 1961 he supervised the construction of the Berlin Wall; he was Ulbricht's chosen successor, but by 1971 he was also Moscow's choice to replace his awkward mentor.

In 1947 Honecker had married a close associate in the FDJ, Edith Baumann (1909–73), and they had one daughter, Erika. The marriage did not last, and in 1953 Honecker married Margot Feist, also an FDJ activist and possibly even more hardline than he. In 1963 she became Minister of Education, and remained so until dismissed and disgraced in 1989. The second Honecker marriage, producing a daughter, Sonja, appeared at times to be at an end, but the two went into enforced retirement together.

Honecker's years in power were characterized by apparent economic success, a much enhanced international profile for the GDR, and fluctuating phases of domestic accommodation and repression. By the mid-1980s the official picture of the GDR economy presented by Honecker and his associates was of a major industrial state enjoying buoyant growth and moving rapidly into modern technologies. Much of this was a deception. Honecker enjoyed the role of international statesman, but his string of prominent visitors and his own visits abroad were intended to impress upon the domestic population the independence and international respectability of the GDR. This did increase as the GDR signed the Basic Treaty with the Federal Republic of Germany in 1972 and entered the United Nations in 1973. Honecker's rapprochement with the Federal Republic culminated in his official visit in September 1987. He also visited Paris, Rome and Brussels, but was not allowed time to fulfil his ambition of being received in London and Washington.

At home Honecker appeared as a tough, ascetic, but not entirely cold character. He was prepared to be conciliatory on occasions, as with the churches from 1978, but individual or collective opposition was stamped on smartly. Honecker took a personal interest in censoring the press and in spying upon suspected dissidents. He claimed to allow collective leadership in the *Politbüro*, but in fact kept a tight rein on his comrades. He associated primarily with Erich Mielke and Günter **Mittag** (although the latter denies that they were close), but deterred the formation of other cliques by at times disgracing even such favoured persons as Egon **Krenz**. Honecker enjoyed hunting, and revelations in 1989–90 of his numerous hunting lodges and other perks of office caused resentment in the GDR.

Honecker's fall from power began when he had to return suddenly from Bucharest in July 1989 for a gall bladder operation. During his enforced absence from the scene, GDR policy drifted in the face of mass exodus of GDR citizens via Hungary and Austria. Growing street protests and police brutality then followed, marring Honecker's triumphant celebration of 40 years of the GDR. His adamant resistance to change was now seen as a liability by *Politbüro* colleagues and on October 17, 1989 a *Politbüro* meeting forced him next day to submit his resignation to the Central Committee "on health grounds". He was replaced by Egon Krenz, the man groomed by him for the succession but by now convinced of the need for change.

At first Honecker's exit seemed fairly dignified, but then he was arrested and expelled from the party. He faced corruption charges, which were later dropped. Forced by his dismissal to leave the luxury party compound at Wandlitz, Honecker and **Margot Honecker** underwent several changes of address, including spells in hospital and detention for Mr Honecker. During early 1990 they were housed by Pastor Uwe Holmer in Lobetal near Bernau, and had to return there when local protest prevented their transfer in March to a government guesthouse at Lindow. On April 3, 1990 the couple were given a flat in Red Army barracks at Beelitz, south of Potsdam. Honecker still stood accused of ordering the shoot-to-kill policy on the GDR border, and an order for his arrest was given on the day of the first all-German elections on December 2, 1990. His Soviet hosts showed reluctance to hand him over and then spirited him away to the Soviet Union. The Federal government protested that it wanted him back, although his trial in Germany would undoubtedly inflame many old wounds.

Extended interviews with Honecker and his wife, published as a book entitled *Der Sturz* (The Fall) in December 1990, showed them unrepentant and bitter and highly critical of those who had ousted them. Honecker had tried but failed to prevent publication of the book.

Because of the threat of extradition, especially after the collapse of communism in the (former) Soviet Union, the Honeckers took refuge in the Chilean Embassy in Moscow, hoping to benefit from the GDR's support of Chilean opponents to the Pinochet regime and the fact that their daughter Sonja is married to a Chilean. The Santiago government prevaricated about giving them asylum, but pressure from the German government and Russian president Yeltsin persuaded it to give Honecker up in July 1992. He now awaits trial in Berlin.

Honecker, Margot (née Feist, b. Halle, 1927), GDR Minister of Education, 1963–89. Having joined the **Communist Party** (KPD) in 1945, Margot Feist married Erich **Honecker** in 1953. She became a minister and a member of the party central committee in 1963. In the crisis summer of 1989 she continued to make hardline speeches denouncing reform. She acted as her husband's spokesperson, accusing the Federal government of hypocrisy in fêting him back in 1987 but now seeking his arrest. She left for Chile in July 1992. (See **Honecker, Erich**)

IFM (*Initiative Frieden und Menschenrechte*). See **Peace and Human Rights Initiative**.

Independent Social Democratic Party of Germany (*Unabhängige Sozialdemokratische Partei Deutschlands* — USPD). *Foundation.* 1917. Refounded February 1990. *History.* The original USPD was a breakaway from the **Social Democratic Party** (SPD) during the First World War. After some initial success, it had dwindled to insignificance by the mid-1920s. The new version of the party, founded at Fürstenwalde on February 16, 1990, was intended as a resurrection of the principles of the earlier one, but in the election of March 1990 it received only 3,891 votes. *Programme.* Radical democratic socialism.

Independent Women's Association (*Unabhängiger Frauenverband* — UFV). *Foundation.* February 1990. *Membership.* 3,030 (August 1990). *Leadership.* Tatjana Böhm, Ina Merkel (spokeswomen). *History.* The UFV had origins in the early 1980s, as attempts were made to form a women's movement separate from the official **Democratic Women's League of Germany** (DFD), although contacts were maintained with the latter. An early group (from 1982) was Women for Peace (*Frauen für den Frieden*). In the autumn and winter of 1989 various women's initiatives were formed to keep women's issues alive in the course of the revolution. They included LILO (*lila offensive*, Lilac Offensive), SOFI (*Sozialistische Frauen-Initiative*, Socialist Women's Initiative, later renamed *Solidarische Fraueninitiative*, Solidary Women's Initiative), and EWA (*Erster weiblicher Aufbruch*, First Female Awakening). Many of the activists involved hoped to bring the various groups into one organization and on December 3, 1989 a "manifesto for an autonomous women's movement" was issued. This was the beginning of the UFV, although the founding congress was not held until February 17, 1990 in East **Berlin**. The UFV had meanwhile sent a total of 20 representatives to the **Round Table** and had provided a minister, Tatjana Böhm, in the reconstituted **Modrow** government. An electoral pact had also been agreed with the **Green Party**. Between them the parties received 226,932 votes (2.0 per cent) and eight *Volkskammer* seats, but the alliance broke up when the Green Party refused to give the UFV one of the seats. In the *Bundestag* election of December 1990 two UFV members, Christina Schenk and Petra Bläss, were elected, but on the lists respectively of the Greens/**Alliance 90** and the Left List/**PDS**. *Organization.* Concentrating on women's issues, the UFV does not prohibit simultaneous membership of another party or organization. *Programme.* Democracy, women's and environmental issues. Two prominent concerns have been growing female unemployment, and the threat to abortion rights in east Germany from the west German paragraph 218.

Kirchner, Martin (b. Weimar, August 9, 1949), General Secretary of the CDU in the GDR, 1989–90. Kirchner joined the **CDU** in 1967 and was active in the party and in the evangelical church. In September 1989 he was a co-signatory of the so-called "Weimar letter" which called upon the CDU to respond to the problems of the GDR. He became General Secretary in December, but in August 1990 was forced to resign because of revelations of previous contacts with the *Stasi*.

Kohl, Helmut (b. Ludwigshafen, Bavarian Palatinate, now Rhineland-Palatinate, April 3, 1930), Federal Chancellor (CDU) since 1982. Kohl studied history, politics and law at the universities of Frankfurt and Heidelberg. He was then employed by the Ludwigshafen branch of the Chemical Industry Association. He had joined the **CDU** in 1947 and played a leading role in the youth section, the Young Union (*Junge Union*). He was chairman of the CDU in the **Rhineland-Palatinate** from 1966 to 1973 and Minister President of the *Land* from 1969 to 1976. From 1969 to 1973 he was deputy chairman of the Federal CDU and thereafter its chairman. In 1976 he stood unsuccessfully for the chancellorship against Chancellor Helmut Schmidt of the **SPD**, and when in 1980 Kohl was superseded as chancellor candidate by Franz Josef Strauss of the **CSU** it appeared that his political career was waning. However, Kohl did become Chancellor after the SPD's coalition partner, the **FDP**, switched sides and Kohl won a *Bundestag* constructive vote of no confidence in the government in October 1982. He then led his CDU/CSU/FDP coalition to election victories in 1983 and 1987.

Before the revolution in the GDR there were signs in West Germany that Kohl was running into electoral danger. When the regime in the GDR changed in October–November 1989 and then the Berlin Wall was opened, Kohl initially seemed wrong-footed. He met a hostile reception in West

Berlin on November 10, 1989. By the end of the month, however, he seemed to have regained the initiative with his 10-point plan for German unity. He visited the GDR in December and received an enthusiastic welcome from the population, especially in Dresden. From that point on his political skills and a degree of good fortune carried him from success to success. During the course of 1990 he negotiated with Mikhail Gorbachev first in February on German unity and then in July on all-German NATO membership. Kohl returned on both occasions in triumph, although Gorbachev's room for manoeuvre was in any case limited.

In Germany itself Kohl, after some prevarication, launched the might of the West German CDU behind the electoral campaign of Lothar **de Maizière**. Kohl undoubtedly won many votes in the east by promising an early introduction of the Deutschemark with an exchange rate for wages, pensions and most savings of 1:1. With the victory of the CDU and its allies in the *Volkskammer* election of March 1990 Kohl had a generally easy ride with his east German partners, although there were some instances of disagreement with de Maizière. Kohl basked in his success as the Chancellor of unity and comfortably won the *Bundestag* election of December 1990.

Since unification Kohl's position has been more difficult. He has had to renege on promises that there would be no tax increases and that nobody would be worse off in a united Germany. Since October 1990 he has not faced an electoral test in east Germany, but the results for his CDU in west German *Land* elections have been almost uniformly bad. The worst moment was probably the loss in April 1991 of Kohl's home state of Rhineland-Palatinate. He has the consolation, however, that the opposition SPD has also not performed robustly in recent elections.

KPD (*Kommunistische Partei Deutschlands*). See **Communist Party of Germany**.

Krause, Günther (b. Halle, September 13, 1953), Federal Minister of Transport (CDU) from January 1991. Of all the politicians to emerge from the crisis of the old GDR, **de Maizière** and Krause made the strongest impression, but the former had to depart from politics. Krause remains Minister of Transport in **Kohl**'s government and was for a time at least well in the Chancellor's favour. Krause studied construction engineering and information technology and was a lecturer at the technical high school in Wismar. He is reported to have had contacts with the **CDU** since 1975 but to have joined only early in 1990. He was elected to the *Volkskammer* for Rostock and, after a close poll, as *Land* chairman of the CDU in **Mecklenburg-West Pomerania**. His rapid advance continued as he became parliamentary chairman of the CDU and parliamentary state secretary to de Maizière with special responsibility for economic affairs. Krause was closely involved in the negotiations toward the first state treaty on economic union and — alongside West German Minister of the Interior Wolfgang **Schäuble** — he was the main negotiator of the second treaty on German unity. He represented a line strongly in favour of rapid unification and the introduction of market structures into the GDR. In August 1990 Krause decided against standing for the premiership of his *Land* and instead looked to a political career in **Bonn**. With German unity he entered the *Bundestag* and Kohl's cabinet as a minister without portfolio. He was elected for Mecklenburg-West Pomerania in December 1990 and in January was appointed Minister of Transport. His career since has been somewhat stormy. In the summer of 1991 he came under intense pressure to resign, accused of having facilitated the purchase of motorway service stations by associates of his. He rejected the charges and retained his post. In the spring of 1992 he then became embroiled in a dispute within the CDU leadership in Mecklenburg-West Pomerania which led to the resignation of the Minister President, Alfred **Gomolka**. Krause is now reported to be less in Kohl's good books than he had been.

Krenz, Egon (b. Kolberg, Pomerania, now Kolobrzeg, Poland, March 19, 1937) General Secretary of the **Socialist Unity Party of Germany**, October–December 1989. Egon Krenz was briefly the third leader of the GDR, succeeding Erich **Honecker** in October 1989, first as General Secretary of the **SED** and then as head of state (Chairman of the State Council). Krenz had been, like Honecker, chairman of the **FDJ** party youth organization (from 1974). He became a full member of the *Politbüro* in 1983 and was made responsible for security and youth affairs. He was regarded as Honecker's designated successor, although Honecker deliberately reduced his prominence in the mid-1980s for fear of him becoming a threat. Krenz reappeared towards the end of the decade but made few friends when he supervised the fraudulent elections of May 1989 and visited Beijing to congratulate the Chinese leadership on its Tiananmen Square operation. During Honecker's illness in the summer of 1989, Krenz chafed at the lack of policy coming from stand-in Günter **Mittag** and began to plot with Günter **Schabowski** and others the removal of Honecker and Mittag. Although known as a hardliner, he initiated the "*Wende*" (turning point) in GDR politics and was responsible for the opening of the Berlin Wall on November 9, 1989. His concessions were never enough, however, and he failed to establish either his own trustworthiness or the legitimacy of the SED. He resigned in December 1989 and was expelled from the party in January 1990. Still living in Pankow, East Berlin, he began to make a living writing for the West German popular press. In the spring of 1990 he published his account of the revolution in the GDR, *Wenn Mauern fallen* (When Walls Fall). Its narrative and interpretations have been contested by his co-conspirator, Schabowski.

Lafontaine, Oskar (b. Saarlouis, September 16, 1943), Minister President (SPD) of the Saarland from 1985. Lafontaine studied physics in **Bonn** and Saarbrücken and joined the **SPD** in 1966. He made his political career primarily in the **Saarland** itself and in 1985 won the *Land* election which made him Minister President. Always a controversial and populist character within the SPD leadership, Lafontaine was adopted as the party's candidate for the chancellorship in the election of 1990. Although Lafontaine might originally have hoped to benefit from Chancellor **Kohl**'s declining popularity in West Germany, the election year was overshadowed by the process of German unity. Lafontaine's suggestion that assistance to incoming East Germans be stopped in order to prevent excessive migration went down very badly in East Germany. The SPD lost the *Volkskammer* election in March 1990 and Lafontaine failed to recoup the position thereafter. He did benefit from a wave of sympathy after he received serious knife wounds from a lone attacker in April 1990, but when he tried to warn of the real costs of German unity, in unemployment for the East Germans and tax rises for the West Germans, he managed only to give the impression that he was half-hearted about or even opposed to German unity. His threatened use of the SPD's majority in the *Bundesrat* to block legislation on German unity won him little support in either east or west. The result was that the SPD vote in the *Bundestag* election in December 1990 fell in west Germany and rose only slightly in east Germany. In the aftermath of the election Lafontaine declined the post of SPD party chairman.

Land (plural *Länder*). One of the states of the Federal Republic, with substantial constitutional powers and with representation at Federal level in the *Bundesrat*. The East German *Länder* were effectively abolished in 1952 and divided up into districts. They were reconstituted by the *Volkskammer* law of July 22, 1990. See **Baden-Württemberg, Bavaria, Berlin, Brandenburg, Bremen, Hamburg, Hesse, Lower Saxony, Mecklenburg-West Pomerania, North Rhine-Westphalia, Rhineland-Palatinate, Saarland, Saxony, Saxony-Anhalt, Schleswig-Holstein** and **Thuringia**.

Landtag (plural *Landtage*). The directly-elected parliament of a *Land*. In the city states of **Berlin, Bremen** and **Hamburg** the designations vary, but the functions are the same.

LDP (*Liberal-Demokratische Partei*). See **Liberal Democratic Party**.

LDPD (*Liberal-Demokratische Partei Deutschlands*). See **Liberal Democratic Party**.

League of Free Democrats — The Liberals (*Bund Freier Demokraten — Die Liberalen —* BFD). *Foundation*. March 27, 1990. *Leadership*. Rainer **Ortleb** (ch.). The BFD was originally an electoral alliance formed in February 1990 by the **Liberal Democratic Party** (LDP), **Free Democratic Party** (FDP) and **German Forum Party** (DFP) to fight the March election, when it won 5.3 per cent of the vote and 21 seats. After the election an LDP conference decided to change the party's name to the BFD. The **National Democratic Party** (NDPD) joined it, but the FDP and DFP, while campaigning with the BFD, maintained their separate identities. In Lothar **de Maizière**'s cabinet the BFD furnished three cabinet ministers, but two of them — Kurt Wünsche and Axel Viehweger — later had to resign because of their activities under the old communist regime. In the May local elections the BFD increased its share of the vote to 6.7 per cent. It and the other liberal parties merged with the West German FDP in August 1990.

Leipzig. Leipzig was the second city of the GDR, with a population of nearly 550,000. It lies in **Saxony** in the central south of the country and has for centuries been a cultural and economic centre. In the spring and autumn it stages the Leipzig trade fair, with wide international participation. It was also the centre for book publishing in the GDR and is the home of the Gewandhaus orchestra. In 1989 Leipzig was crucial in the progress of the revolution in the GDR. From the late summer of that year weekly Monday demonstrations were held to protest at the obduracy of the **Honecker** regime in resisting reform. They were met with violence in October and were in imminent danger of being suppressed by Honecker in imitation of the Chinese in Tiananmen Square in June 1989. Once the regime had been overthrown there was no halt to the weekly marches, as calls for democratization became increasingly overshadowed by demands for German unity.

Liberal Democratic Party (*Liberal-Demokratische Partei* — LDP). *Foundation*. 1945. Renamed LDPD 1945. Renamed LDP February 1990. Renamed BFD March 1990. Merged with West German FDP August 1990. *Membership*. Nil (104,000 in 1987). *Leadership*. Manfred **Gerlach** (ch. 1967–90; b. 1928; acting ch. of Council of State 1989-90); Rainer **Ortleb** (ch. 1990; b. 1944; Minister for Education 1991).

History. Until the upheaval of 1989–90 the Liberal Democratic Party of Germany (LDPD) was one of the National Front parties allied to the ruling **Socialist Unity Party** (SED). It was founded in July 1945 as a liberal initiative with a middle-class constituency, but was rapidly pressured into subordinating itself to the SED. After that it was little more than a means by which the SED could organize and discipline white-collar workers, craftsmen, businessmen and professionals. Its membership, at 199,000, was at its height in 1950 and then fell drastically to 67,000 in the early 1960s. From that point, like the other National Front parties, the LDPD grew, as the SED encouraged organization of non-communists in order to bolster the system. In 1987 its membership was 104,000.

The LDPD managed to retain its leader during the early phase of the revolution. Indeed, Manfred Gerlach was the first leader of any of the subordinate parties to speak out in favour of reform. This contrasted with the rhetoric which he had been using for the previous 20-odd years. He came to be seen as a bridge between the SED and those demanding more thorough changes, and after the resignation of Egon **Krenz** as head of state in December 1989, Gerlach was elected to replace him in a provisional capacity. He resigned as party chairman in February 1990 and declared his intention to retire from politics after the March 1990 elections. Meanwhile three LDP members joined the **Modrow** government of February 1990. Two of them, Peter Moreth and Kurt Wünsche, had before the revolution been members of the political committee of the LDPD.

For the elections the renamed LDP joined with the **Free Democratic Party** (FDP) and the **German Forum Party** (DFP) in an electoral alliance called the **League of Free Democrats** (BFD), which took 5.3 per cent of the vote and 21 seats. After the election the waning **National Democratic Party** (NDPD) decided to dissolve itself and join the LDP. Under the title of BFD they improved their performance in the May 1990 local elections to 6.7 per cent. The final merger of all the liberal parties with the West German FDP took place in August 1990. From January 1991 the LDP still had a continuing legacy in the person of Chancellor Kohl's Minister of Education, Rainer Ortleb, who after Gerlach had been the last chairman of the old party.

Programme. In 1987 the party programme declared that "The LDPD is a party working in and for socialism ... The LDPD directs itself primarily to craftsmen, tradesmen, members of the intelligentsia and white-collar employees ...". By the autumn of 1989 chairman Gerlach was calling for change in the GDR. By December 1989 the party called for a market economy which guaranteed social and ecological security, a process of German unification, and disarmament in Europe. *Affiliations*. Democratic Block (to December 1989). League of Free Democrats (February–August 1990).

Lower Saxony (*Niedersachsen*). *Population*. 7.19 million. *Area*. 47,439 sq km. *Capital*. Hanover (Hannover). *Other cities*. Brunswick (Braunschweig), Göttingen, Hildesheim, Oldenburg, Osnabrück, Salzgitter, Wolfsburg. *Minister president*. Gerhard Schröder (SPD). From 1714 to 1837 the kingdom of Hanover was in personal union with the British crown. In 1866 it succumbed to

Prussian annexation. The state of Lower Saxony was formed in 1946 out of this Prussian province of Hanover and the former *Länder* of Oldenburg, Brunswick and Schaumburg-Lippe. By area it is the second largest of the Federal states and has a varied economy ranging from fishery and agriculture to manufacturing industry. In May 1990 the **CDU**-led coalition government fell from office as a result of the *Landtag* election and the CDU lost its majority in the ***Bundesrat***. This exacerbated the tension between the CDU and the **SPD** in the negotiations leading to German unity.

Maizière, Lothar de (see **De Maizière, Lothar**).

Meckel, Markus (b. Müncheberg, Frankfurt an der Oder, August 18, 1952), GDR Foreign Minister (SPD), April–August 1990. Son of a pastor, and a pastor himself, Meckel was before the *Wende* active in the peace and human rights movement in the GDR. He was a founder member of the **SDP** (later **SPD**), becoming a deputy chairman in February 1990. When Ibrahim **Böhme** was forced to lay down his party offices in March 1990, Meckel took over in a caretaker capacity, and in April he was appointed Foreign Minister in the **de Maizière** government. He was a participant in the **Two-Plus-Four** negotiations, but was eclipsed by his more experienced West German counterpart, Hans-Dietrich **Genscher**. Within the GDR he suffered from criticism for giving posts to friends and family members. In mid-August Meckel resigned from the cabinet in the wake of de Maizière's sacking of other SPD ministers and de Maizière himself took over his responsibilities. Meckel was a member of the *Volkskammer* for Magdeburg. He did not join the *Bundestag* with German unity, but was elected for Prenzlau, **Brandenburg** on December 2, 1990.

Mecklenburg-West Pomerania (*Mecklenburg-Vorpommern*). *Population*. 1.95 million. *Area*. 23,838 sq km. *Capital*. Schwerin. *Other cities*. Greifswald, Neubrandenburg, Rostock, Stralsund, Wismar. *Minister president*. Berndt **Seite** (CDU). Northernmost of the new *Länder* of the Federal Republic, comprising the pre-1933 *Länder* of Mecklenburg-Schwerin, Mecklenburg-Strelitz and part of Prussian Pomerania. Formed in 1945, it was effectively abolished in 1952 and divided up into the districts of Rostock, Schwerin and Neubrandenburg. It was reconstituted by the *Volkskammer* law of July 22, 1990. The two main economic sectors of the region have been agriculture and shipbuilding and both now present great problems. Even under the communist regime the local complaint was that the northern districts were starved of investment by Berlin. Now shipbuilding orders to Rostock from the former Soviet Union have dried up, and associated industries are suffering. Employment is also disappearing in the fishing industry and has gone from the nuclear power station at Greifswald, shut down for safety reasons. One opportunity for expansion is the tourist attraction of the Baltic coast. Mecklenburg-West Pomerania is governed by a **CDU**-led coalition.

Merkel, Angela (b. Templin, **Brandenburg**, 1954), Federal Minister for Women and Youth (CDU) from January 1991. Merkel grew up in a pastor's family, studied physics, and worked at the Academy of Sciences in (East) **Berlin**. In the autumn of 1989 she joined **Democratic Awakening** (DA) and in April 1990 became a deputy spokesperson for the **de Maizière** administration. In the autumn she failed to find a seat to contest in her native Brandenburg, but when she stood in December 1990 for the **CDU** in Stralsund-Rügen-Grimmen in the north-east she won a direct *Bundestag* mandate from the constituency. In January 1991 she joined the **Kohl** cabinet and grew in his estimation as a useful representative of the CDU in the east. She benefited from her DA background, untainted by the complicity of older eastern CDU members in the communist system. In November 1991 Kohl backed her for the chair of the Brandenburg CDU, vacated by de Maizière, but she obtained little more than half the votes registered for her rival, Ulf **Fink**.

Mittag, Günter (b. Stettin, now Szczecin, Poland, October 8, 1926), GDR Party Secretary for the Economy 1962–89. Mittag rose through the **SED** party hierarchy from 1946, becoming a full *Politbüro* member in 1966. His specialism was management of the command economy, and he was party secretary for the economy for most of the period 1962–89, enjoying close contact with Erich **Honecker**. He was responsible for the gross inadequacies of the planning structure, which he tried to disguise by ordering the manipulation of statistics. From time to time he exposed flaws in the economy and demanded changes, but these interventions were largely cosmetic and designed to exert his political control over industry and the regional leaderships of the SED. Despite health problems (diabetes and a partly amputated leg), he was a vigorous representative of the GDR in West German economic circles. When Honecker fell ill in the summer of 1989, Mittag deputized for him, but in his resolution to avoid reform he failed to grasp the depth of the crisis. He was dismissed in October 1989 along with Honecker and party propaganda secretary Joachim Herrmann. Mittag and Herrmann did not even receive the thanks accorded to Honecker. Mittag was later expelled from the SED and charged with corruption and other offences. In 1991 he published his self-justificatory memoirs, *Um jeden Preis: im Spannungsfeld zweier Systeme*. The dust-jacket rather cheekily carried a photograph of Mittag sitting alongside Birgit **Breuel**, head of the *Treuhandanstalt*, although he never had any dealings with her in that capacity.

Modrow, Hans (b. Jasenitz, West Pomerania, January 27, 1928), GDR Prime Minister 1989–90. Appointed in November 1989, Modrow was a key figure in the revolution which overtook the GDR regime in 1989–90, and he could be so because he had not been too closely implicated in the abuses of the past. Although a loyal member of the **SED** from the beginning of the GDR, he was for a long time distrusted by the party leadership and deliberately kept at a distance and out of high office. Modrow joined the **FDJ**, the **FDGB** and the **SED** in 1949. From 1952 to 1961 he was active in the **Berlin** section of the FDJ, thereafter in the party organization in Berlin. His progress was at times unusually slow, indicating that his career was deliberately being restrained. He only became a full member of the Central Committee in 1967, and during his 16 years from 1973 as party secretary for the Dresden district he was not admitted to even candidate *Politbüro* status. By 1989 Modrow had developed a reputation, particularly in the Dresden area itself, as an honest and reform-minded man who spurned the luxuries enjoyed by other party leaders. He was also seen in West Germany as a hope for reform in the GDR. For these reasons he was viewed with distrust by the *Politbüro* and in February 1989 a party commission led by Günter **Mittag** was sent from Berlin to Dresden to deal with "political and economic shortcomings". In other words, Modrow was being investigated and disciplined.

When the crisis broke in the autumn of 1989 and Egon **Krenz** replaced Erich **Honecker** as party secretary, Modrow was increasingly mentioned as a necessary member of any reform government to give it credibility. Although not a close associate of Krenz, Modrow was elected to the *Politbüro* in November and proposed as the new prime minister (Chairman of the Council of Ministers). He took office on November 13, 1989 and appointed a coalition cabinet with some new faces. When Krenz was displaced as SED General Secretary and as head of state, Modrow effectively became the leader of the GDR.

From December 1989 Modrow entered into the **Round Table** discussions with opposition groups and parties, but had difficulty holding them and his coalition together. He had, for instance, to backtrack on his decision to retain a state security service. By late January 1990 Modrow was announcing clearly that the GDR was in deep crisis and that he needed the help of the opposition. It was agreed by most opposition groups and parties that they were willing to participate in a grand coalition government, provided that all ministers, including Modrow himself, temporarily lay aside their party positions. Modrow had already done this in all but name when he said that he was acting on behalf of his country rather than his party. At the beginning of February Modrow took the step which no other SED politician had dared take before: he declared that the two German states should move towards one neutral federal fatherland with its capital in Berlin. The neutrality question remained the stumbling block with **Bonn**. Modrow acquired a generally positive reputation at home and abroad, and this helped his party to more than survive the election of March 1990. The 66 seats and 16.4 per cent of the vote were not enough, however, to allow Modrow to continue, and his was a caretaker administration until Lothar **de Maizière** was charged with forming a new coalition government in April. Despite pressure from the PDS, Modrow failed to be elected president of the *Volkskammer*. In October 1990 he was one of the PDS delegation which joined the *Bundestag*, and he was elected in December on the PDS list for Mecklenburg - West Pomerania. In March 1991 he completed his memoirs of the turbulent time in which he had played such a prominent part. Entitled *Aufbruch und Ende* (Break-up and End), they express his commitment to democratic change in a socialist format and his irritation with the way in which he was treated by the West Germans. It is striking, however, that he does not seem to acknowledge that he never had a democratic mandate himself.

Möllemann, Jürgen (b. Augsburg, **Bavaria**, July 15, 1945), Federal Minister of the Economy (FDP) from January 1991 and Deputy Chancellor from April/May 1992. Originally a member of the CDU from 1962 to 1969, Möllemann joined the **FDP** in 1970. Trained as a teacher, he became a member of the **Bundestag** and the FDP's parliamentary spokesman on education in 1972. His subsequent posts have included the chairmanship of the FDP in **North Rhine-Westphalia** (from 1983), Minister of State in the Foreign Office (1982–87), and Federal Minister of Education and Science (1987–91). With the resignation of Helmut **Haussmann,** Möllemann took over as Federal Minister of the Economy in **Kohl**'s post-election cabinet. Since then he has had to contend with the plight of the east German economy and a downturn in performance in the west. As a strong proponent of the free market economy he has successfully argued for the dismantling of subsidies within the economy as a whole, west as well as east. Möllemann is reported to have ambitions to succeed Otto Graf Lambsdorff as leader of the FDP.

Momper, Walter (b. Sulingen, **Lower Saxony**, February 21, 1945), Governing Mayor of (West) **Berlin** (SPD), 1989–91. Momper was in charge of the city government of West Berlin during the extraordinary events of 1989–90 and hence played an important part in beginning the process of fusion between the two parts of the city. His origins were in Lower Saxony and he went to school in **Bremen**, but he moved to Berlin in the late 1960s. His career was as an historical specialist in academic institutes and archives in West Berlin. He joined the **SPD** in 1967, was elected to the Berlin House of Representatives in 1975, and from 1985 to 1989 was the leader of the SPD opposition in that chamber. The Berlin elections of January 1989 brought him the post of Governing Mayor, at the head of an uneasy coalition with the **Alternative List**. Momper was also President of the ***Bundesrat***. When the Berlin Wall was breached in November 1989 Momper's administration faced the huge logistical problems of the influx of East Germans. Traffic and public transport difficulties were not the least of them. With the barrier between the two parts of the city now removed Momper began to co-operate with his counterparts in East Berlin, especially Tino **Schwierzina**, who was to become SPD mayor of East Berlin in May 1990. From German unity in October Momper and Schwierzina shared the mayoral duties. Momper's own position was under threat, however, because his Alternative List partners took umbrage at the administration's treatment of squatters in Berlin, a city with a severe shortage of accommodation. They abandoned the coalition in November 1990 and increased the likelihood of Momper losing the December election. This he did, on the day when Germany as a whole swung to the **CDU**, and he left office in January 1991. He still plays a part in the city's government, however, since his successor Eberhard **Diepgen** of the CDU rules in coalition with the SPD. Momper has published his memoirs of Berlin in the period of revolution and reunification as *Grenzfall: Berlin im Brennpunkt deutscher Geschichte* (Border Case [or Fall of a Border]: Berlin as the Focus of German History).

Münch, Werner (b. Kirchhellen, now **Lower Saxony**, September 25, 1940), Minister President (CDU) of **Saxony-Anhalt** from July 1991. A university lecturer in politics in West Germany and a **CDU** member of the European Parliament from 1984, Münch embarked upon a new political career in the former GDR. In October 1990 he became Finance Minister in Saxony-Anhalt and in July 1991 he succeeded the disgraced Gerd **Gies** as Minister President.

National Democratic Party of Germany (*National-Demokratische Partei Deutschlands* — NDPD). *Foundation.* 1948. Merged with LDP March 1990. *Membership.* Nil (110,000 in 1987). *Leadership.* Heinrich Homann (acting ch. 1967–72; ch. 1972–89); Günter Hartmann (ch. 1989–90); Wolfgang Gläser (ch. 1990); Wolfgang Rauls (ch. 1990). *History.* Along with the **Democratic Farmers' Party** (DBD), the NDPD was founded in the Soviet occupation zone of Germany in April 1948 on the instigation of the **Socialist Unity Party** (SED), in order to mobilize and control a particular section of society. The NDPD, with its German nationalist aspect, was intended to attract former soldiers, particularly officers, and former members of the Nazi party who were not implicated in serious crimes. It became part of the National Front and thus little more than a mouthpiece for official ideology. Besides its original membership, however, it did develop a role as representative of small private or semi-private traders and professional people.

The NDPD increased its numbers from the mid-1970s to 110,000 in 1987, as part of an SED policy to build up the allied block parties and draw more people into identification with the system. The events of 1989–90, however, threw the NDPD into confusion. Its long-serving chairman, Heinrich Homann, resigned from his post in November 1989 and was expelled from the party in December. His successor, Günter Hartmann, lasted only until January 1990, when he was voted out in favour of Wolfgang Gläser. Gläser resigned shortly afterwards, to be replaced by Wolfgang Rauls on February 11, 1990. The party was torn between its record of complicity in the old regime and its potential role as a mobilizer of the nationalist right. On this latter ground it competed with other groups emerging in the GDR, for instance, the **German Social Union** (DSU). In the March 1990 elections, when it failed in its attempt to ally itself with the **League of Free Democrats** (BFD), the NDPD performed abysmally (0.4 per cent of the vote and only two seats). Thereupon it decided to merge with the **Liberal Democratic Party** (LDP), and thus made its way indirectly into the **Free Democratic Party** (FDP) in August 1990.

Programme. The party programme of 1987 placed the NDPD in the tradition of "nationally-minded petty bourgeois democratic forces" and declared the aim of the party to be "to open up the national question as a class and power question ... so that the citizens of our country can be conscious of their national identity in and with our republic". By the end of 1989 the NDPD favoured democracy, a market economy and German unification.

National People's Army (*Nationale Volksarmee* — NVA). The NVA was the army of the GDR. It was founded in 1955–56 from the ranks of the People's Police in Barracks (*Kasernierte Volkspolizei* — KVP), as the GDR joined the Warsaw Pact. It was placed under the Ministry for National Defence. Military service was 18 months for men (due to be reduced to 12 months), and conscientious objection was discouraged and rewarded with harassment. The NVA in the 1980s was 120,000 men strong, including 71,500 conscripts. In addition were a navy of 16,000 (8,000 conscripts serving 36 months), an airforce of 37,000 (15,000 conscripts), 390,000 reserves, and other armed forces under the authority of the ministries of National Defence, State Security (see *Stasi*) and the Interior. The defence budget (including internal and border security etc.) in 1988 was M 21.7 billion, nearly 8 per cent of Net Material Product. The alleged militarization of society in the GDR was one of the main targets of opposition groups from the early 1980s. Church leaders were critical of military indoctrination of the young and the difficulties faced by those wishing to perform non-military national service. Already before the cut in the period of compulsory national service, the GDR had announced a reduction of 10,000 men by the end of 1990, in line with defence cuts throughout the Warsaw Pact. In the aftermath of the revolution in the GDR, the NVA lost conscripts both to emigration and to desertion and by the spring of 1990 the army faced internal collapse. German unification meant that links with the Warsaw Pact were severed and what was left of the NVA and all its matériel fell to the ***Bundeswehr***. (See *Bundeswehr*)

NDPD (*National-Demokratische Partei Deutschlands*). See **National Democratic Party of Germany**.

Neues Deutschland (New Germany). *Neues Deutschland* was the official party newspaper of the **SED** from its foundation in 1946. It had a daily circulation of over a million in 1982. From 1978 to 1985 it was edited by Günter **Schabowski**, later the political associate of Egon **Krenz**. In the aftermath of the revolution of 1989, Schabowski complained that Erich **Honecker** had demanded to inspect each issue of ND before it appeared. The revolution meant the removal of current editor, Herbert Naumann, and his replacement by Wolfgang Spickermann and a new editorial team. It also meant ND's redesignation in December 1989 first as "Organ of the SED" (previously "Organ of the Central Committee of the SED") and then simply as "Socialist Daily Paper". ND retains its attachment to the **PDS**, but its content has been transformed from dogmatic propaganda into critical comment on current affairs.

New Forum (*Neues Forum* — NF). *Address.* Rosa-Luxemburg-Strasse 19, O-1020 Berlin. *Foundation.* September 1989. *Membership.* 100,000 (March 1990). *Leadership.* Bärbel **Bohley**, Rolf

Heinrich, Sebastian Pflugbeil, Jens **Reich**, Hans-Jochen Tschiche (founders). *History*. Founded in September 1989 and issuing in October a declaration signed by over 200,000 people, New Forum was the first major opposition group to make an impact in the GDR. It was not conceived as a political party, but literally as a "forum" for open discussion. It began with an emphasis on socialist and humanitarian values and environmental concerns. It also concerned itself with the necessity for far-reaching economic reform in the GDR; in late November 1989 it held an international economics conference in East **Berlin**, where matters of currency reform, price subsidies, social ownership, and foreign trade were discussed fully. NF operated at this stage within the context of a GDR still independent in the future.

By January 1990 NF had reached a membership estimated at 150,000 and was publishing its own weekly newspaper, *Die Andere* (The Other One), but it was already falling behind in the political contest. The loose amalgamation found itself competing electorally with new parties linked explicitly with West German counterparts, and falling foul of internal disputes. The issues of German unity and the free market economy forced several of NF's leading figures to renounce the group's new policy. In the elections of March 1990 NF collaborated with **Democracy Now** and the **Peace and Human Rights Initiative** in the **Alliance 90**, but they reached only 2.9 per cent of the vote and 12 seats. Alliance 90 continued to stand in subsequent elections, with better results. NF itself stood separately in the *Landtag* election in **Mecklenburg-West Pomerania** in October 1990, but achieved only 2.9 per cent and split the vote with Alliance 90. NF's loose membership was also falling away rapidly.

Organization. New Forum decided not to become a political party, but to remain a "citizens' movement with a political programme". Part of NF has, however, become a party through its entry into Alliance 90. *Programme*. New Forum was principally concerned with humanitarian issues and the democratization of the GDR. From sections of the movement came calls for the re-establishment of the east German *Länder*, for German unity, and for a market economy. Questions of social justice and the environment were very much to the fore.

North Rhine-Westphalia (*Nordrhein-Westfalen*). *Population*. 16.9 million. *Area*. 34,071 sq km. *Capital*. Düsseldorf. *Other cities*. Aachen, Bielefeld, Bochum, Bonn, Cologne (Köln), Dortmund, Duisburg, Essen, Gelsenkirchen, Hagen, Hamm, Krefeld, Leverkusen, Mönchen-Gladbach, Mülheim, Münster, Paderborn, Recklinghausen, Remscheid, Siegen, Solingen, Wuppertal. *Minister president*. Johannes Rau (SPD). After the defeat of Napoleon in 1815 Prussia acquired the territories in the west of Germany which were to become the heavy industrial power-house of Germany. The coal-mining (Ruhr) and iron- and steel- producing state of North Rhine-Westphalia was a new construct in 1946, consequent upon the break-up of Prussia. It comprises primarily the former Prussian province of Westphalia and the northern portion of the Prussian Rhine Province. Because of its industrial base and its numerous large cities, it is the most populous of the German *Länder* and in fact has more inhabitants than did the entire GDR. The *Landtag* election of May 1990 saw the **SPD** just maintain its hold on an absolute majority, and the **CDU** vote fell back very slightly.

NVA (*Nationale Volksarmee*). See **National People's Army**.

Ortleb, Rainer (b. Gera, June 5, 1944), Federal Minister of Education (FDP) from January 1991. A mathematician by training and a professor in shipping technology, Ortleb steered the old **LDPD** into union with the West German **FDP** and into eventual coalition with **Kohl's CDU**. A member of the LDPD since 1968 and local chairman in Rostock, he was elected chairman of the party on February 10, 1990 to replace Manfred **Gerlach**. He took the party into an electoral alliance with the other liberal parties, as the **League of Free Democrats** (BFD), and was elected to the *Volkskammer* for Dresden. The liberal parties of the GDR merged with the FDP of the Federal Republic on August 12, 1990. Ortleb joined the *Bundestag* in October and his seat was secured by election in December for **Mecklenburg-West Pomerania**. The strong performance of the FDP in the elections helped to win more ministries for the party in Kohl's new cabinet, and Ortleb was put in charge of education on January 16, 1991.

Party of Central German National Democrats (*Partei der Mitteldeutschen Nationaldemokraten*). One of several small ultra-right parties reported to be active in east Germany in 1990. The name of the party hints at its affinity to the west German neo-Nazi National Democratic Party of Germany (*Nationaldemokratische Partei Deutschlands* — NPD), and also at the refusal of the extreme right to accept the loss of Germany's eastern territories after 1945. "Central Germany" in this context means the territory of the former GDR.

Party of Democratic Socialism (*Partei des Demokratischen Sozialismus* — PDS). *Address*. Kleine Alexanderstrasse 28, O-1020 Berlin. *Foundation*. Originally as SED 1946. Renamed SED-PDS December 1989. Renamed PDS February 1990. *Membership*. 185,000 in east Germany (1991); 1,000 in west Germany. Leadership. Gregor Gysi (ch.); André Brie (dep. ch.); Marlies Deneke (dep. ch.); Wolfgang Pohl (dep. ch.); Wolfgang Gehrcke (g.s.); Hans Modrow (hon. ch.).

History. The PDS is since February 4, 1990 the successor to the previous ruling party of the GDR. It is a smaller and much altered version. The **Socialist Unity Party of Germany** (SED) was the Marxist-Leninist political party which ruled the GDR from its inception until the revolutionary changes of 1989–90. It was founded in April 1946 in the Soviet sector of Berlin as an amalgamation of the **Communist Party** (KPD) and the **Social Democratic Party** (SPD), and soon came to pursue a Stalinist line. It was led first by Walter Ulbricht and then from 1971 by Erich **Honecker**. The SED permeated all facets of life in the GDR, either directly or indirectly, and party adherence became a prerequisite for career advancement in many fields. The party grew to a maximum membership (including candidate members) of 2.3 million. The leading role of the party was enshrined in the constitution of the GDR, and in practice the SED was the decisive organ of government in the state.

By October 1989 the crisis in the GDR was evident to many members of the SED, including some *Politbüro* members. Led by Egon **Krenz** and Günter **Schabowski**, they dismissed Honecker. However, even with major concessions, the new leadership of Krenz was unable to halt the challenge to the party. The political suppression, the personal corruption, and the evidence of complete economic mismanagement made it impossible for the SED to continue as before. Krenz was abandoned in December 1989, and the upper echelons and the structures of the old party were swept aside. A provisional party committee of 100 members was led by the new chairman, Gregor **Gysi**, who made it his purpose to regenerate the party as the Party of Democratic Socialism (SED-PDS, then PDS). Meanwhile, however, the membership base had halved and the sole remaining PDS figure with power, prime minister Hans Modrow, was being moved further and further into coalition agreements and the prospect of German unity. Proposals were made on several occasions to dissolve the party entirely, but in the event, Gysi and Modrow managed to salvage something in the March elections. With 16.4 per cent of the vote and 66 seats, the PDS emerged as the third largest party after the **Christian Democratic Union** (CDU) and the SPD. It did so on the votes of those loyal to a separate GDR and fearful of a sell-out of its perceived social and socialist achievements. The PDS's stronghold was East **Berlin**, where it came second to the SPD.

The election result did not mean the end of the PDS, but it did mean the end of its power. Cast into opposition, it failed to find any other party willing to co-operate with it. Attempts were made in 1990 to extend the organization into west Germany, but with scarcely any success. In the ***Bundestag*** election of December 1990 the PDS vote fell to 9.9 per cent in east Germany, meaning only 2.4 per cent in Germany as a whole. 17 PDS members entered the parliament, including Gregor Gysi, who was re-elected Chairman in January 1991. However, at that party congress, reconvened in June, internal party disputes raged between an orthodox majority and a radical reformist minority led by presidium members Rainer Börner and Helga Adler. Gysi appealed for dialogue, and made it clear that he was prepared to resign if harmony were not achieved.

The PDS has many problems. Its membership decline is continuing, albeit at a slower rate; that membership is elderly (48 per cent of pensionable age, 9 per cent under 30 years), and far too heterogeneous for easy compromise; little progress has been made in west Germany, even with the formerly SED-sponsored German Communist Party (*Deutsche Kommunistische Partei* — DKP); and there is evidence of great discontent amongst ordinary party members with the party leadership and *Bundestag* members. These last have petitioned the constitutional court for "fraction" not, as at present, "group" status. The former carries political and financial advantages. The court is also to decide on the PDS's vast financial and property legacy from the SED. In the autumn of 1990 it was revealed that some high-placed PDS members had attempted to spirit large amounts of PDS funds out of the country. In March 1991 the PDS asked for a ruling on whether it could keep 20 per cent of former SED property, disposing of the remainder for social purposes. In June the *Treuhandanstalt* froze the PDS's assets.

Organization. Party congress elects leadership and approves programme. *Programme.* Humane socialism in a market economy (although dispute within the party about the latter). Wide-ranging structural help for the new federal states. *Affiliations.* PDS candidates often campaign together with the Left List (*Linke Liste*).

PDS (*Partei des Demokratischen Sozialismus*). See **Party of Democratic Socialism**.

Peace and Human Rights Initiative (*Initiative Frieden und Menschenrechte* — IFM). *Foundation.* January 1986. *Leadership.* Wolfgang Templin (spokesman); Gerd Poppe (minister without portfolio in Modrow government). *History.* An early opposition group, founded by Templin, Poppe and Bärbel **Bohley**, the IFM derived from the unofficial peace movement of the early 1980s. During the late 1980s it operated illegally and therefore without clear organization, membership or spokespersons. From June 1986 it published the monthly periodical *Grenzfall* ("border incident", "border case" or "fall of the border"). In 1988 five IFM activists, including Bohley and Templin were expelled from the GDR, later to return after protest. Before the "*Wende*" (turning point) IFM comprised only about 30 people, who were then involved in founding other new citizens' movements (Bohley and **New Forum**, for instance). From the winter of 1989–90 IFM itself grew and formed regional groups and project groups throughout the GDR. A committee was elected in February 1990. Poppe, Templin and eight other IFM representatives participated in the **Round Table** discussions from December 1989 to March 1990. In February 1990 the IFM joined New Forum and **Democracy Now** in the **Alliance 90**. Poppe was a member of the **Modrow** government from February to March 1990, and is now the sole IFM representative in the *Bundestag*.

Organization. IFM has an elected committee, but it has throughout its history endeavoured to avoid all hierarchical forms of organization. Since January 1991 IFM has been collaborating organizationally with Democracy Now (DJ) and they publish jointly *Bündnis 2000*. *Programme.* Anti-authoritarian, anti-militarist and pro-disarmament. Anxious to maintain the social achievements of the GDR. *Affiliations.* Alliance 90 (from February 1990).

People's Chamber. See *Volkskammer*.

People's Union(*Volksunion*). One of the 12 groups which formed the **German Social Union** (DSU) in January 1990.

Pöhl, Karl Otto (b. Hanover, December 1, 1929), President of the *Deutsche Bundesbank*, 1980–1991. Pöhl was appointed to the vice-presidency of the *Bundesbank* in 1977 and three years later Chancellor Helmut Schmidt elevated him to the presidency. In 1990, when the terms of German monetary union were being discussed, Pöhl made it clear that he did not favour exchange rates between the Deutschemark and the Mark of the GDR which overvalued the latter for political reasons. He feared for the effect on the Deutschemark and for the health of the east German economy. His view did not prevail against that of Chancellor **Kohl** and exchange rates of 1:1 and 1:2 were introduced. Pöhl and the *Bundesbank* ensured the smooth operation of currency union, but he maintained his criticism of the terms. In May 1991 Pöhl announced that he wished to retire early from the presidency of the *Bundesbank*, saying that this was a career decision with the interests of his family in mind. There was understandably public speculation about the role of his rift with Chancellor Kohl and also about the possible effect of the assassination of the president of the *Treuhandanstalt*, Detlev **Rohwedder**, the month before. Pöhl was succeeded later in the year by his vice-president Helmut Schlesinger, with the expectation that Schlesinger would give way soon on his retirement to Hans Tietmeyer.

Progressive People's Party (*Fortschrittliche Volkspartei* — FVP). *Foundation.* December 1989. *Membership.* 200 (December 1989). *Leadership.* Bernhard Becher (acting spokesman). *History.*

One of the 12 groups which formed the **German Social Union** (DSU) in January 1990. *Programme.* The FVP's main objective was an electoral alliance of all forces in the GDR which rejected a renewed attempt at socialism. It advocated German unity and a market economy.

Red Army Faction (*Rote Armee Fraktion* — RAF). The RAF is a small but lethal terrorist organization which has its origins in the early 1970s. It has claimed responsibility for numerous attacks, including the individual murders of some prominent West German public officials, bankers and businessmen, most notably Siegfried Buback, Jürgen Ponto and Hanns-Martin Schleyer in 1977. Better known internationally as the Baader-Meinhof gang (after Andreas Baader and Ulrike Meinhof, two of its early leaders), the RAF has undergone many changes of personnel. Activists have been imprisoned, been killed, committed suicide (Meinhof and Baader in 1976 and 1977), or disappeared. Many of the last category, it transpired in 1990, had been given refuge and new identities by the *Stasi* in the GDR. In June of that year Susanne Albrecht, wanted for assisting in the murder of Ponto, her godfather, was detained in East **Berlin**. Further arrests followed, and Albrecht gave information against her erstwhile accomplices. She was sentenced in June 1991 to 12 years in gaol, a reduced penalty in recognition of her assistance. Meanwhile, the latest generation of the RAF continued to act. In November 1989 they had murdered Alfred Herrhausen, chief executive of Deutsche Bank, and in April 1991 they intervened directly in the process of German unification by killing Detlev **Rohwedder**, president of the *Treuhandanstalt*. One year later, however, in April 1992 a letter purporting to be from the command of the RAF offered to suspend violence in favour of political action. The Federal authorities treated it with caution.

Reich, Jens (b. March 26, 1939) co-founder of **New Forum**, 1989. Reich was a professor of molecular biology at the Academy of Sciences in East **Berlin**, but he was dismissed for political reasons. He mixed in intellectual and oppositional circles and in 1989 was one of the prime movers of the citizens' movement. Along with Bärbel **Bohley** and others he founded New Forum (NF) and in March 1990 was elected to the *Volkskammer* for **Alliance 90**, the electoral list which included NF. He then became its parliamentary spokesman. Since the decline of the citizens' movement Reich has not been at the political forefront, but he is still very much involved in publishing and in academic organizations.

Republicans, The (*Die Republikaner* — REPs). *Address.* Sandstr. 41, D-8000 Munich 2. *Foundation.* 1983. *Membership.* 25,000 (in west Germany). *Leadership.* Franz Schönhuber (ch. intermittently since 1985). *History.* The Republicans are a party of the extreme right, often accused of neo-Nazism. They originated in west Germany and scored there some significant electoral successes in 1989: 7.5 per cent of the vote in West **Berlin** and 7.1 per cent in the Federal Republic as a whole in the elections to the European Parliament. In **Bavaria** and **Baden-Württemberg** their advance was even more spectacular, causing fears in Germany and elsewhere of a revival of the extreme right. The Republicans' appeal was eclipsed by the events of 1989–90 and, partly because they were banned in the GDR in the run-up to the *Volkskammer* election and their populist chairman Franz Schönhuber was refused entry to the country, their hopes of exploiting the situation were dashed. In the December 1990 election to the new *Bundestag* the Republicans' vote was 2.3 per cent in west Germany and even less (1.3 per cent) in east Germany. In the Berlin elections on the same day their vote fell back sharply in west Berlin to 3.7 per cent and they scored only 1.9 per cent in the eastern part of the city. However, with the growing social discontent and radical rightist activity of 1991–92, the Republicans are trying to assert a presence in the former GDR. They were reported to be organized in Dresden by June 1991, as was a breakaway group calling itself the **German Alternative**. A Republican revival then manifested itself in west Germany in April 1992, when the party scored a remarkable 10.9 per cent in the *Landtag* election in Baden-Württemberg. *Programme.* Ultra-nationalist aspirations of recovering Germany's lost territories and encouraging foreign workers to leave Germany.

Rhineland-Palatinate (*Rheinland-Pfalz*). *Population.* 3.66 million. *Area.* 19,848 sq km. *Capital.* Mainz. *Other cities.* Koblenz, Ludwigshafen. *Minister president.* Rudolf Scharping (SPD). Rhineland-Palatinate is a state formed in 1947 from Prussian, Bavarian and Hessian territories which had not previously belonged together. Its industries include chemicals (BASF Ludwigshafen), engineering, and shoe manufacture (Pirmasens). Wine production (on the Rhine, Mosel and Nahe rivers), forestry and tourism are also crucial to the local economy. The *Land* has been a bastion of the **CDU** since the founding of the Federal Republic, but in April 1991 provided a shock by giving the **SPD** a majority over the CDU. This was a sign of the political disillusionment which set in in west Germany in the wake of unification and gave a personal message to Chancellor **Kohl**, who was born in the area and was Minister President of the *Land* from 1969 to 1976.

Rohwedder, Detlev (b. Gotha, Thuringia, 1932; d. Düsseldorf, April 1, 1991), Supervisory, then Executive President of the *Treuhandanstalt*, July/August 1990–April 1991. In 1969 Rohwedder was appointed state secretary in the Ministry of Economics in **Bonn**, and he served under Ministers Karl Schiller, Helmut Schmidt, Hans Friderichs and Otto Graf Lambsdorff. During this time he had responsibilities for trade relations between the Federal Republic and the GDR. He was a member of the **SPD**. In 1980 Rohwedder was appointed chairman of Hoesch, the steel and engineering concern. At the end of June 1990 GDR Prime Minister **de Maizière** asked him to head the supervisory board of the *Treuhandanstalt*, the holding company of all previously state-owned concerns in the GDR. In August, when the Executive President, Reiner **Gohlke**, resigned in frustration, Rohwedder took over. He helped to move the *Treuhandanstalt* more in the direction of privatization (not its original purpose under the **Modrow** government), but in doing so became the target of hostility in east Germany. He and the *Treuhandanstalt* were accused of failing to salvage east German businesses and of putting hundreds of thousands of people out of work. **Red Army Faction** terrorists, possibly with *Stasi* assistance, thought that they could exploit this resentment by murdering Rohwedder. In April 1991 he was gunned down at his Düsseldorf home, causing shock throughout Germany. A memorial service was held in Berlin, led by the Federal President, Richard von **Weizsäcker**, and the *Treuhandanstalt* headquarters in the city were renamed the Detlev Rohwedder House. A fortnight after the assassination Rohwedder's place was taken by Birgit **Breuel**.

Romberg, Walter (b. Schwerin, December 27, 1928), GDR Finance Minister, April–August 1990. Dr Romberg, a mathematician by profession, was the man who signed the first state treaty between the GDR and the Federal Republic of Germany on May 18, 1990. As Finance Minister of the GDR, he and his West German counterpart Theo **Waigel** (CSU) were responsible for the terms of the economic, currency and social union which came into effect on July 1, 1990. Romberg was an early member of the **SDP** (later **SPD**) in late 1989 and joined the **Modrow** government in February 1990 as a minister without portfolio. In April he became one of the six SPD ministers in **de Maizière**'s new cabinet, and was faced immediately by the worsening economic and budgetary situation in the GDR. He had difficulty appraising the current state of affairs, and this led Waigel to criticize him for not having sufficient information to hand. Despite this, the negotiations toward the state treaty went ahead successfully. After currency union Romberg had to reassess the GDR budget and make further claims on the Federal Republic, alleging that unity had been rushed. Romberg then in the summer of 1990 became a casualty of de Maizière's use of his three economics ministers (the others being Pollack at Agriculture and Pohl at Economics) as scapegoats. They were sacked on August 15 and replaced only by state secretaries. Romberg joined the *Bundestag* on October 3, but was not elected on December 2, 1990.

Round Table (*Runder Tisch*). The round table discussions which took place in the GDR on an irregular but increasingly frequent basis from December 7, 1989 were the forum for the elaboration of the political future of the GDR. For the first time on a formal basis the government of the GDR was exposed to opposition criticism and proposals. The Round Table was in fact rectangular, chaired at one end by church representatives and addressed by government spokespersons. By the end of January 1990 the 39 participants were the **LDPD** (3), **NDPD** (3), **DBD** (3), **CDU** (3), Association of Mutual Peasant Aid (*Vereinigung der gegenseitigen Bauernhilfe*) (2), Sorbian Round Table (1), **SED-PDS** (3), **Democratic Awakening** (2), **Independent Women's Association** (2), **Green League** (2), **Peace and Human Rights Initiative** (2), **Green Party** (2),

New Forum (3), **Democracy Now** (2), **SPD** (2), **United Left** (2), and **FDGB** (2). Other organizations were permitted observer status.

Meeting first in the Dietrich Bonhoeffer House and later in the conference building in the grounds of the Niederschönhausen palace in East **Berlin**, the Round Table had no official parliamentary or governmental function. Its plenary sessions and its numerous working parties soon, however, became crucial in the direction of GDR policy. The sessions were earnest and purposeful, but had many chaotic, angry moments. On occasions the **Modrow** government had to back down on policy (on the proposed state security office, for instance), and by February 1990 several of the new groups represented at the Round Table joined the governmental coalition. As the elections of March 18, 1990 approached, competition between the parties increased and the Round Table was closed down.

Saarland. *Population.* 1.05 million. *Area.* 2,570 sq km. *Capital.* Saarbrücken. *Minister president.* Oskar **Lafontaine** (SPD). Bordering France and possessing an important coal-mining area, the Saar was after both the First and Second World Wars detached from Germany. Since January 1957 it has been a *Land* of the Federal Republic, the smallest apart from the city states. Previously heavily dependent on coal, steel and manufacturing, the Saar has undergone some restructuring to come out of a serious economic crisis. One peculiarity of recent politics was that the leader of the GDR deposed in 1989, Erich **Honecker**, and the **SPD**'s candidate for the chancellorship in 1990, Oskar Lafontaine, both came from the Saar. This fact was used in the campaign against Lafontaine, with the slogan, "One Saarländer is enough!"

Saxony, Free State of (*Freistaat Sachsen*). *Population.* 4.84 million. *Area.* 18,337 sq km. *Capital.* Dresden. *Other cities.* Bautzen, Chemnitz, Görlitz, Hoyerswerda, Leipzig, Plauen, Zwickau. *Minister president.* Kurt **Biedenkopf** (CDU). One of the new *Länder* of the Federal Republic, largely co-terminous with its pre-1933 namesake. Formed in 1945, it was effectively abolished in 1952 and divided up into the districts of Dresden, **Leipzig** and Chemnitz (1953–90 Karl-Marx-Stadt). It was reconstituted by the *Volkskammer* law of July 22, 1990. From the beginnings of industrial development in Germany, Saxony has been one of the core industrial centres and it contributed nearly one-third of the industrial output of the GDR. Major industries have been mechanical engineering, motor cars (Trabant, Zwickau), light industry, textiles, electronics, and lignite and uranium mining. Lignite production is to be greatly curtailed and previously Soviet-controlled uranium extraction is stopping altogether. A local speciality, previously reserved for the élite of the GDR, is the wine produced on the river Elbe near Meissen. During the revolution of 1989 the cities of Leipzig and Dresden played an important role in challenging the old regime, but now Dresden has acquired the unpleasant reputation of being the centre of east German neo-Nazism. Saxony is governed by the **CDU**, which has an absolute majority in the *Landtag*.

Saxony-Anhalt (*Sachsen-Anhalt*). *Population.* 2.92 million. *Area.* 20,445 sq km. *Capital.* Magdeburg. *Other cities.* Dessau, Halle, Halle-Neustadt, Stendal, Wittenberg. *Minister president.* Werner **Münch** (CDU). One of the new *Länder* of the Federal Republic, comprising the pre-1933 Prussian province of Saxony, the *Land* of Anhalt and some territories of Brunswick and **Thuringia**. Initially a province in 1945, it became a *Land* in 1947 but was effectively abolished in 1952 and divided up into the districts of Magdeburg and Halle. It was reconstituted by the *Volkskammer* law of July 22, 1990. Saxony-Anhalt has been dominated economically by chemicals (Halle, Merseburg, Bitterfeld), lignite mining, copper smelting and other heavy industry, but the disastrous environmental consequences mean that many concerns will have to be closed down. The eastern Harz region around Wernigerode is by contrast a popular tourist area, and in the south of the state wine is produced in small quantities in the Saale-Unstrut area. Saxony-Anhalt is governed by the **CDU** in coalition with the **FDP**.

Schabowski, Günter (b. Anklam, West Pomerania, January 4, 1929), GDR spokesman, October–November 1989. Günter Schabowski was editor of the **SED** party newspaper *Neues Deutschland*, before becoming SED First Secretary for **Berlin** and a full *Politbüro* member in 1985. In 1989 he assisted **Krenz** in the ousting of **Honecker** and for a short time was the public spokesman of the new regime. It was Schabowski who gave the laconic announcement on November 9, 1989 that GDR citizens were to be allowed to travel freely. Like Krenz, he failed to master the rapidly changing situation and in the winter of 1989–90 was deprived of office and of his party membership. In November 1990 a series of extended interviews with Schabowski was published as *Das Politbüro: Ende eines Mythos* (The *Politbüro*: End of a Myth). In it Schabowski describes in much greater detail than Krenz the workings of the Honecker regime and on many points contests Krenz's account. He is also much more open than Krenz or Honecker about the failings of the GDR which led to its demise. Schabowski published further memoirs as *Der Absturz* (The Fall) in April 1991.

Schalck-Golodkowski, Alexander (b. Berlin, July 3, 1932), State Secretary in the GDR Ministry of Foreign Trade, 1975–89. Of all the careers which were exposed to the light in the aftermath of the revolution in the GDR, that of Schalck-Golodkowski was the most extraordinary. Although apparently a background figure in the **Honecker** years, he had been the principal agent in the procurement of desperately-needed hard currency for the regime, and simultaneously a senior officer in the *Stasi*. He operated as head of the department of "Commercial Co-ordination" (*Kommerzielle Koordinierung* — KoKo) within the Ministry of Foreign Trade and was involved in many surreptitious machinations, including arms dealing. When his activities came under investigation in late November 1989 he fled the GDR for West **Berlin**. There he was questioned, but released in January 1990. Although Schalck-Golodkowski is suspected of many illegal activities, including embezzlement on his own behalf, he is yet to face charges in court and he lives in comfort in **Bavaria**. This fact has aroused understandable resentment amongst the population of the former GDR.

Schäuble, Wolfgang (b. Freiburg im Breisgau, September 18, 1942), Federal Minister of the Interior (CDU) 1989–91. Schäuble studied law and economics in Freiburg and **Hamburg** and joined the **CDU** in 1965. He had university and state employment and qualified as a lawyer in 1978. A member of the ***Bundestag*** from 1972, he was appointed chief of Chancellor **Kohl**'s office in 1984. He held this post, which was combined with ministerial status, until his move to the Ministry of the Interior in 1989. This put him in a crucial position when in 1990 the negotiations began on the shape of German unity. It was Schäuble who, together with Günther **Krause** on the GDR side, formulated the unification treaty which was signed on August 31, 1990. Schäuble has described the process in his book *Der Vertrag: Wie ich über die deutsche Einheit verhandelte* (The Treaty: How I negotiated German unity). Only shortly after the achievement of German unity, however, Schäuble was the victim of an assassination attempt on October 12, 1990 in Oppenau, Baden. The would-be killer was apparently not connected to any political organization. Schäuble was left wheelchair-bound, but he determined to continue with his political career.

Schleswig-Holstein. *Population.* 2.57 million. *Area.* 15,728 sq km. *Capital.* Kiel. *Other city.* Lübeck. *Minister president.* Björn **Engholm** (SPD). The northernmost of the *Länder* of the Federal Republic, bordering Denmark. Schleswig-Holstein became a Prussian province in 1866 after the military defeat of first Denmark, then Austria. After the First World War northern Schleswig was ceded to Denmark once more. With the break-up of Prussia after the Second World War Schleswig-Holstein became a *Land* in 1946. At this time it experienced a massive inflow of refugees from eastern and central Germany. It is an area dominated by agriculture and the sea, with both North Sea and Baltic coasts. The **CDU** has been politically dominant in the region since the founding of the Federal Republic, but in the 1980s a political scandal arose from the secret political manoeuvres of Minister President Uwe Barschel. He was found dead in mysterious circumstances and the affair led to electoral reverses for his party. The **SPD** achieved an absolute majority in 1988 and although this was lost in April 1992 Minister President Engholm, by now national leader of the SPD, still had a narrow overall majority in the *Landtag*. The same April election also saw a shock surge in the vote for the neo-Nazi **German People's Union** (DVU) which — together with the success of the **Republicans** in **Baden-Württemberg** on the same day — caused consternation amongst senior figures of the mainstream political parties. The results symbolized the economic and social problems which are affecting political behaviour in west as well as in east Germany.

Schnur, Wolfgang (b. Stettin, now Szczecin, Poland, June 8, 1944), chairman of **Democratic Awakening**, 1989–90. Schnur was the first chairman (elected December 17, 1989) of Democratic Awakening (DA), one of the three parties in the conservative Alliance for Germany. He participated in the **Round Table** political discussions in East **Berlin**, and also in the talks with **Kohl**, Ebeling and **de Maizière** in February 1990. On March 14, 1990, just before the *Volkskammer* elections, he resigned, after admitting he had been a collaborator with the *Stasi*. He was replaced by Rainer **Eppelmann**, but the scandal severely weakened the DA. It performed very badly in the *Volkskammer* election (four seats) and in all subsequent votes, losing leading members and eventually disappearing into the **CDU**.

Schwierzina, Tino (b. Kralowska Huta, Poland, May 30, 1927), mayor of (East) **Berlin** (SPD), 1990 and joint mayor of Berlin, 1990–91. A lawyer who worked in the food industry from the 1950s, Schwierzina was a co-founder of the **SDP** (later **SPD**) in the GDR in 1989. He then came to prominence as the last person to hold the post of mayor of the capital of the GDR. He did so from after the local elections in May 1990 until the day of German unity in October, leading an SPD-CDU coalition. Thereafter he shared the honour of being mayor of the united city with Walter **Momper**, his SPD colleague from west Berlin. After the CDU had won the Berlin elections in December 1990, Eberhard **Diepgen** took over as head of a CDU-SPD coalition in January 1991.

SDP (*Sozialdemokratische Partei*). See **Social Democratic Party of Germany** (*Sozialdemokratische Partei Deutschlands* — SPD).

SED (*Sozialistische Einheitspartei Deutschlands*). See **Party of Democratic Socialism** (*Partei des Demokratischen Sozialismus* — PDS).

SED-PDS (*Sozialistische Einheitspartei Deutschlands* — *Partei des Demokratischen Sozialismus*). See **Party of Democratic Socialism** (*Partei des Demokratischen Sozialismus* — PDS).

Seilschaften. A term used in the aftermath of the revolution in the GDR to describe an alleged old-boy network of former communists and *Stasi* members still acting in politics and the economy to protect each others' interests. The word means literally bands of mountaineers roped together.

Seite, Berndt (b. 1940?), Minister President (CDU) of **Mecklenburg-West Pomerania** from March 1992. Much to the displeasure of Chancellor **Kohl**, there was in March 1992 an internal feud within the *Land* **CDU** leadership between chairman and Federal Transport Minister Günther **Krause**, Minister President Alfred **Gomolka** and others. It brought the resignation of Gomolka and his replacement by Seite. Seite was a veterinary surgeon from Röbel on the Müritz, long active in the evangelical-Lutheran church but only recently engaged in politics. In the autumn of 1989 he became a member of **New Forum**, but switched to the CDU in the spring of 1990. One of the reasons for the local political dispute is the dire state of the economy in the *Land*, particularly in the shipyards and construction industry, and Seite now faces further clashes with both CDU and **FDP** colleagues.

Social Civic Union (*Soziale Bürgerliche Union*). One of the 12 groups which formed the **German Social Union** (DSU) in January 1990.

Social Democratic Party of Germany (*Sozialdemokratische Partei Deutschlands* — SPD). *Addresses*. Ollenhauerstrasse 1, D-5300 Bonn 1; Rungestrasse 3–6, O-1020 Berlin. *Foundation*. 1875. Banned 1933-45. Refounded 1945. In Soviet occupation zone merged with **KPD** 1946 to form **SED**. In GDR refounded as **SDP** October 1989. Renamed SPD January 1990. United with west German SPD September 1990. *Membership*. In 1991: 928,000 (including 28,000 in east Germany). *Leadership*. Björn **Engholm** (ch.); Herta Däubler-Gmelin (dep. ch.); Oskar **Lafontaine** (dep. ch.); Johannes Rau (dep. ch.); Wolfgang **Thierse** (dep. ch.); Karlheinz Blessing (g.s.); Willy Brandt (hon. ch.). *Former GDR leadership*. Ibrahim **Böhme** (sec. 1989–90; ch. 1990); Markus **Meckel** (dep. ch. 1990; acting ch. 1990); Wolfgang Thierse (ch. 1990).

History. The original SPD was founded in Gotha in 1875 and adopted a Marxist programme in Erfurt in 1891. By the eve of the First World War it was the largest party and had the largest parliamentary fraction in Germany. It survived various splits, only to be banned by the Nazis in 1933. It was refounded in the Soviet occupation zone in 1945, but was forced to merge with the

Communist Party (KPD) in 1946 to form the **Socialist Unity Party of Germany** (SED). In the Federal Republic the SPD continued, to become one of the major parties of West German politics. SPD chancellors Willy Brandt and Helmut Schmidt governed from 1969 to 1974 and from 1974 to 1982 respectively.

The new form of the SPD in the GDR was founded (originally as the SDP) at Schwante, north-west of **Berlin**, on October 7, 1989. At this stage it was an illegal organization. The 43 people originally involved had by the end of January 1990 become a membership of 45–50,000. At the party's first national delegates' conference in January 1990 it was decided to change the name from SDP to SPD in order to recognize its commitment to German unity and to facilitate links with the SPD in the Federal Republic. Willy Brandt, honorary chairman of the west German SPD, was asked to assume the same position in the GDR party. He attended an emotional meeting in Gotha early in 1990.

The initial leader of the SPD in the GDR was Ibrahim Böhme. He took the SPD into the March 1990 elections, only to be badly disappointed with 21.9 per cent of the vote and 88 seats. Later that month Böhme fell victim to accusations of collaboration with the *Stasi* (state security). He denied these, but then resigned on grounds of ill health, with the announced intent of clearing his name. Despite several attempts to make a comeback, even after German unification, he failed to free himself of the allegations. Böhme was succeeded in a provisional capacity by Markus Meckel, who was appointed Foreign Minister in the **de Maizière** cabinet. The SPD, drawn into the coalition despite its reservations about the **German Social Union**'s (DSU) presence, also furnished five other ministers, including the Minister of Finance, Walter **Romberg**, who negotiated the treaty on economic and currency union. With Meckel and Romberg in such crucial posts, the SPD might have been expected to make a strong mark on the terms of economic and political union, but their freedom of manoeuvre was much restricted. In August de Maizière sacked Romberg and drove the SPD out of the coalition. De Maizière himself took over foreign affairs from Meckel.

In June 1990 Wolfgang Thierse was unexpectedly elected the new chairman of the SPD. When the party united with its west German counterpart in September, Thierse became a deputy chairman. He was confirmed in this post at the SPD congress in May 1991. In the former GDR the SPD has so far suffered at the hands of a buoyant **Christian Democratic Union** (CDU) and the challenge on the left of the **Party of Democratic Socialism** (PDS). In December 1990 under the candidature of Oskar Lafontaine the SPD could only muster 23.6 per cent of the vote in east Germany, compared to 35.9 per cent in the west. Lafontaine's apparent half-heartedness on the question of German unity and his pessimistic, though realistic, prognosis of the fate of the east German economy failed to win him mass support in the east. The SPD's organization in the former GDR has proved relatively weak, with a membership well down on its initial promise. The west German SPD achieved some electoral successes in 1991 at the expense of the CDU, but since then the party, now under the chairmanship of Björn Engholm, appears to be having as much difficulty as the CDU in coping with the problems of German unity.

Organization. The SPD has a large network of local branches. The party congress every two years elects an executive committee, which then elects a presidium. *Programme.* The SDP/SPD in the GDR represented a revitalization of social democratic ideals. They are still embodied in the Godesberg programme of the west German SPD, adopted in 1959. According to this, "The Social Democratic Party of Germany is the party of the freedom of the spirit. It is a community of people from different directions of belief and thought". The SPD aims for social justice within a free but properly regulated market economy. *Affiliations.* Socialist International; Confederation of Socialist Parties of the European Community.

Socialist Unity Party of Germany (*Sozialistische Einheitspartei Deutschlands* — SED). The former communist ruling party of the GDR. (See **Party of Democratic Socialism**)

Spartacist Workers' Party of Germany (*Spartakist-Arbeiterpartei Deutschlands* — SpAD). *Foundation.* January 1990. One of several small parties of the left which tried to retrieve Leninist and Trotskyist socialism from the legacy of the **Socialist Unity Party** (SED). It very shortly lost some of its adherents to a breakaway SpAD-Leninist party and when it stood in the election of March 1990 it won only 2,417 votes.

SPD (*Sozialdemokratische Partei Deutschlands*). See **Social Democratic Party of Germany**.

Stasi (state security). The nickname for the office and personnel of the Ministry for State Security (*Ministerium für Staatssicherheit* — MfS) in the GDR, founded in 1950 and abolished during the revolution of 1989. Led since 1957 by Minister Erich Mielke, it expanded into a vast network of internal and external espionage. By the end it had 86,000 full-time employees, 109,000 informers, 2,000 buildings, and an immense arsenal. The *Stasi* involved itself in surveillance of multifarious kinds and overt suppression of dissent. Its high command structure remains unclear, since Egon **Krenz**, the former party secretary for security, claims that **Honecker** and Mielke took all decisions between them. The internal security budget in 1989 was M 3.6 billion, about 1.3 per cent of total spending, but total financial commitment to the *Stasi* was probably much higher than this.

So feared and hated was the *Stasi* that it was one of the first institutions to be reformed at the end of 1989. It became first of all the Office of National Security, as Mielke was dismissed and arrested, but then **Modrow**'s proposal to revive a state security service was defeated by opposition objections. In January 1990, in one of the few violent incidents of the revolution in the GDR, tens of thousands of East Berliners stormed and ransacked the headquarters of the organization in the Normannenstrasse in Lichtenberg, East **Berlin**, but there are suspicions that incognito *Stasi* officers themselves may have egged on the protesters, in order that compromising files be destroyed. Certainly many files were deliberately shredded in the last days of the old regime.

The damage which the *Stasi* did in the GDR continues to be felt. Accusations have been made of emergent politicians' murky pasts in its service. Wolfgang **Schnur** of **Democratic Awakening** had to resign after admitting involvement. Ibrahim **Böhme** of the **SPD** did so while denying it. Lothar de Maizière repeatedly tried to fend off accusations that as agent "Czerny" he had informed on his legal clients, but in the end he had to forgo all political office. His former colleague, Gregor **Gysi** of the **PDS**, has come under suspicion, as has the SPD Minister President of **Brandenburg**, Manfred **Stolpe**. The activities or alleged activities of these prominent individuals is only part of the story, for when the supervisory body led by Joachim **Gauck** opened up the *Stasi* files relating to individuals in the winter of 1991–92 the true extent of *Stasi* infiltration of everyday life became apparent. The press abounded in reports of husbands spying on wives, of fathers informing on sons, and of friends betraying friends. Another aspect of *Stasi* activity also came to light in 1990, when several terrorists from the **Red Army Faction**, long sought by the police in West Germany, were found to be living under assumed names in the GDR. They had been given refuge and assistance by the *Stasi*.

Stolpe, Manfred (b. Stettin, now Szczecin, Poland, May 16, 1935), Minister President of **Brandenburg** (SPD) from October 1990. Stolpe studied law in Jena and then spent his career in the evangelical church. From 1969 to 1981 he was in charge of the secretariat of the Church League and from 1982 he was consistorial president of the **Berlin**-Brandenburg church. Throughout this time he was engaged in negotiating the difficult relationship between church and state in the GDR, which found a basis in the agreement of March 1978. The churches were permitted a certain degree of autonomy within the socialist system, but the system itself was not to be challenged. Stolpe entered politics after the *Wende* in the GDR, joining the **SPD** and leading it to victory in the *Land* elections in Brandenburg in October 1990. He formed a coalition of SPD, **FDP** and **Alliance 90** and generated a good deal of personal popularity for the way in which he stood up for the people of the former GDR. In the winter of 1991–92, however, it was revealed that he had had contacts with the *Stasi* and had on occasions passed on information. Unlike most of those prominent people faced with such a liability from the past, Stolpe neither resigned nor denied the charges. Instead, he made public the nature of his contacts with the security service and argued that for anyone in a position of responsibility in the GDR such dealings were normal and necessary. He survived the initial onslaught of criticism, but it was revived in April 1992 when new material came to light. Stolpe was under great pressure to resign.

Stoph, Willi (b. Berlin, July 9, 1914), GDR prime minister 1976–89. Willi Stoph joined the **KPD** in 1931, and served in the German army during the Second World War. Subsequently he had a long career in the **SED**, filling numerous functions and joining the *Politbüro* in 1953. For most of the period 1964–89 he was the equivalent of prime minister (Chairman of the Council of Ministers). On Ulbricht's death he became head of state (Chairman of the Council of State) from 1973 to 1976, but in this position as in his other he was subordinate to the General Secretary of the party. For all his long years near the top of GDR politics, Stoph failed to make a strong public impact. Only in March 1970, when he received West German Chancellor Willy Brandt at a pioneering encounter in Erfurt, did he have a high profile and even then the crowds were more appreciative of the West German "Willy" than the East German "Willi". Stoph showed every outward sign of loyalty to **Honecker**, even when the latter notoriously poked fun at him in public. The two never seemed particularly close associates, but Stoph fulfilled a useful role as a dependable undemonstrative anchorman. In the autumn of 1989 Stoph helped to engineer Honecker's demise, but his government resigned on November 7, 1989 and he was replaced on November 13 by Hans **Modrow**. In his memoirs Modrow complains that Stoph refused to vacate his office immediately and forced Modrow to work from a hotel room.

Thierse, Wolfgang (b. Breslau, now Wrocław, Poland, October 22, 1943), chairman of SPD in GDR, June–October 1990. The downfall of **SPD** chairman Ibrahim **Böhme** led to his eventual replacement by Wolfgang Thierse. Son of a lawyer and brought up a Christian, Thierse studied German in East **Berlin**. His protest against the expulsion of the singer Wolf Biermann in 1976 led to dismissal from his post in the Ministry of Culture. Thereafter he worked in the Academy of Science. In 1989 he was first with **New Forum** and then joined the new **SDP** (later **SPD**). In March 1990 he was elected for East Berlin to the *Volkskammer*, and in June was the surprise victor in the election of a new SPD chairman. He joined the *Bundestag* in October 1990, being elected for Berlin in December. With the union of the East and West SPD organizations, Thierse became a deputy chairman of the party.

Thuringia (*Thüringen*). *Population*. 2.65 million. *Area*. 16,251 sq km. *Capital*. Erfurt. *Other cities*. Altenburg, Gera, Gotha, Jena, Suhl, Weimar. *Minister president*. Bernhard **Vogel** (CDU). By area the smallest of the new *Länder* of the Federal Republic, largely co-terminous with its pre-1933 namesake. Formed as a province in 1946 and a *Land* in 1947, it was effectively abolished in 1952 and divided up into the districts of Erfurt, Gera and Suhl. It was reconstituted by the *Volkskammer* law of July 22, 1990. The main industries have been optics (Zeiss, Jena), motor cars (Wartburg, Eisenach), electronics (Robotron, Sömmerda), potassium mining (southern Harz and Werra valley) and Soviet-controlled uranium mining (Ronneburg area). Jobs in all of these have been cut back drastically, and for environmental reasons the mining is to cease. Some western investment has moved in, especially in Eisenach. The Thuringian Forest in the south-west of the state is a tourist attraction, but here too ecological damage has been widespread.

Treuhandanstalt (Trust Agency). *Address*. Leipziger Strasse 5–7, O-1080 Berlin. *President*. Birgit **Breuel**. The *Treuhandanstalt* was established by the **Modrow** government in March 1990 as a public institution subordinate to the government and the new legal owner of all the businesses formerly classified as "people's concerns" (VEB) and "combines" (*Kombinate*). These and other categories within the state-owned economy were transformed either into limited liability companies (GmbH) or joint-stock companies (*Aktiengesellschaften* — AG). Excluded were the public enterprises of the *Deutsche Post* (postal and telephone service), *the Deutsche Reichsbahn* (railways), and the administration of roads and waterways. The *Treuhandanstalt*, initially under the chairmanship of the head of the West German *Bundesbahn*, Reiner **Gohlke**, sat in East **Berlin**, where it was subdivided into five trustee companies: for heavy industry, for the investment goods industry, for the consumer goods industry, for agriculture and forestry, and for trade and the service sector. The *Treuhandanstalt* had regional offices in each of the 15 districts of the GDR. Its remit was a large one. It could order enquiries into the operations and finances of the concerns and it could make funds available to restructure them. In the longer term its purpose was to sell them off. The process moved very slowly to begin with. By mid-July 1990 a quarter of the approximately 8,000 concerns involved had still not been transformed into capitalized companies, and of those now legally GmbH or AG, many did not yet have full complements of chairmen, boards and management. Another problem was that companies put in large claims for restructuring funds.

The *Treuhandanstalt* had to make controversial choices about which businesses were viable in the longer term and should be supported for the time being. For the month of July 1990 alone claims totalled over DM17 billion, of which 41 per cent were approved.

The slow progress made by the *Treuhandanstalt*, the emphasis which it was forced to place on keeping ailing industries going rather than on selling them, and the accusations made that bureaucrats and managers still in place from the old system were hampering advance all took their toll, and only four weeks after his appointment Gohlke resigned. He said that the task of privatization was more difficult than he had originally assumed and that the GDR economy was in chaos. Gohlke was replaced by Detlev **Rohwedder**, chairman of Hoesch steel and already chairman of the *Treuhandanstalt*'s supervisory board. Despite voicing many qualms himself about the efficacy of the *Treuhandanstalt* in the face of its enormous task, Rohwedder was persuaded by the West German government to carry on into 1991. The emphasis shifted much more towards the privatization of concerns, but this brought its own criticism from amongst those in the GDR faced with redundancy. Rohwedder himself fell victim to a terrorist assassination by the **Red Army Faction** in April 1991. He was succeeded by Birgit Breuel.

By March 1992 the *Treuhandanstalt* had disposed of about 5,500 companies to new owners, plus nearly 15,000 retail outlets. This left about 5,800 companies still in the hands of the *Treuhandanstalt*. The total is more than the original 8,000 because the larger concerns were split up for sale and/or restructuring. (See also Jeffries essay in this volume.)

Trust Agency. See *Treuhandanstalt* (previous entry).

Two-Plus-Four talks. The "two" were the Federal Republic and the GDR, and the "four" were the former occupying powers, the USA, the Soviet Union, the United Kingdom and France. The talks were necessary because the four powers still had authority in Berlin and vestiges of it in the remainder of Germany. In the absence of a peace treaty after the Second World War and for German unification to be attained in conditions of full sovereignty, the agreement of the four powers was essential. The process began in Ottawa in February 1990, when it was agreed that negotiations should take place, and after some preliminary discussions the talks ran from May to September 1990 in **Bonn**, **Berlin**, Paris and Moscow. Because of the sensitivity of Germany's future eastern border the Polish foreign minister was invited to the Paris meeting in July 1990. There was initially evidence that the British and French had reservations about immediate German unification, but once Mikhail Gorbachev in July 1990 made it clear that a united Germany could remain part of NATO if it wished, there were few obstacles in the way of agreement. Although the Two-Plus-Four accord had not been fully ratified in the respective countries before the day of German unification, Germany could assume that sovereignty had been regained.

United Left (*Vereinigte Linke* — VL). *Foundation*. October 1989. *Membership*. 1,500–2,000 (January 1990); 300–500 (March 1990). *Leadership*. Marion Seelig, Thomas Klein (spokespersons). *History*. The VL is a socialist group formed in opposition to the old GDR regime. It had various origins, including the groups "Votes against" (*Gegenstimmen*) and "Church from below" (*Kirche von unten*), and the environmental library at the Zion church in East **Berlin** and the Green "Ark Network", both of which had been harassed by the security forces. In its "Böhlen manifesto" of September 1989 it called for a "left, socialist alternative". From December 1989 the VL was represented at the **Round Table** debates. In January it temporarily joined an abortive electoral alliance with, among others, the **Social Democratic Party, Democratic Awakening** (DA) and **New Forum**, and explored links with the **Greens** and the **Independent Women's Association** (UFV), but in the following month it switched to a pact with the **Carnations**, who had previously been a group within VL. In the March election this Action Alliance United Left received 20,340 votes. The VL subsequently shrank in importance but it did not disappear. In December 1990 Jutta Braband of the VL was elected to the ***Bundestag***, but on the Left List/**PDS**. *Programme*. The original aim of the VL was to find a third, socialist path between capitalism and the command socialist economy of the old GDR.

USPD (*Unabhängige Sozialdemokratische Partei Deutschlands*). See **Independent Social Democratic Party of Germany**.

Vertragsgemeinschaft (contractual community). A short-lived term used by political leaders in the winter of 1989–90 to describe a possible means of drawing together the two German states, short of full union.

Vogel, Bernhard *(b. Göttingen, December 19, 1932)*, Minister President *(CDU) of* **Thuringia** from January 1992. Vogel, a close associate of Chancellor **Kohl**, was Minister of Culture in the *Land* of **Rhineland-Palatinate** from 1967 to 1976 and then its Minister President from 1976 to 1988. He became chairman of the **CDU**'s Adenauer Foundation in 1989. In January 1992, when crisis hit the CDU-led government in Thuringia and Minister President **Duchac** resigned, Kohl proposed Vogel as a replacement. Vogel's brother, Hans-Jochen, was also prominent in German politics, latterly as chairman of the **SPD** from 1987 to 1991.

Volkskammer (People's Chamber). The parliament of the GDR, constitutionally the supreme organ of state, but in practice a rubber-stamping body until 1989–90. The provisional *Volkskammer* was constituted with the founding of the GDR on October 7, 1949 and the first elections were held in 1950. These and subsequent elections until March 1990 were based not on free choice but on a pre-determined distribution of seats among official candidates from the block parties and mass organizations. The 500 members of the *Volkskammer* met infrequently in the Palace of the Republic to endorse decisions by the state (and party) leadership. From November 1989 the deliberations of the *Volkskammer* became more influential, and after the March 1990 election the televised debates of the now 400 members, though often criticized for their meanderings, took on real meaning as the GDR reformed and then dissolved itself. All constitutional changes required a two-thirds majority in the *Volkskammer*. From October 3, 1990 until the all-German election in December 144 delegates from the now defunct *Volkskammer* joined the ***Bundestag***. The Palace of the Republic is now closed because of asbestos pollution. It has been suggested that it should be demolished to make way for a reconstruction of the Hohenzollern palace which it replaced.

Waigel, Theo (b. Oberrohr, Bavaria, April 22, 1939), Federal Minister of Finance (CSU) and chairman of CSU in Bavaria. Waigel joined the **CSU** in 1960, studied law in **Bavaria**, and entered the ***Bundestag*** in 1972. From 1982 to 1989 he was deputy chairman of the CDU-CSU parliamentary group and in 1988 he was elected chairman of the CSU. In 1989 Chancellor **Kohl** appointed him Federal Minister of Finance. Waigel's principal role in the preparation of German unity was the negotiation of the state treaty between the Federal Republic and the GDR on currency, economic and social union from July 1, 1990. He conducted the process rapidly, showing signs of impatience with his East German counterpart, Walter **Romberg**. Waigel's criticism of Romberg that the latter did not have the necessary financial information to hand now pales into insignificance in the light of Waigel's own initial underestimation of the costs of German unity. His figure of DM115 billion over five years was from the outset plainly inadequate, and Waigel has since had to renege on the **Bonn** government's pledge not to increase taxes. From July 1, 1991 a temporary package of tax rises came into effect and the following month Waigel announced the necessity of an increase in VAT from 14 to 15 per cent. Waigel's budgets since German unification have had to be augmented by supplementary measures, and the extent of government borrowing has soared.

Warteschleife. The term used to describe the temporary suspension of employees, primarily professional employees, in the former GDR, pending investigation of their past behaviour and affiliations. After the *Warteschleife* many have been dismissed.

Weizsäcker, Richard von (b. Stuttgart, April 15, 1920), Federal President since 1984. Before the Second World War Weizsäcker, the son of a diplomat, was educated in **Berlin** and abroad. He served in the German *Wehrmacht* from 1938 to 1945 and was taken prisoner-of-war. He subsequently studied law and history in Göttingen, and thereafter practised law, particularly in the field of business. He became active both in the evangelical church and in the **CDU**, which he joined in 1954. He was a member of the ***Bundestag*** from 1969 to 1981, and then from 1981 to 1984 Governing Mayor of (West) Berlin. He was then elected Federal President. In the process of German unification Weizsäcker's role had to be a cautious one, since the President's powers are circumscribed, but he did, for instance, make clear his favouring Berlin as the capital of Germany once more.

Wende (turning point or change). The term used generally to describe the changes which came about in the GDR from the autumn of 1989, but also specifically to mean the recognition by the new **SED** leadership under Egon **Krenz** that rigid orthodoxy could no longer control the situation. Although Krenz admitted a greater degree of pluralism in the GDR and opened the borders on November 9, 1989 his conception of the *Wende* did not include the abandonment of socialism, nor of the Warsaw Pact and certainly not of the GDR itself. The term in fact meant a playing down by the SED of the momentous nature of the events.

Young Union (*Junge Union* — JU). One of the 12 groups which formed the **German Social Union** (DSU) in January 1990.

TABLES OF GOVERNMENTS, ELECTION RESULTS AND ECONOMIC INDICATORS

Table 1: *The Federal Republic of Germany: basic facts*

	1988	1989	1990	1991
Area (000 sq km)	249	249	357[1]	357[1]
Population (millions)	61.4	62.0	78.8[1]	79.5[1,2]
GNP at market prices (DM billions)	2,107	2,244	2,429	2,617
Real GNP growth (%)	3.7	3.9	4.5	2.0[1,2]
Consumer price inflation (%)	1.3	2.8	2.7	3.3
Trade balance (DM billions fob-cif)	128.0	134.5	105.2	20.8[1]

[1] including former GDR.
[2] estimates.

Table 2: *The Federal Republic: the Kohl government, as in April 1989*

Chancellor	Helmut Kohl (CDU)
Foreign Affairs and Deputy Chancellor	Hans-Dietrich Genscher (FDP)
Interior	Wolfgang Schäuble (CDU)
Defence	Gerhard Stoltenberg (CDU)
Justice	Hans Engelhard (FDP)
Economy	Helmut Haussmann (FDP)
Finance	Theo Waigel (CSU)
Agriculture, Food and Forestry	Ignaz Kiechle (CSU)
Inner German Relations	Dorothee Wilms (CDU)
Labour and Social Order	Norbert Blüm (CDU)
Youth, Family, Women and Health	Ursula Lehr (CDU)
Transport	Friedrich Zimmermann (CSU)
Environment	Klaus Töpfer (CDU)
Post and Telecommunications	Christian Schwarz-Schilling (CDU)
Construction	Gerda Hasselfeldt (CSU)
Research and Technology	Heinz Riesenhuber (CDU)
Education	Jürgen Möllemann (FDP)
Economic Co-operation	Jürgen Warnke (CSU)
Chancellor's Office	Rudolf Seiters (CDU)
Government Spokesman	Hans Klein (CSU)

Table 3: *The GDR: the Politbüro of the SED, as in August 1989*

Erich Honecker

Hermann Axen, Hans-Joachim Böhme, Horst Dohlus, Werner Eberlein, Kurt Hager, Joachim Herrmann, Werner Jarowinsky, Heinz Kessler, Günther Kleiber, Egon Krenz, Werner Krolikowski, Siegfried Lorenz, Erich Mielke, Günter Mittag, Erich Mückenberger, Alfred Neumann, Günter Schabowski, Horst Sindermann, Willi Stoph, Harry Tisch

(candidates) Ingeburg Lange, Gerhard Müller, Margarete Müller, Gerhard Schürer, Werner Walde

Table 4: *The GDR: the Central Committee Secretariat of the SED, as in August 1989*

General Secretary	Erich Honecker
Agitation and Propaganda	Joachim Herrmann
Agriculture	Werner Krolikowski
Berlin	Günter Schabowski
Culture, Science, Education	Kurt Hager
Economy	Günter Mittag
International Affairs	Hermann Axen
Party Organization	Horst Dohlus
Trade, Supply and Church Affairs	Werner Jarowinsky
Security, Youth and Sports	Egon Krenz
Women's Affairs	Ingeburg Lange

Table 5: *The GDR: the State Council, as in August 1989*
(SED unless otherwise indicated)

Chairman (i.e. Head of State)	Erich Honecker
Deputy Chairmen	Manfred Gerlach (LDPD)
	Gerald Götting (CDU)
	Heinrich Homann (NDPD)
	Egon Krenz
	Günther Maleuda (DBD)
	Günter Mittag
	Horst Sindermann
	Willi Stoph
and 19 other members	

Table 6: *The GDR: the Stoph government (Council of Ministers), as in August 1989*
(SED unless otherwise indicated)

Prime Minister (Chairman of Council of Ministers)	Willi Stoph
First Deputy Chairmen	Günther Kleiber
	Alfred Neumann
Deputy Chairmen	Manfred Flegel (NDPD)
	Hans-Joachim Heusinger (LDPD)
	Wolfgang Rauchfuss
	Hans Reichelt (DBD)
	Gerhard Schürer
	Rudolf Schulze (CDU)
	Horst Sölle
	Herbert Weiz
Chairman of the State Planning Commission	Gerhard Schürer
Agriculture, Forestry and Food	Bruno Lietz
Chemical Industry	Günther Wyschofsky
Coal and Energy	Wolfgang Mitzinger
Construction	Wolfgang Junker
Culture	Hans-Joachim Hoffmann
Defence	Heinz Kessler
District-Managed Industry	Udo-Dieter Wange
Electrical Engineering and Electronics	Felix Meier
Environmental Protection and Water Management	Hans Reichelt (DBD)
Finance	Ernst Höfner
Foreign Affairs	Oskar Fischer
Foreign Trade	Gerhard Beil
General Machinery etc.	Gerhard Trautenhahn
Geology	Manfred Bochmann
Glass and Ceramics	Karl Grünheid
Health	Ludwig Mecklinger
Heavy Machinery and Equipment	Hans-Joachim Lauck
Interior	Friedrich Dickel
Justice	Hans-Joachim Heusinger (LDPD)
Light Industry	Werner Buschmann
Machine Tools etc.	Rudi Georgi
Management of Materials	Wolfgang Rauchfuss
Ore Mining, Metallurgy and Potash	Kurt Singhuber
Post and Telecommunications	Rudolf Schulze
Public Education	Margot Honecker
Science and Technology	Herbert Weiz
State Security	Erich Mielke
Trade and Supply	Gerhard Briksa
Transport	Otto Arndt
University and Technical School Affairs	Hans-Joachim Böhme
and eight others	

Table 7: *The GDR: the Modrow government, November 18, 1989*

Prime Minister	Hans Modrow (SED)
Deputy Prime Minister for Economic Affairs	Christa Luft (SED)
Deputy Prime Minister for Local State Bodies	Peter Moreth (LDPD)
Deputy Prime Minister for Church Affairs	Lothar de Maizière (CDU)
Agriculture, Forestry and Food	Hans Watzek (DBD)
Construction and Housing	Gerhard Baumgärtel (CDU)
Culture	Dietmar Keller (SED)
Defence	Theodor Hoffmann (SED)
Education and Youth	Hans-Heinz Emons (SED)
Employment and Wages	Hannelore Mensch (SED)
Engineering	Karl Grünheid (SED)[1]
Environmental Protection	Hans Reichelt (DBD)[2]
Finance and Prices	Uta Nickel (SED)[3]
Foreign Affairs	Oskar Fischer (SED)
Foreign Trade	Gerhard Beil (SED)
Health and Social Welfare	Klaus Thielmann (SED)
Heavy Industry	Kurt Singhuber (SED)
Internal Affairs	Lothar Ahrendt (SED)
Justice	Hans-Joachim Heusinger (LDPD)[4]
Light Industry	Gunter Halm (NDPD)
Office for National Security	Wolfgang Schwanitz (SED)
Post and Telecommunications	Klaus Wolf (CDU)
Science and Technology	Klaus-Peter Budig (LDPD)
Tourism	Bruno Benthien (LDPD)
Trade and Supply	Manfred Flegel (NDPD)
Transport	Heinrich Scholz (SED)
Chairman of the State Planning Commission	Gerhard Schürer (SED)[5]
Government Spokesman & Head of Press Office	Wolfgang Meyer (SED)

[1] replaced by Hans-Joachim Lauck (SED-PDS), January 11, 1990; Grünheid became Chairman of the Committee on the Economy.
[2] resigned January 9, 1990, replaced by Peter Diederich (DBD).
[3] resigned January 22, 1990.
[4] dismissed January 5, 1990, replaced by Kurt Wünsche (LDPD).
[5] dismissed January 1990.

TABLES OF GOVERNMENTS, ELECTION RESULTS AND ECONOMIC INDICATORS

Table 8: *The GDR: the Modrow Government of National Responsibility, February 5, 1990*

Prime Minister	Hans Modrow (PDS)
Deputy Prime Minister and Economic Affairs	Christa Luft (PDS)
Deputy Prime Minister and Local State Bodies	Peter Moreth (LDPD)
Deputy Prime Minister and Church Affairs	Lothar de Maizière (CDU)
Defence	Theodor Hoffmann (PDS)
Education	Hans-Heinz Emons (PDS)
Employment and Wages	Hannelore Mensch (PDS)
Engineering	Hans-Joachim Lauck (PDS)
Environmental Protection	Peter Diederich (DBD)
Foreign Affairs	Oskar Fischer (PDS)
Foreign Trade	Gerhard Beil (PDS)
Health and Social Welfare	Klaus Thielmann (PDS)
Internal Affairs	Lothar Ahrendt (PDS)
Justice	Kurt Wünsche (LDPD)
Science and Technology	Klaus-Peter Budig (LDPD)
Trade and Supply	Manfred Flegel (NDPD)
Transport	Heinrich Scholz (PDS)
Chairman of the Committee on the Economy	Karl Grünheid (PDS)
Government Spokesman & Head of Press Office	Wolfgang Meyer (PDS)
Without Portfolio	Tatjana Böhm (UFV)
	Rainer Eppelmann (DA)
	Sebastian Flugbeil (NF)
	Mathias Platzeck (GP)
	Gerd Poppe (IFM)
	Walter Romberg (SPD)
	Klaus Schlüter (GL)
	Wolfgang Ullmann (DJ)

Note: The party appellations refer to the political origins of the ministers; officially they were now non-party.

Abbreviations
UFV = Independent Women's Association
NF = New Forum
GP = Green Party
IFM = Peace and Human Rights Initiative
GL = Green League
DJ = Democracy Now

Table 9: *The GDR: the De Maizière Government, April 9, 1990*

Prime Minister	Lothar de Maizière (CDU)
Chief of Prime Minister's Staff	Klaus Riechenbach (CDU)
Government Spokesman	Mathias Dehler (CDU)
Interior and Deputy Prime Minister	Peter-Michael Diestel (DSU)
Foreign Affairs	Markus Meckel (SPD)
Defence and Disarmament	Rainer Eppelmann (DA)
Economy	Gerhard Pohl (CDU)
Finance	Walter Romberg (SPD)
Environment and Energy	Karl-Hermann Steinberg (CDU)
Education and Science	Hans-Joachim Meyer (Ind)
Research and Technology	Frank Terpe (SPD)
Trade and Tourism	Sybille Reider (SPD)
Economic Co-operation	Hans-Wilhelm Ebeling (DSU)
Justice	Kurt Wünsche (BFD)
Labour and Social Affairs	Regine Hildebrandt (SPD)
Post and Telecommunications	Emil Schnell (SPD)
Transport	Horst Gibtner (CDU)
Construction	Axel Viehweger (BFD)
Regional and Local Affairs	Manfred Preiss (BFD)
Agriculture	Peter Pollack (Ind)[1]
Health	Jürgen Kleditzsch (CDU)
Media	Gottfried Müller (CDU)
Culture	Herbert Schirmer (CDU)
Women and Family Affairs	Christa Schmidt (CDU)
Youth and Sport	Cordula Schubert (CDU)

[1] nominated by SPD.

TABLES OF GOVERNMENTS, ELECTION RESULTS AND ECONOMIC INDICATORS

Table 10: *The Federal Republic: the Kohl Government, January 16, 1991*

Chancellor	Helmut Kohl (CDU)
Foreign Affairs and Deputy Chancellor	Hans-Dietrich Genscher (FDP)[1]
Interior	Wolfgang Schäuble (CDU)[7]
Defence	Gerhard Stoltenberg (CDU)[2]
Justice	Klaus Kinkel (FDP)[3]
Economy	Jürgen Möllemann (FDP)
Finance	Theo Waigel (CSU)
Agriculture, Food and Forestry	Ignaz Kiechle (CSU)
Labour and Social Order	Norbert Blüm (CDU)
Family and Old People	Hannelore Rönsch (CDU)
Women and Youth	Angela Merkel (CDU)[6]
Health	Gerda Hasselfeldt (CSU)[4]
Transport	Günther Krause (CDU)[6]
Environment	Klaus Töpfer (CDU)
Post and Telecommunications	Christian Schwarz-Schilling (CDU)
Construction	Irmgard Schwaetzer (FDP)[5]
Research	Heinz Riesenhuber (CDU)
Education	Rainer Ortleb (FDP)[6]
Development	Carl-Dieter Spranger (CSU)

[1] resigned with effect from May 17, 1992, replaced by Klaus Kinkel as Foreign Minister and by Jürgen Möllemann as Deputy Chancellor.
[2] resigned March 31, 1992, replaced by Volker Rühe.
[3] appointed Minister of Foreign Affairs with effect from May 17, 1992, replaced by Sabine Leutheusser-Schnarrenberger (FDP).
[4] resigned April 27, 1992, replaced by Horst Seehofer (CSU).
[5] named as new Minister of Foreign Affairs on Genscher's resignation, but then rejected by FDP parliamentary party.
[6] ministers from the former GDR
[7] resigned November 26, 1991 to become chairman of CDU/CSU parliamentary fraction, replaced by Rudolf Seiters (CDU).

Table 11: *Elections to the* Volkskammer *of the GDR, March 18, 1990*
(turnout 93.4 per cent)

	Valid votes	%		Seats	
CDU ⎤	4,710,598	40.8		163	
DSU ⎬ Alliance for Germany	727,730	6.3	48.0	25	192
DA ⎦	106,146	0.9		4	
SPD	2,525,534	21.9		88	
PDS (= former SED)	1,892,381	16.4		66	
BFD (= liberal coalition)	608,935	5.3		21	
A90 (= New Forum & others)	336,074	2.9		12	
DBD (= farmers' party)	251,226	2.2		9	
Greens/Women's Association	226,932	2.0		8	
NDPD	44,292	0.4		2	
Others	111,307	1.0		2	
TOTAL	11,541,155	100.0		400	

Table 12: *Local elections in the GDR, May 6, 1990*
(turnout c. 80 per cent)

	%	Change from March election
CDU	34.4	−6.4
SPD	21.3	−0.6
PDS	14.6	−1.8
DSU	3.4	−2.9
BFD	6.7	+1.4
A90	2.4	−0.5
Farmers' parties (including DBD)	5.7	+3.5
Others	11.5	+7.3
TOTAL	100.0	

Table 13: *Elections to East German* Landtage, *October 14, 1990*
(% of valid votes cast)

	Brandenburg	Mecklenburg-W. Pomerania	Saxony	Saxony-Anhalt	Thuringia
CDU	29.4	38.3	53.8	39.0	45.4
DSU	1.0	0.8	3.6	1.7	3.3
FDP-Liberals	6.6	5.5	5.3	13.5	9.3
SPD	38.3	27.0	19.1	26.0	22.8
Alliance 90	6.4	2.2	5.6	5.3	6.5
Greens	2.8	4.2			
New Forum	—	2.9	—	—	—
PDS	13.4	15.7	10.2	12.0	9.7
Others	2.1	3.4	2.4	2.6	3.0
Turnout	67.4	65.2	73.5	65.6	72.1

Table 14: *Elections to the Berlin House of Representatives, December 2, 1990*

	Berlin %	Berlin seats	West Berlin %	West Berlin (previous %)	East Berlin %	East Berlin (previous %)
CDU	40.3	100	48.9	(37.7)	25.0	(18.6)
SPD	30.5	76	29.5	(37.7)	32.1	(34.0)
PDS	9.2	23	1.1	(—)	23.6	(30.0)
FDP	7.1	18	7.9	(3.9)	5.6	(2.2)
GAL	5.0	12	6.9	(11.8)	1.7	(—)
A90/G	4.4	11	1.4	(—)	9.7	(9.9)
Reps	3.1	—	3.7	(7.5)	1.9	(—)

Abbreviations
GAL = Greens/Alternative List
A90/G = Alliance 90/Greens
Reps = Republicans

Table 15: *Elections to* Bundestag, *December 2, 1990*
(% of valid votes cast)

	Germany	West Germany	(1987)	East Germany	(March)	Seats in new Bundestag
CDU	36.7	35.0	34.5	43.4	40.8	270
CSU	7.1	9.1	9.8	—	—	49
DSU	0.2	—	—	0.9	6.3	—
SPD	33.5	35.9	37.0	23.6	21.9	239
FDP	11.0	10.6	9.1	13.4	—	79
PDS	2.4	—	—	9.9	16.4	17
Greens	3.9	4.7	8.3	—	—	—
Greens/A90	1.2	—	—	5.9	—	8
Republicans	2.1	2.3	—	1.3	—	—
Others	1.9	2.4	1.3	1.6	14.6	—
TOTAL	100.0	100.0	100.0	100.0	100.0	662
Turnout	77.8	78.5	84.4	74.5	93.4	—

Table 16: *Land elections in western Germany 1990–92*
(% of valid votes)

	Saarland Jan. 1990	Lower Saxony May 1990	North Rhine Westphalia May 1990	Bavaria Oct. 1990	Hesse Jan. 1991
CDU[1]	33.4	42.0	36.7	54.9	40.2
SPD	54.4	44.2	50.0	26.0	40.8
FDP	5.6	6.0	5.8	5.2	7.4
Greens	2.7	5.5	5.0	6.4	8.8
Republicans	3.3	1.5	1.8	4.9	1.7
DVU[2]	—	—	—	—	—

	Rhineland Palatinate April 1991	Hamburg June 1991	Bremen Sept. 1991	Baden Württemberg April 1992	Schleswig-Holstein April 1992
CDU	38.7	35.1	30.7	39.6	33.8
SPD	44.8	48.0	38.8	29.4	46.2
FDP	6.9	5.4	9.5	5.9	5.6
Greens	6.4	7.2	11.4	9.5	4.9
Reps	2.0	—	1.5	10.9	1.2
DVU	—	—	6.2	—	6.3

[1] CSU in Bavaria.
[2] German People's Union.

Table 17: *GDR Net Material Product 1984–89*

	1984	1985	1986	1987	1988	1989
NMP at 1985 prices (M bn)	229.9	241.9	252.2	260.6	268.1	273.7
Official NMP growth %	5.5	5.2	4.3	3.3	2.8	2.1

Source: Statistisches Jahrbuch der DDR 1990.

Table 18: *GDR economic indicators 1989–90 (per cent change on period previous year)*

	1989		1990				
	Q3	Q4	Q1	Q2	Q3	Q4	Year
Gross industrial output	3.8	−1.0	−4.5	−9.5	−48.1	−50.0[1]	−20.0[1]
Retail trade turnover	2.7	2.5	7.0	−0.6	−45.0	n.a.	n.a.

[1] estimate
Sources: Statistisches Amt der DDR, Statistisches Bundesamt.

TABLES OF GOVERNMENTS, ELECTION RESULTS AND ECONOMIC INDICATORS

Table 19: *Unemployment and short-time working in territory of GDR 1990–92*

	Unemployed		Short-time		Total	
	'000s	%	'000s	%	'000s	%
Jan. 1990	7	0.1	—		7	0.1
April	65	0.7	—		65	0.7
July	272	3.1	656	7.4	928	10.5
Oct.	537	6.1	1,704	19.1	2,241	25.2
Jan. 1991	757	8.6	1,841	21.0	2,598	29.6
April	837	9.5	2,019	22.7	2,856	32.2
July	1,069	12.1	1,611	18.1	2,680	30.2
Oct.	1,049	11.9	1,200	13.5	2,249	25.4
Jan. 1992	1,343	16.5	520	5.8	1,863	22.3

Sources: *Monatsberichte der Deutschen Bundesbank*, 1990–92.

Table 20: *Gross industrial output in the GDR by sector, 1990*
(Index: 1989=100)

	May	June	July	Aug.	Sept.
Energy and fuels	92.3	87.9	59.9	52.3	61.6
Chemicals	85.2	79.9	59.8	48.5	49.8
Metallurgy	90.3	77.0	39.7	33.1	34.5
Building materials	97.4	97.3	63.0	40.6	34.3
Water industry	105.8	110.1	89.6	100.8	100.3
Machinery and vehicles	97.5	103.8	71.2	64.2	62.6
Electricals	98.9	93.4	67.3	53.3	53.3
Light industry	87.1	75.2	48.9	44.6	46.2
Textiles	81.2	72.2	48.7	44.9	45.7
Food	86.7	72.0	42.3	38.6	37.9
TOTAL	91.0	84.5	57.9	49.2	48.9

Table 21: *GDR foreign trade turnover 1985–88, according to old GDR statistics*
(billions of Valuta Marks)

	1985	1986	1987	1988	%
Socialist countries	119.0	122.6	121.8	122.5	69.1
(of which: USSR	69.9	70.6	68.5	66.5	37.5)
Industrial capitalist countries	52.9	51.4	48.0	48.9	27.6
(of which: West Germany	15.0	13.1	12.5	12.4	7.0)
Developing countries	8.2	7.9	6.7	5.9	3.3
TOTAL	180.2	182.0	176.5	177.3	100.0

Source: *Statistisches Jahrbuch der Deutschen Demokratischen Republik 1986–9.*

Table 22: *GDR foreign trade 1988-89, according to new GDR statistics*
(hard currency value in billions of Marks)

	1988					1989				
	Exp.	Imp.	Bal.	Turnover	%	Exp.	Imp.	Bal.	Turnover	%
USSR	33.5	34.5	−1.0	68.0	24.5	33.5	31.9	1.6	65.4	22.9
West Germany	29.0	25.7	3.3	54.7	19.7	30.2	28.6	1.6	58.8	20.6
Czechoslovakia	8.0	6.9	1.1	14.8	5.4	7.7	6.7	1.1	14.4	5.0
Poland	6.2	6.1	0.1	12.4	4.5	6.4	6.4	−0.0	12.8	4.5
France	4.0	3.5	0.5	7.4	2.7	4.4	6.1	−1.7	10.5	3.7
Hungary	5.6	4.7	0.9	10.4	3.7	5.6	4.9	0.7	10.5	3.7
Switzerland[1]	2.2	7.1	−4.8	9.3	3.4	3.5	6.8	−3.3	10.3	3.6
Austria	2.3	5.9	−3.5	8.2	2.9	2.4	6.6	−4.2	9.0	3.1
Netherlands	2.3	4.5	−2.2	6.8	2.5	2.7	3.6	−0.9	6.3	2.2
Romania	2.7	2.4	0.3	5.1	1.9	2.9	2.7	0.2	5.5	1.9
United Kingdom	2.6	2.8	−0.3	5.4	1.9	3.0	2.4	0.6	5.4	1.9
Bulgaria	3.1	2.7	0.4	5.8	2.1	2.8	2.7	0.1	5.4	1.9
Yugoslavia	2.2	3.1	−0.9	5.3	1.9	2.2	2.8	−0.6	5.0	1.7
Sweden	2.3	1.9	0.4	4.3	1.5	2.3	1.9	0.3	4.2	1.5
China	2.0	2.0	0.1	4.0	1.4	2.1	2.0	0.1	4.1	1.4
Italy	1.2	2.3	−1.1	3.5	1.3	1.4	2.7	−1.4	4.1	1.4
Belgium[1]	2.1	2.2	−0.1	4.3	1.6	1.9	2.0	−0.2	3.9	1.4
Cuba	1.4	1.2	0.2	2.5	0.9	1.4	1.3	0.1	2.8	1.0
Others	22.6	22.2	0.4	44.8	16.2	24.8	22.6	2.2	47.3	16.6
TOTAL	135.3	141.7	−6.4	277.0	100.0	141.1	144.7	−3.6	285.8	100.0

[1] Switzerland includes Liechtenstein; Belgium includes Luxembourg.
Source: *Statistisches Jahrbuch der Deutschen Demokratischen Republik 1990.*

Table 23: *GDR foreign trade January–July 1990, excluding W. Germany* (DM billions)

	Exp.	Imp.	Bal.	Turnover	%
USSR	9.29	6.96	2.33	16.25	42.1
Czechoslovakia	2.28	1.38	0.91	3.66	9.5
Poland	1.27	1.39	-0.12	2.66	6.9
France	0.44	0.44	-0.00	0.88	2.3
Hungary	1.56	0.98	0.58	2.54	6.6
Switzerland[1]	0.31	0.61	-0.31	0.92	2.4
Austria	0.18	0.57	-0.39	0.75	1.9
Netherlands	0.28	0.39	-0.11	0.66	1.7
Romania	0.85	0.35	0.49	1.20	3.1
United Kingdom	0.34	0.29	0.05	0.62	1.6
Bulgaria	0.91	0.51	0.40	1.42	3.7
Others	3.51	3.54	-0.03	7.05	18.3
TOTAL	21.20	17.40	3.80	38.60	100.0

[1] Switzerland includes Liechtenstein.
Source: Statistisches Amt der Deutschen Demokratischen Republik.

A 10-point plan for overcoming the division of Europe and Germany

Speech by Federal Chancellor Helmut Kohl in the *Bundestag*, Bonn, 28 November 1989

Excerpts

(...)
We all know that we cannot plan the way to German unity simply in theory or with our appointment calendars. Abstract models may be all right for polemical purposes but they help us no further. Today, however, we are in a position to prepare in advance the stages which lead to this goal. These I would like to elucidate with the following 10-point plan:

1. Immediate measures are called for as a result of events of recent weeks, particularly the flow of resettlers and the huge increase in the number of travellers. The Federal Government will provide immediate aid where it is needed. We will assist in the humanitarian sector and provide medical aid if it is wanted and considered helpful.

We are also aware that the welcome money given once a year to every visitor from the GDR is no answer to the question of travel funds. The GDR must itself provide travellers with the necessary foreign exchange. We are, however, prepared to contribute to a currency fund for a transitional period, provided that persons entering the GDR no longer have to exchange a minimum amount of currency, that entry into the GDR is made considerably easier, and that the GDR itself contributes substantially to the fund.

Our aim is to facilitate traffic as much as possible in both directions.

2. The Federal Government will continue its co-operation with the GDR in all areas where it is of direct benefit to the people on both sides, especially in the economic, scientific, technological and cultural fields. It is particularly important to intensify co-operation in the field of environmental protection. Here we will be able to take decisions on new projects shortly, irrespective of other developments.

We also want to extensively increase telephone links with the GDR and help expand the GDR's telephone network. The Federal Minister of Posts and Telecommunications has begun talks on this subject.

Negotiations continue on the extension of the Hanover–Berlin railway line. This is not enough, however, and we need to take a thorough look at transport and rail systems in the GDR and the Federal Republic in the light of the new situation. Forty years of separation also mean that traffic routes have in some cases developed quite differently. This applies not only to border crossing-points but to the traditional East–West lines of communication in central Europe. There seems to be no reason why the classical Moscow–Warsaw–Berlin–Paris route, which always included Cologne and was of great importance at all times, should not be brought into consideration in the age of high-speed trains and just as Europe's transport network is to be extended accordingly.

3. I have offered comprehensive aid and co-operation should the GDR bindingly undertake to carry out a fundamental change in the political and economic system and put the necessary measures irreversibly into effect. By "irreversible" we mean that the GDR leadership must reach agreement with opposition groups on constitutional amendments and a new electoral law.

We support the demand for free, equal and secret elections in the GDR, in which, of course, independent, that is to say, non-socialist, parties would also participate. The SED's monopoly on power must be removed. The introduction of a democratic system means, above all, the abolition of laws on political crimes and the immediate release of all political prisoners.

Economic aid can only be effective if the economic system is radically reformed. This is obvious from the situation in all Comecon states and is not a question of our preaching to them. The centrally-planned economy must be dismantled.

We do not want to stabilize conditions that have become indefensible. Economic improvement can only occur if the GDR opens its doors to Western investment, if conditions of free enterprise are created, and if private initiative becomes possible. I don't understand those who accuse us of tutelage in this respect. There are daily examples of this in Hungary and Poland which can surely be followed by the GDR, likewise a member of Comecon.

Our sincere hope is that the necessary legislation will be introduced quickly, because we would not be very happy if private capital were to be invested in Poland — and with developments progressing so well — even more so in Hungary, which I would also welcome, but not in the middle of Germany. We want as many companies as possible to invest as much as possible.

I wish to emphasize once again that these are not preconditions but simply the foundations needed for effective assistance. Nor can there be any doubt that the people in the GDR want this. They want economic freedom which will enable them at long last to reap the fruit of their labour and enjoy more prosperity.

When I consider how this matter of the GDR's future economic system is being discussed by the SED itself — it will all be heard publicly at its special convention in a few days' time — I cannot for the life of me see how anyone saying this can be accused of meddling in the GDR's internal affairs. I find that rather absurd.

4. Prime Minister Modrow spoke in his government policy statement of a "contractual community". We are prepared to adopt this idea. The proximity of our two states in Germany and the special nature of their relationship demand an increasingly close network of agreements in all sectors and at all levels.

This co-operation will also require more common institutions. The existing commissions could be given new tasks and new ones created, especially for industry, transport, environmental protection, science and technology, health and cultural affairs. It goes without saying that Berlin will be fully incorporated in these co-operative efforts. This has always been our policy.

5. We are also prepared to take a further decisive step, namely, to develop confederative structures between the two states in Germany with a view to creating a federation. But this presupposes the election of a democratic government in the GDR.

We can envisage the following institutions being created after early, free elections:

– an intergovernmental committee for continuous consultation and political co-ordination,

– joint technical committees, and

– many others in the light of new developments.

Previous policy towards the GDR had to be limited mainly to small steps by which we sought above all to alleviate the consequences of division and to keep alive and strengthen the people's awareness of the unity of the nation. If, in the future, a democratically legitimized, that is, a freely elected government, becomes our partner, that will open up completely new perspectives.

Gradually, new forms of institutional co-operation can be created and further developed. Such coalescence is inherent in the continuity of German history. State organization in Germany has nearly always taken the form of a confederation or federation. We can fall back on this past experience. Nobody knows at the present time what a reunited Germany will look like. I am, however, sure that unity will come, if it is wanted by the German people.

6. The development of intra-German relations remains embedded in the pan-European process, that is to say in the framework of East–West relations. The future architecture of Germany must fit into the future architecture of Europe as a whole. Here the West has shown itself to be the pacemaker with its concept of a lasting and equitable peaceful order in Europe.

In our joint declaration of June this year, which I have already quoted, General Secretary Gorbachev and I spoke of the structural elements of a "common European home". They are, for example:

– Unqualified respect for the integrity and security of each state. Each state has the right freely to choose its own political and social system.

– Unqualified respect for the principles and rules or international law, especially respect for the people's right of self-determination.

– The realization of human rights.

– Respect for and maintenance of the traditional cultures of the nations of Europe.

With all of these points, as Mr Gorbachev and I laid down, we aim to follow Europe's long traditions and help overcome the division of Europe.

7. The attraction and aura of the European Community are and remain a constant feature of pan-European development. We want to and must strengthen them further still.

The European Community must now approach the reformist countries of central, Eastern and south-eastern Europe with openness and flexibility. This was also endorsed by the heads of state and government of the EC member states at their recent meeting in Paris.

This of course includes the GDR. The Federal Government therefore approves the early conclusion of a trade and co-operation agreement with the GDR. This would give it wider access to the Common Market, also in the perspective of 1992.

We can envisage specific forms of association which would lead the reformist countries of central and south-eastern Europe to the European Community, thus helping to level the economic and social gradients of our continent. This is one of the crucial issues if tomorrow's Europe is to be a united Europe.

We have always regarded the process leading to the recovery of German unity to be a European concern as well. It must, therefore, also be seen in the context of European integration. To put it simply, the EC must not end at the Elbe but must remain open to the East.

Only in this way can the EC be the foundation for a truly comprehensive European Union — after all, we have always regarded the Twelve as only a part, not as the whole, of the Continent. Only in this way can it maintain, assert and develop the common European identity. That identity is not only based on the cultural diversity of Europe but also, and especially, on the fundamental values of freedom, democracy, human rights and self-determination.

If the countries of central and south-eastern Europe meet the requirements we would also welcome their membership of the Council of Europe, and especially of the Convention for the Protection of Human Rights and Fundamental Freedoms.

8. The CSCE process is a central element of the pan-European architecture and must be vigorously promoted in the following forums:

– the Human Rights Conferences in Copenhagen, in 1990, and in Moscow, in 1991,

– the Conference on Economic Co-operation in Bonn, in 1990,

– the symposium on the cultural heritage in Cracow, in 1991, and

– last but not least the next follow-up meeting in Helsinki.

There we should also think about new institutional forms of pan-European co-operation. We can well imagine a common institution for the co-ordination of East–West economic co-operation, as well as the creation of a pan-European environmental council.

9. Overcoming the division of Europe and Germany presupposes far-reaching and rapid steps in the field of disarmament and arms control. Disarmament and arms control must keep pace with political developments and thus be accelerated where necessary.

This is particularly true of the Vienna Negotiations on the Reduction of Conventional Forces in Europe, and for the Agreement on Confidence-Building Measures and the global Ban on Chemical Weapons, which we hope will materialize in 1990. It also requires that the nuclear potential of the superpowers be reduced to the strategically necessary minimum. The forthcoming meeting between President Bush and General Secretary Gorbachev offers a good opportunity to add new impetus to the current negotiations.

We are doing our best — also in bilateral discussions with the Warsaw Pact countries, including the GDR — to support this process.

10. With this comprehensive policy we are working for a state of peace in Europe in which the German nation can recover its unity in free self-determination. Reunification — that is regaining national unity — remains the political goal of the Federal government. We are grateful that once again we have received support in this matter from our allies in the Declaration issued after the NATO Summit Meeting in Brussels in May.

We are conscious of the fact that many difficult problems will confront us on the road to German unity, problems for which no one has a definitive solution today. Above all, this includes the difficult and crucial question of overlapping security structures in Europe.

The linking of the German question to pan-European developments and East–West relations, as explained in these ten points, will allow a natural development which takes account of the interests of all concerned and paves the way for peaceful development in freedom, which is our objective.

Only together and in an atmosphere of mutual trust will we be able to peacefully overcome the division of Europe, which is also the division of Germany. This calls for prudence, understanding and sound judgement on all sides so that the current promising developments may continue steadily and peacefully. This process cannot be hampered by reforms, rather by their rejection. It is not freedom that creates instability but its suppression. Every successful step towards reform means more stability and more freedom and security for the whole of Europe.

In a few weeks' time we enter the final decade of this century, a century which has seen so much misery, bloodshed and suffering. There are today many promising signs that the 90s will bring more peace and freedom in Europe and in Germany. Much depends, and everyone senses this, on the German contribution. We should all face this challenge of history.

Treaty between the Federal Republic of Germany and the German Democratic Republic establishing a Monetary, Economic and Social Union

May 1990

The High Contracting Parties,

Owing to the fact that a peaceful and democratic revolution took place in the German Democratic Republic in the autumn of 1989,

Resolved to achieve in freedom as soon as possible the unity of Germany within a European peace order,

Intending to introduce the social market economy in the German Democratic Republic as the basis for further economic and social development, with social compensation and social safeguards and responsibility towards the environment, and thereby constantly to improve the living and working conditions of its population.

Proceeding from the mutual desire to take an initial significant step through the establishment of a Monetary, Economic and Social Union towards national unity in accordance with Article 23 of the Basic Law of the Federal Republic of Germany as a contribution to European unification, taking into account that the external aspects of establishing unity are the subject of negotiations with the Governments of the French Republic, the United Kingdom of Great Britain and Northern Ireland and the United States of America.

Recognizing that the establishment of national unity is accompanied by the development of federal structures in the German Democratic Republic.

Realizing that the provisions of this Treaty are intended to safeguard the application of European Community law following the establishment of national unity.

Have agreed to conclude a Treaty establishing a Monetary, Economic and Social Union, containing the following provisions.

Chapter I
Basic principles

Article 1
Subject of the Treaty

(1) The Contracting Parties shall establish a Monetary, Economic and Social Union.

(2) Starting on 1 July 1990 the Contracting Parties shall constitute a monetary union comprising a unified currency area and with the Deutsche Mark as the common currency. The Deutsche Bundesbank shall be the central bank in this currency area. The liabilities and claims expressed in Mark of the German Democratic Republic shall be converted into Deutsche Mark in accordance with this Treaty.

(3) The basis of the economic union shall be the social market economy as the common economic system of the two Contracting Parties. It shall be determined particularly by ownership, competition, free pricing and, as a basic principle, complete freedom of movement of labour, capital goods and services; this shall not preclude the legal admission of special forms of ownership providing for the participation of public authorities or other legal entities in trade and commerce as long as private legal entities are not subject to discrimination. It shall take into account the requirements of environmental protection.

(4) The social union together with the monetary and economic union shall form one entity. It shall be characterized in particular by system of labour law that corresponds to the social market economy and a comprehensive system of social security based on merit and social justice.

Article 2
Principles

(1) The Contracting Parties are committed to a free, democratic, federal and social basic order governed by the rule of law. To ensure the rights laid down in or following from this Treaty, they shall especially guarantee freedom of contract, freedom to exercise a trade, freedom of establishment and occupation, and freedom to form associations to safeguard and enhance working and economic conditions and in accordance with Annex IX, ownership of land and means of production by private investors.

(2) Contrary provisions of the Constitution of the German Democratic Republic relating to its former socialist social and political system shall no longer be applied.

Article 3
Legal Basis

The establishing of a monetary union and the currency conversion shall be governed by the agreed provisions listed in Annex I. Pending the establishment of monetary union, the legislation of the Federal Republic of Germany concerning currency, credit, money and coinage as well as economic and social union referred to in Annex II shall be implemented in the German Democratic Republic; thereafter, it shall apply, as amended, in the entire currency area according to Annex II, unless this Treaty provides otherwise. The Deutsche Bundesbank, the Federal Banking Supervisory Office and the Federal Insurance Supervisory Office shall exercise the authority accorded to them under this Treaty and said legislation in the entire area of application of this Treaty.

Article 4
Legal Adjustments

(1) Legal adjustments in the German Democratic Republic necessitated by the establishment of the monetary, economic and social union shall be governed by the principles laid down in article 2 (1) and the guidelines agreed in the Protocol; legislation remaining in force shall be interpreted and applied in accordance with said principles and guidelines. The German Democratic Republic shall repeal or amend the legislation referred to in Annex III and adopt the new legislation referred to in Annex IV prior to the establishment of monetary union, provided that no other time limit is fixed in the Treaty or in the Annexes.

(2) The proposed amendments to legislation in the Federal Republic of Germany are listed in Annex V. The proposed legislative adjustments in the German Democratic Republic are listed in Annex VI.

(3) In the transmission of personal information, the principles contained in Annex VII shall apply.

Article 5
Administrative Assistance

The authorities of the Contracting Parties shall, subject to the provisions of domestic law, assist each other in the implementation of this Treaty. Article 32 of the Treaty shall remain unaffected.

Article 6
Recourse to the Courts

(1) Should any person's rights guaranteed by or following from this Treaty be violated by public authority he shall have recourse to the

courts. In so far as no other jurisdiction has been established, recourse shall be to the ordinary courts.

(2) The German Democratic Republic shall guarantee recourse to the courts, including recourse for provisional court protection. In the absence of special courts for public-law disputes, special arbitration courts shall be set up at ordinary courts. Jurisdiction for such disputes shall be concentrated at specific regional and district courts.

(3) Pending the establishment of a special labour jurisdiction, legal disputes between employers and employees shall be settled by neutral arbitration bodies to be composed of an equal number of employers and employees and a neutral chairman. Their decisions shall be appealable in a court of law.

(4) The German Democratic Republic shall permit free arbitration in the field of private law.

Article 7
Arbitral Tribunal

(1) Disputes concerning the interpretation or application of this Treaty, including the Protocol and the Annexes, shall be settled by the Governments of the two Contracting Parties through negotiation.

(2) If a dispute cannot thus be settled, either Contracting Party may submit the dispute to an arbitral tribunal. Such submission shall be admissible irrespective of whether a court has jurisdiction in accordance with Article 6 of this Treaty.

(3) The arbitral tribunal shall be composed of a chairman and four members. Within a period of one month following the entry into force of this Treaty, the Government of each Contracting Party shall appoint two regular and two deputy members. Within the same period, the chairman and the deputy chairman shall be appointed in agreement between the Governments of the two Contracting Parties. If the periods specified in the second and third sentences have not been observed, the necessary appointments shall be made by the President of the Court of Justice of the European Communities.

(4) The period of office shall be two years.

(5) The chairman and members of the arbitral tribunal shall exercise their office independently and free from instructions. Before commencing their activities, the chairman and members of the arbitral tribunal shall undertake to carry out their duties independently and conscientiously and to observe confidentiality.

(6) The provisions governing the convening and the procedure of the arbitral tribunal are laid down in Annex VIII.

Article 8
Intergovernmental Committee

The Contracting Parties shall appoint an Intergovernmental Committee. The Committee shall discuss — and where necessary reach agreement on — questions relating to the implementation of the Treaty. The tasks of the Committee shall include the settlement of disputes under Article 7 (1) of the Treaty.

Article 9
Amendments to the Treaty

Should amendments or additions to this Treaty appear necessary in order to achieve any of its aims, such amendments or additions shall be agreed between the Contracting Parties.

Chapter II
Provisions concerning Monetary Union

Article 10
Prerequisites and Principles

(1) Through the establishment of a Monetary Union between the Contracting Parties, the Deutsche Mark shall be the means of payment, unit of account and means of deposit in the entire currency area. To this end, the monetary responsibility of the Deutsche Bundesbank as the sole issuing bank for this currency shall be extended to the entire currency area. The issuance of coin shall be the exclusive right of the Federal Republic of Germany.

(2) Enjoyment of the advantages of monetary union presupposes a stable monetary value for the economy of the German Democratic Republic, while currency stabil-

ity must be maintained in the Federal Republic of Germany. The Contracting Parties shall therefore choose conversion modalities which do not cause any inflationary tendencies in the entire area of the monetary union and which at the same time increase the competitiveness of enterprises in the German Democratic Republic.

(3) The Deutsche Bundesbank, by deploying its instruments on its own responsibility and, pursuant to Section 12 to the Bundesbank Law, independent of instructions from the Governments of the Contracting Parties, shall regulate the circulation of money and credit supply in the entire currency area with the aim of safeguarding the currency.

(4) Monetary control presupposes that the German Democratic Republic establishes a free-market credit system. This shall include a system of commercial banks operating according to private-sector principles, with competing private, cooperative and public-law banks, as well as a free money and a free capital market and non-regulated interest-rate fixing on financial markets.

(5) To achieve the aims described in paragraphs 1 to 4 above, the Contracting Parties shall, in accordance with the provisions laid down in Annex I, agree on the following principles for monetary union:

— With effect from 1 July 1990 the Deutsche Mark shall be introduced as currency in the German Democratic Republic. The bank notes issued by the Deutsche Bundesbank and denominated in Deutsche Mark, and the federal coins issued by the Federal Republic of Germany and denominated in Deutsche Mark or Pfennig, shall be sole legal tender from 1 July 1990.

— Wages, salaries, grants, pensions, rents and leases as well as other recurring payments shall be converted at a rate of one to one.

— All other claims and liabilities denominated in Mark of the German Democratic Republic shall be converted to Deutsche Mark at the rate of two to one.

— The conversion of bank notes and coin denominated in Mark of the German Democratic Republic shall only be possible for persons or agencies domiciled in the German Democratic Republic via accounts with financial institutions in the German Democratic Republic into which the cash amounts to be converted may be paid.

— Deposits with financial institutions held by individuals domiciled in the German Democratic Republic shall be converted upon application at a rate of one to one up to certain limits, there being a differentiation according to the age of the beneficiaries.

— Special regulations shall apply to deposits of persons domiciled outside the German Democratic Republic.

— Action shall be taken against abuse.

(6) Following an inventory of publicly owned assets and their earning power and following their primary use for the structural adaptation of the economy and for the recapitalization of the budget, the German Democratic Republic shall ensure where possible that a vested right to a share in publicly owned assets can be granted to savers at a later date for the amount reduced following conversion at a rate of two to one.

(7) The Deutsche Bundesbank shall exercise the powers accorded it by this Treaty and by the Law concerning the Deutsche Bundesbank in the entire currency area. It shall establish for this purpose a provisional office in Berlin with up to fifteen branches in the German Democratic Republic, which shall be located in the premises of the State Bank of the German Democratic Republic.

Chapter III
Provisions concerning Economic Union

Article 11
Economic Policy Foundations

(1) The German Democratic Republic shall ensure that its economic and financial policy measures are in harmony with the social market system. Such measures shall be introduced in such a way that, within the framework of the market economy system, they are at the same time conducive to price stability, a high level of employment and foreign trade equilibrium, and thus steady and adequate economic growth.

(2) The German Democratic Republic shall create the basic conditions for the development of market forces and private initiative in

order to promote structural change, the creation of modern jobs, a broad basis of small and medium-sized companies and liberal professions, as well as environmental protection. The corporate legal structure shall be based on the principles of the social market economy described in Article 1 of this Treaty, enterprises being free to decide on products, quantities, production processes, investment, employment, prices and utilization of profits.

(3) The German Democratic Republic, taking into consideration the foreign trade relations that have evolved with the member countries of the Council for Mutual Economic Assistance, shall progressively bring its policy into line with the law and the economic policy goals of the European Communities.

(4) In decisions which affect the economic policy principles referred to in paragraphs 1 and 2 above, the Government of the German Democratic Republic shall reach agreement with the Government of the Federal Republic of the Germany within the framework of the Intergovernmental Committee appointed in accordance with Article 8 of this Treaty.

Article 12
Intra-German Trade

(1) The Berlin Agreement of 20 September 1951 concluded between the Contracting Parties shall be amended in view of monetary and economic union. The clearing system established by that Agreement shall be ended and the swing shall be finally balanced. Outstanding obligations shall be settled in Deutsche Mark.

(2) The Contracting Parties shall guarantee that goods which do not originate in the Federal Republic of Germany or the Democratic Republic are transported across the intra-German border in accordance with a customs monitoring procedure.

(3) The Contracting Parties shall endeavour to create as soon as possible the preconditions for complete abolition of controls at the intra-German border.

Article 13
Foreign Trade and Payments

(1) In its foreign trade, the German Democratic Republic shall take into account the principles of free world trade, as expressed in particular in the General Agreement on Tariffs and Trade. The Federal Republic of Germany shall make its experience fully available for the further integration of the economy of the German Democratic Republic into the world economy.

(2) The existing foreign trade relations of the German Democratic Republic, in particular its contractual obligation towards the countries of the Council for Mutual Economic Assistance, shall be respected. They shall be further developed and extended in accordance with free-market principles, taking account of the facts established by monetary and economic union and the interests of all involved. Where necessary, the German Democratic Republic shall adjust existing contractual obligations in the light of those facts, in agreement with its partners.

(3) The Contracting Parties shall cooperate closely in advancing their foreign trade interests, with due regard for the jurisdiction of the European Communities.

Article 14
Structural Adjustment of Enterprises

In order to promote the necessary adjustment of enterprises in the German Democratic Republic, the Government of the German Democratic Republic shall, for a transitional period and subject to its budgetary means, take measures to facilitate a swift structural adjustment of enterprises to the new market conditions. The Governments of the Contracting Parties shall agree on the specific nature of these measures. The objective shall be to strengthen the competitiveness of enterprises on the basis of the social market economy and to build up, through the development of private initiative, a diversified, modern economic structure in the German Democratic Republic, with as many small and medium-sized enterprises as possible, and thereby to create the basis for increased growth and secure jobs.

Article 15
Agriculture and Food Industry

(1) Because of the crucial importance of the European Community rules for the agriculture and food industries, the German Demo-

cratic Republic shall introduce a price support and external protection scheme in line with the EC market regime so that agricultural producer prices in the German Democratic Republic become adjusted to those in the Federal Republic of Germany. The German Democratic Republic shall not introduce levies or refunds vis-à-vis the European Community, subject to reciprocity.

(2) For categories of goods in respect of which it is not possible to introduce a full price support system immediately upon the entry into force of this Treaty, transitional arrangements may be applied. Pending the legal integration of the agricultural and food industry of the German Democratic Republic into the EC agricultural market, specific quantitative restriction mechanisms shall be allowed for sensitive agricultural products in trade between the Contracting Parties.

(3) Without prejudice to the measures to be taken under Article 14 of this Treaty, the German Democratic Republic shall, within the limits of its budgetary means and for a transitional period, take suitable measures to promote the structural adaptation in the agricultural and food industries which is necessary to improve the competitiveness of enterprises, to achieve environmentally acceptable and quality-based production, and to avoid surpluses.

(4) The Governments of the Contracting Parties shall agree on the specific nature of the measures referred to in paragraphs 2 and 3 above.

Article 16
Protection of the Environment

(1) The protection of human beings, animals and plants, soil, water, air, the climate and landscape as well as cultural and other material property against harmful environmental influences is a major objective of both Contracting Parties. They shall pursue this objective on the basis of prevention, the polluter pays principle and cooperation. Their aim is the rapid establishment of a German environmental union.

(2) The German Democratic Republic shall introduce regulations to ensure that, on the entry into force of this Treaty, the safety and environmental requirements applicable in the Federal Republic of Germany are the precondition for the granting of authorization under environmental law for new plant and installations on its territory. For existing plant and installations the German Democratic Republic shall introduce regulations to bring them up to standard as quickly as possible.

(3) The German Democratic Republic shall, along with the development of the federal structure at Land level and with the establishment of an administrative jurisidiction, adopt the environmental law of the Federal Republic of Germany.

(4) In further shaping a common environmental law, the environmental requirements of the Federal Republic of Germany and the German Democratic Republic shall be harmonized and developed at a high level as quickly as possible.

(5) The German Democratic Republic shall harmonize the provisions governing promotion of environmental protection measures with those of the Federal Republic of Germany.

Chapter IV
Provisions concerning Social Union

Article 17
Principles of Labour Law

In the German Democratic Republic freedom of association, autonomy in collective bargaining, legislation relating to industrial action, corporate legal structure, codetermination at board level and protection against dismissal shall apply in line with the law of the Federal Republic of Germany; further details are contained in the Protocol on Guidelines and in Annexes II and III.

Article 18
Principles of Social Insurance

(1) The German Democratic Republic shall introduce a structured system of social insurance, to be governed by the following principles:
1. Pension, sickness, accident and unemployment insurance shall each be administered by self-governing bodies under public law subject to legal supervision by the state.
2. Pension, sickness, accident and unemployment insurance including employment

promotion shall be financed primarily by contributions. Contributions to pension, sickness and unemployment insurance shall, as a rule, be paid half by the employee and half by the employer in line with the contribution rates applicable in the Federal Republic of Germany, and accident insurance contributions shall be borne by the employer.

3. Wage replacement benefits shall be based on the level of insured earnings.

(2) Initially, pension, sickness and accident insurance shall be administered by a single institution; income and expenditure shall be accounted for separately according to the type of insurance. Separate pension, sickness and accident insurance institutions shall be established, if possible by 1 January 1991. The aim shall be to create an organizational structure for social insurance which corresponds to that of the Federal Republic of Germany.

(3) For a transitional period the present comprehensive compulsory social insurance cover in the German Democratic Republic may be retained. Exemption from compulsory social insurance cover shall be granted to self-employed persons and professionals who can prove that they have adequate alternative insurance. In this connection, the creation of professional pension schemes outside the pension insurance system shall be made possible.

(4) Wage-earners whose earnings in the last wage accounting period before 1 July 1990 were subject to a special tax rate under Section 10 of the Ordinance of 11 December 1952 on the Taxation of Earned Income (Law Gazette No. 182, p. 1413) shall receive until 31 December 1990 a supplement to their pension insurance contribution amounting to
— DM30, for monthly wages up to DM600
— DM20, for monthly wages of more than DM600, up to DM700, and
— DM10, for monthly wages of more than DM700, up to DM800.
Earnings from several employments shall be counted together. The supplement shall be paid to the wage-earner by the employer. Upon application the employer shall be reimbursed for these payments from the budget.

(5) The ceilings for compulsory insurance cover and for contribution assessment shall be fixed according to the principles of social insurance law applying in the Federal Republic of Germany.

Article 19
Unemployment Insurance and Employment Promotion

The German Democratic Republic shall introduce a system of unemployment insurance including employment promotion which shall be in line with the provisions of the Employment Promotion Act of the Federal Republic of Germany. Special importance shall be attached to an active labour market policy, such as vocational training and retaining. Consideration shall be given to the interests of women and disabled persons. In the transitional phase, special conditions in the German Democratic Republic shall be taken into account. The Governments of both Contracting Parties shall cooperate closely in the development of unemployment insurance including employment promotion.

Article 20
Pension Insurance

(1) The German Democratic Republic shall introduce all necessary measures to adapt its pension law to the pension insurance law of the Federal Republic of Germany, which is based on the principle of wage and contribution-related benefits. Over a transitional period of five years account shall be taken of the principle of bona fide rights protection in respect of persons approaching pensionable age.

(2) The pension insurance fund shall use its resources exclusively to meet its obligations with regard to rehabilitation, invalidity, old age, and death. The existing supplementary and special pensions schemes shall be discontinued as of 1 July 1990. Accrued claims and entitlements shall be transferred to the pension insurance fund, and benefits on the basis of special arrangements shall be reviewed with a view to abolishing unjustified benefits and reducing excessive benefits. The additional expenditure incurred by the pension insurance fund because of such transfers shall be reimbursed from the budget.

(3) Upon conversion to Deutsche Mark current pension from the pension insurance

fund shall be fixed at a net replacement rate which, for a pensioner who has completed 45 insurance/working years and whose earnings were at all times in line with average earning, shall be 70 per cent of average net earnings in the German Democratic Republic. For a greater or smaller number of insurance/working years, the percentage shall be correspondingly higher or lower. The basis for calculating the upgrading rate for individual pensions shall be the pension of an average wage-earner in the German Democratic Republic, graduated to year of entry, who has paid full contributions to the voluntary supplementary insurance scheme of the German Democratic Republic, over and above his compulsory social insurance contributions. If there is no upgrading on this basis a pension shall be paid in Deutsche Mark which corresponds to the amount of the former pension in Mark of the German Democratic Republic. Survivors' pensions shall be calculated on the basis of the pension which the deceased would have received after conversion.

(4) Pensions from the pension insurance fund shall be adjusted in line with the development of net wages and salaries in the German Democratic Republic.

(5) The voluntary supplementary pension insurance scheme in the German Democratic Republic shall be discontinued.

(6) The German Democratic Republic shall make a government contribution to its pension insurance fund to offset its expenditure.

(7) Persons who have transferred their habitual residence from the territory of either Contracting Party to that of the other Party after 18 May 1990 shall receive from the pension insurance institution hitherto responsible a pension calculated to the regulations applicable to that institution for the period completed there.

Article 21
Health Insurance

(1) The German Democratic Republic shall introduce all necessary measures to adapt its health insurance law to that of the Federal Republic of Germany.

(2) Benefits which have hitherto been financed from the health insurance fund according to the legislation of the German Democratic Republic but which according to the legislation of the Federal Republic of Germany are not benefits covered by the health insurance fund shall, for the time being, be financed from the budget of the German Democratic Republic.

(3) The German Democratic Republic shall introduce continued payment of wages in the event of sickness which is in line with legislation governing continued payment of wages in the Federal Republic of Germany.

(4) Pensioners shall be covered by health insurance. The contribution rate of the relevant health insurance fund shall be applicable. The health insurance contributions of pensioners shall be paid in a lump sum by the pension insurance fund to the health insurance fund. The amount to be paid shall be determined according to overall pension payments before deduction of the proportion of the health insurance contribution payable by pensioners. This shall not affect the net replacement rate envisaged after conversion of pensions.

(5) Investment in in-patient and out-patient facilities of the health service of the German Democratic Republic shall be financed from budget funds and not from contribution revenue.

Article 22
Public Health

(1) Medical care and health protection are of particular concern to the Contracting Parties.

(2) While provisionally continuing the present system, which is necessary to maintain public medical services, the German Democratic Republic shall gradually move towards the range of services offered in the Federal Republic of Germany with private providers, particularly by admitting registered doctors, dentists and pharmacists as well as independent providers of medicaments and remedial aids, and by admitting private providers of independent, non-profit-making hospitals.

(3) The German Democratic Republic shall create the necessary legal framework for the development of the necessary contractual relations — particularly as regards remuneration — between health insurance institutions and providers of services.

Article 23
Accident Insurance Pensions

(1) The German Democratic Republic shall introduce all necessary measures to adapt its accident insurance law to that of the Federal Republic of Germany.

(2) Upon conversion to Deutsche Mark, current accident insurance pensions shall be recalculated and paid on the basis of average gross earnings in the German Democratic republic.

(3) Accident pensions to be determined after the conversion to Deutsche Mark shall be based on the average gross monthly earnings in the twelve months prior to the accident.

(4) The provisions of Article 20 (4) and (7) shall apply mutatis mutandis.

Article 24
Social Assistance

The German Democratic Republic shall introduce a system of social assistance which shall correspond to the Social Assistance Act of the Federal Republic of Germany.

Article 25
Initial Financing

If, during a transitional period, contributions to the unemployment insurance fund of the German Democratic Republic and both the contributions and the government subsidy to the pension insurance fund of the German Democratic Republic do not fully cover expenditures on benefits, the Federal Republic of Germany shall provide temporary initial financing for the German Democratic Republic within the framework of the budgetary aid granted under Article 28 of this Treaty.

Chapter V
Provisions concerning the Budget and Finance

Section 1: The Budget

Article 26
Principles underlying the Fiscal Policy of the German Democratic Republic

(1) Public budgets in the German Democratic Republic shall be drawn up by the relevant national, regional or local authorities on their own responsibility, due to account being taken of the requirements of general economic equilibrium. The aim shall be to establish a system of budgeting adapted to the market economy. Budgets shall be balanced as regards revenue and expenditure. All revenue and expenditure shall be included in the appropriate budget.

(2) Budgets shall be adapted to the budget structures of the Federal Republic of Germany. The following in particular shall be removed from the budget, starting with the partial budget for 1990 as of the establishment of monetary union:

— the social sector, in so far as it is wholly or mainly financed from charges or contributions on the Federal Republic of Germany,

— state undertakings by conversion into legally and economically independent enterprises,

— transport undertakings by making them legally independent,

— the management of the Deutsche Reichsbahn and the Deutsche Post, which will be operated as special funds.

Government borrowing for housing shall be allocated to individual projects on the basis of their existing physical assets.

(3) National, regional and local authorities in the German Democratic Republic shall make every effort to limit deficits in drawing up and executing budgets. As regards expenditure this shall include:

— abolition of budget subsidies, particularly in the short term for industrial goods, agricultural products and food, autonomous price supports being permissible for the latter in line with the regulations of the European Communities, and progressively in the sectors of transport, energy for private households and housing, making allowances for the general development of income,

— sustained reduction of personnel expenditure in the public service,

— review of all items of expenditure, including the legal provisions on which they are based, to determine whether they are necessary and can be financed,

— structural improvements in the education system and preparatory division according to a federal structure (including the research sector).

As regards revenue, the limitation of deficits shall require, in addition to the measures under Section 2 of this Chapter, the harmonization or introduction of contributions and fees for public services corresponding to the system in the Federal Republic of Germany.

(4) An inventory shall be made of publicly owned assets. Publicly owned assets shall be used primarily for the structural adaption of the economy and for the recapitalization of the budget in the German Democratic Republic.

Article 27
Borrowing and Debts

(1) Borrowing authorizations in the budgets of the local, regional and national authorities of the German Democratic Republic shall be limited to 10 billion Deutsche Mark for 1990 and 14 billion Deutsche Mark for 1991 and allocated to the different levels of government in agreement with the Minister of Finance of the Federal Republic of Germany. A borrowing limit of 7 billion Deutsche Mark for 1990 and 10 billion Deutsche Mark for 1991 shall be established for the advance financing of proceeds expected to accrue from the realization of assets currently held in trust. In the event of fundamental change in conditions, the Minister of Finance of the Federal Republic of Germany may permit these credit ceilings to be exceeded.

(2) The raising of loans and the granting of equalization claims shall be conducted in agreement between the Minister of Finance of the German Democratic Republic and the Minister of Finance of the Federal Republic of Germany. The same shall apply to the assumption of sureties, warranties or other guarantees and for the total authorizations for future commitments to be appropriated in the budget.

(3) After accession, debt accrued in the budget of the German Democratic Republic shall be transferred to the assets held in trust in so far as it can be redeemed by proceeds expected to accrue from the realization of the assets held in trust. The remaining debt shall be assumed in equal parts by the Federal Government and the Länder newly constituted on the territory of the German Democratic Republic. Loans raised by Länder and local authorities shall remain their responsibility.

Article 28
Financial Allocations granted by the Federal Republic of Germany

(1) The Federal Republic of Germany shall grant the German Democratic Republic financial allocations amounting to 22 billion Deutsche Mark for the second half of 1990 and 35 billion Deutsche Mark for 1991 for the specific purpose of balancing its budget. Furthermore, initial financing shall be made available from the federal budget, in accordance with Article 25, amounting to 750 million Deutsche Mark for the second half of 1990 for pension insurance as well as 2 billion Deutsche Mark for the second half of 1990 and 3 billion Deutsche Mark for 1991 for unemployment insurance. Payments shall be made as required.

(2) The Contracting Parties agree that the transit sum payable under Article 18 of the Agreement of 17 December 1971 on the Transit of Civilian Persons and Goods between the Federal Republic of Germany and Berlin (West) shall lapse upon the entry into force of this Treaty. The German Democratic Republic shall cancel with effect for the two Contracting Parties the regulations on fees laid down in that Agreement and in the Agreement of 31 October 1979 on the Exemption of Road Vehicles from Taxes and Fees. In amendment of the Agreement of 5 December 1989, the Contracting Parties agree that from 1 July 1990 no more payments shall be made into the hard-currency fund (for citizens of the German Democratic Republic travelling to the Federal Republic of Germany). A supplementary agreement shall be concluded between the Finance Ministers of the Contracting Parties on the use of any amounts remaining in the fund upon establishment of monetary union.

Article 29
Transitional Regulations in the Public Service

The Government of the German Democratic Republic shall guarantee, with due regard for the first sentence of Article 2(1), that in collective bargaining agreements or other settlements in the public administration sector the general economic and financial conditions in the German Democratic Republic and the exigencies of budget consolidation are taken into account, with any new service regulations being of transitional nature only. The Federal Representation of Staff Act shall be applied mutatis mutandis.

Section 2: Finance

Article 30
Customs and Special Excise Taxes

(1) In accordance with the principle set out in Article 11 (3) of this Treaty, the German Democratic Republic shall adopt step by step the customs law of the European Communities, including the Common Customs Tariff, and the special excise taxes stipulated in Annex IV to this Treaty.

(2) The Contracting Parties are agreed that their customs territory shall comprise the area of application of this Treaty.

(3) Equalization at the border between the fiscal territories for excise taxes of both Contracting Parties, except those of tobacco, shall be discontinued. Fiscal jurisidiction shall remain unaffected. Separate agreements shall be made to offset shifts in excise revenue.

(4) The movement of untaxed excisable goods between the fiscal territories shall be permitted as stipulated in the regulations on movements of untaxed goods within one fiscal territory.

(5) Tax relief for export goods shall be granted only upon proof of export to territories other than the two fiscal territories.

Article 31
Taxes on Income, Property, Net Worth and Transactions

(1) The German Democratic Republic shall regulate taxes on income, property, net worth and transactions in accordance with Annex IV to this Treaty.

(2) For the purposes of turnover tax there shall be no tax frontier between the Contracting Parties; in consequence, there shall be no equalization of turnover tax burdens at the frontier. Fiscal jurisdiction shall remain unaffected. The right of input tax deduction shall extend to the tax on turnovers which are subject to the turnover tax of the other Contracting Party. Compensation for the reduced yield resulting from this shall be settled by special agreement.

(3) Where there is unlimited net worth tax liability in the territory of one Contracting Party, that Party shall have the exclusive right to tax; where there is unlimited net worth tax liability in the territories of both Contracting Parties, this shall apply to the Party with which the taxpayer has the closer personal and economic ties (centre of vital interests) or in whose territory he has effective management as a legal person. Property located in the territory of the other Contracting Party shall be assessed according to the regulations for domestic property applying in that territory.

(4) Where there is unlimited inheritance tax or gift tax liability in the territory of one Contracting Party, that Party shall have the exclusive right to tax transfers on which tax is payable after 31 December 1990. Where there is unlimited tax liability in the territory of both Contracting Parties, this shall apply to the Party with which the testator or donor had the closer personal and economic ties when the tax liability was incurred (centre of vital interests), or in whose territory he had effective management as a legal person. Paragraph 3, second sentence, shall apply mutatis mutandis to evaluation.

(5) Paragraph 4 shall apply accordingly to transfers of property by reason of death on which taxes are incurred after 30 June 1990 and before 1 January 1991. Transfers of property by reason of death from citizens of the Contracting Parties who had established residence in the territory of the other Party after 8 November 1990 or who for the first time had their customary abode there and who still had their residence or customary abode there at the time of death cannot be subjected to any higher inheritance tax than would be imposed where there is unlimited tax liability in the territory of the first-mentioned Contracting Party.

(6) Disclosure and notification obligations resulting from the inheritance tax and gift tax legislation of the Contracting Parties shall in each case apply also with regards to the revenue authorities of the other Party.

Article 32
Exchange of Information

(1) The Contracting Parties shall exchange such information as is necessary for the execution of their taxation and monopoly legislation. The Ministers of Finance of the Contracting Parties, together with the authorities empowered by them, shall be responsible for the exchange of information. Any information received by a Contracting Party shall be treated as secret in the same manner as information obtained under the domestic laws of that party and shall be disclosed only to those persons or authorities (including courts and administrative bodies) involved in the assessment or collection of, the enforcement or prosecution in respect of, or the determination of appeals in relation to the taxes and monopolies falling within this Section. Such persons or authorities shall use the information for these purposes only. They may disclose the information in public court proceedings or in judicial decisions.

(2) The provisions of paragraph 1 shall not commit either Contracting Party

— to carry out administrative measures at variance with the laws and administrative practice of that or of the other Contracting Party;

— to supply information which is not obtainable under the laws or in the normal course of the administration of that or of the other Contracting Party;

— to supply information which would disclose any trade, business, industrial, commercial or professional secret or trade process, or information the disclosure of which would be contrary to public policy.

Article 33
Consulting Procedure

(1) The Contracting Parties shall endeavour to avoid double taxation in respect of taxes on income, property, net worth and transactions by reaching agreement on the appropriate delimitation of the tax base. They shall also strive to eliminate by mutual agreement any difficulties or doubts which result from the interpretation or application of their law on the taxes and monopolies that fall within this Section.

(2) To reach agreement as mentioned in paragraph 1 above, the Minister of Finance of the Federal Republic of Germany and the Minister of Finance of the German Democratic Republic may communicate directly with each other.

Article 34
Structure of the Revenue Administration

(1) The German Democratic Republic shall create the legal basis for a three-tier revenue administration in line with the Revenue Administration Act of the Federal Republic of Germany, incorporating the amendments arising from this Treaty, and shall establish the administration accordingly.

(2) Before the establishment of monetary, economic and social union, the first priority shall be to set up efficient tax and customs administration.

Chapter VI
Final provisions

Article 35
International Treaties

This Treaty shall not affect the international treaties which the Federal Republic of Germany and the German Democratic Republic have concluded with third countries.

Article 36
Review of the Treaty

The provisions of this Treaty shall be reviewed in the light of any fundamental changes in the situation.

Article 37
Berlin Clause

Consistent with the Quadripartite Agreement of 3 September 1971 this Treaty will, in accordance with established procedures, be extended to Berlin (West).

Article 38
Entry into Force

This Treaty, including the Protocol and Annexes I–IX, shall enter into force on the date on which the Governments of the Contracting Parties have informed each other that the necessary constitutional and other national requirements for such entry into force have been fulfilled.

Done at Bonn on 18 May 1990 in duplicate in the German language.

For the	For the
Federal Republic of Germany	German Democratic Republic
Dr Theo Waigel	Dr Walter Romberg

Protocol on Guidelines

To supplement the Treaty establishing a Monetary, Economic and Social Union, the High Contracting Parties have agreed on the following guidelines which shall be binding in accordance with the first sentence of Article 4 (1) of the Treaty.

A. General Guidelines

I. General Provisions

1. The law of the German Democratic Republic will be modelled on the principles of a free, democratic federal and social order governed by the rule of law and be guided by the legal regime of the European Communities.

2. Regulations which commit individuals or state institutions, including the legislature and the judiciary, to a socialist system of law, a socialist body politic, the aims and targets of centralized economic control and planning, a socialist sense of justice, socialist convictions, the convictions of individual groups or parties, socialist morality, or comparable notions, will no longer be applied. The rights and obligations of parties to legal relations shall be bounded by public morals, the principle of good faith, and the necessity of protecting the economically weaker party from undue disadvantage.

3. Authorizations should be required only for compelling reasons of the common weal. Their preconditions shall be clearly defined.

II. Economic Union

1. Economic activity should primarily occur in the private sector and on the basis of competition.

2. Freedom of contract will be guaranteed. Intervention in the freedom of economic activity must be kept to a minimum.

3. Business decisions shall be free from planning targets (e.g. regarding production, purchase, deliveries, investment, employment, prices and utilization of profits).

4. Private enterprises and liberal professions will not be subjected to worse treatment than state and cooperative enterprises.

5. Prices will be freely set, except where they are established by the government for compelling reasons in cases where the economy as a whole is affected.

6. For economic activity, the freedom to acquire, dispose of and use land and other factors of production will be guaranteed.

7. Enterprises under direct or indirect state ownership will be managed according to the principles of economic efficiency. They will be organized competitively as quickly as possible and transferred to private ownership as far as possible. The aim is to open up opportunities for small and medium-sized enterprises in particular.

8. In respect of posts and telecommunications, the regulatory and organizational principles contained in the Structure of Posts and Telecommunications Act of the Federal Republic of Germany will be adopted step by step.

III. Social Union

1. Everyone has the right to form or join organizations to safeguard and enhance working and economic conditions, to leave such organizations and to remain outside them. Furthermore, the right to be active within such organizations is guaranteed. All agreements which restrict these rights will be void. Trade unions and employers' associations will be protected as regards their establishment, existence, organizational autonomy and proper activity.

2. Trade unions and employers' associations able to conclude collective agreements must be freely formed, not include members from the other side, be organized on a supra-

company level and independent, and accept existing legislation on collective bargaining as binding; they must also be able to conclude collective agreements by exerting pressure on their bargaining partner.

3. Wages and other working conditions shall not be determined by the state but through free negotiation between trade unions, employers' associations and employers.

4. Legislation providing for special participation rights for the Free German Trade Unions' Federation, company-level union organizations and union management will no longer be applied.

B. Guidelines for Individual Fields of Law

I. Judicial System

1. Regulations providing for the participation of collectives, social organs, trade unions, works, social prosecutors and defenders in the judicial system and their right to be informed about proceedings will no longer be applied; the right of trade unions to advice and legal representation in labour disputes will remain unaffected by this provision.

2. Regulations on cooperation between the courts and local representations of the people and other organs, the duty of judges to inform the latter, as well as criticism of the courts will no longer be applied.

3. Regulations concerning the involvement of public prosecutors in the judicial system will only be applicable in criminal cases and in family law, parent and child and guardianship cases.

4. Principles contained in the Criminal Code of the German Democratic Republic which relate to the socialist system of law and the socialist body politic, as well as regulations which serve to maintain a centrally planned economy, conflict with a future unification of the two German states or are contrary to principles of a free democratic state, will not be applied to offences committed after the entry into force of this Treaty.

5. Provisions of the Criminal Code which relate to socialist property will not be applied to offences committed after the entry into force of this Treaty; regulations concerning personal or private property will also be applied to other property and assets after the entry into force of this Treaty.

6. To this extent that the legislation referred to in Annex II provides for fines or penalties and cannot be incorporated in the system of sanctions of the German Democratic Republic, the German Democratic Republic will adapt it to its own law as far as possible in line with the legislation of the Federal Republic of Germany.

II. Economic Law

1. For the purpose of establishing collateral for credits, rights equivalent to those in the Federal Republic of Germany, especially rights in rem. will be created in the German Democratic Republic.

2. Conditions for a free capital market will be created in the German Democratic Republic. They will include particularly the liberalizations of interest rates and the admission of tradeable securities (stocks and bonds).

3. Conditions will be created so that administrative decisions and other rulings made by authorities referred to the third sentence of Article 3 of the Treaty can be enforced against persons domiciled in the German Democratic Republic, if necessary by compulsion.

4. The existing insurance monopoly in the German Democratic Republic will be abolished, premium control removed from those insurance branches where tariffs are not part of the business statutes, and current legislation and rules on general conditions for insurance companies repealed.

5. Existing barriers in the payment transaction system of the German Democratic Republic will be removed and its structuring under law promoted.

6. Foreign trade and payment will be free. Restrictions shall be permissible only for compelling reasons in cases where the economy as a whole is affected, on the basis of intergovernmental agreements. The German Democratic Republic will abolish its external trade monopoly.

7. In order to achieve a comparable basis, the German Democratic Republic will adjust its statistics to those of the Federal Republic of Germany and, in cooperation with the Federal Statistical Office or the Deutsche Bundesbank, make information available in

accordance with federal statistical standards for the following areas: labour market, prices, production, turnover, foreign trade and payments and retail trade.

III. Building Law

In order to establish a reliable basis for construction planning and investment, the German Democratic Republic will create as soon as possible a legal framework consistent with the Building Code and the Regional Planning Act of the Federal Republic of Germany.

IV. Labour and Social Law

1. Employers in the German Democratic Republic may agree with employees from the Federal Republic of Germany who are temporarily employed in the German Democratic Republic that the labour legislation of the Federal Republic of Germany be applied.
2. Persons in temporary employment may be exempt from compulsory social insurance if they have other cover.
3. The regulations of the German Democratic Republic governing occupational safety and health will be adapted within an appropriate transitional period to the industrial safety laws of the Federal Republic of Germany.
4. In changing its legal minimum period of notice for employment contracts, the German Democratic Republic will not exceed the statutory minimum periods of notice applicable in the Federal Republic of Germany in respect of wage-earners and salaried employees.
5. The German Democratic Republic will create a legal basis for summary dismissal for important reasons in conformity with Sections 626 and 628 of the Civil Code of the Federal Republic of Germany.

Statements for the record

At the signing of the Treaty between the Federal Republic of Germany and the German Democratic Republic establishing a Monetary, Economic and Social Union, the following statements were made with reference to the Treaty:

1. The two Contracting Parties state the following with regards to the second sentence of Article 2(1) of the Treaty: Freedom of movement within the meaning of this provision also includes the entry into the currency area of individuals, including members of ethnic minorities, who are in possession of an identity card, a passport or document in lieu of a passport of the Federal Republic of Germany or the German Democratic Republic.
2. The German Democratic Republic states that it will grant national and enterprises of all members states of the European Communities equal treatment with individuals and enterprises of the Federal Republic of Germany on a reciprocal basis in so far as the jurisdiction of the European Communities might be affected and in so far as nothing to the contrary is explicitly agreed in this Treaty; the protocol (to the EEC Treaty) on German internal trade remains unaffected by this provision.
3. The two Contracting Parties understand the three-month FIBOR within the meaning of the third sentence of Article 8 of Section 4 (1) of Annex I to be the respective interest rate which is determined in Frankfurt/Main every three months on the second business day prior to the beginning of an interest period, according to Section 2 (3) of the Conditions for the Bond of the Federal Republic of Germany of 1990 (Securities Code No. 113–478) without the discount envisaged in it.
4. In connection with Section 1 (3) of Annex IV the German Democratic Republic states: To ensure competition for public contracts appropriate directives will be established without delay and applied by public authorities with effect from 1 January 1991 at the latest.

Bonn. 18 May 1990

For the
Federal Republic of German
Dr Theo Waigel

For the
German Democratic Republic
Dr Walter Romberg

Treaty on Unification of the German Democratic Republic and the Federal Republic of Germany

August 1990

(abbreviated text)

Preamble

The Federal Republic of Germany and the German Democratic Republic resolved to complete the unification of Germany in peace and freedom as an equal member of the community of nations in free self-determination,
— starting from the desire of people in both parts of Germany to live together in peace and freedom in a democratic and federal social state based on a legal order,
— with grateful respect for those who helped freedom break through, who unerringly held on to the task of creating German unity and completing it,
— conscious of the continuity of the German history and mindful of the responsibility resulting from this for a democratic development in Germany which remains committed to respect for human rights and peace,
— in the endeavour to make a contribution to the unification of Europe and to the construction of a European peace-time order by German unity in which borders no longer separate and which guarantees all European nations that they can live together in confidence,
— conscious of the fact that the inviolability of frontiers and the territorial integrity and sovereignty of all states in Europe within their borders is a basic condition for peace, have agreed to conclude a treaty on creating German unity with the following regulations:

Chapter I: The effect of accession

Article 1
Länder

(1) With the coming into effect of the accession of the German Democratic Republic to the Federal Republic of Germany in accordance with Article 23 of the Basic Law on 3rd October 1990 the Länder of Brandenburg, Mecklenburg-Western Pomerania, Saxony, Saxony-Anhalt and Thuringia will become Länder of the Federal Republic of Germany. The rules of the constitutional law on the formation of Länder in the German Democratic Republic of the 22nd July 1990. . . [apply].
(2) The 23 boroughs of Berlin will form the Land of Berlin.

Article 2
Capital

The capital of Germany is Berlin. The question as to the seat of parliament and government will be resolved after the establishment of the unity of Germany.

Chapter II: Basic Law
Article 3

Coming into effect of the Basic Law

With the coming into effect of the accession the Basic Law for the Federal Republic of Germany of 23rd May 1949 in the version of 21st December 1983 will come into force in the Länder of Brandenburg, Mecklenburg-Western Pomerania, Saxony, Saxony-Anhalt and Thuringia, as well as in the part of the Land of Berlin where it was hitherto not in effect, with the alterations resulting from Article 4, in as far as nothing different is specified in this Treaty.

Article 4
Changes to the Basic Law conditional on accession

The Basic Law . . . will be changed as follows:
1. The preamble will be worded as follows: Mindful of its responsibility to God and mankind, filled with the desire to serve peace in the world as an equal member in an united Europe, the German People has made this Basic Law by virtue of its constitutional power. The Germans in the Länder of Baden-Württemberg, Bavaria, Berlin, Brandenburg, Bremen, Hamburg, Hesse, Mecklenburg-Western Pomerania, Lower Saxony, North Rhine-Westphalia, Rhineland-Palatinate, Saarland, Saxony, Saxony-Anhalt, Schleswig-Holstein and Thuringia have completed the unity and freedom of Germany in free self-determination. This Basic Law is valid for the whole of the German people.
2. Article 23 (area of applicability of the Basic Law) will be rescinded.
3. Article 51 Paragraph 2 of the Basic Law will be formulated as follows: "Each Land shall have at least three votes, Länder with more than two million inhabitants shall have four, Länder with more than three million inhabitants shall have five, Länder with more than five million inhabitants shall have six, Länder with more than seven million inhabitants [shall have seven], and Länder with more than twelve million inhabitants eight votes."
4. The previous text of Article 135a (Old liabilities) will become Paragraph 1. The following Paragraph will be added after Paragraph 1:
"Paragraph 1 shall have corresponding application to liabilities of the German Democratic Republic or its legal entities and to liabilities of the Federation or other corporate bodies and institutions under public law, which are connected with the transfer of properties of the German Democratic Republic to the Federation, Länder and communes, and to liabilities which are based on measures taken by the German Democratic Republic or its legal entitites."
5. The following new Article 143 will be added to the Basic Law:
"In the part of Germany which has acceded law can diverge from the stipulations of this Basic Law at the latest until 31st December 1995 in as far as and as long as complete adaption to the constitutional order cannot yet be reached because of the varying conditions. Divergences must not violate Article 19 (Restriction of basic rights), Paragraph 2 and they have to be compatible with the principles cited in Article 79 (Amendment of the Basic Law), Paragraph 3. Article 41 of the Unification Treaty and regulations for its implementation are valid in so far as they envisage that expropriations on the territory named in Article 3 of this Treaty will not be revoked."
6. Article 146 (Duration of validity of the Basic Law) will be formulated as follows:
"This Basic Law, which will be valid for the whole of the German people after the completion of the unity and freedom of Germany, will lose its validity on the day that a new Constitution comes into force, that has been resolved freely by the German people."

Article 5
Future changes to the Constitution

The governments of the two contracting parties recommend that the legislative bodies of the united Germany deal within a period of two years with the issues raised in connection with German unification concerning changes of or amendments to the Basic Law, in particular:
— as regards the relations between the Federation and the Länder in accordance with the Prime Ministerial Joint Resolution of 5th July 1990,

— as regards the possibility of a new structure for the Berlin/Brandenburg region diverging from the provisions of Article 29 of the Basic Law through the agreement of the Länder involved,

— as regards the considerations concerning incorporating provisions on state objectives into the Basic Law, as well as

— with regard to the question of the application of Article 146 of the Basic Law.

Article 6
Special Regulation

Article 131 of the Basic Law (Legal position of former members of the public service) will for the present not be put into force in the area named in Article 3:

— as regards the considerations concerning incorporating into the Basic Law state objective regulations as well as

— concerning the question of applying Article 146 of the Basic Law.

Article 7
Financial Constitution

The Financial Constitution of the Federal Republic of Germany will be extended to the area named in Article 3, in so far as is not determined otherwise in this Treaty.

For the distribution of the tax revenue to the Federation and to the Länder and the communes in the area named in Article 3 the regulations of Article 106 of the Basic Law apply (distribution of tax revenue), with the proviso that:

1. Up to 31st December 1994 Paragraph 3, Clause 4, and Paragraph 4 are not applied;

2. Up to 31st December 1996 the share of the communes in income tax revenue is passed on under Article 106 Paragraph 5 of the Basic Law by the Länder to the communes not on the basis of the income tax payments of their inhabitants but according to the number of inhabitants of the local authorities;

3. Deviating from Article 106, Clause 7 of the Basic Law, an annual share of at least 205 of the Land share of the total revenue from joint taxes and of the total revenue of the Land taxes as well as an annual share of 40% of the Land share from the resources of the German Unity Fund under Paragraph 5 no. 1 shall accrue to the communes by the 31st December 1994.

Article 107 of the Basic Law (fiscal adjustment) applies in the area named in Article 3, with the proviso that up to 31st December 1994 between the present Länder of the Federal Republic of Germany and the Länder in the area named in Article 3 the ruling of Paragraph 1 Clause 4 is not applied and an all-German fiscal adjustment between the Länder does not take place.

The all-German Länder share of the turnover tax will be divided up into an eastern and a western share in such a way that the average turnover tax share per inhabitant in the Länder of Brandenburg, Mecklenburg-Western Pomerania, Saxony, Saxony-Anhalt and Thuringia amounts in the years

1991 to 55%
1992 to 60%
1993 to 65%
1994 to 70%

of the average turnover tax share per inhabitant in the Länder of Baden-Württemberg, Bavaria, Bremen, Hesse, Hamburg, Lower Saxony, North Rhine-Westphalia, Rhineland-Palatinate, Saarland and Schleswig-Holstein. The share of the Land of Berlin will be calculated in advance according to the number of inhabitants.

The area mentioned in Article 3 will be included in the arrangements of Articles 91a (participation of the Federation on the basis of federal legislation), 91b (co-operation of Federation and Länder on the basis of agreements) and 104a (apportionment of tasks to Federation and Länder) paragraph 3 and 4 of the Basic Law including the relevant implementing statutes under the terms of this Treaty with effect from 1st January 1991.

Upon the establishment of German unity the annual payments from the German Unity Fund will be as follows:

1. Eighty-five per cent in special support of the Länder of Brandenburg, Mecklenburg-Western Pomerania, Saxony, Saxony-Anhalt and Thuringia as well as the Land of Berlin to cover their general financial requirement, and distributed to these Länder in proportion to their number of inhabitants without taking into account the number of inhabitants of Berlin (West), as well as

2. Fifteen per cent to meet central public tasks in the area of the aforementioned Länder.

In case of fundamentally changed conditions scope for further assistance for the appropriate equalisation of the financial resources for the Länder in the area named in Article 3 will be examined jointly by the Federation and Länder.

Article 8
Transference of Federal Law

With the coming into effect of the accession, Federal Law will come into force in the area named in Article 3, in so far as it is not restricted in its area of validity to particular Länder or parts of the Federal Republic of Germany and in so far as no other provisions are made by this Treaty, particularly its Appendix I.

Article 9
Continued application of GDR law

The law of the German Democratic Republic which applies at the time of the signing of this Treaty, and which is Land Law according to the listing of competences in the Basic Law, remains in force in so far as it is compatible with the Basic Law, without taking into account Article 143, compatible with the Federal Law that comes into force and with the immediately valid law of the European Communities and in so far as no other provision is made in this Treaty. The law of the German Democratic Republic which is Federal Law under the listing of competences in the Basic Law and which does not affect matters governed in a federally uniform way, applies under the conditions of Clause 1 as Land Law until the federal legislative applies a ruling. ... The church taxation law decreed by the German Democratic Republic applies ... (with the exception of East Berlin) as Land Law.

Article 10
EC Law

With the coming into effect of the accession, the treaties on the European Communities, including changes and additions, and the international agreements, treaties and decisions which have come into force in connection with these treaties apply in the area named in Article 3. ...

Chapter IV: Treaties and Agreements under international law

Article 11
Treaties of the Federal Republic of Germany

The Treaty parties start from the premise that treaties and agreements under international law to which the Federal Republic is a Treaty party, including those treaties that establish membership of international organizations or institutions, will retain their validity and that the rights and obligations resulting from this will also apply to the area cited in Article 3, with the exception of the treaties named in Appendix I. In as far as adjustments are necessary in individual cases the All-German government will contact the respective Treaty partners.

Article 12
Treaties of the German Democratic Republic

The Treaty parties are agreed that the German Democratic Republic's treaties under international law are to be discussed with the Treaty partners of the German Democratic Republic during the establishment of German unity from the standpoint of the protection of confidence, the interests of the states involved and the Treaty obligations of the Federal Republic of Germany, as well as according to the principles of a free, democratic state order under the rule of law in order to settle and/or establish whether they should have continued validity or require adjustment or abolition.

A united Germany will establish its position on the transition of the German Democratic Republic's treaties under international law after consultations with the respective Treaty partners and with the European Communities in so far as their competences are affected.

Should a united Germany intend to join international organizations or other multilateral treaties to which the German Democratic Republic but not the Federal Republic of Germany belongs then agreement will be made with the respective Treaty partners and the European Communities, in so far as their competences are affected.

Article 13
Transfer of Institutions

Administrative bodies and other institutions serving public administration or the administration of justice in the area named in Article 3 shall be subordinate to the government of the Land in which they are located. Institutions with a supra-regional sphere of activity will be transferred to the joint responsibility of the Länder concerned. . . . In so far as the institutions or parts of institutions have fulfilled tasks until the time of the accession coming into effect which under the listing of competences in the Basic Law fall to the Federation, they shall be subordinate to the responsible supreme Federal authorities. They shall settle the transfer or the liquidation.

The named institutions also include cultural, educational, scientific, and sporting institutions, and radio and television institutions, whose legal entity is the public administration.

Article 14

Joint institutions of the Länder . . . will until a final ruling continue to be run as joint institutions of the . . . (five GDR) Länder.

Article 15
Transitional regulations for the Land administration

The Land spokesmen in the Länder (without Berlin) named in Article 1 and the government commissioners in the Areas shall continue to fulfil their tasks from the coming into affect of the accession until the election of the Prime Ministers in the responsibility of the Federal government and shall be subject to its instructions. . . . The other Länder and the Federation will provide administrative help in developing the Land administration . . . at the latest until 30th June 1991.

Article 16
Berlin

Until the creation of an All-Berlin Land government, the Senate of Berlin and the Magistrat [East Berlin Council] will exercise the tasks of the All-Berlin Land government.

Article 17
Rehabilitation

The parties in the Treaty affirm their intention that a legal basis be created without delay so that all persons can be rehabilitated who have been the victims of politically motivated criminal proceedings or other legal decision that was contrary to the rule of law or unconstitutional. The rehabilitation of these victims of the unjust SED regime shall be linked to an appropriate ruling on compensation.

Article 18
Continued validity of judicial decisions

Decisions taken by Courts of the German Democratic Republic before the coming into effect of the accession shall remain effective and can be executed according to the law either adopted according to Article 8 or as it continues to remain in force according to Article 9. This law will also be applied to the examination of the compatibility of decisions and their execution with constitutional principles. Article 17 remains unaffected. Those sentenced by a criminal court of the German Democratic Republic are granted by this Treaty . . . the individual right to bring about final decisions through judicial appeal.

Article 19
Continued application of public administrative decisions

Administrative acts by the German Democratic Republic passed before the coming into effect of the accession remain valid. They may be rescinded if they are incompatible with constitutional principles or with the provisions of this Treaty. As for the rest the regulations concerning the existing force of administrative acts remain unaffected.

Article 20
Legal position of the Civil Service

The legal position of members of the civil service at the time of the accession is as agreed in the transitional arrangements of Appendix I. Public tasks (sovereign authority within the meaning of Article 33 Paragraph 4 of the Basic Law) must be entrusted to public servants as soon as possible. Civil service legislation is to be introduced under the terms of the arrangements agreed in Appendix I. Article 92 of the Basic Law (organization of the courts) remains unaffected. Military law is to be introduced under the terms of the arrangements agreed in Appendix I.

Chapter VI: Public assets and debts

Article 21
Administrative assets

The assets of the German Democratic Republic which serve directly specified administrative tasks will become Federal assets. In so far as . . . they were not primarily intended for administrative tasks which according to the Basic Law are to be carried out by Länder, local authorities or other bodies of public administration. In far as administrative assets were primarily used for tasks of the former Ministry for State Security/Office for National Security, the Trust Agency is entitled to them unless . . . they have already been transferred to new social or public purposes. In as far as administrative assets do not become Federal assets . . . those bodies of public administration are entitled to them which are responsible for that administrative task in accordance with the Basic Law. . . .

Article 22
Financial assets

. . . Financial assets, excluding social insurance assets, will come under Federal trust administration, in as far as it has not been transferred to the Trust Agency. . . . Through Federal law the financial assets are to be shared out to the Federal government and the Länder named in Article 1 in such a way that the Federal government and the Länder each receive a half of the total value of the assets. Assets that the Federal government receives after this are to be used to carry out public tasks in the area cited in Article 3. . . . (That) is not valid for state assets used for the provision of housing which is owned by the state-owned housing enterprises. These assets will be transferred to the ownership of local authorities with the simultaneous taking on of the pro rata debts upon the coming into effect of accession. The local authorities will gradually transfer their housing stock to a market-economy housing sector, taking into account social concerns. During this process privatization is to be carried out at a quicker pace to promote the formation of individuals' ownership of housing. . . .

Article 23
Debt ruling

With the coming into effect of accession the total debts of the national budget of the GDR that have accumulated up to this time will be taken over by a special Federation fund without legal status which will fulfil the debt servicing commitments. The special fund will be empowered to take up credits for the repayment of debts of the special fund, to cover accruing costs of interest and of the procurement of credits and for the purpose of purchasing debt instrument of the special fund as part of market support.

The Federal Finance Minister shall administer the special fund. . . . The Federation is responsible for the liabilities of the special fund. From the day of the coming into effect of the accession until 31st December 1993 the Federation and the Trust Agency will each reimburse half of the interest payments made by the social fund. . . .

With effect from 1st January 1994 the Federation and the Länder named in Article 1 and the Trust Agency will take over the total debts accruing to the special fund on 31st December 1993 according to Article 27 Paragraph 3 of the Treaty of 18th May 1990 on Monetary, Economic and Social Union. . . . The special fund will be dissolved with the expiry of 1993.

With the coming into effect of the accession, the Federal Republic of Germany will enter into the guarantees, warranties and sureties taken on by the German Democratic Republic at the expense of the state budget up until unification. The (GDR) Länder and Berlin . . . shall jointly and severally take on a countersurety of 50% for the guarantees, warranties and sureties transferred to the Federal Republic. . . .

Article 24
Foreign debts

Settlement shall take place on the instructions and under the supervision of the Federal Finance Ministry.

Article 25
Trust Agency assets

The Trust agency law of 17th June 1990 will continue to be valid with the following proviso: In accordance with the Trust Agency law, the Trust Agency will continue to be entrusted with the task of making competitive and privatizing the former publicly-owned enterprises. It will be a direct federal institution under public law. The technical and legal supervision is the job of the Federal Minister of Finance. . . .

The number of the administrative council members of the Trust Agency will be increased from 16 to 20, for the first administrative council to 23. Instead of the two representatives elected from among the People's Chamber the Länder mentioned in Article 1 will be given one seat each on the Trust Agency's administrative council. Notwithstanding Paragraph 4 section 2 of the Trust Agency Law the chairman and the other members of the administrative council will be appointed by the Federal government.

The contracting parties affirm that the publicly-owned assets will be used exclusively and solely for the benefit of measures in the territory mentioned in Article 3, irrespective of the budgetary entity. . . . Within the framework of the structural harmonization of agriculture trust agency proceeds may in individual cases also be used to pay off debts of agricultural enterprises. . . .

The authority granted to the Trust Agency through Article 27 Paragraph 1 of the Treaty dated 18th May 1990 to take up credits is to be increased from a total of up to DM17,000 million to DM25,000 million. The aforementioned credits are to be repaid as a rule by 31st December 1995. . . .

According to the provisions of Article 10 Paragraph 6 of the Treaty dated 18th May 1990 opportunities are to be provided for savers to be allowed later on a guaranteed share in the publicly-owned assets at the reduced conversion rate of 2:1.

Interest and redemption payments for credits taken up before 30th June 1990 are to be suspended until the DM-opening balance sheet has been established. Interest payments due are to be paid to the Deutsche Kreditbank AG via the Trust Agency.

Article 26
Reichsbahn [East German Railways]

The ownership and all other real rights . . . become the Deutsche Reichsbahn assets special fund of the Federal Republic of Germany with the coming into effect of accession. . . . Together with the real rights the obligations and claims connected with them are transferred to the special fund. The Chairman of the Board of the Deutsche Bundesbahn [West German Railways] and the Chairman of the Board of the Deutsche Reichsbahn are responsible for co-ordinating both special funds. They are to work towards the goal of technically and organizationally merging the two railway companies.

Article 27
Post Office

The property and all real rights which are part of the Deutsche Post [East German Post Office] special fund will become assets of the Federal Republic of Germany. They will be merged with the Deutsche Bundespost [West German Post Office] special fund. During this the obligations and claims connected with the real rights will at the same be transferred to the Deutsche Bundespost special fund. The assets which serve sovereign and political aims together with the relevant obligations and claims will not become part of the Deutsche Bundespost special fund. . . .

Article 28
Promotion of the Economy

Upon accession the area named in Article 3 will be included in the existing Federal rules on the promotion of the economy. In this the particular needs of structural adaptation will be into account during a transitional period. . . . Specific programmes of measures will extend to the following areas: regional promotion of the economy, improving economic framework conditions in local areas, the development of medium-sized firms, modernizing the economy and freeing enterprises from debt after examining individual cases.

Article 29
Foreign Trade Relations

The foreign trade relations of the German Democratic Republic which have grown up, in particular existing Treaty obligations to countries of the Council for Mutual Economic Assistance, enjoy protection of confidence. They will be . . . further developed and expanded.

Chapter VII: Employment, Social Affairs, Family, Health, Environmental Protection

Article 30
Employment and Social Affairs

It is the task of the All-German legislator,
— to codify as soon as possible a new and uniform law of contracts of employment, as well as the public law on working hours including the permissibility of working on Sundays and holidays and the particular protection of women at work,
— to reformulate and update public health and safety at work in agreement with European Community legislation and that part of the health and safety at work laws of the German Democratic Republic which conforms to it.

Employees may on completion of the 57th year, in the area mentioned in Article 3, receive a pre-retirement sum for a period of three years, but not longer than the earliest possible receipt of an old-age pension from the statutory retirement pension fund. The amount of the pre-retirement sum is 65% of the final average net emolument. . . . Until 31st December 1990 women, on completion of their 55th year, may receive pre-retirement payment for a maximum period of five years. . . .

Persons whose pension from the statutory pension fund commences in the period from 1st January 1992 to 30th June 1995, will
— receive a pension always at least of the same amount which would have resulted on 30th June 1990 according to the pension law valid until then in the territory mentioned in Article 3 without taking into consideration payments from additional or special pensions systems,
— be granted a pension even if on 30th June 1990 a pension claim had existed according to the pension law in force until then in the territory mentioned in Article 3.

As for the rest the transition is to be characterized by the objective of realizing, with the harmonization of wages and salaries in the territory mentioned in Article 3, also a harmonization of pensions for those in the remaining Länder. . . .

Article 31
Family and Women

It is the task of the all-German legislator to develop further legislation on equality between men and women . . . (and) to structure the legal position from the standpoint of the compatibility of family and profession in face of the different legal and institutional starting points in the employment of mothers and fathers. In order to guarantee the continuation of institutions looking after children during the day in the area named in Article 3 the Federal government will share the cost of these institutions for a transitional period until 30th June 1991.

Article 32
Independent Associations

. . . The building up and expansion of independent welfare institutions and an independent youth support sector in the area named in Article 3 will be promoted within the framework of responsibilities laid down in the Constitution.

Article 33
Health Service

It is the task of the legislator to create the prerequisites for swiftly and lastingly improving the level of in-patient provision of care for the population of the area named in Article 3 and adapting it to the situation in the rest of the territory of the Federation. In order to avoid deficits in expenditure by health insurance institutes on medicines in the area which has acceded the All-German legislator will make rules with a time limit by which the price paid to the manufacturer will be reduced in accordance with the rules on the price of pharmaceuticals by a proportion which corresponds to the difference between income from obligatory contributions in the area which has acceded and the Federal area of today.

Article 34
Environmental Protection

... It (is) the task of the legislator to protect man's natural basis for life, taking into account the principles of precautions, the pollutor [pays] and co-operation and to promote uniformity in ecological living conditions at a high level, or at least at that achieved in the Federal Republic of Germany. Ecological restructuring and development programmes are to be drawn up for the area named in Article 3 for the promotion of the cited goal within the framework of the rules on responsibility laid down in the constitution. Planning measures to prevent dangers to the population's health is a priority.

Article 35
Culture

... The cultural substance in the area named in Article 3 must suffer no harm. The fulfilment of the cultural tasks including the financing of them is to be secured, whereby the protection and promotion of culture and art are the duty of the new Länder and communes in accordance with the allocation of responsibilities in the Basic Law. The hitherto centrally managed cultural establishments will be transferred to the ownership of the Länder or communes in which they are situated. Co-financing by the Federation will not be ruled out in exceptional cases, particularly in the Land Berlin.... The Cultural Fund (of the GDR) will be continued until 31st December 1994 in the area named in Article 3 as a transitional arrangement to promote culture, art and artists. Co-financing by the Federation in the framework of the allocation of responsibilities in the Basic Law is not ruled out ...

Article 36
Broadcasting

The "GDR Radio" and the "German Television" will continue to be run until 31st December 1991 at the latest by the Länder named in Article 1 as a public institution, independent of the state and with legal status.... The bodies of the institution shall be the broadcasting commissioner [German: *Rundfunkbeauftragte*] and the broadcasting advisory council [German: *Rundfunkbeirat*].

The broadcasting commissioner will be elected by the People's Chamber on the suggestion of the Prime Minister of the German Democratic Republic. If no election by the People's Chamber comes about, the broadcasting commissioner will be elected by a majority by the Land spokesman of the Länder named in Article 1 and by the Mayor of Berlin. The broadcasting commissioner will manage the institution and represent it in law and extra-judicially. ... The broadcasting advisory council will consist of 18 recognized personalities from public life as representatives of socially relevant groups ...

The institution will be financed primarily from income from broadcasting licence receipts from listeners and viewers resident in the area named in Article 3.... The institution (is), in line with the federal structure of broadcasting, to be dissolved by a joint State Treaty of the Länder named in Article 1 or to be transferred into institutions of public law of individual or several Länder. Should a State Treaty not come about by 31st December 1991, the institution will then be dissolved with the expiry of that period ...

Article 37
Education

School, vocational and academic qualifications or certificates of competence gained or recognized by the state in the German Democratic Republic will continue to be valid in the area named in Article 3.... Their equivalence will be ascertained on application by the authority responsible in each case. Federal and EC laws on the equivalence of examinations or certificates of competence as well as specific regulations in this Treaty have priority. The right to hold vocational descriptions recognised by the state or academic degrees and titles conferred remains unaffected in any case.

The usual procedure of the Conference of Ministers of Culture for recognizing teacher-training qualifications will be valid. The Conference of Ministers of Culture will make relevant transitional rules. Certificates in accordance with the system of trained vocations and the system of skilled work, final examinations and examinations for apprentices in recognized trained vocations are equal to one another. The regulations required for restructuring the school system in the area named in Article 3 will be made by the Länder named in Article 1. The necessary rules on recognizing certificates from schools will be agreed by the Conference of Ministers of Culture . . .

Students who change colleges before concluding their studies will have their studies and examinations hitherto recognized in accordance with the principles of Paragraph 7 of the General Rules for Degree Examination Regulations (ABD) or within the framework of the rules valid for the admissability to state examinations. The right to matriculation confirmed on final certificates from engineering and vocational colleges in the German Democratic Republic will be valid in accordance with the decision by the Conference of Ministers of Culture of 10th May 1990 and Appendix B to it. Further reaching principles and procedures for the recognition of vocational college and university-level education are to be developed within the framework of the Conference of Ministers of Culture.

Article 38
Science and Research

Science and research will continue to form an important basis for state and society in a united Germany. An assessment of publicly supported institutions by the Scientific Council, which will be concluded by 31st December 1991, will serve the necessary renewal of science and research while retaining high-performance institutions in the area named in Article 3, whereby individual results are to be put into effect step by step beforehand . . .

With the coming into effect of accession the Academy of Sciences as a society of academics will be separated from research institutes and other institutions. The decision on how the Academy's society of academics is to be continued will be taken in accordance with Land law. The research institutes and other institutions will continue to exist in the first instance until 31st December 1991 as Land institutions in the area named in Article 3, in as far as they have not been disbanded beforehand or transformed. . . . Contracts of employment . . . will continue to exist until 31st December 1991 as temporary contracts with the Länder . . .

The intent (of the same regulations) is valid for the Construction Academy and the Academy of Agricultural Sciences as well as institutions coming under the Ministry of Food, Agriculture and Forestry. The Research Council of the German Democratic Republic is disbanded with the coming into effect of the German Democratic Republic's accession.

Article 39
Sport

The sports structures being transformed in the region named in Article 3 will be switched to self-administration. The public authorities will promote sport in both a non-material and a material way.

Top level sport and its development will, insofar as it has proved its worth, continue to be promoted in the region named in Article 3. This promotion will be within the framework of the rules and principles valid in the Federal Republic of Germany. Within this framework the Research Institute for Physical Culture and Sport in Leipzig, the Research and Development Department for Sports Equipment in Berlin (East) and the IOC-recognized Doping Control Laboratory in Kreischa, near Dresden, will be continued or appended to existing institutions.

The Federal government will support disabled sport until 31st December 1992.

Chapter IX: Transitional and final regulations

Article 40
Treaties and Agreements

The obligations from the Treaty of 18th May 1990 on the creation of a Monetary, Economic and Social Union between the Federal Republic of Germany and the GDR continue to be valid, as long as nothing different is set in this Treaty or the agreements become irrelevant in the course of the establishing of German unity.

In as far as rights and obligations from other treaties and agreements between the Federal Republic of Germany or the Federal States and the German Democratic Republic have not become irrelevant in the course of creating German unity they will be taken over, adapted, or carried out by the internal legal entities responsible.

Article 41
Issues concerning assets

The Joint Statement by the government of the GDR and the government of the Federal Republic of Germany of 15th June 1990 on the settling of open questions of property is part of the Treaty. In accordance with specific legal rules there will be no return of property rights over plots of land or buildings if the relevant plot of land and building is required for urgent purposes of investment, which are to be more closely laid down, on a sure planning basis, serves the setting up of a location for a trading enterprise and is of particular value for promoting this investment decision in terms of the national economy, and above all creates or preserves jobs. Compensation for the former owner is also to be regulated in the law. Besides this the Federal Republic of Germany will not pass any laws which contradict the Joint Statement.

Article 42
Bundestag Deputies

Before the accession of the German Democratic Republic comes into effect the People's Chamber will elect 144 deputies as well as a sufficient number of substitutes on the basis of its composition on 1st September 1990 to be sent to the 11th Bundestag. The parliamentary groups represented in the People's Chamber will make relevant proposals . . .

Article 43
Bundesrat

From the formation of the (GDR) Länder until the election of the Prime Minister the Land plenipotentiary can take part in sessions of the Bundesrat with an advisory vote.

Article 44
Upholding of rights

Rights from this Treaty in favour of the German Democratic Republic or the Länder named in Article 1 can be claimed by each of these Länder after the accession comes into effect.

Article 45
The coming into effect of the Treaty

This Treaty, including the protocol enclosed and Appendices I to III, comes into force on the day when the governments of the GDR and the Federal Republic of Germany have informed one another that the required internal state conditions for the coming into force have been fulfilled. After the establishing of German unity the Treaty remains in force as Federal Law.

Protocol notes —

1. On Article 1: The boundaries of the Land of Berlin are stipulated by the law on the establishment of a new Berlin municipality of the 27th April 1920 [as received] with the proviso . . . that all areas in which elections to the House of Representatives or the Berlin City Council have taken place shall form a part of the districts of Berlin. The Länder of Berlin and Brandenburg shall examine and document the resulting boundaries within a year.

2. On Article 9: The two parties to the Treaty shall note the statement by the Land of Berlin that the church tax law applicable in Berlin (West) shall be extended to that part of Berlin in which it was not so far applicable from the 1st January 1991.

3./4. On Article 13: . . . in as far as institutions are wholly or partially transferred to the Federation, suitable staff are to be recruited on the appropriate scale in order to meet the requirements needed to fulfil tasks.

5. On Article 16: The two parties to the Treaty shall note the announcement by the Land of Berlin that the Mayor shall be appointed member of the Bundesrat on the 3rd October 1990 and that the members of the city government as well as other members of the Berlin Land government shall be involved in deputising for the appointed Bundesrat members.

6. On Article 20: The introduction of the civil servant law according to the provisions agreed in Appendix I shall take effect in line with the principles on functions of a permanent nature which are decisive for the staffing levels of the Federal Republic of Germany.

7. On Article 21: The Länder shall be informed about any further appropriation of property under military use. The affected Länder are to be consulted before property hitherto used by the military, which becomes a federal asset, are given over to a new use.

8. On Article 22: The publicly-owned property and land used by housing co-operatives for housing purposes . . . shall ultimately be transferred to ownership by the housing cooperatives while retaining their proper use.

9. On Article 35: The Federal Republic of Germany and the German Democratic Republic declare in connection with Article 35 of the Treaty: There is freedom to affirm Sorb nationality and exercise Sorb culture. The freedom to preserve and continue the development of Sorb culture and Sorb traditions shall be ensured. Members of the Sorb people and their organizations have the freedom to cultivate and to preserve the Sorb language in public life. The allocation of responsibilities in the Basic Law remains untouched.

10. On Article 38: Agreements made by the Academy of Sciences, the Building Academy and Academy of the Agricultural Sciences of the German Democratic Republic with organizations in other states or with international organizations will be examined according to the principles laid down in Article 12 of the Treaty.

11. On Article 40: Cases in which the Federal government has approved the taking over of the costs for the medical treatment of Germans from the area named in Article 3 will be settled by the Federal government.

12. To Appendix II, Chapter II, Section III, no. 2 (party assets) (not yet published): The parties have a claim to equal opportunities in preparation for and competing in elections. Money or assets having a monetary value which have come into the hands of the parties neither via membership subscriptions nor by donations nor by state contributions to election expenses, in particular the assets of former bloc parties and the PDS in the German Democratic Republic, may not be used either for preparation for the election or for the election campaign. The parties are obliged to give affidavits by their treasurers on this and to have the renunciation of the use of such monies confirmed by accountants on 1st December 1990. In as far as parties in the Federal Republic of Germany merge with former bloc parties of the German Democratic Republic they have to provide a final balance and an opening balance at the moment of their merger by 1st November 1990 which correspond to the criteria of Paragraph 24 Section 4 of the law on parties.

Protocol statement to the Treaty: Both parties to the Treaty agree that the commitments in the Treaty are made without detriment to the rights and responsibilities of the Four Powers with reference to Berlin and Germany as a whole which still exist or to the results still to come from the talks on the external aspects of the creation of German unity.

Treaty on the Final Settlement with Respect to Germany, September 12, 1990

(Two-Plus-Four Treaty)

The Federal Republic of Germany, the German Democratic Republic, the French Republic, the Union of Soviet Socialist Republics, the United Kingdom of Great Britain and Northern Ireland, and the United States of America,

Conscious of the fact that their peoples have been living together in peace since 1945;

Mindful of the recent historic changes in Europe which make it possible to overcome the division of the continent;

Having regard to the rights and responsibilities of the Four Powers relating to Berlin and to Germany as a whole, and the corresponding wartime and post-war agreements and decisions of the Four Powers;

Resolved in accordance with their obligations under the Charter of the United Nations to develop friendly relations among nations based on respect for the principle of equal rights and self-determination of peoples, and to take other appropriate measures to strengthen universal peace;

Recalling the principles of the Final Act of the Conference on Security and Co-operation in Europe, signed in Helsinki;

Recognizing that those principles have laid firm foundations for the establishment of a just and lasting peaceful order in Europe;

Determined to take account of everyone's security interests;

Convinced of the need finally to overcome antagonism and to develop co-operation in Europe;

Confirming their readiness to reinforce security, in particular by adopting effective arms control, disarmament and confidence-building measures; their willingness not to regard each other as adversaries but to work for a relationship of trust and co-operation; and accordingly their readiness to consider positively setting up appropriate institutional arrangements within the framework of the Conference on Security and Co-operation in Europe;

Welcoming the fact that the German people, freely exercising their right of self-determination, have expressed their will to bring about the unity of Germany as a state so that they will be able to serve the peace of the world as an equal and sovereign partner in a united Europe;

Convinced that the unification of Germany as a state with definitive borders is a significant contribution to peace and stability in Europe;

Intending to conclude the final settlement with respect to Germany;

Recognizing that thereby, and with the unification of Germany as a democratic and peaceful state, the rights and responsibilities of the Four Powers relating to Berlin and to Germany as a whole lose their function;

Represented by their Ministers for Foreign Affairs who, in accordance with the Ottawa Declaration of February 13, 1990, met in Bonn on May 5, 1990, in Berlin on June 22, 1990, in Paris on July 17, 1990, with the participation of the Minister for Foreign Affairs of the Republic of Poland, and in Moscow on September 12, 1990;

Have agreed as follows:

Article 1

(1) The united Germany shall comprise the territory of the Federal Republic of Germany, the German Democratic Republic, and the whole of Berlin. Its external borders shall be the borders of the Federal Republic of Germany and the German Democratic Republic and shall be definitive from the date on which the present Treaty comes into force. The confirmation of the definitive nature of the borders of the united Germany is an essential element of the peaceful order in Europe.

(2) The united Germany and the Republic of Poland shall confirm the existing border between them in a treaty that is binding under international law.

(3) The united Germany has no territorial claims whatsoever against other states and shall not assert any in the future.

(4) The Governments of the Federal Republic of Germany and the German Democratic Republic shall ensure that the constitution of the united Germany does not contain any provision incompatible with these principles. This applies accordingly to the provisions laid down in the preamble, the second sentence of Article 23, and Article 146 of the Basic Law for the Federal Republic of Germany.

(5) The Governments of the French Republic, the Union of the Soviet Socialist Republics, the United Kingdom of Great Britain and Northern Ireland, and the United States of America take formal note of the corresponding commitments and declarations by the Governments of the Federal Republic of Germany and the German Democratic Republic and declare that their implementation will confirm the definitive nature of the united Germany's borders.

Article 2

The governments of the Federal Republic of Germany and the German Democratic Republic reaffirm their declarations that only peace will emanate from German soil. According to the constitution of the united Germany, acts tending to and undertaken with the intent to disturb the peaceful relations between nations, especially to prepare for aggressive war, are unconstitutional and a punishable offence. The governments of the Federal Republic of Germany and the German Democratic Republic declare that the united Germany will never employ any of its weapons except in accordance with its constitution and the Charter of the United Nations.

Article 3

(1) The Governments of the Federal Republic of Germany and the German Democratic Republic reaffirm their renunciation of the manufacture and possession of and control over nuclear, biological, and chemical weapons. They declare that the united Germany, too, will abide by these commitments. In particular, rights and obligations arising from the Treaty on the Non-Proliferation of Nuclear Weapons of July 1, 1968, will continue to apply to the united Germany.

(2) The government of the Federal Republic of Germany, acting in full agreement with the Government of the German Democratic Republic, made the following statement on August 30, 1990, in Vienna at the Negotiations on Conventional Armed Forces in Europe:

"The Government of the Federal Republic of Germany undertakes to reduce the personnel strength of the armed forces of the united Germany to 370,000 (ground, air, and naval forces) within three to four years. This reduction will commence on the entry into force of the first CFE agreement. Within the scope of this overall ceiling no more than 345,000 will belong to the ground and air forces which, pursuant to the agreed mandate, alone are the subject of the Negotiations on Conventional Armed Forces in Europe. The federal government regards its commitment to reduce ground and air forces as a significant German contribution to the reduction of conventional armed forces in Europe. It assumes that in follow-on negotiations the other participants in the negotiations, too, will render their contribution to enhancing security and stability in Europe, including measures to limit personnel strengths."

The government of the German Democratic Republic has expressly associated itself with this statement.

(3) The governments of the French Republic, the Union of Soviet Socialist Republics, the United Kingdom of Great Britain and Northern Ireland, and the United States of America take note of these statements by the governments of the Federal Republic of Germany and the German Democratic Republic.

Article 4

(1) The governments of the Federal Republic of Germany, the German Democratic Republic, and the Union of Soviet Socialist Republics state that the united Germany and the Union of Soviet Socialist Republics will settle by treaty the conditions for and the duration of the presence of Soviet armed forces on the territory of the present German Democratic Republic and of Berlin, as well as the conduct of the withdrawal of these armed forces which will be completed by the end of 1994, in connection with the implementation of the undertaking of the Federal Republic of Germany and the German Democratic Republic referred to in paragraph 2 of Article 3 of the present treaty.

(2) The governments of the French Republic, the United Kingdom of Great Britain and Northern Ireland, and the United States of America take note of this statement.

Article 5

(1) Until the completion of the withdrawal of the Soviet armed forces from the territory of the present German Democratic Republic and of Berlin in accordance with Article 4 of the present treaty, only German territorial defense units which are not integrated into the alliance structures to which German armed forces in the rest of German territory are assigned will be stationed in that territory as armed forces of the united Germany. During that period and subject to the provisions of paragraph 2 of this Article, armed forces of other states will not be stationed in that territory or carry out any other military activity there.

(2) For the duration of the presence of Soviet armed forces in the territory of the present German Democratic Republic and of Berlin, armed forces of the French Republic, the United Kingdom of Great Britain and Northern Ireland, and the United States of America will, upon German request, remain stationed in Berlin by agreement to this effect between the government of the united Germany and the governments of the states concerned. The number of troops and the amount of equipment of all non-German armed forces stationed in Berlin will not be greater than at the time of signature of the present treaty. New categories of weapons will not be introduced there by non-German armed forces. The government of the united Germany will conclude with the governments of those states which have armed forces stationed in Berlin treaties with conditions which are fair taking account of the relations existing with the states concerned.

(3) Following the completion of the withdrawal of the Soviet armed forces from the territory of the present German Democratic Republic and of Berlin, units of German armed forces assigned to military alliance structures in the same way as those in the rest of German territory may also be stationed in that part of Germany, but without nuclear weapon carriers. This does not apply to conventional weapon systems which may have other capabilities in addition to conventional ones but which in that part of Germany are equipped for a conventional role and designated only for such. Foreign armed forces and nuclear weapons or their carriers will not be stationed in that part of Germany or deployed there.

Article 6

The right of the united Germany to belong to alliances, with all the rights and responsibilities arising therefrom, shall not be affected by the present treaty.

Article 7

(1) The French Republic, the Union of Soviet Socialist Republics, the United Kingdom of Great Britain and Northern Ireland, and the United States of America hereby terminate their rights and responsibilities relating to Berlin and to Germany as a whole. As a

result, the corresponding, related quadripartite agreements, decisions, and practices are terminated and all related Four Power institutions are dissolved.

(2) The united Germany shall have accordingly full sovereignty over its internal and external affairs.

Article 8

(1) The present treaty is subject to ratification or acceptance as soon as possible. On the German side it will be ratified by the united Germany. The treaty will therefore apply to the united Germany.

(2) The instruments of ratification or acceptance shall be deposited with the government of the united Germany. That government shall inform the governments of the other contracting parties of the deposit of each instrument of ratification or acceptance.

Article 9

The present Treaty shall enter into force for the united Germany, the French Republic, the Union of Soviet Socialist Republics, the United Kingdom of Great Britain and Northern Ireland, and the United States of America on the date of deposit of the last instrument of ratification or acceptance by these states.

Article 10

The original of the present treaty, of which the English, French, German, and Russian texts are equally authentic, shall be deposited with the government of the Federal Republic of Germany, which shall transmit certified true copies to the governments of the other contracting parties.

Agreed Minute to the Treaty on the Final Settlement with Respect to Germany of September 12, 1990

Any questions with respect to the application of the word "deployed" as used in the last sentence of paragraph 3 of Article 5 will be decided by the government of the united Germany in a reasonable and responsible way taking into account the security interests of each contracting party as set forth in the preamble.

For the Federal Republic of Germany
HANS-DIETRICH GENSCHER

For the German Democratic Republic
LOTHAR DE MAIZIÈRE

For the French Republic
ROLAND DUMAS

For the Union of Soviet Socialist Republics
EDUARD SHEVARDNADZE

For the United Kingdom of Great Britain and Northern Ireland
DOUGLAS HURD

For the United States of America
JAMES W. BAKER III

Letter from Foreign Minister Hans-Dietrich Genscher (Federal Republic) and Prime Minister Lothar de Maizière (German Democratic Republic) to the foreign ministers of the United States, France, Great Britain, and the Soviet Union, concerning the Treaty on the Final Settlement with Respect to Germany.

Mr. Foreign Minister,

In connection with the signing today of the Treaty on the Final Settlement with Respect to Germany, we would like to inform you that the governments of the Federal Republic of Germany and the German Democratic Republic declared the following in the negotiations:

1. The Joint Declaration of June 15, 1990, by the governments of the Federal Republic of Germany and the German Democratic Republic on the settlement of outstanding property matters contains, inter alia, the following observations:

The expropriations effected on the basis of occupation law or sovereignty (between 1945 and 1949) are irreversible. The governments of the Soviet Union and the German Democratic Republic do not see any means of revising the measures taken then. The government of the Federal Republic of Germany takes note of this in the light of the historical development. It is of the opinion that a final decision on any public compensation must be reserved for a future all-German parliament.

According to Article 41 (1) of the treaty of August 31, 1990, between the Federal Republic of Germany and the German Democratic Republic establishing German unity (Unification Treaty), the aforementioned Joint Declaration forms an integral part of the Treaty. Pursuant to Article 41 (3) of the Unification Treaty, the Federal Republic of Germany will not enact any legislation contradicting the part of the Joint Declaration quoted above.

2. The monuments dedicated to the victims of war and tyranny which have been erected on German soil will be respected and will enjoy the protection of German law. The same applies to the war graves, which will be maintained and looked after.

3. In the united Germany, too, the free democratic basic order will be protected by the Constitution. It provides the basis for ensuring that parties which, by reason of their aims or the behavior of their adherents, seek to impair or abolish the free democratic basic order as well as associations which are directed against the constitutional order or the concept of international understanding, can be prohibited. This also applies to parties and associations with National Socialist aims.

4. On the treaties of the German Democratic Republic, the following has been agreed in Article 12 (1) and (2) of the treaty of August 31, 1990, between the Federal Republic of Germany and the German Democratic Republic establishing German unity:

"The contracting parties agree that, as part of the process of establishing German unity, the international treaties concluded by the German Democratic Republic shall be discussed with the contracting parties in terms of the protection of bona fide rights, the interests of the states concerned and the treaty obligations of the Federal Republic of Germany as well as in the light of the principles of a free democratic basic order founded on the rule of law and taking into account the responsibilities of the European Communities in order to regulate or ascertain the continuance, adjustment, or termination of such treaties.

The united Germany shall lay down its position on the continuance of international treaties of the German Democratic Republic after consultations with the respective contracting parties and with the European Communities insofar as their responsibilities are affected."

Accept, Mr. Foreign Minister, the assurances of our high consideration.

Treaty between the Federal Republic of Germany and the Union of Soviet Socialist Republics on Good-Neighbourliness, Partnership and Co-operation, signed in Moscow, 9 November 1990

The Federal Republic of Germany and the Union of Soviet Socialist Republics,

Conscious of their responsibility for the preservation of peace in Europe and in the world,

Desiring to set the final seal on the past and, through understanding and reconciliation, render a major contribution towards ending the division of Europe,

Convinced of the need to build a new, united Europe on the basis of common values and to create a just and lasting peaceful order in Europe including stable security structures,

Convinced that great importance attaches to human rights and fundamental freedoms as part of the heritage of the whole of Europe and that respect for them is a major prerequisite for progress in developing that peaceful order,

Reaffirming their commitment to the aims and principles enshrined in the United Nations Charter and to the provisions of the Final Act of Helsinki of 1 August 1975 and of subsequent documents adopted by the Conference on Security and Co-operation in Europe,

Resolved to continue the good traditions of their centuries-long history, to make good-neighbourliness, partnership and co-operation the basis of their relations, and to meet the historic challenges that present themselves on the threshold of the third millennium.

Having regard to the foundations established in recent years through the development of co-operation between the Union of Soviet Socialist Republics and the Federal Republic of Germany as well as the German Democratic Republic,

Moved by the desire the further develop and intensify the fruitful and mutually beneficial co-operation between the two States in all fields and to give their mutual relationship a new quality in the interests of their peoples and of peace in Europe,

Taking account of the signing of the Treaty of 12 September 1990 on the Final Settlement with respect to Germany regulating the external aspects of German unity,

Have agreed as follows.

Article 1

The Federal Republic of Germany and the Union of Soviet Socialist Republics will, in developing their relations, be guided by the following principles:

They will respect each other's sovereign equality, territorial integrity and political independence.

They will make the dignity and rights of the individual, concern for the survival of mankind, and preservation of the natural environment the focal point of their policy.

They reaffirm the right of all nations and States to determine their own fate freely and without interference from outside and to proceed with their political, economic, social and cultural development as they see fit.

They uphold the principle that any war, whether nuclear or conventional, must be effectively prevented and peace preserved and developed.

They guarantee the precedence of the universal rules of international law in their domestic and international relations and confirm their resolve to honour their contractual obligations.

They pledge themselves to make use of the creative potential of the individual and modern society with a view to safeguarding peace and enhancing the prosperity of all nations.

Article 2

The Federal Republic of Germany and the Union of Soviet Socialist Republics undertake to respect without qualification the territorial integrity of all States in Europe within their present frontiers.

They declare that they have no territorial claims whatsoever against any State and will not raise any in the future.

They regard and will continue to regard as inviolable the frontiers of all States in Europe as they exist on the day of signature of the present Treaty.

Article 3

The Federal Republic of Germany and the Union of Soviet Socialist Republics reaffirm that they will refrain from any threat or use of force which is directed against the territorial integrity or political independence of the other side or is in any other way incompatible with the aims and principles of the United Nations Charter or with the CSCE Final Act.

They will settle their disputes exclusively by peaceful means and never resort to any of their weapons except for the purpose of individual or collective self-defence. They will never and under no circumstances be the first to employ armed forces against one another or against third States. They call upon all other States to join in this non-aggression commitment.

Should either side become the object of an attack the other side will not afford any military support or other assistance to the aggressor and resort to all measures to settle the conflict in conformity with the principles and procedures of the United Nations and other institutions of collective security.

Article 4

The Federal Republic of Germany and the Union of Soviet Socialist Republics will seek to ensure that armed forces and armaments are substantially reduced by means of binding, effectively verifiable agreements in order to achieve, in conjunction with unilateral measures, a stable balance at a lower level, especially in Europe, which will suffice for defence but not for attack.

The same applies to the multilateral and bilateral enhancement of confidence-building and stabilizing measures.

Article 5

Both sides will support to the best of their ability the process of security and co-operation in Europe on the basis of the Final Act of Helsinki adopted on 1 August 1975 and, with the co-operation of all participating States, develop and intensify that co-operation further still, notably by creating permanent institutions and bodies. The aim of these efforts is the consolidation of peace, stability and security and the coalescence of Europe to form a single area of law, democracy and co-operation in the fields of economy, culture and information.

Article 6

The Federal Republic of Germany and the Union of Soviet Socialist Republics have agreed to hold regular consultations with a view to further developing and intensifying their bilateral relations and co-ordinating their position on international issues.

Consultations at the highest political level shall be held as necessary but at least once a year.

The Foreign Ministers will meet at least twice a year.

The Defence Ministers will meet at regular intervals.

Other ministers will meet as necessary to discuss matters of mutual interest.

The existing mixed commissions will consider ways and means of intensifying their work. New mixed commissions will be appointed as necessary by mutual agreement.

Article 7

Should a situation arise which in the opinion of either side constitutes a threat to or violation of peace or may lead to dangerous international complications, both sides will immediately make contact with a view to co-ordinating their positions and agreeing on measures to improve or resolve the situation.

Article 8

The Federal Republic of Germany and the Union of Soviet Socialist Republics have agreed to substantially expand and intensify their bilateral co-operation, especially in the economic, industrial and scientific-technological fields and in the field of environmental protection, with a view to developing their mutual relations on a stable and long-term basis and deepening the trust between the two States and peoples. They will to this end conclude a comprehensive agreement on the development of co-operation in the economic, industrial and scientific-technological fields and, where necessary, separate arrangements on specific matters.

Both sides attach great importance to co-operation in the training of specialists and executive personnel from industry for the development of bilateral relations and are prepared to considerably expand and itensify that co-operation.

Article 9

The Federal Republic of Germany and the Union of Soviet Socialist Republics will further develop and intensify their economic co-operation for their mutual benefit. They will create, as far as their domestic legislation and their obligations under international treaties allow, the most favourable general conditions for entrepreneurial and other economic activity by citizens, enterprises and governmental as well as non-governmental institutions of the other side.

This applies in particular to the treatment of capital investment and investors.

Both sides will encourage the initiatives necessary for economic co-operation by those directly concerned, especially with the aim of fully exploiting the possibilities afforded by the existing treaties and programmes.

Article 10

Both sides will, on the basis of the Agreement of 22 July 1986 concerning Economic and Technological Co-operation, further develop exchanges in this field and implement joint projects. They propose to draw on the achievements of modern science and technology for the sake of the people, their health, and their prosperity. They will promote and support parallel initiatives by researchers and research establishments in this sphere.

Article 11

Convinced that the preservation of the natural sources of life is indispensable for prosperous economic and social development, both sides reaffirm their determination to continue and intensify their co-operation in the field of environmental protection on the basis of the agreement of 25 October 1988.

They propose to solve major problems of environmental protection together, to study harmful effects on the environment, and to develop measures for their prevention. They will participate in the development of co-ordinated strategies and concepts for a transborder environmental policy within the international, and especially the European, framework.

Article 12

Both sides will seek to extend transport communications (air, rail, sea, inland waterway and road links) between the Federal Republic of Germany and the Union of Soviet Socialist Republics through the use of state-of-the-art technology.

Article 13

Both sides will strive to simplify to a considerable extent, on the basis of reciprocity, the procedure for the issue of visas to citizens of both countries wishing to travel, primarily for business, economic and cultural reasons and for purposes of scientific and technological co-operation.

Article 14

Both sides support comprehensive contacts among people from both countries and the development of co-operation among parties, trade unions, foundations, schools, universities, sports organizations, churches and social institutions, women's associations, environmental protection and other social organizations and associations.

Special attention will be given to the deepening of contacts between the parliaments of the two States.

They welcome co-operation based on partnership between municipalities and regions and between Federal States and Republics of the Union.

An important role falls to the German-Soviet Discussion Forum and co-operation among the media.

Both sides will facilitate the participation of all young people and their organizations in exchanges and other contacts and joint projects.

Article 15

The Federal Republic of Germany and the Union of Soviet Socialist Republics, conscious of the mutual enrichment of the cultures of their peoples over the centuries and of their unmistakable contribution to Europe's common cultural heritage, as well as of the importance of cultural exchange for international understanding, will considerably extend their cultural co-operation.

Both sides will give substance to and fully exploit the agreement on the establishment and work of cultural centres.

Both sides reaffirm their willingness to give all interested persons comprehensive access to the languages and cultures of the other side and will encourage public and private initiatives.

Both sides strongly advocate the creation of wider possibilities for learning the language of the other country in schools, universities and other educational institutions and will for this purpose assist the other side in the training of teachers and make available teaching aids, including the use of television, radio, audio-visual and computer technology. They will support initiatives for the establishment of bilingual schools.

Soviet citizens of German nationality as well as citizens from the Union of Soviet Socialist Republics who have their permanent abode in the Federal Republic of Germany and wish to preserve their language, culture or traditions will be enabled to develop their national, linguistic and cultural identity. Accordingly, both sides will make possible and facilitate promotional measures for the benefit of such persons or their organizations within the framework of their respective laws.

Article 16

The Federal Republic of Germany and the Union of Soviet Socialist Republics will advocate the preservation of cultural treasures of the other side in their territory.

They agree that lost or unlawfully transferred art treasures which are located in their territory will be returned to their owners or their successors.

Article 17

Both sides stress the special importance of humanitarian co-operation in their bilateral relations. They will intensify this co-operation with the assistance of the charitable organizations of both sides.

Article 18

The Government of the Federal Republic of Germany declares that the monuments to Soviet victims of the war and totalitarian rule erected on German soil will be respected and be under the protection of German law.

The same applies to Soviet war graves; they will be preserved and tended.

The Government of the Union of Soviet Socialist Republics will guarantee access to the graves of Germans on Soviet territory, their preservation and upkeep.

The responsible organizations of both sides will itensify their co-operation on these matters.

Article 19

The Federal Republic of Germany and the Union of Soviet Socialist Republics will intensify their mutual assistance in civil and family matters on the basis of the Hague Convention relating to Civil Procedure to which they are signatories. Both sides will further develop their mutual assistance in criminal matters, taking into account their legal systems and proceeding in harmony with international law.

The responsible authorities in the Federal Republic of Germany and the Union of Soviet Socialist Republics will co-operate in combating organized crime, terrorism, drug trafficking, illicit interference with civil aviation and maritime shipping, the manufacture or dissemination of counterfeit money, and smuggling, including the illicit transborder movement of works of art. The procedure and conditions for mutual co-operation will be the subject of a separate arrangement.

Article 20

The two Governments will intensify their co-operation within the scope of international organizations, taking into account their mutual interests and each side's co-operation with other countries. They will assist one another in developing co-operation with international, especially European, organizations and institutions of which either side is a member, should the other side express an interest in such co-operation.

Article 21

The present Treaty will not affect the rights and obligations arising from existing bilateral and multilateral agreements which the two sides have concluded with other States. The present Treaty is directed against no one; both sides regard their co-operation as an integral part and dynamic element of the further development of the CSCE process.

Article 22

The present Treaty is subject to ratification; the instruments of ratification will be exchanged as soon as possible in Moscow.

The present Treaty will enter into force on the date of exchange of the instruments of ratification.

The present Treaty will remain in force for twenty years. Thereafter it will be tacitly extended for successive periods of five years unless either Contracting Party denounces the Treaty in writing subject to one year's notice prior to its expiry.

Done at Bonn on 9 November 1990 in duplicate in the German and Russian languages, both texts being equally authentic.

For the	For the
Federal Republic	Union of Soviet
of Germany	Socialist Republics

BIBLIOGRAPHY

This is a structured selection from the vast amount of material which has appeared on the final phase of the GDR and German reunification. In view of the relative paucity of titles in English on very recent events, some items announced as forthcoming are also listed and are marked as such. Further titles (mainly in German) are to be found in: P. Bryson, "The economics of German reunification: a review of the literature", in *Journal of Comparative Economics* 16, No. 1 (1992), pp.118–49; and in: H. Buck and H. Bauer (eds.), *Transformation der Wirtschaftsordnung der ehemaligen DDR. Wirtschaftliche Erneuerung in den neuen Bundesländern. Literaturführer* (Gesamtdeutsches Institut: Bonn, 3rd edn 1991).

Germany in the twentieth century

V. Berghahn, *Modern Germany: Society, economy and politics in the twentieth century* (Cambridge University Press: Cambridge, 2nd edn 1987).

M. Fulbrook, *The Fontana History of Germany 1918–1990: The Divided Nation* (London: Fontana, 1991).

The two German republics before 1989

D. Bark and D. Gress, *A History of West Germany*, 2 vols. (Basil Blackwell: Oxford, 1989).

D. Childs, *The GDR: Moscow's German Ally* (Unwin Hyman: London, 2nd edn 1988).

D. Childs, T. Baylis and M. Rueschemeyer (eds.), *East Germany in Comparative Perspective* (Routledge: London, 1989).

D. Conradt, *The German Polity* (Longman: London, 4th edn 1989).

DDR Handbuch (Wissenschaft und Politik: Cologne, 3rd edn 1985), ed. by H. Zimmermann for Federal Ministry for Inner-German Relations.

M. Dennis, *The German Democratic Republic: Politics, Economics and Society* (Pinter: London, 1988).

G. Edwards, *GDR Society and Institutions* (Macmillan: London, 1985).

M. Fulbrook, *The Two Germanies, 1945–1990: Problems of Interpretation* (Macmillan: Basingstoke and London, 1992).

E. Kolinsky (ed.), *The Federal Republic of Germany: The End of an Era* (Berg: Oxford, 1991).

G. Kloss, *West Germany: An Introduction* (Macmillan: Basingstoke and London, 2nd edn 1990).

M. McCauley, *The German Democratic Republic since 1945* (Macmillan: London, 1983).

M. Rueschemeyer and C. Lemke (eds.), *The Quality of Life in the German Democratic Republic* (Sharpe: Armonk, New York, 1989).

J. Thomaneck and J. Mellis (eds.), *Politics, Government and Society in the German Democratic Republic: Basic Documents* (Berg: Oxford, 1989).

H. Weber, *Geschichte der DDR* (DTV: Munich, 1985).

Political memoirs

R. Andert and W. Herzberg, *Der Sturz: Erich Honecker im Kreuzverhör* (Aufbau: Berlin and Weimar, 1990).

S. Bergmann-Pohl, *Abschied ohne Tränen: Rückblick auf das Jahr der Einheit* (Ullstein: Berlin and Frankfurt/Main, 1991).

M. Gerlach, *Mitverantwortlich: Als Liberaler im SED-Staat* (Morgenbuch: Berlin, 1991).

G. Gysi and Thomas Falkner, *Sturm aufs Grosse Haus: Der Untergang der SED* (Fischerinsel: Berlin, 1990).

C. -H. Janson, *Totengräber der DDR: Wie Günter Mittag den SED-Staat ruinierte* (ECON: Düsseldorf, Vienna and New York, 1991).

E. Krenz, *Wenn Mauern fallen: Die friedliche Revolution: Vorgeschichte — Ablauf — Auswirkungen* (Paul Neff: Vienna, 1990).

G. Mittag, *Um Jeden Preis: Im Spannungsfeld zweier Systeme* (Aufbau: Berlin and Weimar, 1991).

H. Modrow, *Aufbruch und Ende* (Konkret Literatur: Hamburg, 1991).

W. Momper, *Grenzfall: Berlin im Brennpunkt deutscher Geschichte* (Bertelsmann: Munich, 1991).

G. Schabowski, *Der Absturz* (Rowohlt: Berlin, 1991).

G. Schabowski, *Das Politbüro: Ende eines Mythos* (Rowohlt: Berlin, 1990), ed. F. Sieren and L. Koehne.

W. Schäuble, *Der Vertrag: Wie ich über die deutsche Einheit verhandelte* (DVA: Stuttgart, 1991).

M. Wolf, *In eigenem Auftrag: Bekenntnisse und Einsichten* (Schneekluth: Munich, 1991).

Politics in the GDR

S. Berglund, "The Breakdown of the German Democratic Republic", in S. Berglund and J. Dellenbrant (eds.), *The New Democracies in Eastern Europe: Party Systems and Political Cleavages* (Edward Elgar: Aldershot, 1991), pp.107–35.

V. Gransow and K. Jarausch (eds.), *Die deutsche Vereinigung: Dokumente zu Bürgerbewegung, Annäherung und Beitritt* (Wissenschaft und Politik: Cologne, 1991).

G. -J. Glaessner and I. Wallace (eds.), *The German Revolution of 1989: Causes and Consequences* (Berg: Oxford, forthcoming 1992).

P. Ködderitzsch and L. Müller, *Rechtsradikalismus in der DDR* (Lamuv: Göttingen, 1990).

P. Lapp, *Die "befreundeten Parteien" der SED: DDR-Blockparteien heute* (Wissenschaft und Politik: Cologne, 1988).

K. Löw (ed.), *Ursachen und Verlauf der deutschen Revolution 1989* (Duncker & Humblot: Berlin, 1991).

H. Müller-Enbergs, Marianne Schulz and Jan Wielgohs (eds.), *Von der Illegalität ins Parlament: Werdegang und Konzept der neuen Bürgerbewegungen* (LinksDruck: Berlin, 1991).

J. Osmond, "Germany", in S. White (ed.), *Handbook of Reconstruction in Eastern Europe and the Soviet Union* (Harlow: Longman, 1991), pp.59–111.

J. Osmond, "Germany", in B. Szajkowski (ed.), *New Political Parties of Eastern Europe and the Soviet Union* (Harlow: Longman, 1991), pp.95–127.

P. Przybylski, *Tatort Politbüro: Die Akte Honecker* (Rowohlt: Berlin, 1991).

W. Seiffert and N. Treutwein, *Die Schalck Papiere: DDR-Mafia zwischen Ost und West. Die Beweise* (Zsolnay: Vienna, 1991).

U. Thaysen, *Der Runde Tisch. Oder: Wo blieb das Volk? Der Weg der DDR in die Demokratie* (Westdeutscher Verlag: Opladen, 1990).

C. Wuttke and B. Musiolek (eds.), *Parteien und politische Bewegungen im letzten Jahr der DDR* (BasisDruck: Berlin, 1991).

The *Stasi*

J. Gauck, *Die Stasi-Akten: Das unheimliche Erbe der DDR* (Rowohlt: Reinbek, 1991).

BIBLIOGRAPHY

D. Gill and U. Schröter, *Das Ministerium für Staatssicherheit: Anatomie des Mielke-Imperiums* (Rowohlt: Berlin, 1991).

J. von Lang, *Erich Mielke: Eine deutsche Karriere* (Rowohlt: Berlin, 1991).

M. Müller and A. Kanonenberg, *Die RAF-Stasi Connection* (Rowohlt: Berlin, 1992).

R. Popplewell, "The Stasi and the East German Revolution of 1989", in *Contemporary European History* 1 (1992), pp.37–63.

M. Schell and W. Kalinka, *Stasi und kein Ende: Die Personen und Fakten* (Ullstein: Frankfurt/Main and Berlin, 1991).

Stasi Intern: Macht und Banalität (Forum: Leipzig, 2nd edn 1991), ed. Bürgerkomitee Leipzig.

Parties, elections and political structures in united Germany

T. Ammer, "The emerging democratic party system in the GDR", in *Aussenpolitik* 4 (1990), pp.377–87.

K. von Beyme, "Electoral unification: the first German elections in December 1990", in *Government and Opposition* 26 (1991), pp.167–84.

C. Clay, "Helmut Kohl's CDU and German unification: the price of success", in *German Politics and Society* 22 (1991), pp.33–44.

R. Dalton (ed.), *Germany Votes 1990: Reunification and the Creation of a New German Party System* (Berg: Oxford, forthcoming 1992/93).

U. Feist and H. -J. Hoffmann, "Landtagswahlen in der ehemaligen DDR am 14. Oktober 1990: Föderalismus im wiedervereinten Deutschland - Tradition und neue Konturen", in *Zeitschrift für Parlamentsfragen* 22 (1991), pp.5–34.

M. Fulbrook, "Wir sind ein Volk? Reflections on German unification", in *Parliamentary Affairs* 44 (1991), pp.389–404.

V. Gransow and K. Jarausch (eds.), *Die deutsche Vereinigung: Dokumente zu Bürgerbewegung, Annäherung und Beitritt* (Wissenschaft und Politik: Cologne, 1991).

D. Grosser (ed.), *Uniting Germany: The Unexpected Challenge* (Berg: Oxford, forthcoming 1992).

R. Irving and W. Paterson, "The 1990 German general election", in *Parliamentary Affairs* 44 (1991), pp.353–72.

C. Jeffrey, "Voting on unity: the German election of 1990", in *International Relations* 10 (1991), pp.329–46.

W. Kaltefleiter (with B. Lübcke), "Die Struktur der deutschen Wählerschaft nach der Vereinigung", in *Zeitschrift für Politik* 38 (1991), pp.1–32.

J. McAdams, "Towards a new Germany? Problems of unification", in *Government and Opposition* 25 (1990), pp.304–16.

S. Padgett (ed.), *Party Politics in the New Germany* (ASGP/Dartmouth: Aldershot, 1992).

P. Pulzer, "The German federal election of 1990", in *Electoral Studies* 10 (1991), pp.145–54.

G. Roberts, "'Emigrants in their own country': German reunification and its political consequences", in *Parliamentary Affairs* 44 (1991), pp.378–88.

U. Schmidt, "Die Parteienlandschaft in Deutschland nach der Vereinigung", in *Gegenwartskunde. Gesellschaft, Staat, Erziehung* 4 (1991), pp.515–44.

D. Southern, "The Constitutional Framework of the New Germany" in *German Politics* 1 (1992), pp.31–49.

S. Suckut and D. Staritz, "Alte Heimat oder neue Linke? Das SED-Erbe und die PDS-Erben", in *Deutschland Archiv* 10 (1991), pp.1038–51.

R. Wildenmann, *Volksparteien. Ratlose Riesen?* (Nomos: Baden-Baden, 1989).

G. Wuthe, "Einheit der Nation — Traum oder Trauma der Sozialdemokratie?" in *Deutschland Archiv* 11 (1991), pp.1170–9.

The economy

G. Akerlof, A. Rose, J. Yellen and H. Hessenius, "East Germany in from the Cold: The Economic Aftermath of Currency Union", in *Brookings Papers on Economic Activity* 1 (1991), pp.1–105.

R. Bentley, *Research and Technology in the former GDR* (Westview: Boulder, San Francisco, Oxford, forthcoming 1991).

B. Breuel, "A social market economy cannot be introduced overnight", in *European Affairs* 6 (1991), pp.28–32.

H. Brezinski, "Private agriculture in the GDR: limitations of orthodox socialist agricultural policy", in *Soviet Studies* 3 (1990), pp.535–53.

P. Bryson, "The economics of German reunification: a review of the literature", in *Journal of Comparative Economics* 16, No. 1 (1992), pp.118–49.

P. Bryson and M. Melzer, *The End of the East German Economy* (Macmillan: Basingstoke and London, 1991).

P. Christ and R. Neubauer, *Kolonie im eigenen Land: Die Treuhand, Bonn und die Wirtschaftskatastrophe der fünf neuen Länder* (Rowohlt: Berlin, 1991).

I. Collier, "On the first year of German monetary, economic and social union", in *Journal of Economic Perspectives* 5, No. 4 (1991), pp.179–86.

Eastern Europe: Long Way Ahead to Economic Well-Being (CIA: Washington D.C., 1990).

Economic Assistance in the new German Länder (Federal Ministry of Economics: Bonn, 1991).

I. Jeffries (ed.), *Industrial Reform in Socialist Countries: from Restructuring to Revolution* (Edward Elgar: Aldershot, 1992).

I. Jeffries and M. Melzer (eds.), *The East German Economy* (Croom Helm: London, 1987).

R. Kurz, *Honeckers Rache: Zur politischen Ökonomie des wiedervereinigten Deutschlands* (Bittermann: Berlin, 1991).

L. Lipschitz and D. McDonald (eds.), *German Unification: Economic Issues* (IMF: Washington D.C., 1990), IMF Occasional Paper, No. 75.

R. Pohl (ed.), *Handbook of the Economy of the German Democratic Republic* (Saxon House: Farnborough, 1979).

H. Schmieding, *German Unification: the Economics of Transition*, working paper 468 (Kiel Institute of World Economics: Kiel, 1991).

G. Schneider, *Wirtschaftswunder DDR: Anspruch und Realität* (Bund: Cologne, 1988).

H. Siebert, "German unification: the economics of transition", in *Economic Policy* 13 (1991), pp.287–340.

H. Siebert and H. Schmieding, *Restructuring Industry in the GDR* working paper 431 (Kiel Institute of World Economics: Kiel, 1990).

O. Singer, "The Politics and Economics of German Unification: from Currency Union to Economic Dichotomy", in *German Politics* 1 (1992), pp.78–94.

Statistisches Jahrbuch der Deutschen Demokratischen Republik 1990 (Rudolf Haufe: Berlin, 1990).

H. Suhr, *Der Treuhand Skandal: Wie Ostdeutschland geschlachtet wurde* (Eichborn: Frankfurt/Main, 1991).

V. Vincentz, *Privatization in Eastern Germany: Principles and Practice*, working paper 146 (Eastern Europe Institute: Munich, 1991).

M. Wilson, *Germany at the Crossroads: The Costs of Reunification* (Financial Times: London, 1991).

Wirtschaftsreport: Daten und Fakten zur wirtschaftlichen Lage Ostdeutschlands (Die Wirtschaft: Berlin, 1990).

Trade unions and the labour market

Arbeitsmarkt in Zahlen. Aktuelle Daten für das Beitrittsgebiet (Federal Institute for Labour: Nuremberg, monthly 1991–2).

M. Fichter, "From Transmission Belt to Social Partnership? The Case of Organised Labour in Eastern Germany", in *German Politics and Society* 23 (1991), pp.1–19.

U. Gill, *FDGB: Die DDR-Gewerkschaft von 1945 bis zu ihrer Auflösung 1990* (Bund: Cologne, 1991).

M. Kittner (ed.), *Gewerkschaftsjahrbuch 1991* (Bund: Cologne, 1991).

A. S. Markovits and C.S. Allen, "The Trade Unions", in G. Smith, W. E. Paterson and P. Merkl (eds.), *Developments in West German Politics* (Macmillan: London, 1989).

Die Neuen Gewerkschaften: Repräsentativ-Erhebung bei Arbeitnehmerinnen und Arbeitnehmern in den neuen Bundesländern (IFEP: Munich and Cologne, 1991).

T. Pirker, H. H. Hertle, J. Kädtler and R. Weinert, *Wende zum Ende: Auf dem Weg zu unabhängigen Gewerkschaften?* (Bund: Cologne, 1990).

R. Zoll, H. Brauer and M. Springhorn-Schmidt (eds.), *Arbeitlose und Gewerkschaft: Untersuchung einer schwierigen Beziehung* (Bund: Cologne, 1991).

Women

Beratung, Fortbildung, Umschulung, Arbeitsbeschaffung für Frauen in den neuen Bundesländern (Federal Ministry for Women and Youth: Bonn, 1991).

I. Doelling, "Between hope and helplessness: women in the GDR after the 'Turning Point'", in *Feminist Review*, Special Issue 39 (1991), pp.3–15.

B. Einhorn, "Where have all the women gone? Women and the women's movement in east central Europe", in *Feminist Review*, Special Issue 39 (1991), pp.16–36.

Frauen in den neuen Bundesländern im Prozess der deutschen Einigung (Infas: Bad Godesberg, 1991).

E. Kolinsky, *Women in West Germany: Life, Work and Politics* (Berg: Oxford, 1989).

H. Shaffer, *Women in the Two Germanies* (Pergamon: New York, 1981).

G. Winkler (ed.), *Frauenreport '90* (Die Wirtschaft: Berlin, 1990).

The environment and Green politics

M. Haendcke-Hoppe and K. Merkel (eds.), *Umweltschutz in beiden Teilen Deutschlands* (Duncker & Humblot: Berlin and Munich, 1986).

C. Hager, "Environmentalism and Democracy in the Two Germanies", in *German Politics* 1 (1992), pp.95–118.

W. Hülsberg, *The German Greens: A Social and Political Profile* (Verso: London and New York, 1988).

E. Kolinsky (ed.), *The Greens in West Germany: organisation and policy making* (Berg: Oxford, 1989).

U. Petschow, J. Meyerhoff and C. Thomasberger (eds.), *Umweltreport DDR: Bilanz der Zerstörung — Kosten der Sanierung — Strategien für den ökologischen Umbau* (Fischer: Frankfurt/Main, 1990).

The international context

E. Arnold, "German foreign policy and unification", in *International Affairs* 67 (1991), pp.453–71.

"The European Community and German unification", in *Bulletin of the European Communities*, supplement 4 (Luxembourg, 1990).

R. Fritsch-Bournazel, *Europe and German Unification* (Berg: Oxford, 1992).

V. Gransow and K. Jarausch (eds.), *Die deutsche Vereinigung: Dokumente zu Bürgerbewegung, Annäherung und Beitritt* (Wissenschaft und Politik: Cologne, 1991).

E. Kirchner and J. Sperling "The future Germany and the future of NATO", in *German Politics* 1 (1992), pp.50–77.

B. Kohler-Koch (ed.), *Die Osterweitung der EG: Die Einbeziehung der ehemaligen DDR in die Gemeinschaft* (Baden-Baden: Nomos, 1991).

H. Kurz and T. Heuss (eds.), *United Germany and the New Europe* (Edward Elgar: Aldershot, forthcoming 1992).

F. Larrabee (ed.), *The Two German States and European Security* (Macmillan: London, 1989).

C. Menges, *The Future of Germany and the Atlantic Alliance* (AEI Press: Washington D.C., 1991).

J. Osmond, "German Unification and its Implications for Europe", in *European Community: Economic Structure and Analysis* (Economist Intelligence Unit: London, 1991), vol.2, pp.12–18.

A. Pittman, *From Ostpolitik to Reunification: West German–Soviet Political Relations Since 1974* (Cambridge University Press: Cambridge, forthcoming 1992).

J. Rollo (ed.), *The New Eastern Europe: Western Responses* (Pinter: London, 1990).

A. Rotfeld and W. Stützle (eds.), *Germany and Europe in Transition* (Oxford University Press: Oxford, 1991).

D. Spence, *Enlargement Without Accession: The EC's Response to German Unification* (Royal Institute of International Affairs: London, 1991).

INDEX

bold type indicates an entry in the DIRECTORY

abortion rights, 192–3
Abwicklung, **201**
Adenauer, Konrad, 17, 94
Adler, Helga, 230
agriculture, 79–80, 109–11, 153–4, 167–8, 264–5
Ahrendt, Lothar, 246–7
Albrecht, Hans, 42
Albrecht, Susanne, 9, 13, 232
Alliance 90, 150, **201**, 249–51
Alliance for Germany, 57, **201**, 249
Alternative List, **202**, 251
Alternative Youth List, 57, **202**
Arndt, Otto, 245
Association of Mutual Peasant Aid (*Vereinigung der gegenseitigen Bauernhilfe*), 233
Association of Working Groups for Employee Politics and Democracy, **202**
Aurich, Eberhard, 202, 215
Austria, 3–4, 15–17, 25, 27, 50, 58, 83, 95, 235
  and trade with GDR, 254–5
Axen, Hermann, 32, 34, 244

Baader–Meinhof gang, *see* Red Army Faction
Baden, 15
Baden-Württemberg, 11, 12, 14, **202**, 207, 208, 232, 235, 252
Baker, James, 290
Bangemann, Martin, 100–2, 106
Barschel, Uwe, 213, 235
Bartscher, Rainer, 206
Bauernverband der DDR, *see* Farmers' Association of the GDR
Baumann, Edith, 219
Baumgärtel, Gerhard, 246

Bavaria, 15, 52, **202**, 208, 209, 232, 252
Becher, Bernhard, 231
Becher, Johannes R., 64
Beil, Gerhard, 45, 245–7
Benthien, Bruno, 246
Berghofer, Wolfgang, 4–7, 14, 28, 52, **202**
Bergmann-Pohl, Sabine, 8–9, 11, 60, 69, 139, 141, **203**
Berlin, 16–17, 18, 20–21, 31–32, 33–5, **203**, 257, 271, 275, 277–9, 283, 285–6
  building of Wall in (1961), 20–21, 203
  elections in, 70–1, 88, 251
  opening of Wall in (1989), 43–4, 227
BFD, *see* League of Free Democrats
Biedenkopf, Kurt, 11, 140, 143, 175, **203**, 234
Biermann, Wolf, 27, 203, 239
Bismarck, Otto von, 16
Bizonia, 17
Bläss, Petra, 57, 221
Blessing, Karlheinz, 236
Blüm, Norbert, 243, 249
Bochmann, Manfred, 245
Bohley, Bärbel, 27, 42, **203–4**, 228, 231, 232
Böhm, Tatjana, 221, 247
Böhme, Hans-Joachim (minister), 245
Böhme, Hans-Joachim (SED secretary), 33–5, 244
Böhme, Ibrahim, **204**, 236–7
Bonn, **204**, and *passim*
Börner, Rainer, 230
Braband, Jutta, 240
Brandenburg, **204**, 250, and *passim*
Brandt, Willy, 7, 21, 58, 67, 94, 124, 129, 170, 236–7, 239
Breit, Ernst, 173, 178
Bremen, 13, 132, **204**, 215, 216, 223, 252
Breuel, Birgit, 12, 77, 165, 167, **204–5**, 226, 233, 239–40
Brie, André, 230
Briksa, Gerhard, 245
Brittan, Leon, 107
Brüning, Heinrich, 19

303

Brunner, Gerd, 13, 145
Buback, Siegfried, 232
Budig, Klaus–Peter, 246–7
Bund der Evangelischen Kirchen in der DDR (BEK), *see* Federation of Evangelical Churches in the GDR
Bund Freier Demokraten, *see* League of Free Democrats
Bundesbahn, 80, 281
Bundesbank, *see* Deutsche Bundesbank
Bundesrat, 63, 69, 133, **205**, 223, 227, 285
Bundestag, **205**
 elections to, 70–1, 115–16, 118, 126–9, 251
Bundeswehr, **205–6**, 228, 288–9
Bündnis 90, see Alliance 90
Buschmann, Werner, 245
Bush, George, 9, 67, 259

Carnations, The, **206**, 208
CDU, *see* Christian Democratic Union of Germany
Chemnitz, *see* Karl–Marx–Stadt
Chemnitzer, Johannes, 37
Chequers seminar (March 1990), 94–5
Christian Democratic Social Union, **206**
Christian Democratic Union of Germany (CDU), 116–21, 141–5, **206–8**, and *passim*
Christian League, **208**
Christian Social Association, **208**
Christian Social Party of Germany, **208**
Christian Social Union, **208**
Christian Social Union in Bavaria (CSU), **208**, 251–2
churches in the GDR, 28, 147
citizens' movements (*Bürgerbewegungen*), 40–2
 see also Alliance 90, Democracy Now, Democratic Awakening, Green League, Green Party, Independent Women's Association, New Forum, Peace and Human Rights Initiative, United Left
Collins, Gerry, 101
Commercial Co-ordination (*Kommerzielle Koordinierung* — KoKo), 235
Committees for Justice, 88
Communist Party of Germany (KPD), 18–20, **208**

Council for Mutual Economic Assistance (CMEA), 82–4, 99, 101, 105–6, 109–12, 152, 154, 163–4, 257, 264, 282
Crespo, Enrico Baron, 104
CSU, *see* Christian Social Union in Bavaria
Customs Union of 1834, 16
Czechoslovakia, 6, 13, 16, 21, 25, 33, 41, 73, 82, 84, 89, 99, 114, 152, 163
 and trade with GDR, 254–5
Czollek, Michael, 206

DA, *see* Democratic Awakening
Dämmrich, Karl, 213
DBD, *see* Democratic Farmers' Party of Germany
De Maizière, Lothar, **209**
 government of, 60–5, 157, 248
 and *passim*
Dehler, Mathias, 248
Delors, Jacques, 68, 94–6, 100, 104
Demba, Judith, 217
Democracy Now (DJ), **210**
Democratic Awakening (DA), **210–11**, 249
Democratic Farmers' Party of Germany (DBD), **211**
Democratic Women's League of Germany (DFD), 57, 58, **211**, 221
Demokratie Jetzt, *see* Democracy Now
Demokratische Bauernpartei Deutschlands, *see* Democratic Farmers' Party of Germany
Demokratischer Aufbruch, *see* Democratic Awakening
Demokratischer Frauenbund Deutschlands, *see* Democratic Women's League of Germany
Deneke, Marlies, 230
Deutsche Alternative, *see* German Alternative
Deutsche Biertrinker Union, *see* German Beer Drinkers' Union
Deutsche Bundesbank, 61, 71, 75, 96–7, 157–60, **211–12**, 231, 260–3
Deutsche Forumpartei, *see* German Forum Party
Deutsche Freiheitsunion, *see* German Freedom Union
Deutsche Post, 268, 281
Deutsche Reichsbahn, 80, 268, 281

INDEX

Deutsche Soziale Union, see German Social Union
Deutsche Volksunion, see German People's Union
DFD, *see* Democratic Women's League of Germany
DFP, *see* German Forum Party
DGB (*Deutscher Gewerkschaftsbund*), *see* German Trade Union League
Dickel, Friedrich, 245
Diederich, Peter, 211, 246, 247
Diepgen, Eberhard, 12, 70, 203, **212**, 227, 236
Diestel, Peter-Michael, 8, 9, 52, 62, 65, 88–9, 139–40, **212**, 217, 248
Dohlus, Horst, 244
Dohnanyi, Klaus von, 179, 180
Donnelly, Alan, 100
Dresden
  neo-Nazism in, 86
  SED organization in, 31, 52
  violence at railway station in, 25–6
DSU, *see* German Social Union
Duchac, Josef, 11, 14, 71, 140, 144, **212**, 241
Dumas, Roland, 290
DVU, *see* German People's Union

Ebeling, Fred, 210
Ebeling, Hans-Wilhelm, **212**, 216–17, 248
Eberlein, Werner, 244
economy of GDR/eastern Germany, 71–84, 152–69, 252–5
education
  and German unification, 283–4
Eichel, Hans, 12, 219
elections, 57–60, 115–32, 249–52
  to Berlin House of Representatives, 70–1, 251
  to *Bundestag*, 70–1, 126–9, 251
  to *Landtage*, 69, 250, 252
  to local assemblies in GDR, 62, 250
  to *Volkskammer*, 57–60, 121–6, 249
Emons, Hans-Heinz, 246–7
energy in GDR, 81
Engelhard, Hans, 243
Engholm, Björn, 11, 13, **213**, 235, 236–7
environmental issues, 40, 81–2, 108, 217–18, 265, 283, 294
Eppelmann, Rainer, 8, 61, 62, 139, 143, 210, **213**, 236, 247–8

European Community
  and German reunification, 68–9, 93–114, 258, 260, 264, 268, 270, 272, 278, 282, 291

families
  conditions in east Germany, 190–6
Farmers' Association of the GDR, **213**
FDGB, *see* Free German Trade Union League
FDJ, *see* Free German Youth
FDP, *see* Free Democratic Party
Federal Constitutional Court (*Bundesverfassungsgericht*), Karlsruhe, 11, 66, 70, 76, 193
Federation of Evangelical Churches in the GDR, 28
Fernandez-Albor, Gerardo, 100
Fink, Ulf, 13, 89, 143–4, **213**, 225
Fischbek, Hans-Jürgen, 210
Fischer, Oskar, 45, 245–7
Flegel, Manfred, 245–7
Flugbeil, Sebastian, 247
Forck, Gottfried, 48
foreign trade
  of GDR, 82–4, 154–5, 254–5
Forum Party of Thuringia, **213**
Four Power Agreement on Berlin (1971), 21, 65, 203
France
  and trade with GDR, 82, 254–5
  and Two-Plus-Four-Treaty, 287–91
Free Democratic Party (FDP), 116–21, 145, **213–14**, and *passim*
  see also Genscher, Hans-Dietrich
Free Democratic Union of Germany, **214**
Free German Trade Union League (FDGB), 171–5, **214**, 273
Free German Union, **214**
Free German Youth (FDJ), 19, 31, 32, 34, 57, 85, 172, 202, **214–15**, 219, 222, 226
Freie Demokratische Partei, see Free Democratic Party
Freie Deutsche Jugend, see Free German Youth
Freie Deutsche Union, see Free German Union
Freier Deutscher Gewerkschaftsbund, see Free German Trade Union League
Frey, Gerhard, 216

305

Friderichs, Hans, 233
Friedrich, Walter, 31

Gauck, Joachim, 85, **215**, 238
Gehrcke, Wolfgang, 230
Gemeinschaftswerk Aufschwung Ost (Joint Programme for Eastern Regeneration), 176–7, 183
Genscher, Hans–Dietrich, 4, 14, 25, 58, 62, 67–70, 94, 97, 113–14, 128, 145, 156, 166, **215**, 225, 243, 249, 290–1
Georgi, Rudi, 245
Gerlach, Manfred, 4, 5, 6, 37, 45, 60, 211, **215**, 224, 229, 244
German Alternative, **215–16**, 232
German Beer Drinkers' Union, 57, **216**
German Communist Party (*Deutsche Kommunistische Partei* — DKP), 230
German Empire (1871–1918), 16
German Forum Party (DFP), 7, 8, 58, 214, 216, 223, 224
German Freedom Union, **216**
German People's Union (DVU), 13, 14, 86, 95, 204, **216**, 235, 252
German Social Union (DSU), 7, 8, 9, 51–2, 57–62, 69, 70, 88, 139, 141–2, 201, **216–17**, 248–51
German Trade Union League (*Deutscher Gewerkschaftsbund* — DGB), 171–84, 214
German Unity Fund, 61, 75, 176, 277
Gibtner, Horst, 248
Gies, Gerd, 11, 13, 71, 140, 143, **217**, 227
Gläser, Wolfgang, 227
Goethe, Johann Wolfgang von, 16
Gohlke, Reiner, 10, 77, 165, **217**, 233, 239–40
Gomolka, Alfred, 11, 14, 71, 140, **217**, 222, 236
Gorbachev, Mikhail, 23–4, 33–4, 38, 65–6, 240
Götting, Gerald, 5, 13, 42, 206–7, 209, 244
governments
  of Federal Republic of Germany, 243, 249
  of German Democratic Republic, 244–8
Great Britain, *see* United Kingdom
Green League, **217–18**, 233
Green Party, 5, 7, 40, 48, 57, 58, 60, **217–18**, 221, 233

Greens, 150, **217–18**, and *passim*
Grehn, Klaus, 183
Grotewohl, Otto, 19, 20
Grüne Liga, *see* Green League
Grüne Partei, *see* Green Party
Grünen, die, *see* Greens
Grünheid, Karl, 245–7
Gueffroy, Chris, 3, 14
Gysi, Gregor, 6, 8, 11, 45, 59, 69, 88–9, 138, 209, **218–19**, 230, 238
Gysi, Klaus, 218

Hager, Kurt, 24, 30, 33, 35, 244
Halle, 33, 35, 70, 145, 164, 217–18, 234
Halm, Gunter, 246
Hamburg, 13, 132, 173, 202, 204, 207, **219**, 223, 252
Hanover, 15
Hartmann, Günter, 227–8
Häse, Andreas, 216
Hasselfeldt, Gerda, 243, 249
Haussmann, Helmut, 11, 168, **219**, 227, 243
Havel, Václav, 6, 41, 51
Heilmann, Friedrich, 217
Heinrich, Ingo, 14
Heinrich, Rolf, 228–9
Herger, Wolfgang, 29
Herrhausen, Alfred, 6, 232
Herrmann, Joachim, 4, 25, 29, 32, 35–40, 46, 226, 244
Hesse, 12, 15, 132, **219**, 252
Heusinger, Hans-Joachim, 45, 47, 245–6
Hildebrandt, Regine, 139, 248
Hindenburg, Paul von, 19
Hintze, Peter, 89
Hitler, Adolf, 16–19, 33, 43, 53, 58, 95, 219
Hoffmann von Fallersleben, August Heinrich, 16, 64
Hoffmann, Hans-Joachim, 245
Hoffmann, Theodor, 246–7
Höfner, Ernst, 245
Holy Roman Empire, 15–16
Homann, Heinrich, 5, 42, 227–8, 244
Honecker, Erich, **219–20**
  overthrow of, 32–9
  regime of, 21–2
  and *passim*
Honecker, Margot, 5, 29, 42, 219, **220**, 245

Hornhues, Karl-Heinz, 97
Hoyerswerda, 86, 234
Huber, Erwin, 183, 208
Hungary, 15, 41, 48, 73, 99, 110, 114, 163, 220, 257
   and opening of border to Austria, 25, 27, 29, 33
   and trade with GDR, 254–5
Hurd, Douglas, 290

IFM, *see* Peace and Human Rights Initiative
IG Metall (metalworkers' union), 164, 173, 181–4
Independent Social Democratic Party of Germany, 18, 57, **221**
Independent Women's Association, 7, 41, 48, 57, 60, 218, **221**, 233, 240, 247
Initiative Frieden und Menschenrechte, *see* Peace and Human Rights Initiative
Interflug, 79, 166

Jahn, Günther, 37
Jarowinsky, Werner, 35, 244
judicial system
   after German monetary union, 273
   after German unification, 278
Junge Union, *see* Young Union
Junker, Wolfgang, 245

Kahlwald, Brigitte, 206
Kant, Hermann, 31
Karl-Marx-Stadt (now Chemnitz), 9, 33, 35, 37, 216, 234
Keller, Dietmar, 246
Keller, Reinhard, 216, 217
Kessler, Heinz, 12, 30, 36, 39, 244–5
Kiechle, Ignaz, 243, 249
Kimmel, Annelis, 172, 214
Kinkel, Klaus, 14, 249
Kirchner, Martin, 10, 207, **221**
Kleditzsch, Jürgen, 248
Kleiber, Günther, 244–5
Klein, Hans, 243
Klein, Thomas, 240
Klemm, Volker, 30
Kohl, Helmut, **221–2**
   and de Maizière, 61–3
   and Gorbachev, 66
   and Modrow, 53–4
   and opening of Berlin Wall, 50–1
   and Poland, 67–8

   and *Volkskammer* election, 59–60
   and *passim*
Kombinate (combines), 153
König, Hartmut, 31
Köppe, Ingrid, 138
KPD, *see* Communist Party of Germany
Krase, Joachim, 11
Krause, Günther, 11, 12, 13, 61, 63, 65, 69, 71, 76, 80, 139–44, 207, 217, **222**, 235, 236, 249
Krenz, Egon, **222–3**
   and overthrow of Honecker, 35–9
   regime of, 39–40, 42–5
   and *passim*
Krolikowski, Werner, 33, 38, 244
Krüger, Thomas, 192
Kuschl, Hans-Dieter, 105

Lafontaine, Oskar, 8, 9, 11, 59, 62, 64, 70, 74–5, 120, 124, 127, 129, 146, **223**, 234, 236–7
Lambsdorff, Otto Graf, 6, 14, 62, 214, 227, 233
Länder, 63, 67, 69, 71, 75, **223**, 275, 276–8, and *passim*
Landtage, **223**
   elections to, 250–2
Lange, Ingeburg, 244
Lauck, Hans-Joachim, 245, 246, 247
LDP, *see* Liberal Democratic Party
LDPD, *see* Liberal Democratic Party
League of Free Democrats (BFD), 53, 57–8, 61–3, 122, 214, 216, **222–3**, 224, 228, 229, 248, 249, 250
Left List (*Linke Liste*), 231
Lehr, Ursula, 243
Leich, Werner, 48
Leipzig, **224**
   demonstrations in, 26–8, 40–1, 224
Leutheusser-Schnarrenberger, Sabine, 249
Liberal Democratic Party (LDP), 4, 5, 6, 7, 8, 19, 37, 45, 47, 50, 57, 60, 136–7, 142, 145, 215, 223, **224**, 227–8, 229, 233, 244–7
Liebknecht, Karl, 24, 206
Liebrenz, Viktor, 217
Lietz, Bruno, 245
Lorenz, Siegfried, 32, 33, 35, 37, 244
Lower Saxony, 9, 69, 204, 205, **224–5**, 252
Luft, Christa, 45, 155–6, 246–7

Lufthansa, 79, 166
Lühr, Uwe-Berndt, 145, 214
Luxemburg, Rosa, 24, 206

Maastricht summit (December 1991), 93, 113
Maaz, Hans–Joachim, xi, 26
Maizière, Lothar de, *see* De Maizière, Lothar
Maleuda, Günther, 5, 45, 211, 244
Masur, Kurt, 4
Matthaei, Walter, 215–16
Mausch, Helga, 172–3, 214
Mazowiecki, Tadeusz, 25
Meckel, Markus, 8, 10, 67, 138–9, 209, **225**, 236–7, 248
Mecklenburg–West Pomerania, 11, 14, 69, 74, 140, 142–3, 181, 193, 194, 217, 222, **225**, 229, 236, 250
Mecklinger, Ludwig, 245
media
  in GDR/eastern Germany, 86–7, 228, 283
Meier, Felix, 245
Mensch, Hannelore, 246–7
Menzel, Bruno, 214
Merkel, Angela, 71, 141–4, 207, 213, **225**, 249
Merkel, Ina, 221
Meyer, Christian, 155
Meyer, Hans-Joachim, 248
Meyer, Heinz–Werner, 178–9, 182–4
Meyer, Wolfgang, 246–7
Michelis, Gianni de, 104
Mielke, Erich, 5–6, 14, 24, 29–30, 33, 35, 38–9, 42, 220, 238, 244–5, *see also Stasi*
Mittag, Günter, 3–6, 24, 29–40, 45, 46, 82, 220, 223, **225–6**, 244
Mitterrand, François, 6, 9, 51, 96
Mitzinger, Wolfgang, 245
Modrow, Hans, **226–7**, 257
  government of, 45–56, 155–7, 246–7
  and *passim*
Möllemann, Jürgen, 12, 13, 74, 76, 145, 176, 181–2, 219, **227**, 243, 249
Momper, Walter, 3, 5, 70, 212, **227**, 236
monetary, economic and social union of Germany (July 1990), 61–2, 157–64, 260–74
Moreth, Peter, 224, 246–7
Mückenberger, Erich, 244

Müller, Gerhard, 244
Müller, Gottfried, 248
Müller, Margarete, 244
Münch, Werner, 13, 143, 217, **227**, 234
Murmann, Klaus, 182

National Defence Council, 29–30
National Democratic Party of Germany (NDPD), 5, 19, 37, 42, 58, 60, 136–7, 214, 223, 224, **227–8**, 233, 244–7, 249
National People's Army (NVA), 20, 206, 210, 213, **228**
National Socialists (Nazis), 16–19, 216, 218, 227, 291
NATO (North Atlantic Treaty Organization), 9, 10, 20, 22, 37, 53, 65–7, 71, 93, 96, 113, 205–6, 216, 222, 240
Naumann, Herbert, 87, 228
NDPD, *see* National Democratic Party of Germany
Nelken, die, *see* Carnations, The
neo-Nazism, 86, 215–6, 232
Nessing-Stranz, Dorrit, 217
Neubert, Jürgen, 214
Neue Heimat, 175
Neues Deutschland, 5, 23, 36, 39, 46, 48, 53, 87, **228**, 234
Neumann, Alfred, 4, 32–8, 244–5
New Forum, 4–7, 37, 41–2, 47–50, 57, 60, 62, 122–5, 138, 150, 172, 201, 204, 210, 215, 216, **228–9**, 231, 232, 234, 236, 239, 240, 247, 249–50
Nickel, Uta, 45, 246
Niedersachsen, *see* Lower Saxony
North Rhine–Westphalia, 9, 190, 203, 227, **229**, 252
Nuschke, Otto, 206
NVA, *see* National People's Army

Odewald, Jens, 165
Ortleb, Rainer, 11, 12, 69, 71, 139–40, 214, 215, 223, 224, **229**, 249
Ottawa declaration (February 1990), 7, 67, 240, 287
ÖTV (Public Services and Transport Workers' Union), 173, 175, 181

Parteienverdrossenheit, 119
Party of Central German National Democrats, **230**

INDEX

Party of Democratic Socialism (PDS), 148–50, **230–1**, 286, and *passim*
Peace and Human Rights Initiative (IFM), 7, 41, 48, 57, 201, 210, **231**, 233, 247
People's Union, **231**
Peplowski, Werner, 172
Pflugbeil, Sebastian, 229
Pieck, Wilhelm, 19–20
Platzeck, Mathias, 247
Pohl, Gerhard, 10, 63, 233, 248
Pöhl, Karl Otto, 12–13, 59, 75, 159–60, 164, 168, 176, 211–12, **231**
Pohl, Wolfgang, 230
Poland, 67–8, 257, 288
  and trade with GDR, 254–5
Pollack, Peter, 10, 63, 233, 248
Pomerania, 17, 67, *see also* Mecklenburg-West Pomerania
Ponto, Jürgen, 232
Poppe, Gerd, 231, 247
Poppe, Ulrike, 210
Portugal, 97, 101, 105, 110–12
Prague, 25
Preiss, Manfred, 248
privatization of east German economy, 76–8, 165–8
Progressive People's Party, **231–2**
property claims in east Germany, 78, 166–7
Prussia, 15–18, 67, 203, 204, 229, 235

Ramin, Lothar, 216
Rappe, Hermann, 183
Rau, Johannes, 236
Rauchfuss, Wolfgang, 245
Rauls, Wolfgang, 227
Red Army Faction, 62, 77, 202, **232**, 240
Reich, Jens, 42, 229, **232**
Reichelt, Hans, 30, 45, 211, 245–6
Reider, Sybille, 248
Republicans, 3, 14, 60, 70–1, 86, 95, 117, 121, 134, 202, 216, 217, **232**, 235, 251–2
Rhineland–Palatinate, 12, 15, 132, 144, 205, 207, 221–2, **232–3**, 241, 252
Ridley, Nicholas, 95
Riechenbach, Klaus, 248
Riesenhuber, Heinz, 243, 249
Rohwedder, Detlev, 9–10, 12, 62, 77, 165, 204–5, 212, 217, 231, 232, **233**, 240
Romberg, Walter, 8–10, 61, 63, 75, 139–40, 157, **233**, 237, 241, 247–8

Rönsch, Hannelore, 192, 249
Rote Armee Fraktion, *see* Red Army Faction
Rothe, Peter, 173
Round Table, 47–50, **233–4**
Rühe, Volker, 142–3, 205, 206, 249
Rühle, Heide, 218

Saarland, 9, 16–17, 120, 124, 219, 223, **234**, 252
Saxony, 9, 11, 15, 18, 51, 59–60, 69, 140, 143, 175, 203, 208, 212, 217, 224, 227, **234**, 250
Saxony–Anhalt, 11, 13, 69, 140, 143, 145, 217, 227, **234**, 250
Sbrzesny, Klaus, 208
Schabowski, Günter, 4–7, 24, 30–9, 42–4, 52, 223, 228, 230, **234–5**, 244
Schalck-Golodkowski, Alexander, 44, **235**
Scharping, Rudolf, 12, 232
Schäuble, Wolfgang, 11, 51–2, 61–5, 89, 222, **235**, 243, 249
Schenk, Christina, 221
Schiller, Friedrich von, 16
Schiller, Karl, 233
Schirmer, Herbert, 248
Schlesinger, Helmut, 13, 168, 211–12, 231
Schleswig-Holstein, 11, 14, 213, 216, **235**, 252
Schleyer, Hanns–Martin, 232
Schlüter, Klaus, 247
Schmidt, Christa, 248
Schmidt, Helmut, 58, 213, 221, 231, 233, 237
Schmieder, Jürgen, 216
Schnell, Emil, 248
Schnur, Wolfgang, 6, 8, 58, 59, 61, 138, 209, 210, 212, 213, **236**, 238
Scholz, Heinrich, 246–7
Schönhuber, Franz, 232
Schorlemmer, Friedrich, 210
Schramm, Henry, 217
Schröder, Birgit, 202
Schröder, Gerhard, 224
Schubert, Cordula, 248
Schulze, Rudolf, 245
Schürer, Gerhard, 45, 244–6
Schwaetzer, Irmgard, 14, 101, 249
Schwanitz, Wolfgang, 246
Schwarz-Schilling, Christian, 243, 249
Schwierzina, Tino, 227, **236**

SDP, *see* Social Democratic Party of Germany
SED, *see* Socialist Unity Party of Germany
SED-PDS, *see* Socialist Unity Party of Germany and Party of Democratic Socialism
Seehofer, Horst, 249
Seelig, Marion, 240
Seilschaften, **236**
Seite, Berndt, 14, 217, 225, **236**
Seiters, Rudolf, 5, 6, 243
Shevardnadze, Eduard, 290
Silesia, 15–17, 67
Sindermann, Horst, 5, 30–3, 244
Singhuber, Kurt, 245–6
Single European Act (1986), 95
Skubiszewski, Krzysztof, 68
Social Civic Union, **236**
social consequences of unification, 84–7, 164, 170–1, 175–84
Social Democratic Party of Germany (SPD), **236–7**
  in coalition government, 62–3, 247–8
  election performance of, 57–60, 115–32, 249–52
  history of, 18–20
  and politics since 1989, 146–8
  in West Germany, 116–21
  and *passim*
social insurance and pensions, 265–8, 282
Socialist Unity Party of Germany (SED), 257, 279
  and crisis of 1989, 23–50, 230
  history of, 19–22, 136–7, 230
  party leadership and governments of, 244–7
  and *passim*
  see also Party of Democratic Socialism
Solidarity, 24–5, 41
Sölle, Horst, 245
Sonntag, Rainer, 13
Sorbs, 15, 49, 233, 286
Soviet Union
  and German reunification, 65–7, 287–91, 292–6
  and *passim*
Spain, 69, 97, 105, 110–12
Spartacist Workers' Party of Germany, **237**
Späth, Lothar, 12, 202

SPD, *see* Social Democratic Party of Germany
Spickermann, Wolfgang, 87, 228
Spranger, Carl-Dieter, 249
Sputnik, 24
Stalin, Joseph, 18–20, 24
Stasi, 26–7, 29–30, 42, 49, 138–49, **238**, 280, and *passim*
Steinberg, Karl-Hermann, 248
Steinkühler, Franz, 182, 184
Stihl, Hans-Peter, 78, 181
Stolpe, Manfred, 11, 71, 140, 143, 204, **238**
Stoltenberg, Gerhard, 14, 243, 249
Stoph, Willi, 4–5, 12, 21–2, 30, 32, 34–5, 38–9, 42–3, 45, **238–9**, 244–5
Strauss, Franz Josef, 202, 208, 221
Streletz, Fritz, 30, 37
Super, 87
Süssmuth, Rita, 9, 170, 203

taxation, 270–1, 277
telecommunications, 256, 272
Templin, Wolfgang, 231
Ten-point plan for German unity, 95–7, 256–9
Terpe, Frank, 248
Teufel, Erwin, 12, 202
Thälmann, Ernst, 18, 19
Thatcher, Margaret, 94–7
Thielmann, Klaus, 246–7
Thierse, Wolfgang, 9, 236–7, **239**
Thietz, Peter, 214
Third Reich (1933–45), 16, 19, 53, 78
Thuringia, 11, 14, 18, 59–60, 69, 140, 144, 193, 212, 213, 217, 218, **239**, 241, 250
Tiananmen Square massacre, 3, 26, 223, 224
Tietmeyer, Hans, 13, 61, 102, 211–12, 231
Tisch, Harry, 4–6, 13, 32, 35–8, 42, 45–6, 171–2, 214, 244
Töpfer, Klaus, 12, 81, 243, 249
Törkowsky, Frank, 202
trade unions, 85, 170–84, 272–3
  membership of, 174
transport, 80, 108, 256
Trautenhahn, Gerhard, 245
Treuhandanstalt, 55–6, 165–7, **239–40**, 280–1, and *passim*
Trojan, Carlo, 102
Trumpf, Jürgen, 100

INDEX

Tschiche, Hans-Jochen, 229
Two-Plus-Four treaty, 67, **240**, 287–91

Ulbricht, Walter, 19–21, 153, 203, 219, 230, 239
Ullmann, Wolfgang, 138, 210, 247
Unabhängiger Frauenverband, see Independent Women's Association
unemployment, 160–3, 175–82, 252
 of women, 187–9
unification, treaty of (1990), 275–86
Union of Mutual Peasant Aid (*Vereinigung der gegenseitigen Bauernhilfe — VdgB*), 48, 211, 213
United Kingdom
 and German unification, 67–9, 93–7, 287–91
 and trade with GDR, 254–5
United Left (*Vereinigte Linke*), 48, 50, 208, 234, **240**
United States
 and German unification, 67, 287–91
uprising of June 1953, 20, 69
USA, *see* United States
USPD, *see* Independent Social Democratic Party of Germany
USSR, *see* Soviet Union

Vereinigte Linke, *see* United Left
Vereinigung der gegenseitigen Bauernhilfe — VdgB, *see* Union of Mutual Peasant Aid
Versailles Treaty (1919), 16
Vertragsgemeinschaft, 50, **241**, 257
Vertrauensschutz, 99, 105, 109–10, 278
Viehweger, Axel, 10, 139, 145, 223, 248
Vogel, Bernhard, 14, 144, 212, 239, **241**
Vogel, Hans–Jochen, 9, 11, 13, 241
Volkskammer, **241**
 election to (March 1990), 57–60, 121–6, 249
Volksparteien (CDU–CSU and SPD), 116–32
Voscherau, Henning, 13, 219

wages, 164, 175–82

Wagner, Herbert, 202
Waigel, Theo, 9, 13, 61, 75–6, 157–9, 208, 216, 233, **241**, 243, 249
Walde, Werner, 33, 37, 244
Wałęsa, Lech, 41
Walther, Hansjoachim, 11, 69, 139, 216–17
Wandlitz, 6, 30, 35, 37–8, 220
Wange, Udo-Dieter, 245
Warnke, Jürgen, 243
Wars of Liberation (1813–14), 16
Warsaw, 25, 27, 68
Warsaw Treaty Organization (Warsaw Pact), 9, 12, 20, 53, 65–6, 94, 205, 228, 259
Warteschleife, **241**
Watzek, Hans, 246
Wedemeier, Klaus, 204
Weimar Republic (1919–33), 16–17
Weiske, Christine, 217
Weiss, Heinrich, 73
Weiss, Konrad, 210
Weiz, Herbert, 245
Weizsäcker, Richard von, 6, 9, 212, 233, **241**
Wende, 40, **242**, and *passim*
Willerding, Jochen, 31
Williamson, David, 100, 102
Wilms, Dorothee, 243
Wisser, Martin, 214
Wolf, Klaus, 246
Wolf, Markus, 3
Wollenberger, Vera, 26, 89
women, 185–97, 282
work creation schemes (*Arbeitsbeschaffungsmassnahmen — ABM*), 188
Wünsche, Kurt, 10, 139, 223, 224, 246–8
Württemberg, 15
Wyschofsky, Günther, 245

Yeltsin, Boris, 23, 220
Young Union, **242**

Ziegenhahn, Herbert, 42
Zimmermann, Friedrich, 243

311

REFERENCE

ELIHU BURRITT LIBRARY
CENTRAL CONNECTICUT STATE UNIVERSITY
NEW BRITAIN, CONNECTICUT

WITHDRAWN